Shipping Finance
3rd Edition

Prepared by Stephenson Harwood

EUROMONEY BOOKS

Published by
Euromoney Institutional Investor Plc
Nestor House, Playhouse Yard
London EC4V 5EX
United Kingdom

Tel: +44 (0) 20 7779 8999 or USA +1 800 437 9997
Fax: +44 (0) 20 7779 8300
www.euromoneybooks.com
E-mail:hotline@euromoneyplc.com

Reprinted 2008, 2009

ISBN 10: 1 84374 265 9
ISBN 13: 978 1 84374 265 4

This publication is designed to provide accurate and authoritative information with regard to the subject matter covered. In the preparation of this book, every effort has been made to offer the most current, correct, and clearly expressed information possible. The materials presented in this publication are for informational purposes only. They reflect the subjective views of authors and contributors and do not necessarily represent current or past practices or beliefs of any organization. In this publication, none of the contributors, their past or present employers, the editor, or the publisher is engaged in rendering accounting, business, financial, investment, legal, tax, or other professional advice or services whatsoever and is not liable for any losses, financial or otherwise, associated with adopting any ideas, approaches, or frameworks contained in this book. If investment advice or other expert assistance is required, the individual services of a competent professional should be sought.

Printed and bound in Great Britain by
CPI Antony Rowe, Chippenham and Eastbourne

Shipping Finance

3rd Edition

Contents

Contents

Contents

Foreword

Dagfinn Lunde
Chairman and CEO, DVB Bank N.V.

There has been a great deal of change in both the shipping industry and in the shipping finance market since the publication of the second edition of this book some eleven years ago. Although bank debt remains the dominant source of capital in the industry, we have seen a significant increase in alternative capital sources in recent years. Debt and equity from the public markets, the Norwegian KS and German KG systems, tonnage tax schemes and tax lease finance can all now be regarded as commonplace in the shipping finance market. Bank debt structures have also become considerably more complex and the use of financial markets products in shipping finance transactions is now standard.

Freight rates and vessel values across all major shipping sectors have reached unprecedented levels in the last couple of years following a period of relatively depressed activity through the late 1990s and into the early part of the new millennium. A five year old Panamax bulk carrier, for example, could be purchased for US$13.5m and achieve freight rates of US$5,500 per day in 1999 while a similar profile vessel was worth US$46m and achieved freight rates in excess of US$46,000 per day in 2004/2005. This recent period of prosperity has seen the profile of shipping raised and resulted in a successful foray into the public equity markets by a number of owners. It has also raised the awareness of individual investors and shipowners alike to the benefits of tax partnerships and tax leases. More recently we have seen the tax leasing structures give way to new structures based on real economic risk. In most countries this is in the form of the more popular tonnage tax regimes. These regimes offer a favourable outcome when compared with investments made in land-based transportation activities.

The future of shipping continues to see one name at the forefront of all discussions: China. Not only is it significant in world trade, but its significance to the shipping industry as a whole continues to grow apace. The shipbuilding industry is a prime example. China, which accounted for no more than 5 per cent of the shipbuilding industry 2 years ago, now accounts for 19 per cent. This escalates them to third in the ranks of shipbuilding nations behind South Korea and Japan. The momentum shows no sign of abating, with China set to become the number one shipbuilding nation within the next couple of years. At the same time however, Japan and Korea show no sign of conceding capacity to compensate. It is a fair assumption therefore that shipbuilding capacity will be in abundance in the coming years. The ongoing imbalance between supply and demand will therefore continue to contribute to the volatility of the shipping market and continue to provide opportunities to those that are financially and economically aware.

The wide range of topics covered in this text book makes it an invaluable tool for all involved in shipping finance. Written and updated by experts in their fields, each chapter deals with the many issues faced by practitioners on a daily basis. This new edition covers not only the basics of shipping finance – with chapters on financing new and second hand vessels, standard security documents and sale and purchase – it also looks at the hot topics of the day including IPOs, derivatives and Islamic financing. Probably the most practical chapters are the two dealing with vessel and mortgage registration. Set out in a question and answer format for ease of comparison, these two chapters now contain contributions from both Indian and Chinese lawyers, in addition to updated contributions from lawyers in all major maritime jurisdictions, making this a must have manual for bankers, owners, brokers, lawyers and indeed all those involved in shipping finance.

July 2006

Preface

Over ten years have passed since the second edition of this book was published and a great deal has happened in the world of ship finance since then. We at Stephenson Harwood have written the third edition in order to ensure that it is still the practical ship finance manual it was designed to be.

The areas covered by the previous edititons of the book have been reviewed. The chapter on environmental issues has been omitted, not because this is no longer relevant, but simply because the Oil Pollution Act of 1990 has been around for some 16 years now and is so much part of shipping that it is no longer the hot topic it was in 1995. Ship finance is a global subject and we have therefore replaced the chapter on UK tax issues (which we felt was unlikely to be of interest to a large number of our readers) with a chapter on Islamic finance – an area of great interest at present.

The last few years have been great years for shipping, with historical highs achieved in the tanker, bulk and liner charter markets. Shipping has also made an impact on Wall Street thanks to the high volume of shipping IPOs, especially since 2004. We are delighted that we are able to include an updated chapter on the US Capital Markets, contributed by an expert in his field, Gary Wolfe, a man who has been involved in some form or another with almost every shipping IPO in recent years.

The shipping industry has become far more regulated in the past decade with the introduction, amongst other things, of the ISM Code in 1993 and the ISPS Code in 2002. The day-to-day impact of these far-reaching regulations can be seen in our updated questionnaire section in the chapter on vessel registration. The list of registries contributing to our chapters on vessel and mortgage registration has been updated to reflect current trends and we are very pleased that we have been able to include two new up-and-coming registries in our questionnaire sections – China and India.

Graham Burns did a wonderful job in editing the first two editions of this book and, indeed, wrote several of the chapters. We have been very fortunate to have such a strong foundation on which to build and for this, we owe Graham a huge debt of gratitude (and forgive him for declining our request to come out of 'retirement' to edit this 2006 edition).

Our thanks also to all the contributors to this third edition – to those lawyers who have provided detailed information on their respective flags and shipbuilding industries, to Doug Garnsey for rewriting the chapter on derivatives in shipping finance and Graham Barnes for updating his chapter on insurances and to Peter Illingworth and Alan Brauner for writing the chapter on the Banker's Perspective. Thanks also to all the other contributors within Stephenson Harwood – not only to those named as such in each chapter but especially to Philippa Sharratt, who helped to edit the various questionnaires, to June Pun who carried out a great deal of painstaking legal research and to Michael Bundock, whose comments and advice on many chapters were invaluable.

Finally we must repeat the word of warning with which Graham Burns ended the preface to the first and second editions. Any book of this nature can only contain advice in very general terms. Every transaction involves different considerations, both legal and commercial, and no book can be an adequate substitute for taking full and detailed professional advice in each individual situation. We have attempted to state the law at July 2006, unless otherwise indicated.

Lucy French and Jonathan Ward
Stephenson Harwood
One St. Paul's Churchyard
London
EC4M 8SH

July 2006

Author biographies

Graham Barnes

Graham Barnes is the founding Director of BankServe Insurance Services Ltd, Lloyds brokers, providing confidential insurance broking, claims recovery and insurance consultancy services to banks and financial institutions in respect of their ship, rig and aircraft financing operations. BankServe now acts for the majority of all shipping banks. Previously founder, Chairman and Managing Director of BankAssure Insurance Services Ltd when it operated as an autonomous company within Aon. Prior to that he was one of the founders and Managing Director of Bankscope Insurance Services Ltd which was eventually absorbed into BankAssure. Graham had the leading role in providing Certificates of Financial Responsibility under the US Oil Pollution Act 1990 and views the latest Athens Protocol 2002 as an even larger challenge for the International Group of Protection & Indemnity clubs.

Alan Brauner

Alan Brauner was formally Head of Shipping for Midland Bank in London, which was merged into HSBC in the early 1990's. He retired from HSBC in early 1994 but has remained working within the shipping industry in one form or another. A career banker for 39 years he joined Chase Manhattan Bank, London in 1955 where he established the European Shipping Division twelve years later. He left Chase in 1981 to join Midland Bank. Following retirement Alan became a consultant to Sinclair Roche & Temperley, which merged with Stephenson Harwood in May 2002. In December 1993 he was appointed a Non-Executive Director of F T Everard & Sons Ltd, a long established UK shipping company operating 35 vessels in the dry and wet coastal trades.

David Brookes

David Brookes is a senior assistant solicitor in the Banking and Asset Finance Department of Stephenson Harwood. He specialises in all forms of non-contentious shipping and has extensive experience in sale and purchase work and debt finance and leasing matters. He has previously spent three years in the Firm's Piraeus office. He is fluent in Norwegian.

Arlene Dourish

Arlene Dourish joined Stephenson Harwood from Sinclair Roche and Temperley in 1995 and became a partner in 2000. She acts for banks, lending institutions and shipowners in a wide variety of ship finance transactions including structured finance and leasing. She has specialised more recently in projects involving Islamic finance, through the second Shari'a compliant shipping fund set up in 2004.

Lucy French

Lucy French graduated in law from St Edmund Hall, Oxford in 1994, joined Stephenson Harwood the following year and was admitted as a solicitor in 1997. On qualification, she joined Stephenson Harwood's shipping department and has specialised since then in all aspects of ship finance work, including sale, purchase and registration of second hand vessels and the financing of both newbuildings and second hand vessels. She acts for both lenders and borrowers. Lucy became a partner in Stephenson Harwood's Banking and Asset Finance Department in 2005.

Douglas Garnsey

Douglas Garnsey joined the Corporate Risk Solutions Shipping team within the Markets Division of The Royal Bank of Scotland plc in July 2001. He works within a team dedicated to providing risk management solutions to the bank's global shipping client base. He specifically advises the bank's shipping clients based in Greece and Asia with regards to interest rate risk management.

Peter Illingworth

Peter Illingworth is General Manager and Head of Shipping in DVB Bank AG's London Branch. He joined DVB Bank in 1998. He started his career with ANZ Investment Bank in 1986 before moving to Kleinwort Benson and then Long Term Credit Bank of Japan (LTCB), where he was Head of Shipping Finance. He joined DVB following its acquisition of the LTCB Transportation business. After DVB's acquisition of Nedship Bank NV in 2000, he acted as Deputy Managing Director and Head of Risk Management at DVB Bank NV in Rotterdam for 2 years. Since 2002 he has been General Manager and Head of Shipping Finance in DVB's London Branch. He has 20 years of experience in banking, in 16 of which he has specialised in shipping finance. He holds a Master's degree from Pembroke College, Cambridge University.

Dora Kokota

Dora Kokota is of Greek origin. She studied for her LLB at the University of Sheffield and has an LLM from Cambridge University where she specialised in finance law. She joined Stephenson Harwood in 2004 as a trainee solicitor. In September 2006 she will qualify into the Banking and Asset Finance Department, where she will specialise in shipping finance.

Ian Mace

Ian Mace is an assistant solicitor in the Banking and Asset Finance Department of Stephenson Harwood. He graduated in law with European law from The University of Hull in 1999 and subsequently completed the Legal Practice Course at Nottingham Law School. He trained with Stephenson Harwood and qualified into their Banking and Asset Finance Department in 2004. He specialises in all aspects of ship finance.

Sheila Obhrai

Sheila Obhrai has specialised in Ship Finance since qualification and is a Senior Associate at Stephenson Harwood. She advises international banks and financial institutions on all aspects of bilateral and syndicated lending and in particular has advised a number of international banks on high profile complex syndicated transactions. Sheila has extensive experience in relation to all types of financing arrangements for new buildings and second hand vessels as well as vessel related project financings. Sheila acts for banks as well as shipowners including first class banks and owners in the Middle East.

Struan Robertson

Struan Robertson has practised in the maritime field for more than thirty years. He is Deputy Chairman of the International Maritime Industries Forum, a member of the Steering Committee of the London Shipping Law Centre and past chairman of the City of London Law Society Sub-Committee on Shipping and Aerospace law. He specialises in sale and purchase, shipbuilding, finance and cross-border leasing and has a particular interest in the C.I.S. and in the Gulf States due largely to an involvement with the tanker industry as a result of some years spent with a leading tanker owner in the Far East.

Mark Russell

Mark Russell is the head of Stephenson Harwood's Banking and Asset Finance Practice Group. He acts for a range of banks and other lending institutions, as well as shipowners and North Sea operators, in a wide variety of ship finance, leasing and sale and purchase matters, and in connection with oil and gas exploration and project financing.

Jonathan Ward

Jonathan Ward is a partner in the Banking and Asset Finance Department of Stephenson Harwood. He specialises in all aspects of ship finance including ship registration, sale and purchase, shipbuilding, structured ship finance and leasing matters, domestic and cross border. Jonathan represents ship finance institutions, lessors, shipowners, shipyards and contractors world-wide. Jonathan is a regular speaker at finance and shipping seminars and has lectured in the UK and abroad.

Gary J Wolfe

Gary J Wolfe is a partner of New York City law firm Seward & Kissel LLP, where he heads that firm's capital markets group. He represents domestic and international clients mainly in securities, corporate and maritime matters. Mr Wolfe graduated from Cornell University and Yale Law School, where he was a founding editor of the Yale Journal of World Public Order. Mr Wolfe has served as President of the US Business Council for South Eastern Europe, Chairman of the Admiralty and Maritime Law Committee of the New York County Lawyers Association and a member of the Admiralty and Maritime Law Committee of the Association of the Bar of the City of New York.

List of abbreviations

BIMCO	Baltic and International Maritime Counsel
CEXIM	The Export-Import Bank of China
CIRR	Commercial Interest Reference Rate
COFR	Certificate of Financial Responsibility
Dwt	deadweight
EBITAD	Earnings before Interest, Tax and Depreciation
ECGD	Export Credits Guarantee Department
FFE	forward foreign exchange
FFA	forward freight agreement
FFABA	Forward Freight Agreement Brokers Association
FRA	forward rate agreements
grt	gross registered tonnage
gt	gross tonnage
HSCGS	Home Shipbuilding Credit Guarantee Scheme
IMO	International Maritime Organisation
IOPC Funds	International Oil Pollution Compensation Funds
IPO	Initial Public Offering
IRS	Interest rate swap
ISDA	International Swaps and Derivatives Association
ISM Code	International Safety Management Code
ISPS Code	International Ship and Port Facility Security Code
ITF	International Transport Workers' Federation
KEXIM	The Export-Import Bank of Korea
LIBOR	London Interbank Offered Rate
LMAA	London Maritime Arbitrators' Association
MarAd	US Maritime Administration
MOA	memorandum of agreement
MTM	mark-to-market
MVC	mimimum value covenant
NIS	Norwegian International Ship Register
NOS	Norwegian Options Exchange
nrt	net registered tonnage

NSF	Norwegian Sale Form
NYMEX	New York Mercantile Exchange
NYSE	New York Stock Exchange
P&I clubs	protection and indemnity clubs
QIB	Qualified Institutional Buyer
SDR	Special Drawing Rights
SEC	Securities and Exchange Commission
SGA	Sale of Goods Act
SMFC	Ship Mortgage Finance Company plc
SOLAS	Safety of Life at Sea
SUECS	Sector Understanding on Export Credits for Ships
UCC	Uniform Commercial Code
US GAAP	US Generally Accepted Accounting Principles
VLCC	very large crude carrier

Chapter 1

Introduction

Updated by Lucy French

> *The method of obtaining finance for ships…may be summarised in these words. The bank advances to one or more owning companies a large sum of money. It of course requires security. It will take a mortgage on the ship for that security. It may take other mortgages on other ships for the same security. If the ship, as often happens, is about to be time chartered, then the bank will take an assignment of the time charter in order that the bank as assignee can benefit from the time charter in order to reduce the mortgage debt. In addition it will…take an assignment of insurance policies and P and I Club cover in order that in the event of total or partial loss of the ship the bank as the lender may be suitably secured…The effect of this is to ensure that the lending bank is completely secured against the insolvency of the borrower who intends that the bank shall obtain complete priority over the claims of other creditors against the borrower.[1]*

In general terms then, that is what ship finance and hence this book is all about. The bottom line of any ship finance deal is that a bank or some other lender advances money to a shipowner to assist the owner to build a new ship; buy a second-hand ship; convert, repair or alter a ship; or refinance existing indebtedness secured on a ship. The lender must be secured and looks, for his principal (though by no means only) security, to the ship itself.

Of course, there are many permutations, many refinements, many factors to be taken into account, and the aim of this book is to explore some of them. It is not intended to be a fully comprehensive textbook on shipping or banking. Rather, it is intended to highlight the particular factors that make ship finance different from other types of lending. One general topic not covered in this third edition is tax – not because it is no longer relevant, far from it. A discussion on the tax aspects of shipping finance, to be of any real value, would require an entire book. A single chapter would not do justice to such a huge subject.

Ship finance is no more a fixed science than is any other sort of finance. Financial terms and conditions change – especially in a cyclical industry such as shipping – and banks and owners become ever more sophisticated. Different types of vessel require lenders to take into account different considerations. Ultimately, though, the starting point is the same. The bank lends and the borrower secures the repayment of the loan by mortgaging his ship to the bank. Invariably there will be other security. What and why will be explored later.

The international element

More than most other forms of finance, ship finance is international. A ship is an unusual asset. Most ships move – or are capable of moving – all over the world. The financing of large ocean-going ships is undertaken by banks all over the world, by no means just for owners in

1

their own country. On the contrary, and certainly for larger ships and larger owners, one is more likely to find, for example, an American bank, acting through its London office, lending to a Greek-controlled owning company and securing itself on a Liberian registered ship. There may be a degree of patriotism – but if a foreign bank can offer better terms, then owners, accustomed to international dealings in the everyday operation of their ships, will not be troubled about dealing with foreign lenders.

There are two common elements. First, the universal currency of international shipping is the US dollar. Loans in other currencies, except to owners who operate their vessels within narrow geographical confines, such as ferry operators, and therefore have the bulk of their income in local currency, are relatively rare. For ships that trade worldwide, income will almost invariably be in US dollars and ships will be bought and sold in US dollars; hence, to limit exposure to currency fluctuations, loans (and loan repayments) will be in US dollars. (Although multi-currency options appear in facilities from time to time, they tend normally to be dollar based.)[2]

The second common element is the importance of English law. London remains one of the world's major shipping centres. Although major British owners are now few and far between, and the importance of the Baltic Exchange for fixing employment for ships has diminished as technology has advanced, a very large proportion of the world's fleet is insured or reinsured through the London insurance market and much financing is still done by banks in London. English law, and London arbitration, are common choices of parties to shipping contracts, such as charterparties, even where those parties have no obvious connection with England and where the ship may never come near an English port. This is not to play down the role of other legal systems: it is simply that historically English law has attained an ascendancy in the world of shipping which other legal systems have yet to succeed in shaking off.

Ship registration

Assets, generally speaking, fall into three categories. There are immovables (principally land); tangible movables (for example, ships, cars or furniture); and intangibles (for example, bank balances and trade creditors). Commonly, immovables are subject to some form of registration system – for example, in England title to most land is registered at HM Land Registry – but movables are not. Ships, however, are an exception to this general rule.

There are several reasons for this. First, ships travel the world. For a large part of their life they are on the high seas, outside the jurisdiction of any particular country. Secondly, they are more valuable assets than many other tangible movables and lenders will normally want to take security over them (which is difficult to do in many legal systems on an unregistered asset without physical possession). Thirdly, they are strategic assets, of great value in time of war. Fourthly, for economic and political reasons countries may wish to restrict certain types of trade to their own flag ships.

Not surprisingly, with a view to controlling the numerous national systems of registration and preventing a complete free for all, international law has intervened, chiefly by a series of United Nations (UN) conventions, mostly in the 1980s, including the 1982 UN Convention on the Law of the Sea (the 1982 Convention). Now signed by approximately 150 countries, the 1982 Convention only came into force on 16 November 1994, one year after it had been ratified by the required minimum of 60 countries.

Article 90 of the 1982 Convention provides that every state has the right to have a merchant fleet under its flag, and vessels in that fleet are entitled to the use of the high seas. Article 91 provides that 'every state shall fix the conditions for the grant of nationality to ships, for the registration of ships in its territory, and for the right to fly its flag. Ships have the nationality of the state whose flag they are entitled to fly. There must be a genuine link between the state and the ship'.'

The 1982 Convention stops there and does not tell us what constitutes a 'genuine link'. The 1986 UN Convention on Conditions for Registration of Ships tries to help by describing the requirement of a genuine link as meaning that nationals of the flag state must participate in the ownership, manning or management of the vessel. This Convention has not yet been signed by a sufficient number of countries to come into force and it is unlikely that it will. Certainly, it has not been signed by many important ship registry jurisdictions.

As anyone with any involvement with the shipping industry will know, this is not how ship registration works in practice.

The different types of registry

Traditionally, a ship owned by a national of a particular country was registered in that country and crewed by nationals of that country. It was subject to the jurisdiction of the authorities of that country, and was liable to requisition by those authorities in time of war. In many countries, the owner had no say in the matter and registration was obligatory. In the United Kingdom, registration of British ships was compulsory from the Navigation Acts of 1660 onwards. Section 2 of the Merchant Shipping Act 1894, which codified the previous law and held sway for over 90 years, made it mandatory for a British ship (subject to certain minor exemptions) to be registered in accordance with the Act. Although not specifically defined in the Act, the term 'British ship' meant, in summary, any ship owned by a British subject or a body corporate established under the laws of some part of Her Majesty's dominions, with a principal place of business in those dominions.

Only in 1989, with the coming into force of the Merchant Shipping Act 1988, did the rules change so that a British ship was entitled to be registered, and was the only type of ship entitled to be registered, in the United Kingdom, but was no longer under any obligation to be registered. Now, under the Merchant Shipping Act 1995, the test is that a majority of the shares in the ship must be owned by someone with 'a British connection'.[3]

Since the middle of the twentieth century there has been a marked change in the operation of ship registries and the expression 'flag of convenience' is now well known. The historical background is that, before and after the Second World War, several countries began to open up their ship registers to all comers. Beginning with the use of the Panamanian flag by US cruise ship operators during the prohibition years, the trail blazers were the so-called PanLibHon registers – Panama, Liberia and Honduras. Although Honduras has declined dramatically in importance (it is now only just inside the top 50 registries in terms of gross tonnage), Panama and Liberia have had sufficient success to make them, by gross registered tonnage, the world's two largest fleets. More recently, other countries have joined the club, including Cyprus, the Bahamas and the Marshall Islands.

The chief distinguishing characteristic of these open registers is their lack of restriction. As will be seen in more detail later, anyone can, broadly speaking, register his ship on one of

3

these registers, as long as the ship satisfies the register's requirements as to, for example, age and technical standards. Sometimes, as in Cyprus, it is necessary to set up a locally registered company to own the ship, but normally a shelf company can be acquired in a matter of hours and usually there are no restrictions on the nationality or identity of the directors or shareholders. Chapter 11 deals in more detail with vessel registration and the ownership requirements for various flags.

As well as being unrestricted as to ownership, the open registers for the most part impose no restrictions on the nationality of the officers and crew employed on vessels registered on them, though officers must normally satisfy certain technical standards. Again, this compares with the traditional national registers, where strict requirements for officers and crews, either as to nationality or as to pay rates, are frequently imposed. This has a dramatic impact on the running costs of a vessel, for the obvious reason that crews from less developed countries come much cheaper than those from developed nations. Some national registers have fought back, with the introduction by their governments of tonnage tax schemes. In addition to providing strong tax incentives for owners to enter the scheme and thereby boost that country's maritime industry, many tonnage tax schemes have made a commitment by the prospective tonnage tax company to seafarer training a compulsory requirement for acceptance of that company on the scheme. Such a requirement helps to expand the pool of qualified officers in that country.

Nevertheless, crews from developing countries have become, to a large extent, the norm. Many owners will say, not without some justification, that without the latitude to employ cheap crew they would have been forced out of business long ago. Their arguments have not found much favour with the International Transport Workers' Federation (ITF) which has waged a long and vigorous campaign to protect these seamen from exploitation. One result of the campaign has been the designation by the ITF of certain registers – principally the open registers – with the supposedly pejorative term 'flag of convenience'. Any ship registered under a flag of convenience is liable to be subject to action such as blacking by members of ITF-affiliated unions unless it can produce a certificate that it has satisfied the ITF that its crew's conditions of employment meet certain minimum standards.

The ITF has another concern, which brings us to another criticism often made of the open registers. The ITF is not just concerned with the financial well-being of seafarers, but also their physical well-being, and continues to campaign against what it sees as unacceptably low safety standards on ships. The safety standards applicable on board ships are ultimately a matter for the flag state, which may or may not adhere to certain internationally accepted standards. Safety concerns and a desire to raise standards worldwide, resulted in the International Maritime Organisation (the United Nations' agency responsible for improving, among other things, maritime safety) introducing the International Safety Management Code (ISM Code) in the mid-1990s.[4] The ISM Code has made it compulsory since 1 July 1998 for ships and their owners and managers to have adequate safety management systems in place, both on board and ashore. Governments are responsible for carrying out ISM audits and for issuing certificates showing that the ISM Code has been complied with by a ship and its owners and managers. Ships without valid ISM Code certification are prevented from trading. Owners (and their lenders) will therefore avoid registries who fail to monitor these international standards to an acceptable level and have neither the resources nor the technical expertise under their control to meet their obligations under the ISM Code.

Similarly, following the terrorist attacks of 11 September 2001, governments recognised the need to put in place a worldwide set of security rules for both ships and ports, to make the shipping industry less vulnerable to terrorist attack. The International Ship and Port Facility Security Code (ISPS Code) came into force on 1 July 2004[5] and, with a very few exceptions, applies to all passenger and cargo ships and to all port facilities servicing such ships, engaged in international voyages. Ship registries are responsible for setting the security levels and requirements for ships entitled to fly their flag and for monitoring compliance. A ship without valid ISPS Code documentation will not be able to trade and, as with the ISM Code, open registries who are unable to carry out their ISPS Code obligations will find that no matter how attractive a choice they may otherwise be, they will not be acceptable to either owners or lenders.

As well as the traditional open registers, such as Liberia and Panama, two other types of register have developed. The offshore register is typically a register established in a colony or dependency of a particular country, with a view to attracting the registration of ships from that country which might otherwise go to an open register. The United Kingdom led the way, with offshore registers in places as diverse as Bermuda, Gibraltar, the Isle of Man and the Cayman Islands and Dutch shipping has taken advantage of the Netherlands Antilles.

In many cases, these dependencies are well established as centres for offshore finance and the use of their ship registers has followed almost accidentally. Their general approach is to allow owners to fly the flag of the home country (such as the Red Ensign), while imposing less strict requirements for ownership and crewing than the home register. There may also be tax advantages in operating in a tax haven jurisdiction with low, or no, corporation tax and, very possibly, no obligation to deduct income tax or national insurance at source from officers' and crews' wages. Many of the offshore registers are also classified as flags of convenience by the ITF, either completely or on a vessel-by-vessel basis depending on the nationality of the vessel's ultimate owner.

The other type of register is the international register. This is much the same as the offshore register but does not rely for its existence on the accident of a convenient dependency and is set up in the home country and run parallel to the domestic register. Much the most successful example of this species is the Norwegian International Ship Register (NIS), set up in 1987. Other countries with international registers are Denmark, Turkey and Italy. At the time of writing, Russia is also about to set up a second register and France is replacing its offshore register (Kerguelen) with a second register. Conditions of entry differ, but the principal aim is similar to that of the offshore register: the national flag may be flown without some of the restrictions that otherwise entails. However, unlike the accidental development of some of the offshore registers in established offshore financial centres, the international registers are entirely creatures of expediency, established in a conscious effort to attract tonnage back from the open registers.

Statistics reveal the rise of the open registers. Exhibit 1.1 shows the world's 10 largest fleets, by gross registered tonnage (grt), at five-yearly intervals since 1974.[6] The rise of the open registers will be apparent, though it is worth noting the continuing significant market shares of some of the traditional maritime nations, notably Greece, Japan and, until recently, the United States. The Greek situation is worthy of note, for some time ago Greece took positive steps to arrest the trend towards flagging out. Although Greek owners have been no more immune than others to the economic pressures of the shipping industry since the Second World War, and many Greek owners have flagged out, particularly to Cyprus, successive Greek governments have sought, by the use of fiscal incentives, to maintain the use of the Greek flag by Greek owners.

Exhibit 1.1

The world's top 10 registered fleets by grt – 1974 to 2004

1974

1	Liberia	55,321,641
2	Japan	38,707,659
3	UK	31,566,298
4	Norway	24,852,917
5	Greece	21,759,449
6	USSR	18,175,918
7	USA	14,429,076
8	Panama	11,003,227
9	Italy	9,722,015
10	France	8,834,519

1979

1	Liberia	81,528,175
2	Japan	39,992,925
3	Greece	37,352,597
4	UK	27,951,342
5	USSR	22,900,201
6	Norway	22,349,337
7	Panama	22,323,931
8	USA	17,542,220
9	France	11,945,837
10	Italy	11,694,872

1984

1	Liberia	62,024,700
2	Japan	40,358,749
3	Panama	37,244,233
4	Greece	35,058,593
5	USSR	24,492,469
6	USA	19,291,868
7	Norway	17,662,916
8	UK	15,874,062
9	PRC	9,300,358
10	Italy	9,157,867

(Continued)

Exhibit 1.1 *(Continued)*

1989

1	Liberia	47,892,529
2	Panama	47,365,362
3	Japan	28,030,425
4	USSR	25,853,712
5	Greece	21,324,340
6	USA	20,587,812
7	Cyprus	18,134,011
8	Norway	15,596,900
9	PRC	13,513,578
10	Bahamas	11,578,891

1994

1	Panama	64,170,219
2	Liberia	57,647,708
3	Greece	30,161,758
4	Cyprus	23,292,954
5	Bahamas	22,915,349
6	Japan	22,101,606
7	Norway (NIS)	19,976,489
8	Russia	16,503,871
9	PRC	15,826,688
10	Malta	15,455,370

1999

1	Panama	99,749,102
2	Liberia	57,179,231
3	Malta	25,518,507
4	Bahamas	25,478,573
5	Greece	24,251,781
6	Cyprus	22,239,967
7	Singapore	21,126,078
8	Norway (NIS)	18,428,456
9	Japan	14,538,938
10	USA	14,252,729

2004

1	Panama	127,753,074
2	Liberia	52,229,133
3	Bahamas	32,706,405
4	Greece	32,035,847
5	Hong Kong	25,405,871
6	Singapore	24,975,904
7	Malta	21,972,693
8	Marshall Islands	21,949,834
9	Cyprus	20,525,024
10	PRC	18,015,105

Sources: Lloyd's Register of Shipping Statistical Tables 1991 and 1992; Lloyd's Register of Shipping World Fleet Statistics 1993 and 1994; Lloyds Register Fairplay data, 2006.

Exhibit 1.2

The world's four largest open registers by grt 1974–2004

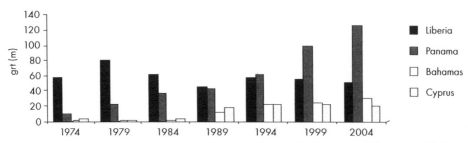

Sources: Lloyd's Register of Shipping Statistical Tables 1991 and 1992; Lloyd's Register of Shipping World Fleet Statistics 1993 and 1994; Lloyd's Register of Fairplay Data, 2006.

Exhibit 1.3

Four traditional maritime nations grt 1974–2004

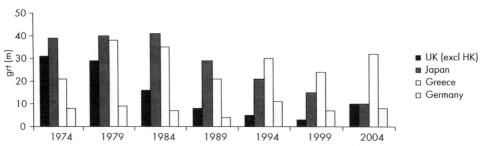

Sources: Lloyd's Register of Shipping Statistical Tables 1991 and 1992; Lloyd's Register of Shipping World Fleet Statistics 1993 and 1994; Lloyd's Register of Fairplay Data, 2006.

Exhibit 1.2 shows, by way of illustration, the record of the four largest open registers – Liberia, Panama, Cyprus and the Bahamas. The dramatic rise of the Bahamas is very noticeable, as is the continuing rise of Panama. By way of contrast, Exhibit 1.3 shows the relative performance of four traditional maritime nations; Japan, the United Kingdom, Greece and the Federal Republic of Germany. The relative stability of the Greek flag, under generally pro-shipping governments has already been noted; the demise of UK flag shipping, under a series of governments which have consistently adopted a non-interventionist shipping policy, is readily apparent although there has been a marked growth in the last five years shown, perhaps due to the UK tonnage tax scheme. In each case, the figures shown are for the gross registered tonnage registered under that flag in the years in question.

Exhibit 1.4 compares all eight nations in terms of percentage of the world fleet (again by grt) and, for the sake of completeness, Exhibit 1.5 shows the changing size of the world fleet during the same period. The moral is clear. The economics of lower operating costs prevail over the fine words of the UN Conventions. It is also of interest to note the average

Exhibit 1.4

Comparative percentage of world fleet by grt 1974–2004

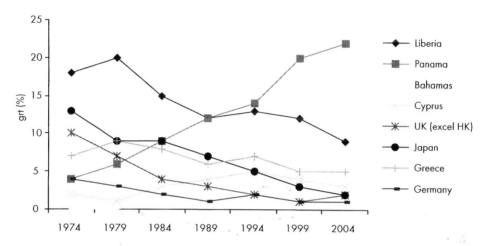

Sources: Lloyd's Register of Shipping Statistical Tables 1991 and 1992; Lloyd's Register of Shipping World Fleet Statistics 1993 and 1994; Lloyd's Register of Fairplay Data, 2006.

Exhibit 1.5

Changing size of world fleet by grt 1974–2004

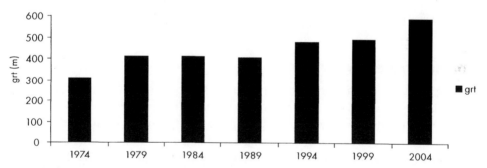

Sources: Lloyd's Register of Shipping Statistical Tables 1991 and 1992; Lloyd's Register of Shipping World Fleet Statistics 1993 and 1994; Lloyd's Register of Fairplay Data, 2006.

age of vessel on the world's registers. Singapore (11 years) and Liberia, Hong Kong and the Marshall Islands (12 years) have the youngest fleets. Traditional national registers such as Sweden (30 years), Finland (31 years) and Canada (29 years) are among the oldest, and the Isle of Man (10 years) is the youngest of all. An understanding of these basic facts of shipping life is essential for anyone operating in shipping finance. Later on, we will look at some of the more detailed requirements of the various registries.[6] What, though, is the significance of the flag of a ship for a lender?

The basic answer is that the law of the flag will invariably govern the mortgage which will be a fundamental part of the lender's security. Again, detailed consideration of the mortgage laws of the principal ship registration jurisdictions will come in Chapter 7, but the crucial question for a lender will always be whether the mortgage will give the lender the security he requires. A lender will also always be concerned to ensure that the ship satisfies the requirements of the flag state. If it does not, the registration will be liable to be avoided and with it may go the lender's mortgage. Other factors for a lender will be the extent of any regulatory requirements with which the owner will need to comply as a result of having his ship registered on the flag in question – for example, a Cyprus ship must be owned by a Cypriot or a Cypriot company, and the lender will be concerned to ensure that a Cypriot owning company has suitable offshore status to allow it to service foreign currency debt.

The policy adopted by lenders differs. Some will have no concern about the flag flown by the vessel, so long as they are convinced, perhaps on the strength of an opinion from a local lawyer, that their security by way of registered mortgage is adequate. Others, with the same end in mind, will turn down without question ships not registered on certain registers with a proven track record of security enforcement by mortgagees.

Lenders should, however, look rather further than this. For example, a lender should consider whether the vessel's flag state will impose and enforce acceptable safety and technical standards. This is especially true, as we have seen, following the introduction of first the ISM Code and then the ISPS Code. A lender will, generally speaking, be looking to the ship's earning capacity as the primary source of the debt service, and will be none too keen to have the ship delayed or detained because of failure to meet acceptable technical standards. He will also need to consider the way in which the legal system of the flag state deals with maritime liens: in some countries a wide range of claims against the vessel will take priority to the rights of a mortgagee on a forced sale.[7] Lastly, the political stability of the flag state may be an issue.

Bareboat charter registration

Bareboat or demise charter registration, frequently known as parallel registration, is a system that has developed in certain (though by no means all) countries. It allows the registration of a vessel in that country to be temporarily suspended for the duration of a bareboat, or demise charter, with the vessel being registered in the name of the charterer on an alternative register for the duration of the charter, during which time it may fly the flag of the charterer's chosen register.

The precise conditions on which different countries permit bareboat charter registration out from, or in to, their ship registers vary, and are detailed in Chapter 11. However, some of the relevant features are listed below.

- The owner's title remains registered on the primary register, his registration being not terminated, but merely suspended.
- Similarly, mortgages will remain registered on the primary register. Mortgagees' consent will usually be required for any bareboat charter registration, but there is frequently no procedure for the mortgage to be registered or even noted on the secondary register – as the vessel will be flying the flag of the country of the secondary register third parties will be

unaware of the country of the primary register. This lack of transparency can create concern for lenders, even though their security rights should not be adversely affected.

- As mentioned above, the vessel will fly the flag of the country of the secondary register for the duration of the bareboat charter (though sometimes subject to periodic renewal of the temporary registration during the life of the charter).

Charterers of vessels let on bareboat charter may require the vessel to be temporarily registered on the register of their choice. This is particularly important (a) where specific cargoes or geographical trades are limited to vessels flying certain flags; (b) in leasing transactions where the lessee/charterer will not want the choice of the vessel's flag to be determined by any mandatory requirements of the lessor's country of incorporation; and (c) where the country of the charterer's chosen register does not have a system of mortgage registration considered adequate by international banks – financing through bareboat charter registration (that is, lending to a single ship company in an acceptable jurisdiction then permitting bareboat charter registration by the ultimate shipowner, as bareboat charterer, in a less acceptable jurisdiction) can resolve this issue.

The one-ship company

Apart from 'flag of convenience', the other shipping term with which many laymen will be familiar is 'one-ship company'. Commonly, though by no means invariably, a shipowner will establish a separate company to own each ship in his fleet. Occasionally, this will be dictated by the requirements of the flag – for example, the requirement (generally speaking) for a Liberian ship to be owned by a Liberian company will mean that the ship will necessarily be in separate ownership from a Cyprus flag ship in the same ultimate ownership, which must be owned by a Cypriot company. There may be administrative or fiscal advantages. However, the main reason relates to arrest.

The International Convention relating to the Arrest of Seagoing Ships was signed on behalf of the United Kingdom in 1952. Article 3 of the convention provides that 'a claimant may arrest either the particular ship in respect of which the maritime claim arose, or any other ship which is owned by the person who was, at the time when the maritime claim arose, the owner of the particular ship'. Article 3 was introduced into English law by the Administration of Justice Act 1956. The current English law on what has come to be known commonly as 'sister ship arrest' is found in Section 21 of the Supreme Court Act 1981. This provides that:

[...] in the case of any such claim as is mentioned in Section 20 (2) (e) to (r),[8] where:

(a) the claim arises in connection with a ship; and
(b) the person who would be liable on a claim on an action *in personam* ('the relevant person') was, when the cause of action arose, the owner or charterer of, or in possession or control of, the ship, an action *in rem*[9] may (whether or not the claim gives raise to a maritime lien on that ship) be brought in the High Court against:
    (i) that ship, if at the time when the action is brought the relevant person is either the beneficial owner of that ship as respects all the shares in it or the charterer of it under a charter by demise; or

>   (ii) any other ship of which, at the time when the action is brought, the relevant
>   person is the beneficial owner as respects all the shares in it.

In other words a claimant is not restricted to arresting the ship against which his claim arose, but may also arrest any other ship in the same beneficial ownership when the action was brought. Most other maritime jurisdictions have similar provisions. Some, for example South Africa, have even more extensive sister ship arrest rights.

The obvious solution, therefore, is to register each ship in a particular owner's fleet in the name of a different company, each company being a subsidiary of the parent company or owned by the individual shipowner. Certainly in English law, the separate legal personality of each company is sufficient to prevent a ship owned by one of these one-ship companies being arrested for claims against other ships in the same group. This was tested as recently as 1988, when the Court of Appeal gave judgment in the case of the 'EVPO AGNIC'.[10] The then Master of the Rolls, Lord Donaldson of Lymington, summarised the position as follows.

> The truth of the matter, as I see it, is that Section 21 [of the Supreme Court Act 1981] does not go, and is not intended to go, nearly far enough to give the plaintiffs a right of arresting a ship which is not the 'particular ship' or a sister ship, but the ship of a sister company of the owners of the 'particular ship'.[11]

He drew an important distinction between the beneficial ownership of the ship and the beneficial ownership of the shares in the owning company, holding that the ship (owned by a traditional one-ship company) was both legally and beneficially owned by that company and that:

> [...] any division between legal and equitable interests occurs in relation to the registered owner itself, which is almost always a juridical person. The legal property in its shares may well be held by A and the equitable property by B, but this does not affect the ownership of the ship or of the shares in that ship. They are the legal and equitable property of the Company.[12]

The use of the one-ship company has two principal implications for lenders. The first is an advantage. It makes the mortgaged ship immune from arrest for claims against other ships in the owner's fleet (though if the lender has secured himself by mortgages on all the ships in the fleet this advantage disappears). No lender wishes the earning capacity of a mortgaged ship to be adversely affected as a result of a claim totally unrelated to that ship.

The second implication is that the lender will be lending to a borrower with no assets of any consequence other than the ship. Apart from the ship (and its insurances and earnings) the borrower will be unable to offer any other assets to the lender by way of security or as a source of income for debt repayment and service.

This makes the enforceability of the mortgage of crucial importance. It also means that the lender must look elsewhere for additional security, often by way of a guarantee from the ultimate parent of the one-ship company, perhaps backed by security over its assets. An alternative approach, sometimes used for large corporate groups, is for the lender to lend to the parent and to take guarantees from each shipowning subsidiary, those guarantees being backed by mortgages over the owning companies' vessels. Where one-ship companies are used, shipping finance is asset finance in the narrowest sense of the term because if the ship, for whatever reason, disappears the lender will, for all practical purposes, have no recourse to the borrower and will be left to look to his secondary lines of security.

[1] Lord Justice Roskill, the 'PANGLOBAL FRIENDSHIP' [1978] 1 Lloyd's Rep. 368 @ 371.

[2] See Chapter 2.

[3] See Section 9 of The Merchant Shipping Act 1995 and Regulations 7 and 8 of The Merchant Shipping (Registration of Ships) Regulations 1993, Regulation 7 as amended by The Merchant Shipping (Registration of Ships) (Amendment) Regulations 1998, which came into force on 1 January 1999 and the British Overseas Territories Act 2002, which came into force on 26 February 2002 and Regulation 8 as amended by The Merchant Shipping (Registration of Ships) (Amendment) Regulations 1994.

[4] The International Management Code for the Safe Management of Ships and for Pollution Prevention, as adopted by the Assembly of the International Maritime Organisation on 4 November 1993 by Resolution A.741 (18) and incorporated on 19 May 1994 as Chapter X of the Safety of Life at Sea Convention 1974.

[5] The International Ship and Port Security Code as adopted by the Conference of Contracting Governments to the Safety of Life at Sea Convention 1974 on 13 January 2002 and incorporated as Chapter XI-2 of the Safety of Life at Sea Convention 1974.

[6] See Chapter 11.

[7] For further details see Chapter 7.

[8] These categories include (among others) claims such as claims for general average, disbursements, crew wages, salvage, towage, damage done by the ship and loss or damage to goods carried on board.

[9] Hence the right to arrest.

[10] [1988] 2 Lloyd's Rep. 411.

[11] Ibid., 415.

[12] Ibid., 415.

Chapter 2

The financing of second-hand ships

Updated by Mark Russell

From 2004 onwards, reflecting the boom times in the shipping market, there has been considerable activity in the newbuilding markets and in large fleet refinances, where owners have locked into the comparatively cheap pricing available in the bank market in 2004/2006, but traditionally the financing of second-hand ships remains the bread and butter of a shipping bank's business.

Self-evidently, bank finance for second-hand ships is generally used to assist an owner in purchasing a second-hand ship, but it is also often used in refinancing existing facilities secured on ships already owned by the borrower. Refinancing is largely the result of competition between lenders – owners will generally approach more than one lender to finance a new acquisition and it is not uncommon for owners to switch lenders during the life of a facility where a different lender is able to offer better terms, particularly to refinance balloon instalments at the end of the life of a loan.

Types of lender

Most of the analysis contained in this chapter, as elsewhere in this book, is specifically directed at bank lending. That is not to say that many of the general principles are not equally applicable to, for example, inter-company borrowing or borrowing from institutions other than banks. Except perhaps in financing through tax-based leasing and, for some larger owners, financing through the issue of debt securities and IPOs (Initial Public Offerings) on a stock exchange there is little institutional lending to the shipping industry other than by banks and, to a relatively minor extent except in their own particular geographical market, by the Japanese trading houses. Where companies other than banks are lending, it is important always to check their constitutional documents and to take appropriate local legal advice, in order to ensure that the lending company has the corporate capacity to lend and take security, and that any local restrictions (for example, as to exchange control) are complied with.

The majority of shipping lending is carried out by large international commercial banks, for which shipping lending will be just one of a vast range of products offered to customers. This has both advantages and disadvantages for borrowers. On the plus side, the major international banks will have a substantial capital base and will generally be able to offer the borrower their own in-house treasury products, electronic banking and other facilities which are becoming increasingly important as shipowner borrowers become more sophisticated. On the minus side, large banks may see shipping as something of a backwater and simply a training ground for bank executives, with the result that there can be a lack of continuity of personnel and expertise. In a specialised and cyclical industry such as shipping, personnel with experience and proven track records are just as important on the bank's side as they undoubtedly are on the borrower's; after all, a bank would be very wary about lending to an owning company whose executives have changed constantly at three- or four-year intervals or who have no practical experience of working through the issues raised by market downturns.

At the other end of the banking spectrum there are the specialist shipping banks such as those found in Germany and the Netherlands. Here the pros and cons are exactly the reverse of those of the large international banks. Bankers in the specialist banks will frequently have been in shipping finance for many years and it is not uncommon for them to have a background of sea-faring or working for shipowners. Either of these backgrounds will give the banker a valuable insight into the workings of the shipping industry. Set against this, however, is the vulnerability of the specialist banks to industry-driven market forces (the 'all the eggs in one basket' syndrome). Outlooks may be too narrow – specialist banks are often perceived as the most traditional and least innovative. Often, too, the lack of a substantial capital base leads to a requirement to syndicate from the start facilities which other banks would underwrite themselves.

Between the two extremes are certain smaller domestic or international banks which have traditionally had a shipowning customer base, and lastly, there are government owned or backed banks in many countries, which generally limit their lending to support their domestic owners or domestic shipbuilding.

Which type of lender should a borrower choose? The answer depends very much on what the borrower wants from his lender – each type has its own particular attraction. Some borrowers will appreciate the stability and personal nature of their dealings with the small specialist banks. Others will prefer the, perhaps, greater flexibility of dealing with the big boys. The upturn in vessel values in 2003–2006 brought some new names into the ship finance market, at a time when margins fell strongly and (in some cases) covenants were relaxed. Those without a strong background in shipping may find it harder to deal with downturns in the freight markets and in asset values.

Loan and guarantee facilities

The term loan

Most lending secured on second-hand ships is by way of term loan or reducing revolving credits. In other words, the lender will lend to the shipowner a fixed amount repayable over a set period of time – the 'term'. In its simplest form, the loan will be available to the borrower in one drawing only and will be repayable in equal instalments over the duration of the term, either by way of repayments (in the case of a term loan) or by repayments and redrawings against reducing availability amounts (in the case of a revolver) most likely payable every three or six months. As has already been seen, the US dollar is the almost universal currency of shipping, and loans (other than those made by the domestic branches of US banks and the less common loans made in other currencies) will therefore generally be funded in the Eurodollar markets in western Europe and, most commonly, in London.

Interest will almost invariably be fixed by reference to the London Interbank Offered Rate (Libor), now frequently by reference to the Reuters ISDA page or its Telerate equivalent rather than to any actual cost of funds to the particular lending bank. The bank's return on the facility thus derives from the margin over Libor which it is able to charge the borrower (and any fees payable by the borrower to the bank). The size of the margin that the bank is able to charge is very much a reflection of the standing and bargaining position of the borrower, of the perceived risk to the bank in doing the particular deal and of the number of banks chasing that borrower's business. Prime shipping names, whose accounts are sought by several banks, are able to borrow at a very fine margin – in the current competitive climate at significantly less than 1 per cent over Libor. Owners whose track record is less established or who have a lower reputation in the market will pay higher margins.

The actual interest rate will be fixed periodically during the term of the loan, with the borrower usually given the option of fixing his interest rate for three- or six-month periods throughout the term. Frequently one month (sometimes at a higher margin), nine months and 12 months will also be available options. The borrower is normally permitted to select the length of each interest period two or three banking days before the interest period begins, to enable the bank to borrow matching funds in the money market if necessary and to enable the borrower to form an on-the-spot assessment about future interest rate movements. Loan documents will contain provisions fixing the length of the interest periods if the borrower fails to make his selection. Interest will be payable at the end of each interest period, and it is normal for borrowers to be required to pay interest at least every six months, even if the interest period is longer. Borrowers may, if they wish, protect themselves from extreme interest rate movements or fix interest rates for longer periods by using some of the increasingly developed and tailored treasury products on offer from most lenders, for example, interest rate swaps, caps, collars and floors (see Chapter 5), and increasingly banks are requiring some or all of the interest exposure on a transaction to be fixed by means of such an instrument.

The length of the term can vary enormously. Somewhere between four and 10 years is probably commonest in second-hand ship financing and up to 12 years for newbuilding finance. Equal quarterly or half yearly repayments have the attraction of simplicity but there is no point in fixing repayment instalments that bear no relation to the earning capacity of the vessel or vessels being financed. Hence many facilities, particularly when second-hand ship values are high, provide for a 'balloon' repayment, that is, a significantly larger final repayment, the intention being that the borrower will finance the repayment of the balloon either by refinancing with the same, or another, lender, or by selling the vessel. For certain types of vessel, for example, fishing or cruise vessels, where income does not arise at a constant rate over the course of a year, a seasonally adjusted repayment profile may be more appropriate.

Making the loan available in a single drawing is obviously appropriate where the loan is being made to assist the borrower to purchase a vessel. However, banks will often offer term loan facilities to groups of companies to enable them to purchase more than one vessel, or to refinance facilities secured on more than one vessel. In those circumstances, the bank may wish to allow multiple drawings up to the maximum amount of the facility. Drawings will be subject to a minimum amount, and there will be a cut-off date after which no further drawings will be permitted.

The revolving facility

Term loan facilities will provide that amounts repaid cannot be re-borrowed. In a revolving facility, amounts repaid are made available for re-borrowing, up to the maximum amount of the facility. Revolving facilities are particularly appropriate for shipowning groups that buy and sell ships on a regular basis, allowing them to repay on selling vessels and draw on the revolving facility to purchase new tonnage (approved by the bank) without having to negotiate a new facility. Revolving facilities can also be useful where the loan is being made available for working capital purposes rather than for buying vessels into the group.

Apart from allowing repayments to be redrawn, a revolving facility differs little from a multiple drawdown term loan. Normally the whole facility will still need to be repaid by a fixed date, interest will be calculated and fixed in much the same way, and the loan documents will contain identical representations and warranties, covenants, conditions precedent, events of default and so on.

The guarantee facility

Although banks may be asked to issue guarantees in connection with the financing of newbuildings, it is unusual for second-hand ships to be sold on credit terms. On the rare occasions when a seller will be prepared to deliver a ship to a buyer without being paid in full, the seller will rarely rely on the credit of a one-ship company and will normally require comfort from a third party, usually a bank, unless the buyer can produce a satisfactory guarantee from, for example, its parent company.

In structural terms, a guarantee facility is straightforward. The bank agrees to issue the required guarantee when called on to do so, while the owner agrees to counter-indemnify the bank for any sums that the bank is called on to pay under the guarantee and pays the bank a commission, usually calculated on an annual basis, for its services. The owner will secure the counter-indemnity in the same way as a loan, by mortgaging the ship to the bank and by granting some or all of the other security discussed later. Although historically there were doubts in some jurisdictions about the ability of a shipowner legally to grant a mortgage to secure a contingent obligation, those doubts have now been resolved in all major ship registration jurisdictions.

In a guarantee facility, the critical factor for the bank is to ensure that it will be able to enforce the counter-indemnity as soon as it has paid under its guarantee. Counter-indemnities will, therefore, contain many of the protective clauses found in guarantees[1] and, most importantly, will contain provisions imposing liability on the owner as soon as the bank makes a payment in good faith under the guarantee, even if the bank is subsequently shown not to have been under a legal obligation to do so.

Syndicated loans

Historically, as ship values rose it became increasingly common for individual banks to wish to share their lending obligations with others. Sometimes this derived from regulatory requirements, either external or internal, limiting banks' ability to lend, or perhaps to lend to a particular country or in a particular industry such as shipping. At other times it derived purely from a commonsense desire to spread risk. Hence, particularly with large loan facilities to groups, syndicated lending became more common. In a syndicated loan a group of banks will each commit themselves to make part of the loan. One bank (the agent) will administer the facility on behalf of the syndicate, dealing with the fixing of interest rates, receiving repayments and accounting to the other syndicate members. Frequently, though not invariably, the agent role will be taken by the bank making available the largest share of the total loan.

Syndicated loan agreements will make clear that each bank's obligation to lend is entirely separate from the obligations of the others. In other words, if one bank, for any reason, fails to make its part of the loan available, the other members of the syndicate are not obliged to step in. Syndicated loan agreements will also contain a series of provisions regulating the relationship between the syndicate members and the agent. (This is sometimes contained in a separate agreement.)

For a borrower, borrowing from a syndicate presents few changes from borrowing from a single bank because the borrower's everyday relationship will normally be with the agent alone. The banks, however, must agree between themselves at the outset whether such decisions as amendments to the facility, the enforcement of security and the giving of consents are to be made by the agent alone, by the banks acting unanimously or by a specified majority (by number or value) of the banks. Generally, unanimity will be required for the most major decisions, such as the release or variation of any security, the waiver of any payments, the extension of any repayment or interest payment dates, or any step that may increase the obligations of any of the banks. A syndicated loan agency clause (or agreement) will also contain provisions protecting the agent, for example, clauses putting the onus for credit assessments onto each lending bank and making clear that the agent is only obliged to account to the other syndicate members for amounts actually received. It is, however, important for a borrower from a syndicate to appreciate that although he may only deal directly with the agent, the agent's relationship with the other lenders is likely to give the agent less flexibility in dealing with the borrower than a sole lender would have. Problems have arisen, particularly with syndicates containing numerous or less-experienced banks, when one bank has effectively been able to hold the others to ransom by vetoing, for example, a planned restructuring, although as banks take bigger 'tickets', even with increasing loan sizes the number of banks in a typical syndicate has probably reduced over the last few years.

One question that often arises in syndicated shipping loans is whether the security should be taken in favour of all the banks or simply in favour of the agent (or another bank as security agent or trustee) on behalf of the members of the syndicate. So long as the agency clause or agreement, or a separate security trust deed, properly deals with the relationship of the syndicate members both to each other and to the security agent or trustee, and so long as security documents make clear that they are taken by the security agent or trustee on behalf of the syndicate members, it is much neater and administratively easier (for example, when it comes to the discharge or variation of the security) for the security documents to be in favour of one bank only.

However, care must be taken to ensure that ship mortgages, which will be governed by the law of the flag, may, according to their local law, be taken in favour of a security agent or trustee. A Liberian mortgage, for example, may be taken in favour of one bank acting as trustee for others, but not acting as agent only, hence the need both for an express declaration of trust of the benefit of the mortgage by the trustee bank in favour of the syndicate members, and for the mortgage to state on its face that the mortgagee acts as trustee.

Multi-currency options

Although most owners will want to borrow in US dollars to match their operating income, borrowers will occasionally wish to have the option to convert their loans into other currencies. While this can be done by using such treasury products as currency swaps, multi-currency options are sometimes specifically written into loan agreements. The borrower will be permitted (usually when selecting his interest period) to specify an alternative currency in which the loan – and hence the repayments – will be denominated for the duration of that interest period. This will allow the borrower to take advantage of lower interest rates applicable to certain currencies, though it will also expose him to currency fluctuations if he selects a currency other than that in which his operating income arises.

The risk for the bank is that the selected currency will move too far from the US dollar (or other base currency) during the interest period, potentially throwing into disarray both the bank's expected return on the facility and the borrower's ability to service the loan. Hence, loan agreements containing multi-currency options normally require the borrower to make additional repayments to ensure that the outstanding balance of the loan in the base currency remains within a certain tolerance of what the outstanding balance would be had the loan repayments remained in the base currency. The loan agreement may restrict the optional currencies available to the borrower or allow him to denominate the loan in any currency that the bank is readily able to obtain in the market.

The importance of the international element

It is a rare ship finance facility where lender and borrower are incorporated in the same country which also happens to be both the vessel's country of registration and the jurisdiction governing the loan agreement. A more common situation would be for, say, a German bank to lend to a Liberian incorporated borrower, secured on a Panamanian flag ship, with a Greek personal guarantor and a loan agreement governed by English law. The lender will, therefore, need to ensure not only that his loan agreement is valid and enforceable under English law, but also that the borrower has the necessary capacity under Liberian law to enter into the agreement and meet its obligations and to grant security over its assets; that the vessel and the mortgage are properly registered under Panamanian law, and the mortgage valid under Panamanian law; and that the personal guarantor is entitled, as a matter of Greek law, to enter into the personal guarantee. The lender will need to consider not only corporate capacity and directors' and shareholders' powers but also exchange control, withholding tax, registration of security, any formalities required by the local law of the place where the documents are executed[2] and many other matters.

In ship finance transactions, therefore, probably more than in any other sort of lending, banks are heavily dependent on a wide range of legal advisers. In our hypothetical situation, the bank will probably rely on its English solicitors to draw up the loan agreement and security documents (even the Panamanian mortgage – most English solicitors who specialise in ship finance will be able to draft mortgages governed by the laws of most major ship registration jurisdictions). In turn, however, the bank will require formal legal opinions to be issued by lawyers in all other relevant jurisdictions confirming that, to the extent relevant, their local laws have been satisfied.

The obtaining of legal opinions by lenders can sometimes be treated rather casually, almost as a ritual. A lender should, however, always ensure before the loan is drawn that all legal opinions will be given in satisfactory terms. While this is often made a condition precedent in loan agreements, lenders frequently overlook this requirement and rely on the lawyers issuing satisfactory opinions after the event. This is a dangerous course, for obvious reasons. Legal opinions will not normally be issued before the loan and security documents have been executed because the lawyers will need to see the documents (or copies) in their executed form to give a meaningful opinion, but the lender would be well advised to agree the terms of the opinion which his lawyers expect to be able to give at the earliest possible stage of the transaction. Sometimes agreed draft documents are opined on but this too can create difficulty if last minute amendments are made. A sample legal opinion appears as Annex A.

Most legal opinions are heavily qualified, for the simple reason that in all legal systems there are so many variables that no lawyer will give a 100 per cent categorical assurance that a certain state of affairs could never be open to challenge under local law. They are nevertheless worthwhile, because no reputable lawyer will risk his or his firm's name on a formal opinion letter without using reasonable care to address the relevant issues and deal with them adequately. The bank should ensure that the opinion letter is addressed to it and paid for (initially) by it, enabling it to sue the lawyer for breach of contract if the lawyer, in giving his opinion, fails to comply with the implied term (at least in English law) that the lawyer will use reasonable care and skill in giving the opinion. In many legal systems – including the English – the bank would also have a tortious claim against the lawyer if the lawyer acted negligently in giving the opinion.

In crude commercial terms any legal opinion is only as good as the financial standing of the lawyer giving it. There is little benefit to a bank in lending US$20m on the strength of a legal opinion from a sole practitioner in a remote part of the world where professional indemnity insurance is unheard of. Yet few countries have the large, well-insured law firms commonly found in England and the United States. The bank is, therefore, forced to rely on the integrity and ability of a lawyer it has probably never met, with no adequate insurance cover for a substantial negligence claim and no alternative source of specialist advice with sufficient assets and/or cover.

Another issue of increased importance in ship finance, owing to the international nature of business, is withholding tax. It is not proposed to deal with tax issues in this book but it is worth noting here that borrowers are sometimes required to withhold or deduct tax from interest payments made to a foreign lender. Any well-drafted loan agreement will contain provisions ensuring that the lender does not suffer as a result. These provisions are, in practice, largely aimed at changes in law – few banks will want to lend in the first place if they know that withholding tax will bite, and even fewer borrowers will want to borrow. It is normally possible for a borrower to obtain his finance from a lender (perhaps a subsidiary or associated company of his original lender) in an alternative jurisdiction where withholding tax will not apply. With the increasing popularity of Singapore as a maritime jurisdiction, and because of withholding taxes applying to payments of interest from Singapore companies to many other countries, a structure of lending through Singapore entities, sometimes on a back-to-back or 'conduit' basis, is now commonly used.

The international element also makes choice of law important. Chapter 1 dealt with the importance of English law in ship finance. Irrespective of the nationality of the parties, a large number of loan agreements in international shipping are expressly governed by English law. As long as the choice is not made in bad faith and is not contrary to public policy, the parties' express choice of English law to govern their contractual relations will be given effect by the English courts.[3]

Similarly, most security documents will be governed by English law. It makes obvious sense for the security documents to be governed by the same system of law as the loan agreement. There are, however, some exceptions. Ship mortgages are almost invariably governed by the law of the flag, quite simply because most jurisdictions require this as a prerequisite to registration, and registration is the cornerstone of the bank's protection. In countries with an English-style form of statutory mortgage[4] there is no reason (except in Cyprus where the deed of covenants is also registered) why the collateral deed of covenants should not be governed by English law.

It is important to distinguish between choice of law and choice of jurisdiction. It does not necessarily follow that the courts of the country whose legal system is to govern the relationship between the parties will automatically have jurisdiction to do so, unless the agreement contains a submission to the jurisdiction of those courts. It is a reflection of the relative bargaining powers of lenders and borrowers that a lender will invariably require his borrower to submit to the jurisdiction of the English courts if the loan agreement is governed by English law, but will look askance at any suggestion by the borrower that the lender (if it does not have a place of business in England) make an equivalent submission.

Generally, an English court will give effect to a contractual submission to its jurisdiction, so long as the claim is one that the English courts would, in principle, have jurisdiction to hear. All contractual claims, except perhaps those relating to land abroad, are thus included. This rule is modified by the 1968 Brussels Convention on Jurisdiction and the Enforcement of Judgments in Civil and Commercial Matters (Brussels Convention) which applies to Denmark only, the Convention on Jurisdiction and Enforcement of Judgments in Civil and Commercial Matters (Lugano Convention) which applies to Iceland, Norway, Poland and Switzerland and Council Regulation (EC) 44/2001 (2001 Regulation) which applies to the remaining European Union Member States. The common principle shared by these three instruments is that with regard to choice of jurisdiction clauses, if the parties to a contract, at least one of which is domiciled in a contracting state, agree that the courts of a contracting state are to have jurisdiction to settle disputes arising in connection with that contract, the courts of the contracting state chosen will have exclusive jurisdiction, and the courts of the other contracting states must decline jurisdiction. If neither party is domiciled in a contracting state, but the parties select the jurisdiction of the courts of a contracting state, the courts of all other contracting states must similarly decline jurisdiction unless the courts of the selected contracting state have themselves declined jurisdiction.

These provisions are not particularly convenient for lenders, who naturally wish to retain the widest possible range of jurisdictions in which to commence proceedings against borrowers, depending on where the assets of the borrowers may be at the relevant time. While in English law agreements lenders will wish to ensure the borrower's submission to the English courts, they will equally not wish thereby to prevent themselves from commencing proceedings in the courts of other contracting states if assets of the borrowers can be traced to those states. Prior to 1 March 2002, where matters of jurisdiction between Member States of the European Convention were governed by Article 17 of the 1968 Convention, there was a loophole for lenders, providing that if an agreement conferring jurisdiction is concluded for the benefit of only one of the parties to the contract, that party retains the right to commence proceedings against the other in any other court that would have jurisdiction by virtue of the convention. However, this wording has not been retained in the 2001 Regulation. It does apply to the states listed above which are still governed by the Brussels Convention and Lugano Convention.

As a result, therefore, most jurisdiction clauses in loan agreements and security documents will expressly stipulate that the choice of jurisdiction is made for the benefit of the lender. Although, on a very strict construction of the words of Article 17, a jurisdiction clause for the benefit of more than one party to a contract (for example, a syndicate of banks) would not come within the exception in Article 17, it is generally accepted that the Article 17 exception will apply to a jurisdiction clause for the benefit of a number (though presumably not all) of the parties to a multipartite contract.[5]

A well-drafted submission clause will contain an express waiver by the borrower of any right to claim that the action has been commenced in an inconvenient or inappropriate court,[6] and, importantly, will designate an address in England or Wales where process can be served. If no address for service is designated, the lender will need the permission of the court to serve proceedings out of the jurisdiction.[7] Although this will almost invariably be granted where the defendant has submitted to the jurisdiction, applying for permission adds unnecessary cost and delay both in making the application and in then effecting service, particularly if the borrower is being evasive.

Loan agreement provisions of particular significance

It is perhaps instructive to consider the following sample contents page from a fairly standard simple shipping term loan agreement.

Clause	Heading
1	Definitions and interpretation
2	The loan and its purpose
3	Conditions precedent and subsequent
4	Representations and warranties
5	Repayment and prepayment
6	Interest
7	Flag
8	Fees
9	Security documents
10	Covenants
11	Events of default
12	Set-off and lien

(Continued)

Clause	Heading *(continued)*
13	Assignment, syndication and sub-participation
14	Payments, mandatory prepayment, reserve requirements and illegality
15	Notices
16	Miscellaneous
17	Law and jurisdiction
18	Headings and contents page
19	Letter of offer
Appendix A	Form of drawdown notice
Appendix B	Form of mortgage
Appendix C	Form of deed of covenants
Appendix D	Form of assignment
Appendix E	Form of guarantee

Most shipping term loan agreements will contain a similar list of clauses, though perhaps arranged or subdivided differently.

It will be seen that a shipping term loan agreement differs little in structure from any other, nor is it the purpose of this book to deal in detail with areas covered in standard texts on banking law. This section will, therefore, look at these clauses in general terms and address the provisions peculiar to shipping finance.

1   Definitions and interpretation

Curiously, the most complex part of the loan agreement is often the clause that defines a wide range of terms used elsewhere in the documents. Most of these are relatively standard in any form of loan agreement but in shipping loans additional definitions often appear, covering the vessel or vessels being financed or refinanced, and earnings, insurances and requisition compensation.[8]

2   The loan and its purpose

This clause will contain the bank's commitment to make the loan and, again, will be in standard banking terms. It is normal to provide (assuming it to be the case) that the loan is to be used to assist the borrower in financing (or refinancing) part of the purchase price of the vessel(s), though with a proviso that the bank is not obliged to ensure that the loan is actually used for that purpose. This leaves the bank treading a tightrope – since it wants to be sure that the loan is used for the proper purpose and certainly does not want to find its right to repayment compromised by any argument (however spurious) that it knew all along that the loan was intended for something different.

3   Conditions precedent and subsequent

Before being committed to advancing the loan the lender will normally look for a large amount of information and a large number of documents to be made available in form and substance satisfactory to the lender and its lawyers. These will include the following.

- The constitutional documents (that is, certificate of incorporation and memorandum and articles of association or equivalent) of the borrower and of any corporate guarantor. This is to ensure that the borrower has the corporate power to own the vessel, grant security over it and borrow money, and to enable the bank to see any restrictions on the powers of the directors. This is particularly important in the context of guarantees by companies incorporated in some parts of the UK.[9] There is an argument for United Kingdom companies, based on Section 35(1) of the Companies Act 1985,[10] that a third party, such as a lending bank, need no longer be concerned with the company's constitutional documents, but the drafting of the section is ambiguous[11] and generally accepted best practice remains to check.
- A certificate of goodstanding for the borrower and any corporate guarantor, if available in their country of incorporation.[12] This will confirm that no steps are being taken to wind up the borrower (or guarantor) and will confirm the payment of all outstanding corporate fees.
- A company search against the borrower and any corporate guarantor, if available in their country of incorporation, to confirm the identity of shareholders (if required to be registered) and directors, and, again, to verify that no steps have been taken to lead to the winding up or receivership or administration of the company. The extent of the information available from such a search can vary markedly depending on the county of incorporation.
- Minutes of meetings of the directors and, possibly, shareholders of the borrower and of any corporate guarantor. Precisely what is required will depend on the country of incorporation and the constitutional documents of the company, and it is essential to take local advice as to the precise requirements and any necessary formalities. For example, an English company will not normally need shareholder approval to buy or sell ships (subject always to the contents of its memorandum and articles of association); a Liberian company will generally require shareholder approval of the disposal of a substantial part of its assets or for the giving of a guarantee, and it is generally accepted practice to require shareholders' resolutions to be produced for the purchase and financing of ships, although for practical reasons this cannot be readily satisfied for a publicly traded company. It is important to ensure that any required waivers of notice of meetings or consents to short notice are also produced.
- Any powers of attorney under which the loan agreement or any other relevant documents are to be executed. Most foreign companies execute deeds (such as ship mortgages) by attorney. Again, it is imperative to take local advice as to precise requirements, both substantive and formal.
- A copy, perhaps certified by an officer of the borrower, of the memorandum of agreement by which the borrower agrees to buy the vessel; for newbuildings this will be a copy of the shipbuilding contract, together (usually) with the original refund guarantees granted to the shipowner, which will be assigned to the financing bank.
- A copy of the bill of sale transferring title in the vessel to the borrower.
- The result of a search at the relevant ship's registry confirming that the vessel is owned by the seller (or, in the case of a refinancing, the borrower) free of registered encumbrances. This search should be carried out at the last possible moment, as nearly as possible simultaneously with drawdown of the loan. The lender may also wish to be supplied with an

official certificate or transcript of registry prior to drawdown, but it is the last-minute search that is all important.

- Evidence that the vessel is (or will be from delivery) satisfactorily insured. This will normally take the form of written confirmations from the brokers or insurers summarising the principal terms of cover, most notably insured values and deductibles. Due to the complexity of insurance arrangements, lenders very regularly wish to have this confirmation reviewed before drawdown by outside insurance consultants.[13]
- A recent certificate of confirmation of class for the vessel, free of recommendations affecting class.
- Copies of the vessel's current safety construction, safety radio, safety equipment and load line certificates and any other certificates required depending on the type of vessel.
- A copy of any charterparty of the vessel. This is particularly important if the lender is looking to a long-term charterparty as the primary source of repayment and is essential if the lender is taking a specific assignment of the charterparty.[14]
- A survey report on the condition of the vessel and/or a valuation of the vessel by an independent surveyor or valuer.
- If the vessel is to be registered under a new flag, a deletion certificate from the vessel's old flag, or (if acceptable to the registration authorities of the new flag) an undertaking to provide a deletion certificate within a set period of time.
- An export licence for the vessel, if required.
- Confirmation that all legal opinions which the bank requires will be given in the form required.[15]
- All necessary bank mandates and drawdown notices.

This list is by no means exhaustive. Other conditions precedent may be called for in any particular transaction. The bank will also require any commitment or other front-end fees to be paid before advancing any funds.

This clause will probably also commit the borrower to produce to the bank as soon as practicable after drawdown evidence of registration of the bank's mortgage, evidence of any registrations required at companies or other public registries and appropriate letters of undertaking[16] from the vessel's insurers.

4   Representations and warranties

Most of these will be standard representations and warranties found in normal corporate term loan agreements, for example, as to the borrower's corporate status, absence of any insolvency proceedings and so on. Any representations and warranties specifically relating to the vessel will normally be contained in the mortgage or deed of covenants,[17] although the loan agreement will often contain a warranty that the bank has been provided with a full copy of documentation relating to the purchase and chartering of the vessel.

5   Repayment and prepayment

Repayment has been discussed in general terms above and, apart from taking into account the matters mentioned there, the fact that the loan is a shipping loan will have no effect on the details of the repayment terms. This clause will probably also deal with prepayment rights, including break cost indemnities and any required notice period.

6 Interest

This will set out the mechanics for fixing the interest rate and paying interest on the loan, as discussed earlier. It will also probably include a provision increasing the margin payable if an event of default occurs. Under English law there is a risk that the increased margin will be held unenforceable as a penalty, but it is generally considered acceptable so long as the increase is kept within reasonable bounds (for example, an additional 1–2 per cent).

7 Flag

This clause will contain an obligation on the borrower to keep the vessel registered under the flag approved by the bank. The borrower may ask for the agreement to be drafted in a way that enables the borrower to change the flag of the vessel, primarily to give the borrower an escape route in the event of political instability in the country of the chosen flag. Banks will often agree to a suitable proviso being inserted as long as it is clear that the bank's approval of the new flag must be obtained and that consent to a change of flag is conditional on the borrower executing and registering such further security documents – principally a new mortgage in the form appropriate for the new flag – as the bank may require, together with relevant corporate papers and subject to the bank obtaining a clean legal opinion.

8 Fees

As with any other loan agreement, this will set out the fees that are payable by the borrower to the bank. Alternatively, details of the fees will be set out in a separate letter, particularly if the lender wishes to syndicate or grant sub-participations in the loan, when the lender will often wish to take a turn on the fees rather than simply pass on a proportion of them to the participants. Even in those circumstances, the borrower's contractual commitment to pay the fees specified in the fee letter will generally be contained in the loan agreement.

9 Security documents

This clause will set out the security documents that the bank will require.[18]

10 Covenants

In addition to normal financial and other covenants relating to the borrower, this clause may contain certain of the major covenants relating to the vessel (for example, as to insurance). Alternatively, and more logically, all covenants specifically relating to the vessel, as opposed to the borrower, will be included in the mortgage or deed of covenants. One covenant likely to be included in the loan agreement is the important covenant by the borrower to ensure that the value of the vessel always exceeds a certain percentage of the loan outstanding – maybe 120–130 per cent. (This may sometimes be seen in reverse, that is, a covenant that the amount

26

of the loan outstanding will never exceed, say, 60 or 70 per cent of the value of the vessel.) The precise ratio may depend on the age and type of ship–there will obviously be a readier market for a newer, less specialist ship, so the lender may be content with a higher loan-to-value ratio.

This clause will probably also contain a mechanism for assessing the value of the vessel for the purpose of the agreement. Commonly, agreement will be reached that both bank and borrower will appoint a valuer, and that for the purpose of the agreement the value of the vessel will be the mean of their two valuations. The clause will also contain a requirement for the borrower to make an appropriate prepayment or provide additional security (often cash) if the loan-to-value ratio is too high. The clause should also contain a mechanism whereby any such top-up security may be released if the loan-to-value ratio is met without the need for the additional security.

11   Events of default

Unless the loan is repayable on demand, most term loan agreements contain a comprehensive list of events of default whose occurrence will entitle the bank to declare the outstanding balance of the loan, accrued interest and any other sums due under the loan agreement to be immediately repayable. A well-drafted agreement will make clear that it is not the event itself that accelerates the loan, but the bank's declaration or notice. This is because, if the occurrence of the event of default itself accelerates the loan, it will start the limitation period running. If the bank does not commence proceedings within six years of the event (12 years if the loan agreement is executed as a deed) the borrower will be able to plead limitation as a defence to the bank's claim. Although most banks will act well before six years, let alone 12, have passed, it is sensible to leave the commencement of the limitation period in the bank's hands – that is, the date of the bank's demand for repayment. Shipping loan agreements will contain the usual range of events of default – the most obvious being failure to repay the loan or to pay interest, but others including breach of covenant, breach of any of the security documents, insolvency of the borrower, material misrepresentation, material adverse change and so on. The two most likely events particularly related to the ship are:

- if the ship is sold or encumbered without the bank's consent; and
- if the ship becomes a total loss.

The latter is regularly the subject of negotiation by borrowers who, with some justification, point out that a total loss will almost invariably be covered by insurance assigned to the bank. If the bank will ultimately receive the insurance proceeds, why should it accelerate the loan and put the borrower into default, potentially triggering cross-default provisions in other loan documents, while the insurance claim is being processed? This is an argument with which most banks have sympathy. It is generally possible for a borrower to negotiate a proviso that no event of default will occur if the insurance proceeds are paid to the bank in full within a set period after the casualty giving rise to the total loss – between 90 and 180 days is common – so long as the insurers have not refused to pay the claim and, perhaps, are not disputing the claim.

Other vessel-related incidents will indirectly be events of default by constituting breaches of the mortgage or deed of covenants. Examples are failure to insure in accordance with the lender's requirements, loss of classification, the imposition of maritime liens taking priority to the mortgage and challenges to the registration of the vessel or the mortgage.[19]

Due to the use of one-ship companies, shipping loans will often also include cross-default provisions making it an event of default under one facility if an event of default occurs under other facilities secured on other vessels or companies in the same group or under other facilities to the same borrower.

12   Set-off and lien

This will be a standard clause enabling the bank to set-off against the indebtedness after an event of default any credit balances or other property of the borrower that it holds, and giving the bank a lien on any property of the borrower which it may hold until the indebtedness is repaid.

The recent case of *National Westminster Bank plc v Spectrum Plus Limited*,[20] which went to the House of Lords, has changed the position on the creation of charges over bank accounts. The position prior to this case, as set out in *Siebe Gorman v Barclays Bank* Limited,[21] was that a debenture was effective to create a fixed charge over book debts, and this was also the unanimous view of the Court of Appeal in *Spectrum*. What the House of Lords has now said is that whether a charge over book debts operates as a fixed or floating charge will depend on the level of control over the account retained by the account holder (and whether the document describes it as 'fixed' or 'floating' is immaterial). To be certain of having the benefit of a fixed charge it seems that any payments out of the account need to be individually sanctioned by the chargee; while this is practical for a retention account it would not work for a traditional operating account.[22]

13   Assignment, syndication and sub-participation

There are no special requirements for assigning, syndicating or granting sub-participations in shipping loans, though many owners feel strongly about their personal relationships with their bankers and will seek to restrict the bank's ability to allow other banks to become involved in the relationship. This is very much a matter for negotiation, but banks will often agree to seek the borrower's consent (not to be unreasonably withheld) to an assignment, syndication or sub-participation outside the bank's group. Most banks will want to preserve their ability to assign, syndicate or sub-participate freely to their own parent, subsidiary or sister companies.

Another concern felt by borrowers is that the bank will transfer all or part of the loan to a lender in a jurisdiction where withholding tax becomes a problem and the borrower becomes obliged to gross-up his interest payments. Sometimes borrowers will allow banks unlimited rights to transfer if any increased cost is not passed on to the borrower. Similar considerations apply to transfers by banks of their lending office to a branch in another jurisdiction.

14   Payments

This clause sets out the details of where payments under the loan agreement should be made, and will include standard loan agreement provisions such as:

- requiring all payments to be made free and clear of deduction, withholding, counterclaim or set-off;

- requiring payments to be grossed up, if any withholding tax or other deduction has to be made;
- requiring the borrower to indemnify the bank against any increased costs arising from changes in law, taxation or central bank or governmental requirements;
- providing a mechanism for renegotiating the interest rate (or its method of calculation) if the bank is unable to fix a rate in the market; and
- cancelling the bank's commitment to make or maintain the loan if it becomes illegal or practically impossible for it to do so.

15   Notices

This will be a standard notices clause, setting out where and how notices are to be given by one party to the other.

16   Miscellaneous

This clause will contain a series of boiler-plate provisions that do not easily fit in elsewhere in the agreement. Most will be standard provisions with no particular shipping emphasis. One of the most important for the bank will be its indemnity from the borrower for legal and other costs.

17   Law and jurisdiction

This will contain the agreement of the parties to English governing law and the borrower's submission to the jurisdiction of the English courts. The borrower will also waive any objection to the jurisdiction of the English courts, on the grounds of convenience or otherwise, and will designate an address in England or Wales at which proceedings can be effectively served on the borrower. This last provision is not necessary if the borrower is an English company, as service of proceedings at the company's registered office is deemed good service there.[23]

18   Headings and contents page

This will simply provide that the headings and contents page used in the agreement are for reference only and not to be taken into account in interpreting the agreement.

19   Letter of offer

Most loan agreements follow an offer letter from the bank to the borrower. Although the offers contained in such letters are invariably made subject to the execution of satisfactory documentation, it is often expressly provided that the agreement supersedes the offer letter, and any other correspondence between the parties (or their agents) relating to the facility. This is aimed at avoiding disputes should there subsequently be any inconsistency between the offer letter and the final agreement.

Execution

In English law there is no reason why a loan agreement needs to be executed as a deed. There is, by the nature of the transaction, adequate consideration moving both ways to make the agreement a valid contract. The only possible advantage to the bank in having the agreement executed as a deed would be to provide the bank with a 12-year, rather than a six-year, limitation period. This is not a substantial advantage – six years is normally quite adequate for a bank to reach a decision on enforcement and, as has already been seen, if the loan agreement has been properly drafted, the limitation period will not begin to run until the bank declares an event of default. Once the bank has reached a decision to do that, it is rarely likely to wish to defer enforcement for a further six years.

Standard security in ship finance transactions

Traditionally, the shipping banker was happy if he had a loan of, say, 60 per cent of the value of the vessel (the exact percentage depending on the type of vessel and the likely market on a forced sale) secured by a first mortgage, together with the usual collateral assignment of the vessel's insurances and earnings. When the late 1970s arrived and with them the realisation that world shipping was labouring under serious over-capacity, ship values fell, in many cases quite dramatically. Many banks with their comfortable 60 per cent mortgages suddenly found that, even if they were to enforce the mortgage and sell the ship, their only market was to the scrap merchants. While a loan of 60 per cent of the value of a profitably trading ship was fine, a loan of 200 per cent of the value of a pile of rusting scrap metal meant that some bankers had some hard talking to do to their internal and external regulators.

So the confidence of the banker in the ship mortgage as the be-all and end-all of his security took something of a knock. Nevertheless, few bankers operating in ship-related lending (other than to the large, blue-chip owners where loans are constructed more on the basis of a corporate credit than a shipping loan) will be prepared to lend without a mortgage on the ship. As well as the positive security that the mortgage offers, it also gives the bank a form of negative security in preventing other creditors establishing a priority claim on what is likely to be the only substantial asset of the borrower. Rather, bankers began to look more closely at the additional security available.

Most particularly, banks began to look in more detail at the sources of repayment of their loans, paying a good deal of attention to projected cash flows and often only lending either to owners with undoubted long-term track records in successful ship operation through good and bad markets, or secured on ships where a good long-term or medium-term charter was in place, the hire from which would be the principal source of the bank's repayment. Effectively, name lending became the order of the day. If the borrower or those behind him had traded through the lean years either by time chartering or (though less attractive to banks) trading on the spot markets, with a satisfactory outcome then the banks felt understandably happier. Alternatively, if the charterer was an oil major, bankers would breathe large sighs of relief. This latter option is still name lending – but lending against the good name of a charterer rather than the good name of an owner. Only the brave banks were inclined to lend to new operators who had not yet proved themselves. Sometimes that bravery was well rewarded, at other times not.

Another of the traditional forms of security for ship-related lending has been coming under attack. Perhaps symptomatic of the rising markets of the late 1980s was the willingness of some banks to accede to borrowers' requests to dispense with personal or parent company guarantees, which previously would have been thought of as indispensable security for facilities to one-ship companies. The reasons for taking parent company or personal guarantees are looked at in detail in Chapter 9 and are fairly self-evident. Without them, banks lose any recourse to those behind the shipowning company – when the chips are down the ship and/or her earnings will be the bank's only source of repayment. It is too easy to rely on a moral obligation, whether encapsulated in a non-binding comfort letter or not. When times are hard, a moral obligation without a legally enforceable guarantee is of little tangible value to a lender.

The following are principal types of security for which a bank will look in a ship-based transaction:

- a first priority mortgage over the ship or ships concerned;
- an assignment of all the insurances of that ship;
- an assignment of all the earnings of the ship, possibly including a specific assignment of a particular charterparty;
- an assignment of any requisition compensation of the ship;
- a personal or parent company guarantee and indemnity;
- a charge over or pledge of the shares of the borrower (used frequently but not invariably); and
- some form of security over either a cash deposit and/or earnings and retention accounts (again, used frequently but not invariably).

This list is by no means exhaustive and Chapter 9 will look at some of the other principal types of security commonly taken. No two transactions are ever identical and the lending bank must be discriminating about the security it calls for in any particular case. The ultimate aim must be to give the bank the maximum protection consistent with allowing the borrower to operate his business and maximise his earning capacity without undue restraint.

The fear of banks taking too much security is a more recent phenomenon. Concern has been expressed in the United States that lending banks could make themselves liable under the Oil Pollution Act 1990, and other environmental legislation, if the range of security that they take is so extensive as to constitute them, in the eyes of the US courts, controllers of mortgaged vessels. Particularly vulnerable, it is argued, are banks with security over the shares in the vessel-owning company, whether or not they have actually exercised their rights under their security. For this reason some banks now prefer to have an option to take a share charge at a later date, rather than taking it initially. The risk is that at the moment they wish to exercise the option the cooperation of the borrower and its shareholders may not be forthcoming. Ultimately it is a balance between taking the security at the start of the transaction (where there is a slight risk that the bank could be deemed an 'operator' in relation to liability issues) or taking the risk that the pledge may not be granted when requested.

Secondly, banks that take out Mortgagees' Additional Perils – Pollution insurance (MAP)[24] are likely, in the event of an insured event happening, to be hampered in establishing their 'net loss' if they have a wide range of security to realise or need to convince an independent lawyer that realisation is not commercially practicable. The message for lending banks must be to consider whether it realistically expects in a default situation to have to rely on every item of security that it takes. If not, why incur the expense and potential drawbacks of taking it?

Registration of security

Shipping lenders must not forget that, as well as registration of mortgages at the appropriate ship's registry, some jurisdictions will require certain security documents created by companies incorporated in them to be registered in companies' or other public registries. This principally applies to the common law jurisdictions which have taken their company law from England – in shipping terms Cyprus, Malta, Hong Kong and Singapore are the most significant.

In English law the position is governed by Part XII of the Companies Act 1985, as amended by the Insolvency Act 1985. Under English law a charge created by a company registered in England and Wales and covering any of the types of property listed in Section 396 of the Companies Act 1985, will, so far as any security on the company's property is concerned, be void against a liquidator or administrator and any creditor of the company unless the prescribed particulars of the charge and the original charge document are delivered to, or received by, the Registrar of Companies within 21 days after the creation of the charge.[25] Although the obligation to register is strictly that of the company, most banks will understandably wish to protect their own interests by handling the registration themselves. In shipping terms, the obligation to deliver particulars to the Registrar of Companies will extend to the mortgage, the deed of covenants (if any), the assignment of insurances, earnings and so on (to the extent that it potentially could be interpreted as creating a charge), any charge over, for example, a retention account and any (arguably) charge created by a company over shares in another company. It may also apply to extended set-off rights in loan agreements or guarantees.

The consequences for a lender of non-registration are serious. Failure to deliver the particulars of the charge in due time will mean that the charge will be void against any liquidator or administrator, who will be able to deal with the asset that is the subject of the charge as if the charge did not exist. Similarly, any other creditor of the company will, to all intents and purposes, be able to ignore the charge. The underlying debt will not be affected by failure to deliver particulars,[26] but that is likely to be of little comfort to a lender forced to compete in the insolvency of the borrower with the borrower's other unsecured creditors.

One of the decided English cases known to most shipping bankers is Slavenburg's case.[27] By virtue of Section 409 of the Companies Act 1985, the obligation to deliver particulars of charges to the Registrar of Companies extends to charges on property in England or Wales created by a company incorporated outside England or Wales if that company has an established place of business in England or Wales. In the Slavenburg case, the English High Court held that a charge created by a Bermudan company in favour of a Dutch bank, and governed by Dutch law, was void for want of registration. This was so because the Bermudan company was found, as a matter of fact, to have a place of business in England, even though it had not registered that place of business under the predecessor of Part XXIII of the Companies Act 1985.[28] The court additionally found that Section 409 applied to property brought into England or Wales after the creation of the charge, whether or not the company still then had a place of business in England or Wales.

The potential for difficulty for ship mortgagees as a result of this decision will be apparent. On the face of it, if the ship calls at an English port the ship mortgage will, in principle, be registerable if the owning company is held, as a matter of fact, to have a place of business in the United Kingdom, perhaps by virtue of being managed from within the country. As a result, the practice has developed of delivering particulars of all ship-related security taken in England to the Registrar of Companies, irrespective of the position of the ship at the time, or of whether the owner or other person giving the security is incorporated, or has an obvious place of business, in England or Wales. Invariably, the Registrar of Companies will return the documents unregistered (how could he do otherwise?) but the obligation in Section 395 to deliver particulars will have been satisfied, irrespective of registration, and the mortgagee should be protected. Additionally, it is normal market practice to obtain representations and warranties from all security parties that they do not have a place of business in the United Kingdom (or, indeed, in the USA, where similar filing requirements arise under the Uniform Commercial Code (UCC)); although this offers little protection if the warranty is breached, it does at least focus the borrower's mind on this issue.

The illogicality of the Slavenburg situation was recognised by parliament and the Companies Act 1989 (Section 105 and Schedule 15) amends Section 409 of the 1985 Act substantially. The only difficulty is that this part of the 1989 Act is still not in force and may never come into force, at least in its current form.

The reasons for this are not directly connected with Section 409 and Slavenburg's case, but rather with other proposed amendments to the regime for registration of company charges contained in the 1985 Act. Consultation periods have been and gone. All that can be said at this stage is that some reform of the regime for registration of charges looks likely in the medium term. The Law Commission has published final recommendations but these have not been incorporated in the Company Law Reform Bill as expected. However, the Company Law Reform Bill does provide scope for such provisions to be introduced at a later stage. It is unfortunate that the opportunity to put the position of charges created by overseas companies on a sensible footing has been lost (or at least delayed) in the wider exercise.

Nevertheless, it remains a serious possibility that any new rules regarding charges created by overseas companies will largely reflect the Companies Act 1989 proposals, so it is worth summarising them briefly. If and when those provisions (intended to become Sections 703A to 703N of the 1985 Act) come into effect, particulars of a charge created by a company incorporated outside the United Kingdom will only need to be delivered if the company has registered an established place of business in some part of the United Kingdom under Section 691 of the 1985 Act and if the property charged is then situated in the United Kingdom or subsequently remains there for a continuous period of four months.[29] A lender will, therefore, be able to check the register of overseas companies to establish whether or not his charges need to be registered. Whether or not the charge requires registration will be determined at the date of its creation or at the date of registration of the company under Section 691, whichever is the later.[30]

This, of course, still presents the difficulty that the charge may become registerable after its creation if the company subsequently registers a place of business under Section 691. Fortunately this difficulty has also been recognised, and failure to deliver particulars in those circumstances will only make the company liable to a fine; charges will not be rendered void[31]. Equally, the four month provision should not cause lenders undue concern –

Section 703L expressly provides that a ship is only to be regarded as situated in the United Kingdom if registered there. A lender should, however, beware of agreeing to changes of flag if the vessel is to move onto the British registry – he should at least check to ensure that the owner has not registered under Section 691.

Equity

Although this chapter has concentrated on shipping finance through borrowing, it would be wrong to ignore completely the role of equity. Traditionally, equity finance for shipping has come from within the shipping industry, principally from retained earnings from vessel operation and retained profit on ship sales. These sources remain the principal source of shipping finance equity to this day, though increasingly there have been efforts to attract equity into shipping from sources outside the industry, most notably by the listing of shipping shares on the stock exchanges in countries such as Norway and the USA. Chapter 6 explains some of the requirements of these issues in more detail.

Prior to 2004, these efforts have had (with certain exceptions) only limited success, at least outside the United States. Relatively few shipping companies had their shares quoted on a stock exchange. Those that did tended on the whole, to be the largest blue chip names. However, during 2004 and 2005 there was a rush of IPOs, principally on Nasdaq, AIM and the Oslo Bourse, reflecting the historically high asset and freight markets. Owners were able to realise some of these high values through a listing, and institutional investors showed (for a limited period) significant appetite for these issues. However, due at least in part to a perception that some owners were using the market for personal gain and structuring issues so that connected companies of the owners were awarded management and other contracts at very favourable prices, this market cooled in the autumn of 2005.

Additionally, shipping is (rightly) perceived as a cyclical industry. Pressure on quoted companies to produce a relatively steady, rather than fluctuating, dividend stream does not lie easily with the ups and downs of the shipping world unless the bulk of a fleet is committed on long-term charters. By the same token, owners can be remarkably reluctant to share their gains with outsiders.

This risk perception is also reflected in the inability of the majority of shipowners to tap into the capital markets as a source of finance. Only a very few large names, such as the major cruise lines, have a sufficiently high and accepted credit rating to enable them to issue Eurobonds and similar instruments.

A number of shipping funds have also been launched. Some of these are established within specialist shipping banks, others are not, but they all serve to widen the pool of capital available to the shipping industry.

Mezzanine finance

Lastly, mention should be made of mezzanine finance. Simply speaking, this is a form of debt which will be subordinated to the owner's principal (or senior) bank borrowing. In return for the higher risk involved in being postponed to the senior debt when it comes to repayment and security, the lender will demand a significantly higher interest margin and will often receive some form of equity kicker, that is, a right to take an equity stake in the borrowing company at a future date, usually at a fixed or ascertainable future price. The use of mezzanine finance in shipping has generally been too limited to merit detailed consideration in a book of this nature, although by 2006 it is being incorporated into lending structures more. However, rather than separate junior debt it is often structured as a split of the facility amount whereby a conservative portion of the loan (say a 60 or 65 per cent advance ratio) is conventionally priced senior debt and the 'top up' of maybe another 20 per cent takes the form of junior debt, from many of the same banks, at a higher coupon.

---

[1] See Chapter 9.

[2] Under English conflict of law rules, a contract will, in principle, be validly executed if executed in accordance either with the law of the place of execution or the governing law – see Article 9 of the Rome Convention of 1980 enacted in English law by the Contracts (Applicable Law) Act 1990. It is good practice to endeavour, as far as possible, to satisfy both, though a compromise between the two that satisfies neither is, of course, unacceptable.

[3] Article 16 of the 1980 Rome Convention–Schedule 1 Contracts (Applicable Law) Act 1990.

[4] See Chapter 7.

[5] The exclusive jurisdiction provisions are set out in Article 23 of Council Regulation (EC) 44/2001 and Article 17 of the Brussels and Lugano Conventions.

[6] See *Spiliada Maritime Corporation v Cansulex Ltd* [1987] AC 460 for a discussion by the House of Lords of the circumstances where proceedings before the English courts may be stayed on the ground that there exists a more convenient or more appropriate forum.

[7] Civil Procedure, 6.20.

[8] See Chapter 8.

[9] See Chapter 9.

[10] This provides that 'the validity of an act done by a company shall not be called into question on the ground of lack of capacity by reason of anything in the company's memorandum'. Note that the Company Law Reform Bill will reform this area and is expected to come into force no sooner than 2007.

[11] For example, does it protect third parties if the relevant powers are omitted from the memorandum?

[12] For example, Liberia or Panama.

[13] See Chapter 12.

[14] See Chapter 8.

[15] See Annex A–thanks to David Lacey for preparing the sample opinion.

[16] See Chapter 8.

[17] See Chapter 7.

[18] See Chapters 7 to 9.

[19] See Chapter 7.

[20] *National Westminster Bank plc v Spectrum Plus Ltd* [2005] 4 All ER 209.

[21] *Siebe Gorman & Co Ltd v Barclays Bank Ltd* [1979] 2 Lloyd's Rep. 142.

[22] See Chapter 9.

[23] Section 725 Companies Act 1985.

[24] See Chapter 13.

[25] Section 395(1) Companies Act 1985.

[26] Its repayment will, in fact, be accelerated (Section 395(2) Companies Act 1985).

[27] *Slavenburg's Bank NV v Intercontinental Natural Resources Ltd* [1980] 1 WLR 1076.

[28] Section 691 Companies Act 1985 provides that, when a company incorporated outside the United Kingdom establishes a place of business there, it must within one month of doing so deliver certain prescribed documents to the Registrar of Companies.

[29] Section 703D.
[30] Section 703B.
[31] Section 703F(2).

Annex A

Sample legal opinion

[Name of Bank]
[Address of Bank]

[date]

Dear Sirs

US$[ ] Loan Facility (the '**Facility**')
[Name of Borrower] (the '**Borrower**')

You, [Name of Bank] (the '**Bank**') have asked us to give a legal opinion in connection with a secured loan facility of up to [ ] United States Dollars (US$[ ]) granted by you to the Borrower, a company incorporated under the laws of [ ].

We have acted as [ ] legal advisers to you in connection with this transaction. This opinion is limited to the law of [ ] as at the date of this opinion and as currently applied by the courts of [ ]. It is given on the basis that it will be governed by and construed in accordance with the law of [ ].

1 Documents
  1.1 For the purpose of this opinion we have examined the following documents:-
    (a) loan agreement dated [date] (the '**Agreement**') made between the Borrower and the Bank;
    (b) a statutory mortgage dated [date] (the '**Mortgage**') executed by the Borrower in favour of the Bank in respect of m.v. '[Name of Vessel]' (the '**Vessel**');
    (c) a deed of covenant dated [date] (the '**Deed of Covenant**') executed by the Borrower in favour of the Bank;
    (d) a deed of assignment dated [date] (the '**Assignment**') executed by the Borrower in favour of the Bank assigning to the Bank all insurances, earnings and requisition compensation of the Vessel;
    (e) the Certificate of Incorporation and Memorandum and Articles of Association of the Borrower;
    (f) written resolutions of all of the directors of the Borrower approving the execution of the Documents; and
    (g) a Power of Attorney granted by the Borrower under which the Documents were executed on behalf of the Borrower.
  1.2 '**Document**' means each document referred to in paragraphs 1.1(a) to (d).

2 Searches
  2.1 We have carried out the following searches:
    (a) a search against the Borrower at the Registry of Companies of [ ]; and
    (b) a search against the Borrower in the company winding-up register kept by the Supreme Court of [ ]; and

(c) a search against the Vessel and the Borrower at the Supreme Court of [ ] to establish the existence or otherwise of proceedings commenced against the Vessel or the Borrower in the courts of [ ]; and

(d) a search against the Vessel at the Registry of Ships of [ ].

2.2 Each of the searches referred to above was carried out on [date].

3 Assumptions

3.1 In giving this opinion we have assumed:

(a) the genuineness of all signatures on the Documents;

(b) the authenticity of all Documents submitted to us as originals; and

(c) the Agreement, the Deed of Covenant and the Assignment create valid binding and enforceable obligations under English law.

3.2 We have not taken any steps to verify any of these assumptions.

4 Opinion

On the basis of the assumptions set out above and subject to the qualifications set out below, we are of the opinion that:

(a) the Borrower is:

(i) duly incorporated in [ ];

(ii) validly existing under the laws of [ ];

(iii) a separate legal entity with limited liability; and

(iv) capable of suing and being sued in its corporate name.

(b) no steps have been taken by any person which could lead to or result in the insolvency, bankruptcy, liquidation, dissolution or analogous circumstance of the Borrower, or the appointment of a liquidator, administrator, receiver, administrative receiver, manager, custodian, trustee or similar officer or analogous person of the Borrower or any of its assets;

(c) the Borrower has:

(i) the corporate power to own its assets and to carry on its business as it is currently being conducted and to enter into the Documents and to perform and observe its obligations under them; and

(ii) taken all action required on its part to authorise the execution, delivery, performance and observance of the Documents;

(d) the obligations of the Borrower under the Documents are legal, valid, binding and enforceable in accordance with their terms;

(e) the execution and delivery of the Documents by the Borrower, and the performance and observance of its obligations under them, does not contravene any law or the constitutional documents of the Borrower or exceed any limit on its power or authority or of any or its officers;

(f) no consent, permit, licence, approval, authorisation or exemption is required in connection with the execution, delivery, performance, observance, validity or enforceability of the Documents;

(g) the Documents have been validly executed and delivered by the Borrower;

(h) it is not necessary or advisable in order to ensure or facilitate the legality, validity, enforceability, performance, observance or admissibility in evidence of any of the obligations of the Borrower under or in connection with the Documents that:
  (i) the Documents or any other document be filed, registered, lodged, recorded, authorised, notarised or delivered in or to any public office or elsewhere other than registration of the Mortgage with the Registrar of Companies of [ ] and with the Registrar of Ships of [ ], each of which has been done;
  (ii) any tax, duty or other levy or impost be paid; or
  (iii) any other action be taken or formality observed.

(i) there is no withholding or other tax, duty, levy or impost to be deducted from any payment to be made by, under or in connection with the Documents;

(j) any moneys payable under or in connection with the Documents and the proceeds of any judgment obtained in respect of the Documents in the courts of [ ] may be remitted out of [ ] without limit or restriction and without the need to obtain any consent, permit, licence, approval, authorisation or exemption from any person;

(k) the Borrower is not entitled to claim any immunity in relation to itself or any of its assets or in the courts of [ ] in connection with any legal proceedings relating to the Documents;

(l) the Documents are in proper form for enforcement in the courts of [ ];

(m) the Bank will not be deemed to be resident, domiciled or carrying on business or subject to taxation in [ ] by reason only of the negotiation, preparation, execution, delivery, registration, performance, observance or enforcement of, or receipt of any payment or repayment under, the Documents;

(n) there is no stamp duty or other documentary tax or impost of any nature payable in respect of the execution, delivery, registration, performance, observance or enforcement of the Documents nor to render them admissible in evidence;

(o) the choice of English law to govern the Agreement, the Deed of Covenant and the Assignment will be upheld as a valid choice of law in any action in the courts of [ ];

(p) the submissions in the Documents by the Borrower to the jurisdiction of the courts of England and the irrevocable appointment of an agent in England to accept service of process are both valid and binding and not subject to revocation and will be given effect by the courts of [ ];

(q) the Bank may enforce a conclusive and unsatisfied judgment which is enforceable by execution in England and obtained in relation to the Documents in a superior court of England having jurisdiction to give that judgment without bringing separate proceedings in the appropriate courts of [ ] and those courts will recognise and accept the judgment without re-trial or examination of the merits of the case;

(r) the Bank will be entitled without limit or restriction and without the need to obtain any consent, approval, licence or permission from any person to exercise all or any of its rights under the Documents (without having to establish a place of business in [ ] or to carry out any other requirement and without limit or restriction) and to bring an action in the courts of [ ] to enforce its rights under or pursuant to the Documents;

(s) there is no applicable usury or interest limitation law which may restrict its rights of the Bank under the Documents or the observance or performance by the Borrower of its obligations under the Documents;

(t) the obligations of the Borrower under the Documents rank at least equally in priority of payments and in all other respects with all other unsecured obligations of the Borrower present and future (other than obligations mandatorily preferred by law);

(u) the Vessel is owned by the Borrower; and

(v) the Mortgage constitutes a first priority security interest on the Vessel enforceable against a liquidator or analogous office-holder of the Borrower and all other third parties and is subject to no prior or equal security interest, other than any maritime liens existing from time to time.

5 Qualifications

This opinion is subject to the following qualifications:

(a) the enforceability of the rights and remedies provided for in the Documents:

(i) is limited by laws relating to bankruptcy, insolvency, liquidation, moratoria, reorganisation and other laws of general application relating to or affecting the rights of creditors;

(ii) may be limited by general principles of equity which are in the discretion of the courts; and

(iii) may become barred or may be or become subject to defences of set-off or counter-claim;

(b) where obligations are to be performed in a jurisdiction outside [ ], those obligations may not be enforceable in [ ] to the extent that performance of them would be illegal or contrary to public policy under the laws of that other jurisdiction;

(c) a certificate, determination, notification or opinion given by the Bank as to any matter provided for in the Agreement or in connection with the Documents may be held by the [ ] courts not to be conclusive if shown to have an unreasonable or arbitrary basis or in the event of manifest error; and

(d) interest provided for under the Agreement may not be recoverable if it amounts to a penalty.

6 Reliance

This letter is addressed to you for your benefit alone and may not, without our prior written consent be:

6.1 relied upon by any other person;

6.2 disclosed, except to your legal advisers and to persons who in the ordinary course of your business have access to your records on the basis that they will make no further disclosure;

6.3 filed with any person; or

6.4 quoted or referred to in a public document.

Yours faithfully

[*Name of law office issuing the opinion*]

Chapter 3

The financing of newbuildings

Updated by Jonathan Ward and Dora Kokota

Any consideration of newbuilding finance as opposed to the financing of second-hand tonnage must examine a combination of financial, commercial and political factors. For many years shipbuilding played a significant role in the economies of many of the world's industrialised nations, and the decline of traditional 'heavy' industries in the Western world, coupled with the advance of technological developments and the availability of cheap and increasingly skilled labour in the Eastern Asia, led many governments to look at ways of subsidising or otherwise supporting domestic shipbuilding activity. This has been particularly true of those nations whose poorly performing shipyards have been located in areas of economic deprivation where unemployment is high and traditional industrial activity has declined.

Many governments have considered it politically desirable to take steps to support their domestic yards and any owner wishing to have a new ship built would have been wise to consider the possible availability of some form of governmental support, either directly or indirectly, for the financing of their project. In the late 1980s and 1990s Western governments sought to provide governmental financial support in various forms to prop up their ailing shipbuilding industry. In the new millennium the governments of Eastern Asia began to recognise the benefits of export credits. Of course, there are many other important factors that a buyer will have to consider, not least the technical expertise available in any particular yard, the reputation of that yard for reliability and punctuality, and the stability of the political regime in the country in question, but the effect of governmental or quasi-governmental support either on the price or the payment terms on offer has been, and will continue to be, a material consideration.

The range and nature of the subsidies and other support available in certain of the principal shipbuilding nations of the world are considered in this chapter. The data suggest, however, that the various support offered by Western governments has had little effect in encouraging newbuilding orders to be placed in Western Europe as opposed to the yards of Asia Pacific where, in Korea and more recently China, concerted efforts have been made to attract newbuilding work from the West. The rise of Asia Pacific as a force in world shipbuilding is graphically illustrated in Exhibit 3.1.[1] This shows, for five-yearly intervals from 1974 to 1994 and for two-yearly intervals from 1994 to 2004, the world's five largest shipbuilding nations by gross tonnage (gt) completed. It can be seen from this table that the dominant nation throughout this period has been Japan, but the decline of shipbuilding in Western Europe is clear: only Germany survives from the 1974 table into the 2004 table and Germany's figures were certainly boosted by reunification and the inclusion of the yards of the former East Germany, which received substantial government aid since reunification. Denmark only survives from the 1974 table into the 2002 table but not into the 2004 table; the decline is obvious. The former Yugoslavia's rise during the 1980s was dramatically curtailed by political events, but from the figures in the 2004 table it appears that perhaps the Croatian yards are now more confident and able to raise their own finance and provide refund guarantees within the context of a more stable political environment.

Exhibit 3.1

Ships completed (ranked by gt)

1974		gt (m)
1	Japan	16.89
2	West Germany	2.14
3	Spain	1.56
4	UK	1.19
5	Denmark	1.07
1979		
1	Japan	4.69
2	USA	1.35
3	France	0.7
4	UK	0.6
5	Brazil	0.6
1984		
1	Japan	9.7
2	Korea	1.4
3	Taiwan	0.8
4	West Germany	0.5
5	Denmark	0.4
1989		
1	Japan	5.36
2	Korea	3.1
3	Yugoslavia	0.5
4	West Germany	0.4
5	Taiwan	0.4
1994		
1	Japan	8.6
2	Korea	4.08
3	Germany	1.0
4	People's Republic of China	0.7
5	Denmark	0.6
1996		
1	Japan	10.15
2	Korea	7.37
3	Germany	1.20
4	People's Republic of China	0.65
5	Denmark	0.49

(Continued)

Exhibit 3.1 *(Continued)*

1998		gt (m)
1	Japan	10.2
2	Korea	7.1
3	Italy	0.8
4	People's Republic of China	0.4
5	Spain	0.3
2000		
1	Japan	11.9
2	Korea	11.9
3	Germany	0.9
4	People's Republic of China	0.6
5	Denmark	0.4
2002		
1	Korea	12.9
2	Japan	11.9
3	Germany	1.2
4	People's Republic of China	0.6
5	Denmark	0.4
2004		
1	Korea	14.7
2	Japan	14.5
3	Germany	0.9
4	Croatia	0.8
5	People's Republic of China	0.7

Sources: Lloyd's Register of Shipbuilding Statistics 1996–2005; Lloyd's Register of Shipping Statistical Tables 1991 and 1992; Lloyd's Register of Shipping World Fleet Statistics 1993–2004.

The other obvious trend is the rise of Korea and Taiwan. From very nearly a standing start in 1972, Korea is now the largest shipbuilding nation in the world. Taiwan, on the other hand, rose to a peak in the mid-1980s, and has since dropped back, losing its place in the table to its communist neighbour.

Exhibit 3.2 shows the overall gt completed in the world for each year since 1974 and displays dramatically the decline in world shipbuilding from the mid-1970s to the late 1980s. However, Exhibit 3.2 also shows that a modest upturn in the early 1990s has now given its turn to a dramatic increase in world shipbuilding by the beginning of the twenty-first century. Indeed, figures in 2004 are similar to the ones reached before the decline in the mid-1970s, despite earlier forecasts suggesting that the heights of the early 1970s were unlikely to be reached again. Not surprisingly, it is predominately the rise of Korea and the solidarity of Japan as shipbuilding nations that have led to this increase.

Very similar general trends appear if one considers the comparative figures for the actual number of ships completed, as opposed to gt. Here, when compared with Exhibit 3.1, the dominance of the East in building larger ships is even more emphasised (see Exhibit 3.3). These figures illustrate the continued use of domestic yards to build short sea or coastal vessels or vessels used on inland waterways, but that the yards of Asia Pacific have secured the lion's share of newbuilding work for major ocean-going tonnage.

Exhibit 3.2

Gt (m) completed between 1974–2005

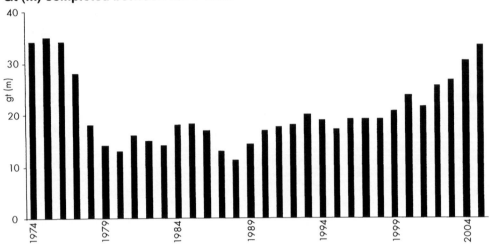

Sources: Lloyd's Register of Shipbuilding Statistics 1996–2005; Lloyd's Register of Shipping Statistical Tables 1991 and 1992; Lloyd's Register of Shipping World Fleet Statistics 1993–2004.

Exhibit 3.3

Ships completed (ranked by number)

1974		No of ships
1	Japan	1,045
2	US	233
3	Spain	230
4	Norway	129
5	West Germany	128
1979		
1	Japan	993
2	US	182
3	Norway	113
4	Spain	99
5	Netherlands	98
1984		
1	Japan	902
2	West Germany	109
3	Spain	92
4	Korea	87
5	US	73
1989		
1	Japan	640
2	Spain	130
3	Korea	102
4	West Germany	54
5	Netherlands	33

(Continued)

Exhibit 3.3 *(Continued)*

1994		No of ships
1	Japan	597
2	Korea	118
3	Germany	93
4	Netherlands	70
5	Malaysia	56
1996		
1	Japan	604
2	Korea	192
3	Spain	100
4	Germany	91
5	Denmark	1
1998		
1	Japan	597
2	Korea	183
3	Germany	72
4	Netherlands	43
5	Spain	1
2000		
1	Japan	634
2	Korea	213
3	Germany	64
4	People's Republic of China	3
5	Denmark	1
2002		
1	Japan	549
2	Korea	276
3	Germany	51
4	People's Republic China	4
5	Denmark	2
2004		
1	Japan	583
2	Korea	302
3	Germany	44
4	Netherlands	36
5	Denmark	2
2005		
1	Japan	401
2	Korea	256
3	Germany	48
4	Netherlands	33
5	Denmark	2

Sources: Lloyd's Register of Shipbuilding Statistics 1996–2005; Lloyd's Register of Shipping Statistical Tables 1991 and 1992; Lloyd's Register of Shipping World Fleet Statistics 1993–2004.

Exhibit 3.4
Ships completed worldwide by number

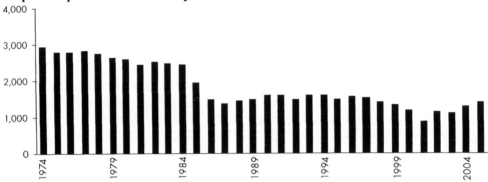

Sources: Lloyd's Register of Shipbuilding Statistics 1996–2005; Lloyd's Register of Shipping Statistical Tables
1991 and 1992; Lloyd's Register of Shipping World Fleet Statistics 1993–2004.

The financing options

For a buyer wishing to finance the purchase of a newbuilding by borrowing, there have been
two sources of traditional finance. Either the buyer obtained bank finance to pay for the ship
in full on delivery (and/or to refinance its payment of the pre-delivery instalments) ('buyer's
credit') or the buyer agreed to purchase the vessel on deferred payment terms with credit provided by the builder ('seller's credit'). In the past building contracts gave buyers the option to
pay cash on delivery or to take yard credit, with the buyer having the right to nominate his
preferred payment terms. A number of factors, such as the decreasing willingness of governments and commercial banks to provide funds to enable builders to provide seller's credit, the
increasing number of banks willing to provide newbuilding finance, the greater flexibility of
lending banks, and, perhaps most importantly, low US dollar interest rates which made the
generally fixed-rate government subsidised schemes unattractive, combined to make yard
credit much less widely available today than previously although they are still used from time
to time.

Shipbuilding contracts will normally provide for the buyer to pay for the construction and
delivery of the ship in instalments over the duration of the contract. Payments of contract price
will fall due at specific contract milestones. A typical seller's credit contract might provide for
an instalment schedule as follows:

Signing of contract	5%
6 months after contract	4%
Beginning of keel laying	4%
Launching	4%
Delivery	3%
Post-delivery (yard credit)	80%
	100%

On a cash contract, a possible split would be:

Signing of contract	15%
Cutting of first steel plate	15%
Beginning of keel laying	10%
Launching	10%
Delivery	50%
	100%

In the case of a seller's credit contract, the buyer will normally be expected to find the first 20 per cent or so of the contract price (that is, the first pre-delivery instalment) from his own resources. The balance will then be treated as an advance from the builder, repayable at regular intervals with interest (fixed or floating) in much the same manner as a normal commercial loan although, as explained below, there may be interest or other subsidies available. The terms of the yard financing may be set out in the shipbuilding contract itself or may be contained in a separate credit agreement, and will provide for repayment of the seller's credit over a set period after delivery, usually at equal half-yearly intervals. The terms of the seller's credit will generally be very similar to those contained in loan agreements used in financing second-hand ships, which are discussed in more detail in Chapter 2, with certain obvious differences.

Where the builder agrees to provide a seller's credit to the buyer the shipbuilder will require security from the buyer for the repayment of that credit in the same manner as any commercial lender will require security. This it may take by way of mortgage over the vessel on delivery coupled with an assignment of insurances and earnings. Alternatively, in the days when yards were able to offer buyers better credit terms than banks, the yard would often require a bank guarantee of the buyer's obligations to be issued in its favour by the buyer's bank. In that event, the buyer's bank would normally look to take a mortgage over the vessel, and other standard security, to secure the buyer's counter-indemnity.

Where seller's credit is involved, it is normal for the builder and the buyer to agree the forms of the security documents when the building contract is signed and to annex drafts of those security documents to the building contract. Alternatively, if a bank guarantee is called for, the bank may well be required to issue a commitment letter to the yard when the building contract is signed, or within a short period afterwards, committing it to issue its guarantee in the agreed form when called on to do so. Additionally, the yard may require a bank guarantee of future instalments of the purchase price, which may cause the bank issuing the guarantee security problems, (for reasons discussed below), unless the buyer has other assets available to be used as security.

Where a seller's credit is on offer, many yards will require the buyer to issue the builder with a series of promissory notes, one in respect of each of the post-delivery instalments of principal plus interest. This is a particularly American practice in origin and has little real advantage in English law other than as evidence of the debt under the shipbuilding contract or other seller's credit agreement. It does allow the builder easily to assign the benefit of the seller's credit by assigning or endorsing the notes to a third party, often the government-owned or government-sponsored bank financing the builder. The bank guarantee from the buyer's bank will then guarantee payment of the promissory notes as and when they fall due. A specimen promissory note, bank commitment letter and bank guarantee appear as Annex A. It should be stressed that these are only specimens. Individual builders and banks all have their preferred forms and, ultimately, the final form will need to be agreed by all the parties concerned.

The majority of shipbuilding contracts currently employed worldwide are financed on buyer's credit terms. Payments of pre-delivery contract price are treated as advances under the contract. If the builder fails to complete the construction of the ship in accordance with the shipbuilding contract by the contractual delivery date, or if he is otherwise in breach of the shipbuilding contract so as to entitle the buyer to terminate the shipbuilding contract, the buyer will be entitled to terminate the shipbuilding contract and require repayment of the pre-delivery instalments of contact price.

Where the building contract provides for payment in full by instalments on or before delivery, the buyer will commonly finance the payments by bank debt. Here, the bank will normally require the buyer to pay the first part – perhaps 20–30 per cent – of the purchase price from its own resources, advancing the balance, again on normal commercial terms. In this structure, the loan (and the loan agreement) will substantially follow their equivalents in second-hand financing, except only that the loan will be made available for drawing in tranches to meet the later building contract instalments as they fall due, and the bank will require, as a condition precedent to each drawing, evidence from the builder that the instalment to be financed by that drawing has become payable, coupled with a certificate from the classification society that the milestone credit, for example, keel laying, has occurred. It would be common for the loan not to become repayable until after delivery, when the vessel's earnings come on stream, and sometimes a borrower can persuade the bank to allow interest to be rolled up (or capitalised) in the meantime.

Lending in order to finance vessel construction causes banks particular security problems. This is because in many jurisdictions it is not possible for the lending bank to take a mortgage over a vessel under construction. In any event, title to the vessel will frequently, by the terms of the building contract, remain with the yard until delivery, so that the vessel under construction will not be an asset of the buyer over which the buyer can grant security. Even if, as is sometimes the case, title to materials used in the construction of the vessel passes to the buyer as the materials are appropriated to the vessel, the builder will retain a lien on the vessel until payment (or delivery if a seller's credit is to be provided) and any form of security which the buyer could grant its bank (for example, by way of a fixed and floating charge over its assets generally) would be of limited value. This position should be contrasted to that where the bank lends on delivery of the new vessel, either simply to finance the delivery instalment or to refinance earlier instalments paid by the buyer from other sources. A mortgage over the ship in the usual way is then perfectly possible, and financing techniques and documents are almost identical to those used in the financing of second-hand tonnage.

Under English law, a registered mortgage over a ship under construction is an impossibility, even to the extent that title has passed to the buyer. A statutory mortgage can only be taken over a registered ship and, to be eligible for registration, a ship must be 'used in navigation'[2] and, as a precondition to registration, a builder's certificate must be produced.[3] This inability to take a registered mortgage during construction is not limited to the United Kingdom, but is relatively common throughout the world, though with exceptions such as Germany, where the builder will frequently mortgage the vessel under construction to its bank until delivery, making it important for a buyer and his bank to ensure that any mortgage granted by the builder is, indeed, discharged on delivery. As a result, a financing bank will generally need to look elsewhere for security, perhaps to guarantees and to security over other assets of the buyer or of its parent or associated companies.

One form of security commonly taken by ship finance banks lending for newbuilding construction is an assignment of the benefit of the building contract and refund guarantee. This will enable the bank, in the event of the buyer's default, to continue with the construction of the vessel, take delivery, and then sell the vessel to satisfy the outstanding debt. It is not an entirely satisfactory security for several reasons. First, while the assignment will not of itself make the bank liable for unpaid instalments of the contract price, in practice if the buyer defaults the bank will have little option but to continue to pay those instalments from its own resources in order to complete the construction of the vessel. The bank may be able to negotiate a price reduction with the builder but it will still be tying itself to a possibly substantial ongoing commitment, all the time relying on the market for the type of vessel concerned staying sufficiently firm to allow it to sell the vessel on completion for a sufficient amount to satisfy the outstanding debt.

Secondly, enforcing its rights as assignee after default creates ongoing administrative and operational difficulties for a lender. While before default the lender will normally be content to allow the buyer and its representatives to supervise the construction of the ship, after default – when cooperation from the buyer is likely to be limited or non-existent – the lender will not normally have the technical expertise necessary properly to supervise the construction and will have to rely on employing (and paying) outside advisers. There may be ongoing insurance obligations, and pending delivery the lender will have a non-performing asset on its books and an increasing debt. The only way out is for the lender to find a third party prepared to take a further assignment of the contract – in effect, to sell the contract.

The weaknesses of an assignment of the shipbuilding contract need to be countered by the strengths of an assignment of a refund guarantee. As has already been seen, the buyers will normally be required to part with a substantial proportion of the contract price before delivery takes place and, not unnaturally, will usually require security to be provided by the yard for the repayment of those instalments (together with interest) if they become repayable under the terms of the building contract – for example, if the yard fails to deliver the vessel on time or becomes insolvent. It is commonly accepted practice for such security to be provided by means of a bank guarantee from the yard's bank in favour of the buyer. A specimen form of refund guarantee is included as Annex B, though the precise form will be subject to negotiation in each individual case and does vary from yard to yard. Annex B is very favourable to the buyer: yards will generally require that payment under the refund guarantee be postponed if the yard's obligation to refund pre-delivery instalments is disputed, perhaps until a final arbitration award under the building contract has been obtained.

An assignment of the refund guarantee will be another form of security available to a bank during the construction period and will almost invariably be required by both the buyer and his financier. A buyer should, therefore, ensure at the outset that the form of refund guarantee and the identity of the refund guarantor are acceptable to the financing bank. Many yards will prefer to tender guarantees from their local (often state-owned) banks, which may not be considered acceptable credit risks. Indeed, it was the inability of Western shipbuilders to persuade Western banks or export credit institutions to issue refund guarantees which was one of the major factors behind the decline in the 1990s in the order books of yards in Europe, particularly Eastern Europe.

It is important for a buyer to ensure that the building contract and refund guarantee are freely assignable, or that any necessary consents to assignment will be forthcoming. If they are not, the buyer may well have difficulty putting together an acceptable security package during the construction period. Where the vessel is built on seller's credit terms this is not a relevant consideration, assuming that the buyer is financing the pre-delivery instalments from its own resources, and where cash contracts are concerned yards will generally appreciate that it is in their interests to allow the assignment of the building contract and refund guarantee to a reputable lender to facilitate the buyer's financing arrangements, if the alternative would be to lose the order.

Finally, buyers and their financiers will need to ensure payments can be made abroad by refund guarantors and all requisite consents, licences and approvals are obtained.

Government support – the OECD and the EU[4]

Despite the considerable increase in new orders received by European shipyards during the 1990s, the continuing imbalance between supply and demand and increased international competition has been creating some difficulty for the European shipbuilding market. Against this background, the shipbuilding aid policy of the European Community (EC) has aimed to pursue the following broad objectives:

- to provide a defensive instrument against unfair competition through injurious pricing;
- to maintain a sufficient level of EC activity in those segments where EC yards will remain competitive under normal competitive conditions;
- to encourage the development of higher value-added specialised ships; and
- to provide a level playing field so that competition within the EC in shipbuilding is conducted on a fair and equitable basis.

Furthermore, when considering the subject of government support to European shipbuilding, it is essential to bear in mind the EC's participation in the international OECD effort to re-establish normal competitive conditions in the world market.

As part of this effort, in the early 1990s the 'Agreement Respecting Normal Competitive Conditions in the Commercial Shipbuilding and Repair Industry' was agreed under the auspices of the OECD. The said Agreement was opened for signature on 21 December 1994 and was scheduled to enter into force in 1996 but was not ratified by the United States and, accordingly, failed to become effective.

In light of the above, negotiations took place within the OECD which led to the conclusion of the 'Sector Understanding on Export Credits for Ships' (SUECS), which became effective on 15 April 2002. Australia, Japan, Korea, Norway, Poland, the Slovak Republic and the member states of the EC are parties to the SUECS. Indeed, by virtue of Decision 2002/634/EC the Council of the European Union has incorporated the SUECS into European legislation, thus giving effect to the SUECS over previous EC rules in this area.

The SUECS

The principal aim of the SUECS is to set out guidelines for officially supported export credits relating to export contracts.

Under the SUECS, subsidised credit schemes for newbuildings should meet the following criteria:

- the maximum newbuilding loan repayment period should be 12 years from delivery;
- repayment of principal should be in equal instalments at regular intervals of 6 to 12 months;
- there should be a minimum cash payment of 20 per cent of the contract price upon delivery of the vessel; and
- the interest rate should be determined by the CIRR (Commercial Interest Reference Rate).

The SUECS only applies to export contracts relating to:

- sea-going vessels of more than 1,000 grt used for the transportation of goods or persons or the performance of specialised services and which are self-navigable in the high seas;
- tugs of 365 kW and over;
- unfinished shells of ships that are afloat and mobile; and
- sea-going vessels of more than 1,000 grt which are converted.

In further meetings of the OECD since 2002 the participants of the OECD Arrangement on Guidelines for Officially Supported Export Credits under the auspices of which all the relevant agreements and/or understandings are reached, have agreed to take further steps in order to bring about 'normal competitive conditions' in the global shipbuilding market by virtue of a new international shipbuilding agreement to be prepared and brought on by a Special Negotiating Group within the Arrangement. The ultimate objective according to the Arrangement participants is to 'encourage competition for export sales based on their price and quality of the goods and/or services being exported rather than the cost of official export credit financing'.[5] In light of the failure of the relevant parties to implement the 1994 Agreement this might be a rather long and complicated process.

Government support in the United Kingdom[6]

Support for UK domestic shipbuilding is given, within the parameters of the OECD understanding, by the Department of Trade and Industry, acting through the Export Credits Guarantee Department (ECGD) and only in respect of sellers situated in the UK selling to overseas buyers.

It must be noted, that the potential for obtaining support for UK domestic shipbuilding has been significantly narrower since April 2005 when the Home Shipbuilding Credit Guarantee Scheme (HSCGS) also operated by the Department of Trade and Industry, acting through the Ship Mortgage Finance Company plc (SMFC) was abolished. The HSCGS provided support in respect of domestic buyers.

Under Section 10 of the Industry Act 1972 (as amended) the Secretary of State for Trade and Industry is given power to guarantee the repayment of loans granted to United Kingdom bodies (that is, persons resident in, or companies incorporated under the law of, some part of the UK, the Isle of Man or the Channel Islands) for the purpose of financing the construction, completion or alteration of ships and mobile off-shore installations. The seller carrying out the work and the relevant lending institution must both be approved by the Secretary of State. Where guarantees are given by the Secretary of State, finance, repayable at half-yearly intervals from delivery, will be available at a fixed rate. In addition to any repayments and interest payable, a fee, or premium is payable to ECGD for the issue of a guarantee; this is not fixed and may be quite substantial, but may be payable by instalments, with the instalments guaranteed by a bank.

ECGD have been engaged by the Secretary of State to conduct enquiries and negotiations in respect of any loans. They will advise on the creditworthiness of the applicant, the nature and extent of the security required and the documentation, and will report on applications to an advisory committee consisting of at least two directors of ECGD and a third member nominated by the Secretary of State.

Guarantees will only be available for the construction, completion and equipment of (a) a ship, other than a tug, of at least 100 grt; (b) a tug of not less than 500 bhp; or (c) a mobile off-shore installation weighing not less than 100 tons excluding fuel and water; or for the radical alteration of (d) a ship of at least 1,000 grt; or (e) a mobile off-shore installation weighing not less than 1,000 tons excluding fuel and water. Guarantees will not be available for repairs unless those repairs involve radical alteration to the ship or installation. Orders for the completion of partially constructed ships or installations may qualify for a guarantee.

In addition, guarantees will only be available where the relevant loan is made in support of a shipbuilding contract with a value of at least £1m (alternative finance products are available in respect of contracts with a value of less than £1m but these are not particularly suitable for shipbuilding contracts). The relevant lending institution must either be an authorised person for the purposes of the Financial Services and Markets Act 2000 (as amended from time to time) or have the benefit of an 'EEA authorisation' as this is defined in the said Act. Finally, in technical terms, the application to obtain a guarantee from ECGD must be made by the seller.

The maximum loan to be covered by a government guarantee will be 85 per cent of the approved contract price for ships and mobile offshore installations. Loans will be repayable by half yearly instalments from delivery over a maximum term of $8\frac{1}{2}$ years. Any grants obtained by the buyer from other UK or EU sources must be applied towards reduction of the guaranteed loan.

Loans will generally be secured by an assignment of the building contract during construction, followed by a first priority mortgage during the post-delivery credit period (or by a first priority mortgage on a ship or mobile off-shore installation being altered) together, where required, with security over other assets and/or third-party (sometimes bank) guarantees. Security may also be taken over other existing vessels or installations.

The documents required will include: (a) loan agreement between lending bank and buyer; (b) shipbuilding contract; (c) premium agreement between ECGD and seller in respect of the premium payment and other obligations of the seller; and (d) guarantee agreement between the Secretary of State and the lending bank. There will also be an interest equalisation agreement between the Secretary of State and the lending bank, whereby the Secretary of State will agree to make up to the bank the difference between the interest rate charged to the buyer and a commercial rate. The documents will be drawn up by solicitors instructed by ECGD and will be in the standard forms used by ECGD, rather than those of the actual lending bank concerned. Few amendments to the standard forms are likely to be accepted, and any renegotiations would inevitably involve additional legal costs, whether or not accepted. An estimate of likely legal costs is given at the time of the initial offer.

Japan[7]

In Japan, builders' credit is generally available for both domestic and foreign buyers and there are no specific requirements laid down by Japanese law. Rather, the terms of any yard credit are a matter for negotiation between the buyer and the builder. Government support is available from the Development Bank of Japan under the Loan Program for the Promotion of Foreign Direct Investment in Japan and (for overseas buyers) from the Japan Bank for International Cooperation. Again, the precise requirements and procedure vary from transaction to transaction. While it is possible, under Japanese law, to take a mortgage over a ship under construction, in practice this is rarely done and a mortgage will only be used as security post-delivery.

Korea[8]

In Korea, yard credit for ships to be exported overseas is commonly available, backed by The Export-Import Bank of Korea (Kexim) mainly under two initiatives: the Export Loan to Korean Shipyards and the Direct Loan to Foreign Buyers.

In respect of the Export Loan, the maximum loan amount made available by Kexim will be 90 per cent of the balance of the contract price (net of advance payments which should themselves be at least 20 per cent of the total contract price) in the case of pre-delivery financing, and 100 per cent of the contract price in the case of post-delivery financing. Interest will be the Base Rate plus the Margin (in respect of Korean Won) and the London Interbank Offered Rate (Libor) plus Margin (in respect of foreign currency) for pre-delivery financing. In the case of post-delivery financing interest will be generally fixed according to CIRR plus Margin or the equivalent Libor plus Margin.

During the construction period, the yard will require a payment guarantee for the pre-delivery instalments and Kexim will, in turn, require the yard to provide a *yangdo-tambo* security on the ship under construction. The effect of this is to pass legal ownership of the ship under construction to Kexim, and the *yangdo-tambo* security will be released at the time of delivery to the buyer. In the case of post-delivery credit the security required by Kexim will include a promissory note or trade bills related to the transaction in question and a letter of guarantee or letter of credit issued or confirmed by a creditworthy international bank.

A ship under construction cannot be registered under Korean law, and yards are reluctant to provide for title to ships under construction to pass progressively to the buyer, because of the need to transfer title to Kexim by way of the aforementioned *yangdo-tambo* security. If a *yangdo-tambo* security were not taken by Kexim, such a security would be available to a buyer or a third-party financier, as would be the possibility of a mortgage on the ship under construction. This is of little practical significance, first because the *yangdo-tambo* security is almost invariably established in favour of Kexim and, secondly, because of the ready availability of satisfactory refund guarantees from banks for Korean builders.

53

In respect of the Direct Loan, this is an export credit service that helps foreign buyers purchase Korean goods and services with repayment terms of two years or more. Under this program, Kexim enters directly into loan agreements with the foreign buyers and provides them with loans that are used to pay the Korean shipyards. The maximum loan amount made available by Kexim will be 100 per cent of the contract price. An exposure fee charged according to the OECD Guidelines, a commitment fee of no less than 0.3 per cent per annum and a management fee charged around 0.3 per cent of the approved loan amount will be chargeable. Interest rate will be fixed according to the CIRR plus Margin or the equivalent Libor plus Margin. Currently the maximum repayment term in respect of vessels is 12 years. The security required by Kexim in respect of this kind of arrangement will be similar to that required in respect of post-delivery credit under the Export Loan.

The Structured Finance for Ships, a new scheme for the Direct Loan, is also extended to foreign shipping companies which intend to buy vessels from Korean shipyards. The maximum loan amount made available by Kexim, in principle, will be 80 per cent in the case of the total debt amount not exceeding US$200m and 70 per cent in the case of the total debt amount exceeding US$200m and the balance may be raised by co-financing banks with Kexim. Fees payable, interest rate and maximum repayment term will be the same as those of the Direct Loan stated above. Kexim will require a first priority mortgage over the relevant vessel, a corporate guarantee or support letter of the sponsor, a first priority assignment of charter, earnings and insurance and other securities reasonably required as security.

It will be clearly seen from the above that, although Korea does not officially provide any government subsidies, grants or other support to the shipbuilding industry or to owners of ships built in Korea, at any rate, the facilities provided by Kexim have been very useful financing methods for both Korean shipyards and foreign buyers.

China[9]

In China, yard credit for ships to be exported overseas is available and is backed by The Export-Import Bank of China (CEXIM) through export seller's credit. Export seller's credit refers to the loans provided by CEXIM to Chinese shipbuilders and trading houses for financing their manufacturing and export of ships, or for their repair and reconstruction of ships registered in foreign countries. The advance payments made by the buyers under the shipbuilding contracts should generally be at least 20 per cent of the contract price. CEXIM will require the shipbuilders and trading houses to provide security in relation to their repayment obligations under the loans.

A foreign buyer can obtain finance from CEXIM directly through export buyer's credit, which refers to the medium- and long-term credit offered by CEXIM to foreign buyers to support the export of Chinese-built ships. The operations of the export buyer's credit generally follow the Arrangement on Guidelines for Officially Supported Export Credits as developed by OECD.

There are various requirements which have to be met before export buyer's credit can be granted to foreign buyers. For instance, the price of the shipbuilding contract should be over US$2m, the loan amount provided by CEXIM should not generally exceed 80 per cent of the contract price and the foreign buyer may be required to provide security to CEXIM.

The maximum repayment period for export buyer's credit is 15 years from the date of the first drawdown of the loan. The interest rate could be either fixed at the CIRR as monthly announced by OECD, or floating on the basis of six months Libor plus a Margin.

The United States[10]

In 1938, the US Congress enacted a system of federally insured ship financing, where, in the event of default, the US government would repay funds that had been loaned by a private lender. This programme evolved from what was essentially an insurance policy issued by the US government to a full faith and credit guarantee by the US government for the purpose of promoting the growth and modernisation of the US Merchant Marine and US shipyards. This programme is generally known as 'Title XI' since it is found in the eleventh title of the US Merchant Marine Act 1936.

This insurance and later guarantee programme was used extensively and successfully during the Second World War and for nearly 30 years thereafter with relatively few defaults. However, the Title XI programme began to suffer losses from defaults in the mid-1970s. Steadily, it has fallen into disuse due in large part to a decline in the construction of US-built commercial vessels and the Reagan administration, which was generally opposed to government guarantees and subsidies, despite the efforts of the Clinton administration to extend and renew the old policy under the National Shipbuilding and Shipyard Conversion Act of 1993 (the Shipbuilding Act).

The Shipbuilding Act added Sections 1111 and 1112 to Title XI of the Merchant Marine Act 1936. These sections authorise the Secretary of Transportation, acting through the US Maritime Administration (MarAd), to guarantee obligations issued to finance the construction, reconstruction or reconditioning of eligible export vessels and for shipyard modernisation and improvement. The major change made by these new sections to the old guarantee programme was to open it, for the first time, to non-US flag vessels – vessels built for export. This was a dramatic change from previous policy which had made Title XI financing available only for US flag vessels built for and operated by US citizens. Under the present programme, non-US citizens may qualify for Title XI financing for vessels built for export.

Section 1111 allows the Secretary of Transportation to guarantee obligations for eligible export vessels in accordance with the terms and conditions of Title XI. Alternatively, MarAd may guarantee *more favourable* terms than already provided under Title XI. These terms are compatible with the export credit terms offered by foreign governments for the sale of vessels built in foreign shipyards.

Section 1112 of the Act allows the Secretary to guarantee the payment of the principal of, and interest on, obligations for modern and advanced shipbuilding technology.

The revised and expanded Title XI programme currently administered by MarAd provides for a full faith and credit guarantee by the US government of debt obligations issued by:

- US or foreign shipowners for the purpose of financing or re-financing either US flag vessels or eligible export vessels constructed, reconstructed or reconditioned in US shipyards; and
- US shipyards for the purpose of financing advanced shipbuilding technology and modern shipbuilding technology of a privately owned general shipyard facility located in the United States.

Financing is available up to 87.5 per cent of the actual cost of the project. Most transactions, however, will probably involve financing of no more than 75 per cent of the project. The term of the financing can be as long as 25 years, depending upon the economics of the project involved. The interest rate and most terms of the debt to be guaranteed by the government are set by the private sector lender.

All types of vessels are eligible for consideration. This includes not only ocean-going vessels intended for international commerce but tugs and barges used on inland waterways, supply boats used in the offshore drilling industry and even drilling rigs registered as vessels. However, MarAd has made clear that it will closely scrutinise the economics of any proposed project in order to determine whether the guarantees should be granted, and each project must be justified on strict economic terms.

The application itself is a MarAd form which requires detailed information as to the identity and corporate structure of the applicant as well as extensive documentation as to the design of the vessel or vessels involved and the economics of the project.

A non-refundable filing fee of US$5,000 is required to accompany the application. Prior to MarAd's issuance of a binding commitment to guarantee, the applicant will have to pay an investigation fee of $\frac{1}{2}$ per cent of 1 per cent on the debt to be guaranteed up to US$10m and $\frac{1}{8}$ per cent of 1 per cent on all debt in excess of US$10m.

MarAd prescribes its standard forms of mortgages and other security documents that must be suitably modified and executed by each applicant.

Annex A

Promissory note

US$[ ]   Date: [ ]

No: [1] of [13]

For value received, [Buyer] a corporation duly organised and existing under the laws of [ ] having its registered office at [ ] hereby unconditionally promises to pay, on the [ ] day of [ ] to [Builder] a corporation duly organised and existing under the laws of [ ] having its registered office at [ ] the principal sum of United States Dollars [ ] and to pay interest on the said principal sum from and including the date hereof, at the rate of [ ] per cent per annum, the first payment of interest to be due and payable six (6) months after the date hereof (namely [ ]) and thereafter payable semi-annually on the [ ] day of [ ] and on the [ ] day of [ ] of each and every year, until maturity (whether by acceleration or otherwise) and thereafter at the rate of [ ] per cent ([ ]) per annum until the principal sum and the interest thereon are fully paid.

Interest shall be calculated on the basis of the actual days elapsed and a year of three hundred and sixty (360) days. Both principal and interest shall be payable in United States Dollars in immediately available funds at the account of [ ] without any deduction or withholding for or on account of any present or future taxes or other charge.

This note is one of a series of [thirteen (13)] promissory notes in the aggregate principal amount of United States Dollars [ ] of like form and tenor except for their respective numbers, principal amounts and dates of maturity. Each of the said notes is secured by a Letter of Guarantee issued by [ ].

In the event that default shall be made in the payment of interest on this note, or in the payment of the principal of or interest on any of the other notes of this series as and when the same shall become due and payable, and such default shall continue for a period of fifteen (15) days, the holder of this note may at its option declare the principal of and accrued interest on this note to be forthwith due and payable, whereupon the same shall be forthwith due and payable, and the holder hereof shall have the other remedies herein or by law provided.

The holder of this note shall be under no obligation to make presentment for payment, demand or notice of any kind whatsoever.

The maker and the endorsers of this note hereby waive the right to interpose any defence, set-off or counterclaim of any nature or description in any action or proceeding arising on, out of, under or by reason of this note.

The maker of this note may at its option prepay the whole of this note without premium or penalty on the due date of the next forthcoming interest payment of this note by payment of the principal hereof together with accrued interest thereon to and including the date of pre-payment. The maker of this note shall give the holder of this note notice of such prepayment not less than thirty (30) days prior to the date of such proposed prepayment. Notice of prepayment shall identify this note by number, shall specify the intended date of prepayment and shall be irrevocable.

This note shall be governed by the laws of the State of New York, USA. The maker and the endorsers hereby consent to any legal action or proceeding in relation to this note being brought in the State of New York, USA or in London, England and hereby irrevocably waive any immunity from suit, attachment (before or after judgment) or execution on a judgment to which they or their property may be entitled.

The maker and the endorsers hereby irrevocably submit to the non-exclusive jurisdiction of the courts of the State of New York and the federal courts of the United States of America located in the City and State of New York, United States of America or of the courts of England as any holder of this note may elect and hereby irrevocably consent to the service of process out of the said courts by registered air mail, postage prepaid, to the maker or the endorser as the case may be or in any other manner permitted by law.

The maker hereby certifies and declares that all acts, conditions and things required to be done and performed and to have happened precedent to the creation and issue of this note, and to constitute this note the legal, valid and binding obligations of the maker in accordance with its terms, have been done and performed and have happened in due and strict compliance with all applicable laws and regulations.

In witness whereof the undersigned has caused this note to be signed in its corporate name by its representative thereunto duly authorised this [ ] day of [ ].

For and on behalf of [*Buyer*]

Letter of commitment

By:
Name:
Title:

TO: [*Builder*]   Date: [ ]

LETTER OF COMMITMENT

In consideration of the execution by you ('the Builder') of a Shipbuilding Contract with [*Buyer*] ('the Buyer') for the construction and sale of one (1) [ ] having Hull No [ ] (hereinafter called the 'Vessel') and in consideration of the sum of one (1) United States Dollar (USD1) paid by you to us (the receipt and sufficiency of which we hereby acknowledge) we hereby irrevocably and unconditionally undertake that we will execute and deliver to you a letter of guarantee (the 'Letter of Guarantee') in the form of the draft annexed hereto simultaneously with delivery and acceptance of the Vessel against the presentation to us of:

1 a duplicate original Protocol of Delivery and Acceptance signed by an officer or attorney of the Builder and by an officer or attorney of the Buyer; and
2 a photocopy of each of the Promissory Notes referred to in the Letter of Guarantee signed and completed by an officer or attorney of the Buyer; and
3 a duplicate original copy of the Builder's Certificate and Declaration of Warranty for the Vessel;

and we confirm that, for the presentation of the foregoing documents, we shall make our duly authorised representative available at the time and place such documents are signed.

The Letter of Guarantee will be in respect of the Buyer's obligations in the principal amount of USD [ ] and interest thereon. We shall be under no obligation whatsoever to execute and deliver to you the Letter of Guarantee after [ ].

This letter of commitment shall be governed by and construed in accordance with English law.

Yours faithfully,

Letter of guarantee

TO: [*Builder*]   Date: [ ]

Gentlemen:

LETTER OF GUARANTEE NO [ ]

In consideration of your completing and delivering one (1) [ ] known as [ ], your Hull No [ ] (hereinafter called the 'Vessel') to [ ] (hereinafter called the 'Buyer'), on deferred payment terms under a Shipbuilding Contract dated [ ] as amended (the 'Contract'), entered into by you and the Buyer, the undersigned, as primary obligor and not merely as surety, hereby irrevocably and unconditionally guarantees the due and punctual payment whether at the stated maturity, by acceleration or otherwise, by the Buyer of a series of [ ] promissory notes (together the 'Promissory Notes' and individually 'Promissory Note'), respectively numbered one (1) to [ ] inclusive, each in the principal amount specified in the schedule of payments below, the first Promissory Note to be due and payable [ ] months after the date of delivery and acceptance of the Vessel under the Contract and the successive Promissory Notes to be due and payable at intervals of six (6) months thereafter, issued by the Buyer to the order of yourself upon delivery and acceptance of the Vessel under the Contract, and also guarantee the due and punctual payment by the Buyer of interest on the principal amount of each Promissory Note, the first such payment of interest to be due and payable six (6) months after the date of delivery and acceptance of the Vessel under the Contract and thereafter payable semi-annually, within a period of [ ] years from the date of delivery and acceptance of the Vessel under the Contract, at the rate of [ ] per cent per annum until maturity (by acceleration or otherwise) of such Promissory Note, then thereafter at the rate of [ ] per cent per annum until full payment.

Interest shall be calculated on the basis of the actual days elapsed and a year of three hundred and sixty (360) days.

Below is the schedule of payments due under the Promissory Notes:

Promissory		Principal Amount	
Note (No)	Date	US Dollars	Due Date

Interest is payable on the principal amount of each Promissory Note semi-annually on the [ ] and on the [ ] in each and every year, until maturity (by acceleration or otherwise) at the rate of [ ] per cent per annum and thereafter at the rate of [ ] per cent per annum until full payment.

The undersigned hereby waives the right to interpose any defence, set-off or counter-claim of any nature or description in any action or proceedings arising on, out of, under or by reason of the Promissory Notes or this letter of guarantee.

In the event that the Buyer fails to pay any one or more of the Promissory Notes and/or interest thereon covered by this letter of guarantee on the due date for each payment or upon acceleration in accordance with the terms of the Promissory Notes, the undersigned will pay to you or your assignee the amounts due and payable and covered by this letter of guarantee immediately upon receipt by the undersigned of written demand from you or your assignee including a statement that the Buyer is in default of payment of any of the Promissory Notes and/or interest thereon and specifying the amount(s) in default and the subject of demand hereunder, without requesting you to take any further procedure or step against the Buyer or with respect to the Promissory Notes and/or interest thereon in default and the undersigned shall itself pay interest on any such amounts demanded by you as aforesaid from the due date thereof until the payment in full of such amounts at the rate of [ ] per cent per annum together with all costs and expenses incurred in the enforcement or attempted enforcement of this letter of guarantee.

Neither the Promissory Notes nor any indebtedness represented thereby may be extended, renewed, varied or changed without the prior written consent of the undersigned (such consent not to be unreasonably withheld if the undersigned is satisfied that its obligations hereunder will not be in any way adversely affected thereby), except that (i) the maturity of the principal or interest on any Promissory Note may be extended for a period not exceeding three (3) months and (ii) any typographical and/or clerical errors in the Promissory Notes may be corrected, in either case with notice to the undersigned.

The undersigned hereby agrees that this letter of guarantee and undertaking hereunder shall be assignable to and shall inure to the benefit of [ ] without our prior written consent and, with our prior written consent (such consent not to be unreasonably withheld), to any other subsequent holder of any one or more of the Promissory Notes PROVIDED HOWEVER that in the event of any such assignment (whether or not our prior written consent is required as aforesaid) (i) the liability of the undersigned under this letter of guarantee shall be no greater than it would have been if no assignment had been made and (ii) the undersigned shall not be bound by any such assignment unless and until it shall have received written notice thereof.

All payments by the undersigned under this letter of guarantee shall be made in United States Dollars in immediately available funds by telegraphic transfer to [ ] or, in the case of any assignment as hereinbefore mentioned, to the account designated by the assignee, without deduction or withholding on account of any present or future taxes and without set-off. In the event that any deduction or withholding is imposed on any payment to be made hereunder by law or by any taxing authority on account of any present or future taxes (other than taxes on, or calculated by reference to, the overall net income of the beneficiary hereof for the time being), the undersigned agrees to pay such additional amount as may be necessary in order that the actual amount received after deduction or withholding shall be equal to the amount that would have been received if such deduction or withholding were not required after allowance for any increase in taxes or charges payable by virtue of the receipt of such additional amount.

Notwithstanding anything to the contrary herein contained the undersigned's liability hereunder at any relevant time shall, subject to the second sentence of the preceding paragraph, be limited, in the case only of principal and interest payable under the Promissory Notes, to the aggregate of the following:

(1) in respect of principal, an amount equal to the aggregate of the respective principal amounts of the Promissory Notes remaining unpaid at such time PROVIDED ALWAYS

that any Promissory Note which the Buyer shall have failed to pay on the due date thereof and in respect of which you or your assignee shall have failed to make demand hereunder within a period of three (3) months following such due date, shall, for the purpose of this letter of guarantee, be deemed to have been paid by the Buyer in full and the undersigned's maximum liability hereunder reduced accordingly; and

(2) in respect of interest, an amount equal to six (6) months' interest at the rate of [ ] per cent ([ ]) per annum and an amount equal to one (1) month's default interest at the rate of [ ] per cent per annum on the amount specified in paragraph (1) above.

This letter of guarantee shall come into full force and effect upon delivery of the Vessel by you to, and acceptance of the Vessel by, the Buyer under the Contract and shall continue in force and effect until the earlier of (i) [date] (being three (3) months after the maturity date of the last Promissory Note to mature) and (ii) the full payment of the Promissory Notes and (to the extent guaranteed under this letter of guarantee) interest thereon.

Notwithstanding the foregoing, the undersigned shall be discharged of any further liability under this letter of guarantee if at any time the undersigned pays to you or your assignee at the aforesaid account an amount in United States Dollars in immediately available funds equal to the aggregate of the respective principal amounts of the Promissory Notes remaining unpaid at such time together with interest accrued thereon at the rate of [ ] per cent ([ ]) per annum and at the rate of [ ] per cent if applicable as specified above from the last date of payment of such interest up to and including the date of such payment by the undersigned PROVIDED HOWEVER that the undersigned shall give at least thirty (30) days' irrevocable prior written notice of such prepayment to you or your assignee.

The obligation of the undersigned hereunder is absolute and unconditional irrespective of any legal limitation, disability, incapacity or other circumstances relating to the Buyer or any other person or the Promissory Notes or any other document, instrument or agreement contemplated therein or of the genuineness, legality, validity, regularity or enforceability of the Promissory Notes or any other documents, instruments or agreements contemplated therein.

This letter of guarantee shall be continuing and shall, subject as provided herein, cover and secure any ultimate balance owing under the Promissory Notes, but you shall not be obliged to exhaust your recourse against the Buyer or the securities which you may hold before being entitled to payment from the undersigned of the obligations hereby guaranteed.

The undersigned hereby represents and warrants that (i) the undersigned is a limited company duly organised and validly existing and in full compliance with the laws of [ ] and has full legal right, power and authority to execute this letter of guarantee and to perform its obligations hereunder, (ii) the undersigned has taken all appropriate and necessary corporate action to authorise the issue of this letter of guarantee and the performance by it of its obligations hereunder, (iii) the execution, delivery and performance of this letter of guarantee and the covenants herein contained do not, to the knowledge and belief of the undersigned, violate or contravene any provisions of any existing treaty, law or regulation or any judgment, order or decree of any court or governmental agency applicable to the undersigned, or violate or result in a default under any mortgage, contract or agreement to which the undersigned is a party,

(iv) this letter of guarantee constitutes the legal, valid and binding obligations of the under-signed, and (v) the undersigned has obtained all necessary consents, licences, approvals, authorisations, registrations or declarations with any governmental authority in [ ] required, if any, in connection with the validity and enforceability of this letter of guarantee, and the same are in full force and effect.

This letter of guarantee shall be governed by and construed in accordance with English law. The undersigned hereby irrevocably consents that any legal action or proceeding against the undersigned, or any of its property, with respect to this letter of guarantee may be brought in the English courts, and, by execution and delivery of this letter of guarantee, the undersigned hereby accepts in regard to any such action or proceeding, for itself and in respect of its prop-erty, generally and unconditionally, the non-exclusive jurisdiction of the aforesaid courts. The undersigned hereby consents to the service of process out of the said courts by registered air mail, postage prepaid, to the undersigned, or in any other manner permitted by law.

The undersigned represents and warrants that this letter of guarantee is a commercial act and that the undersigned is not entitled to claim immunity from legal proceedings with respect to itself or any of its properties or assets on the grounds of sovereignty or otherwise under any law. To the extent that the undersigned or any of its properties or assets has or hereafter may acquire any right to immunity from set-off, legal proceedings, attachment prior to judgment, other attachment or execution of judgment on the grounds of sovereignty or otherwise, the undersigned for itself and its properties and other assets hereby irrevocably waives such right to immunity in respect of its obligations under this letter of guarantee.

After this letter of guarantee shall have expired or been discharged as aforesaid, you or your assignee will return the same to the undersigned without any request from the undersigned.

IN WITNESS WHEREOF, the undersigned has caused this letter of guarantee to be executed and delivery by its duly authorised representative the day and year above written.

Yours very truly,
for and on behalf of

[ ]

By

Name:

Title:

Annex B

Refund guarantee

[Date]

TO: [*Buyer*]

Dear Sirs,

IRREVOCABLE LETTER OF GUARANTEE NO [ ]

At the request of [*Builder*] (hereinafter called 'the Seller') and in consideration of you agreeing to pay the Seller the instalments before delivery of the vessel under the contract concluded by you and the Seller dated [ ] (hereinafter as amended from time to time called 'the
Contract') for the construction of one (1) [ ] to be designated as Hull No [ ] (hereinafter called
'the Vessel') we, the undersigned, hereby irrevocably and unconditionally guarantee to you
that the Seller will repay to you a principal amount up to a total of United States Dollars [ ]
representing the aggregate amount of the first, second, third and fourth instalments of the
Contract Price (as referred to and defined in Article [ ] of the Contract) which have been paid
by you to the Seller under the Contract prior to the delivery of the Vessel, as and when the
same become liable for repayment as provided under Article [ ] of the Contract. Should the
Seller fail to make such repayment, we will forthwith, upon your first demand (which
demand shall include a certificate signed by one of your duly authorised officers that the
Seller is obliged to make such payment) pay to you the aforesaid amount of such instalments
which have been paid by you to the Seller prior to delivery of the Vessel together with interest at the rate of [ ] per cent per annum on each of the said instalments from the time that you
paid each of the said instalments to the Seller until the full amount of such instalments is
repaid to you.

Our liability under this letter of guarantee shall not exceed the maximum principal sum of
United States Dollars [ ] representing the aggregate amount of the instalments of the Contract
Price paid by you to the Seller prior to delivery of the Vessel, plus interest at the rate of [ ] per
annum calculated on the amount of each instalment of the Contract Price paid under the contract from the date of receipt of the same by the Seller until the date on which the same is
repaid under this letter of guarantee.

Payment under this letter of guarantee shall be made in United States Dollars to your account
with [ ]. All payments under this letter of guarantee shall be made in full and without deduction for or on account of any taxation or any other deduction or withholding whatsoever. If
such deductions are required to be made by law then payments under this letter of guarantee
shall be increased so that the net amount received under this letter of guarantee will be the full
amount which would have been paid but for such deduction or withholding.

Our obligations under this letter of guarantee shall not be affected by the bankruptcy or insolvency of the Seller or any breach of or default under the Contract, it being intended that our

obligations under this letter of guarantee shall only be discharged if any of the following events has occurred:

(i) the Vessel is delivered to you as provided in Article [ ] of the Contract; or
(ii) the Seller refunds to you all moneys paid by you under the Contract; or
(iii)payment of the full amount guaranteed hereunder is made by us to you.

Any claim or demand shall be made on us in writing, signed by one of your duly authorized officers and may be served on us by hand or by post, and if sent by post to [ ] (or such other address as we may notify to you in writing) or by tested telex (telex no) via [ ].

This letter of guarantee is to be governed by and construed in accordance with the laws of England and, for your benefit, we hereby submit to the non-exclusive jurisdiction of the English courts and agree that service of proceedings under this letter of guarantee may be effected on our branch office in London. We further hereby waive and disclaim all rights what-soever to claim sovereign immunity for ourselves or our assets in respect of any claim or pro-ceedings brought under this letter of guarantee, and waive and disclaim any claim that any proceedings brought against us under or in respect of this letter of guarantee have been brought in an inconvenient or inappropriate forum.

Yours truly,

[1] Sources for statistics in this chapter are as follows: *Lloyd's Register of World Shipbuilding Statistics 1996* to *2005*; *Lloyd's Register of Shipping Statistical Tables 1991* and *1992* and *Lloyd's Register of Shipping World Fleet Statistics 1993* to *2004*.

[2] Section 313(1) Merchant Shipping Act 1995.

[3] Regulation 28 of The Merchant Shipping (Registration of Ships) Regulations 1993.

[4] Sources for the information in this part of the chapter are as follows: http://www.oecd.org; OJ No L 206, 3.8.2002, p. 16 and OJ No L 32, 2.2.2001, p. 1.

[5] http://www.oecd.org/document/29/0,2340,en_2649_34169_1844765_1_1_1_1,00.html

[6] We are indebted to John Smith and Malcolm Tate of ECGD and Nick Evans of SMFC for the information provided in respect of this part of the chapter.

[7] Sources for the information in this part of the chapter are as follows: http://www.dbj.go.jp and http://jbic.go.jp.

[8] Sources for the information in this part of the chapter are as follows: http://www.koreaexim.go.kr. We are indebted to H. S. Yoon of Kim & Chang, Korea for his comments in respect of this part of the chapter.

[9] Sources for the information in this part of the chapter are as follows: http://www.eximbank.tw. We are indebted to our colleague, Hongkai Zhou for compiling this part of the chapter.

[10] Sources for the information in this part of the chapter are as follows: http://www.marad.dot.gov/TitleXI.

Chapter 4

The banker's perspective

Alan Brauner and Peter Illingworth

The shipping market

Shipping is a highly capital-intensive industry in constant need of large amounts of capital funds to upgrade and expand the fleet – generally estimated between US$30–45bn annually. For the years 2003–2005 the sum invested has been substantially in excess of the norm (see Exhibit 4.1). According to Clarkson Research Services the value of newbuilding deliveries will leap from US$34bn in 2005 to US$55bn in 2006 and US$72bn in 2007.

Exhibit 4.1
Investment Trends

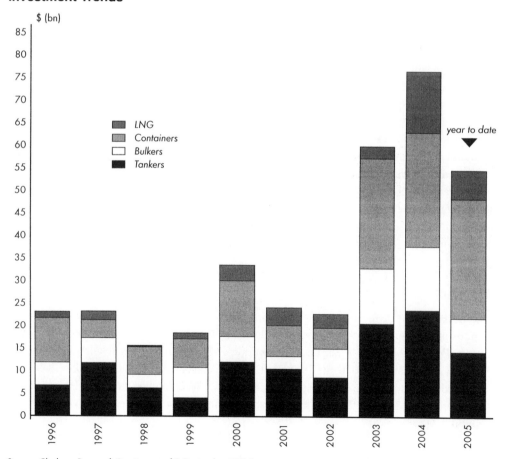

Source: Clarkson Research Services as of 1 September 2005.

The history of ship finance can be traced back to the sixteenth century when vessels were financed by wealthy individuals under a limited liability structure. It was in the mid-nineteenth century when the shipping community started to use debt, mainly to finance maintenance of their fleet, that mortgage finance came into being. The use of debt was limited to small amounts and conservative leverage (loan to value). Generally, the industry's borrowing requirements were modest and many of the older established owners financed investments from retained earnings. This situation remained basically the same until the 1950s.

In the 1950s and 1960s the rapidly growing industrial economies of the USA, Europe and Japan led to a significant development in both the demand for ships and the size and types of vessels. Shipping moved towards becoming a capital-intensive industry in need of external capital as the financing of new investments from cash flow became increasingly difficult. Initially, banks continued lending on a conservative basis. Loans were for three to five years, with period time-charter cover or advances around 50 per cent of the hull value against a first mortgage on modern ships. The 1950s to the early 1970s saw a dramatic increase in charter-backed finance, both period time-charters (up to seven or even 15 years) and longer term bare-boat charters (for example Shikumizen deals between Hong Kong-based shipowners and Japanese charterers). In the 1960s deferred shipyard credit with government involvement was introduced and became very popular. It offered an 80 per cent advance at an artificially low fixed interest and was used by shipyards to assist in obtaining new orders for ships. Thus financing during this period was dominated by banks and shipyard credit (most of which was arranged and funded by banks with credit backed by governments). Shipyard credit lost its appeal in the mid-1980s as market interest rates fell below the OECD agreed fixed rate for the eight-year term of $8\frac{1}{2}$ per cent per annum.

It is only in the last 20 years that there has been any significant development in alternative sources of capital available to shipping. These sources include both debt and equity from the public markets, tax-based partnerships such as the K/S in Norway and KG in Germany, tax lease finance, equity funds and so on (see Exhibit 4.2). Some of these financial products only become available periodically depending upon conditions in both the shipping and financial markets. At the time of writing, bank debt finance remains the dominant source of capital, providing over 70 per cent of the industry's external finance needs. This is unlikely to change much in the foreseeable future, especially for bulk shipping, although much will depend upon how the shipping markets perform in the future.

The fleet

The development of the fleet over the period since 1963 has changed greatly and includes periods of rapid growth, stagnation and decline. The fleet has grown from around 200 million deadweight (dwt) in 1963 to just under one billion dwt today. According to Clarkson Research Services as at 1 January 2006, the dry bulk fleet consisted of 6,127 ships, the tanker fleet 4,024 ships and the fast-growing container fleet 3,600 ships. The combined bulk fleet at over 10,000 ships has doubled since 1970, while the first container ship commenced trading in 1966 (see Exhibit 4.3).

The fleet is comprised of several different ship types. The major sectors listed by size (dwt) are oil tankers, bulk carriers, general cargo, container, chemical carriers, liquefied gas,

Exhibit 4.2
Sources of capital for shipping

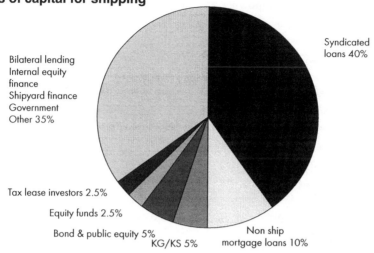

Source: Lloyd's Shipping Economist; DVB internal resources.

Exhibit 4.3
Fleet age profile in deadweight

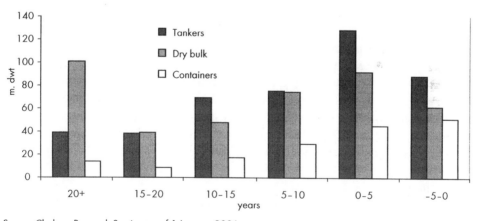

Source: Clarkson Research Services as of 1 January 2006.

ro-ro carriers and refrigerated cargo. Thus, shipping consists of several different businesses and markets. The cruise fleet has also grown rapidly over the last 30 years. Although an entirely different business, cruise ships are a significant part of several shipping banks' portfolios.

Another feature of the world fleet during the last 30 years has been the rapid escalation of ship sizes, particularly in the bulk sector. Economies of scale are an important element of unit transport costs. Therefore, it is not too surprising that the sizes of merchant ships has grown. The average size of ships has grown gradually across all sizes, whether Handy size, Panamax or Capesize. Merchant ships take several years to build and this introduces a time-lag into the shipowner's response to an upsurge in demand, new technology or size increments.

The major sources of cash flowing into the shipping markets come from the freight market, the sale and purchase market, ship demolition, bank loans and capital market activities. The main outflows arise from the purchase of newbuildings, (for second-hand sale and purchase funds usually flow from one shipowner to another and, therefore, stay in the market), operational costs, voyage costs, (variable costs associated with specific voyage(s)), periodic maintenance costs (dry-docking/special surveys), capital costs (debt service principal and interest) and dividends (which are discretionary).

Operating costs

The typical breakdown for a bulk carrier's operation costs are as follows:

Crew matters	40%
Repairs/maintenance	16%
Insurance	21%
Stores/provisions/lubs	16%
Overheads	7%
	100%

Plus loan principal, interest and depreciation.

Relative costs depend on many factors that may change over time. For example, crew matters will vary according to the number of crew personnel used and the level of wages. When structuring a cash flow forecast, it is a straightforward exercise to calculate what is needed by way of daily charter hire to cover operating cost, voyage costs, debt servicing and to provide an acceptable return on capital invested. The difficulty is the many variables particularly on the revenue side. The shipowner can play the spot market and accept full market risk, or can time-charter the vessel, which shifts that risk to the charterer. Earnings also depend on the productivity of the ship, which includes its carrying capacity and performance (for example, days off-hire).

Obviously, ships of different size and age have a completely different cost structure. As a ship ages its capital costs reduce but its operating and voyage costs increase relative to newer ships. This is due to the effects not only of ageing but also due to technical improvements (for example, more efficient engines) to new ships.

Assessing shipping risk

Among ship finance banks, history over the past 35 years has demonstrated the dangers of relying on asset values. This has reinforced not only credit standards among banks but also the importance of sound security documentation.

Why is shipping subject to more financial speculation than other asset-based cyclical industries? The key issue in shipping is the credit risk – namely the shipowner's ability to meet all its financial obligations over the medium to long term, even in adverse conditions. The four characteristics that make ship finance distinctive are:

- *Capital intensity* – The amounts borrowed are large, not only in absolute terms but also as a percentage of total asset value. For new investments, lenders generally insist upon an infusion of cash equity which eats up liquidity. In a highly cyclical business such as shipping, maintaining a proper level of liquidity is crucial.
- *Mobility of assets* – Unlike aircraft which can be regarded as homogeneous assets, there are numerous types and specifications of ships and the overall perception is that the physical condition of these vessels can be highly disparate. Ships trade in a perilous environment and move continually from one jurisdiction to another. Lenders tend to treat ships as 'stand alone' assets with wide swings in value that occur; ship finance has strong asset-based financing characteristics.
- *Volatility* – the shipping industry is exposed to volatile and unpredictable market conditions that frequently experience wild swings in revenues and asset values. All industries face economic risk, but some of the risks in shipping are unique to the industry. As an example, much of the volatility is due to over-ordering of ships and in certain sectors timing can be crucial. While bankers are used to handling volatility the basic problem with ship lending is that it combines volatility with medium- to long-term lending which is very risky.
- *Business structures* – the industry is dominated by entrepreneurs. Most ships are owned through single purpose companies, often with bearer shares belonging to disparate groups with the overall perception of secrecy on both operational and financial matters.

These four factors make it difficult to carry out the conventional credit analysis on which most bank lending relies. As a result, shipping is often difficult to appraise – even for experienced bankers.

Ship finance is fundamentally about appraising and securing shipping risk and a bank's priority is to secure its investment. If the sources of collateral are examined the central role of the freight market becomes apparent – it dominates the two main sources of collateral, the asset value of the ship and its earnings. A third source of security is the balance sheet, but to the extent that this contains substantial non-shipping assets then we are moving away from shipping risk towards corporate lending.

It follows that shipping financiers cannot avoid taking a view of the freight market and in bulk shipping this means the 'Shipping Market Cycle' (see Exhibit 4.4). Perhaps the most important feature of the cycle is that for much of the time it is far too unpredictable to provide bankers or anyone else with much guidance on the future earnings or the collateral value of the vessels they finance.

The unpredictability of shipping revenues resulting in falling asset values impacts on the creditworthiness of the industry in general, often making it difficult for shipping companies to compete for capital in certain areas of the financial markets.

Past history has resulted in the financial markets considering shipping as a specialised and unpredictable business. Shipping breaks down into many sectors each with its own sub-sectors,

Exhibit 4.4

The shipping market cycle

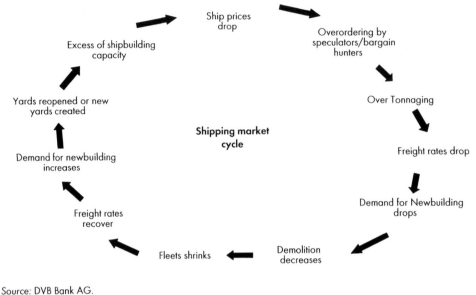

Source: DVB Bank AG.

with very different characteristics. Most sectors act independently of each other. The major bulk sectors tend to be the most volatile, while smaller, more specialised sectors, tend to be less fragmented and so suffer less volatility.

In the container/liner sector, rates are much less volatile but volumes can fluctuate widely depending on the supply/demand cycle. From an economic viewpoint, the service has three important differences:

- The business of transporting many small units requires a much larger and more complex administrative overhead.
- The obligation to sail to a timetable makes capacity inflexible. The supply of capacity is not continuous but a series of ship sized increments. This means that when trade is growing, new ships are ordered in multiples (sometimes 10 or 12) dictated by the service frequency.
- In a downturn, tramp owners respond quickly to supply/demand imbalances (by slow steaming or laying-up ships). Liner companies, however, have to stick to the service schedules and substantial operating losses can accrue very quickly.

It is important to remember that different shipping sectors will have different risk profiles and therefore be more suited to certain forms of financing. In addition to the risk factors there are also issues of time scale, flexibility and cost, which the shipowner will have to take into account when choosing which form of financing will suit its particular needs.

Exhibit 4.5a
Dry cargo market cycles

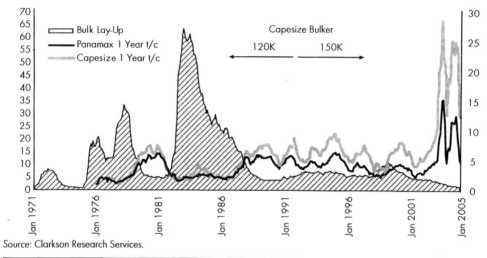

Source: Clarkson Research Services.

Some of the characteristics of the shipping business do not easily meet the requirements of banks. Bankers like predictable earnings, a belief in the future values of the assets financed and transparency in both financial and operational matters. Shipping companies do not always satisfy these criteria.

Cyclicality is an inherent part of the shipping business. Market cycles pose problems for both shipping investors and lenders and are the primary driving force behind both investment and chartering. Changes in the demand and supply of ships lead to a shortage or surplus in tonnage capacity, which in turn leads to an increase or decrease in freight rates (see Exhibit 4.5). The demand side is not the difficult part to understanding the shipping business. While quite a few sectors are subject to seasonal patterns these annual cycles are, to a large degree, foreseeable (for example, the reefer trade). The major cause of the prolonged imbalances in many shipping sectors is the fleet capacity, which results from the past investing behaviour of the shipowners. Activity in the sale and purchase market reflects a change of ownership of already existing assets – it is the newbuilding order book that has a major influence on market sentiment. Shipping cycles are also irregular. History has shown that while the average cycle during the twentieth century is seven years, in reality, cycles range from three years to 10 years, with none actually being seven years.

The major factors that influence shipping markets are freight rates, economic growth, ship supply and shipbuilding prices. Statistics show that there is a close correlation between GDP and ship demand. History has shown, however, that invariably economic forecasts can be radically wrong. Much of the volatility in shipping must be attributed to supply-side management. Over-ordering of new ships has been the major cause of high volatility in most sectors. Owners tend to order ships in a rising market and take delivery in a falling market.

73

Exhibit 4.5b
Crude tanker market cycles

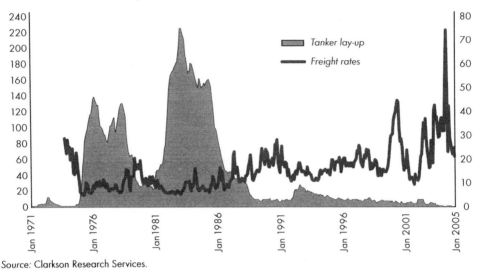

Source: Clarkson Research Services.

Similarly, the banks' lending activity increases significantly in a good market and is cut back in a downturn. The level of freight rates is not just set by the fundamentals of supply and demand but is also heavily influenced by events (for example, canal closure) and market sentiment.

While corporate risk often occurs in shipping finance, more often than not financing is against a single ship or a series of ships. When looking at a corporate shipping company, it is a question of the extent to which the company is subject to the vagaries of the market that is considered.

The standard lending mnemonics for banks applies as much in shipping as in any other form of lending. A widely used mnemonic is the four Cs of credit.

CHARACTER – Shipowner, management, business integrity, track record, strategy (in particular investment and financing), market sector(s), vessel employment, market share, client base, operational and technical management, loss and risk management.
Basic rule – who you do business with can be important.

CAPITAL AND CAPACITY – Shipowner, shareholder(s), access to capital, financial structure, capitalisation, debt, gearing ratio, earnings, cash flow, liquidity.
Basic rule – don't lend too much relative to cash flow (earnings often difficult to forecast).

COLLATERAL – Fleet composition – type, age, condition of vessels, securities, mortgages, assignment of earnings and insurances, personal and corporate guarantees. Where the vessel is trading, how it is trading, quality of charter, how marketable the asset is, future value, enforced value.
Basic rule – it's a problematic industry – securities are important.

CONDITIONS – Economic conditions, shipping markets, where we are in the cycle, other events (for example, political, regulatory, specific commodities (for example, oil market), financial markets).

Basic rule – knowing how to read the markets, monitor loans and deal with problems is part of a shipping banker's skill.

It is important for both lenders and investors to take the time to do the research and the credit work, to understand the risks and to consider the down-side. The way that bank analysts and investment analysts look at shipping risk is very similar. The basic difference is that the investment analyst looks more closely at profitability and return and whether the company can meet its obligations going forward. The bank, while looking at the same things, is also concerned with default and potential loss.

Banks do not lose money solely because the initial decision to lend was wrong. In shipping, where the perceived risks and cyclicality are greater, losses normally occur if warning signs are ignored. When market fundamentals do get shaky, companies with too much leverage or a flawed strategy begin to suffer financial difficulties very quickly. The earlier a problem is spotted, the better the chances are of avoiding a loss, as it usually allows for more opportunities to resolve the situation. Banks have developed systems for monitoring credits that are both industry and client specific. As part of the early warning system, covenants play an important role.

Shipping relies on bank finance. Those banks committed to ship financing base their lending on their personal knowledge of the industry and relationships with owners based on many years' experience.

Shipping has developed an image in financial circles as a very specialised high-risk business where the unexpected can happen. Notorious for its boom-and-bust cycles, it is also a business where the rewards do not match the risks for much of the time. The 1970s and 1980s were both dominated by long and deep recessions in bulk shipping, resulting in numerous bankruptcies among shipowners and substantial losses for banks. The last three years (2003–2005) has been the best period for shipping in the last 50 years. It is the longest period of sustained profits within the industry with freight rates and vessel prices reaching record highs.

It is in the peak of the cycle when the biggest mistakes are made. High ship prices mean that it is much harder to put together sensible deals. Without a fixed-period charter, it is a gamble on spot rates remaining firm for some time to justify an investment and a high percentage finance.

It is very difficult to forecast the future markets, especially the bulk sectors. It is important to take notice of the signs which indicate that the market may be turning up or down. One certainty is that rates will not remain at the high levels prevailing at the time of writing and will fall to more normal levels, albeit with short peaks along the way. The question is what will constitute 'normal levels' and how deep and for how long will the next cycle be?

During the current boom, many shipping companies have been able to build strong balance sheets and are in a much stronger position to trade through a downturn. The stronger bulk shipping companies will be better placed to choose slow steaming and lay-up practices to combat falling freight rates.

Choice of finance for shipowners

The financial markets are a loose cooperation between numerous banks, financial institutions, brokers and so on. The markets are generally divided into commercial banks and the capital markets. Banks deal on a bilateral basis with borrowers, whereas the capital markets are made up of buyers and sellers trading in packaged investments so that buyers know what they are getting without the need for too much research.

Shipowners have a constant concern – when and how to expand or renew the fleet. A major factor in their consideration will be how best to finance their plans. The capital costs of ships account for a major part of the total costs of operating a ship and the choice of financing is important and can be crucial to the success of the project. Not surprisingly, few vessel purchases are paid for in cash generated from a shipowner's own resources. Choosing the right financial structure can be crucial to the success of the acquisition. The most important issue for both lender and borrower is to achieve the right balance between debt and equity from both a risk and reward consideration.

There are three main groups of sources of shipping finance.

- *Equity finance*: which includes owners' private equity, retained earnings, equity offerings either public or private (includes tax partnerships such as K/S and KGs).
- *Mezzanine finance*: preference shares, hybrids (warrants and convertibles) and subordinated loans.
- *Debt finance*: bank loans, export finance, public issues, private placements, and leasing.

Mezzanine finance is a generic term that encompasses the broad spectrum of financing that lies between pure equity and senior debt. For shipping, mezzanine finance is mostly a structure with debt and equity features or subordinated debt with an equity related return.

A shipping transaction can be a very simple arrangement (conventional first mortgage debt) or much more complex. Increasingly, banks are taking a more sophisticated approach to credit risk – leading to an increasing number of complex structures, which cross different risk categories.

The more stable conditions for international shipping markets in recent times have led to an increasing variety of finance options, each with unique characteristics and consequences for the business. The different sources of capital offered have advantages and disadvantages and contain specific parameters in terms of:

- deal or company specific;
- percentage advance rate;
- term and repayment schedule;
- secured or unsecured;
- covenants;
- timing/ease of access/flexibility; and
- cost of capital.

The other categories of financing structures used in ship finance today are listed here.

- Project finance – is a transaction which involves no or limited recourse to sponsors and where there are several distinct risk components.
- Structured finance – is defined as structuring the financial profile of a company or a deal and tailoring the finance sources used to reflect more closely the needs of the borrower and the risks involved.
- Financial engineering – is the use of financial instruments to restructure an existing financial profile into one having more desirable properties. The tools used comprise the new financial instruments created over the past two decades: forwards, futures, options and swaps and so on.

Risk is normally associated with the unexpected and the undesirable, financial engineering reduces or replaces risk with certainty. Financial engineering tools and techniques can be assembled in various ways to create novel financial structures. (Most basic conversion between fixed and floating rates of interest.)

The financial instruments used in project and structured finance are not new but they are used in a more sophisticated way. Generally speaking, project finance is raising money for the purchase, development or use of an asset where the only source to repay the investor/lender is the asset's cash flow. The financing structure usually consists of debt/equity hybrid structures. However, in ship finance an initial project approach rather than a corporate finance approach is often used in the risk analysis.

Structured finance usually involves more than one tranche. The credit will vary by tranche, as will the pricing, and use other types of finance in addition to or as an alternative to bank debt. The first tranche reflects the lowest risk and pricing would reflect normal pricing for that risk. The second tranche would be based upon a mix of asset valuation, cash flow, other collateral such as guarantees, residual value cover and may involve equity or profit sharing arrangements. In the wider context, tax-based leasing is a major form of structured finance used in shipping.

There is no set way for financing a ship and there is often more than one type of finance that is suitable. It is for the shipping company to choose the form of financing that suits it best. The company must, however, pay proper attention to the level and predictability of future cash flow as well as cost minimisation.

Ideally, the shipowner will seek to tailor the finance to match the economic life of the vessel, allow for the shipping market cycles and provide an acceptable return (see Exhibit 4.6). The lender is looking to tailor the finance to its evaluation of the credit risk and protect itself against downturns in the shipping cycles. At the time of writing, the competitive conditions in the financial markets, with a glut of money available combined with the more stable conditions in the shipping industry, allow for more creativity and innovation in financing structures.

It is important to the shipowner to have maximum control over the operation of the vessel and the cash flow. The lender, on the other hand, is looking to restrict the degree of control over its main sources of collateral – the vessel and its earnings.

Usually, before making an investment in a new ship, a shipowner will gather information on what is available and obtain a clear indication or a commitment for financing the acquisition. Many shipowners tend to look to an objective then seek to find a structure that fits.

Exhibit 4.6

Borrower and lender objectives

Flash points are related to return on equity, cash and covenant controls and recourse	
Borrower's objectives	**Lender's objectives**
High leverage	Low leverage
Back ended repayment (profile)	Rapid repayment
Long term	Short term
Low price	High price
Freedom to pay dividends	Dividend restrictions
Limited recourse (walk away option)	Full recourse
Payment default only	Financial and VMC covenant triggers
Free movement of cash	Ring fenced cash
High certainty of cash drawdown	Conditionality on drawdown (conditions precedent)

Source: DVB Bank AG.

However, the financing structure that a particular shipowner may be offered will be determined by:

- the credit standing of the borrower;
- the level of security offered;
- the cash flow cover; and
- the return.

It follows that the better credits have greater opportunities for obtaining finance and the widest choice of financing options. The larger shipping companies have the necessary scale to tap the whole range of products. Consequently, the financing methods used at the top end of the market can be very different from those available among the middle- and lower-tier owners.

The term sheet and risk analysis

There are three components to shipping finance – the asset, its cash flow and the corporate recourse enjoyed by the transaction. You will see at least two and often all three components in most transactions. As a consequence the shipping banker combines the skills of three quite distinct disciplines – those of the asset financier, who is focused on asset values, the project financier who is focused on cash flow and the various causes for its interruption and the corporate banker who is focused on corporate credit.

Exhibit 4.7
'Traditional' shipping finance structure

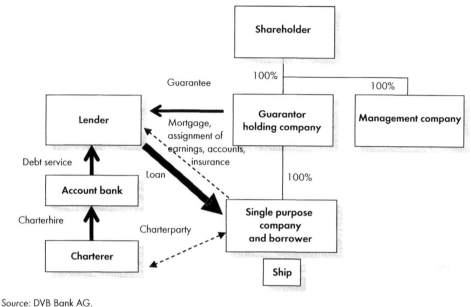

Source: DVB Bank AG.

The typical transaction includes a ship or ships over which the bank holds a mortgage, an assignment over earnings (the subject of spot, time-charter or bareboat charter earnings), and a guarantee from one or more corporate entities (see Exhibit 4.7).

In this section we will consider aspects of the practical application of ship finance – the term sheet which is used to negotiate the transaction structure (and which is, itself, the basis for loan documentation), and the techniques used by banks to analyse shipping risk. Finally, we will look at the implications of new banking regulation – 'Basel II'.

The term sheet is the key document for negotiations between bank and borrower. This document is normally drafted by the bank in response to a financing request. The first draft is normally indicative, that is, issued prior to credit approval. If this document is agreed with the borrower, the bank proceeds to its credit committee and, on approval, issues a committed term sheet, which the borrower is asked to sign. By signing this committed term sheet, the borrower agrees to underwrite costs incurred (especially legal costs) and both parties agree to complete the transaction outlined, subject to legal documentation. Legal documentation can expose ambiguities in the most carefully drafted term sheets (and often they are very broadly drafted), and subsequent negotiations can include 'deal breaker' discussions.

Exhibit 4.8 gives a broad summary of the headline terms and conditions in most term sheets. It should be emphasised that structure and preference will vary between banks. Many institutions require standard clauses, but all term sheets are tailored to the deal. Our discussion of term sheets will necessarily be generalised and heavily qualified with 'commonly,' 'generally' and 'normally,' because in truth, there is no such thing as a universal term sheet.

Exhibit 4.8

The Term Sheet

Disclaimer	Rubric at the head of the Term Sheet will usually specify whether the terms are subject to Credit Approval and/or Loan Documentation
Parties to the Transaction	Borrowers, Guarantors, Lenders, Arrangers, Underwriters, Trustees will be specified.
Loan Amount	Commonly both a maximum amount and a maximum percentage finance will be specified
Purpose	To purchase specific ships, to refinance existing debt, or for general purposes ...
Availability and Drawdown	Generally limits on availability period and number of drawings
Final Maturity	Normally an end date will be specified or is calculable from the final Availability or Drawdown dates.
Repayment	Standard repayments expressed as amounts or percentages of the Loan Amount and their frequency.
Prepayment	How proceeds from asset sales, insurance claims or entirely optional payments are applied to the loan.
Interest, Margin	Borrower may have the option of choosing interest periods (1,3 or 6 months is common). Interest cost will normally be calculated as a percentage based on LIBOR plus a margin in Basis
Commitment Fees	Periodic fees charged on undrawn loan commitments, traditionally 50% of Margin to create a comparable return on capital under the BIS capital adequacy rules
Facility Fees	"Front End" Fees payable to all Lenders on documentation or drawdown
Underwriting Fees*	Front End Fees for banks taking an underwriting risk
Arrangement Fees*	Front End Fees for leading bank/s
Agency Fees*	Annual Fees for banks acting as agent in a syndicated deal
Financial Information	Financial Statements and other financial information required, which will specify which companies on what frequency
Financial Covenants	Eg: Covenants on the financial structure of the Borrower and/or Guarantor 1. Maximum Leverage 2. Minimum Net Worth 3. Minimum Liquidity/Cash 4. Minimum Cashflow
Security	Ship Mortgages Cash Accounts, Retentions Accounts Insurance, Earnings and Charter Assignments
Insurance	Requires acceptable terms for Hull & Machinery, War Risks, P&I, MII, MAP
Minimum Value Covenant("MVC")/ Value Maintenance Covenant ("VMC")	Leverage covenant on Loan to Ship Value
Conditions Precedent	Requirements to be met prior to draw down of the loan
Affirmative Covenants	Compliance with laws Maintenance of Vessel/s Maintenance of acceptable Class, Flag, Management

(Continued)

Exhibit 4.8 *(Continued)*

Negative Covenants	Negative Pledge
	Restrictions on 3rd party debt
	Restrictions on cash and dividends
	Restrictions on mergers and acquisitions
	Restrictions on change of ownership
Events of Default	Non compliance with any of the above, insolvency, cross default with other obligations, material adverse change etc
Transferability	Terms under which lenders can transfer loan to 3rd parties
Clear Market	Designed to prevent simultaneous syndication of deals for the same borrower/group
Market Flex	Ability of the arranger to "flex" the terms and conditions in the event that it is unable to meet syndication targets
Taxes, Increased Costs etc	Unforeseen lender costs payable by borrower
Law	Eg: Documentation under English law, subject to English Court jurisdiction

*For reasons of commercial confidentialilty, usually covered in a side letter.

Source: Authors' own.

A copy of the term sheet is normally attached to the bank's credit application, and will be the basis for internal approval. It follows that any deviations from the approved terms will generally require fresh approval.

We will now look in detail at particular clauses to examine the ways in which the transaction is structured to meet the (often conflicting) objectives of both borrower and lender.

Loan amount

Theory suggests that borrowers should ask for the highest leverage (loan to value) possible. Debt is cheaper than equity (in 2006, average debt cost is around 6–7 per cent, equity costs (or expects to earn) 10–15 per cent). Assuming a successful project, the higher loan to value ratio will generate the highest equity return.

The banker sees the risk side. Debt is a fixed obligation – failure to service interest and repayments represents a default. Dividends to equity can be suspended. So a highly leveraged transaction has higher fixed costs and less flexibility in a weak market.

While borrowers generally seek to arbitrage the lower cost of debt to leverage their transactions as highly as possible, bankers will seek a premium on higher loan to value ratios. This is seen in premium-priced junior or mezzanine tranches and the increasingly popular leases offered by banks which offer 100 per cent finance with pricing based on a blend of debt and equity.

Ship finance loans are normally subject to loan to value tests at drawdown, especially when there is a time gap between commitment and drawdown. A typical loan will offer a fixed sum subject to a maximum percentage of ship market valuation. This transfers an element of risk to the shipowner, who may have to source additional equity to fund the vessel on delivery, if values have fallen.

At the time of writing, ship values are at historic highs and many market players anticipate price falls – much of the discussion is on the timing or degree of those declines. Some borrowers are cash rich and have very modest expectations in leverage; others are committed to buying at elevated prices and are pressing for the highest level of debt.

Availability and drawdown

Where pre-delivery finance is offered for newbuilding ships, these can be important clauses. Typically, shipyards will require five payment instalments; the first on signing of contract and the last on vessel delivery. The percentages for each instalment are negotiable and are likely to have an impact on the contract price. Bank and borrower usually negotiate whether the equity should be contributed in advance of or pro rata with the debt. Borrowers will also seek flexibility on the availability period in case of delays in ship delivery.

Repayment

The majority of ship finance loans are term loans – they can be drawn once (though often in a series of tranches, for instance to meet shipbuilding instalments) and are repaid according to a fixed schedule, usually at three- or six-month intervals. They will have a fixed term, generally up to 12 years (up to 15 years including the pre-delivery period for newbuildings), and will generally end with a balloon payment payable with the last instalment, which the borrower will seek to refinance.

The rate of repayment is a key negotiating point. One common benchmark is the 'profile', the period required to repay the loan in full. Assuming regular and equal ('straight line') repayments, a 10-year loan without balloon has a 10-year profile, but a 10-year loan with a balloon of 33 per cent of the initial amount has a 15-year profile. The banker will seek to agree a rate of repayment well in excess of the likely diminution of the value of the ship in order to allow for future market volatility and the risk of technological obsolescence. This has been a crucial discussion for borrowers in recent years as low interest rates have made repayments and not interest costs the main component in debt service. 'Back-ending' of repayment has a significant effect on equity cash flows and thus returns.

Annuity profiles, in which debt service is level over the loan term (meaning that repayments increase over the term of the loan as the interest cost declines), are usually only seen in transactions with long-term charters to strong counterparties.

With values at historic highs in the years 2004 and 2005, bankers have sought to balance the risk of value declines by accelerating repayment in the early years. Shipyards, the argument goes, will build enough ships to correct any supply deficit and return prices and charter rates to 'normal' levels, but the lag of at least three years from order to delivery gives a window for higher earnings. These earnings, banks feel, should be used to return them to a normal loan to value on normal values. Such acceleration has been widely accepted by borrowers who share a bullish outlook for the medium term and are reluctant to accept the alternative – lower debt. We will look at a working example of a VLCC (very large crude carrier) resale in our risk analysis section.

Interest margin and fees

Shipping banks generate their profits through a range of services, from corporate advisory services, treasury, payments and cash management to loans. The pricing structure of loans has evolved into a mixture of upfront and periodic payments. Facility fees (also known as upfront fees or front end fees) are usually paid on signing of the loan documentation and can be seen as a reimbursement of the bank's set up costs – the credit, approval and documentation process. Where the deal is syndicated to other banks, the facility fees will be subdivided. Arrangement fees reward the arranger for originating, structuring and distributing the deal and normally take the form of a variable skim after payment of fees to participating banks. In larger deals, separate underwriting fees compensate arrangers and co-arrangers who commit to hold larger exposures if they cannot be sold to other banks.

Interest margin is the principal periodic payment, which is paid as a premium to the cost of funds (normally US$ Libor (London Interbank Offered Rate)) and quoted as a percentage (or commonly as hundredths of a percent, or 'basis points').

Commitment fees are effectively margin on undrawn loan amounts. Under international banking regulations, banks are required to maintain capital for undrawn loans equal to 50 per cent of the requirement on drawn loans, so they would like to price commitment fees at 50 per cent of the margin. They do not always achieve this however.

The final category is agency fees, which are designed to compensate the agent for administrative tasks relating to the syndicate of banks and acting as a one-stop shop for the borrower. This will be an annual fee, determined by the size of the facility, number of participating banks or number of vessels.

Covenants

Covenants on the borrower will generally restrict changes of ownership, ship registration, vessel management and enforce minimum operating standards. For the purpose of this 'bankers' view', however, we will focus on the main financial covenants.

Minimum Value Covenant

It is common to have a periodic or continuous obligation to maintain a minimum ratio between ship market value and loan outstanding (a minimum value covenant (MVC)). Many borrowers are resistant to MVC clauses, because they are only likely to be triggered when cash is short, but bankers generally waive the requirement only where there is a full payout charter, or in non-recourse operating lease financings, where there is no obvious remedy for breach.

Financial covenants

In most loans, there will also be financial covenants – commonly these are financial ratios or absolute amounts required at the holding company/guarantor level, as the borrower is normally a single-purpose company. Lending banks are not interested in measures of financial efficiency such as return on equity or asset turnover for this purpose and focus instead on equity, leverage and cash flow in an attempt to give early warning of deterioration of credit quality. Typical covenants are:

- *Leverage*: This is a measure of the percentage of a company's capital provided by debt. Highly leveraged companies are perceived to be vulnerable to cash flow volatility or raised interest rates. (There are companies with very stable and high quality cash flows which can sustain high leverage, but it is considered to be aggressive for a shipping company operating in the short-term charter or spot market). Leverage ratio covenants are normally expressed as 'Total Liabilities' or 'Net Debt' divided by 'Total Assets'. The shipping industry has the advantage of an established secondary market for all but the most specialised vessels, and adjustment for fleet market values is commonly added. This has the positive effect of eliminating variations in accounting for depreciation, and gives full value to 'hidden equity' on long term assets. In a market downturn, however, it creates a risk of dramatic increases in leverage and a breach that may be difficult to remedy.
- *Minimum equity*: This is the most common covenant measure of company scale and the amount of shareholders' capital at risk which could be used to repay debt in a crisis. Again, it is normal in ship finance to apply a minimum test to 'Value Adjusted Equity', being the equity position of the company after adding any ship market values in excess of book value.
- *Minimum cash*: Banks will covenant a large enough float of cash to meet contingencies such as short-term cash flow shortages. Variants include 'Free Cash' (excluding cash already pledged to lenders) and the broader definition of 'Cash and Marketable Securities'.
- *Cash flow*: A favourite ratio is 'Interest Coverage' – 'Earnings before Interest, Tax and Depreciation (EBITAD)/Interest Expense'. Interest Coverage is simple to calculate from the financial statements but lacks the impact of debt repayment, which variants sometimes include.
- *Working capital*: In all types of corporate finance, 'Current Ratio' (Current Assets/Current Liabilities) is commonly used, with the maintenance of a ratio of at least 1:1 being the usual requirement. The typical shipowning company, with minimal inventory, low trade receivables and heavy annual debt repayments, habitually has negative working capital. As a consequence, the ratio is often significantly relaxed by excluding the current portion of long-term debt from current liabilities.

All of the above covenants are tested on receipt of financial information from the borrower or guarantor. Most depend on periodic balance sheets or profit and loss accounts, causing a lag of between three and six months.

Syndication wording

Around 50 per cent of all ship finance deals are 'bilateral' (that is, there are two parties – one bank and one client), and the balance are syndicated – arranged by one or more banks and sold down to others. Of these deals, some are syndicated on a 'best efforts' basis (that is, if they cannot be sold it is the client's problem and the deal will not close) and the rest are 'fully

Exhibit 4.9

How banks assess a transaction – cash flow, asset, recourse

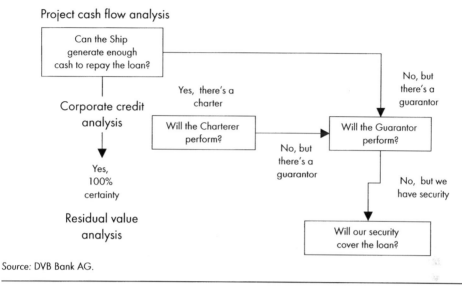

Source: DVB Bank AG.

underwritten' (that is, if they cannot be sold, it is the underwriter's (typically the arranging bank or banks) problem, and a premium is added to fees to cover this risk). We have included two examples of clauses related to loan syndication in Exhibit 4.8. The first is 'Clear Market', which is designed to prevent two arrangers selling two deals in the bank market at the same time, leading to failure of one or both to meet their target selldown. Generally, the client will agree a fixed period to complete the syndication, after which other transactions can be marketed. 'Market Flex' is a clause that has become popular in recent years, but remains controversial – it allows arrangers to change price or other terms on transactions that prove difficult to syndicate. While this might sound like a contradiction in a fully underwritten deal, it is now a frequent requirement for larger or more aggressive deals.

Analysis of cash flow and 'residual value risk'

As we have said, ship financiers usually consider three factors – cash flow, asset value and corporate recourse. The priority given to these factors, and their relative strengths will vary depending on the nature of the transaction. Exhibit 4.9 gives a representation of the way shipping banks think.

Ship finance transactions often benefit from recourse to a corporate entity, usually in the form of a guarantee. We have touched on this and highlighted the significant financial covenants which are designed to give early warning of the deterioration of the credit of the guarantor. However, it is the analysis of the volatility of the earnings and value of the ship on a standalone basis that distinguishes this discipline and is the basis for the structure of transactions. We will focus on this analysis now.

Cash flow analysis

Cash flow is considered to be the first means of repaying a loan and a shortfall in cash flow the most likely source of default. As mentioned previously in this chapter, the freight markets are notoriously unpredictable and can suffer wild swings over a 12-month period. Bankers, therefore, attempt to structure loans so that debt service is sustainable in 'normal' circumstances and default unlikely.

Banks have, over time, developed increasingly sophisticated cash flow models. The model used may cover a single ship, a fleet of ships or a corporate. A shipping cash flow is simple to construct – it is the assumptions that are difficult. It is very difficult to forecast future markets and the level of freight rates. To assist in the modelling some banks use Monte Carlo analysis, which uses stochastic analysis to calculate the probability that a transaction will be able to meet its financial obligations. Others contract out the forecasting to a third-party analyst, who is at least impartial.

Exhibit 4.10
Cash flow risk analysis I

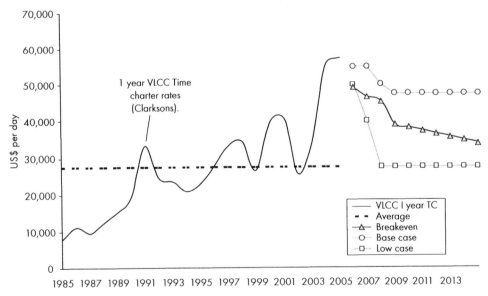

Source: Clarksons Research Services; DVB Bank AG.

Most banks analyse cash flow risk by considering debt service breakevens (the daily sum of operating costs, interest and repayments) against historical time-charter rates over at least one full market cycle. The historical period chosen for this analysis varies according to the asset type, but 20 years certainly provides a good perspective for the more common dry bulk vessels and crude tankers.

Many shipping banks would profess themselves 'counter cyclical' lenders. This may be reflected in their lending through greater generosity in weak markets (anticipating an upturn) and more caution in strong markets. At the time of writing, the shipping markets are very high in historical terms and lenders have been devising strategies to prepare for the downturn. The most common is an acceleration of repayments in the initial years of a transaction in order to bring down breakevens to a more modest level for the remaining loan period.

In order to illustrate this, Exhibit 4.10 shows a typical cash flow analysis chart, using the example of a resale VLCC, acquired at the end of 2005 for the record price of US$140m, and financed at 70 per cent loan to value (a, in historical terms, staggering US$98m).

The plain black line shows the historical 1 year time-charter rates recorded by Clarkson Research Services, which have clearly been very volatile – this is what delights value-driven ship investors and leads risk managers to despair. Commentators are divided on the future of time-charter rates – some believe in a 'paradigm shift' towards permanently higher rates and ship prices, but lending bankers (because they rarely share in the upside or the exuberance) tend to believe that what goes up, in a booming market, will come down to 'normal' levels (also known as 'mean regression').

Exhibit 4.11

Cash flow risk analysis II

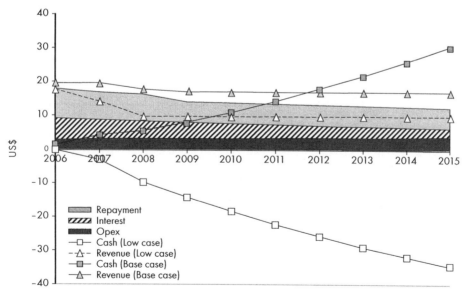

Source: Clarksons Research Services; DVB Bank AG.

As part of his or her credit application, the shipping banker will provide two scenarios – a base case and a low case for future earnings – and will compare these to loan breakeven levels. The base case will be an optimistic case, the low case conservative. The breakeven will in most amortising transactions reduce over time as the repayment of the debt reduces the future interest cost (assuming fixed rate interest).

Exhibit 4.10 illustrates the historical plausibility of the loan cash flows, but another chart is required to illustrate the impact of the two earnings scenarios on accumulated cash.

In Exhibit 4.11, each of the areas illustrates one of the three cost components – operating costs, interest and repayments. The two lines with triangles illustrate total annual revenues from the base and low case scenarios. The lines with squares show accumulated cash in the two scenarios, with a steady divergence leading to a surplus of US$30m in the base case and a deficit of US$35m in the low case. Cash flow is only one part of this story – our next theme is the value of the asset and in particular its future or residual value over the course of and at maturity of the loan.

Residual value analysis

Price movements of ships are influenced by freight rates, newbuilding prices, liquidity of investors and market expectations. In particular the market values of ships are closely correlated to freight rates and display similar volatility.

Exhibit 4.12
Loan to value development analysis

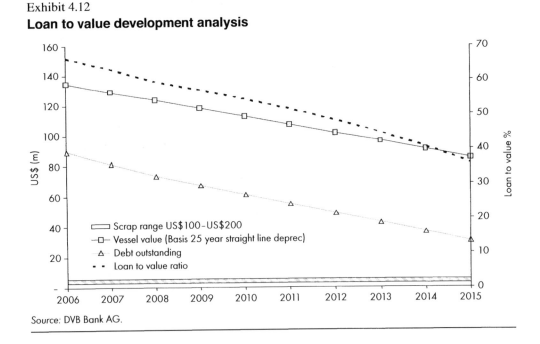

Source: DVB Bank AG.

As mentioned in our term sheet section, the banker has two defences against this volatility – the first is the equity buffer provided by the shipowner. The second is the rate of repayment. The banker will normally seek to negotiate loan repayments well in excess of the rate of asset depreciation. Exhibit 4.12 illustrates this. As the loan progresses, the gap (equity value) between the debt outstanding and the depreciated value of the asset widens, and the leverage falls from the initial 70 per cent to below 40 per cent by the end of the 10-year term.

Exhibit 4.12 only addresses loan to value development against depreciating values. The pessimistic banker (or his credit department) may fear decline of values to historical lows – for this, a comparison of future loan outstandings to historic values is required. Clarkson's Research Services provide data based on reported sale and purchase transactions over at least the last 20 years, in the form of five- and 10-year-old benchmark vessels in the main sectors and sizes. Some data providers are also able to show the range of historical values throughout the term of the loan. The simplest approach is to compare loan and historic values at a fixed point, which in the case of our VLCC resale project, is year five.

In Exhibit 4.13 the dotted line represents the loan outstandings at the end of the fifth year, while the solid line shows values for five-year-old VLCCs over the last 20 years as reported by Clarksons. As mentioned, this loan has a modest initial leverage at 70 per cent and accelerated repayment for the first three years. Although time will tell whether this would have been a good transaction for bank or borrower, it is interesting to note that the value of a five-year-old VLCC has exceeded the US$61m projected loan outstandings in only seven of the last 20 years.

Exhibit 4.13

Asset value risk analysis

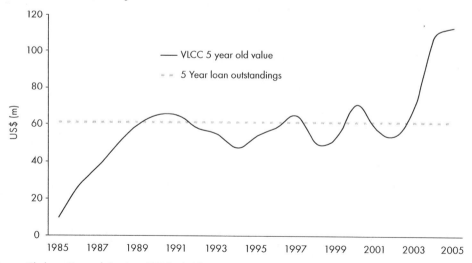

Source: Clarksons Research Services; DVB Bank AG.

Country risk

Banks are required to categorise loans by country. This can be straightforward where the borrower is a manufacturer in Belgium, serving the local market, but shipping companies have a truly global quality. Most deep sea ships trade globally, and will often be owned and flagged through offshore structures. The ship's earnings will almost certainly be in US dollars and it has the potential to earn those dollars from hundreds of different charterers in a variety of countries. From the lender's perspective, though repossession is the last resort, ship mortgages are enforceable worldwide (some locations are much easier than others).

For these reasons, ship financiers are usually among the first to structure commercial cross-border finance transactions in emerging markets.

It can be argued that shipping is supranational, although for internal and regulatory purposes, banks will usually assign location based on ownership, management or borrower domicile, with special consideration given to dependence on particular guarantees or charters.

The Basel Accord and its effect on ship finance

The Bank of International Settlements (BIS), the central bank for central banks, based in Basel, Switzerland, has taken a leading role in setting standards for the regulation of international banks. One of its key achievements has been the two Basel Accords; agreements between the world's principal central banks on the capital requirements for banks. There are many aspects to these Accords, but we will focus on their effect on loan transactions.

The first of these Accords, Basel I, was agreed in 1988 and established a very simple principle – that for every US$100 of loans or similar assets held by a bank, it required US$8 of risk capital to provide a buffer against customer default. This was a good start but meant that the highest quality corporate credits had the same capital requirements as the riskiest speculator.

Basel II adds risk sensitivity to the 1988 standards, requiring higher levels of capital for those borrowers thought to present higher levels of credit risk and potential capital relief for lower risk transactions. Two questions follow: who determines risk and how?

Let's take 'how' first – the BIS says that risk (and thus capital required) is a product of the Probability of Default (PD), Exposure at Default (EAD) and Loss Given Default (LGD). This seems logical – if I have a 20 per cent chance of default on a US$10m exposure and expect to recover only 50 per cent of the loan, my expected loss is 20% × US$10m × 50% = US$1m.

Now 'who' – perhaps surprisingly, banks are being invited to calculate their own capital requirements. According to Basel II they have three options.

- The 'Standardised Approach', which relies on external credit ratings for PD and has prescribed factors for EAD and LGD. This is of limited value for shipping companies, very few of which are externally rated.
- The 'Foundation Approach', which allows banks to calculate the PD themselves with an Internal Rating Model, but again prescribes factors for EAD and LGD. Neither of these first two approaches is attractive for asset-based lenders as they do not give any additional value to secured lending, which has significantly lower LGD.
- The 'Advanced Approach', under which banks will determine all three factors themselves.

Exhibit 4.14

Basel II advanced approach – Three step calculation of Expected Loss and Capital Requirement

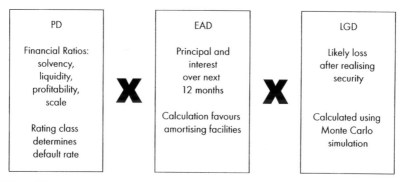

Source: DVB Bank AG.

This is the method most leading shipping banks are seeking to adopt, for the sole reason that it is likely to save them capital.

The Advanced Approach methodology used by banks (see Exhibit 4.14) is subject to many rules and regulations under Basel II. Ideally, the regulators would like banks to calculate PD and LGD from actual experience. In big ticket sectors such as shipping finance, actual default incidence is statistically insignificant, so proxies are expected to be used to project probability; which will be very similar to the analytical steps outlined above – an analysis of the credit of the corporate and of the sustainability of vessel cash flows to determine default probability, a projection of loan amortisation and its comparison to the probable development of vessel value. Vessel value projections may be generated by so-called Monte Carlo simulations but are likely to be based on two factors – past volatility and historical mean values – which means that falls from current values will be expected. These projected values will be subject to various 'haircuts' or discounts to simulate recovery costs.

The significance of Basel II for shipping finance is that it will prompt many banks to adopt compliant rating and pricing models. Banks have a three-year period to collect data on default performance in order to test their models and a two-year transitional period will follow before the new capital calculation methods have full effect – at the earliest from 2010. That means that long-term shipping deals currently being closed belong more to the Basel II era and there is a growing realisation that the rules of the game have changed. The result may be felt in a flight to quality counterparties and more discriminatory pricing.

Many banks will hope to gain competitive advantage by using the most sophisticated systems, subject to the scrutiny of their local regulators. On the face of it, the favourable treatment of secured lending under the Advanced Approach bodes well for shipping and particularly favours specialised banks or those for whom shipping is a significant activity, who will be able to invest in customised rating systems. However, the syndicated loan market, which accounts for about 50 per cent of all shipping debt, will continue to be priced to sell, which might mean borrowers accepting margins to satisfy Standardised or Foundation Approach participants, or those with more generalised Advanced Approach models.

What if capital increases on shipping loans? One of the subjects for legal debate is whether Increased Cost clauses, standard in most English law loan agreements, could be used to increase margin if Basel II increases capital requirements for lenders. It might not be tactful for a bank to suggest to a borrower that his margin be raised as a consequence of the bank's own internal calculations under the Advanced Approach but the possibility remains.

Conclusion

Ship finance has had an excellent run since 1995. Shipowners have done well and the incidence of default has been low. As memories of the 1980s fade, shipping has slowly shed its bad reputation for long slumps, when newbuildings were delivered straight to the scrap yards. Since 2003, most sectors have experienced very high charter rates. Writing this third edition of *Shipping Finance* we are hostages to the hindsight of readers – are we on a cliff edge or on a new paradigmatic plateau – will our comments appear rash or absurdly conservative? Time will tell, but our guess is that ship finance will remain a fascinating and vibrant area, with high volatility, political surprises, fortunes won and lost and some great characters. Bankers will do well to keep grounded and learn from the long history of ship finance.

Chapter 5

Financial markets products

Doug Garnsey

Introduction

A ship finance loan is a long-term obligation between the owner and the financing bank or banks and through the life of this loan the owner is subjected to certain financial risks. Many of these risks can be effectively hedged using financial derivatives. The modern shipowner is able to construct a portfolio of derivative hedges that can help in all or in part to offset any negative economic effect from adverse market movements.

Over the course of the last 10 years, the use of financial market products within the shipping industry as a means for both managing financial risk and maximising returns has increased exponentially. Derivatives are now a common tool among the shipowning community. They have developed far from the traditional currency and interest rate hedging tools to derivatives that reference indices would traditionally have been. They were the preserve of shipowners rather than financial institutions. The modern shipowner can not only hedge its interest rate and currency exposure, but the cost of bunkering and also its freight revenue through the use of derivative structures. Increasingly we are seeing ship finance facilities packaged in a way that offers the owner the ability to manage all of its financial risks in a cost effective and efficient way. Owners are also able to employ a whole host of similar products to maximise the return on any income generated.

The arguments for actively managing financial market risks are many and it is perhaps beyond the scope of this chapter to put forward all of these arguments. Suffice to say we live in a world where financial markets are dominated by volatility. The drivers of this volatility can be economic but it is an unfortunate fact that we live in an era where exogenous factors, such as war and terrorism force huge shifts in financial markets and with this unstable geopolitical climate, the argument to expect further financial markets volatility is strong. The traditional view that risk management was a 'zero sum game' is now more than ever redundant. The cost to the shipowner of not hedging its financial risks in the modern world could be disastrous. As with most things, however, timing is critical.

As the ability of financial institutions to price and quantify the risk on increasingly more complex products has grown, so has the ability of the owner to build a portfolio of products that will better meet their needs and hedging goals.

Through the course of this chapter we will discuss some of the many types of derivative products that have developed in recent years to manage risk and maximise revenue and how they can be applied to good effect in the shipping industry. Although the main focus on the product discussions is with regards to interest rate hedging, the principles and products employed are transferable across most asset classes.

Interest rate hedging products

The goal of any interest rate hedging programme is to create a product that will generate a series of cash flows designed to offset in full or in part an adverse movement in interest rates. In the context of a ship finance loan, the most common goal is to offer some form of protection against rising interest rates. The decision as to what product is used depends greatly on the risk profile of the owner. The risk/reward pay off is something that will be mentioned several times throughout this chapter and is centred on the premise that in order to be 100 per cent hedged against adverse market movements one has to give up flexibility to take advantage of favourable market movements. Whether that lost flexibility comes from being locked into a fixed rate or in terms of a lost premium depends on the type of product used. Conversely, by giving up some of the protection (increasing the risk) one is able to create a structure that allows some flexibility to take advantage of favourable market movements.

As a general rule, interest rate hedging products fall into two categories; fixed rate or options-based products that allow the borrower some flexibility in terms of interest costs. It has, however, become increasingly common to use a combination of these two types of product to create a 'hybrid' structure that better suits the needs of the shipowner.

Fixed rate products

Interest rate swap (IRS)

The IRS in its most simple or 'vanilla' form is a derivative contract where one party exchanges or 'swaps' a series of floating rate interest payment obligations for a series of fixed rate interest payment obligations. The IRS is a stand alone instrument that can be tailored to match the profile of the loan perfectly in terms of settlement dates, repayment profile and tenor.

The IRS allows the owner to convert its floating rate borrowings into fixed rate borrowings (or vice versa) but it operates as a stand alone instrument and therefore offers a number of benefits over a fixed rate loan in terms of flexibility. It allows the holder the ability to restructure the hedge if, for example, the debt was partially pre-paid, or to move the hedge and apply it to another loan in the case of a complete repayment or sale of the vessel.

The single fixed rate at which the IRS is executed is calculated at the time of dealing and is derived from a series of 'Forward Forward' rates. These 'Forward Forward' rates are themselves derived from the 'swap yield curve' which is, in simple terms, the rate at which banks of good credit grade are willing to lend to each other for a range of maturities (otherwise known as the term structure of interest rates).

The swap itself can be executed at any time during the life of a loan and it is the decision of the shipowner as to whether it hedges all or just a percentage of the loan and for what term it wishes to execute the hedge. It can be matched perfectly to the loan or can be executed as a 'proxy' hedge to general group debt (see section on accounting considerations).

The borrower still has to meet its floating rate interest obligations with the lending bank. As Exhibit 5.1 demonstrates, the floating rate cash flow is effectively paid by the swap bank in return for receipt of fixed interest rate payments. By entering into the IRS, the owner has removed its exposure to rising short-term interest rates during the life of the transaction.

Exhibit 5.1
Cash flow diagram for swap and debt

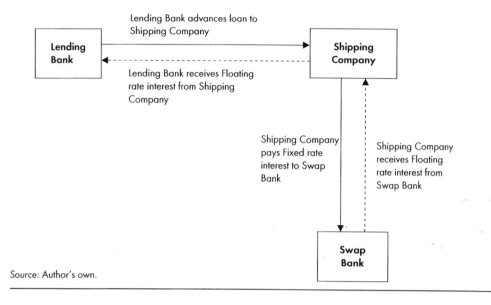

Source: Author's own.

Exhibit 5.2
Net interest cash flows on swap and debt

Period	Interest rate applied to loan (%)	Net settlement on IRS (%)	Net interest paid (excluding lending margin) (%)
1st 6 months	4.75	5.05 – 4.75 = 0.30	5.05
2nd 6 months	4.95	5.05 – 4.95 = 0.10	5.05
3rd 6 months	5.05	5.05 – 5.05 = 0.00	5.05
4th 6 months	5.25	5.05 – 5.25 = -0.20	5.05
5th 6 months	5.50	5.05 – 5.50 = -0.45	5.05
6th 6 months	5.75	5.05 – 5.75 = -0.70	5.05

Source: Author's own.

To illustrate this example we can consider a shipowner who has a 10-year US$10m non amortising loan (see Exhibit 5.2). He hedges this loan for a period of three years, using an IRS and achieves a rate of 5.05 per cent on the IRS (excluding lending margin).

The shipowner has fixed its interest rate on the hedged portion of debt and any increases in the interest rate applied to the loan are offset by a receipt of interest under the swap. Similarly for any period where the interest rate applied to the loan is lower then the swap rate, the shipowner has an additional payment of interest under the swap. As you can see, during the life of the IRS the net interest rate paid when the floating rate loan and the IRS are looked at together is 5.05 per cent.

Forward rate agreements (FRA)

In effect, an FRA is a single period interest rate swap. However, unlike conventional interest rate swaps, the FRA settlement is calculated on a discounted basis, because payment is made at the beginning of the period (as opposed to an interest in arrears calculation on conventional borrowings), with the interest rate differential applied to the notional amount of the transaction. The notional amount used to calculate the cash flow could represent all or part of the outstanding debt on the vessel during a given period. FRAs are not as commonly used by the shipowner wishing to hedge the financing costs of a vessel because to do so would involve buying a 'string' of FRAs which would give rise to a hefty administrative burden. Also because the underlying interest on the loan will be calculated in arrears and the FRA is discounted upfront they do not give the shipowner a perfect hedge.

Options-based products

In general, options-based hedging tools offer protection against pre-defined worst case scenarios while allowing the buyer of protection to benefit should market conditions remain favourable. There is usually a premium associated with such protection, although in the majority of hedging scenarios, the trade is structured in such a way as to avoid the payment of this premium upfront.

Interest rate cap

The interest rate cap affords the purchaser protection against rising interest rates, while allowing it to benefit if, over time, interest rates do not rise. It can be structured to match the profile of the underlying debt obligation in the same way that the IRS can be. Like the swap, it is also a contract for difference, in that the settlement on any given period is the difference between the cap level and the underlying LIBOR (London Interbank Offered Rate) rate applied to that period. After settlement of the premium, it becomes a one-way obligation. The seller of the cap reimburses the purchaser for any interest period during the life of the trade where the LIBOR applied to the loan exceeds the pre-defined 'strike' rate on the option. If LIBOR remains below the strike rate during any interest period then no cash flow takes place under the cap. The purchaser, once it has paid the premium, has no further obligations to the seller of the cap.

Exhibit 5.3 provides an example of interest flows for a shipowner who purchases a cap, with a notional profile that matches its underlying debt and a strike rate of 6 per cent.

Interest rate floor

The interest rate floor is the exact opposite of the cap in that the purchaser is protected against falling interest rates. For this reason as a stand alone instrument it has little use in the world of ship finance where owners are concerned with rising interest rates. It is, however, used in tandem with a cap to create an interest rate collar.

Exhibit 5.3

Interest cash flows under interest rate cap

Interest rate applied to loan (%)	Interest flow under cap (%)	Net funding cost (%)
4.50	0.00	4.50
5.50	0.00	5.50
6.50	0.50	6.00
7.50	1.50	6.00

Source: Author's own.

Exhibit 5.4

Interest cash flows under interest rate collar

Interest rate applied to loan (%)	Interest flow under floor (%)	Interest flow under cap (%)	Net funding cost (%)
4.50	0.50	0.00	5.00
5.50	0.00	0.00	5.50
6.50	0.00	0.50	6.00
7.50	0.00	1.50	6.00

Source: Author's own.

Interest rate collar

The collar is structured using a combination of 'bought cap' and 'sold floor' to create a band or 'collar' to interest rates. From a borrower's perspective, the rationale for creating such a structure is usually to offset the upfront cost of purchasing a cap.

Let us take the previous example of the shipowner purchasing a cap with a strike at 6 per cent but in order to offset the premium associated with this, the shipowner simultaneously sells an interest rate floor with a strike of 5 per cent (see Exhibit 5.4). The net effect is that maximum and minimum funding costs are locked in. Depending on the levels at which the floor and cap strikes are set, the interest rate collar may be executed for zero cost or for a reduced premium compared to a stand alone cap.

Binary interest rate options

Binary or 'digital' interest rate options are caps or floors that differ from traditional caps and floors in the way that they settle. With a traditional cap the purchaser is compensated for the net difference between the strike rate and LIBOR for that period. Hence the term 'contract for difference'. With a digital cap, the purchaser receives a fixed cash flow if the strike rate is reached.

For example, the purchaser of a digital cap with a strike of 6 per cent and a fixed pay out of 1 per cent, will receive the same level of compensation (1 per cent) from the seller regardless of whether LIBOR sets at 6 per cent or 10 per cent for the relevant period.

They have a number of uses in the non ship finance world, where the purchaser is exposed to one-off fixed costs if certain interest rate levels are reached. In the world of ship finance, however, they are used commonly to create hybrid hedging products as will be described later in this chapter.

Swaptions

The 'swaption' is an option that provides the purchaser the right but not the obligation to enter into an interest rate swap, at a future point in time, at a rate agreed at the time the swaption is purchased. Depending on the needs of the purchaser, swaptions can be structured as either a 'payer' (the right to pay fixed interest on the underlying swap) or a 'receiver' (the right to receive fixed interest on the underlying swap). They can also be structured so that the purchaser has the right to exercise the option on a single date ('European') or on a number of dates ('Bermudan').

Any shipowner considering the purchase of a newbuilding will have to consider its interest rate risk. Entering into a fixed interest rate obligation via an IRS or an option structure may not be attractive for a number of reasons. The owner may, for example, feel that the current level of interest rates are too high and that it would prefer to wait until the ship is delivered before locking in its interest costs. The risk that during this delivery period it is wrong in its views and interest rates actually increase greatly rather than fall is one that the owner may want to protect itself against.

Such an owner could purchase a 'payers' swaption which, on the vessel delivery date, gives it the right but not the obligation to enter into an interest rate swap for the whole or part of the debt obligation. If, on delivery of the vessel, the prevailing market swap rate is lower than the strike rate of the swaption then the owner will let the swaption expire and will execute a swap at the prevailing market rate. The premium associated with the purchase of the swaption is all or partially offset by the fact that the owner is able to execute the swap at the time of delivery at a lower rate. Conversely if at the time of delivery the market swap rate is higher than the swaption strike, the owner will exercise the swaption and enter into the underlying IRS.

Hybrid products

Although all of the products listed above are used in their own right as hedging tools, they can also be considered as building blocks that can be used to create much more tailored hedging products. The scope for creating such hybrid products is vast. Detailed in the following paragraphs are some of the more commonly used structures. With all of these hybrid structures there is a risk/reward pay off and it is a matter for the shipowner and the hedging bank to work together to build a product that matches the owner's appetite for risk and desire for protection.

Swaps with sold caps, discount swaps and capped discount swaps

The shipowner may be keen to lock in its funding costs by way of an IRS because it feels that interest rates are likely to rise but it could also hold the view that this rise during the life of the trade will not be limitless. A vanilla IRS, by its very nature, will protect against any rise in interest rates above the swap rate. If the shipowner feels that some of this protection is not necessary then it can 'sell' it to achieve a discounted swap rate. The following are all variations of this concept of selling some of the swap protection. Aside from vanilla IRS, these products are probably the most widely used hedging tools among shipowners looking to hedge interest rate exposures.

The *swap with sold cap* provides the borrower with fixed rate funding provided that interest rates do not exceed the pre-defined strike rate. If interest rates increase above this strike rate, then the borrower will revert to floating rate funding but at a discount to the prevailing market LIBOR. The borrower enters into an IRS but also sells an interest rate cap that matches the swap in terms of notional amount, interest periods and so on. The premium generated from the sale of this cap is embedded into the IRS to achieve a discount to the prevailing vanilla swap rate.

For example, a shipowner wishes to hedge the exposure on a 10-year loan and decides that the market 10-year swap rate of 5 per cent is undesirable. It simultaneously sells an interest rate cap with a strike of 6.5 per cent. The premium generated is used to create a discounted swap rate of 4.6 per cent.

For any period where LIBOR sets below 6.5 per cent: the borrower funds at 4.6 per cent. For any period where LIBOR sets above 6.5 per cent: the borrower funds at LIBOR minus 1.9 per cent.

The *discount swap* is similar but with this product the borrower reverts to floating rate funding for any period where LIBOR exceeds the strike rate. On a risk/reward basis, the discount swap will offer a greater discount to the vanilla swap rate than could be achieved with a 'swap with sold cap' of matching size, profile and strike. This is because the risk or interest cost to the borrower if LIBOR exceeds the strike is higher. The borrower enters into an IRS but also sells an interest rate cap and a digital cap which match the swap in terms of notional amount, interest periods and so on. The premium generated from the sale of these caps is embedded into the IRS to achieve a discount to the prevailing vanilla swap rate.

For example, a shipowner wishes to hedge the exposure on a 10-year loan and decides that the market 10-year swap rate of 5 per cent is undesirable. It simultaneously sells a combination of interest rate cap and digital cap with a strike of 6.5 per cent. The premium generated is used to create a discounted swap rate of 4.5 per cent.

For any period where LIBOR sets below 6.5 per cent: the borrower funds at 4.5 per cent. For any period where LIBOR sets above 6.5 per cent: the borrower funds at LIBOR.

The *capped discount swap* involves entering into a discount swap but also purchasing a further interest rate cap that limits the worst case funding cost.

For example, a shipowner wishes to hedge the exposure on a 10-year loan and decides that the market 10-year swap rate of 5 per cent is undesirable. It simultaneously sells a combination of interest rate cap and digital cap with a strike of 6.5 per cent. It also purchases a cap with a strike of 8 per cent. The net premium generated is used to create a discounted swap rate of 4.75 per cent.

For any period where LIBOR sets below 6.5 per cent: the borrower funds at 4.75 per cent.
For any period where LIBOR sets above 6.5 per cent but below 8 per cent: the borrower funds at LIBOR.
For any period where LIBOR sets above 8 per cent: the borrower funds at 8 per cent.

Discounted and value collar structures

In the same way that options can be sold to achieve more desirable swap rates, they can also be used to improve the levels of interest rate collars. Discount and value collars come in many variations, but the underlying concept in each of them is similar; to sell some of the protection from extreme scenarios in return for more attractive levels of protection against likely scenarios.

The 'Knock Out Collar' is a way for shipowners to improve the terms of a vanilla collar by removing some of the cap protection. We have already described how the shipowner can sell a floor to offset the upfront premium normally associated with purchasing a cap. By selling the right combination of options, the shipowner can create a structure whereby it has a best and worst case funding rate as with the collar, but if LIBOR increases to certain pre-defined levels the cap protection is 'knocked out' for that period. The level at which the protection is knocked out can be set at a level that the owner feels LIBOR is unlikely to reach for any sustained period of time during the life of the hedge.

Cancellable and extendible swaps

The combination of a vanilla swap with a swaption can create a range of different products to suit various needs and views. These products can be created either to provide the shipowner with the flexibility to terminate or extend all or part of its hedge, or to provide the shipowner with a discount to the vanilla swap rate in return for giving the swap bank the right to terminate or extend the swap at some point in the future. Any premium associated with this flexibility is embedded into the swap rate and amortised over time.

An example of their use would be the shipowner who has committed to a 10-year finance facility and wants to hedge its interest rate exposure, but is concerned that it may want to sell the vessel at some point in the future and does not want to be exposed to potential break costs on the swap agreement if it terminates it. The owner could enter into a 10-year swap where it has the right to cancel it at year five for zero cost. As noted previously, the cost of this optionality is embedded into the swap rate and amortised over time. The alternative to this product would be for the owner to enter into a five-year swap affords it the right to extend it for a further five years if the vessel is not sold.

The flip side of this type of product is for the shipowner to give the swap bank the right to cancel or extend the hedge. These sorts of products can be extremely attractive in certain interest rate environments and if tailored correctly, can provide the shipowner with a significant discount to the vanilla swap. The important issue from the shipowner's perspective is to make sure that it is comfortable with the risk associated with the product. For example, if the trade is extendible, is it at a level that the owner can live with?

It is worth noting at this stage that entering into any form of derivative contract can give rise to potential breakage costs, should either party to the transaction decide to terminate the contract prior to maturity, unless there is an inbuilt option to cancel.

Currency hedging products

The majority of ship finance facilities are still predominantly US dollar-based transactions and in most cases the charter income received is also in US dollars. This does not, however, mean that the shipowner is not exposed to currency risks in one form or another. During the trading life of the asset, the shipowner may incur non US dollar expenses in relation to the vessel's time in port or for the vessel's maintenance. The most common exposure, however, for the traditional European owner is the fact that all income is received in US dollars but the cost of running and staffing its offices on land are usually met in euros.

As with interest rate hedging, currency hedging tools can generally be divided into the category of fixed rate or option-based structures.

Forward foreign exchange (FFE) contracts

The FFE contract allows the borrower to lock in the rate at which it is able to exchange one currency for another at a future point in time. They can be traded as a single contract or as a series or 'strip' of contracts. The rate at which one can buy or sell a currency at a certain point in the future is defined as the 'forward rate'. It is calculated by adding or subtracting 'forward points' from the spot rate. The spot rate is the rate at which one currency can be exchanged for another for immediate delivery, which in most currency pairs, means for delivery in two days' time. Forwards deal at either premiums or discounts. Premium forward points are added to the spot rate, making the forward rate higher than the spot rate. Discount forward points must be subtracted, making the forward rate lower.

It is a common misconception that a currency's 'forward rate' is a prediction of where the market thinks the spot rate will move to over time. The forward points that are used to adjust the 'spot' rate into a forward rate are, in fact, calculated using the principle of 'Interest Rate Parity'. Namely, that there should be no arbitrage opportunity between a currency pairs spot rate, the forward rate and the term structure of interest rates for the two currencies.

Let us imagine the case of a shipowner who needs to hedge the purchase of €1m in six months' time. In order to fund this purchase the owner will sell US dollars and there are two ways the owner can achieve this purchase (ignoring options-related structures):

- buy the euros today at the spot rate and hold them on deposit for six months; or
- buy the euros six months forward at the forward rate agreed today.

The cost of each method must be the same, otherwise an arbitrage opportunity will exist. At the time of writing, US dollar interest rates are higher than euro interest rates. Therefore it is beneficial for the owner to hold dollars on deposit rather than convert them to euros and hold these for the six months until they are required. The forward rate at which the owner can purchase the euros is calculated so as to cancel out any benefit derived from theoretically holding the higher yielding currency on deposit during the time to expiry of the forward contract.

In the above theoretical example we can calculate the forward rate as follows:

6-month € interest rate	= 2.93%
6-month US$ interest rate	= 5.06%
Spot €/US$ exchange rate	= 1.2050

Forward points
$$= \frac{(2.93\% - 5.06\%) \times 1.2050 \times 182/360}{(2.93\% \times 182/360) + 1}$$

$$= 0.01276$$

Forward rate $\quad = 1.2050 + 0.01276 = 1.2178$

The above example is simplified as, in reality, there are bid offer spreads to take into account, in both the spot FX and the interest rate market but it does serve to highlight the principles involved.

Options-related structures

The two main building blocks of currency option structures are puts and calls. The buyer of a put option, in return for paying a premium, has the right but not the obligation to sell a specific amount of a currency for another at a certain point in the future, for a pre-agreed exchange rate. Conversely, the buyer of the call option holds the right but not the obligation to purchase a currency. The benefit over the forward contract is the flexibility to take advantage of favourable currency moves rather than being locked into an exchange rate. The downside is the requirement to pay an upfront premium.

As with interest rate options, the majority of currency options used by shipowners are traded as a combination of products to create a bespoke hedging product and to avoid any up front premium. They are also frequently used to create yield enhancing deposit structures.

The concepts and the type of products that can be used are very similar to interest rate products so there is little need to repeat the ideas again. Suffice to say that the principle when building currency-based structures is, again, one of risk versus reward.

Freight hedging products

So far in this chapter, we have focused on the products available in the more mature derivative arenas, principally the interest rate and FX markets. Due to the depth and liquidity of these markets, they have developed to the extent that the more complex second- and third-generation derivatives are now commonplace.

The freight derivative market is a different beast altogether. While the first trades were completed in the early 1990s, there is still nowhere near the depth or liquidity available to make these more complex products viable. At present, the freight derivative market is limited to the traditional swap and the occasional call or put option. While it is not within the scope of this chapter to describe the minutiae of the freight derivative market, we will try to capture the broad themes and issues impacting this market.

Exhibit 5.5

Sample contract specifications

Market	Dry bulk	Tankers
Contract type	Capesize, Panamax or Supramax, several possible voyage routes or Average of Time Charter Routes	Route ie, TD3 (VLCC Arabian Gulf to Japan) or TC4 (Mid Range Clean Product Tanker, Rotterdam to New York)
Amount	Minimum $\frac{1}{2}$ vessel (1 for Supramax)	Usually a multiple of 5,000 tonnes per month
Fixed rate	Time charter ($ per day) or Voyage (US$ per tonne)	WS Rate
Floating rate	As published by the Baltic Exchange daily (average of whole month for Time charter, or last seven days for Voyage)	As published by the Baltic Exchange Daily
Settlement	Usually monthly in arrears, on the fifth business day of the preceding month	
Period	Monthly, quarterly or calendar year, up to 3 years forward in the more liquid routes/contracts	
Buyer or seller	The buyer pays the fixed rate and receives floating that is, benefits from a rising spot (floating) rate. The seller receives the fixed rate and pays the floating.	
Contract type	Either ISDA (International Swaps and Derivatives Association) style or FFABA (Forward Freight Agreement Brokers Association)	

Source: Author's own.

A forward freight agreement (FFA) is a form of swap whereby one party pays to the other a fixed rate and receives a floating rate. Like the interest rate swap, it is a contract for difference, which ordinarily settles on a monthly basis. The parameters of this swap will incorporate all of the elements shown in Exhibit 5.5.

This is best illustrated by way of an example.

A Panamax owner believes that freight rates will fall next year and wishes to hedge against this eventuality using the FFA market. It would therefore look to sell an appropriate contract to profit from a falling market. In this instance, the appropriate contract may be the average of the 4 Panamax Time Charter Routes for calendar year 2007. The owner approaches a buyer for a price, who shows them a fixed rate of US$15,000 per day. The owner takes this price and the buyer sends an ISDA style confirmation detailing the key terms (see section on documentation).

On 5 February 2007, the first month's settlement is due. The shipowner's view has proved to be correct and the market has fallen in the intervening period. The average of the 4 Panamax Time Charter Routes for the month of January, as contributed by the broker panel and published by the Baltic Exchange, is US$13,500 per day. The net settlement from the buyer to the shipowner would therefore be US$1,500 × 31 days = US$46,500. As a calendar trade, there would be a further 11 settlements for each of the remaining months of 2007.

For the shipowner, as the market has fallen, we can expect that it received approximately US$13,500 per day of charter income for the Panamax during the month. If we add the US$1,500 per day received under the FFA to its vessel income, we can see that it has 'locked in' its income at US$15,000 per day.

In reality, there is substantial basis risk between actual earning from the vessel and the floating rate paid under the FFA, unless the physical charter is referenced against the Baltic Exchange published prices. However, it is fair to say that an FFA should give the shipowner a reasonable proxy hedge to capture significant market movements.

Vanilla call and put options are now also being more commonly used in freight hedging, although there are substantially more buyers than sellers. Pricing therefore does not necessarily match what would be expected when the parameters are fed into a traditional option pricing model.

More sophisticated users of FFAs (both shipowners and charterers) will have a managed book of bought and sold FFAs and options, combined with physical charters. The advantage of the derivative over a physical fixture is that it allows the user to act quickly to take advantage of a specific view or perceived arbitrage opportunity. Trades can be broken up into part cargoes, and transaction costs are low. On the flip side, however, the basis risk between paper and physical is often high, and users potentially take on substantial counterparty credit risk. In addition, privately owned shipping companies, which are often domiciled in flag of convenience jurisdictions, may have some difficulty in finding counterparties willing to trade with them due to the usual lack of disclosure of financial information.

It is this credit risk issue that has spurred the development of a 'Cleared' FFA Market. Originally NOS (the Norwegian Options Exchange) and latterly the London Clearing House and NYMEX (New York Mercantile Exchange) have offered a clearing service for FFAs. Participants pledge an initial margin to the clearing house and subsequently the daily mark-to-market (MTM) movement in the net value of trades is paid or received between the clearing house and the counterparty. This has the advantage of removing the credit risk but participants may need deep pockets in order to satisfy some of the margin calls in a very volatile market. This has led to a slight imbalance as smaller players remain on the sidelines.

Some banks have sought to correct this imbalance by offering freight hedging facilities to their shipowning clients, generally by linking it (via an ISDA agreement) to the ship mortgage security. The bank acts as counterparty to the owner, and then takes out its own trading risk by booking an equal and opposite trade with another counterparty, who would generally be happy to take the credit risk of an international bank.

The role of the FFA broker in this market must not be overlooked. Unlike most established derivative markets, the broker is still very much an essential player in bringing FFA parties together. As spreads are still generally quite wide, the broker brings an essential aspect of price discovery, particularly on the dry freight side. On the tanker side, a reasonable amount of business is conducted directly between parties (specifically between financial institutions and energy companies) but the broker still gets the lion's share. This explains the substantial increase in the number of broking firms involved in the FFA market in recent years.

While the FFA market is still relatively illiquid, it is at least heading in the right direction as more participants get involved, volume increases and spreads narrow. Shipping companies now have another way to manage what is undoubtedly the biggest risk they face–that of freight rate volatility. It should be pointed out, however, that for many owners, this is the one risk they want to keep, as it is the reason why they are in the shipping market in the first place.

Tying in hedging products to a ship finance facility
Credit lines

With the exception of options, where the entire premium has been paid upfront, many of the products discussed create a two-way credit exposure. With an interest rate cap, for example, once the seller has received the premium it no longer has any exposure to the buyer. The buyer of the cap does, however, have an ongoing credit exposure to the seller. This is because, over time, the buyer of the cap will expect to be paid any compensation for periods where LIBOR exceeded the cap strike. With an interest rate swap, there is an ongoing two-way credit exposure between the two parties to the transaction. At each settlement date on the swap, the two parties will exchange the net difference between the fixed rate and the floating rate. For any period where the floating rate is lower than the fixed rate, the floating rate payer will receive the difference. For any period where the fixed rate is lower than the floating rate, the fixed rate payer will receive the difference. The party due to receive the net interest settlement on the swap is at risk that the other party defaults.

The exposure on swaps is measured by calculating the current MTM value of the swap (which represents the termination value of the swap) and adding to this an amount that estimates the potential future exposure (as the credit exposure on the swap could continue to rise due to further interest rate movements). In order to determine the termination value of a swap, the bank has to calculate the MTM value of the swap. This value can either be negative or positive depending on where the interest rates are in relation to where they were when the transaction was originally undertaken. The relevant interest rate in this context is the prevailing rate that will cancel out the remaining transaction.

For structured products, the valuations process becomes more complex, although the principle described still holds good in that the MTM value of a transaction is essentially the difference between the original trade and the level at which an equal and opposite trade can be transacted in the market at the time of valuation.

Added to any MTM exposure is a measure of the potential future changes in the MTM. The potential future exposure component is calculated to a statistically significant level. Therefore, not only is the bank able to assess the current exposure (close-out risk) of a given transaction, it can also tell within a statistically significant confidence level what the maximum exposure is likely to be over any given time frame.

The ability of banks to accurately quantify the credit exposures of all of the hedging products described, means that they are able to offer these facilities to the shipowner packaged into the ship finance facility. The mortgage that secures the debt obligations can also be used to secure the hedging facility with a limited amount of additional documentation. The modern shipowner can use the underlying asset as security for the finance, the interest rate hedges and for the forward freight agreements. This is a highly cost efficient way of operating a hedging programme for the shipowner.

Of course, in some circumstances, the financing bank may not be able to offer the full suite of hedging products and in such circumstances it may be necessary for the shipowner to enter into its hedges with another institution. The ability of that institution to quantify the risk, allows owners to set up cash (or alternative assets) secured facilities relatively cheaply.

Documentation

All of the derivative instruments discussed in this chapter give rise to a legal contract between two parties. The form of contract that has become the market standard is the ISDA Master Agreement, which has, since 1987, become the internationally accepted standard agreement between banks and their customers. The Master Agreement is in the form of a master document whereby the parties set out terms on which all types of derivative transactions specified in the Master Agreement undertaken between them will be effected. The Master Agreement covers: obligations of the parties to make payments; basic representations and warranties; events of default/termination; settlement procedures on default/termination; netting and settling of payments; and methods of sending formal notices.

A supplementary Schedule sets out in more detail the exact nature of the business relationship between the parties. The Schedule covers: the precise definitions of the parties and the transactions to be covered; the agreed method of calculation of settlement amounts on termination; and assurances about the ability of the parties to make payments without deducting tax. Further sections deal with administrative matters such as the production of documents, board resolutions and authorities and the addresses for settlements and notices. Finally, part five of the Schedule allows for variations to the Master Agreement. The Schedule includes a number of additional representations and warranties, further termination events related to the corporate/business constitution of the bank's counterparty and linkages to existing or new loan agreements and security.

It should be noted that the Master Agreement and Schedule together form a single agreement and, by signing of the Master Agreement, the parties are also accepting the terms of the Schedule.

Individual trades undertaken under the umbrella of the Master Agreement, and as agreed by telephone, are evidenced by a confirmation which is sent by the bank to its counterparty immediately after a deal is concluded. Counterparties are asked to check and return a signed copy of the confirmation by way of agreement to the terms of the transaction.

The normal process in a packaged ship finance facility is for the vessel mortgage to secure the debt and also all liabilities under the prevailing ISDA.

Accounting issues

One issue that has become much more relevant for shipowners in recent years is the accounting treatment of derivatives under IAS 39 and FAS 133. Following a number of highly publicised financial reporting scandals involving derivatives in the 1980s and 1990s, FAS 133 and IAS 39 were introduced to provide greater transparency as to companies' use of derivatives and other financial instruments. All listed companies in the EU are now required to report under IAS 39 and an increasing number of countries are extending this requirement to smaller private companies.

In the US, all companies must apply FAS 133 with a few limited exceptions. Many private shipping companies based in Europe are also accounting under either IAS 39 or FAS 133.

Hedge accounting

All derivatives must be marked-to-market on the balance sheet.

Changes in derivative fair value are taken to the profit and loss account ('P&L') as they arise, which can result in significant P&L volatility, unless the derivative qualifies for hedge accounting and the company elects to apply hedge accounting. Hedge accounting is a privilege that must be earned by satisfying certain criteria – it is not an automatic right.

Hedge accounting is the method by which gains and losses on the derivative are recognised in the same P&L period as the related loss or gain on the hedged item: that is, matching the accounting impact with the economic objective of the transactions and avoiding P&L volatility.

Faced with the complexity of the accounting regulations, companies are having to strike a balance between sound economic hedging practices and the desire to apply hedge accounting.

Some companies will amend their economic hedging strategies such that they can always apply hedge accounting, whereas others choose to continue with their existing approach of hedging with the most appropriate economic solution. The latter group of companies have decided that the economic benefits of the hedging strategy outweigh the accounting volatility resulting from not applying hedge accounting.

What are the different types of hedge accounting?

- *Fair value hedge accounting*: hedge of changes in fair value of a recognised asset or liability or an unrecognised firm commitment; for example, a receive fixed/pay floating interest rate swap used to hedge a fixed rate liability.
- *Cash flow hedge accounting*: hedge of variability in cash flows on a recognised asset or liability or a highly probable forecast transaction; for example, a pay fixed/receive floating interest rate swap used to lock in the cost of a floating rate liability, or a forward foreign exchange contract used to hedge highly probable forecast revenue denominated in a foreign currency.
- *Net investment hedge accounting*: hedge of the domestic-currency equivalent value of a parent company's investment in an overseas subsidiary; for example, a forward foreign exchange contract used to hedge the net asset value of a foreign subsidiary.

What are the criteria that must be satisfied to apply hedge accounting?

Formal designation and documentation of the hedge relationship is required. This documentation must be completed at the inception of each hedge relationship and must contain or cross-reference the entity's risk management objective and strategy for undertaking the hedge. It will also detail the derivative employed as the hedging instrument, the underlying hedged item or transaction, the nature of the risk being hedged, and how hedge effectiveness will be assessed.

The entity must be able to reliably assess the effectiveness of the hedge and have an expectation that the hedge will be 'highly effective'. At the end of the period, the entity must also prove that the hedge has been 'highly effective' in offsetting changes in the fair value/cash flows of the underlying item.

A hedge will generally be considered 'highly effective' where the derivative is a good economic hedge of the underlying item; that is, the cash flows on the derivative offset the changes in cash flows or value of the hedged asset, liability or transaction. For hedge accounting to be applied, the derivative cash flows must be between 80 and 125 per cent effective in offsetting changes in the underlying item.

In the case of a cash flow hedge, the hedged forecast transaction must be probable (FAS 133) or highly probable (IAS 39) of occurring. This is a subjective and often controversial definition that an entity will need to discuss with its auditors to determine what constitutes a probable or highly probable forecast transaction.

There are also a number of restrictions around what can be designated as a hedging instrument or hedged item. For example, a net written (sold) option cannot be a hedging instrument in an IAS 39-compliant hedge relationship and forecast foreign currency intercompany dividends are not an eligible hedged item (although declared dividends will qualify).

What is hedge effectiveness and how is it measured?

Hedge effectiveness is assessed by comparing the change in fair value of the derivative to the change in fair value or cash flows of the underlying hedged item. As noted above, the hedge is considered 'highly effective' if the change in fair value of the derivative offsets between 80 and 125 per cent of the change in the underlying hedged item.

IAS 39 and FAS 133 require hedge effectiveness to be assessed on both a prospective basis (that is, based on simulated market data, how will the hedge relationship behave over time in the future?) and a retrospective basis (that is, how has the hedge relationship actually performed over the period it has been outstanding?). A company has to prove that its hedges should be effective and that they actually have been effective.

A simple ratio analysis of the change in fair value of the derivative divided by the change in fair value of the underlying item will often be sufficient to generate a result within the 80–125 per cent effectiveness boundaries. More complex hedge relationships will, however, require the use of more advanced statistical techniques (for example, regression analysis) to prove the hedge is 80–125 per cent effective. Regression analysis can also be used on the more vanilla hedge relationships to improve the effectiveness testing result.

Conclusion

As we indicated in the introduction of this chapter, the management of financial risks is paramount in the modern shipowning world. With the correct documentation in place, the shipowner is able to employ a vast array of hedging products and the hedging bank is able to secure the transactions in a way that is cost effective for the shipowner. Derivatives and hedging in general should be viewed as a dynamic process. The flexible nature of derivatives allows for ongoing management as the shipowner's risk profile changes over time. In many cases the shipping company may have no need to employ personnel to manage these products on a full time basis, however, even the smallest of owners should be able to call on the support of the hedging bank to help manage these risks as and when the need arises. Ultimately, it is the decision of the shipowner as to whether or not to hedge and, if so, what products should be employed, but this decision-making process can be aided greatly with the support of its hedging bank.

Chapter 6

The US capital markets

Gary Wolfe

Until the mid-1990s, the US capital markets had virtually no exposure to the international shipping industry. As of March 2006, over 20 international shipping companies have raised money in the US through initial public offerings.

The first part of this chapter presents an overview of the primary actions that both existing and newly established foreign shipowning companies would need to take in connection with the offering of their shares publicly in the United States pursuant to a registration statement filed with the Securities and Exchange Commission (SEC), and the listing of those shares on the New York Stock Exchange (NYSE) and the NASDAQ National Market (NASDAQ). The second part of this chapter looks at methods of offering to US investors without registering with the SEC.

Initial public offering and NYSE or NASDAQ listing

This section gives an overview of procedures for an initial US public offering (IPO) and listing on the NYSE or NASDAQ of shares of an existing or newly established shipowning company.

United States public offerings

Under the Securities Act of 1933 (the Securities Act), the public offering of shares of a company, called an 'issuer' for securities law purposes, whether domestic or foreign, requires the filing with the SEC of a registration statement that contains the form of prospectus which must be delivered to investors. When its shares are offered publicly and listed on a national securities exchange such as the NYSE or on the NASDAQ, the issuer must also register with the SEC and become a reporting company under the Securities Exchange Act of 1934 (Exchange Act).[1]

Foreign private issuers

If the issuer qualifies as a 'foreign private issuer', in order to register the IPO, the issuer files a Securities Act Registration Statement on Form F-1. The 'private' in 'foreign private issuer' denotes a company that is privately, as opposed to governmentally, owned. SEC rules define a 'foreign private issuer' in the negative. A corporation organised outside the United States is not a foreign private issuer if:

- more than 50 per cent of its outstanding voting securities are held of record, either directly or through voting trust certificates or depositary receipts, by persons for whom a US address appears on the records of the issuer, its transfer agent, voting trustee or depositary; and

- any of the following factors are present: (a) the majority of the executive officers or directors of the issuer are US citizens or residents; (b) more than 50 per cent of the assets of the issuer are located in the United States; or (c) the business of the issuer is administered principally in the United States.

Thus, a privately owned company with a substantial US presence could be a foreign private issuer at the commencement of the process, because a majority of its shareholders are not US, and then lose its foreign private issuer status once its US IPO closes.

Public shipowning companies that are foreign private issuers currently include Diana Shipping, Inc. (NYSE:DSX), Frontline Ltd (NYSE:FRO), Ship Finance International Ltd (NYSE:SFL), Golar LNG Ltd (NasdaqNM:GLNG), Torm (NasdaqNM:TRMD), Top Tankers Inc. (NasdaqNM:TOPT), Aries Maritime Transport Limited (NasdaqNM:RAMS), DryShips Inc. (NasdaqNM:DRYS), Knightsbridge Tankers Ltd (NasdaqNM:VLCCF), Omega Navigation Enterprises, Inc. (NasdaqNM: ONAV) and Nordic American Tanker Shipping Ltd (NYSE: NAT).

In recent years, the SEC has revised the contents of the Form F-1 to resemble more closely the contents of European disclosure documents. The Form F-1 contains detailed information about the issuer including:

- a detailed description of its assets, business and operations;
- a description of any pending litigation involving the issuer;
- a discussion of the trading markets for its securities;
- a discussion of exchange controls and any other limitations affecting US holders;
- the identities of all 5 per cent beneficial shareholders;
- shareholdings by management (executive officers and directors);
- a discussion of taxes, including withholding, to which US holders may be subject;
- a description of its shares and their voting rights under applicable corporate documents and the corporate law of its home country and its corporate governance;
- a description of management including compensation of management as a group;
- disclosure of any debt of which the issuer or one of its significant subsidiaries is in default;
- description of related party transactions;
- information with respect to the offering and the underwriting;
- use of proceeds;
- capitalisation; and
- dilution to new investors in the offering.

While these items may take significant time to prepare, they generally should not present any significant problems for the foreign issuer.

Form F-1 also requires that the foreign issuer include income statements for its three most recent fiscal years and balance sheets for its two most recent fiscal years. These financial statements must either be prepared according to US Generally Accepted Accounting Principles (US GAAP) or be reconciled to US GAAP.[2] In some cases, the audited financial statements must be no older than 12 months. In others, the minimum age of audited financials may not exceed 15 months.

In addition, Form F-1 includes selected financial data for the issuer's past five fiscal years. Form F-1 also requires the inclusion of a management's discussion and analysis of financial condition and results of operations, including liquidity and capital resources (MD&A) which is intended to help US investors understand the financial statements included in the Form F-1. The MD&A is prepared in conjunction with the auditors and counsel before the Form F-1 submission is made. In recent years, the SEC has ascribed increasing importance to well and broadly written MD&As. Preparation of both the audited financial statements and related MD&A can take a lot of time. They are probably the key 'gating' items in any IPO.

Until mid-2005, many shipowning companies that had acquired vessels on time charter faced a serious accounting problem. The SEC in many cases took the view that a vessel acquired with a time charter attached constituted an 'acquired business'. An acquired business, in turn, required the inclusion of historical financial statements for that business. In the shipping world, hardly any seller of a vessel is willing to supply financial performance data to a buyer. Shipowners seeking to go public, then, met an impasse.

In mid-2005, the SEC Accounting Staff informally resolved that impasse by agreeing to allow companies to treat an acquired vessel as an asset, not as a business, thereby eliminating the need for historical financial statements of the acquired vessel. In exchange, the SEC staff required disclosure in the MD&A of a sensitivity analysis of how vessel acquisitions along with changes in charter rates or operating expenses may affect a company's performance. Shipowners that had acquired vessels on time charter were able to provide this information, and a number of shipping IPOs that had faced this issue were then completed.[3]

Exhibits and confidentiality

Most investors read just the prospectus for an offering. However, the prospectus is only one part of the SEC Registration Statement. The Registration Statement on file with the SEC and accessible on the SEC's website, www.sec.gov, also contains exhibits. These exhibits include the issuer's:

- articles of incorporation and bylaws;
- form of share certificate;
- underwriting agreement with its investment bankers;
- list of subsidiaries; and
- material contracts for the past two years *not* in the ordinary course of business.

Material contracts may include sensitive information and issuers often face the dilemma of whether to try to withhold a material contract as not being in the ordinary course. While the SEC does have a procedure for requesting confidential treatment of portions of exhibits, that procedure is (purposely) not speedy. In addition, the market practice on whether to file every one-vessel loan agreement, as opposed to a company-wide fleet agreement, varies. However, an issuer wishing to go public in the US should be prepared to disclose what it would otherwise have considered confidential information, such as charter rates or loan details. That is a consequence of being a public company.

Other issuers

If the foreign issuer has any substantial US presence, then it will probably not qualify as a foreign private issuer. In such a case, the foreign issuer will be treated for all practical purposes as a domestic issuer. Like a domestic issuer, the foreign issuer will file a Registration Statement on Form S-1 in order to register its shares under the Securities Act. A Form S-1 calls for information almost identical to that in a Form F-1, except that detailed disclosure must also be made as to compensation of senior management as individuals. That can be a major issue for foreigners who are used to keeping their compensation private. Examples of shipowning companies that are not foreign private issuers are: Overseas Shipholding Corp. Inc. (NYSE:OSG), General Maritime Corporation (NYSE:GMR), Genco Shipping & Trading Ltd (NasdaqNM:GSTL); OMI Corp. (NYSE:OMM), International Shipholding Group, Inc. (NYSE:ISH) and Eagle Bulk Shipping Inc. (NasdaqNM: EGLE).

The fee for filing a Securities Act registration form (whether Form F-1 or Form S-1) has been declining in recent years. As of 15 March 2006, the fee is 0.0107 per cent of the aggregate expected gross proceeds of the offering.

The offering and underwriting process

In a typical public offering, the process from retaining counsel to the offering of the securities to the public and their pricing will take somewhere between four and five months. The process may take longer in the case of an IPO by a foreign issuer if it has not previously prepared US GAAP financial statements. Issuers that have been particularly well prepared have priced offerings between three to four months of retaining counsel.

Billions of Dollars on a Handshake

In US practice, the issuer does not formally enter into an underwriting agreement with the underwriter until the night before or the morning when the offered shares start to trade. This contrasts with the European practice where a binding underwriting agreement is signed earlier. In some cases, in the United States, the issuer and the underwriter commence the underwriting process by first entering into an engagement letter. The engagement letter usually provides that the underwriter will have only a non-binding intent to enter into the underwriting arrangement and market the shares. In contrast, the engagement letter will bind the issuer to reimburse the underwriter's expenses, perhaps choose counsel and accountants acceptable to the underwriter, and reimburse fees of counsel to the underwriter insofar as those fees relate to US state 'blue sky' securities registration compliance. These terms are subject to negotiation. Recently, as potential underwriters have become more competitive, they have ceased to require engagement letters for public offerings. That signifies their willingness to do months of work and incur hundreds of thousands of dollars of expenses 'on the come'.

Once the process begins, the issuer and issuer's counsel prepare the draft prospectus and registration statement, and issuer's counsel then coordinates the entire registration and listing process. Again, this contrasts with the procedure in Europe where the underwriter and underwriter's counsel generally assume primary responsibility for the drafting of the prospectus.

Under the Securities Act, the underwriter may have a defence from liability with respect to disclosure matters if it has conducted due diligence into the matters set forth in the prospectus. Therefore, the underwriter and underwriter's counsel engage in a due diligence investigation of the issuer, interview officers and key employees of the issuer, learn the issuer's operations and business, review basic corporate documents (for example, articles of incorporation, bylaws and shareholders' agreements) and agreements with major customers or suppliers and acquaint themselves with any material litigation, applicable governmental regulation and the issuer's major shareholders. This process can take several weeks or months and usually occurs while the issuer and issuer's counsel are drafting the prospectus and the registration statement. Since conducting due diligence may also protect the issuer's directors and officers from liability under the Securities Act, issuer's counsel will also conduct its own due diligence.

After the first draft of the prospectus is ready, the issuer, the underwriter and their respective counsel engage in a series of drafting sessions in which changes to the prospectus are made. Some of these meetings may also involve the issuer's auditors. Depending on the underwriter's comfort with the issuer and the riskiness of the offering, these drafting sessions can take several weeks. When the issuer and the underwriter are satisfied with the draft prospectus, the issuer files the registration statement, which includes a form of preliminary prospectus, with the SEC.

Once the Registration Statement is filed with the SEC, the SEC Division of Corporation Finance reviews the Form and invariably makes comments and suggestions with respect to the disclosures in the prospectus to which the issuer must respond. The SEC does not conduct a merit review of the offering, as the SEC is not charged with determining whether or not the offering is beneficial for investors. The SEC's role is to determine whether full disclosure of all material facts relating to the issuer and the offering has been made. In this connection, as mentioned above, the SEC staff pays special attention to the MD&A and other financial data.

The SEC usually responds with its initial comments to the prospectus within 30 days of filing. These comments will cover both disclosure and accounting points. Issuer's counsel usually will coordinate formal, written responses, together with filed revisions to the disclosure documents. Issuer's counsel and auditors may also have informal telephone discussions with the SEC Staff to discuss particular items. If necessary, albeit more rarely, meetings can be held with the SEC staff in Washington to discuss the SEC's comments. Most IPO filings involve at least two rounds of comments. In the case of an initial US offering by a foreign issuer, a meeting with the SEC Office of International Corporate Finance may be desirable even before the registration statement is filed in order to identify potential disclosure and accounting issues.

Special procedure for foreign private issuers

The SEC Office of International Corporate Finance (the 'Office') has established a special procedure for reviewing IPOs of foreign private issuers. The Office allows foreign private issuers to submit draft Registration Statements on Form F-1 for confidential review, without payment of the filing fee or filing on the SEC's website. The SEC Staff otherwise treats filings by foreign private issuers completely seriously, and provides comments within the same time periods as it does for domestic issuers. Once the issuer has satisfied the SEC's comments, the issuer then pays its filing fee, files its 'official' Registration Statement containing a red herring prospectus with a price range, and the marketing of the issue begins.

This confidential review procedure allows a foreign private issuer to 'test the waters' with the SEC. If the issuer determines not to proceed before filing its red herring Registration Statement, then it can do so without ever having made its intention to file public.

Concurrently with the filing with the SEC, filings are made in each state where the securities are being offered and where they also must be registered. Some states have disclosure review, while others have merit review of the offering. Nevertheless, under US federal law, the states no longer review offerings that have been approved for listing either on the NYSE or the NASDAQ National Market. Underwriter's counsel generally handles any negotiations with the various state blue sky securities authorities.

Road shows generally take ten days to two weeks. The time is used for meetings with potential investors, while the underwriters 'build a book' for the offering. If the road show has been successful, then the issuer's chief executive officer and chief financial officer will typically negotiate with the underwriter on the evening preceding trading to price the issue. While there will have been an initial price range for the shares set forth in the registration statement filed with the SEC and the preliminary prospectus delivered to potential buyers of the securities, the underwriter, based on its book of indications of interest, will determine a final price for the offering and endeavour to have the issuer agree to it.

Concurrently, any remaining comments of the SEC are satisfied (and those comments may come up until the last minute), and the SEC declares the Registration Statement effective, allowing sales to take place.

When the underwriter and issuer have reached agreement on the price, the underwriting agreement, a form of which will already have been negotiated during the period following the initial filing with the SEC, is executed. The issue goes to market the next morning, the shares are listed on the NYSE or the NASDAQ National Market, as applicable, and begin to trade. The closing takes place three business days afterwards. At the closing, the underwriter wire transfers the proceeds of the offering against the underwritten securities which are delivered to a depositary used by US broker-dealers.

Up to the signing of the underwriting agreement, the underwriter has no obligation to buy the shares, and the issuer has no obligation to sell them.

When an issuer lists its shares on the NYSE or the NASDAQ National Market, it is also required to register under the Exchange Act. It does so, simultaneously with having its Form F-1 declared effective, by filing a simple Form 8-A. Since the issuer has become a reporting company under the Exchange Act, the Exchange Act reporting requirements will then apply to it.[4]

NASDAQ National Market System requirements

The quantitative listing requirements for inclusion of a security in the NASDAQ National Market System do not differentiate between 'foreign private issuers' and other issuers.

In addition to being registered under the Exchange Act, the securities of an issuer must meet the following quantitative listing requirements.

Quantitative requirements

Alternative 1

1 The issuer of the security had annual income from continuing operations before income taxes of at least US$1m in the most recently completed fiscal year or in two of the last three most recently completed fiscal years.

2 There are at least 1.1 million publicly held shares.

3 The market value of publicly held shares is at least US$8m.

4 The minimum bid price per share is at least US$5.

5 The issuer of the security has stockholders' equity of at least US$15m.

6 The issuer has at least 400 round lot shareholders.

7 There are at least three registered and active market makers with respect to the security.

Alternative 2

1 The issuer of the security has stockholders' equity of at least US$30m.

2 There are at least 1.1 million publicly held shares.

3 The market value of the publicly held shares is at least US$18m.

4 The minimum bid price per share is at least US$5.

5 There are at least 400 round lot holders (shareholders of 100 shares or more).

6 There are at least three registered and active market makers with respect to the security.

7 The issuer has an operating history of at least 2 years.

Alternative 3

1 The issuer has:

    (a) a market value of listed securities of US$75m (currently traded issuers must meet this requirement and the bid price requirement for 90 consecutive trading days prior to applying for listing); or

    (b) total assets and total revenue of US$75m each for the most recently completed fiscal year or two of the last three most recently completed fiscal years.

2 There are at least 1.1 million publicly held shares.

3 The market value of the publicly held shares is at least US$20m.

4 The minimum bid price per share is at least US$5.

5 There are at least 400 round lot holders (shareholders of 100 shares or more).

6 There are at least four registered and active market makers with respect to the security.

Qualitative listing standards

The following is a description of the corporate governance requirements for standard issuers with securities listed on the NASDAQ National Market.

Standard Issuers

1 Distribution of Annual and Interim Reports

    (a) The issuer must distribute to shareholders copies of an annual report containing audited financial statements of the company and its subsidiaries. The report must be distributed to shareholders within a reasonable period of time prior to the company's annual meeting of shareholders and must be filed with NASDAQ at the time it is distributed to shareholders.

(b) Issuers listed on the NASDAQ National Market that receive an audit opinion that contains a going concern qualification must make a public announcement through the news media disclosing the receipt of such qualification. If a company receives an audit opinion while undergoing its initial public offering, this public announcement is not required.

2 Each issuer must make available copies of quarterly reports including statements of operating results to shareholders either prior to or as soon as practicable following the company's filing of its Form 10-Q with the SEC.

3 Independent directors

(a) A majority of the board of directors must be comprised of independent directors. The company must disclose in its annual filings those directors that the board of directors has determined to be independent.

(b) Independent directors must have regularly scheduled meetings at which only independent directors are present. These meetings are commonly referred to as 'executive sessions'.

(c) An issuer listing in connection with its initial public offering is permitted to phase in its compliance with the independent committee requirements as follows: (1) one independent member at the time of listing; (2) a majority of independent members within 90 days of listing; and (3) all independent members within one year of listing.

4 Compensation of officers

(a) Compensation of the chief executive officer of the company must be determined, or recommended to the board of directors for determination, either by:

(i) a majority of the independent directors; or

(ii) a compensation committee comprised solely of independent directors. The chief executive officer may not be present during voting or deliberations.

(b) Compensation of all other executive officers must be determined, or recommended to the board of directors for determination, either by:

(i) a majority of the independent directors; or

(ii) a compensation committee comprised solely of independent directors.

5 Nomination of directors

(a) Director nominees must either be selected, or recommended for the board of directors' selection, either by:

(i) a majority of the independent directors; or

(ii) a nominations committee comprised solely of independent directors.

(b) Each issuer must certify that it has adopted a formal written nominations process.

(c) Independent director oversight of director nominations shall not apply in cases where the right to nominate a director legally belongs to a third party.

6 Audit committee

(a) Audit committee charter

(i) Each issuer must adopt a formal written audit committee charter that the audit committee reviews and reassesses the adequacy of the formal written charter on an annual basis. The charter must specify:

(1) the scope of the audit committee's responsibilities, and how it carries out those respon-sibilities, including structure, processes, and membership requirements; and (2) the com-mittee's purpose of overseeing the accounting and financial reporting processes of the issuer and the audits of the financial statements of the issuer.

(b) Audit committee composition

(i) Each standard issuer must have, at all times, an audit committee of at least three independent members. None of the members may have participated in the prepara-tion of the financial statements of the issuer during the past three years and must be able to read and understand fundamental financial statements.

(c) Audit committee responsibilities and authority

(i) The audit committee must have specific audit committee responsibilities relating to: (1) registered public accounting firms, (2) complaints relating to accounting, inter-nal accounting controls or auditing matters, (3) authority to engage advisors, and (4) funding as determined by the audit committee.

7 Shareholder meeting

(a) Each issuer listing common stock or voting preferred stock shall hold an annual meet-ing of shareholders no later than one year after the end of the issuer's fiscal year-end.

8 Quorum

(a) Each issuer shall provide for a quorum as specified in its bylaws for any meeting of the holders of at least 33⅓ per cent of the outstanding shares of common stock.

9 Solicitation of proxies

(a) Each issuer shall solicit proxies and provide proxy statements for all meetings of share-holders and shall provide copies of such proxy solicitation to NASDAQ.

10 Conflicts of interest

(a) Each issuer shall conduct an appropriate review of all related party transactions for potential conflict of interest situations on an ongoing basis and all such transactions shall be approved by the company's audit committee or another independent body of the board of directors.

11 Shareholder approval

(a) Each issuer shall require shareholder approval in connection with the establishment of, or material amendment to, a stock option plan and prior to the issuance of designated securities (i) which will result in a change of control, (ii) in exchange for assets or stock of another company in which insiders have substantial stakes or (iii) which will result in the increase of the outstanding common stock by 20 per cent or more.

12 Listing Agreement

(a) Each issuer shall execute a NASDAQ Listing Agreement.

13 Auditor registration

(a) Each listed issuer must be audited by an independent public accountant that is registered as a public accounting firm with the Public Company Accounting Oversight Board.

14 Direct Registration Program

(a) If an issuer establishes or maintains a Direct Registration Program for its shareholders, the issuer must participate in an electronic link with a registered securities depository to facilitate the electronic transfer of securities held pursuant to such program.

15 Notification of material noncompliance
    (a) An issuer must provide NASDAQ with prompt notification after an executive officer
        of the issuer becomes aware of any material noncompliance by the issuer with any of
        the above mentioned requirements.
16 Code of conduct
    (a) Each issuer shall adopt a code of conduct applicable to all directors, officers and
        employees, which shall be publicly available.

Foreign Private Issuers:
Foreign private issuers are exempt from nearly every requirement that standard issuers must
adhere to. Their sole NASDAQ requirements are:

1 Issuers listed on the NASDAQ National Market that receive an audit opinion that contains
   a going concern qualification must make a public announcement through the news media
   disclosing the receipt of such qualification. If a company receives an audit opinion while
   undergoing its initial public offering, this public announcement is not required.
2 The audit committee is permitted to have fewer than three members, but each member must
   meet the criteria for independence.
3 The audit committee must have the necessary audit authority and responsibilities relating
   to: (i) registered public accounting firms, (ii) complaints relating to accounting or internal
   controls, (iii) authority to engage advisors, and (iv) funding.
4 A foreign private issuer must provide NASDAQ with prompt notification after an executive officer of the issuer becomes aware of any material noncompliance by the issuer with
   the NASDAQ Marketplace Rules.
5 Foreign private issuers shall publish interim balance sheet and income statement as of the
   end of its second quarter in a press release.
6 Any of the corporate governance standards that a foreign private issuer chooses not to follow, other than requirements outlined in this section, must be disclosed in its annual reports
   and registration statements. Further, the practice followed in lieu of these requirements
   must also be disclosed.

There are less stringent listing and corporate governance requirements for NASDAQ securities which are not part of the National Market System.

Fees

The entry fee payable for inclusion in the NASDAQ system (including the National Market
System) is no less than US$100,000 with a maximum of US$150,000. There are also annual
maintenance fees no less than US$24,500 with a maximum of US$75,000. All fee calculations
are based on the total number of shares outstanding.

Reporting and other requirements

Foreign private issuers have a much lighter ongoing reporting requirement regime than
domestic issuers. Once an issuer has become a reporting company under the Exchange Act, if

it is a foreign private issuer, SEC rules require it to provide an annual updated disclosure report on Form 20-F, including financial statements prepared according to or reconciled with US GAAP, within six months of the close of each fiscal year.[5] In addition, a foreign private issuer must provide to the SEC on Form 6-K copies of all material information translated into English that it provides to home country regulators, stock exchanges and its shareholders. Foreign private issuers are not required to file quarterly reports with the SEC. Similarly, foreign private issuers are not required to comply with the SEC proxy and shortswing rules mentioned below.

The annual report on Form 20-F also contains certifications from the company's chief executive officer and chief financial officer as to the company's financial statements and systems of internal control. Foreign private issuers are required to obtain attestations from their auditors as to their internal controls (so-called 'Sarbanes-Oxley 404' compliance) commencing with their annual report on Form 20-F covering the fiscal year ended 31 December 2006.

A foreign issuer that does not qualify as a foreign private issuer is treated like any domestic reporting company. A company that is in its first year of having gone public must file an annual updated disclosure on Form 10-K within 90 days of the close of its fiscal year, and quarterly financial reports on Form 10-Q within 45 days of the close of each quarter. Accelerated deadlines may apply after that time. The information contained in Form 10-K generally mirrors and updates that contained in the Form S-1. The Form 10-K also includes audited annual financial statements containing balance sheets, results of operations and statements of cash flows prepared in accordance with US GAAP. The issuer must also file special reports on Form 8-K with respect to major corporate events such as mergers, acquisitions, dispositions and changes in the issuer's accountants, fiscal year chief executive officer and chief financial officers. Domestic issuers must also comply with 'fair disclosure' rules aimed at assuring that market professionals do not receive material nonpublic information before the investing public at large.

In addition, reporting companies that are *not* foreign private issuers must also comply with shareholder proxy solicitation and disclosure of 'short-swing profits' rules applicable to directors, officers and 10 per cent shareholders concerning profits realised from short-swing purchases and sales of stock within any six-month period. There are exemptions from the proxy and short-swing rules for foreign private issuers even where the issuer's securities are listed on the NYSE or the NASDAQ National Market.

Non-SEC registered offerings

Until recently, many foreign companies, especially shipowners and operators, have avoided the US capital markets. While the US public markets offer perhaps the greatest liquidity in the world, the reason for their avoidance has been the expressed fear of the complication, cost and litigation risk of registering an offering to US investors with the SEC. Such foreign companies, especially the shipowners and operators, have had a point. An initial public offering in the United States usually takes four to five months to execute and can easily cost over US$2m in fees and expenses, aside from the underwriters' discount. For an industry that is still oriented around strong, entrepreneurial individuals and families and in which secrecy is prized, the public continuous disclosure and loss of control entailed in a US public offering are negatives.

There are alternatives. The United States has a massive private placement market of institutions looking for places to invest their money. Foreign stock exchanges, particularly the Oslo Stock Exchange, have made a speciality of listing offerings by shipowners and operators. This section presents some of the alternatives for offering and sale of securities to US institutional investors, together with the relevant registration requirements and exemptions from registration contained in the Securities Act and the related regulations adopted by the SEC.

As we will discuss, it is possible to conduct concurrent unregistered offshore public offerings and US private placements. When such offerings are structured correctly, a US institutional buyer in a US private placement may immediately resell its securities through, for example, the Oslo, Stockholm, Helsinki, DAX or London stock exchanges, even though that buyer executes a subscription agreement which contains all the usual restrictions on resale that are contained in subscription agreements generally used in US private placements.

Private offerings

Under the Securities Act, all public offerings of securities for which no specific exemption is set forth in the Securities Act must be registered with the SEC. Literally taken, the registration requirements apply to offerings worldwide, so long as some jurisdictional means and connection with the United States, such as use of the mails or telephone calls, is present. The registration requirements apply to issuers, underwriters and dealers. The issuer is the company that raises money by selling equity such as shares, or debt such as debentures or notes, and, in the case of shipowners, secured mortgage notes. The underwriter is the broker-dealer that distributes the securities and raises money for the issuer. A dealer is a professional that buys and sells securities as a business.

The basic exemption from registration contained in the Securities Act is the exemption for persons other than the issuer itself, underwriters and dealers. Offerings of an issuer's shares by dealers, in turn, are exempt from the registration requirements after expiration of the applicable seasoning period following the offering of shares to the public or filing of a registration statement with the SEC.

In addition, private placements are exempt from registration under Section 4(2) of the Securities Act. The private placement exemption has been given a safe harbour by the SEC for offerings that comply with the SEC's Regulation D. Many private placements, however, do not comply with the exact requirements of Regulation D but, rather, conform to commonly accepted practices for private placements to institutional investors which have developed in the securities industry. These practices include limiting the placements to institutional investors and using disclosure documents more or less meeting the standards for prospectuses used in registered public offerings, subscription agreements containing restrictions on resale, and restrictive legends on the securities themselves. The SEC has also adopted Rule 144A, which exempts from registration initial private placements for immediate resale to Qualified Institutional Buyers (QIBs), and permits a market for trading unregistered securities to exist among QIBs. In essence, QIBs are major institutional investors.

Starting in the early 1970s, as international capital markets grew the SEC tried to find a way to deal with offerings abroad by issuers who may or may not have markets for their securities in the United States. For years the SEC focused on whether the securities were offered to US investors, no matter where they were located geographically. With the adoption of Regulation S, which exempts from registration 'offerings conducted outside the United States', the SEC changed its focus to one of geography.

With the use of a combination of the private placement exemption, Rule 144A and Regulation S, it should be possible for a foreign issuer to conduct a public offering which is styled for US regulatory purposes as a Regulation S offering abroad, and a private placement in the United States. The SEC has specifically stated (in Regulation D) that concurrent Regulation S offerings outside the United States and private placements within the United States are permitted.

Regulation S and concurrent US private placements

Let us assume that a Scandinavian shipowner wishes to offer shares, and that the offering will include US institutional investors. A foreign broker-dealer (foreign underwriter), acting as underwriter, will solicit purchasers outside the United States and a US registered broker-dealer (US underwriter, placement agent or 'initial purchaser') will solicit institutional investors in the United States, but without the shares being registered with the SEC.[6]

First, under Regulation S and Regulation D, this is perfectly permissible so long as the foreign offering and the US offering are conducted separately, and the US offering is structured as a private placement. To comply both with the Regulation S and private placement exemptions, there should be no efforts to condition the market in the United States for the shares, such as general advertisements, planted articles and public statements in newspapers and magazines with general circulation in the United States, and the like. Regulation S refers to such acts as 'directed selling efforts in the United States'. Directed selling efforts in the United States will vitiate both the Regulation S exemption outside the United States and the private placement exemption within the United States. However, this does not prohibit road shows or other solicitation of potential buyers from taking place in the United States. Soliciting a buyer is not the same as making a directed selling effort, which requires a general conditioning of the market. Secondly, the offers and sales pursuant to Regulation S should take place outside the United States. Such offerings and sales are referred to as 'offshore' offerings.[7]

In order to comply with Regulation S, the offering materials for the offshore offering should contain appropriate legends stating that the shares have not been registered under the Securities Act, and that resales are not allowed to US persons without such registration or an exemption from registration. The typical foreign shipowner will not have substantial US market interest for its securities in the United States. That is, there will be no large trading markets for the shipowner's securities in the United States. In such a case, Regulation S imposes no requirement that the underwriting agreement or agreements with dealers or other distributors contain any provision limiting sales or resales to US persons. Similarly, in situations involving offerings by foreign issuers without substantial US market interest, Regulation S does not require that the securities themselves be legended.

By contrast, in the case of issuers with substantial US market interest, the issuer and any underwriters or other distributors in the offshore offering should undertake in their underwriting and distribution agreements that they will not offer the shares in that offering to US persons for a certain period. For foreign issuers that report to the SEC, the period is 40 days, and the certificates for the securities need not be legended. For foreign issuers offering equity securities with substantial US market interest that do not report to the SEC, the period is one year, and the share certificates must also be legended.[8]

Concurrently, the US underwriter will conduct a private placement aimed at US institutional investors. The offering documents should be subject to review by US counsel to determine that their disclosure level complies with standards for offering documents used in the US market. The reason is that the antifraud provisions of the securities laws will apply to the disclosure notwithstanding that the offering is not registered.

The US institutional investors in the private placement will execute a subscription agreement which, among other things, will state that they will not resell the securities other than pursuant to registration under the Securities Act or an exemption from registration. If the trading market for the shares is in Scandinavia or another recognised market such as the London Stock Exchange, this will have no practical effect on the institutional investors' ability immediately to resell the shares on any of the Oslo, Stockholm, Helsinki, DAX or London stock exchanges. The reason is that Regulation S contains an exemption for resales (a) in offshore transactions (that is, outside the United States) and (b) without 'directed selling efforts' in the United States. For this purpose, an offshore transaction means either that at the time the resale is originated the seller or its broker reasonably believe that the buyer is outside the United States or the transaction is executed through the facilities of the Oslo, Stockholm, Helsinki, DAX or London Stock Exchanges and neither the seller nor any person acting on its behalf knows that the transaction has been prearranged with a buyer in the United States. In effect, resales on recognised foreign exchanges which have not been prearranged with US buyers will be freely permitted.

The US institutional buyers, however, will be restricted from reselling the shares in the United States. However, subject to the usual requirements for resales of privately placed securities, they will not be restricted from reselling their shares abroad under Regulation S or to other QIBs in the United States pursuant to Rule 144A.

Regulation S and Rule 144A

In this connection, it would be perfectly permissible to have the shares of a foreign shipowner that are not listed on a US exchange or on NASDAQ offered concurrently offshore pursuant to Regulation S and in the United States pursuant to Rule 144A for resale to QIBs.[9] There is no reason why the shares could not flow out to the Scandinavian or London stock exchanges and back to QIBs in the United States, so long as the issuer complied with the information delivery requirements of Rule 144A. Again, it would be desirable to have the disclosure document given to US offerees meet US disclosure standards.[10]

The information requirements under Rule 144A are relatively simple. The issuer must agree to furnish holders of its Rule 144A securities with (a) a very brief statement of the nature of the issuer's business and the products and services it offers and (b) the issuer's most recent balance sheet and profit and loss and retained earnings statement, and similar financial statements for such part of the two preceding fiscal years as the issuer has been in operation. The financial statements should be audited to the extent reasonably available. They need not conform to US GAAP.

Conclusion

Many US institutional investors and fund managers are expressing interest in shipping. Foreign shipowners should not forego those investors. The US capital markets are open to anyone who can make a good case and who has nothing material to hide.

---

[1] There are other national securities exchanges such as the American Stock Exchange, but the overwhelming number of shipping IPOs take place on the NYSE or NASDAQ.

[2] The SEC has a project to 'converge' US GAAP with IFRS, but that project is still in process.

[3] This was an informal SEC Accounting Staff action. The SEC Staff has the discretion to withdraw or change it in the future.

[4] The Exchange Act reporting requirements are discussed below.

[5] Form 20-F is substantially similar to Form F-1, discussed under the offering and underwriting process.

[6] For a broker-dealer, the concept of solicitation is very broad. Therefore, if institutional investors in the United States are to be telephoned or sent promotional materials about the offering, so that the foreign underwriter will not be deemed to be conducting broker-dealer activities in the United States, we would strongly recommend that the offering be formally structured as a concurrent Regulation S offering outside the United States through the foreign underwriter and a private placement in the United States through the US placement agent or 'initial purchaser'.

[7] There is the question of whether sales to offshore funds managed in the United States are sales 'in the United States'. The SEC's adopting release for Regulation S specifically states that sales to a non-US person (such as an offshore fund) will be included within the Regulation S safe harbour for offshore offerings even if that person has an agent (such as a fund manager) in the United States and the securities are delivered in the United States. We assume for this purpose that the offshore fund is deemed to be located outside the United States. Also, the presence of a broker in the United States to sell to offshore funds through their United States fund managers will not necessarily vitiate the offshore quality of the offering.

[8] 'Substantial US market interest' means:

For equity securities:

- US securities exchanges or NASDAQ constituted the single largest market for the class of equity securities being offered in the issuer's prior fiscal year; or
- in the prior fiscal year, 20 per cent or more of the trading in that class of equity securities took place through US exchanges or NASDAQ and less than 55 per cent of such trading took place through the facilities of the securities markets of a single foreign country.

For debt securities:

- the issuer's debt securities plus its non-convertible non-participating preferred shares plus its asset backed securities are held of record by 300 or more US persons;
- US$1bn or more of the outstanding amount of the issuer's debt securities plus the liquidation preference or par value of its non-convertible non-participating preferred shares plus the outstanding principal amount or principal balance of its asset backed securities is held of record by US persons; and
- 20 per cent or more of the outstanding principal amount of its debt securities, plus the liquidation preference or par value of its non-convertible non-participating preferred shares plus the principal amount or balance of its as set backed securities, is held of record by US persons.

[9] Rule 144A is an exemption for resales to QIBs. The original placement in a Rule 144A offering should be structured as a private placement.

[10] Preparation of a US-style disclosure document may not pose a great practical problem for most foreign issuers. Foreign prospectuses have already begun to approach US standards. Such prospectuses can simply be 'wrapped by' extra disclosures (for example, risk factors) for use in the United States.

Chapter 7

The ship mortgage

Updated by Lucy French with international contributions

Introduction

The ship mortgage remains the cornerstone upon which lenders build a ship finance transaction, despite the availability of different kinds of security. The important provisions of mortgages will be considered in more detail below, but it is worth noting at this point the essential features of a ship mortgage, namely:

- it gives the lender *in rem* rights against the mortgaged vessel (that is, rights against the vessel itself, and not just personal rights against the owner);
- it gives the lender priority over unsecured creditors of the shipowner;
- it enables the lender to take possession of the ship in the event of a default by the owner; and
- it allows the lender to sell the ship to realise funds to satisfy the lender's debt.

The origins of the ship mortgage, at least in English law, are generally thought to stem from the use of bottomry bonds. English law has long recognised the right of the master of a vessel to pledge the vessel, by way of a bottomry bond, in circumstances of necessity or distress, in order to secure the provision of funds to enable the voyage to continue. The use of bottomry bonds (and their counterparts, respondentia, where the cargo was pledged) became obsolete many years ago, largely as a result of improved communications. In the UK, they were replaced, from the early nineteenth century onwards, by a system of ship mortgages. (The first UK Act of Parliament dealing with ship mortgages was in 1825.) In certain other of the major maritime nations, a sophisticated ship mortgage system was not developed until earlier this century.

Types of mortgage

Almost invariably, a ship mortgage will be required to be governed by the law of the flag if it is to be registered against the vessel. As a result, the form which the mortgage takes will be dictated by the legal system appropriate to the jurisdiction in which the vessel is registered. Broadly speaking, mortgages in the principal ship registration jurisdictions fall into two types, which can perhaps conveniently be distinguished as the *statutory mortgage* and the *preferred mortgage*. Under English law, a registered ship mortgage must be in one of the forms prescribed by regulations made under the Merchant Shipping Act 1995. Those jurisdictions, principally of the former British Empire, which have a legal system based on the English, tend to have largely adopted the system of the prescribed statutory form of mortgage, though there are some relatively minor differences in the forms themselves. The Bahamas, Bermuda, Cyprus, Hong Kong, Malta and Singapore are, perhaps, the most significant jurisdictions for these purposes.

The UK statutory forms, and those of the jurisdictions that have followed English law, are very brief, doing no more than: setting out the registered particulars of the vessel; reciting in general terms the basis of the debt or other obligation secured by the mortgage; and providing for the mortgage of the vessel by the owner to the mortgagee. Two alternative forms are prescribed in the UK, the mortgage to secure 'Principal Sum and Interest' and the mortgage to secure 'Account Current/other obligation'. As a matter of practice, the 'Principal Sum and Interest' form is rarely used, securing, as its name implies, only principal and interest, and not any of the other sums, for example, costs, or insurance premiums paid by the mortgagee, which mortgagees will usually wish to be secured. The vast majority of mortgages registered over British flag ships will, accordingly, be in the account current form.

By contrast, most of the principal ship registration jurisdictions that do not base their legal systems closely on English law allow the parties, perhaps subject to certain mandatory requirements as to what must be included, to dictate their own form of mortgage. This is the case, for example, in major ship registration jurisdictions such as Liberia, Marshall Islands and Panama. Inevitably, this form of mortgage will be considerably longer than the UK statutory forms and will contain a wide range of detailed provisions to protect the mortgagee's security interests. (Additionally, in a few jurisdictions, notably the Nordic countries (such as Norway), a standard printed form of mortgage is used which is longer and more detailed than the UK forms.)

As a result of this difference in approach, the practice has developed in the United Kingdom and related jurisdictions of the owner and mortgagee entering into a separate agreement, normally known as a deed of covenants. This will be expressed to be collateral to the statutory mortgage and will contain all the protective provisions for mortgagees normally found in the forms of mortgage used in other jurisdictions. The deed of covenants will not be registered at the ship's registry (except in Cyprus where it should be bound in with the statutory mortgage form and will be registered together with the statutory mortgage).

The deed of covenants may well itself also contain a charge over the vessel, and, if it does, it, as well as the statutory mortgage, will in principle be registerable under Section 395 Companies Act 1985 (as amended)[1] if the owner is a United Kingdom registered company, or under any similar statutory provisions in other jurisdictions. The deed of covenants may also contain an assignment in favour of the mortgagee of the insurances, earnings and requisition compensation of the vessel, though this is more often contained in a separate document and is dealt with in more detail in Chapter 8.

In order to give a mortgagee the optimum protection, the mortgage must be registered against the vessel at the relevant ship registry. Nevertheless, a mortgage that is not registered may be legally valid between the parties and, indeed, enforceable against a subsequent purchaser of the vessel, even if that purchaser had no knowledge of the mortgage because of the lack of registration.[2] It will, however, in almost all jurisdictions, be postponed to a registered mortgage and may not provide the mortgagee with *in rem* rights against the vessel. In the

UK, and in most other jurisdictions, mortgages take their priority from the date and time of registration. An unregistered mortgage will, therefore, be postponed to one that has been duly registered, even though (whether or not it is in the statutory form) it may create a valid security interest over the vessel.

The basic rights required by a mortgagee

Most legal systems automatically confer certain statutory or common law rights on registered mortgagees of ships, and the rights conferred by individual jurisdictions are dealt with in more detail below. Enforcement of ship mortgages is a topic which alone could occupy an entire book, and there is not room to deal with it in any detail here, but the basic rights which a mortgagee will invariably look for, either by operation of law or by the express terms of the mortgage, will include those given below.

The right to take possession of the vessel

A mortgagee will require the right to take possession, principally to enable it to arrange for the vessel to be sailed to an amenable jurisdiction where the vessel can be conveniently arrested to provide security for the mortgagee's claim. (In theory at least, however, the mortgagee could simply operate the vessel in the same way as an owner for as long as he liked.[3]) In English law, possession may be taken either actually – by the mortgagee or its agent dismissing the master and crew and appointing a new master and crew – or constructively, by the mortgagee doing an act indicating an intention to assume the rights of ownership or by giving notice to the owner and any charterer. As will be appreciated, neither of these methods of taking possession is entirely satisfactory unless the owner's cooperation is forthcoming.

In practice, mortgagees rarely take possession, because to do so can be very much a two-edged sword. A mortgagee who has taken possession will be entitled to receive all earnings due to the owner in respect of the vessel (though, as the earnings will invariably have been assigned to the mortgagee in any event, this is of little additional benefit). The mortgagee will also be responsible for all expenses of operating the vessel, which, in a default situation, may well exceed the earnings. In addition, a mortgagee in possession will also potentially be liable to the owner for any losses arising from the mortgagee's imprudent use of the vessel, though a mortgagee who has taken possession of a mortgaged vessel is under no implied duty to sell the vessel.[4]

The right of sale

Probably the most important right for a mortgagee is his right, in a default situation, to sell the mortgaged vessel. This is often given to a mortgagee by statute (for example, in the UK, by Schedule 1 paragraph 9 (1) of the Merchant Shipping Act 1995), but is regularly expanded by express agreement in the mortgage or deed of covenants itself. The extent to which any expansion is effective will depend on the governing law of the mortgage, that is, the law of the flag, which may lay down certain requirements, (for example, as to the length of notice of any sale which must be given to the owner, from which the parties, even by agreement, may not derogate).

Ideally, a mortgagee should have the right to sell the vessel either at auction (with or without judicial supervision) or by private treaty; in any currency; with or without a minimum price; and with the right to bid at auction or purchase the vessel itself. The mortgagee should, if possible, be given complete freedom to dictate the timing and terms of the sale, to sell on deferred payment terms and to make a new loan to a potential purchaser. Whether such extensive terms will be recognised, even if contained in the mortgage itself, will, as already stated, depend on the law of the flag and also on the law of the jurisdiction where the mortgagee attempts to enforce the mortgage.

In practice, most mortgagees will prefer to sell the vessel through a judicial auction sale, after arresting the vessel in an amenable jurisdiction, rather than selling privately. This has the advantage for a purchaser that a judicial sale will generally give the purchaser a clean title to the vessel free of liens and other encumbrances, a fact which will no doubt be reflected in the price. A judicial sale will 'clear off' all maritime liens and other claims (the holders of which will shift their claims to the proceeds of sale) and will give the purchaser confidence that he can deal with the vessel without his right to do so subsequently being challenged. On a private sale, maritime liens may survive to follow the vessel into the hands of a purchaser.

For the selling mortgagee, a judicial sale has the benefit of removing any requirement for any warranties (for example, as to freedom from liens) to be given. It also avoids the possibility of a claim by the owner for damages for breach of the mortgagee's obligations to obtain the best price reasonably obtainable, and to exercise its power of sale 'as a reasonable man would behave in the realisation of his own property, so that the mortgagor may receive credit for the fair value of the property sold'.[5]

Several jurisdictions now accept the concept of 'hybrid' sales which have the advantages of both private and judicial sales. With a hybrid sale, the mortgagee is able to find a purchaser (as with a private sale) but the sale itself will be carried out through the court and, like a judicial sale, will ensure that the purchaser obtains clean legal title, free of encumbrances, maritime liens and other claims. The main requirement for the sale to be carried out through the court is that the sale price should be the market value of the vessel.

Receivership

A mortgagee will generally require the right to appoint a receiver of the mortgaged vessel, to enable the mortgagee to take possession of the ship and receive her income through a professional agent. This potentially has much the same risks as the mortgagee taking possession. The appointment of a receiver by a mortgagee is unusual, but retaining the right to appoint can be important.[6] Again, the law of the flag as the governing law of the mortgage will dictate the extent to which contractual receivership provisions are enforceable.

Foreclosure

In certain jurisdictions, a mortgagee may be permitted to foreclose, that is, to forfeit the mortgaged vessel and assume absolute title to it.[7] This remedy, again, is rarely used by mortgagees, who will usually prefer to arrest the vessel. In England a court order is required, and, when compared with the procedure leading to a vessel's arrest and sale, the procedure in a foreclosure action is cumbersome and complex.

Arrest

A mortgagee will, under most legal systems, have the right to arrest the vessel to secure its claim. In English law, Section 20 (2) (c) of the Supreme Court Act 1981 gives this right to a mortgagee irrespective of whether the mortgage is registered. This is consistent with the notion than an unregistered mortgage still operates as a valid and enforceable mortgage. As noted above, however, lack of registration may defeat the validity, at least as regards the creation of rights *in rem*, of mortgages of non-British flag vessels. In that event, a mortgagee of a non-British vessel seeking to arrest in the UK would not be able to take advantage of this section.

In most jurisdictions, an arresting party will be able to apply for the arrested vessel to be sold and for the sale proceeds to be held by the court and ultimately distributed to the various claimants. A mortgagee will often be able to take advantage of summary judgment type procedures, with the result that the mortgagee should be able to procure the payment out of court of its share of the sale proceeds without too much delay. However, a period when the vessel is unable to trade while still incurring mooring, insurance and other costs (which the mortgagee, at least in the first instance, will have to bear) will be inevitable.

The question of priorities of various types of claim (which, in the case of arrest, will include court fees and the like), and factors that a mortgagee should consider when deciding where to arrest, are discussed below. Because of certain inherent risks for a mortgagee in taking possession or attempting to sell a mortgaged vessel without the assistance of the court, this is the method of enforcement preferred by most mortgagees (unless they know that they have a ready purchaser of the vessel the sale to whom is unlikely to be attacked by an aggrieved owner or a liquidator or third-party creditor).

Whether or not they are available at law, most forms of mortgage or deed of covenants will contain these, and perhaps other, rights which the mortgagee will be able to exercise in a default situation. It is important for a mortgagee to ensure that the mortgage or deed of covenants does not limit or restrict the rights to which the mortgagee would be entitled at law. On the other hand, it is important to remember that the governing law may not permit a mortgagee to exercise certain rights even if expressly contained in the mortgage, or may impose certain requirements to safeguard the interests of the mortgagor. In English law, for example, a mortgagor always has the right to redeem the mortgaged property by satisfying the underlying debt, and the English courts will not permit this right of redemption to be fettered.[8]

Maritime and possessory liens

In most jurisdictions, certain species of claims against vessels will entitle their holders to assert a maritime lien against the vessel. A maritime lien entitles its holder to satisfy his claim against the vessel itself, irrespective of change of ownership; in other words, it confers a right which operates *in rem* rather than *in personam*.

A maritime lien (unlike a possessory lien – see below) does not rely on the holder of it having physical possession of the vessel. It is often described as 'inchoate': that is to say it does not bite until the lienor commences an action *in rem* against the vessel to enforce the lien.

In English law, the only liens that are recognised as maritime liens in the strict sense are liens in respect of:

- damage done by the vessel;
- salvage;
- wages of the vessel's master and crew;
- master's disbursements; and
- bottomry and respondentia (see above).

In certain other jurisdictions, perhaps most notably the United States, the list of possible maritime liens is considerably more extensive.

Often confused with the maritime lien is the possessory lien. This is a form of lien that arises in favour of a person who has possession of a vessel and has incurred expenditure for the account of the vessel's owner. It allows the lienor to retain possession of the vessel until the owner's liability is satisfied. The most important example of a strict possessory lien is the lien that arises in favour of a ship-repairer for the cost of work done on the ship. Rights largely equivalent to possessory liens may also arise by statute in favour of port authorities in respect of unpaid port dues. These statutory rights may also include a power of sale,[9] whereas the holder of a possessory lien is not (in English law) entitled to sell the vessel, at least without a court order. Unlike a maritime lien, a possessory lien will be lost as soon as the lienor gives up the physical possession of the vessel. Again, in certain jurisdictions, liens that are merely possessory in nature in English law are characterised as maritime liens.

For a lender, the principal significance of the maritime lien is that in most jurisdictions its holder will have priority over the claims of a mortgagee, whether the maritime lien arose before or after the date of the mortgage. When the mortgagee seeks to enforce his mortgage, any maritime lienors will generally have prior claims to the proceeds of sale, as will possessory lienors if they remain in possession of the vessel. The ranking of maritime liens, both among themselves and as between themselves and the claims of mortgagees or holders of possessory or statutory liens, can raise difficult questions.

It is, of course, quite likely that maritime and possessory liens will arise in different jurisdictions from either the country of the flag, or the country in whose courts the enforcement action is begun. In English law, these questions of priorities are characterised as procedural matters and are therefore resolved, in actions before the English courts, according to English law (though the validity of a mortgage, for the purpose of determining priorities, will be determined by the governing law of the mortgage, that is, the law of the flag). Determining priorities in this way may involve parties with the benefit of maritime liens according to their own local law finding those liens lost or postponed.

An example of this occurred in the case of the 'HALCYON ISLE'.[10] Here, the question to be resolved was the priority between a registered mortgage and a lien in favour of an unpaid ship-repairer. The repairer was American, and, in the United States, an unpaid repairer is entitled to a maritime lien, not merely a possessory lien. The case reached the Privy Council, on appeal from the courts of Singapore where the action *in rem* had been begun. The Privy Council board, after stressing that English law was, for all material purposes, identical to Singapore law, held, by a three to two majority, that, as a ship-repairer was not entitled to assert a maritime lien under Singapore law, and as the question of priority was to be governed by the law of the forum (that is, Singapore law), the mortgagee took priority. It was irrelevant that the repairer was entitled to a maritime lien under his own local law.

The English method of determining priorities should be contrasted with that used in other jurisdictions, which may apply quite different rules. It is relatively common for priority to be determined according to the law of the flag, for example in South Korea. This at least has the advantage of certainty; adopting the English approach, a vessel may attract and lose maritime liens on a regular basis as she travels the world. While efforts have been made on an international basis to create a uniform approach (resulting in three international conventions on maritime liens and mortgages in 1926, 1967 and 1993) no real consensus has emerged. Indeed, many of the world's leading maritime nations, including the United States and the United Kingdom, have failed to ratify any of the conventions.

It will be clear, therefore, that the question of where to arrest a mortgaged vessel can be crucial for a mortgagee. The important factors will be as follows:

- Can the arrest be accomplished quickly and easily?
- What are the costs of arresting, and can they be recovered from the proceeds of sale of the vessel in priority to other claims?
- How quickly can the vessel be sold and the proceeds of sale distributed?
- How high a priority is afforded to mortgagees as against other claimants against the vessel?

Most mortgages and deeds of covenants will attempt to prohibit the creation of liens, whether maritime or possessory, without the mortgagee's consent. In practice, of course, a mortgagee will rarely be in a position to give or withhold consent, for example in the event of a lien in respect of damage done by the vessel in a collision or of the vessel needing to be salved. In those circumstances, the mortgage or deed of covenants will normally require the owner to discharge the lien within a fairly short period of time, usually done by putting up security in respect of the lienor's claim in a form satisfactory to the lienor. Many claims which are likely to lead to a maritime lien will be covered by insurance, and the insurers or P&I club will normally be prepared to provide a satisfactory letter of undertaking or guarantee to enable the lien to be discharged and any arrest by the lienor lifted. As a result, the mortgagee is unlikely to be seriously prejudiced.

The existence of other maritime liens, for example that in respect of master's and crew's wages, is much more within the control of the owner and it is not unreasonable for a mortgagee to attempt to prohibit their creation. Failure to pay crew is all too often one of the first signs of an owner in financial difficulty. Similarly, a mortgagee will also normally require any ship-repairer, or other person likely to obtain a possessory lien, to undertake not to exercise that lien before the vessel is put into his possession. Again, this normally involves the owner, or his insurers, providing security for the cost of the repairs.

Standard mortgage provisions

Due to the fact that the British-style form of statutory mortgage is so brief, the deed of covenants will differ little in structure and content from the forms of mortgage used in jurisdictions which adopt the preferred mortgage format, save only to the extent that other jurisdictions may have certain mandatory or desirable provisions that must be included to ensure the validity or priority of the mortgage under their local law. These are discussed below in relation to several important registration jurisdictions. The purpose of this Section is to look at the structure and content of a straightforward mortgage or deed of covenants, assuming for these purposes that any assignment of insurances or earnings contained in a separate document.[11]

It is important first of all to note that most mortgages and deeds of covenants will cross-refer extensively to the underlying facility agreement. Frequently, a copy of the facility agreement will be attached to the mortgage as an alternative to setting out at length the repayment and interest provisions of the facility which many jurisdictions will require to be included in a mortgage. The mortgage or deed of covenants and the facility agreement must, however, be read together. It is also important to recognise that a mortgage may secure obligations other than loan repayments and interest, for example, obligations under a guarantee or counter-indemnity. In that event, it is likely that a copy of the guarantee or counter-indemnity will be attached to the mortgage instead of a copy of the facility agreement. The comments below will, as a general rule, apply equally to mortgages taken to secure contingent obligations as to mortgages to secure loan repayment obligations. (In looking at some of the standard provisions below, the term 'mortgage' will be used generically to refer both to mortgages (other than statutory mortgages) and deeds of covenants, unless an express distinction is drawn.)

Recitals

The mortgage will generally begin by reciting the basis of the underlying facility and the owner's agreement to grant the mortgage. A deed of covenants will also recite the contemporaneous execution of the statutory mortgage, and may recite the opening by the owner of an 'account current' with the mortgagee.

Definitions

The mortgage is most likely to incorporate by reference the extensive range of definitions and interpretation provisions usually contained in the facility agreement. It will include any additional necessary definitions not found in the facility agreement, and may contain an expanded definition of the vessel, to refer to registration details, tonnages, measurements and so on, and to provide that the mortgage encompasses the vessel's engines, machinery, fuel, stores and spares. The inclusion of registration details, tonnages, dimensions and so on may be a requirement of the law of the flag, but in any event is a convenient way of ensuring beyond doubt that the vessel is properly identified. A deed of covenants will probably define the 'account current' referred to in the statutory mortgage, usually to encompass all accounts kept by the owner with the mortgagee relating to the facility or the vessel.

Representations and warranties

Most facility agreements will contain an extensive list of representations and warranties by the owner to the lender. However, certain representations and warranties specifically related to the vessel or the mortgage itself may be included instead (or as well) in the mortgage. These may include assurances that:

- there are no approvals, consents or registrations (other than at the relevant ships' registry or companies' registry) necessary to ensure the validity and enforceability of the mortgage – aimed principally at exchange control consents and the like;
- the owner is the legal and beneficial owner of the whole of the vessel;
- the vessel is free from encumbrances, liens and claims (other than in favour of the mortgagee) and not under arrest; and
- the vessel is insured and classed in accordance with the requirements of the mortgage.

Charging clause

The most important clause of a mortgage (though not of a deed of covenants), the charging clause will grant the mortgagee the mortgage over the vessel as security for the indebtedness due from time to time under the facility agreement. It is essential for a mortgagee to ensure that the wording used satisfies the law of the flag to create a valid mortgage capable of registration. In some jurisdictions (for example, Greece) it has to include a statement of the maximum amount secured by the mortgage, preventing the use of 'all moneys' security over ships registered in those countries. A deed of covenants may also contain an express charge over the vessel, though this is not strictly necessary given the existence of the statutory mortgage.

Repayment

The mortgage will contain a covenant to repay the loan and all other sums due under the underlying facility agreement. Some jurisdictions require the mortgage to contain full details of the interest rate and repayment schedule. As noted above, while this can be done by repeating the relevant provisions of the facility agreement, it is frequently effected by annexing to the mortgage a copy of the relevant facility agreement and by the owner simply covenanting to repay (and pay interest) in accordance with the terms of that agreement. A deed of covenants will include an authority by the owner to the mortgagee to debit all sums due to the 'account current'.

Insurance

It is essential for a mortgagee to ensure that the mortgaged vessel is adequately insured. This clause is therefore likely to set out in some detail the mortgagee's insurance requirements. These will include:

- the hull and machinery of the vessel be kept insured for at least a certain percentage of the amount of the loan – perhaps 120 per cent – and insured against protection and indemnity

133

risks, war risks, pollution risks and any other specific risks relevant to the type of vessel or required by the mortgagee, coupled with a covenant to maintain the insurance cover and pay the premiums punctually;

- a requirement that the terms of the insurance cover meet with the approval of the mortgagee – and also that the cover be placed in markets and by brokers approved by the mortgagee;
- a covenant not to vary the terms of the insurances without the mortgagee's consent;
- a covenant to provide the mortgagee from time to time with information about the insurances, including copy policies and evidence of payment of premiums;
- an undertaking to indemnify the mortgagee for the premium paid by the mortgagee in taking out mortgagees' interest insurance and, if required, additional perils (pollution) insurance;[12]
- a covenant to procure that letters of undertaking are issued in favour of the mortgagee by the insurance brokers and P&I club;[13]
- an agreement by the owner that, after an event of default, the mortgagee can negotiate the settlement of insurance claims directly with the insurers and an agreement by the owner not in any event to settle any insurance claim over a certain threshold amount without the mortgagee's consent; and
- the right for the mortgagee to insure the vessel itself and claim reimbursement of the premiums if the owner should fail in its obligations. (It is worth noting that, at least in English law, while a mortgagee has an insurable interest in the mortgaged vessel by virtue of Section 14(1) Marine Insurance Act 1906, this does not of itself extend to a right to add on the premiums to the mortgage debt, unless expressly agreed by the parties, at least while the mortgagee is not in possession of the vessel.[14])

General covenants

While the facility agreement will contain many of the owner's covenants, those most closely related to the operation and maintenance of the vessel will usually be contained in the mortgage. These will include the obligations detailed below.

- The owner must keep the vessel seaworthy.
- The vessel must continue to be registered under the approved flag, and the owner must not prejudice that registration.
- The vessel must be kept in class and generally comply with class requirements.
- All laws and regulations applicable to the vessel must be complied with. This will include specific covenants relating to compliance with the ISM Code[15] and the ISPS Code[16] and may also include specific covenants with regard to environment laws and regulations.
- No substantial alteration to the vessel is permissible without the mortgagee's consent.
- The mortgagee or its representatives must be allowed on board to inspect the condition of the vessel and to carry out (at the owner's expense) any necessary repairs.
- The mortgagee must be notified immediately of any arrest, detention or seizure of the vessel and to procure the release of the vessel within a set (usually rather short) period of time.
- The vessel may not be sold nor any other encumbrances be created on her, or on her insurances or earnings.

- The mortgagee must be provided with information about the vessel and her employment on request.
- The vessel must not be used to carry any prohibited cargo or taken beyond the geographical limits contained in the vessel's insurances.
- The vessel must not be let on bareboat or long-term time charter without the consent of the mortgagee. (This would remove too much control from the owner and may make the enforcement of the mortgagee's rights difficult, resulting in a dispute as to the respective rights of the mortgagee and the charterer.) In addition, the vessel must not be let on charter at all after the occurrence of an event of default. Under English law, a mortgagor has an unlimited right to charter the mortgaged vessel, in the absence of any agreement to the contrary, so long as he does not materially impair the mortgagee's security: if the security is impaired, the mortgagee will be entitled to take possession of the vessel free of the charterparty.[17] This should be contrasted with the position where the charterparty is in existence at the date of the mortgage, to the mortgagee's knowledge, where the rights of the charterer may prevail over the rights of the mortgagee, and an injunction may be granted restraining the mortgagee from exercising its rights in such a way as to interfere with the charterparty.[18]
- The vessel's earnings must not be shared with any third party.
- All taxes and other financial obligations applicable to the owner or the vessel must be paid.
- The mortgagee must be kept informed of legal proceedings involving the vessel or the owner (where the amount at stake is over a specified threshold).
- Only managers approved by the mortgagee can be employed as managers of the vessel, and neither managers nor the terms of the management agreement may be changed without the mortgagee's consent.
- No liens may be permitted to arise on the vessel. Any that do arise must be removed within a set, usually short, period of time.
- If appropriate, a notice of the mortgage should be placed in the mortgagee's required terms and a copy of the mortgage kept on board the vessel.[19]
- If appropriate, the mortgage should be registered at any applicable companies' registry within the period prescribed by statute.

Indemnity

The mortgage will probably contain a general indemnity by the owner to the mortgagee in respect of any loss suffered by the mortgagee as a consequence of an event of default or in maintaining or enforcing the mortgagee's rights under the mortgage, including any insurance premiums paid by the mortgagee. The clause may include specific provision for interest to accrue on any indemnity liabilities.

Default

The mortgage will set out that the mortgagee will be entitled to exercise its rights on the occurrence of any of the events of default contained in the facility agreement. It may also include some additional vessel-related events, for example loss of class, but these are more likely to be treated as events of default under the terms of the facility agreement as being breaches of covenant.

Mortgagee's rights

As already mentioned, the mortgage will probably list the mortgagee's rights in a default situation in some detail, even if certain of those rights may arise automatically by operation of law. It may be appropriate here to exclude, to the extent possible, any limits on the mortgagee's rights imposed by the law of the flag. The rights conferred on the mortgagee will generally include:

- the right to take possession of the vessel;
- the right to discharge the master and crew and appoint replacements and to direct the course of the vessel (with a view to the vessel sailing to a port in an amenable jurisdiction for arrest);
- the right to sell the vessel on terms and at a time dictated by the mortgagee, at auction or by private treaty, with or without the benefit of any charterparty, and with the power to make a loan to a prospective purchaser;
- the right to repair or alter the vessel;
- the right to charter the vessel out; and
- the right to buy the vessel in.

The clause may also contain protective provisions for any purchaser from the mortgagee.

Receiver

The mortgagee's right to appoint a receiver of the vessel on default may be contained in a separate clause which will cover the following:

- the method of appointing the receiver – usually in writing signed by an authorised signatory of the mortgagee;
- the mortgagee's right to appoint joint receivers and to remove and replace receivers;
- the right to fix the receiver's remuneration without being subject to any limit imposed by law;
- the receiver's status as an agent, not of the mortgagee, but of the owner, who is therefore responsible for the receiver's acts and defaults; and
- the authority of the receiver, who is to have unlimited power to deal with the vessel, her insurances, earnings and so on, without attracting any liability to the mortgagee (or to the receiver himself) as mortgagee in possession.

Appropriation

The mortgage is likely to set out how sums recovered by the mortgagee are to be applied. The usual order is:

- costs, expenses and indemnity liabilities;
- accrued but unpaid interest;
- principal.

Under English law, in the absence of such a clause, the owner would have the right to determine when making any payment how it should be appropriated.[20]

Power of attorney

The mortgage will contain an irrevocable Power of Attorney granted by the owner in favour of the mortgagee, enabling the mortgagee to do anything in connection with the vessel which the owner could do. The mortgagee will normally agree not to exercise its rights as attorney unless an event of default has occurred. The principal use of the Power of Attorney is to enable the mortgagee, when exercising its power of sale, to execute a bill of sale in favour of a purchaser.

Notices, law and jurisdiction

The mortgage will contain the usual range of notices, law and jurisdiction clauses, either in full or by cross reference to the equivalent provisions in the underlying facility agreement. Although the mortgage will be governed by the law of the flag, the mortgagee will often require a submission to the courts of another country, if only for consistency with the facility agreement and other security documents. A deed of covenants, on the other hand, as a private agreement between the parties, need not be governed by the law of the flag, except in respect of a Cyprus flag ship where, as noted above, the deed of covenants is registered at the ship registry together with the statutory mortgage. There are different views as to whether it is preferable for a deed of covenants to be governed by the same legal system as the statutory mortgage to which it is collateral, or whether it should be governed by the same legal system as the facility agreement and other security documents, again for the sake of consistency. In the author's view, the latter is preferable.

Discharge

The mortgage may contain an undertaking by the mortgagee to discharge the mortgage on satisfaction of all the secured liabilities, though, under English law at least, this is not strictly necessary.

Miscellaneous

Like most security documents, the mortgage will contain a range of standard 'boiler-plate' clauses. For example:

- a severability clause, in case any individual provision of the mortgage is deemed illegal or unenforceable;
- provisions as to precedence in the event of any unintentional conflict between the terms of the mortgage and those of the facility agreement or, if the mortgage is to be translated into

another language for registration purposes (for example, in Panama), between the two languages;

- provisions as to the mortgagee's right to transfer the benefit of the mortgage, possibly linked to any restrictions on assignment contained in the facility agreement; or
- other provisions aimed at protecting the mortgagee and ensuring, so far as possible, that nothing done by the mortgagee inadvertently prejudices the mortgagee's position.

Other matters

For certain flags, other clauses may be required dealing, for example, with the maturity date of the mortgage or the maximum amount secured, or appointing a local agent for service of notices relating to the vessel.

Mortgages in the most important ship registration jurisdictions

The remainder of this chapter is devoted to a study of the mortgage requirements of certain of the world's major ship registration jurisdictions, and looks at the laws and practices of those jurisdictions with regard to, first, the form and content of mortgages; secondly, the rights given to mortgagees; and thirdly, the registration practices and procedures in those jurisdictions. For ease of comparison, the information is set out in question and answer format.[21]

---

[1] See Chapter 2.

[2] *The SHIZELLE* [1992] 2 Lloyd's Rep. 444, where a purportedly legal mortgage taken over a yacht which was too small to require to be registered was held to constitute a legal mortgage enforceable against a purchaser, even though that purchaser had no way of discovering the existence of the mortgage. The yacht was owned by an individual, so no question of registration under Section 395 of the Companies Act 1985 arose. It is not absolutely clear what the position would have been had the yacht been owned by a company and particulars of the mortgage not been delivered to the Registrar of Companies. In the author's view, this would not have affected the position, because Section 395 only renders unregistered charges void against a liquidator, administrator or creditors of the company in question, and it is stretching the English language to consider a purchaser from a company to be a creditor of the company.

[3] *European & Australian Royal Mail Co. Ltd v Royal Mail Steam Packet Co.* (1858) 4 K&J 676.

[4] See, for example, *the CALM C* [1975] 1 Lloyd's Rep. 188, a decision of the Canadian Court of Appeal.

[5] Per Lord Moulton in *McHugh v Union Bank of Canada* [1913] AC 299. See also *Cuckmere Brick Co. Ltd v Mutual Finance Limited* [1971] Ch 949 and *AIB Finance Ltd v Debtors* [1998] 2 All ER 929; *Standard Chartered Bank Ltd v Walker* [1982] 1 WLR 1410 extending the duty to apply to a guarantor also.

[6] See Chapter 9.

[7] Note that the term 'foreclosure' is often, inaccurately, used to refer to enforcement generally – in fact, foreclosure in the strict sense has a much narrower meaning.

[8] See, for example, *Fletcher and Campbell v City Marine Finance Ltd* [1968] 2 Lloyd's Rep. and *Banque Worms v Owners of the Ship or Vessel 'MAULE' and another* [1997] 1 Lloyd's Rep. 419.

[9] See Sections 44 and 56 Harbours, Docks and Piers Clauses Act 1847.

[10] *Bankers Trust International v Todd Shipyards Corporation* [1981] AC 221.

[11] See Chapter 8.

[12] See Chapter 12.

[13] See Chapter 12.

[14] *The BASILDON* [1967] 2 Lloyd's Rep. 134.

[15] The International Management Code for the Safe Management of Ships and for Pollution Prevention, as adopted

by the Assembly of the International Maritime Organisation on 4 November 1993 by resolution A.741 (18) and incorporated on 19 May 1994 as Chapter X of the Safety of Life at Sea Convention 1974.

[16] The International Ship and Port Security Code as adopted by the Conference of Contracting Governments to the Safety of Life at Sea Convention 1974 on 13 January 2002 and incorporated as Chapter XI-2 of the Safety of Life at Sea Convention 1974.

[17] *The HEATHER BELL* [1901] P143.

[18] See *De Mattos v Gibson* (1858) 4 De G & J 276; *Swiss Bank Corporation v Lloyds Bank Limited* at first instance [1979] Ch. 548; an injunction will, however, not be granted against the mortgagee if it is shown that, even if an injunction were granted, the owner would not be able, for financial or other reasons, to perform the charterparty.

[19] This is a requirement of certain legal systems, for example, Liberia.

[20] *Deeley v Lloyds Bank Limited* [1912] AC 756.

[21] I am enormously indebted to my colleague, Philippa Sharratt, for her assistance in collating and editing the information contained in the remainder of this chapter.

Bahamas*

A   Form and contents

1   Does the legal system in the Bahamas prescribe a set form of mortgage?

2   If not, does the legal system in the Bahamas lay down any specific requirements as to the content of mortgages, to ensure either their validity or their priority?

3   Must mortgages for registration in the Bahamas be in any particular language?

4   What are the requirements of the legal system in the Bahamas with regard to:
   4.1   execution of the mortgage by the mortgagor?
   4.2   execution of the mortgage by the mortgagee?
   4.3   notarisation?
   4.4   legalisation?

The Bahamas has a prescribed statutory form of mortgage and must be in English and signed by the mortgagor or its duly appointed attorney. The mortgagee need not sign the mortgage which must be notarised and, if executed in a country other than the Bahamas or England, legalised.

B   Mortgagees' rights

1   Does the legal system in the Bahamas provide mortgagees with the rights which they would normally expect, that is, the right to take possession of and sell the vessel on default, (a) by law and/or (b) only if included expressly in the mortgage?

With respect to the right to take possession of and sell the vessel on default, the legal system in the Bahamas provides mortgagees with the rights that they would normally expect by virtue of the Merchant Shipping Act 1976.

2   Are there any limits (and if so, what are they) on the right of the mortgagee on default:
   2.1   to take possession of the vessel?
   2.2   to sell the vessel at auction?
   2.3   to sell the vessel privately?

Beyond what may be necessary for making the mortgaged ship or share available as security for the mortgage debt, registered mortgagees are not deemed to be the owners of the ship or share in respect of which they are registered. Registered mortgagees do, however, have the absolute power to dispose of the ship and give effectual receipt for the purchase money. Such power is limited in that where there is more than one registered mortgagee of the same ship or share, subsequent mortgagees are unable to sell the ship or share without the concurrence of every prior mortgagee unless the sale is being made pursuant to an order of a court of competent jurisdiction.

C   Registration

1   Where may registration of mortgages take place:
1.1   in the Bahamas?
1.2   abroad?

Mortgages may be registered in the following places:

1.1   In Nassau: Bahamas Maritime Authority, Gold Circle Building, East Bay Street, PO Box N 4891, Nassau, Bahamas
Telephone No.: (242)-394-0445
Fax No.: (242)-394-3014

1.2   In London: Bahamas Maritime Authority, 2nd Floor, Latham House, 16 Minories, London EC3N 1EH, England
Telephone No.: 011-44-207-264-2550
Fax No.: 011-44-207-264-2589
In New York: Bahamas Maritime Authority, Bahamas House, 231 East 46th Street, New York, NY 10017
Telephone No.: 212-829-0221
Fax No.: 212-829-0356
In Japan: Bahamas Maritime Authority, c/o Mitsui Foko Co. Ltd, Kanto Branch, Ships & Registry Team, 3-22-23 Kaigan, Minato-ku, Tokyo, 108-0022, Japan
Telephone No.: 011-813-6400-8521
Fax No.: 011-813-6400-8539

2   If mortgages may be executed and presented for registration in a foreign language, what, if any, are the translation requirements and when must they be completed?

A mortgage must be presented in the English language.

3   How many originals of the mortgage must be presented for registration? How many are retained by the registering authority?

Only one original mortgage is presented for registration. A notation is made at the Registrar's office and the mortgage is returned to the mortgagee.

4   What other documents must be produced to the registering authority when registering the mortgage? Which will be retained?

The only other document that will be presented at the time of registration of the mortgage will be a Power of Attorney in respect of the signing authority.

5   Must original documents be submitted or will photocopies or fax copies of some or all documents be accepted? If so which? Are there any requirements for copies to be verified?

An original mortgage must be submitted, photocopies will not be accepted.

6   What fees are currently payable on mortgage registration?

The fees on filing the mortgage are as follows:
(a)   Below 1,600 nrt: US$200.00
(b)   Above 1,601 nrt: US$400.00

D   Amendment

1   Can registered mortgages be amended and or supplemented?
Registered mortgages may not be amended or supplemented.

E   Discharge

1   What documents are required by the registering authority to discharge a registered mortgage?
Mortgages are discharged by completion of the discharge of mortgage on the reverse side of the statutory form.

2   Please answer the questions listed above as if references to mortgages were references to mortgage discharges.
Fees payable for discharge of mortgage are as follows:
   (a)   Below 1,600 nrt: US$200.00
   (b)   Above 1,601 nrt: US$400.00

F   General

1   Please identify the principal statute in the Bahamas governing the registration of mortgages on ships
The principal statute is the Merchant Shipping Act 1976.

2   Must notice of mortgage and/or a certified copy of the mortgage be placed on board the ship?
There is no requirement that a certified copy or notice of the mortgage be placed on board the vessel.

----

*   Contributed by Paul Knowles of McKinney Bancroft and Hughes, Nassau, Bahamas.

Bermuda*

A Form and contents

1 Does the legal system in Bermuda prescribe a set form of mortgage?
Legal registered mortgages must be in one of the statutory forms approved by the Minister of Transport.

2 If not, does the legal system in Bermuda lay down any specific requirements as to the content of mortgages, to ensure either their validity or their priority?
Where the statutory form to secure account current is used, there is no requirement for the form to state the maximum amount secured.

3 Must mortgages for registration in Bermuda be in any particular language?
The statutory forms should if possible be completed in English. If any of the information is in a language other than English then a certified translation must also be provided. It is advisable to submit a draft copy of the mortgage to the Registrar of Shipping for pre-approval prior to registration.

4 What are the requirements of the legal system in Bermuda with regard to:
    4.1 execution of the mortgage by the mortgagor?
    4.2 execution of the mortgage by the mortgagee?
    4.3 notarisation?
    4.4 legalisation?

4.1   The mortgagor should execute the mortgage under seal or appoint an attorney-in-fact to execute it under his personal seal on behalf of the mortgagor (unless sealing is unnecessary under the laws of the mortgagor's domicile). Where the document is executed under a Power of Attorney, the Registrar of Ships will require sight of the original Power of Attorney.

4.2   The mortgagee is not required to execute the mortgage.

4.3   Documentation executed outside Bermuda should be notarised.

4.4   Though preferable, legalisation is not generally required.

B Mortgagees' rights

1 Does the legal system in Bermuda provide mortgagees with the rights which they would normally expect, that is, the right to take possession of and sell the vessel on default, (a) by law and/or (b) only if included expressly in the mortgage?
The mortgagee is statutorily empowered to sell a mortgaged vessel, without further express provision in the mortgage if the mortgagor is in financial default under the mortgage or if the security is imperilled.

2 Are there any limits (and, if so, what are they) on the right of the mortgagee on default:

2.1   *to take possession of the vessel?*

2.2   *to sell the vessel at auction?*

2.3   *to sell the vessel privately?*

2.1   There is no express statutory right for a mortgagee to enter into possession, although a mortgagee is likely to have a right to enter into possession through a collateral deed to the mortgage. There are also statutory provisions the effect of which confers an implied right to take possession in certain circumstances.

2.2   There is no statutory right of auction. Such rights will likely be contained within a deed collateral to the mortgage.

2.3   See comments above regarding statutory power of sale. A contractual right of sale may exist if the deed collateral to the mortgage is so drafted.

C   Amendment

1   Can registered mortgages be amended and/or supplemented?

There are statutory provisions which contemplate that regulations may be enacted to allow for corrections or the addition of supplemental information to a mortgage, but to date, those regulations have not been enacted.

2   If so, what documents are required by the registering authority?

See comment above.

D   Registration

1   Where may registration of mortgages take place:

     1.1   in Bermuda?

     1.2   abroad?

1.1   At the Department of Maritime Administration, Hamilton, Bermuda.

1.2   Nowhere.

2   If mortgages may be executed and presented for registration in a foreign language, are there any translation requirements and when must they be completed?

See Section A3 above.

3   How many originals of the mortgage must be presented for registration? How many are retained by the registering authority?

One, which is returned to the mortgagee after registration.

4   What other documents must be produced to the registering authority? Which will be retained?

Any Power of Attorney under which the mortgage is executed. It should be noted that the Power of Attorney will need an accompanying notarial attestation confirming that the signatories are authorised to sign for the mortgagor. The original will be returned.

5   *Must original documents be submitted or will photocopies, faxed copies or pdf copies of some or all documents be accepted? If so, which? Are there any requirements for copies to be verified?*

The original mortgage must be submitted. The Registrar of Shipping will need either the original Power of Attorney or a notarised, certified copy.

6   *What are the fees currently payable on mortgage registration?*

Registration of each mortgage, transfer or discharge of mortgage
Yachts not exceeding 24 metres in registered length: US$110
Yachts exceeding 24 metres in registered length: US$220
Other ships: US$440

7   *Can a mortgage be registered over a vessel currently under construction? If so, please provide details of the documents to be submitted and the fees payable.*

A statutory mortgage will only be possible where the proposed mortgagor has legal title in the vessel and registration formalities are followed. There is provision in the regulations providing for registration by a proposed mortgagee of a priority interest in advance of entering into a statutory mortgage in respect of vessels still under construction, vessels registered elsewhere and vessels not registered.

E   Discharge

1   *What documents are required by the registering authority to discharge a registered mortgage?*

The original, duly executed discharge of mortgage must be completed, as contained within the statutory mortgage form, and executed by the mortgagee.

2   *Where may registration of mortgages take place:*
     2.1   in Bermuda?
     2.2   abroad?

2.1   At the Department of Maritime Administration, Hamilton, Bermuda.
2.2   Nowhere.

3   *If a discharge of mortgage may be executed and presented for registration in a foreign language, are there any translation requirements and when must they be completed?*

See Section A3 above.

4   *How many originals of the discharge of mortgage must be presented for registration? How many are retained by the registering authority?*

The original statutory mortgage must be presented, which is returned after entry of the discharge of mortgage.

5   *What other documents must be produced to the registering authority? Which will be retained?*

Any Power of Attorney under which the mortgage discharge is executed. It should be noted that the Power of Attorney will need an accompanying notarial attestation confirming that the signatories are authorised to sign for the mortgagee. The original will be returned.

6   *Must original documents be submitted or will photocopies, faxed copies or pdf copies of some or all documents be accepted? If so, which? Are there any requirements for copies to be verified?*

The original mortgage must be submitted. The Registrar of Shipping will need either the original Power of Attorney or a notarised, certified copy.

7   *What are the fees currently payable on a discharge of mortgage?*

See list above under Section D6.

* Contributed by Timothy Counsell and Clive Langley, Appleby Spurling Hunter, Hamilton, Bermuda.

The People's Republic of China*

A   Form and contents

1   Does the legal system in the PRC prescribe a set form of mortgage?
No.

2   If not, does the legal system in the PRC lay down any specific requirements as to the content of mortgages, to ensure either their validity or their priority?
A mortgage must contain:
> (a)   name or designation and address of the mortgagee and the name or designation and address of the mortgagor of the ship;
>
> (b)   name and nationality of the mortgaged ship and the authorities that issued the certificate of ownership and the certificate number thereof; and
>
> (c)   amount of debt secured, the interest rate and the period for the repayment of the debt.

3   Must mortgages for registration in the PRC be in any particular language?
They must be in Chinese.

4   What are the requirements of the legal system in the PRC with regard to:
> *4.1   execution of the mortgage by the mortgagor?*
> *4.2   execution of the mortgage by the mortgagee?*
> *4.3   notarisation?*
> *4.4   legalisation.*

No specific requirements. If the contract of mortgage is signed by a natural person as one party, his or her signature is sufficient. If the contract of mortgage is with a company as one party, the signature of the legal representative of the company is required and the company stamp must be affixed.

B   Mortgagees' rights

1   Does the legal system in the PRC provide mortgagees with the rights which they would normally expect, that is, the right to take possession of and sell the vessel on default, (a) by law and/or (b) only if included expressly in the mortgage?
On default, the mortgagee can, upon a separate agreement with the mortgagor, directly take possession of the ship at a price agreed, or sell the vessel through auction or sell the ship privately to get the credit right secured by the mortgage satisfied. Failing agreement with the mortgagor, the mortgagee can bring a suit before the court for realising the mortgage. It is not allowed to agree in the mortgage that the mortgagee can directly take possession of the ship on default.

2   Are there any limits (and, if so, what are they) on the right of the mortgagee on default:
> *2.1   to take possession of the vessel?*
> *2.2   to sell the vessel at auction?*
> *2.3   to sell the vessel privately?*

See the preceding point.

C   Registration

1   *Where may registration of mortgages take place:*
    1.1   *in the PRC?*
    1.2   *abroad?*
Mortgage registration may only take place in the PRC.

2   *If mortgages may be executed and presented for registration in a foreign language, what, if any, are the translation requirements and when must they be completed?*
The mortgage must be in Chinese. Any translation produced by an intermediary who has the legal qualification for producing translations must be submitted at the same time as the application for registration.

3   *How many originals of the mortgage must be presented for registration? How many are retained by the registering authority?*
The mortgage application must be submitted in two originals. The contract of mortgage is required to be submitted in one original. The ship registration authority will retain one copy while the original will be returned to the applicant after verification.

4   *What other documents must be produced to the registering authority when registering the mortgage? Which will be retained?*
In addition to the contract of mortgage, the following documents shall also be submitted:
    (a)   application for mortgage registration signed by mortgagee and mortgagor;
    (b)   document evidencing the identity of the mortgagor and mortgagee;
    (c)   principal contract to be secured by the mortgage;
    (d)   ship building contract (applicable in case the ship to be mortgaged is under construction);
    (e)   document evidencing that a notice has been given to the charterer if the ship has been demise-chartered;
    (f)   written consent from joint owners with 2/3 majority shares or other number of agreed shares (applicable if the ship is joined owned); and
    (g)   document evidencing other mortgage (applicable if there is other mortgage on the ship).
Copies of all these documents will be retained by the Ship Registration Authority.

5   *Must original documents be submitted or will photocopies, faxed copies or pdf copies of some or all documents be accepted? If so, which? Are there any requirements for copies to be verified?*
Original documents shall be submitted for verification. Fax copy or pdf copies are not acceptable.

6   What are the fees currently payable on mortgage registration?
A fee of 0.5 per cent of the amount secured by the mortgage is payable.

*7   Can a mortgage be registered over a vessel currently under construction? If so,
         please provide details of the documents to be submitted and the fees payable.*
Yes. See Points C4 and C6 above.

D   Amendment

1   Can registered mortgages be amended and/or supplemented?
Yes.

2   If so, what documents are required by the registering authority?
After a mortgage is registered, if the principal contract secured by the mortgage is amended, the
registered mortgagee shall be amended accordingly by submitting the following documents:
      (a)   application for amending the registered mortgage;
      (b)   certificate of ownership;
      (c)   original certificate of ship mortgage; and
      (d)   document evidencing the amendment of the contract of mortgage.

*3   If so, please answer the questions listed under the sections A and C as if references
         to mortgages were references to amending and/or supplementing instruments.*
The procedure is very similar.

E   Discharge

*1   What documents are required by the registering authority to discharge a registered
         mortgage?*
In order to discharge a registered mortgage the following documents are required:
      (a)   application for discharge the registered mortgage;
      (b)   certificate of mortgage registration;
      (c)   document evidencing the need for discharging the mortgage, such as the
            certificate from the mortgagee that debts secured by the mortgage and inter-
            est thereon have been paid in full or the agreement between the mortgagee
            and the shipowner for discharging the mortgage;
      (d)   certificate of ownership; and
      (e)   principal contract and contract of mortgage.

*2   Please answer the questions listed above in sections A and C as if references to mort-
         gages where references to mortgage discharges.*
The procedure is very similar.

F   General

*1   Please identify the principal statutes and regulations in the PRC governing the reg-
         istration of mortgages on ships.*

Maritime Code of the PRC, with effect from 1 July 1993;

Guarantee Law of the PRC;

Ship Registration Regulations of the PRC promulgated by the State Council, with effect from 1 January 1995;

For mortgage established on a ship in favour of a foreign party, the following regulations shall also be applied:

Regulations on Provision of Guarantee by a Domestic Institution to a Foreign Party and their implementing rules.

2   *Must notice of mortgage and/or a certified copy or original mortgage be placed on board the mortgaged ship? Is there any time limit for doing so?*

No.

3   *Are there any other matters in the context of mortgages on ships under the legal system in the PRC which you feel should be emphasised?*

As China has foreign exchange controls, if the mortgagee is a foreign company, the shipowner shall first obtain approval from the local branch of the State Administration for Foreign Exchange if the mortgage is established to secure satisfaction of the debts of a third party (or for amending such an existing registered mortgage), and then the owner shall report the mortgage to the local branch of the State Administration for Foreign Exchange for recording in addition to registration with the Ship Registration Authority. The amount of debt secured by the mortgage in such circumstances shall not exceed the owner's income in foreign exchange for the preceding year.

If the mortgage is established to secure the owner's own debts (or for amending such an existing registered mortgage), prior approval is not necessary but the mortgage must still be reported to the local branch of the State Administration for Foreign Exchange for recording in addition to registration with the Ship Registration Authority. If the shipowner is a Chinese-capitalised enterprise other than a foreign invested company, when filing is made to the State Administration for Foreign Exchange for recording, evidence documents showing that the State Administration for Foreign Exchange has approved the owner to incur such debts (those debts secured by the mortgage) towards the foreign party shall be presented.

---

*   Contributed by Shen Xiangman of Wang Jing & Co., Guangzhou, PRC.

Cyprus*

Introductory note

Cyprus law draws a distinction between:

(a)   a mortgage (or mortgage deed), as the instrument creating the security on the ship, which is executed only by the mortgagor; and

(b)   a collateral deed of covenants, containing the detailed stipulations of the mortgage agreed between the parties, which in essence constitutes a contract between the mortgagor and the mortgagee and is executed by both.

Unlike other Anglo-Saxon law jurisdictions, the collateral deed of covenants must, under Cyprus law, be attached to the mortgage as a matter of statutory requirement, thus forming a composite mortgage document known as 'statutory mortgage and deed of covenants'.

Consequently, the answers to the questionnaire from a Cyprus law standpoint must necessarily refer to (a) the mortgage (or mortgage deed), (b) the deed of covenants and (c) the composite document, that is, the mortgage and deed of covenants, as the case requires.

A   Form and contents

1   Does the legal system in Cyprus prescribe a set form of mortgage?

Cyprus law prescribes two particular forms of mortgage deed which are set out in the schedule to the relevant statute (hence the name 'statutory mortgage') and are the following:

(a)   mortgage to secure principal sum and interest; and

(b)   mortgage to secure account current.

No set form of deed of covenants collateral to the mortgage is provided for in the Cyprus legal system.

2   If not, does the legal system in Cyprus lay down any specific requirements as to the content of mortgages, to ensure either their validity or their priority?

In addition to the prescribed form of mortgage Cyprus law lays down an additional requirement as to the contents of the mortgage, namely that there must be a loan or other valuable consideration to support the valid creation of the security. A gratuitous mortgage is void under Cyprus law.

As regards the collateral deed of covenants the Cyprus statute (see F1 below) provides that this document is to deal with any matter relating to the mortgage, including the following:

(a)   the mode of the payment of interest and the repayment of principal;

(b)   insurances and renewals thereof and application of policy money;

(c)   limitations on employment of ship;

(d)   definition of default on which statutory or other powers may be exercised;

(e)   powers exercisable by the mortgagee including power to take possession of the ship, assume her management and sell the ship by private deal; and

(f)   any other matter ancillary or incidental thereto.

3   Must mortgages for registration in Cyprus be in any particular language?

For purposes of registration the mortgage and deed of covenants must be drawn up in one of the official languages of the Republic of Cyprus, namely, Greek or Turkish, or in the English language. See also answer to question C2 below.

4   *What are the requirements of the legal system in Cyprus with regard to:*

      4.1   execution of the mortgage by the mortgagor?

      4.2   execution of the mortgage by the mortgagee?

      4.3   notarisation?

      4.4   legalisation?

4.1   With regard to execution of the mortgage and deed of covenants by the mortgagor Cyprus law and practice prescribes the following:

      (a)   the statutory mortgage must, as a matter of law, be executed by the mortgagor:

            (i)   as a deed, that is, under seal; and

            (ii)   before an attesting witness; and

      (b)   the deed of covenants is, as a matter of practice, executed by the mortgagor in the same mode as the mortgage, that is, as a deed and before an attesting witness.

4.2   With regard to execution of the mortgage and deed of covenants by the mortgagee Cyprus law and practice prescribes the following:

      (a)   execution of the statutory mortgage by the mortgagee is not required; and

      (b)   the deed of covenants should be executed by the mortgagee in the same mode as by the mortgagor, namely, as a deed and before an attesting witness.

4.3   Notarisation of a Cyprus mortgage and deed of covenants is not legally required. However mortgage documents executed in the Republic of Cyprus are usually signed and sealed before a Certifying Officer (the nearest equivalent to a notary public) who may act as an attesting witness and is authorised by law to certify the genuineness of signatures and seals. Alternatively they may be executed before the Registrar of Cyprus Ships or an authorised officer of the Department of Merchant Shipping on his behalf. Mortgage documents executed outside Cyprus should, preferably, be notarised with the notary confirming the power and authority of the person(s) executing the documents to do so.

4.4   Mortgage documents (that is, a statutory mortgage and deed of covenants) executed outside Cyprus may be:

      (a)   executed before a Consular Officer of the Republic of Cyprus as an attesting witness (without the need for further legalisation); or

      (b)   notarised and then legalised by a Cyprus Consular Officer; or

      (c)   notarised and then apostilled, Cyprus being a signatory to the Hague Convention abolishing the Requirement of Legalisation for Foreign Public Documents, 1961.

B   Mortgagees' rights

I   Does the legal system in Cyprus provide mortgagees with the rights which they would normally expect, that is, the right to take possession of and sell the vessel on default, (a) by law and/or (b) only if included expressly in the mortgage?

The Cyprus legal system confers on or recognises in mortgagees the following rights and powers exercisable in the event of default (unless otherwise stated, see (a)(ii) below).

(a)   by statute:
    (i)   the power absolutely to dispose of the ship and to give effectual receipts for the purchase money (statutory power of sale by auction or private treaty);
    (ii)   the power to take possession of the ship where the mortgagor allows the ship to remain burdened with a maritime lien which impairs the security of the mortgage, even in the absence of default in the payment of interest or repayment of principal;

(b)   by contract (that is, if expressly included in the deed of covenants collateral to the statutory mortgage):
    (i)   the power to take possession of the ship and assume her management upon the happening of an event of default (cf. (a)(ii) above);
    (ii)   the power to sell the ship by private deal (regulating in detail and expanding on the statutory power); and
    (iii)   any other additional or supplemental power agreed to between the parties as exercisable by the mortgagee in the event of default.

2   *Are there any limits on the right of a mortgagee on default:*
    2.1   *to take possession of the vessel?*
    2.2   *to sell the vessel at auction?*
    2.3   *to sell the vessel privately?*

The following limits on or conditions to the mortgagee's rights in the event of default exist under Cyprus law.

2.1   To take possession of the vessel:
    (a)   not exercisable by a mortgagee unless the entire ship is mortgaged;
    (b)   notice of assumption of management of the ship by the mortgagee must be given to the Registrar of Cyprus Ships.

2.2   To sell the vessel at auction.

2.3   To sell the vessel privately:
    (a)   not exercisable by a mortgagee unless the entire ship is mortgaged;
    (b)   subsequent mortgagees cannot sell the ship, except under a court order, without the concurrence of every prior mortgagee.

3   *Does the legal system, in Cyprus give mortgagees any specific rights not generally found in well drafted standard forms of mortgage?*

The Cyprus legal system does not give mortgagees any specific rights not generally found in well drafted standard forms of mortgage and collateral deeds of covenants.

C   Registration

Preliminary note

Cyprus law provides for a dual system of registration for a mortgage on a ship in public registers. Thus:
    (a)   under the Merchant Shipping Law a mortgage is registrable in the Register of Cyprus Ships as a charge on the ship;

(b)   under the Companies Law a mortgage is registrable as a charge on the Cyprus company which may own the ship, in the Register of Charges of the mortgagor company which is kept by the Registrar of Companies in Cyprus.

Registration of the mortgage in the Register of Ships is imperative for the purpose of acquiring priority and limiting the effect of acts of bankruptcy by the mortgagor, but is not essential to the validity of the mortgage. If not registered, a mortgage has the legal effect of a valid equitable mortgage.

Failure to register the mortgage with the Registrar of Companies within the time limited by law renders the charge void against the liquidator or any creditor of the mortgagor company.

1   Where may registration of mortgages take place:

    1.1   in Cyprus?

    1.2   abroad?

Registration of a mortgage as a charge on the ship may take place:

1.1   in Cyprus, with the Registrar of Ships;

1.2   abroad, with a Cyprus Consular Officer on the prior written authority of the Registrar of Ships.

Registration of a mortgage as a charge on the Cyprus mortgagor company can only take place in Cyprus with the Registrar of Companies.

2   If mortgages may be executed and presented for registration in a foreign language, what, if any, are the translation requirements and when must they be completed?

A mortgage and deed of covenants may be executed in a foreign language and may be presented for registration if accompanied by a sworn or certified translation. Mortgages and deeds of covenants drawn up in the English language need not be translated in one of the official languages of the Republic of Cyprus for purposes of registration.

Translation requirements of mortgages and deeds of covenants in a foreign language (other than English) must be completed:

(a)   prior to registration with the Registrar of Ships, or a Cyprus Consular Officer on the Registrar's authority; and

(b)   prior to registration with the Registrar of Companies and within 42 days of the creation of the charge.

3   How many originals of the mortgage must be presented for registration? How many are retained by the registering authority?

For registration of a mortgage with the Registrar of Ships three originals (or more if desired by the parties) are presented, only one of which is retained by the Registrar. The other(s) are returned with a memorandum endorsed thereon stating the day and hour of the record in the Register.

For registration of a mortgage with a Consular Officer of the Republic abroad four originals (or more if desired) are presented, two of which are retained by the Consular Officer.

For registration of a mortgage with the Registrar of Companies one original (or certified copy) is presented which after registration is returned by the Registrar to the person filing the charge.

4   *What other documents must be produced to the registering authority? Which will be retained?*

For registration of a mortgage with the Registrar of Ships or a Cyprus Consular Officer on the authority of the Registrar there must also be produced Powers of Attorney if the mortgage documents (namely, statutory mortgage and deed of covenants) have been executed by attorneys acting on behalf of the mortgagor and the mortgagee. Directors' resolutions of the mortgagor company are also required. For registration of a second (or subsequent) mortgage, the Registrar of Ships also requires the written consent of the first (or other prior) mortgagee(s).

For registration of a mortgage with the Registrar of Companies there must be produced with the mortgage document: the company form containing the prescribed particulars of the charge.

5   *Must original documents be submitted? If not, will photocopies or fax copies of some or all documents be required? If so, which? Are there any requirements for copies to be verified?*

The mortgagor's Power of Attorney (if any) must be submitted in the original. A photocopy or fax copy of the mortgagee's Power of Attorney may be accepted pending receipt and deposit of the original or certified copies. The directors' resolutions can be submitted in a certified copy. A fax copy of the prior mortgagee's consent is sufficient. Copies verified by, say, a notary public are also acceptable.

6   *What fees are currently payable on mortgage registration?*

For the registration of a mortgage with the Registrar of Ships or a Consular Officer of the Republic:
(a)   For each ton gross up to 10,000 gt: 2 cents
(b)   For each additional ton gross in excess of 10,000 gt: 1 cent
(c)   Minimum fee: C£30
       Note: C£1 (one Cyprus pound) = 100 cents.

For the registration of a ship mortgage with the Registrar of Companies where the amount secured is:
(a)   A sum up to C£50,000: C£45
(b)   A sum over C£50,000 but not exceeding C£100,000: C£97.50
(c)   A sum over C£100,000 but not exceeding C£250,000: C£142.50
(d)   A sum over C£250.000 but not exceeding C£500,000: C£187.50
(e)   A sum over C£500,000 (or where no secured amount is fixed, as in the case of an account current mortgage without a ceiling): C£300

D   Amendment

1   Can registered mortgages be amended and/or supplemented?
No registered statutory mortgage can be amended and/or supplemented under Cyprus merchant shipping law.

However the deed of covenants collateral to a statutory mortgage, being essentially a contract between the mortgagor and the mortgagee, can be amended and/or supplemented under the general principles of contract law, provided that the registrable particulars of the statutory mortgage (for example, the maximum amount secured) which have been entered in the Register, are not affected thereby.

2   If so, what documents are required by the registering authority?
There is no procedure to record in the Register of Cyprus Ships the fact of amending and/or supplementing the deed of covenants collateral to a registered statutory mortgage.

The Registrar of Companies may, as a matter of practice, accept a Deed of Amendment for registration as an amended charge.

3   If so, please answer the questions listed under sections A and C above as if references to mortgages were references to amending and/or supplementing instruments.

(A1, 2)   No set form and lays down no specific requirements as to the content of amending and/or supplementing instruments.

(A3)   For purposes of registration with the Registrar of Companies the amending and/or supplementing instrument must be in one of the official languages of the Republic of Cyprus (that is, Greek or Turkish) or in the English language.

(A4)   (a)   The requirements of Cyprus law and practice with regard to execution of the deed of amendment (or supplemental deed) to the deed of covenants by the mortgagor and the mortgagee are identical to those for the execution of the original deed of covenants.

(b)   Re notarisation and legalisation – see answers 4.3 and 4.4 under Section A above.

(C1)   Registration of the deed of amendment (or supplemental deed) to the deed of covenants can only take place with the Registrar of Companies in Cyprus.

(C2)   If the deed of amendment (or supplemental deed) to the deed of covenants is drawn up in a foreign language other than English, it must be translated for purposes of registration into one of the official languages of the Republic of Cyprus (that is, Greek or Turkish) within 42 days of its execution.

(C3)   One original or certified copy of the deed of amendment or supplemental deed must be presented for registration and will be returned by the Registrar of Companies after registration.

(C4)   The company form containing the prescribed particulars of the amended charge.

(C5)   The company form must be an original.

(C6)   Same fees are payable for the registration of a deed of amendment or supplemental deed as are payable for the registration of a ship mortgage with the Registrar of Companies.

E   Discharge

1   What documents are required by the registering authority to discharge a registered mortgage?

To discharge a ship mortgage registered with the Registrar of Cyprus Ships the following documents are required:

(a)   the mortgage deed with a memorandum of discharge endorsed thereon, duly executed and attested (although the Registrar will, as a matter of practice, accept in lieu a certificate of release of mortgage in the form normally used by the mortgagee bank);

(b)   Power of Attorney granted by the mortgagee, if the discharge of mortgage is to be executed by an attorney on its behalf.

To discharge a ship mortgage registered with the Registrar of Companies in Cyprus there must be delivered to them the prescribed company form incorporating a memorandum of complete satisfaction of a registered charge and the declaration verifying the same sworn and signed by a director and the secretary of the mortgagor company. In addition, the Registrar of Companies requires that the company form be accompanied by a copy of the memorandum of discharge of the mortgage or other document evidencing the discharge to his satisfaction.

2   Please answer the questions listed under Sections A and C above as if references to mortgages were references to mortgage discharges.

(A1, 2)   No set form is prescribed by Cyprus law, nor are any specific requirements laid down as to the content of discharges of mortgages to ensure their validity.

(A3)   Discharges of mortgages may be either in one of the official languages of the Republic (Greek or Turkish) or in English.

(A4)   The requirements of Cyprus law and practice with regard to (a) execution of a discharge of mortgage by the mortgagee, (b) notarisation and (c) legalisation are the same as for a mortgage and deed of covenants (see 4.2, 4.3 and 4.4 under main Section A above).

(C1)   Registration of a discharge of mortgage registered with the Registrar of Cyprus Ships may take place either:

(a)   in Cyprus, with the Registrar of Ships; or

(b)   abroad with a Consular Officer of the Republic of Cyprus on the prior written authority of the Registrar of Ships.

Registration of a discharge with the Companies Registry must take place in Cyprus.

(C2)   Discharges of mortgages may be executed and presented for registration in English without any translation requirement. If in any other foreign language, the document must be accompanied by a sworn translation in one of the official languages of the republic prior to registration.

(C3)   One original of the discharge of mortgage needs to be presented for registration which will be retained by the Registrar of Cyprus Ships or the Consular Officer of the Republic.

(C4)   A Power of Attorney granted by the mortgagee must also be produced and will be retained by the registering authority if the discharge of mortgage is to be executed by an attorney on behalf of the mortgagee.

(C5)   The discharge of mortgage must be an original. The Power of Attorney may be either an original or a true copy verified by a notary public.

(C6)   No fees are payable for the registration of a discharge of mortgage.

F   General

1   Please identify the principal statutes and regulations in Cyprus governing the registration of mortgages on ships.

The principal statutes and regulations in Cyprus governing the registration of mortgages on ships are:

      (a)   The Merchant Shipping (Registration of Ships, Sales and Mortgages) Laws, 1963 to 1995;

      (b)   The Companies Law, Cap. 113 as amended; and

      (c)   The Companies Regulations.

2   Must notice of mortgage and/or a certified copy or original mortgage be placed on board the ship? Is there any time limit for doing so?

It is not required under Cyprus law for notice of mortgage and/or a certified copy or original mortgage to be placed on board the mortgaged ship.

3   Are there any other matters in the context of mortgages on ships not referred to above which you feel should be emphasised?

3.1   Transfer of mortgage:
Cyprus law lays down a simple but precise procedure for the transfer of a registered mortgage and the assignment of the benefit of its security from the registered mortgagee to another. A set form of instrument of transfer of mortgage is prescribed in the statute and should be endorsed on the original mortgage deed.

3.2   Negative pledge/Section 30 injunction:
It is now standard practice for a well drafted deed of covenants collateral to a statutory mortgage to incorporate a negative pledge, that is, a restrictive covenant on the mortgagor's part not to sell or otherwise dispose, further mortgage or charge the ship, without the prior written consent of the mortgagee.

Under Section 30 of the Cyprus Merchant Shipping (Registration of Ships, Sales and Mortgages) Law an injunction may be obtained on the application of the mortgagee, to which the mortgagor invariably consents, converting the negative pledge from a contractual undertaking into a court order. This may then be served on the Registrar of Cyprus Ships and entered in the Register as an encumbrance.

However the current invariable practice of the Registrar of Cyprus Ships is to demand the written consent of every prior mortgagee before accepting a second (or subsequent) mortgage for registration, provided a negative pledge is incorporated in the collateral deed of covenants. In the light of this, the consensus of opinion among leading ship finance lawyers in Cyprus is that a Section 30 injunction should only be obtained by a mortgagee in rare cases and for valid reasons (for example, where a mortgage secures future advances or a revolving loan).

3.3 Agent and trustee/holding a ship mortgage in trust:

    3.3.1 It has now become increasingly usual in syndicated loan transactions to have one of the participating lenders acting as agent and trustee for the others.

    3.3.2 It is legally feasible under Cyprus law for the agent and trustee to hold the ship mortgage (and other collateral securities) in its own name, in trust for and for the benefit of itself and the other lenders.

    3.3.3 In such a case no notice of the trust would be entered in the Register of Cyprus Ships and the agent and trustee would alone be registered as mortgagee and be entitled to exercise the statutory and contractual rights and powers of such mortgagee should the need arise.

    3.3.4 However, the equitable rights of the participating lenders would be recognised and if need be enforced by virtue of both express statutory provisions and the principles of equity which are applicable in Cyprus.

---

* Contributed by Acis Montanios and Adam Montanios, of Montanios and Montanios, Nicosia, Cyprus.

Greece*

A   Form and contents

1   Does the legal system in Greece prescribe a set form of mortgage?
No.

2   If not, does the legal system in Greece lay down any specific requirements as to the content of mortgages, to ensure either their validity or their priority?
Distinction should be made between:

(a)   a ship's mortgage (hereinafter 'the mortgage') made pursuant to the provisions of the Greek Code of Private Maritime Law (hereinafter 'CPML') as supplemented by the relevant provisions of the Greek Civil Code (hereinafter 'CC');

(b)   a ship's preferred mortgage (hereafter 'preferred mortgage') made pursuant to the provisions of Legislative Decree 3899/58 concerning preferred mortgages (hereafter 'LD 3899/58'); and

(c)   a preferred mortgage on a vessel registered under Greek flag pursuant to LD 2687/53 by virtue of the Approval, (hereinafter 'LD 2687/53 preferred mortgage'). See Chapter 11 for an explanation of the importance of the Approval.

The mortgage

A mortgage is made either by contract (agreement) between the parties (mortgagor and mortgagee) or by unilateral declaration of the mortgagor. It is always made in the form of a notarial instrument. It must contain:

(a)   the particulars required under the CC, namely, particulars of the mortgagor and the mortgagee, the total amount of the claim secured and the date of maturity of the claim secured;

(b)   express provision as to whether the principal amount of the claim secured is interest bearing and whether costs and expenses are also covered;

(c)   description of the ship including her registration number; and

(d)   appointment of a resident agent (for each of the parties) who shall be authorised to accept service of process in respect of the mortgage.

A mortgage comes into existence upon its recordation with the ship mortgage register of the vessel's home port.

Priority among mortgagees is determined by reference to the chronological order of recordation of their mortgages. Mortgagees whose mortgages were recorded on the same date shall be satisfied pro rata.

The preferred mortgage

A preferred mortgage can only be made by contract (agreement) between the parties (preferred mortgagor and preferred mortgagee).

If the contract of constitution of a preferred mortgage is executed in Greece it must be in the form of a notarial instrument. If it is executed abroad it may also be in the form prescribed by the law of the place of its execution.

As regards the contents of a preferred mortgage, in addition to the particulars referred to above, the contract which constitutes a preferred mortgage must contain:

(a)   particulars of the document of title whereby the ownership of the ship was acquired by the preferred mortgagor;

(b)   the name of the ship, her international call sign, her official number and port of registration, her dimensions and tonnage according to official measurement, her means of propulsion and horsepower of her engine(s);

(c)   the appointment of a resident agent as in (d) above; and

(d)   express provision to the effect that it is a preferred mortgage constituted pursuant to the provisions of LD 2687/53 and that the preferred mortgagee is entitled to assume the management of the ship as soon as his claim becomes due and payable.

A claim secured by a preferred mortgage includes principal, all accrued interest and expenses, even where there is no express provision to this effect in the deed of constitution of the preferred mortgage, subject however to the total amount secured by the preferred mortgage.

As in the case of mortgages, a preferred mortgage comes into existence upon its recordation with the ship mortgage register of the vessel's home port. Priority among preferred mortgagees is determined by the chronological order of the recordation of their respective preferred mortgages. Preferred mortgages registered on the same date rank in accordance with the order in which they have been registered and this order is determined by the order in which the respective applications were filed with the Registrar of Ship Mortgages.

The principal feature that distinguishes a preferred mortgage from a mortgage is that under a preferred mortgage the preferred mortgagee is entitled to assume the management of the ship as soon as his claim becomes due and payable. The preferred mortgagee can also assume the management of the ship in any other case provided for in the preferred mortgage. Under a preferred mortgage additional rights may be stipulated between the parties for the purpose of increasing the preferred mortgagee's security, including the right to sell/transfer the ship without complying with the formalities of public auction (that is, by private sale).

In accordance with the provisions of LD 3899/58 a preferred mortgage can be granted only on ships exceeding 500 grt.

The LD 2687/53 preferred mortgage

The comments above relating to the preferred mortgage apply in respect of an LD 2687/53 preferred mortgage subject to the following remarks.

(a)   Express provision must be made in the relevant deed of constitution of the LD 2687/53 preferred mortgage to the effect that same is constituted pursuant to the provisions of LD 2687/53 and of the Approval which governs the vessel.

(b)   The rights of a mortgagee under the LD 2687/53 preferred mortgage are those stipulated in the relevant deed of constitution of the mortgage and can be in addition to and/or in deviation from the provisions of any other Greek law in force.

(c)   The rights of the owner of a vessel registered pursuant to the Approval, deriving from LD 2687/53 and/or from the Approval, may be assigned to the mortgagee as additional security for his claim.

(d)   LD 2687/53 preferred mortgages which are registered on the same date do not have the same rank; they rank in accordance with the order in which they have been registered and this order must be the same as the one in which the respective applications were filed with the Registrar of Ship Mortgages.

(e)   An LD 2687/53 preferred mortgage may be granted only on ships exceeding 1,500 grt.

3   Must mortgages for registration in Greece be in any particular language?
They must be in the Greek language if executed in Greece. They can be in a foreign language if executed abroad. In order to be submitted for recordation in the Ship Mortgage Register they must be accompanied by a certified Greek translation.

4   What are the requirements of the legal system in Greece with regard to:
4.1   execution of the mortgage by the mortgagor?
4.2   execution of the mortgage by the mortgagee?
4.3   notarisation?
4.4   legalisation?

4.1   Execution by the mortgagor is always necessary. If the mortgagor is an individual, subscription of his name is required. If the mortgagor is a legal entity, subscription of the name of the individual acting for and on behalf of the legal entity is necessary. Express provision in the mortgage (which expression hereinafter shall include a mortgage, a preferred mortgage and an LD 2687/53 preferred mortgage) must be made to the effect that the said individual is acting for and on behalf and in the name of a legal entity.

4.2   Execution by the mortgagee is necessary in the case of a preferred mortgage and an LD 2687/53 preferred mortgage. A mortgage can be made by unilateral declaration of the mortgagor. As regards subscription please see 4.1 above.

4.3   A mortgage must always be in the form of a notarial instrument irrespective of the place or country of its execution. A preferred mortgage and an LD 2687/53 preferred mortgage must be in the form of a notarial instrument if executed in Greece. If executed abroad the mortgage can be executed in any form required or approved by the law of the country where execution takes place.

4.4   Legalisation is required where a mortgage is executed abroad. Legalisation can be made by a local notary public and/or by any other local public authority; such legalisation must thereafter be authenticated by a local Greek consular authority or by way of apostille under the Hague Convention.

B   Mortgagees' rights

1   Does the legal system in Greece provide mortgagees with any rights which they would normally expect, that is, the right to take possession of and sell the vessel on default, (a) by law and/or (b) only if included expressly in the mortgage?
In the case of a mortgage, the mortgagee has the right by law to pursue satisfaction of his claim by the forced sale of the vessel, that is, by sale of the vessel at public auction. The right to take possession of and sell the vessel by private sale is not recognised by the law applicable to a mortgage and cannot therefore be included in the mortgage. In the case of a preferred mortgage

and/or in the case of an LD 2687/53 preferred mortgage the right to take possession of and sell the vessel by private sale is accorded by law but only if expressly provided for in the relevant contract of constitution of the preferred mortgage or the LD 2687/53 preferred mortgage.

2   *Are there any limits on the right of a mortgagee on default:*
   2.1   *to take possession of the vessel?*
   2.2   *to sell the vessel at auction?*
   2.3   *to sell the vessel privately?*

The limits are:

   (a)   In all cases of mortgages (which expression includes a mortgage, a preferred mortgage and an LD 2687/53 preferred mortgage) there are those limits imposed by the general principles of law, namely good faith, abuse of right and similar concepts.

   (b)   In the case of a mortgage, the mortgagee cannot take possession of the vessel and cannot sell her privately. He can only sell the vessel at public auction pursuant to and in strict conformity with the procedure prescribed by Greek law.

   (c)   As regards the rights of a preferred mortgagee and/or an LD 2687/53 preferred mortgagee to take possession of the vessel and/or to sell the vessel privately there are only limits that may be stipulated between the parties in the relevant contract of constitution of a preferred mortgage or an LD 2687/53 preferred mortgage.

3   *Does the legal system in Greece give mortgagees any specific rights not generally found in well drafted standard forms of mortgage?*

No.

C   Registration

1   *Where may registration of mortgages take place:-*
   1.1   *Greece?*
   1.2   *Abroad?*

Registration of a mortgage must take place at the registry of the vessel's home port. It can take place abroad only in the case where initial registration of a Greek flag vessel has taken place at any one of the Greek Mercantile Marine Services of London, New York or Tokyo and always before transcription to a Greek port has been made.

2   *If mortgages may be executed and presented for registration in a foreign language, what, if any, are the translation requirements and when must they be completed?*

Please see A3 above. A certified Greek translation of the mortgage must accompany the original of the mortgage deed upon its submission to the registry of the vessel's home port.

3   *How many originals of the mortgage must be presented for registration? How many are retained by the registering authority?*

One notarially attested copy of the mortgage or (in the case of a preferred mortgage and an LD 2687/53 preferred mortgage executed abroad) one properly legalised original of the mortgage must be presented for registration. Such notarially attested copy or legalised original (together with one certified Greek translation where required) is retained by the Registrar of Ship Mortgages.

4   *What other documents must be produced to the registering authority when register-ing the mortgage? Which will be retained?*

Other documents which must be produced to the registering authority for the purpose of register-ing the mortgage are:

(a)   summary of the mortgage in the form prescribed by Greek law (in two copies);

(b)   tax clearance certificate of the vessel; and

(c)   application.

All of the above documents are retained by the registering authority except one copy of the summary which is returned to the applicant after recordation with a notation thereon that the recordation of the mortgage has been effected.

5   *Must original documents be submitted or will photocopies, faxed copies or pdf copies of some or all documents be accepted? If so, which? Are there any requirements for copies to be verified?*

Originals or notarially attested copies of the mortgage must be submitted. Originals of the documents referred to under C4 above must be submitted.

6   *What are the fees currently payable on mortgage registration.*

No fees are payable on mortgage registration.

7   *Can a mortgage be registered over a vessel currently under construction? If so, please provide details of the documents to be submitted and the fees payable.*

In accordance with the provisions of the CPML, LD 3899/58 and the Approval, a mortgage can be registered on a ship under construction provided she is registered. The same principles apply as per A2 above and the same documents must be submitted as per C5 above and in addition a certified true copy of the shipbuilding contract is required. No fees are payable on mortgage registration.

D   Amendment

1   Can registered mortgages be amended and/or supplemented?

Yes, they can be amended and/or supplemented.

2   *If so, what documents are required by the registering authority?*

The deed of amendment of the mortgage along with the documents referred to under C4.

Note: The vessel's tax clearance certificate need not be produced to the registering authority when there is no increase in the amount secured by the mortgage in the relevant deed of amendment.

3   *If so, please answer the questions listed under Sections A and C above as if refer-ences to mortgages were references to amending and/or supplementing instruments.*

The answers provided in Sections A and C above apply in the cases of amending or supplementing instruments, except that in the case of a mortgage the deed of amendment cannot be made by unilateral declaration where the mortgagee's rights are being thereby reduced. In such a case it must be in the form of an agreement with the mortgagee. A deed of amendment can be recorded at the Greek Mercantile Marine Services of London, New York or Tokyo only if the vessel has not been transcribed to a port office in Greece.

E   Discharge

1   What documents are required by the registering authority to discharge a registered mortgage?

A deed of discharge and an application are required.

2   Please answer the questions listed above in Sections A and C above as if references to mortgages were references to mortgage discharges.

The deed of discharge of a mortgage needs to be executed by the mortgagee only. It must be in the form of a notarial instrument. In the case of a deed of discharge of a preferred mortgage or an LD 2687/53 preferred mortgage executed abroad it suffices that it be in the form prescribed by the laws of the place of its execution. Full description of the mortgage which is being discharged and also of the ship must be contained in the deed of discharge; express provision must be made in the deed to the effect that the mortgage is thereby discharged.

F   General

1   Please identify the principal statutes and regulations in Greece governing the registration of mortgages on ships.

Principal statutes and regulations include but are not limited to the following:
(a)   the CPML (articles 195–204);
(b)   LD 3899/1958;
(c)   the CC (articles 1257–1340);
(d)   LD 2687/53;
(e)   Royal Decree of July 17, 1910 on ship mortgage registers as amended;
(f)   the Greek Code of Public Maritime Law (article 20); and
(g)   Compulsory Law 612/1968 on 'the alteration of mortgage rank'.

2   Must notice of mortgage and/or a certified copy or original mortgage be placed on board the ship? Is there any time limit for doing so?

A certified copy of the mortgage must be placed on board the ship under the custody of the master. The master should also keep a mortgage book provided for by LD 3899/58 in which annotations regarding the registrations or deletions of mortgages must be made by the Registrar of Mortgages or by a Greek consular or port authority upon the Registrar's request.

There is no time limit for the certified copy to be placed on board the ship, but this should take place as soon as possible in order to comply with the law.

3   *Are there any other matters in the context of mortgages on ships not referred to above which you feel should be emphasised?*

       (a)   In the case of assignment of mortgage the deed of assignment must be submitted to the Ship Mortgage Registrar and a relevant notation must be entered in the Ship Mortgage Register.

       (b)   The Registrar will not accept the recordation of a mortgage if a court order prohibiting any change in the legal status of the vessel has been registered against the vessel.

       (c)   The registration of a mortgage made after the registration of an arrest against the vessel is void as regards the claimant who recorded the arrest.

           (i)   In accordance with the provisions of the CPML the following liens have priority over a mortgage and/or a preferred mortgage:

               (1)   legal costs incurred in the common interest of the creditors, dues and charges on the ship, taxes in connection with navigation and also the costs of supervision and preservation from the time the ship enters the last port;

               (2)   claims arising out of the contracts of employment of the master and crew, and also charges of the Seamen's Pension Fund consequent upon their engagement;

               (3)   expenses and remuneration due on account of assistance at sea, salvage and refloating; and

               (4)   compensation owed to ships, passengers and cargo by reason of collision of ships.

           (ii)   LD 2687/53 preferred mortgages rank in priority over all maritime and other liens notwithstanding the above provisions and/or any other provisions of law in force, with the sole exception of the liens provided in Article 2 of the 1926 Brussels Convention regarding the unification of certain rules relating to maritime liens and mortgages, provided the said liens are also recognised as such by Greek law.

---

* Contributed by Nigel Bowen-Morris and Alexandros Damianidis of Stephenson Harwood Consultants OE, Piraeus, Greece.

Hong Kong* **

A   Form and contents

1   Does the Hong Kong legal system prescribe a set form of mortgage?

The Merchant Shipping (Registration) Ordinance ('MSRO') provides that where a mortgagor grants a mortgage over all or part of his interest in a ship, the mortgage instrument must be in a specified form. Forms can be obtained from The Shipping Registry, Marine Department, 21/F Harbour Building, 38 Pier Road, Hong Kong. The specified form requires the following information to be inserted:

(a)   mortgagor's name, address and place of incorporation;

(b)   mortgaged ship's official number and name;

(c)   mortgagee's name, address, place of incorporation and fax and telex details; and

(d)   particulars of the documents or transactions creating the obligations secured by the mortgage.

While it is stated in the MSRO that the mortgage instrument must be in a specified form, instructions issued in December 1990 to the Registrar of Ships by the Director of Marine pursuant to Section 5 of MSRO (the 'Instructions') provide that it can be as near to the specified form as circumstances permit. Therefore, if there are several owners of shares or parts in a ship and the mortgagee will only accept a mortgage covering the whole ship contained in one deed, the specified form of mortgage may be suitably amplified to cover the facts and allow for proper attestation in respect of each of the parties involved.

It is stated in the Instructions that if the specified form has been so completed or amended as to suggest that the essential requirements of the approved form of mortgage have been departed from (being essentially a document in which the mortgagor in consideration of some valuable consideration (usually a loan) covenants with the mortgagee to observe certain terms or other consideration and, as security for such, mortgages to the mortgagee the ship or part of which he is the owner), it should not be accepted for registration, and the deed should be forwarded for consideration by the Department of Justice (paragraph 6.6 of the Instructions).

It is stated in the Instructions that extraneous matters and conditions attaching to the mortgage should be inserted in a separate document between the mortgagor and mortgagee and not in the mortgage. The practice that existed prior to the implementation of the MSRO of mortgagors and mortgagees entering into deeds of covenant (which do not appear on the ship register other than by reference in the mortgage) dealing with insurance of the mortgaged ship and other matters pertaining to the operation, management and condition of the vessel, therefore, continues.

2   If not, does the Hong Kong legal system lay down any specific requirements as to the content of mortgages, to ensure either their validity or their priority?

As mentioned in A1 above, the mortgage must be in a specified form. Validity and priority do not, however, depend only upon content. Priority depends on the order of registration of the mortgages under the MSRO and not on the order of creation. The consent of all existing registered mortgagees is needed before a later mortgage may be registered. Ship mortgages must also be registered under the Companies Ordinance (Sections 80 and 91). Failure to lodge the mortgage with the Hong Kong Registrar of Companies within five weeks of its creation will render it void against a liquidator or any creditor of the mortgagor.

3   Must mortgages for registration in Hong Kong be in any particular language?
To facilitate entries into the Register, the mortgage form should be completed in English. See
also C2.

4   What are the requirements of the Hong Kong legal system with regard to:
     4.1   execution of the mortgage by the mortgagor?
     4.2   execution of the mortgage by the mortgagee?
     4.3   notarisation?
     4.4   legalisation?

The prescribed form of mortgage must be executed under seal of the registered shipowner
(paragraph 6.8(b) of the Instructions). Individual mortgagors should seal their mortgages in
the presence of a witness who must attest the signature of the mortgagor by signing his name
and stating his address and occupation legibly. Corporate mortgagors should execute under
common seal in accordance with their articles of association. If a corporate mortgagor does
not possess a common seal, the mortgage should be executed under the hand and seal of a person purporting to be authorised by the mortgagor to execute on its behalf (such as a director
or the secretary) and such person is required to make a declaration that such corporate mortgagor does not possess a common seal. If the declaration is made outside Hong Kong, the declaration should be made before a notary public practising in that jurisdiction.

    Mortgages may also be executed by a lawful attorney on behalf of the mortgagor under
seal and duly witnessed (namely, signed by a named witness). In such cases the original Power
of Attorney (or a copy certified as true by a notary public) must be produced to the Registrar
with the mortgage instrument. Powers of attorney executed outside Hong Kong must be certified by a notary public practising in the country where the Power of Attorney was given
(paragraph 6.8(b) of the Instructions). A mortgagee is not required to execute the prescribed
form of mortgage. There is no requirement for legalisation.

B   Mortgagees' rights

*1   Does the Hong Kong legal system provide mortgagees with the rights which they
     would normally expect, that is, the right to take possession of and sell the vessel on
     default, (a) by law and/or (b) only if included expressly in the mortgage?*

Section 47(1) of the MSRO gives mortgagees a power 'absolutely' to dispose of the ship and to
give effectual receipts in respect of the disposal. The drafting of section 47(1) is very similar to
its predecessor, Section 35 of the Merchant Shipping Acts 1894 to 1987 ('MSA'), and there is
no suggestion in the Ordinance that it constitutes an exclusive regime for the powers which a
mortgagee may exercise where there is a default under the mortgage by the mortgagor. Common
law powers such as foreclosure, orders for sale and rights to possession and the appointment of
a receiver continue, therefore, to be available to mortgagees. In addition, most mortgagees will
supplement these powers by contract in the deed of covenant pertaining to the mortgage.

    A mortgagee holding an unregistered mortgage in the prescribed form will not enjoy the
statutory power of sale under Section 47(1) of the Ordinance. However, such a mortgagee's
security will constitute an equitable charge. While such a mortgagee's equitable rights (including the power to seek an order for sale) will be postponed to those of a registered mortgagee,

they will nevertheless be enforceable against the mortgagor. The fact that Section 53 of the MSRO permits 'beneficial interests' (an expression which includes equitable interests) to be enforced by or against the mortgagee of a ship underscores this conclusion. On the question of equities, it should be noted that notice of a trust, whether express, implied or constructive, shall not be entered in the register or be receivable by the Registrar.

The form of mortgage is usually supplemented by a deed of covenant containing covenants by the mortgagor as to such matters as insurance, repairs, limits within which the ship may trade, repayment terms, and events of default which entitle the mortgagee to exercise its power to take possession and sell the mortgaged vessel. Such deeds of covenant are not registrable at the Shipping Registry but will invariably be required to be registered at the Companies Registry (as will the mortgage) if such deed of covenants contains a registrable charge and is created over a vessel registered in Hong Kong by a Hong Kong incorporated company or an overseas company registered under the Companies Ordinance.

2   *Are there any limits (and, if so, what are they) on the right of the mortgagee on default:*
       2.1   *to take possession of the vessel?*
       2.2   *to sell the vessel at auction?*
       2.3   *to sell the vessel privately?*

As stated in B1 above, a mortgagee has the power absolutely to dispose of the ship in order to enforce his security. The mortgagee can therefore take possession of the ship and sell it either privately or at auction. Whether the mortgagee is entitled to exercise such power is, however, a different matter. As mentioned above, the mortgagee takes his security subject to other encumbrances which the common law may impose (most notably, maritime liens for crew's wages and other expenses such as dock dues). In addition, in particular cases other limits may be implied by the common law and principles of equity; for example if a mortgagee exercises his power to take possession wrongfully (for example, the power contained in the mortgage documents may only be properly exercisable in limited circumstances) then he may be liable in damages to the mortgagor. Similarly, if the vessel is sold at auction or privately and the mortgagee fails to fulfil its common law duty to the mortgagor to achieve the best price reasonably possible, then liability may arise notwithstanding that Section 47(1) MSRO provides that every registered mortgagee has a power 'absolutely' to dispose of the ship or share in respect of which he is registered as mortgagee. In addition, Section 47(1) expressly provides that the exercise of a power of sale is subject to the concurrence of every prior mortgagee (except under an order of the court).

C   Registration

1   Where may registration of mortgages take place?
       1.1   in Hong Kong?
       1.2   abroad?

A mortgage secured against a ship registered in Hong Kong may be registered only in Hong Kong by the Registrar of Shipping at the Shipping Registry.

If the mortgage is created by a Hong Kong incorporated company or an overseas company (or non-Hong Kong company) registered under Part XI of the Companies Ordinance the mortgage should also be submitted for registration at the Companies Registry in Hong Kong within five weeks of the date of its creation (Sections 80 and 91 of the Companies Ordinance). As mentioned above, the deed of covenants must also be submitted to the Companies Registry for registration if it contains a registrable charge.

2   *If mortgages may be executed and presented for registration in a foreign language, what, if any, are the translation requirements and when must they be completed?*

There is no provision in MSRO allowing a ship mortgage to be created in a foreign language. A legal mortgage must be in the specified form as stated in Section 44(2)(a) MSRO (which is in both the English and the Chinese language).

3   *How many originals of the mortgage must be presented for registration? How many are retained by the registering authority?*

Only one original mortgage deed needs to be presented for registration. After endorsement on the register book the deed will be returned to the mortgagee for retention.

4   *What other documents must be produced to the registering authority when registering the mortgage? Which will be retained?*

Where the mortgagor executes the ship mortgage under a Power of Attorney then the original Power of Attorney must be produced to the Registrar. The relevant Power of Attorney, if executed outside Hong Kong, must be certified by a notary public practising in the country in which the power is given. If the ship is only provisionally registered, the Registrar requires a confirmation by the mortgagee dated the same day on which the mortgage is presented to the Registrar for registration that (i) the mortgagee has sighted the original Bill of Sale and (ii) knows that the original Bill of Sale will not be produced to the Registrar. The confirmation can be, but is not necessary to be, in the specified form. If there are already mortgages registered against the ship, written consent from all the holders of such mortgages must also be submitted. None of these further documents are retained by the Registrar.

5   *Must original documents be submitted or will photocopies or fax copies of some or all documents be accepted? If so which? Are there any requirements for copies to be verified?*

The original mortgage deed and written consents from prior mortgagees (if any) must be submitted. Fax or other copies are not sufficient. If the mortgage is executed by an attorney, the original Power of Attorney should be produced.

6   *What fees are currently payable on mortgage registration?*

The fee chargeable for registering a ship mortgage is HK$440.

D   Amendment

1   Can registered mortgages be amended and/or supplemented?
There is no provision in the MSRO governing procedure for amendment of a registered ship mortgage other than in respect of a transfer or transmission by operation of law. Each time an amendment affecting the registered particulars, other than those of the parties, is proposed, a new mortgage deed reflecting these changes should be executed and registered as a further mortgage.

2   If so, what documents are required by the registering authority?
In the case of a transfer of mortgage, under Section 48 MSRO an instrument of transfer, in specified form setting out the name and address or place of incorporation of the transferee and duly executed by or on behalf of each mortgagee, needs to be lodged with the Registrar.

If the interest of a mortgagee in a mortgage of a registered ship is transmitted by any lawful means other than by transfer under Section 48 MSRO, the recipient needs to make and sign a declaration of transmission setting out the details of the ship and the transmitting and receiving parties. This declaration and such evidence of the transmission as may be required should be lodged with the Registrar.

3   If so, please answer the questions listed under Sections A and C above as if references to mortgages were references to amending and/or supplementing instruments.
See D1 and 2 above. The answers to Sections A and C apply where the context allows. In particular, the fees payable upon the registration of a transfer or transmission of a mortgage are the same as those specified in C6.

E   Discharge

1   What documents are required by the registering authority to discharge a registered mortgage?
Section 50 MSRO provides that when a registered mortgage is discharged, the Registrar shall, on the production of the mortgage instrument with a memorandum of discharge in the specified form endorsed thereon or firmly affixed thereto, duly executed by each mortgagee, make an entry in the register to the effect that the mortgage has been discharged and, on that entry being made, any interest of the mortgagee under the mortgage vests in the mortgagor or in subsequent mortgagees (if any). If the mortgage instrument cannot, for any reason, be lodged with the Registrar, there shall be lodged by the mortgagor or mortgagee, in substitution for the mortgage instrument and memorandum of discharge, a declaration by the mortgagee that the mortgage has been discharged and setting out the name and official number of the ship, the name and address of each mortgagor and mortgagee, the date of the mortgage and the date and time of entry of particulars of the mortgage in the register.

2   Please answer the questions listed under Section A and C above as if references to mortgages were references to mortgage discharges.
The memorandum of discharge must be in the specified form or as near thereto as circumstances permit (paragraph 6.25 of the Instructions).

Where the context allows, the answers provided in Section A and C above apply equally to mortgage discharges. The fees payable upon mortgage discharge are identical to those payable upon registration.

F   General

1   Please identify the principal statutes and regulations in Hong Kong governing the registration of mortgages on ships.

The principal statutes and regulations relating to ship mortgages in Hong Kong are the Merchant Shipping (Registration) Ordinance (Cap. 415), the Merchant Shipping (Registration) (Fees and Charges) Regulations and the Companies Ordinance. Instructions to the Registrar issued pursuant to Section 5 MSRO in December 1990 provide useful information relating to the MSRO and also contain many of the forms necessary for registration. The Companies Ordinance requires that, where the mortgagor is a company incorporated in Hong Kong (Section 80) or a registered overseas company (Section 91), registration of the ship mortgage should also be effected at the Companies Registry within five weeks of its creation. It is pursuant to this Ordinance that deeds of covenant are also required to be registered if such instruments create a registrable charge over the ship and/or book debts of the mortgagor.

2   Must notice of mortgage and/or a certified copy or original mortgage be placed on board the mortgaged ship? Is there any time limit for doing so?

There is no requirement under the MSRO that a notice or copy of the mortgage deed of the ship must be placed on board. However, deeds of covenants sometimes require this to be done.

3   Are there any other matters in the context of mortgages on ships under the Hong Kong legal system which you feel should be emphasised?

There are no restrictions under the MSRO on who may be the mortgagee of a registered ship; foreign lenders can therefore be registered as mortgagees. In addition, Section 32 MSRO indicates that mortgages may now be registered over provisionally registered ships. However, if the ship is not subsequently fully registered, and the provisional registration lapses, or if the registration of a ship is closed for any reason, the registration of any undischarged mortgages will be unaffected. The register will be marked to show that the closure is qualified to the extent that such mortgages are unaffected, with the closure only becoming final upon production of the appropriate memorandum of discharge.

Prior to the MSRO coming into force, the applicable legislation provided for two different types of mortgage, namely, the account current mortgage and the principal and interest mortgage. The legislation no longer makes such a distinction. Instead, it provides that the mortgage can be security for any present or future obligation of the mortgagor. The scope of the obligations which are actually secured will therefore depend on the documents named in the mortgage as creating them. Generally, this will be a loan agreement and a deed of covenants.

---

*   Contributed by Chooi Ling Lau and Ben Harris of Stephenson Harwood and Lo, Hong Kong.

**   The information in this section is based on the law in Hong Kong as at 28 November 2005.

India*

A   Form and contents

1   Does the legal system in India prescribe a set form of mortgage?

The set form of mortgage has been provided in Schedule I of The Merchant Shipping (Registration of Indian Ships) Rules, 1994 read with Rule 38 thereof. Furthermore, according to Section 47(1) of the 1958 Act, the mortgage has to be in the prescribed form. The relevant forms prescribed for the purposes of mortgage in Schedule I of The Merchant Shipping (Registration of Indian Ships) Rules, 1994 are:

(a)   mortgage of secure principal sum and interest (individuals or joint owners): Form 10;

(b)   mortgage to secure principal sum and interest (company): Form 11;

(c)   mortgage to secure account current (individuals or joint owners): Form 12; and

(d)   mortgage to secure account current (company): Form 13.

2   If not, does the legal system in India lay down any specific requirements as to the content of mortgages, to ensure either their validity or other priority?

Not applicable.

3   Must mortgages for registration in India be in any particular language?

The application for registration of a mortgage has to be in the correct prescribed form. All such prescribed forms are in English. Also, any documents to be submitted along with the mortgage form have to be in English. In case such documents are not in English, an English translation will be required.

4   What are the requirements of the legal system in India with regard to:

4.1   execution of the mortgage by the mortgagor?

4.2   execution of the mortgage by the mortgagee?

4.3   notarisation?

4.4   legalisation?

The mortgage form must be executed by the mortgagor by affixing the common seal of the company in the presence of one or two authorised signatories of the company. If there is only one authorised signatory then such signature must be witnessed. The mortgage does not need to be executed by the mortgagee.

B   Mortgagees' rights

1   Does the legal system in India provide mortgagees with the rights which they would normally expect, that is, the right to take possession of and sell the vessel on default, (a) by law and/or (b) only if included expressly in the mortgage?

The legal system in India provides mortgagees with the rights generally available to the mortgagees in other common law jurisdictions, including the right to take possession of and sell the vessel on default. These rights arise by law.

2   *Are there any limits (and, if so, what are they) on the right of the mortgagee on default:*

       2.1   *to take possession of the vessel?*

       2.2   *to sell the vessel at auction?*

       2.3   *to sell the vessel privately?*

2.1   In the event of the mortgagee taking possession of the vessel, without the consent of the mortgagor, then the usual restriction upon the mortgagee is to do it in a peaceful manner and not in violation of law and order, that is, through use of force.

2.2   In the case of one or more mortgages, the mortgagee can approach the High Court for the purposes of getting the vessel or share therein sold at auction.

2.3   In the case of one mortgage, the mortgagee can sell the vessel or share therein upon fulfilling the following conditions:

      (a)   the mortgagee has to give 15 days' advance notice to the Registrar of the vessel's Port of Registration relating to such sale; and

      (b)   the mortgagee has to ensure that such a notice sent to the Registrar of the vessel's Port of Registration relating to sale is accompanied by proof of payment of wages and other amounts to seamen in connection with their employment.

C   Registration

1   *Where may registration of mortgage take place:*

      1.1   *in India?*

      1.2   *abroad?*

According to Section 47(1) of the 1958 Act, the instrument of mortgage has to be produced before the Registrar of the vessel's Port of Registry so that the Registrar can record the same in the register book.

2   *If mortgages may be executed and presented for registration in a foreign language, what, if any, are the translation requirements and when must they be completed?*

The mortgage forms are in the English language. However, if any documents submitted along with the mortgage are in a language other than English, then such documents have to be accompanied by an English translated copy.

3   *How many originals of the mortgage must be presented for registration? How many are retained by the registering authority?*

One original needs to be presented for registration. Such form is duly returned after it is endorsed.

4   *What other documents must be produced to the registering authority when registering the mortgage? Which will be retained?*

The following documents must be produced:

      (a)   The original mortgage, duly affixed with the common seal of the owner. It will be returned after being duly endorsed by the Registrar.

      (b)   Original board resolution of the owner, with common seal of the company affixed. This will be retained by the Registrar.

(c)   Original letter from the mortgagee to the Registrar requesting the registra-
        tion the mortgage. This will be retained by the Registrar.

(d)   Original unconditional no objection certificate from existing mortgagees, if
        any. This will be retained by the Registrar.

(e)   Copy of mortgage registered with the Registrar of Companies (attested by
        authorised signatory). Please note that a mortgage must be registered with
        the Registrar of Companies before it can be registered over a vessel. This
        will be retained by the Registrar.

5   *Must original documents be submitted or will photocopies, faxed copies or pdf copies
        of some or all documents be accepted? If so, which? Are there any requirements for
        copies to be verified?*
Please see our response to C4 above.

6   *What are the fees currently payable on mortgage registration?*
The fees for registration of a mortgage will be INR0.1 for every INR1,000.00 of the value of
the mortgage. If mortgages are being registered on more than one vessel to secure the same
obligations, the fee chargeable for entering the mortgage on second and subsequent vessels
would be INR500.00 only.

7   *Can a mortgage be registered over a vessel currently under construction? If so,
        please provide details of the documents to be submitted and the fees payable.*
There is no provision in the 1958 Act to permit the registration of a mortgage over a vessel
currently under construction.

D   Amendment

1   Can registered mortgages be amended and/or supplemented?
Yes, registered mortgages can be amended and/or supplemented.

2   If so, what documents are required by the registering authority?
The amended mortgage itself and the documents set out in C4 are required.

*3   If so, please answer the questions listed under sections A and C as if reference to
        mortgages were references to amending and/or supplementing instruments.*
The answers given above in A and C apply equally here. However, the fees for mortgage
amendments are based purely on the increased amount of the mortgage.

E   Discharge

*1   What documents are required by the registering authority to discharge a registered
        mortgage?*
According to Section 48 of the 1958 Act, the following documents are required by the registering authority to discharge a registered mortgage:

(a) the mortgage deed; and

(b) receipt for the mortgage money endorsed thereon, duly signed by the mortgagee and attested.

2 *Please answer the questions listed above in Section B as if reference to mortgages were references to mortgage discharges.*

The obligation is imposed upon the Registrar under Section 48 to make an entry in the Register Book to the effect that the mortgage has been discharged. The said entry can only be made at the vessel's port of registry.

The document to be submitted to the Registrar at the Port of Registry of the ship for discharge has to be in English. However, if it is in any foreign language, then the same has to be accompanied by an English translated copy. The fee payable to the Registrar is INR500.

---

* Contributed by Pankaj Prakash of International Law Group, New Delhi, India.

Isle of Man*

A   Form and contents

1   Does the legal system in the Isle of Man prescribe a set form of mortgage?

Yes, there is a prescribed form of Isle of Man mortgage as Section 2(2) of Schedule 1 to the Act requires the instrument creating security over any registered vessel (or share in such vessel) to be in such form as is approved by the Marine Administration. The prescribed form of ship mortgage is similar to the English form of ship mortgage and is a short form document.

Mortgagees generally require a collateral deed of covenants to be granted as additional security. Mortgages are registered in the order in which they are presented for registration and it is the date and time of registration which determines priority of mortgages over Isle of Man registered vessels.

It is possible for an intending mortgagee of a vessel or a share in a vessel to notify the Registrar of its intended interest under a proposed mortgage and the Registrar will record this interest on the register. The form of notice of intent must be in a form approved by the Registrar and once registered no other mortgage may be registered against the vessel in priority to the proposed mortgage. The notification is valid for a period of 30 days but is renewable by the intended mortgagee by notice in writing to the Registrar before the end of the 30 day period. The current fee payable for the registration of the notice of intent is £37 for each 30-day period.

2   If not, does the legal system in the Isle of Man lay down any specific requirements as to the content of mortgages to ensure their validity or their priority?

Not applicable – see above.

3   Must mortgages for registration in the Isle of Man be in any particular language?

As the form of mortgage is in prescribed form it should be in English.

4   What are the requirements of the legal system in the Isle of Man with regard to:
    4.1   execution of the mortgage by the mortgagor?
    4.2   execution of the mortgage by the mortgagee?
    4.3   notarisation?
    4.4   legalisation?

4.1   The mortgage must be executed by the mortgagor as a deed in the presence of a witness. The mortgagor may execute the mortgage itself or by an attorney who has been duly appointed under Power of Attorney.

4.2   The mortgage does not require to be executed by the mortgagee.

4.3   If the mortgage is executed outside of the United Kingdom the mortgage must be notarised.

4.4   Legalisation is not currently a requirement.

B Mortgagees' rights

1   Does the legal system in the Isle of Man provide mortgagees with the rights which they would normally expect, that is, the right to take possession of and sell the vessel on default, (a) by law and/or (b) only if included expressly in the mortgage?

Isle of Man law and practice of ship mortgages is largely based upon and follows English law. The Act sets out an express power for any registered mortgagee, if the mortgage money or any part of it is due, to sell the vessel or share in respect of which he is registered and to give effectual receipts for the purchase money. This power is in addition to any power set out in any security documents.

The exercise by a mortgagee of its power of sale must be exercised with reasonable care and discretion. The conduct of the mortgagee in exercising its power of sale should not be unfair, unreasonable and prejudicial to the interests of the mortgagor.

Where two or more mortgagees are registered in respect of the same vessel or share, a subsequent mortgagee cannot, except under an order of a court of competent jurisdiction, sell the vessel or share without the concurrence of every prior mortgagee.

2   Are there any limits (and, if so, what are they) on the right of the mortgagee on default:
  2.1   to take possession of the vessel?
  2.2   to sell the vessel at auction?
  2.3   to sell the vessel privately?

2.1   The mortgagee is entitled to take possession of the vessel if the costs of the mortgagor materially impair the security of the mortgagee or if the mortgagor defaults on the sums due under the mortgage. The mortgagee may not take possession of or sell or arrest the vessel so as to cause interference with a contract under performance which is able to be performed and which is not prejudicing the mortgagee's interest.

2.2   No restrictions or requirements save that the mortgagee must act with reasonable care as set out in E1 above.

2.3   No restrictions or requirements save that the mortgagee must act with reasonable care as set out in E1 above.

C Registration

1   Where may registration of mortgages take place:
  1.1   in the Isle of Man?
  1.2   abroad?

There is currently no facility for the registration of mortgages other than in the Isle of Man.

2   If mortgages may be executed and presented for registration in a foreign language, what, if any, are the translation requirements and when must they be completed?

Not applicable as mortgages should be in English.

3   How many originals of the mortgage must be presented for registration? How many are retained by the registering authority?

Only one executed original need be presented for registration as the Registry do not retain the original on file. They simply keep copies for their records.

4   What other documents must be produced to the registering authority when register-
       ing the mortgage? Which will be retained?

If the mortgage is executed under Power of Attorney, the original Power of Attorney should
also be produced to the Registrar. The Registry will retain a copy for their files.

5   Must original documents be submitted or will photocopies, faxed copies or pdf copies
       of some or all documents be accepted? If so, which? Are there any requirements for
       copies to be verified?

The original mortgage and any Power of Attorney must be submitted. In exceptional circumstances the Registry may allow a copy of the Power of Attorney to be produced if it is accompanied by an undertaking to produce the original. The Registrar cannot register a mortgage
unless the original is produced.

6   What are the fees currently payable on mortgage registration?

The current fee per mortgage registered is £210. Any transcript of ship register evidencing the
registration of the mortgage currently costs £37 per transcript.

7   Can a mortgage be registered over a vessel currently under construction? If so,
       please provide details of the documents to be submitted and the fees payable.

No, the Isle of Man does not have a register for vessels under construction.

D   Amendment

1   Can registered mortgages be amended and/or supplemented?

Registered mortgages cannot be amended or supplemented.

2   If so, what documents are required by the registering authority?

Not applicable.

3   If so, please answer the questions listed under sections A and C as if references to
       mortgages were references to amending and/or supplementing instruments.

Not applicable.

E   Discharge

1   What documents are required by the registering authority to discharge a registered
       mortgage?

The original registered mortgage must be provided on discharge of the mortgage. The
section on the reverse of the original mortgage entitled 'Discharge of Mortgage' must be
completed and executed by the mortgagee. The Registry will also require any original
Power of Attorney (duly notarised if executed outside of the United Kingdom) issued by
the mortgagee if the discharge of mortgage is executed on behalf of the Mortgagee by an
attorney.

2   *Where may registration of discharge mortgages take place:*
        2.1   *in the Isle of Man?*
        2.2   *abroad?*

The Registry do not permit the registration of discharges of mortgages other than in the Isle of Man.

3   *If the discharge of mortgages may be executed and presented for registration in a foreign language, what, if any are the translation requirements and when must they be completed?*

The discharge is in prescribed form and so should be in English. If however the execution provision (or any notarisation) is in a foreign language an official translation will be required and must be submitted when the discharge of mortgage is presented to the Registry.

4   *How many originals of the discharge of mortgage must be presented for registration? How many are retained by the registering authority?*

Only the original mortgage that was registered may be presented to the Registry for discharge. If the original mortgage is not available, for example, it has been lost, mislaid or destroyed, statutory declarations will be required from both the mortgagor and mortgagee before the mortgage discharge will be registered. The Registry retains a copy of the discharged mortgage for their files and the original is returned.

5   *What other documents must be produced to the registering authority when registering the discharge of mortgage? Which will be retained?*

If the discharge of mortgage has been executed under Power of Attorney, the original Power of Attorney (duly notarised if executed outside of the United Kingdom) must be produced. The original is not retained by the Registry, they simply take a copy for their files. If an authorised signatory of the mortgagee has executed the discharge of mortgage, a copy of any authorised signatory list should be provided to the Registrar.

6   *Must original documents be submitted or will photocopies, faxed copies or pdf copies of some or all documents be accepted? If so, which? Are there any requirements for copies to be verified?*

The original of the mortgage and any Power of Attorney must be submitted. The authorised signatory list need only be a copy.

7   *What are the fees currently payable on registration of a discharge of mortgage?*

The current fee payable on registration of a discharge of mortgage is £210 per mortgage discharge registered.

8   *Can a discharge of mortgage be registered over a vessel currently under construction? If so, please provide details of the documents to be submitted and the fees payable.*

Not applicable. The Isle of Man does not have a 'newbuild' register.

F   General

1   Are there any other matters in the context of registration of mortgages under the legal system in the Isle of Man which you feel should be emphasised here?

If the owner of the vessel is an Isle of Man incorporated company, the mortgage and any other charge documents such as a collateral deed of covenants must be registered against the owner at the Isle of Man Companies Registry. Such registrations must be completed within one month of the creation of the charges. If any registrable charges are not registered against the owner at the Companies Registry they would be void as against any subsequent liquidator of the Company.

Where the owner is not an Isle of Man incorporated company but is a body corporate, the mortgage, any deed of covenants and assignment of earnings may be submitted to the Isle of Man Companies Registry as Slavenburg registrations.

* Contributed by Robyn Wood of Dickinson Cruickshank, Douglas, Isle of Man.

Liberia*

A   Form and contents

1   Does the Liberian legal system prescribe a set form of mortgage?
No, there is no prescribed form of mortgage.

*2   If not, does the Liberian legal system lay down any specific requirements as to the
content of mortgages, to ensure either their validity or their priority?*
A preferred mortgage must contain the following:

(a)   clear identification of the mortgagor and the mortgagee and the vessel(s) covered thereby;

(b)   designation as a 'preferred' mortgage;

(c)   specific indication of the title or status of the persons executing the mortgage;

(d)   the mortgagor's interest in the vessel and the interest so mortgaged;

(e)   if the mortgage secures interest, the formula by which interest is calculated;

(f)   express conveyance language, that is, that the mortgagor does grant, convey and mortgage the vessel to the mortgagee;

(g)   a statement that the mortgage indebtedness is secured by the whole of the vessel or vessels;

(h)   a recording clause stating the total amount intended to be secured by the mortgage,

(i)   including principal, interest and performance of mortgage covenants.

A mortgage which includes property other than a vessel need not contain a separate discharge amount for such property and shall constitute a lien on the vessel on the full amount of the outstanding mortgage indebtedness.

Where the mortgage secures an obligation in respect of which one or more advances or repayments may be made from time to time in the future and the maximum amount outstanding under the obligation at any time is limited to a certain amount, the amount to be recorded may be either:

(a)   the maximum amount that may be outstanding under the mortgage at any one time; or

(b)   the aggregate of all possible advances that may be made and secured by the mortgage.

Where the mortgage secures an agreed-upon maximum amount representing all the debts and obligations arising or that may arise between the mortgagor and the mortgagee within a specified period, such period should be specified on the mortgage and only indebtedness incurred during such period will be covered by the mortgage. In this instance a maturity date should be stated on the mortgage.

Where a mortgage secures an obligation in one or more specified units of account and there is an option to have a unit of account altered from time to time, the principal amount of the mortgage shall be denominated in one or more of the said specified units of account. The recordation may include as additional words 'or an equivalent amount in any alternate unit of account', or similar language, and if such additional words are recorded, no change in the recorded amount shall be required to reflect the fact that the obligation or any proportion thereof is subsequently denominated in a different unit or units of account, unless the parties otherwise agree. Such a mortgage may additionally secure any loss up to a specified amount arising out of fluctuations between a specified unit of account and any alternate unit of account in which the obligation amount may be denominated from time to time, and such specified amount shall also be recorded.

A mortgage may also be granted as a continuation of a prior recorded mortgage, hypothecation or similar charge on a vessel, whether granted under the laws of Liberia or the laws of another jurisdiction in which the vessel was documented at the time such prior mortgage was recorded, if the vessel covered by the mortgage was covered by the prior mortgage, the obligations secured are the same and such mortgage is granted by the current owner of the vessel, whether or not such owner granted the prior mortgage.

There should not be any language which waives the preferred status of the mortgage.

A recordable mortgage must be signed by a duly authorised officer or agent of the mortgagor and contain either an acknowledgement or other proof of due execution subscribed by a person (such as a notary public) authorised to administer oaths or take acknowledgements or certify that the mortgage was duly executed by the person signing it. In the case of a mortgage executed on behalf of a corporation, the acknowledgement should be in substantially one of the following forms:

If the corporate seal is affixed:

On this day of [ ], 200[ ] before me personally appeared [ ] to me known, who being by me duly sworn did depose and say that he/she resides at [ ], that he/she is the [*title*] of [*name of corporation*], the corporation described in and which executed the foregoing instrument; that he/she knows the seal of said corporation; that the seal affixed to said instrument is such corporate seal; and that it was affixed by order of the Board of Directors of said corporation and that he/she signed his/her name thereto by like order.

If the corporate seal is not affixed:

On this [ ]day of [ ], 200[ ] before me personally appeared [ ] to me known, who being by me duly sworn did depose and say that he/she resides at [ ], that he/she is the [*title*] of [*name of corporation*], the corporation described in and which executed the foregoing instrument; and that he/she signed his/her name thereto pursuant to authority granted to him/her by the Board of Directors of said corporation.

3   Must mortgages for registration in Liberia be in any particular language?
All instruments must be in the English language, with the sole exception of foreign mortgages on vessels bareboat charter registered onto the Liberian register pursuant to Section 89 of the Liberian Maritime Law, where only the cover page and execution page need be translated into English.

4   What are the requirements of the Liberian legal system with regard to:
      4.1   execution of the mortgage by the mortgagor?

4.2   *execution of the mortgage by the mortgagee?*

4.3   *notarisation?*

4.4   *legalisation or apostille?*

4.1   Execution of a mortgage by the mortgagor is required.

4.2   Execution of a mortgage by the mortgagee is not required.

4.3   Each mortgage must contain either proof of due execution or an acknowledgement in substantially the form set forth above.

4.4   No legalisation or apostille is necessary.

B   Mortgagees' rights

1   Does the Liberian legal system provide mortgagees with the rights which they would normally expect, that is, the right to take possession of and sell the vessel on default, (a) by law and/or (b) only if included expressly in the mortgage?

Section 112 of the Liberian Maritime Law provides that the lien of a preferred mortgage may be enforced in Liberia by a suit *in rem* in admiralty upon the default of any term or condition thereof. The lien of a preferred mortgage may also be enforced by a suit *in rem* in admiralty or otherwise in any foreign country in which the vessel shall be found, pursuant to the procedure of said country for the enforcement of ship mortgages constituting maritime liens on vessels documented under the laws of said country. In addition to the foregoing, the mortgagee may bring suit *in personam* against the mortgagor in any court of competent jurisdiction for the amount of the outstanding mortgage indebtedness of for any deficiency in the full payment thereof.

2   Are there any limits (and, if so, what are they) on the right of the mortgagee on default:

2.1   to take possession of the vessel?

2.2   to sell the vessel at auction?

2.3   to sell the vessel privately?

The Liberian Maritime Law and Regulations do not specify any limits on the right of the mortgagee to take possession of the vessel and to sell the vessel at auction or privately. Such rights and any conditions on their exercise are normally set forth in detail in the mortgage itself. As a practical matter, the exercise by the mortgagee of such rights is likely to be affected by the actions taken by any other lienors of the vessel as well as by the rights of any charterer thereof.

C   Registration

1   Where may registration of mortgages take place:

1.1   in Liberia?

1.2   abroad?

Mortgages are recorded at the office of the Liberian Deputy Commissioner of Maritime Affairs (the 'Libdepcom') located at 99 Park Avenue, Suite 1700, New York, New York, 10016-1601 USA, or at its foreign offices in (1) Piraeus, Greece, (2) London, England, (3) Hamburg, Germany, (4) Tokyo, Japan and (5) Hong Kong. Throughout this book, references to the Libdepcom shall mean its New York office or any of its foreign offices.

2   *If mortgages may be executed and presented for registration in a foreign language,*
        what, if any, are the translation requirements and when must they be completed?
Except as indicated in A3 above, all mortgages must be in the English language. Translation
must precede recordation.

3   *How many originals of the mortgage must be presented for registration? How many*
        are retained by the registering authority?
Six executed originals must be presented for recordation, three of which are retained by the
Libdepcom.

4   *What other documents must be produced to the registering authority when register-*
        ing the mortgage? Which will be retained?
In addition to the mortgage, the following documents must also be presented to the
Libdepcom:

      (a)   if the underlying mortgage debt is not contained in the mortgage, the docu-
              ment evidencing such debt;

      (b)   an original or a certified copy of evidence of authorisation of the person
              signing the mortgage (customarily in the form of an original Power of
              Attorney or certified board of directors' resolutions);

      (c)   the written consent of any prior mortgagees;

      (d)   a memorandum of particulars setting forth:

          (i)   the name, official number, and gross and net tonnage of the vessel
                 mortgaged;

          (ii)   the type and date of the instrument to be recorded;

          (iii)   the name of the mortgagor;

          (iv)   the name of the mortgagee;

          (v)   the maturity date, if necessary, as rated on A2; the total amount of
                 indebtedness secured by the mortgage;

          (vi)   a description of the document(s), evidencing, the indebtedness or
                 the commitment to any future debts or obligations, including the
                 date(s) and amount(s) thereof;

          (vii) the separate discharge amounts, if any;

         (viii) the intended effect of the instrument;

          (ix)   if the instrument is a foreign mortgage upon a vessel under
                 Liberian Bareboat Charter Registration, the date, book and page
                 number or other identification to the registration of the mortgage
                 in the foreign state of registration of the vessel.

Each of the aforementioned documents will be retained by the Libdepcom.

5   *Must original documents be submitted or will photocopies or fax copies of some or*
        all documents be accepted? If so which? Are there any requirements for copies to
        be verified?

Originals of the mortgage and the memorandum of particulars must be submitted at the time of recordation. Photocopies or faxed copies of the evidence of the signatory's authority and consent of prior mortgagees are generally accepted with the undertaking by the mortgagor to provide originals promptly. There is no requirement that any documents be verified.

6   What fees are currently payable on mortgage registration?
Mortgage: US$525 (the fee is the same for all Instruments including Mortgages, Amendments, Coordinations, Assignments and Subordinations).
Fleet Mortgage fee: US$525 per vessel that is mortgaged.
Certificate of Ownership and Encumbrances (evidencing vessel ownership and all mortgages): US$100 (unless issued at the time of the recordation of an instrument (that is, a mortgage), in which case it is free).
Off-hours business fee: US$525 (1st two hours) and an additional fee of US$350 for each additional 2 hours of the transaction or any portion thereof. If closing takes place on weekend or holidays, the fee is US$650 (1st two hours) and an additional fee of US$450 for each additional 2 hours of the transaction or any portion thereof.

D   Amendment

1   Can registered mortgages be amended and/or supplemented?
Registered mortgages may be amended or supplemented.

2   If so, what documents are required by the registering authority?
Six executed originals of the amendment or supplement each duly acknowledged or accompanied by proof of due execution by all parties thereto.

3   If so, please answer the questions listed under Sections A and C above as if references to mortgages were references to amending and/or supplementing instruments.

Form:
(a)   there is no prescribed form for an amendment or supplement;
(b)   the amendment or supplement must identify the mortgagor, the mortgagee, the vessel and the mortgage thereon;
(c)   the amendment or supplement must refer to the recording data of the original mortgage;
(d)   the amendment or supplement must be in the English language;
(e)   the amendment or supplement must be executed by a duly authorised signatory of each of the mortgagor and the mortgagee and be duly acknowledged or accompanied by proof of due execution; and
(f)   legalisation or apostille of the amendment or supplement is not required.

Recordation:
(a)   recordation of an amendment or supplement is performed at the office of the Libdepcom;

(b)   six executed original amendments or supplements must be submitted to the Libdepcom, three of which are retained by the Libdepcom;

(c)   evidence of the authorisation of the person signing on behalf of the mortgagor and mortgagee must be submitted to the Libdepcom;

(d)   a memorandum of particulars must be submitted to the Libdepcom (see C4); and

(e)   recordation fees for all amendments is US$525.

E   Discharge

1   What documents are required by the Liberian registering authority to discharge a registered mortgage?

Four executed original discharges of mortgage each duly acknowledged or accompanied by proof of due execution by all parties thereto.

2   Please answer the questions listed under Sections A and C above as if references to mortgages were references to mortgage discharges.

Form:

(a)   there is no prescribed form for a discharge;

(b)   the discharge must identify the mortgagor, the mortgagee, the vessel and the mortgage thereon;

(c)   the discharge must refer to the recording data of the original mortgage;

(d)   the discharge must be executed by a duly authorised signatory of the mortgagee and be duly acknowledged or accompanied by proof of due execution; and

(e)   legalisation or apostille of the discharge is not required.

Recordation:

(a)   recordation of a discharge is performed at the office of the Libdepcom;

(b)   four executed original discharges must be provided to the Libdepcom, three of which are retained by the Libdepcom;

(c)   evidence of the authorisation of the person signing on behalf of the mortgagee must be submitted to the Libdepcom; and

(d)   the fee for recording a discharge of mortgage is US$250 per discharge.

F   General

1   Please identify the principal statutes and regulations in Liberia governing the registration of mortgages on ships.

The principal statutes with respect to the registration of mortgages on vessels are Title 21 (Maritime Law) of the Liberian Code of Laws of 1956, as amended, and the Liberian Maritime Regulations made by The Commissioner of Maritime Affairs under the authority vested in him by the Liberian Maritime Law.

2   Must notice of mortgage and/or a certified copy or original mortgage be placed on board the mortgaged ship? Is there any time limit for doing so?

A certified copy of the mortgage and of any amendment or supplement thereto must be placed on board the vessel. There is no time limit for doing so but the law provides that the mortgagor must use due diligence to retain such copy on board the vessel and cause such copy and the document of the vessel to be exhibited by the master to any person having business which may give rise to a maritime lien or to the sale, conveyance or mortgage of the vessel. In addition, mortgages customarily contain a covenant requiring the mortgagor to post notices of mortgages on board the vessel.

3   *Are there any other matters in the context of mortgages on ships under the Liberian legal system which you feel should be emphasised?*
Under Section 113 of the Liberian Maritime Law, a preferred mortgage lien has priority over all claims against the vessel, except liens arising prior in time to the recording of the mortgage, tort liens, liens for specified Liberian governmental charges, liens for crew's wages, general average and salvage, and expenses and fees allowed and costs taxed by the court.

---

* Contributed by Hadley S. Roe, assisted by Kassandra L. Slangan and Mira Trifunovic, all of Seward & Kissel, New York, United States of America.

Malta*

A   Form and contents

1   Does the legal system in Malta prescribe a set form of mortgage?

The Merchant Shipping Act provides for a statutory form of mortgage. There is only one form which has to be used for all types of mortgages whether principal and interest or account current.

2   If not, does the legal system in Malta lay down any specific requirements as to the content of mortgages to ensure either their validity or their priority?

Not applicable.

3   Must mortgages for registration in Malta be in any particular language?

The mortgage must be in English or in Maltese.

4   What are the requirements of the legal system in Malta with regard to:
*   4.1   execution of the mortgage by the mortgagor?*
*   4.2   execution of the mortgage by the mortgagee?*
*   4.3   notarisation?*
*   4.4   legalisation?*

4.1   The mortgagor is usually a company and so the person signing must have authority to do so by virtue of the memorandum and articles of the company or by virtue of resolutions of the board of directors or by virtue of a Power of Attorney issued in pursuance to the resolutions or the memorandum. The mortgagor must execute the mortgage in the presence of a named witness.

4.2   The mortgagee does not execute the mortgage.

4.3   Board resolutions and Powers of Attorney should be notarised.

4.4   Notarised documents should also be legalised by apostille.

Note: Where one of the above is not possible, the Registrar may accept lawyers as witnesses to signature, identity and authority and Honorary Consuls of Malta for legalisation but one should verify the position in each case.

B   Mortgagees' rights

1   Does the legal system in Malta provide mortgagees with the rights which they would normally expect, that is, the right to take possession of and sell the vessel on default, (a) by law and/or (b) only if included expressly in the mortgage?

In the event of default of any term or condition of a registered mortgage or of any document or agreements referred to therein, the mortgagee shall, upon giving notice to the mortgagor:

(a)   be entitled to take possession of the ship or share therein in respect of which he is registered; but except so far as may be necessary for making a mortgaged ship or share available as a security for the mortgage debt, the mortgagee shall not by reason of the mortgage be deemed to be the owner of the ship or share, nor shall the mortgagor be deemed to have ceased to be the owner thereof;

(b)   have power absolutely to sell the ship or share in respect of which he is registered; but where there are more persons than one registered as mortgagees of the same ship or share, a subsequent mortgagee shall not, except under the order of a court of competent jurisdiction, sell the ship or share without the concurrence of every prior mortgagee; and if the proceeds of sale, after discharging the mortgage debt show a surplus in his hands, the mortgagee shall deposit the same for the benefit of other creditors and of the mortgagor; and

(c)   have power to apply for any extensions, pay fees, receive certificates, and generally do all such things in the name of the owner as may be required in order to maintain the status and validity of the registration of the ship.

For the purposes of the proceedings above, the debtor shall be deemed to be served if the application or other act is served on the master of the vessel, or if he is absent from these Islands on the local agent appointed for the vessel by the owners or their agent, or in the absence of such local agent or a curator appointed by the court to represent the debtor and the ship.

2   *Are there any limits (and, if so, what are they) on the right of the mortgagee on default:*

    2.1   to take possession of the vessel?

    2.2   to sell the vessel at auction?

    2.3   to sell the vessel privately?

As seen above, there are no limits except practical ones. In Malta if the owner refuses to allow the mortgagee to take possession, then recourse to the courts will be necessary but that results from the procedural and criminal law, not the Merchant Shipping Act.

C   Registration

1   Where may registration of mortgages take place:

    1.1   in Malta?

    1.2   abroad?

Mortgages may only be registered at the Registry of Ships in Malta.

2   If mortgages may be executed and presented for registration in a foreign language, what, if any, are the translation requirements and when must they be completed?

Not possible.

3   How many originals of the mortgage must be presented for registration? How many are retained by the registering authority?

Only one original form is delivered and registered. A copy is retained by the Registrar and certified copies are issued in any number. The original is returned to the mortgagee.

4   What other documents must be produced to the registering authority when registering the mortgage? Which will be retained?

No other documents, apart from the corporate authorities and written consents, if applicable, need to be filed at the time of the registration of the mortgage in the vessel's Register. The registry is also requiring a good standing certificate from the company registry stating the names of directors and shareholders, issued as of the date of the relevant resolutions.

5   *Must original documents be submitted or will photocopies or fax copies of some or all documents be accepted? If so which? Are there any requirements for copies to be verified?*

Fax copies of the corporate authorities are accepted as long as the originals are notarised and legalised.

6   *What fees are currently payable on mortgage registration?*

The fees payable for mortgage registration are LM200.

7   *Can a mortgage be registered over a vessel currently under construction? If so please provide details of the documents to be submitted and the fees payable.*

A vessel currently under construction may be registered under the Malta flag as long as when built or equipped it would qualify as a ship registrable under the Merchant Shipping Act. In the case where a Declaration of Ownership has been completed in the registration of a vessel under construction, and registration has occurred under the ownership of a particular party, a mortgage may be registered over such vessel while it is still under construction. In cases where no Declaration of Ownership has been made in respect of the vessel registered under the Malta flag, no mortgage may be registered.

The documents required are the same as those required for the registration of a mortgage on a Malta flagged vessel.

The fees applicable are LM200.

D   Amendment

1   *Can registered mortgages be amended and/or supplemented?*

Yes, the amendment of a mortgage may be effected for any purpose, but it must, at law, be effected for any one or more of the following purposes:

    (a)   to increase the amount secured by such mortgage; and/or

    (b)   to extend such mortgage to secure any other obligation of the mortgagor, whether as principal or as surety for any other person, in favour of the mortgagee.

In order to affect the amendment a new instrument of mortgage is executed containing the amendment, together with the written consent on the said instrument, of the mortgagee whose mortgage has been amended. This instrument is executed by the mortgagor and counter-signed by the mortgagee in the presence of witnesses.

    Where any mortgages other than the mortgage that it is intended to amend are entered in the register of the ship, an amendment shall not be noted unless the consent in writing of all the other mortgagees whose interests may be prejudiced by the amendment, is produced to the Registrar.

2   *If so, what documents are required by the registering authority?*

The documents are the same as those of a new mortgage in addition to the above-mentioned consents where applicable.

3   If so, please answer questions listed in Sections A and C above as if references to
mortgages were references to amending and/or supplementing instruments.

The amendment must be in the statutory form of mortgage as in A1, either in English or in Maltese.

Registration may only occur in Malta. One original form is delivered and registered. A copy is retained by the Registrar and certified copies are issued in any number. The original is returned to the mortgagee.

No other documents apart from the mortgage form, the required corporate authorities to execute the amendment mortgage and a good standing certificate dated as per the corporate authorities are required. Fax copies of the corporate authorities are accepted as long as the originals are notarised and legalised.

The fees are LM200.

E   Discharge

1   What documents are required by the registering authority to discharge a registered
mortgage?

The original mortgage deed with a receipt for mortgage money endorsed thereon, duly signed and attested in the requisite part, specifically reserved for discharge on the back of the mortgage deed is all that is required to discharge a mortgage. If the mortgage is not already signed, a Power of Attorney appointing a Maltese representative to sign for and on behalf of the mortgagee will be required. The Power of Attorney must be notarised and apostilled or legalised. The discharge mortgage is substantially a receipt for monies paid.

The discharge is executed by the mortgagee and should be witnessed (preferably by a notary public, Honorary Malta Consul or lawyer).

In practice two systems are usually followed for the purpose of effecting mortgage discharges:

    (a)   in some cases, the mortgagee executes the discharge through his authorised representative at the mortgagee's place of business, which documents are notarised and apostilled and the original form of mortgage is then sent to the local mortgagee's representative for registering at the appropriate moment; and

    (b)   in others, the mortgagee issues a Power of Attorney to his Maltese representative, duly notarised and legalised and the latter attends to the discharge formalities at the appropriate moment and registers such discharge. A specimen Power of Attorney is reproduced.

Fax copies of the Power of Attorney are accepted as long as the originals are notarised and legalised.

SPECIMEN DRAFT POWER OF ATTORNEY

KNOW ALL MEN BY THESE PRESENTS that we [...**Mortgagee's name**...] of [...address...] (hereinafter called 'the Mortgagee') DO HEREBY constitute and appoint [...Attorneys...] (hereinafter each called 'the Attorney') each one severally as its true and lawful attorney with full power of substitution for it and in its name, place and stead to do all or any of the following acts, deeds or things, that is to say:

1.   To sign, execute, register and generally to effect on behalf of the Mortgagee the discharge of:

    a) A [...no. of priority...] Priority Statutory Mortgage '[...letter of mortgage...]' dated the [...date of mortgage...] executed in our favour by [...Mortgagor's name...], (hereinafter called 'the Owner') over its Malta Flag vessel [...**vessel name**...] Registration Number [...registration number...] and registered on the same Vessel on the [...date of registration...] at [...time of registration...] hrs.

2.   Generally to execute, make, sign, and do any such instruments and to make such acts or things as each and any of the Attorneys may, in his absolute discretion, deem desirable or expedient for the carrying out of any of the purposes or acts hereby authorised.

3.   The Mortgagee hereby grants to each of the Attorneys the power to nominate and appoint one or more substitutes as attorney/s for all and any of the purposes aforesaid and the same at pleasure to revoke.

The Mortgagee gives and grants to each of the Attorneys and to his substitute or substitutes full power and authority in the premises hereby ratifying, allowing and confirming and agreeing to ratify, allow and confirm whatsoever shall lawfully be done in the premises by virtue hereof.

IN WITNESS WHEREOF the Mortgagee has executed this Power of Attorney this [ ] day of [ ], 20[ ].

Signed: — — — — — — —

[*name in block letters*]

for and on behalf of

[*name of Bank/Mortgagee*]

(Please note that this Power of Attorney is to be Notarised and Legalised).

I the undersigned ...., notary public, hereby certify that the above is the true signature of Mr ...., Director of .... , and I further certify that the said Mr .... is authorised by .... to execute this Power of Attorney and binds the Company by his signature.

Discharges may be effected quite quickly after instructions are given by the mortgagee. Certified true copies of the discharges are issued by the Registry. Transcripts of Register with a free from encumbrances notation may be ordered or simultaneous issuance but arrangements must be made beforehand, time limitations at the Registry of Shipping permitting.

F   General

1   Please identify the principal statutes and regulations in Malta governing the registration of mortgages on ships.

The Merchant Shipping Act, Chapter 234 of the Laws of Malta is the only act regulating the registration of mortgages.

2   Must notice of mortgage and/or certified copy or original mortgage be placed on board the mortgaged ship? Is there any time limit for doing so?

There is no statutory obligation to display a copy of the mortgage on board the vessel, but this usually forms the object of a specific contractual stipulation usually found in the Deed of Covenants ancillary to the mortgage.

3   Are there any other matters in the context of mortgages on ships under the legal system in Malta which you feel should be emphasised?

A registered mortgage shall be deemed to be an executive title where the obligation it secures is a debt certain liquidated and due and not consisting in the performance of an act.

The rights of a mortgagee apply to all registered mortgages which secure debts resulting from any account current or overdraft or other credit facility.

Upon the registration of any mortgage in the register, the rights of any mortgagee shall not be affected by:

(a)   the creation of any separate privilege or charge on any part, appurtenance or accessory of a ship which may attach in virtue of any law; or

(b)   the reservation of ownership rights by a seller of any part, appurtenance or accessory sold to a shipowner under a contract of sale, hire purchase or any similar contract.

---

*   Contributed by Dr David Galea of Ganado & Associates, Valletta, Malta.

Marshall Islands*

A   Form and contents

1   Does the legal system in the Marshall Islands prescribe a set form of mortgage?
There is no prescribed form of mortgage.

*2   If not, does the legal system in the Marshall Islands lay down any specific require-
         ments as to the content of mortgages, to ensure either their validity or their priority?*
A preferred mortgage must contain the following:

(a)	clear identification of the mortgagor and the mortgagee and the vessel(s) covered thereby;
(b)	designation as a 'preferred' mortgage;
(c)	specific indication of the title or status of the persons executing the mortgage;
(d)	the mortgagor's interest in the vessel and the interest so mortgaged;
(e)	if the mortgage secures interest, the formula by which interest is calculated;
(f)	express conveyance language, that is, that the mortgagor does grant, convey and mortgage the vessel to the mortgagee;
(g)	a statement that the mortgage indebtedness is secured by the whole of the vessel or vessels; and
(h)	a recording clause stating the total amount or amounts of the direct or contingent obligations intended to be secured by the mortgage, including principal, interest and performance of mortgage covenants.

A mortgage which includes property other than a vessel need not contain a separate discharge amount for such property but all constitute a lien on the vessel in the full amount of the outstanding mortgage indebtedness.

Where the mortgage secures an obligation in respect of which one or more advances or repayments may be made from time to time in the future and the maximum amount outstanding under the obligation at any time is limited to a certain amount, the amount to be recorded may be either:

(a)	the maximum amount outstanding under the mortgage at any one time; or
(b)	the aggregate of all possible advances that may be made under the mortgage.

Where the mortgage secures an agreed-upon maximum amount representing all the debts and obligations arising or that may arise between the mortgagor and the mortgagee within a specified period, such period should be specified on the mortgage and only indebtedness incurred during such period will be covered by the mortgage. In this instance a maturity date should be stated on the mortgage.

Where a mortgage secures an obligation in one or more specified units of account and there is an option to have a unit of account altered from time to time, the principal amount of the mortgage shall be denominated in one or more of the said specified units of account. The recordation may include as additional words or an equivalent amount in any alternate unit of account, or similar language, and if such additional words are recorded, no change in the recorded amount shall be required to reflect the fact that the obligation or any proportion thereof is subsequently denominated in a different unit or units of account, unless the parties otherwise agree. Such a mortgage may additionally secure any loss up to a specified amount arising out of fluctuations between a specified unit of account and any alternate unit of account in which the obligation amount may be denominated from time to time, and such specified amount shall also be recorded.

There should not be any language which waives the preferred status of the mortgage.

A recordable mortgage must be signed by a duly authorised officer or agent of the mortgagor and contain either an acknowledgement or other proof of due execution subscribed by a person (such as a notary public) authorised to administer oaths or take acknowledgements or certify that the mortgage was duly executed by the person signing it. In the case of a mortgage executed on behalf of a corporation, the acknowledgement should be in substantially one of the following forms:

If the corporate seal is affixed:
On this [ ] day of [ ], 200[ ] before me personally appeared [ ] to me known, who being by me duly sworn did depose and say that he/she resides at [ ]; that he/she is the [*title*] of [*name of corporation*], the corporation described in and which executed the foregoing instrument; that he/she knows the seal of said corporation; that the seal affixed to said instrument is such corporate seal; and that it was affixed by order of the Board of Directors of said corporation and that he/she signed his/her name thereto by like order.

If the corporate seal is not affixed:
On this [ ] day of [ ], 200[ ] before me personally appeared [ ] to me known, who being by me duly sworn did depose and say that he/she resides at [ ]; that he/she is the [*title*] of [*name of corporation*], the corporation described in and which executed the foregoing instrument; and that he/she signed his/her name thereto pursuant to authority granted to him/her by the Board of Directors of said corporation.

3   Must mortgages for registration in the Marshall Islands be in any particular language?
All instruments must be in the English language, with the sole exception of foreign mortgages on vessels bareboat charter registered with the Marshall Islands Register pursuant to Section 264 of the Marshall Islands Maritime Act 1990, as amended, where only the cover page, background/whereas clauses and execution page need be translated into English.

4   What are the requirements of the legal system in the Marshall Islands with regard to:
    4.1   execution of the mortgage by the mortgagor?
    4.2   execution of the mortgage by the mortgagee?
    4.3   notarisation?
    4.4   legalisation or apostille?
4.1   Execution of a mortgage by the mortgagor is required.
4.2   Execution of a mortgage by the mortgagee is not required.
4.3   Each mortgage must contain either proof of due execution or an acknowledgement in the form set forth above.
4.4   No legalisation or apostille is necessary.

B Mortgagees' rights

*1   Does the legal system in the Marshall Islands provide mortgagees with the rights
which they would normally expect, that is, the right to take possession of and sell the
vessel on default, (a) by law and/or (b) only (included expressly in the mortgage)?*

Section 316 of the Marshall Islands Maritime Act 1990, as amended, provides that the lien of
a preferred mortgage may be enforced by a suit *in rem* in the High Court of the Republic of
the Marshall Islands, sitting in admiralty upon the default of any term or condition thereof.
The lien of a preferred mortgage may also be enforced by a suit *in rem* in admiralty or otherwise in any foreign country in which the vessel shall be found, pursuant to the procedure of
said country for the enforcement of ship mortgages constituting maritime liens on vessels documented under the laws of said country. In addition to the foregoing, the mortgagee may bring
suit *in personam* against the mortgagor, maker, co-maker or guarantor in any court of competent jurisdiction for the amount of the outstanding mortgage indebtedness or for any deficiency in the full payment thereof.

*2   Are there any limits (and, if so, what are they) on the right of the mortgagee on
default:*
2.1   to take possession of the vessel?
2.2   to sell the vessel at auction?
2.3   to sell the vessel privately?

The Marshall Islands Maritime Act 1990, as amended, and the Maritime Regulations do not
specify any limits on the right of the mortgagee to take possession of the vessel and to sell the
vessel at auction or privately. Such rights and any conditions on their exercise are normally
set forth in detail in the mortgage itself. As a practical matter, the exercise by the mortgagee
of such rights is likely to be affected by the actions taken by any other lienors of the vessel as
well as by the rights of any charterer thereof.

C Registration

1   Where may registration of mortgages take place:
1.1   in the Marshall Islands?
1.2   abroad?

Mortgages may be recorded at the office of the Marshall Islands Maritime & Corporate
Administrators, Inc. ('MIMCA') located at 437 Madison Avenue, 32nd Floor, New York, New
York 10022, USA or at any one of its other offices located in Reston (Virginia), Fort Lauderdale
(Florida), London, Tokyo, Rotterdam, Piraeus, Shanghai, Singapore or Hong Kong.

*2   If mortgages may be executed and presented for registration in a foreign language,
what, if any, are the translation requirements and when must they be completed?*

Except as indicated in A3 above, all mortgages must be in the English language. Translation
must precede recordation.

3   *How many originals of the mortgage must be presented for registration? How many are retained by the registering authority?*

Four executed originals must be presented for recordation, one of which is retained by MIMCA. If additional copies of the mortgage are brought to closing, MIMCA will certify them as filed for no additional cost.

4   *What other documents must be produced to the registering authority when registering the mortgage? Which will be retained?*

In addition to the mortgage, the following documents must also be presented to MIMCA:

(a)   if the underlying mortgage debt is not contained in the mortgage, the document evidencing such debt;

(b)   an original or a certified copy plus three copies of evidence of authorisation of the person signing the mortgage (customarily in the form of an original Power of Attorney or certified board of directors' resolutions);

(c)   the written consent of any prior mortgagees;

(d)   a memorandum of particulars setting forth:

(i)   the name, official number, and gross and net tonnage of the vessel mortgaged;

(ii)   the type and date of the instrument to be recorded;

(iii)   the name of the mortgagor;

(iv)   the name of the mortgagee;

(v)   the maturity date, if necessary, as noted in A2;

(vi)   a description of the document(s), evidencing the indebtedness or the commitment to any future debts or obligations, including the date(s) and amount(s) thereof;

(vii)   the intended effect of the instrument; and

(viii)   if the instrument is a notice of a foreign mortgage upon a vessel under Marshall Islands Bareboat Charter Registration, the date, book and page number or other identification to the registration of the mortgage in the foreign state of registration of the vessel along with a certified copy of the foreign mortgage and a memorandum of particulars referencing the particulars in the mortgage, signed by the person who executed the mortgage.

Each of the aforementioned documents will be retained by MIMCA.

5   *Must original documents be submitted or will photocopies of fax copies of some or all documents be accepted? If so, which? Are there any requirements for copies to be verified?*

Originals of the mortgage and the memorandum of particulars must be submitted at the time of recordation. Photocopies or faxed copies of the evidence of the signatory's authority and consent of prior mortgagees are generally accepted with the undertaking by the mortgagor to provide originals promptly. There is no requirement that any documents be verified.

6   What fees are currently payable on mortgage registration?
Mortgage: US$475.
Certificate of Ownership of Encumbrances (evidencing vessel ownership and all mortgages): US$100 (unless issued at the time of the recordation of an instrument (that is, a mortgage), in which case it is free).
All other instruments, including amendments and supplements also have a fee of US$475. Overtime fees: these depend on when the closing takes place, but the fees for the first two hours before or after normal business hours is US$415.

D   Amendment

1   Can registered mortgages be amended and/or supplemented?
Registered mortgages may be amended or supplemented.

2   If so, what documents are required by the registering authority?
Four executed originals of the amendment or supplement each duly acknowledged or accompanied by proof of due execution by all parties thereto. MIMCA retains one original.

3   If so, please answer the questions listed under Sections A and C above as if references to mortgages were references to amending and/or supplementing instruments.
Form:
(a)	there is no prescribed form for an amendment or supplement;
(b)	the amendment or supplement must identify the mortgagor, the mortgagee, the vessel and the mortgage thereon;
(c)	the amendment or supplement must refer to the recording data of the original mortgage;
(d)	the amendment or supplement must be in the English language;
(e)	the amendment or supplement must be executed by a duly authorised signatory of each of the mortgagor and the mortgagee and be duly acknowledged or accompanied by proof of due execution; and
(f)	legalisation or apostille of the amendment is not required.

Recordation:
(a)	recordation of an amendment or supplement may be performed at any of the offices of MIMCA referred to in C1 above;
(b)	four executed original amendments or supplements must be submitted to MIMCA, three of which are retained by MIMCA;
(c)	evidence of the authorisation of the person signing on behalf of the mortgagor and mortgagee must be submitted to MIMCA;
(d)	a memorandum of particulars must be submitted to MIMCA (see C4); and
(e)	recordation fees for all amendments are US$475.

E   Discharge

1   What documents are required by the registering authority to discharge a registered mortgage?

Two executed original discharges of mortgage each duly acknowledged or accompanied by proof of due execution by all parties thereto.

2   Please answer the questions listed under Sections A and C above as if references to mortgages were references to mortgage discharges.

Form:

    (a)   there is no prescribed form for a discharge;

    (b)   the discharge must identify the mortgagor, the mortgagee, the vessel and the mortgage thereon;

    (c)   the discharge must refer to the recording data of the original mortgage;

    (d)   the discharge must be executed by a duly authorised signatory of the mortgagee and be duly acknowledged or accompanied by proof of due execution; and

    (e)   legalisation or apostille of the discharge is not required.

Recordation:

    (a)   recordation of a discharge may be performed at any office of MIMCA;

    (b)   two executed original discharges must be provided to MIMCA, one of which is retained by MIMCA;

    (c)   evidence of the authorisation of the person signing on behalf of the mortgagee must be submitted to MIMCA; and

    (d)   the fee for recording a discharge of mortgage is US$100 per discharge.

F   General

1   Please identify the principal statutes and regulations in the Marshall Islands governing the registration of mortgages on ships.

The principal statutes with respect to the registration of mortgages on vessels are the Marshall Islands Maritime Act 1990, as amended, and the Maritime Regulations made by The Trust Company of the Marshall Islands, Inc., under the authority vested in it as the duly appointed Marshall Islands Maritime Administrator by the Maritime Act 1990, as amended.

2   Must notice of mortgage and/or a certified copy or original mortgage be placed on board the mortgaged ship? Is there any time limit for doing so?

A certified copy of the mortgage and of any amendment or supplement thereto must be placed on board the vessel. There is no time limit for doing so but the law provides that the mortgagor must use due diligence to retain such copy on board the vessel and cause such copy and the document of the vessel to be exhibited by the Master to any person having business which may give rise to a maritime lien or to the sale, conveyance or mortgage of the vessel. In addition, mortgages customarily contain a covenant requiring the mortgagor to post notices of mortgages on board the vessel.

3   *Are there any other matters in the context of mortgages on ships under the legal system in the Marshall Islands which you feel should be emphasised?*

Under Section 318 of the Maritime Act 1990, as amended, a preferred mortgage lien has priority over all claims against the vessel, except liens arising prior in time to the recording of the mortgage, tort liens, liens for specified Marshall Islands governmental charges, liens for crew's wages, general average and salvage, and expenses and fees allowed and costs taxed by the court.

---

* Contributed by Hadley S. Roe, assisted by Kassandra L. Slangan and Mira Trifunovic, all of Seward & Kissel, New York, United States of America.

Norwegian International Ship Register*

A   Form and contents

1   Does the legal system in Norway prescribe a set form of mortgage for NIS registration?
No particular set form of mortgage is prescribed by law. However, a standard form ship mortgage deed prepared by the Norwegian commercial banks and savings banks is customarily used.

2   If not, does the legal system in Norway lay down any specific requirements as to the content of mortgages, to ensure either their validity or their priority?
The Maritime Act of 24 June 1994 No. 39 and the Mortgage Act of 8 February 1980 No. 2 prescribe that the mortgage form must identify the mortgagor, the mortgagee and the mortgaged vessel. Furthermore, the mortgage deed must state the maximum amount of the mortgaged debt. The amount shall be indicated in Norwegian Kroner or any foreign currency that is customarily quoted in Norway.

3   Must mortgages for registration in the NIS registry be in any particular language?
Pursuant to Section 17 of the Regulations Concerning Registration of Vessels in NIS of 30 July 1992, the mortgages must as a general rule, be written in Norwegian, Danish, Swedish or English. If deemed necessary, NIS has the right to require translation of the mortgage into Norwegian. NIS accepts to record mortgages written in a language other than those mentioned above, if a certified translation is enclosed and the Registrar has no doubt about the contents.

4   What are the requirements of the legal system in Norway with regard to:
  4.1   execution of the mortgage by the mortgagor?
  4.2   execution of the mortgage by the mortgagee?
  4.3   notarisation?
  4.4   legalisation?
4.1 The mortgage must be signed by an authorised signatory of the mortgagor.
4.2 There are none. The mortgage is executed by the mortgagor only.
4.3 The mortgagor's signature has to be certified.
   If the mortgagor is a Norwegian company, the certification may be given by either two witnesses of age, resident in Norway or by a Norwegian judge, lawyer or a Norwegian or foreign notary public.
   If the mortgagor is a non-Norwegian company, the certification must be obtained by way of a notarial certificate, which must include a confirmation by the notary that the person signing the mortgage deed on behalf of the relevant non-Norwegian company is duly authorised to do so.
   The Registrar may, in his sole discretion, approve a mortgage deed for registration if a signature has not been certified in a manner as described above.
4.4 If the notarial certification is given by a non-Norwegian notary public, his or her signature must normally be legalised by a Norwegian Embassy, or, if the country in question has ratified the Hague Convention of 5 October 1961 on Abolishing the Requirements of Legalisation for Foreign Public Documents, by apostille.

B   Mortgagees' Rights

1   Does the legal system in Norway provide mortgagees with the rights which they would normally expect, that is, the right to take possession of and sell the vessel on default, (a) by law and/or (b) only if included expressly in the mortgage?

Enforcement in Norway will always be subject to the mandatory provisions of the Norwegian Enforcement Act of 26 June 1992 No. 86 (the 'Enforcement Act') irrespective of the particular provisions of the mortgage deed. The Enforcement Act gives the mortgagee the right to request enforcement of the mortgage on default. This right need not be reflected in the mortgage deed. The mortgagee must file a claim for enforcement with the relevant Norwegian court at the port where the vessel may be at the time of commencement of enforcement proceedings. The court decides whether the manner of enforcement shall be by way of a sale through brokerage channels or a sale through forced auction. The court may also decide that enforcement shall be effected by the mortgagee being granted forced use or the vessel, although this alternative is seldom applied in practice.

2   Are there any limits (and, if so, what are they) on the right of the mortgagee on default:
2.1   to take possession of the vessel?
2.2   to sell the vessel at auction?
2.3   to sell the vessel privately?

If an agreement on enforcement alternatives is made between the owner and the mortgagor after the occurrence of the relevant event of default, such an agreement will be considered valid and binding. However, such agreements are subject to certain restrictions safeguarding the interests of the owner and its other creditors. As a common rule the mortgagee has an obligation to protect the interests of the owner and other creditors of the owner as long as that is compatible with his own interests (commonly referred to as 'the mortgagee's duty of care').

Any agreement on enforcement alternatives made before the occurrence of the relevant event of default, will be considered null and void, and the rights of the mortgagee will be limited to those provided pursuant to the Enforcement Act (please see B1 above).

C   Registration

1   Where may registration of mortgages take place:
1.1   in Norway?
1.2   abroad?

1.1   Yes
1.2   No

2   If mortgages may be executed and presented for registration in a foreign language, what, if any, are the translation requirements and when must they be completed?

Please see A3 above.

3   How many originals of the mortgage must be presented for registration? How many are retained by the registering authority?

One original mortgage and a copy of the mortgage should be presented for registration. After registration the NIS will return the original and retain the copy.

4   *What other documents must be produced to the registering authority when register-*
        ing the mortgage? Which will be retained?

If the mortgagor is a Norwegian company, an original of its updated company certificate ('Firmaattest') is required.

If the mortgagor is a foreign registered company, the signature(s) on the mortgage deed must be notarised and legalised as described in A4.3 and A4.4 above.

5   *Must original documents be submitted or will photocopies, faxed copies or pdf copies*
        of some or all documents be accepted? If so, which? Are there any requirements for
        copies to be verified?

The original mortgage deed must be submitted to NIS.

6   *What are the fees currently payable on mortgage registration.*

As of 1 July 2005, the fee for registering a new mortgage is NOK1,901. The fee for register-ing a mortgage amendment is NOK1,521. A complete list of registration fees along with bank-ing details is available on the NIS home page www.nis-nor.no

7   *Can a mortgage be registered over a vessel currently under construction? If so,*
        please provide details of the documents to be submitted and the fees payable.

Pursuant to Section 31 of the Maritime Act, vessels under construction in Norway may be reg-istered in a separate section of the ship registries called the Shipbuilding Registry if the over-all length of the vessel to be constructed is 10 metres or more. If the vessel under construction is registered in the Shipbuilding Registry, a mortgage can be registered over that vessel pur-suant to Section 41. The regulations for ordinary mortgage registration will apply corre-spondingly to the extent applicable.

D   Amendment

1   *Can registered mortgages be amended and/or supplemented?*

Yes.

2   *If so, what documents are required by the registering authority?*

If the amendment/supplement involves an increase of the mortgagor's obligations, the amend-ment must be endorsed on or attached to the original mortgage deed, and be signed by the owner of the vessel.

If the amendment/supplement involves a reduction of the mortgagor's obligations, the amendment must also be signed by the mortgagee.

3   *If so, please answer the questions listed under Sections A and C as if references to*
        mortgages were references to amending and/or supplementing instruments.

The answers to Section A apply where the context allows.

As of 1 July 2005 the fee for registering a mortgage amendment is NOK1,521.

E   Discharge

1   What documents are required by the registering authority to discharge a registered mortgage?

The original mortgage deed must be endorsed by the mortgagee for deletion. The signature and authority of the person(s) signing the endorsement on behalf of the mortgagee must be certified in the same manner as those which are applicable to the mortgagor. Please see A4.3 and A4.4 above.

2   Please answer the questions listed under Sections A and C as if references to mortgages were references to mortgage discharges.

Please see E1 above.

---

* Contributed by Bernhard Haukali and Gry Bratvold of Wikborg Rein, Oslo, Norway.

Panama*

A   Form and contents

1   Does the Panamanian legal system prescribe a set form of mortgage?
No.

2   If not, does the Panamanian legal system lay down any specific requirements as to the content of mortgages, to ensure either their validity or their priority?
A ship mortgage must contain the following requirements as prescribed by Article 1515 of the Code of Commerce of Panama, to wit:

(a)   The name and domicile of the party granting the mortgage and of the mortgagee.

(b)   The fixed or maximum amount secured. The mortgage is deemed to secure, in addition to the principal, all of the interest accrued, court costs, collection expenses, the amounts arising from fluctuations of currency or of other means of payment and all other sums agreed upon for any other reason in the mortgage contract. It is presumed, both between the parties and with respect to third persons, unless there is evidence to the contrary, that the sums owed, be it in concept of principal, interest or other sums secured by the mortgage, are those expressed in the complaint.

(c)   The dates of payment of principal and interest, or the manner to determine such dates, unless the mortgage is executed to secure obligations due on demand, future obligations or obligations subject to a condition precedent.

(d)   To the extent applicable, the parties must determine in the mortgage contract the interest rate agreed upon or the manner to calculate the same. Among others, the rate may be stipulated with reference to the rate prevailing in a determined market or to the bank rate granted to selected borrowers in any market. The rate may be stipulated by reference to the rate existing at the time of execution of the contract, or in accordance with the fluctuations which it may undergo within the term of the contract. The sums secured by a ship mortgage shall not be subject to a maximum interest rate and therefore the provisions of Law 5 of 1933 and Law 4 of 1935, shall not apply. Nevertheless, the National Banking Commission may establish a maximum interest rate to these credits when the mortgage is granted upon vessels of interior service.

(e)   Name, navigation licence number, radio call letters, and registered dimensions and tonnages. If the vessel is under construction, the circumstances required by Article 1518 of the Code of Commerce shall be indicated.

(f)   In case several vessels are mortgaged to secure a single credit, the amount or part of the mortgage for which each vessel is liable may be stated. If said statement has not been made, the creditor can collect the totality of the sum guaranteed from any of the vessels or from all of them.

3   Must mortgages for registration in Panama be in any particular language?
A ship mortgage may be constituted in any language and should be in writing whether in private or authentic form, or in accordance with the laws of the place of execution, and may be preliminarily registered in such form.

Thereafter, for purposes of final registration at the Public Registry Office in Panama, the corresponding document must be translated into Spanish and protocolised through a notary public in Panama.

4   *What are the requirements of the Panamanian legal system with regard to:*
     4.1   execution of the mortgage by the mortgagor?
     4.2   execution of the mortgage by the mortgagee?
     4.3   notarisation?
     4.4   legalisation?

4.1   The execution of the ship mortgage is accomplished through the signature by the mortgagor or the mortgagor's representative.

4.2   There is no express reference to the execution of the ship mortgage by the mortgagee, but in practice, the ship mortgage is accepted by the mortgagee.

4.3   The signature of the parties to the ship mortgage must be authenticated by a notary public or by a Panamanian Consul in exercise of notarial functions, both as to the identity of the signatories and as to their authority to act.

4.4   The signature of the notary public who authenticates the signature of the parties to the ship mortgage must be legalised by a Panamanian Consul or by way of apostille, to the extent that the ship mortgage is executed abroad.

B   Mortgagees' rights

1   Does the Panamanian legal system provide mortgagees with the rights which they would normally expect, that is, the right to take possession of and sell the vessel on default, (a) by law and/or (b) only if included expressly in the mortgage?

The Panamanian legal system provides a mortgagee with rights to take possession and sell the ship upon default by allowing the parties to a ship mortgage to include terms to that effect in the mortgage contract.

2   Are there any limits (and, if so, what are they) on the rights of a mortgagee on default:
     2.1   to take possession of the vessel?
     2.2   to sell the vessel at auction?
     2.3   to sell the vessel privately?

2.1   The mortgagee is under an obligation to render accounts to the owner every three (3) months and at the end of the period of possession and management, unless otherwise agreed upon. In addition, if there are mortgagees of different ranks, the right to take possession and management of the vessel shall be exercised in accordance with the order of priority of the respective mortgages.

2.2   An auction resulting in a non-judicial sale is subject to notice. The mortgagee must give notice to the owner that he will proceed to sell the mortgaged ship at least 20 calendar days prior to the date in which the sale is to take place. If there are other registered mortgagees, such notice should be given to such registered mortgagees.

2.3 A private sale by a mortgagee on default is subject to notice. The mortgagee must give notice to the owner that he will proceed to sell the mortgaged ship at least 20 calendar days prior to the date in which the sale is to take place. If there are other registered mortgagees, such notice should be given to such registered mortgagees.

C Registration

1 Where may registration of mortgages take place:
    1.1 in Panama?
    1.2 abroad?

1.1 Yes. The owner of a ship that has been provisionally registered under the flag of Panama may constitute a mortgage on the ship and may proceed with preliminary registration thereof through a notary public in Panama, and such registration produces full legal effects for six (6) months thereafter.

Thereafter, within such six (6) months period the ship mortgage must be filed for its permanent or final registration at the Public Registry Office in Panama and upon such registration the security created thereby becomes effective retroactively to the date of preliminary registration.

1.2 Yes. The owner of a ship that has been provisionally registered under the flag of Panama may constitute a mortgage on the ship and proceed with preliminary registration thereof through a Panamanian Consulate with maritime functions, and such registration produces full legal effects for six (6) months thereafter.

Thereafter, within such six (6) months period the ship mortgage must be filed for its permanent or final registration at the Public Registry Office in Panama and upon such registration the security created thereby becomes effective retroactively to the date of preliminary registration.

2 If mortgages may be executed and presented for registration in a foreign language, what, if any, are the translation requirements and when must they be completed?

A ship mortgage may be constituted in any language and should be in writing whether in private or authentic form, or in accordance with the laws of the place of execution, and may be preliminarily registered in such form.

Thereafter, for purposes of final registration at the Public Registry Office in Panama, the corresponding document must be translated into Spanish and protocolised through a notary public in Panama.

3 How many originals of the mortgage must be presented for registration? How many are retained by the registering authority?

At least two (2) originals of the ship mortgage are required for both preliminary and permanent or final registration. One is retained by the notary public or Panamanian Consulate that assists in the preliminary registration thereof, and one is protocolised with a notary public in Panama and the corresponding instrument is then filed and registered at the Public Registry Office in Panama.

*4   What other documents must be produced to the registering authority? Which will be
       retained?*

An application for preliminary registration is filed with the notary public or the Panamanian Consulate together with the ship mortgage. A tax clearance certificate evidencing that the ship is tax cleared with the Panamanian government should also be filed for final or permanent registration at the Public Registry. Furthermore, a copy of the franchise tax receipt evidencing payment of said tax for the current year would also have to be filed if any of the parties to the ship mortgage are Panamanian corporations. These documents are also retained.

*5   Must original documents be submitted or will photocopies or fax copies of some or
       all documents be accepted? If so, which? Are there any requirements for copies to be
       verified?*

Original documents must be submitted.

6   What fees are currently payable on mortgage registration?

(a)   A government charge ranging from US$450 to US$1,200 is payable for preliminary
       registration, and the amount thereof depends on the amount secured.

(b)   Government duties for final registration are calculated at US$0.10 per net ton up to
       a maximum of US$500.00.

(c)   Decree No. 75 of 1990 authorised consular charges for assistance in preliminary reg-
       istration and which can be calculated at US$750. Additional charges may be levied on
       account of legalisations and communication charges incurred at a given Consulate.

D   Amendment

1   Can registered mortgages be amended and/or supplemented?

Yes.

2   If so, what documents are required by the registering authority?

A supplemental ship mortgage agreement.

3   Does the Panamanian legal system prescribe a set form of supplemental mortgage?

No.

*4   If not, does the Panamanian legal system lay down any specific requirements as to the
       content of supplemental mortgages, to ensure either their validity or their priority?*

There are no express requirements, but the corresponding document should at least contain the following information:

(a)   the name and domiciles of the parties to the corresponding document;

(b)   a description of the vessel as included in the original mortgage, together with regis-
       tration data in respect of the original mortgage; and

(c)   details of the items to be amended or supplemented on account of the supplemental
       mortgage agreement.

5   *Must supplemental mortgages for registration in Panama be in any particular language?*
A supplemental mortgage may be constituted in any language and should be in writing whether in private or authentic form, or in accordance with the laws of the place of execution, and may be preliminarily registered in such form.
Thereafter, for final registration at the Public Registry Office in Panama, the corresponding document must be translated into Spanish and protocolised through a notary public in Panama.

6   *What are the requirements of the Panamanian legal system with regard to:*
    6.1   execution of the supplemental mortgage by the mortgagor?
    6.2   execution of the supplemental mortgage by the mortgagee?
    6.3   notarisation?
    6.4   legalisation?

6.1   The execution thereof is accomplished through the signature by the mortgagor or the mortgagor's representative.

6.2   There is no express reference to the execution of the supplemental mortgage by the mortgagee, but in practice it should be accepted by the mortgagee.

6.3   The signature of the parties must be authenticated by a notary public or by a Panamanian Consul in exercise of notarial functions, both as to the identity of the signatories and as to their authority to act.

6.4   The signature of the notary public who authenticates the signature of the parties must be legalised by a Panamanian Consul, or by way of apostille to the extent that the it is executed abroad.

7   *Where may registration of supplemental mortgages take place:*
    7.1   in Panama?
    7.2   abroad?

7.1   Yes. A supplemental mortgage may be preliminarily registered through a notary public in Panama, and such registration produces full legal effects for six (6) months thereafter.
Thereafter, within such six (6) months period the supplemental mortgage must be filed for its permanent or final registration at the Public Registry Office in Panama.

7.2   Yes. A supplemental mortgage may be preliminarily registered through a Panamanian Consulate with Maritime functions, and such registration produces full legal effects for six (6) months thereafter.
Thereafter, within such six (6) months period the ship mortgage must be filed for its permanent or final registration at the Public Registry Office in Panama.

8   *If supplemental mortgages may be executed and presented for registration in a foreign language, what, if any, are the translation requirements and when must they be completed?*
A supplemental mortgage may be constituted in any language and should be in writing whether in private or authentic form, or in accordance with the laws of the place of execution, and may be preliminarily registered in such form.

Thereafter, for purposes of final registration at the Public Registry Office in Panama, the corresponding document must be translated into Spanish and protocolised through a notary public in Panama, and be filed for permanent or final registration at the Public Registry Office in Panama within six (6) months of preliminary registration.

9   *How many originals of the supplemental mortgage must be presented for registration? How many are retained by the registering authority?*

At least two (2) originals of the supplemental mortgage are required for both preliminary and permanent or final registration. One is retained by the notary public or Panamanian Consulate that assists in the preliminary registration thereof, and one is protocolised with a notary public in Panama and the corresponding instrument is then filed and registered at the Public Registry Office in Panama.

10   *What other documents must be produced to the registering authority? Which will be retained?*

An application for preliminary registration is filed with the notary public or the Panamanian Consulate together with the supplemental mortgage. A tax clearance certificate evidencing that the ship is tax cleared with the Panamanian government is also filed for final or permanent registration at the Public Registry. Furthermore, a copy of the Franchise tax receipt evidencing payment of said tax for the current year would also have to be filed if any of the parties to the supplemental mortgage are Panamanian corporations. These documents are also retained.

11   *Must original documents be submitted or will photocopies or fax copies of some or all documents be accepted? If so, which? Are there any requirements for copies to be verified?*

Original documents must be submitted.

12   *What fees are currently payable on supplemental mortgage registration?*

A minimal government duty is to be paid, that is, US$3.05, and consular charges for assistance in preliminary registration and which can be calculated at US$100. Additional charges may be levied on account of legalisations and communication charges incurred at a given Consulate.

E   Discharge

1   *What documents are required by the registering authority to discharge a registered mortgage?*

An instrument of discharge of mortgage properly executed by the mortgagee.

2   *Does the Panamanian legal system prescribe a set form of discharge of mortgage?*

No.

3   *If not, does the Panamanian legal system lay down any specific requirements as to the content of discharges of mortgages, to ensure either their validity or their priority?*

There are no express requirements, but in practice the corresponding documents should contain:

(a)   the name and domicile of the party granting the mortgage and of the mortgagee;

(b)   name, Navigation Licence number, Radio Call Letters, and registered dimensions and tonnages, as well as details concerning the date of the mortgage and registration details thereof; and

(c)   an express declaration that the mortgagee discharges and releases the owner from the obligations secured by the ship mortgage.

4   *Must discharges of mortgages for registration in Panama be in any particular language?*

A discharge of mortgage may be constituted in any language and should be in writing whether in private or authentic form, or in accordance with the laws of the place of execution, and may be preliminarily registered in such form.

Thereafter, for final registration at the Public Registry Office in Panama, the corresponding document must be translated into Spanish and protocolised through a notary public in Panama.

5   *What are the requirements of the Panamanian legal system with regard to:*
       5.1   *execution of the discharge mortgage by the mortgagor?*
       5.2   *execution of the discharge mortgage by the mortgagee?*
       5.3   *notarisation?*
       5.4   *legalisation?*

5.1   None.

5.2   The execution thereof is accomplished through the signature by the mortgagee or the mortgagee's representative.

5.3   The signature of the parties to the discharge of mortgage must be authenticated by a notary public or by a Panamanian Consul in exercise of notarial functions, both as to identity of the signatories and as to their authority to act.

5.4   The signature of the notary public who authenticates the signature of the parties to the discharge of mortgage must be legalised by a Panamanian Consul, or by way of apostille to the extent that the discharge of mortgage is executed abroad.

6   *Where may registration of discharges of mortgages take place:*
       6.1   *in Panama?*
       6.2   *abroad?*

6.1   Yes. A discharge of mortgage may be preliminarily registered through a notary public in Panama, and which registration produces full legal effects for six (6) months thereafter.

       Thereafter, the discharge of mortgage must be filed for its permanent or final registration at the Public Registry Office in Panama.

6.2   Yes. A discharge of mortgage may be preliminarily registered through a Panamanian Consulate with Maritime Functions. Thereafter, the discharge of ship mortgage must be filed for its permanent or final registration at the Public Registry Office in Panama.

7   *If discharges of mortgages may be executed and presented for registration in a for-*
       eign language, what, if any, are the translation requirements, and when must they be
       completed?

A discharge of mortgage may be constituted in any language and should be in writing whether in private or authentic form, or in accordance with the laws of the place of execution, and may be preliminarily registered in such form.

Thereafter, for purposes of final registration at the Public Registry Office in Panama, the corresponding document must be translated into Spanish and protocolised through a notary public in Panama, and must be filed for its permanent or final registration at the Public Registry Office in Panama within six (6) months of preliminary registration.

8   *How many originals of the discharge of mortgage must be presented for registration?*
       How many are retained by the registering authority?

At least two (2) originals are required for both preliminary and permanent or final registration. One is retained by notary public or Panamanian Consulate that assists in the preliminary registration thereof, and one is protocolised with a notary public in Panama and the corresponding instrument is then filed and registered at the Public Registry Office in Panama.

9   *What other documents must be produced to the registering authority? Which will be*
       retained?

An application for preliminary registration is filed with the notary public or the Panamanian Consulate together with the discharge mortgage. A tax clearance certificate evidencing that the ship is tax cleared with the Panamanian government is also filed for purposes of final or permanent registration at the Public Registry. These documents are also retained.

10   *Must original documents or will photocopies or fax copies of some or all documents*
       be accepted? If so, which? Are they any requirements for copies to be verified?

Original documents must be submitted.

11   *What fees are currently payable on mortgage registration?*

A minimal government duty is to be paid, that is, US$3.05 and consular charges for assistance in preliminary registration which can be calculated at US$750. Additional charges may be levied on account of legalisations and communication charges incurred at a given Consulate.

F   General

1   *Please identify the principal statutes and regulations in Panama governing the reg-*
       istration of mortgages on ships.

Articles 1512 to 1533 of the Code of Commerce of Panama refer specifically to Ship Mortgages granted on Panamanian flag vessels. Reference is made therein to the provisions of the Civil Code on Mortgages of Inmovables (Real Estate) and these provisions apply to the extent that they are not in contradiction with the special provisions of the Code of Commerce. In addition, reference should also be made to the provisions of the Civil Code concerning the

Public Registry. In particular, the provisions of the Code of Commerce were amended with the passing of Law No. 14 of 1980 in respect of the preliminary registration of mortgages, and further with the passing of Law No. 43 of 1984.

2 *Must notice of mortgage and/or a certified copy or original mortgage be placed on board the ship? Is there any time limit for doing so?*
No. However, in practice, there is a covenant in the mortgage which so requires.

3 *Are there any other matters in the context of mortgages on ships not referred to above which you feel should be emphasised?*
Law No. 43 of 1984 modified and added various provisions to the Code of Commerce dealing with vessels registered under the flag of Panama and mortgages thereon. The objectives of the law were to improve the provisions dealing with the preliminary registration of documents, that is, Bills of Sale, mortgages, and discharges, through the Consular offices of Panama abroad as well as locally through notaries in Panama City, and to modernise the provisions of the Code to reflect current financial realities.

Among the salient features of the said law, we can find the following:

(a) Mortgages may now be executed by private document in any language both in Panama and abroad. Previously, a mortgage had to be executed in Public Instrument form in Spanish if execution was to take place in Panama, or before a government official abroad or alternatively, in accordance with the laws of the place of execution if executed outside of Panama.

(b) Preliminary registration of the above named documents can now take place in Panama directly through attorneys in Panama, and the same can take place upon execution of the corresponding document in private form and in any language in Panama. Basically, parties can designate attorneys-in-fact to execute a given document or alternatively send the executed document, and through the preparation of an extract with a notary public, the corresponding documents can be filed for preliminary registration at the Public Registry.

(c) While the mortgage deed should reflect the maximum amount of principal secured, the law provides that the mortgage will also cover interests, costs, collection expenses, increments resulting from currency fluctuations and other sums agreed to in the corresponding document.

(d) Several of the provisions were introduced to clarify matters which would appear to have been resolved by commercial practice, but over which there were differences of opinions among the lawyers in Panama, to wit:

    (i) a mortgage may be constituted to secure future obligations or those subject to condition precedent without the need of marginal annotations or amendments, that is, revolving credit facilities, options to convert to a different currency;

    (ii) the law provides that variations in currencies, interests, dates of payment or mode of payment do not extinguish a mortgage, nor would complete repayment of funds advanced as in the case of a revolving credit facility.

In addition, the law provides that the substitution of the debtor does not cause the principal obligation, nor the mortgage, to be extinguished.

(e)   Article 1515 of the Code of Commerce has been modified and as a result thereof there is no longer a ceiling on the maximum amount of interest that may be charged in respect of credits concerning vessels engaged in international service, and furthermore, the need to fix a value for the vessel in the event of a public auction has been eliminated.

(f) Two articles have been added to the Code of Commerce in respect of the taking of possession and administration of a vessel, as well as in respect of a private sale thereof in an event of default and which have been referred to before.

---

*   Contributed by Brett R. Patton of Patton, Moreno and Asvat, Panama and London, England.

Singapore*

A Form and contents

1 Does the legal system in Singapore prescribe a set form of mortgage?
Mortgages of Singapore vessels must be made in one of four statutory forms:

(a) mortgage (to secure principal sum and interest) (body corporate) ('Format A');

(b) mortgage (to secure account current) (body corporate) ('Format B');

(c) mortgage (to secure principal sum and interest) (individual or joint owners) ('Format C'); or

(d) mortgage (to secure account current) (individual or joint owners) ('Format D').

As their names suggest, Formats A and C secure only principal and interest, and not other amounts such as swap payments, guarantee fees, enforcement fees, legal expenses and so on. This means that Formats A and C are nowadays hardly ever used and almost all mortgages are made using either Format B or Format D.

2 If not, does the legal system in Singapore lay down any specific requirements as to the content of mortgages, to ensure either their validity or their priority?
Not applicable.

3 Must mortgages for registration in Singapore be in any particular language?
Mortgages must be made in the English language.

4 What are the requirements of the legal system in Singapore with regard to:
    4.1 execution of the mortgage by the mortgagor?
    4.2 execution of the mortgage by the mortgagee?
    4.3 notarisation?
    4.4 legalisation?

Only the mortgagor needs to execute the mortgage. If the mortgage is executed outside Singapore, it must be notarised and legalised at the Singapore embassy in the place of execution.

B Mortgagees' rights

1 Does the legal system in Singapore provide mortgagees with the rights which they would normally expect, that is, the right to take possession of and sell the vessel on default, (a) by law and/or (b) only if included expressly in the mortgage?
At law, every registered mortgagee has the right to sell the mortgaged vessel by auction or by private treaty and to give an effectual receipt for the purchase price, save that if there is more than one mortgagee, a subsequent mortgagee may not sell the vessel without the agreement of all prior mortgagees or an order of the court. A registered mortgagee may enforce its mortgage by commencing an action *in rem* in admiralty. Prior to executing a mortgage, the mortgagor has a statutory obligation to disclose in writing to the mortgagee the existence of any maritime liens, prior mortgages or other liabilities in respect of the vessel to be mortgaged of which it is aware. If the mortgagor fails to comply with this requirement, the mortgage debt shall, at the election of the mortgagee, become immediately due and payable, notwithstanding

any terms to the contrary in the mortgage. A mortgagee may take possession of a vessel and/or exercise its power of sale of a vessel under the mortgage but a mortgagee would usually prefer a judicial sale *via* the court system as such a sale would likely be more attractive to a buyer as the buyer would take the vessel free from any claims. Further, under a court sale, the mortgagee has less reason to concern itself with whether it has exercised due fiduciary duty of care in obtaining the 'best' price for the vessel.

2   *Are there any limits (and, if so, what are they) on the right of the mortgagee on default:*

      2.1   *to take possession of the vessel?*

      2.2   *to sell the vessel at auction?*

      2.3   *to sell the vessel privately?*

There are certain statutory provisions under the Conveyancing and Law of Property Act (Chapter 61) which have the effect of limiting the right of the mortgagee to take any of such action, for example, Clause 25 thereof requires a mortgagee to have served notice of demand on the mortgagor and default has been made in payment for three months after such service. However, such statutory rights are, as a matter of practice and documentation, expressly waived by the mortgagor in the deed of covenants collateral to the mortgage.

C   Registration

1   *Where may registration of mortgages take place:*

      1.1   *in Singapore?*

      1.2   *abroad?*

All mortgages of Singapore vessels must be registered at the Registry in Singapore. The Registry does not have offices outside Singapore.

2   *If mortgages may be executed and presented for registration in a foreign language, what, if any, are the translation requirements and when must they be completed?*

Not applicable (mortgages must be made in the English language).

3   *How many originals of the mortgage must be presented for registration? How many are retained by the registering authority?*

Only one original of the mortgage needs to be presented for registration. The original mortgage will be returned after registration and the Registry has made an endorsement on the mortgage (that is, as to the date and time of the mortgage registration).

4   *What other documents must be produced to the registering authority when registering the mortgage? Which will be retained?*

The mortgagee or its solicitors must provide a letter to the Registry requesting the registration of the mortgage. If the mortgage is executed by the mortgagor pursuant to a Power of Attorney, the original (and a photocopy) of the Power of Attorney must also be provided. The original of the Power of Attorney will be returned after registration. If, at the time of mortgage registration, the original of the Builder's Certificate or the Bill of Sale, as the case may be, has not yet been submitted to the Registry, the mortgagee must confirm in writing to the Registry that the mortgagee (or its representative) has sighted the original Builder's Certificate or Bill of Sale before the mortgage will be accepted for registration.

5   *Must original documents be submitted or will photocopies, faxed copies or pdf copies of some or all documents be accepted? If so, which? Are there any requirements for copies to be verified?*

Original documents must be submitted.

6   *What are the fees currently payable on mortgage registration.*

The mortgage registration fee is calculated at the rate of S$48 plus S$1 per 100 grt (to the nearest ton) plus GST.

7   *Can a mortgage be registered over a vessel currently under construction? If so, please provide details of the documents to be submitted and the fees payable.*

No.

D   Amendment

1   Can registered mortgages be amended and/or supplemented?

There is no prescribed format or mechanism for the amendment of a mortgage. If necessary, a further mortgage may be registered over the vessel.

It is possible for a mortgagee to transfer a registered mortgage to another person. This is done by the mortgagee executing the prescribed transfer format on the reverse page of the original mortgage and presenting the mortgage to the Registry for registration. A mortgage registration fee is payable as if a new mortgage is registered over the vessel.

2   *If so, what documents are required by the registering authority?*

Not applicable.

3   *If so, please answer the questions listed under Sections A and C as if references to mortgages were references to amending and/or supplementing instruments.*

Not applicable.

E   Discharge

1   What documents are required by the registering authority to discharge a registered mortgage?

The mortgagee must execute the prescribed discharge of mortgage format on the reverse page of the original mortgage. The mortgagee or its solicitors must provide a letter to the Registry enclosing the original signed discharge of mortgage and requesting the discharge of the mortgage. If the discharge of mortgage is executed pursuant to a Power of Attorney, the original (and a photocopy) of the Power of Attorney must also be provided. The original of the Power of Attorney will be returned after registration. In the cases of general Powers of Attorney granted by banks and financial institutions in Singapore and which have been registered with the High Court of Singapore, the Registry will require and retain a certified copy of the general Power of Attorney for the first registration requested by a particular bank. Thereafter, for subsequent registrations by the same bank, the bank (or its solicitors) does not need to provide further copies of the general Power of Attorney and will only need to confirm that the discharge has been signed pursuant to the same general Power of Attorney and that it has not been revoked.

2 *Please answer the questions listed under Sections A and C as if references to mortgages were references to mortgage discharges.*

The answers to Sections A and C apply, *mutatis mutandis*, to applications for mortgage discharges.

F General

1 *Please identify the principal statutes and regulations in Singapore governing the registration of mortgages on ships.*

The Merchant Shipping Act (Chapter 179).

2 *Must notice of the mortgage and/or a certified copy or original mortgage be placed on board the mortgaged ship? Is there a time limit for doing so?*

No, although the deed of covenants usually imposes a contractual obligation on the Mortgagor to place a notice of the mortgage onboard the vessel.

3 *Are there any other matters in the context of mortgages on ships under the legal system in Singapore which you feel should be emphasised here?*

Where a mortgage over a Singapore vessel is already registered with the Registry, it is not a legal requirement for the prior mortgagee to give its written consent before the Registry will register a subsequent mortgage. It is therefore important for the deed of covenants, collateral to the prior mortgage, to provide that it shall be an event of default if the mortgagor creates a subsequent mortgage over the vessel without the prior mortgagee's prior written consent.

Where there is more than one mortgage registered in respect of a Singapore vessel, the mortgagees shall, notwithstanding any express, implied or constructive notice, be entitled in priority one over the other, according to the date and time of the record of each mortgage with the Registry and not according to the date of each mortgage. The time of registration with the Registry is therefore paramount in deciding priority.

If the mortgagor is a Singapore company, the particulars of the security created by the mortgage and the collateral deed of covenants must be registered with ACRA within 30 days of the creation of such security or (if the documents are executed outside Singapore) 37 days of the creation of such security.

A registered mortgage over a Singapore vessel will rank in priority after all statutory liens, maritime liens (for example, wages, collision and salvage claims) and any possessory liens.

Although a vessel may be provisionally registered, the mortgage, when registered over such vessel, is a permanent mortgage.

---

* Contributed by Harold Or of Allen & Gledhill, Singapore.

United Kingdom*

A   Form and contents

1   Does the legal system in the United Kingdom prescribe a set form of mortgage?
The register of British ships and mortgages over them (the 'Register') is the responsibility of the centralised Registry of Shipping and Seamen based in Cardiff (the 'Registry') under the supervision of the Registrar General (the 'Registrar').

A mortgage over a British ship or a share in a British ship must be in the form approved by the Registrar. There are two forms, one to secure sums due on an account current (MSF 4736) and the other to secure principal and interest (MSF 4737).

2   If not, does the legal system in the United Kingdom lay down any specific require-
         ments as to the content of mortgages, to ensure either their validity or their priority?
Not applicable.

3   Must mortgages for registration in the United Kingdom be in any particular lan-
         guage?
They must be completed in English.

4   What are the requirements of the legal system in the United Kingdom with regard to:
         4.1   execution of the mortgage by the mortgagor?
         4.2   execution of the mortgage by the mortgagee?
         4.3   notarisation?
         4.4   legalisation?
The mortgage must be executed as a deed by the mortgagor. The mortgage does not need to be executed by the mortgagee.

Where the mortgagor is a company incorporated in England and Wales, execution of the mortgage should be done under the company seal or by a duly appointed attorney in the presence of a witness. If the company does not have a seal the mortgage should be executed by either two directors or by a director and the company secretary.

Where the mortgagor is an individual he must sign and deliver the mortgage as a deed or appoint an attorney to do so on his behalf.

Any Power of Attorney used should be executed as a deed and should be presented to the Registrar for inspection.

Notarisation and legalisation of the mortgage are not required.

B   Mortgagees' rights

1   Does the legal system in the United Kingdom provide mortgagees with the rights
         which they would normally expect, that is, the right to take possession of and sell the
         vessel on default, (a) by law and/or (b) only if included expressly in the mortgage?
Under statute, every registered mortgagee has the power, if the mortgage money or any part of it is due, to sell the ship or shares in respect of which he is registered and to give effectual receipts for the purchase money. Where there are two or more mortgagees registered,

a subsequent mortgagee is not able to sell the ship or any share in it without the agreement of every prior mortgagee except with an order of the court.

Under common law, the mortgagee has the right to take possession of the vessel if the mortgagor is in default of payment obligations in connection with the principal or interest secured by the mortgage, or the mortgagor otherwise acts to impair the security provided by the mortgage.

The deed of covenants which is usually entered into collateral to the statutory mortgage would normally expressly set out the statutory and common law rights of a mortgagee and will expand on those rights.

2   *Are there any limits (and, if so, what are they) on the right of the mortgagee on default:*
      2.1   to take possession of the vessel?
      2.2   to sell the vessel at auction?
      2.3   to sell the vessel privately?

The mortgagee's rights are subject to prior encumbrances and maritime liens but otherwise are not subject to any limits in the event of a default by the mortgagor. A mortgagee in possession will be liable for expenses incurred in operating the ship and has a duty to operate the ship in the manner consistent with a prudent owner and on any sale has a duty to achieve the best price reasonably obtained. For a more detailed discussion on this please see the body of Chapter 7 of this book.

C   Registration

1   Where may registration of mortgages take place:
      1.1   in the United Kingdom?
      1.2   abroad?

Mortgages may only be registered in the United Kingdom at the Registry. The Registry's address is: The Registry of Shipping and Seamen, PO Box 420, Cardiff CF24 5XR

2   If mortgages may be executed and presented for registration in a foreign language, what, if any, are the translation requirements and when must they be completed?

Not applicable.

3   How many originals of the mortgage must be presented for registration? How many are retained by the registering authority?

There is only one original of the mortgage and this original must be presented for registration. It will be endorsed by the Registry with the date and time of its registration and will then returned to the mortgagee.

4   What other documents must be produced to the registering authority when register-ing the mortgage? Which will be retained?

If the mortgage has been executed under a Power of Attorney (see A4 above) the original of that Power of Attorney should be presented to the Registry for inspection and will be returned.

5   *Must original documents be submitted or will photocopies, fax copies or pdf copies of some or all documents be accepted? If so, which? Are there any requirements for copies to be verified?*

Fax or pdf copies of the mortgage (and Power of Attorney if applicable) may be acceptable with the prior agreement of the Registrar. The original documents will have to be forwarded to the Registry as soon as possible after the fax/pdf copies.

6   *What fees are currently payable on mortgage registration?*

The fees on mortgage registration are currently:

(a)   one mortgage: £105.00;

(b)   where more than one mortgage in relation to the same loan over the same ship is lodged at the same time:

      (i)   two mortgages: £200.00;

      (ii)   three mortgages: £275.00;

      (iii)   four mortgages: £340.00;

      (iv)   five mortgages or more: £400.00;

(c)   registration of notice of intended mortgage: £25.00

7   *Can a mortgage be registered over a vessel currently under construction?*

No.

D   Amendment

1   Can registered mortgages be amended and/or supplemented?

A registered mortgage cannot be amended or supplemented. Any changes would involve the execution and registration of a new mortgage.

The deed of covenants collateral to the mortgage is a contract between the parties and therefore can be amended at any time if all parties agree.

A registered mortgage may be transferred by completion of the form of transfer appearing on the mortgage form and then lodging the mortgage at the Registry. The Registrar will enter the name of the transferee in the Register and will endorse the date and time of transfer on the mortgage.

2   *If so, what documents are required by the registering authority?*

As the deed of covenants is not recorded at the Registry, nothing needs to be submitted to it in the event of amendment. However, if the amendment creates a new charge over assets of any United Kingdom company the document will need to be registered at the relevant companies registry (see F3 below).

3   *If so, please answer the questions listed under Sections A and C above as if references to mortgages were references to amending and/or supplementing instruments.*

Not applicable, see above.

E   Discharge

1   What documents are required by the registering authority to discharge a registered mortgage?

The statutory mortgage form has a discharge section on the back of the mortgage and this needs to be completed by the mortgagee and the form returned to the Registry. The Registry will then register the discharge and will return the endorsed mortgage deed. There is no fee payable to the Registry for effecting a discharge.

2   Please answer the questions listed under Sections A and C above as if references to mortgages were references to mortgage discharges.

See above.

F   General

1   Please identify the principal statutes and regulations in the United Kingdom governing the registration of mortgages on ships.

The Merchant Shipping Act 1995 and the Merchant Shipping (Registration of Ship) Regulations 1993 both as amended.

2   Must notice of mortgage and/or a certified copy or original mortgage be placed on board the mortgaged ship? Is there any time limit for doing so?

There is no legal requirement for a certified copy or the original of the mortgage to be placed on board the vessel but there may be a specific contractual requirement contained in the deed of covenants.

3   Are there any other matters in the context of mortgages on ships under the legal system in the United Kingdom which you feel should be emphasised?

Priority notices

There is a system of priority notices by which any intending mortgagee can notify the Registrar of his interest in a registered ship as a proposed mortgagee and the Registry will record that interest.

The form of application is called a 'Notice of Mortgage Intent' and is in a set form (MSF 4739) and needs to contain the name and official number of the ship, the name and address and signature of the intending mortgagor, the number of shares in the ship to be mortgaged and the name and address of the intending mortgagee.

Where, at the time of submission of the notice, the ship is not presently on the British register, the Registrar will record the interest on the Register and if the ship is subsequently registered, the Registrar will register the ship subject to the interest or if the mortgage has by then been executed, subject to that mortgage.

A priority notice has effect for a period of 30 days. If the mortgage is executed and registered within that period and in the meantime another mortgagee has registered an interest, the holder of the priority notice will take priority over that mortgage. The period of 30 days can be extended by notice in writing to the Registry.

Registration of charges

If a company incorporated in the United Kingdom creates a charge over a ship the document creating the charge must be presented to the relevant companies registry together with a completed form of application for registration of the charge within 21 days of the date of creation of the charge.

---

* Contributed by Philippa Sharratt of Stephenson Harwood, London, England.

Chapter 8

The assignment of insurances and earnings

Updated by Ian Mace

Importance of the assignment to the lender

An invariable part of a financing bank's security package is an assignment of the earnings and of the benefit of the insurances of a mortgaged vessel. The reasons for this will be obvious. It is probable, as we have seen, that the bank will be lending to a one-ship company, with no source of income other than from the operation of the vessel. The lender will, therefore, want to be able to exercise some control over the earnings flow. More importantly, it will want to be sure that, on default, the charterers, and any others from whom earnings may be due, can be called on to pay those earnings to the lender free of any claim from the borrower or its liquidator. Similarly, it will want to be sure that, in the event of a major accident involving the vessel, the proceeds of any insurance claim will be paid directly to the lender towards payment of the outstanding debt.

A lender should, however, be wary of placing too much importance on the assignment. While it is vital, it will be of no use to a lender if the ship stops trading (for example, if a charterer defaults) or if an insurance claim is not met. While there may be other sources of repayment available to a lender in such circumstances (for example, loss of earnings insurance or mortgagees' interest insurance – see Chapter 12), he may nevertheless need to look to his other security for full repayment of the outstanding indebtedness.

It is a cardinal principle of English law that an assignee can be in no better position than the assignor. Thus, if the owner/borrower is in breach of a charterparty in a manner that entitles the charterer to stop paying freight or hire, the lender cannot (unless he has reached a separate agreement with the charterer) ignore that breach and demand payment of hire directly to him. If the charterer was entitled to withhold payment from the owner, then, as a general rule, he will be entitled to withhold payment from the assignee lender too.

In this context, however, the case of the vessel 'TRIDENT BEAUTY',[1] decided by the House of Lords, in early 1994, warrants examination. While it is not in the strict sense an exception to the general proposition, it shows how a lending bank can, in certain circumstances, find itself in a better position than the borrower assignor.

In the 'TRIDENT BEAUTY' case, the borrower had entered into a time charter under which hire for the vessel was payable 15 days in advance. Hire was duly paid to the lender, as assignee, but the vessel subsequently went off hire, so that none of the advance hire payment which had been made was, in fact, earned. In the event, the vessel was off hire for a period of time sufficiently long to entitle the charterers to claim a repudiation of the charterparty by the owners.

The time charter provided, as is normal, that where hire was paid but not earned, the owners were under an obligation to refund it to the charterers. The question that arose for determination by the courts was whether the lender, in its capacity as assignee, was under a similar obligation.

On the face of it, the case brings into conflict two well-established principles of English law. First, the proposition that the assignee can be in no better position than the assignor would seem to suggest that, if the assignor had to refund the hire, then so should the assignee. On the other hand, it is also well-established law that only the benefit of a contract can be assigned, and not the burden. The burden of a contract can only be transferred by novation which would, among other things, involve the charterer joining into the transfer documents and agreeing to accept the lender, rather than the borrower, as its counterparty. In the context of a charterparty, this would clearly be a commercial nonsense.

In effect, the crucial question in the case was whether the obligation to refund unearned hire was an obligation independent of the right to receive the hire, or (looked at another way) whether the payment of hire was in some way conditional, or impressed with some sort of trust in favour of the charterer, if the hire proved not to have been earned. At first instance, it was held that the payment was conditional, and that, if the owner had to refund hire to the charterer, so did an assignee. When the case eventually reached the House of Lords, however, this decision was overruled and the court decided that the obligation to refund hire was independent of the right to receive it, and, as only the benefit of the charterparty had been transferred to the lender by the assignment, the assignee could keep the hire which it had received, even though the assignor was obliged to give the charterer a refund. The charterer was left to pursue its remedy against the assignor which, presumably, had no assets, having mortgaged its ship, and assigned its earnings, to the lender. This is clearly a comforting decision for lenders who might otherwise receive and apply hire (and possibly even release security) in ignorance of the possibility of the hire subsequently becoming refundable to the charterer.

What is normally assigned?

An assignment will generally encompass three categories of income: earnings, insurances and requisition compensation. These are likely to be defined in wide-ranging terms in the facility documents (usually either in the assignment itself or in the underlying facility agreement). Sample definitions are given below.

- *Earnings*: all hires, freights, pool income and other sums payable to or for the account of the borrower and/or the bareboat charterer in respect of the vessel, including (without limitation) all remuneration for salvage and towage services, demurrage and detention moneys; contributions in general average; compensation in respect of any requisition for hire and damages and other payments (whether awarded by any court or arbitral tribunal or by agreement or otherwise) for breach, termination or variation of any contract for the operation, employment or use of the vessel.
- *Insurances*: all policies and contracts of insurance (including all entries in protection and indemnity or war risks associations) which are from time to time taken out or entered into in respect of the vessel or the increased value or her earnings and (where the context permits) all benefits thereof, including all claims of any nature and returns of premium.

- *Requisition compensation*: all compensation or other money which may from time to time be payable to the borrower and/or the bareboat charterer as a result of the vessel being requisitioned for title or in any other way compulsorily acquired (other than by way of requisition for hire).

The assignment may be contained in a separate document, though (for British and similar flag vessels) it is sometimes contained in the deed of covenants. There is no great advantage in either course, though using a separate document means that the whole of the deed of covenants will not need to be produced in any enforcement proceedings. For other flags, it is preferable to take the assignment in a separate document. This is because the mortgage will be governed by the law of the flag, and the lender will normally prefer the assignment to be governed by the same law as the facility agreement. This could be of particular importance in Liberian and certain other mortgages where the preferred status of the mortgage may be adversely affected if the mortgage covers property other than the ship.

In some jurisdictions, a mortgage will perforce encompass either the vessel's insurances or earnings, or both. It is, however, suggested that a lender should normally take a separate assignment, and rely on the additional protection of the law of the flag state as a back up.

English law requirements

In English law, the benefit of a contract (such as a charterparty or a policy of insurance) falls within the category of personal property known as choses in action. Section 136 of the Law of Property Act 1925 sets out detailed rules for the assignment of choses in action. In summary, to be effective under Section 136 as a legal assignment (as opposed to an equitable assignment only, the disadvantages of which are discussed below) an assignment must be:

- in writing;
- signed by the assignor; and
- absolute, and not purporting to be by way of charge only.[2]

Additionally, written notice of the assignment must be given to the debtor (that is, in the case of earnings, the charterer; in the case of insurances, the insurer).

An assignment that satisfies all the above tests transfers to the assignee, from the date of the notice to the debtor:

- the legal right to the debt or other chose in action;
- all legal and other remedies for the recovery of the debt or the enforcement of the chose in action; and
- the power to give a good discharge without involving the assignor.

This is not to say that an assignment that fails any of the above tests is invalid: rather, it is likely to operate as an equitable assignment.[3] For a lender, however, an assignment which is only equitable, rather than legal, has two potential disadvantages. First, the lender cannot give a good discharge for the debt (for example, a receipt for a settled insurance claim) without the

227

agreement of the borrower (though an assignee is frequently given a general power to settle insurance claims without reference to the assignor, at least in a default situation). Secondly, he cannot sue the debtor (for example, a charterer) without joining the borrower into the action, either as a joint-claimant or (if the borrower will not cooperate) as a defendant, both of which are potentially cumbersome. Neither of these two disadvantages is insurmountable, and any assignment will in any event always be equitable as regards any future rights assigned, but a full, legal assignment is preferable where possible.

Statutory requirements

In writing, signed by the assignor

This requirement is self-explanatory. No particular form is required, though in ship finance transactions a formal deed is generally used to ensure that there is no risk of the assignment not being contractually binding for lack of consideration. Note that there is no statutory requirement for signature by the assignee. It is important, however, always to check (so far as it is practicable to do so) that the benefits which are being assigned are freely assignable and that, for example, consent to assign is not required. If the benefits are not freely assignable and any requisite consent is not obtained, there is a risk that the assignment will be completely ineffective.[4]

Absolute and not by way of charge

It should not matter that the assignment is, as in the normal ship finance situation, taken as, in effect, security for the repayment of a loan, so long as the assignment itself is clearly absolute.[5] Care must, however, be taken to look at all the surrounding circumstances and the precise terms of the assignment. For example, an assignment that appears on its face to be absolute may be held not to be so if it reserves certain rights over the assigned property to the assignor.[6] On the other hand, so long as the assignment is itself absolute, it does not matter that it is taken on terms that there will be a reassignment once, for example, the loan has been repaid. The crucial test is that the debtor must know, from the moment he is given notice, that he must pay the assignee.[7] He must not be required to enquire into the state of the account between the assignor and the assignee.

This should be contrasted with the situation where the assignee and the assignor have reached a separate arrangement (for example, in a facility agreement) as to how the assignee will deal with payments which it receives. That does not affect the debtor and will not prevent the assignment being absolute,[8] nor will a proviso for reassignment after a certain time, or on the happening of a certain event, though it must be remembered that the debtor is entitled to be given notice of reassignment before his obligation to pay the assignee ends.[9]

Notice to the debtor

Subject to any additional requirements imposed by the underlying contract, the benefit of which is being assigned, the only requirement is that the notice to the debtor must be in writing.[10] No other formality is required, nor need it be signed by either party. It can be given by assignor or assignee, and can be either in a separate document or contained in the body of an agreement to which the debtor is a party. There is no time limit in which notice must be given, so long as it is given after the assignment and before any reassignment.

The effective date of the notice, and thus of the assignment itself, is the date on which notice is received by the debtor. Ensuring receipt is therefore vital for the assignee, who will be well advised to adopt a policy, wherever possible, of personal delivery of notices of assignment, unless the notice is being given to a debtor of undoubted repute. If a debtor ignores a notice of assignment and pays the assignor, he can be compelled to make a second payment to the assignee.[11] Notices of assignment will often call for acknowledgement by the debtor that he has received the notice and will make payments to the assignee: although of useful evidential value in the event of a dispute with the debtor, this is not strictly necessary.

Although there are no legal time limits for giving notice of assignment, a lender will normally wish to give notice to insurers as soon as funds have been advanced to the borrower. Imagine the consequences for the lender if the vessel were to be destroyed by fire the day after drawdown, when the lender's solicitor had filed the notice of assignment in his pending tray. Notice of assignment of earnings may not always be given so promptly, for reasons that will be explained below.

As more than one assignment of a particular chose in action can exist at any given time, and as priority between assignments, whether legal or equitable, will normally be governed by the order in which written notice is given to the debtor (unless the second assignee, at the time of taking his assignment, knew of the first assignment), prompt giving of notice of assignment is also important to prevent a subsequent assignee obtaining priority.[12] Any further assignment by the borrower of the vessel's earnings, insurances or requisition compensation without the consent of the lender will, almost invariably, be an event of default, though this may be a case of closing the stable door after the horse has bolted.

It is important also to remember that the assignment, to be a valid legal assignment under Section 136, must be of the whole of the chose in action. Part only of a debt cannot be legally assigned as this would amount to a charge only,[13] though an outstanding balance can.

The assignment of insurances

Aside from the general rules in Section 136 of the Law of Property Act 1925, the assignment of a marine insurance policy is expressly dealt with by the Marine Insurance Act 1906. A marine insurance policy (or, strictly speaking, a 'contract of marine insurance') is defined in that Act as 'a contract whereby the insurer undertakes to indemnify the assured ... against marine losses, that is to say, the losses incident to marine adventure'.[14]

It is not the purpose of this chapter to look closely at the principal types of marine insurance, which are dealt with in detail in Chapter 12, but simply to note that all of the types of insurance normally assigned to a lender will be contracts of marine insurance for the purposes of the 1906 Act, if they are governed by English law.

Section 50 of the 1906 Act provides that a marine policy is assignable, unless assignment is expressly prohibited by the terms of the policy, either before or after loss. Where a policy is assigned and the whole beneficial interest passes to the assignee, the assignee is entitled to sue on the policy in his own name, and the insurer is entitled to take any defence against the assignee which he could have taken against the insured. There is no set form of assignment, though the established practice of the London market (as reflected in the Institute Time Clauses) is to require notice of assignment to be signed by the assignor (the insured).

A standard insurance assignment, using a definition of 'insurances' along the lines of that set out at the beginning of this chapter, will operate as a legal assignment of all insurances in being when the assignment is made, and an equitable assignment of all future insurances covered by the terms of the assignment.

An important example of a marine insurance where assignment is normally expressly prohibited is the P&I club entry (see Chapter 12). Here, the insurance will be subject to the rules and regulations of the club in question which will generally prohibit assignment without consent, which is rarely, if ever, given to an assignment to a lender. Nevertheless, clubs and their managers will generally acknowledge assignments to lenders and will agree, by reason of the assignment, not to terminate the vessel's entry. The terms of the loss payable clause and letter of undertaking on offer (see below) will, however, be more limited in scope than those available in the hull market, though this is partly a reflection of the nature of P&I insurance as insurance of third-party liabilities.

A lender will always make it a condition precedent to his loan that he be satisfied as to the insurance cover that will be in place from drawdown. He will require acceptable letters of undertaking from the relevant brokers and clubs as soon as possible after drawdown. Again, the terms of, and reasons for, the letters of undertaking are discussed in detail in Chapter 12. Additionally, a lender will also take from the borrower an undertaking to have endorsed on the policy, or P&I club certificate of entry, a loss payable clause. This sets out the terms on which insurance claims are to be paid as between the owner and the lender. The Annex to this chapter contains typical specimens of a notice of assignment, loss payable clauses and letters of undertaking.

Fleet cover

One important point for a lender is to check whether any of the vessels against the security of which he is lending is covered by any form of fleet insurance (that is, as opposed to being the subject of a separate insurance in its own right). If the vessel is insured under any form of fleet cover, the insurers may well have the right, under the terms of the policy, to set-off claims in respect of any of the insured vessels against premiums outstanding in respect of any of the vessels covered by the fleet policy. The risk to the lender is that the benefit of an insurance assigned to him can be substantially reduced because the owner is behind with premiums due in respect of other vessels in his fleet in which the lender has no interest. A lender will, therefore, generally require the vessels against which he lends to be separately insured, unless the insurers are prepared to give acceptable undertakings not to exercise rights of set-off in respect of other vessels.

Joint insurance

An alternative to an assignment which is sometimes proposed is for the vessel to be insured in the joint names of owner and mortgagee. There is no problem about the mortgagee's insurable interest – that is conferred on him expressly by Section 14(1) of the Marine Insurance Act 1906.

230

Joint insurance gives the mortgagee a degree of control over the terms of the cover and of any changes in cover. This advantage is, however, outweighed by the fact that joint insurance will generally place on the mortgagee a liability for unpaid premiums. As a result, joint insurance is rarely acceptable to lenders and, in any event, will often be resisted by owners.

Most assignments of insurances contain an express acknowledgement by the owners that the mortgagees are not, by reason of the assignment, to be liable for premiums. As, under English law, only rights, and not obligations, can be transferred by assignment (as opposed to novation with the consent of the debtor) this is probably not strictly necessary, but it is accepted practice to spell it out.

The assignment of reinsurances

Occasionally, the vessel's insurances will be placed through a state-owned insurance company or through the owner's own captive insurer. In either of these cases, a lender is likely to be concerned about the ability of the insurers to satisfy claims. He will normally insist on the cover being reinsured in an acceptable market on satisfactory terms and will require the primary insurer to assign the benefit of the reinsurances to the lender. The principles governing the assignment of reinsurance are identical to those that apply to the assignment of insurances, save only that the wording of the loss payable clause and the reinsurer's letter of undertaking will be slightly different. A lender in this position will also wish to ensure that the reinsurance documents contain a cut-through clause.[15]

The assignment of earnings

The principal source of earnings for the owner of a commercial vessel will be sums payable to the owner for the use of the vessel by charterers. It is these earnings to which a lender will normally primarily look as the source of repayment of his loan and interest. Charterparties fall into three basic categories:

- the voyage charterparty, where the ship is let to the charterer for as long as it takes to carry out a specified voyage, or perhaps series of voyages, with the charterer paying a sum known as freight, either set as a lump sum or calculated by reference to the size of cargo carried;
- the time charterparty, where the ship is let to the charterer for a set period of time (or, more usually, within a fairly narrow range of times), with the charterer paying hire, usually at a daily rate during the charter period; or
- the demise or bareboat charterparty which is essentially a species of long-term time charter where the charterer hires literally the 'bare boat' and (unlike the standard voyage or time charterparty) is responsible for the entire operation of the vessel during the charter period, including the provision of crew and the insurance of the vessel.

Voyage charters, time charters and bareboat charters will often be on the standard Baltic and International Maritime Counsel Uniform General Charter (BIMCO)[16] which, in most cases, will be supplemented by a range of additional clauses. Additionally, certain types of cargo call for specific types of charter, and a wide range of standard forms exist for oil, grain, coal and other cargoes. The major oil companies also tend to have their own particular standard forms.

As we have seen, in addition to the freights and hires payable under charterparties, the standard definition of earnings will also include other, largely one-off, payments, that an owner may receive out of the operation of the vessel, for example damages payable to the owner for breach of a charterparty, and any money that may be paid to the owner as a result of the vessel having rendered salvage or towage services to another vessel. These are obviously not reliable sources of income, and certainly should not be taken into account by a lender in making his assessment of the likely operating income of a vessel.

In the ordinary course, a lender will be unlikely to give notice of assignment to a voyage charterer or a short-term time charterer. This is because the owner will require the freight and hire income to pay the vessel's running expenses, and lenders generally will not wish to become too closely involved in the vessel's day-to-day management (unless there is concern about the owner's financial position). Indeed, a lender may be persuaded specifically to agree not to give notice unless an event of default has occurred. Unless notice is given, charterers will be entitled to pay freights and hires to the owner, though, as a matter of practice, lenders will probably require them to be paid to an account with the lender, as a means of monitoring the vessel's income.

With a long-term time or bareboat charter, however, notice will normally be given from the outset to convert the assignment into a full legal assignment. In these situations, the mortgage will generally require the mortgagee's consent to be given before the owner can enter into the charterparty, and the mortgagee's consent will normally be conditional on obtaining certain undertakings from the charterer. These will include:

- an undertaking to pay the hire to the mortgagee, free of set-off or counterclaim;
- an acknowledgement of the existence of the mortgage and a general subordination of the charterer's rights against the vessel to the rights of the mortgagee; and
- an acknowledgement that, in the event of a default by the owner towards the mortgagee, the mortgagee may terminate the charterparty and deal with the vessel free of it.

Whether a charterer is prepared to accept these terms will be a matter for commercial negotiation, but a mortgagee should insist on them, so far as possible. Otherwise, he risks seeing his right to receive hire or to enforce his mortgage in a default situation frustrated by the acts of the charterer.

Where the charterparty is a bareboat charter, a lender will ideally also require the owner and the charterer to join in a tripartite agreement with the lender. In this agreement, in addition to the undertakings taken from time charterers, the bareboat charterer will assign to the mortgagee all his interest in the vessel's insurances and earnings under sub-charterparties, and will give the lender covenants with regard to the endorsement of loss payable clauses on policies in like terms to those given by the owner. Often, such a tripartite agreement will contain a general undertaking by the bareboat charterer to be bound by all the obligations of the owner under the mortgage, with the exception only of the covenants to repay the loan and to pay interest. Where the tripartite agreement contains an assignment by the charterer, the same legal requirements will, of course, apply as to the owner's assignment, and appropriate notices of assignment will need to be given.

Again, whether these terms are commercially acceptable to a bareboat charterer will be a matter of negotiation. Some charterers may seek undertakings from the mortgagee not to interfere with the charterer's operation of the vessel. Given that the management and control of the vessel will pass to the charterer for the duration of the charterparty, and that the hire will be assigned to the lender as his source of repayment, a lender will normally wish to run fairly close credit checks on a bareboat charterer. In fact, it is often the case that although the owner is the nominal borrower, the charterer is the true borrower, on whom the primary credit risk lies.

Assuming, as is often the case, that they are in place at the time (or will be in place from drawdown) both bareboat and long-term time charters will be expressly mentioned in facility agreements and a specific assignment of their benefits in favour of the mortgagee will be taken. Although probably not strictly necessary if a wide definition of earnings is used, it helps concentrate the minds of the parties on what will be an important element of the deal. Express reference to the charterparty in the facility agreement will also remove from the borrower the uncertainty that the lender will refuse to approve the charter. It also offers the lender advantages in that it ensures the charterparty contains no restriction on assignment by the owner, and permits the charterer to be tied into appropriate agreements and undertakings before the loan is advanced.

As mentioned above, however, it remains the case that, if the charterer is excused from performance towards the owner, he will also be excused from performance towards the lender/assignee, unless he has given a direct undertaking (effectively a guarantee) to the lender. For this reason, lenders will frequently insist on bareboat charters being on a 'hell and high water' basis; in other words on terms that hire will continue to be payable in just about every conceivable circumstance, even if the bareboat charterer is deprived of the use of the vessel.

Earnings and retention accounts

A lender will often take from a borrower a covenant to pay the earnings of the mortgaged vessel into a specific account with the lender. This account may be specifically secured in favour of the lender (though see Chapter 9 for discussion of some of the difficulties with this type of security) as security for the repayment of the loan. In any event, the lender will normally have both a contractual lien on it granted by his facility agreement and an implied lien at common law.

Facility agreements will frequently specify in some detail how sums standing to the credit of earnings accounts (sometimes known as 'operating accounts') are to be applied. Normally, the borrower will need the day-to-day running expenses of the vessel paid first, while the lender's primary interest is in ensuring the repayment of the loan and the payment of interest. This is very much a matter for negotiation, but it is worth remembering that the lender has a vested interest in ensuring the continued operation of the vessel to generate the earnings to service the loan.

Where earnings or operating accounts are used, the lender will normally require the borrower to make regular (usually monthly) transfers of funds from the earnings account into a retention account. The amount to be transferred monthly will be calculated as the amount of the next due instalment of principal, divided by the number of months between instalment repayment dates, plus the amount of interest due for the current interest period divided by the number of months in that interest period. For example, if the principal were repayable every six months and the current interest period was of three months, the monthly transfers to the retention account would be one-sixth of the next instalment of principal and one-third of the next interest payment. Other periodic payments (such as guarantee commission) may also be required to be transferred and built up in this way.

As mentioned above, whether or not the borrower is allowed to withdraw operating expenses from the earnings account before the transfers to the retention account are made is very much a matter for negotiation. Otherwise, after transfers to the retention account, sums standing to the credit of an earnings account are generally released to the borrower, though sometimes a minimum balance will be required to be maintained or further transfers made to another reserve, perhaps on account of future repairs to the ship.

The facility agreement will usually give the lender express authority to apply the balance of the retention account towards repayment of the loan or payment of interest, making clear that, if the balance is insufficient to meet the borrower's obligations, those obligations remain unaffected and must be satisfied from other sources. Normally, repayment instalments will be calculated with a view to their being met from the retention account, often leaving a final balloon repayment, significantly larger than the others, to be repaid either from the sale of the vessel or by refinancing.

A retention account will invariably be secured in favour of the lender, and will normally bear interest at commercial rates. Again, it is a matter for negotiation whether any surplus arising in the retention account (for example, by the application of interest) after application towards repayment and interest payment, is to be released to the borrower or retained in the retention account on account of the next transfers of earnings, thus building up a reserve against future failure to generate sufficient earnings to make the required transfers.

Requisition compensation

In wartime, states often assume power, either by statute or in the exercise of royal or executive prerogative, to acquire vessels compulsorily, either to assist in the war effort as troop carriers or to ensure the continued supply of essential goods to the country concerned. This requisition can be of two types: requisition for title, and requisition for hire. The distinction is self-explanatory. If a vessel is requisitioned for title, the state assumes the outright ownership of the vessel. If requisitioned for hire, the state effectively compels the owner to charter the vessel to the state or a state agency.

In both cases, compensation will generally be payable to the vessel's owner, often fixed by a tribunal following a set formula.[17] As the vessel will have been removed from the control of the borrower, the lender will want to receive that compensation on account of his loan. Hire paid under requisition for hire will normally be covered by the general definition of earnings, but compensation for requisition for title will not, hence the separate definition normally used. It is important that, as soon as a lender receives notice of any requisition, he should give notice of assignment to the state agency by which the compensation will become payable in order to perfect his assignment. Although requisition is rare, a lender should not ignore the possibility completely. We have seen in recent years that some of the major open registry states do not enjoy the greatest of political stability, and, as recently as 1982, certain British ships became liable to requisition during the Falklands conflict.[18]

Requisition is not covered by the standard war risk terms available on the London market (Institute War and Strikes Clauses 1 October 1983) and therefore not caught by the assignment of insurances.

Registration

An assignment of insurances, earnings and requisition compensation is generally considered eligible for registration under Section 395 of the Companies Act 1985 (see Chapter 2) as creating a security interest on book debts of the assignor, if the assignor is incorporated in England and Wales or has a place of business here. In the event, however, that the assignor is incorporated in a jurisdiction other than England and Wales, it is advisable in view of the decision in *NV Slavenburg's Bank v Intercontinental National Resources Limited and others*[19] that such assignments be registered. Consideration should also be given to the question of registration in any other relevant jurisdiction – normally the jurisdiction where the owner is incorporated or carries on business.

---

[1] *Pan Ocean Shipping Ltd v Creditcorp Ltd* [1994] 1 All ER 470.

[2] See *Raiffeison Zentralbank Osterreich AG v Fire Star General Trading LLC* and others [2001] 3 All ER 257, in relation to circumstances when an assignment of insurances will be considered an equitable assignment as opposed to a legal assignment.

[3] *Raiffeison Zentralbank Osterreich AG v Fire Star General Trading LLC* and others [2001] 3 All ER 257.

[4] See *Linden Gardens Trust Ltd v Lenesta Sludge Disposals Ltd* [1994] AC 85, though also *Orion Finance Ltd v Crown Financial Management Ltd* [1994] 2 BCLC 607, where an assignment in breach of a prohibition was held effective when the debtor received and acknowledged notice of the assignment without raising any objection to it.

[5] *Hughes v Pump House Hotel Co Ltd* [1902] 2 KB 190.

[6] *Mercantile Bank of London v Evans* [1899] 2 QB 613.

[7] There is authority (*Gatoil Anstalt v Omennial Ltd* [1980] 2 Lloyd's Rep. 489) that notice of assignment which provided that the charterer could continue to pay hire to the assignor until notice to the contrary from the assignee failed to comply with section 136 Law of Property Act, though the logic of this is difficult to follow.

[8] *Comfort v Betts* [1891] 1 QB 737.

[9] *Tancred v Delagoa Bay and East Africa Railway Co.* [1889] 23 QBD 239.

[10] Section 136 Law of Property Act 1925.

[11] *Brice v Bannister* [1878] 3 QBD 569.

[12] *Dearle v Hall* [1828] 3 Russ 1.

[13] *Mercantile Bank of London v Evans* [1899] 2 QB 613.

[14] Section 1 Marine Insurance Act 1906.

[15] See Chapter 12.

[16] BIMCO standard form documents are available from www.bimco.dk.

[17] For example, in the UK during the Second World War under the Compensation (Defence) Act 1939.

[18] Requisition of Ships Order 1982.

[19] [1980]1 All ER 955 *NV Slavenburg's Bank v Intercontinental Natural Resources Ltd and others.*

Annex

Notice of assignment

(For attachment by way of endorsement to all policies, contracts and cover notes)

We, [*Name of Owner*] of [*Address of Owner*], the owners of the m.v. '[*Name of Vessel*]' GIVE NOTICE that, by an assignment in writing dated [ ], we assigned to [*Name of Assignee*] acting through its branch at [*Address of Assignee*], all our rights, title and interest in and to all insurances effected or to be effected in respect of the above vessel, including the insurances constituted by the policy on which this notice is endorsed, and including all monies payable and to become payable thereunder or in connection therewith (including returns of premium).

Signed
For and on behalf of
[*Name of Owner*]

Dated: [ ]

Loss payable clause

(Hull and machinery)

It is noted that, by an assignment in writing collateral to a first preferred mortgage dated [ ] ('the Mortgage') [*Name of Owner*] of [*Address of Owner*] ('the Owner'), owner of the vessel '[*Name of Vessel*]' ('the Vessel'), assigned absolutely to [*Name of Assignee*] acting through its branch at [*Address of Assignee*] ('the Mortgagee'), this policy and all benefits of this policy, including all claims of any nature (including return of premiums) hereunder.

Claims payable under this policy in respect of a total or constructive total or an arranged or agreed or compromised total loss or unrepaired damage, and all claims which (in the opinion of the Mortgagee) are analogous thereto, shall be payable to the Mortgagee up to the Mortgagee's mortgage interest.

Subject thereto, all other claims, unless and until underwriters have received notice from the Mortgagee of a default under the Mortgage, in which event all claims under this policy shall be payable directly to the Mortgagee up to the Mortgagee's mortgage interest, shall be payable as follows:

(i) a claim in respect of any one casualty where the aggregate claim against all insurers does not exceed FIVE HUNDRED THOUSAND UNITED STATES DOLLARS (US$500,000) or the equivalent in any other currency, prior to adjustment for any franchise or deductible under the terms of the policy, shall be paid directly to the Owner for the repair, salvage or other charges involved or as a reimbursement if the Owner has fully repaired the damage and paid all of the salvage or other charges;

(ii) a claim in respect of any one casualty where the aggregate claim against all insurers exceeds FIVE HUNDRED THOUSAND UNITED STATES DOLLARS (US$500,000) or the equivalent in any other currency prior to adjustment for any franchise or deductible under the terms of the policy, shall, subject to the prior written consent of the Mortgagee, be paid to the Owner as and when the vessel is restored to her former state and condition and the liability in respect of which the insurance loss is payable is discharged, and provided that the insurers may with such consent make payment on account of repairs in the course of being effected, but in the absence of such prior written consent shall be payable directly to the Mortgagee up to the Mortgagee's mortgage interest.

Insurer's letter of undertaking
Lloyd's brokers

[Name of Assignee]
[Address of Assignee]

Date:

Dear Sirs,

m.v. '[*Name of Vessel*]' – [*Name of Owner*]

We confirm that we have effected insurances for the account of the above owners as set out in Appendix 'A' attached.

Pursuant to instructions received from the above owners and/or their authorised managers or agents, and in consideration of you approving us as the appointed brokers in connection with the insurances covered by this letter, we hereby undertake:

1 to hold the insurance slips or contracts, the policies when issued, and any renewals of such policies or new policies or any policies substituted therefor with your consent as may be arranged through ourselves and the benefit of the insurances thereunder to your order in accordance with the terms of the loss payable clause(s) set out in Appendix 'B' attached; and

2 to arrange for the said loss payable clause (s) to be included on the policies when issued; and

3 to have endorsed on each and every policy as and when the same is issued a notice of assignment in the form of Appendix 'C' hereto dated and signed by the owners and acknowledged by underwriters in accordance with market practice; and

4 to advise you promptly if we cease to be the broker for the assured or in the event of any material changes of which we are aware affecting the said insurance;

5 following a written application received from you not later than one month before expiry of these insurances to notify you within 14 days of the receipt of such application in the event of our not having received notice of renewal instructions from the owners and/or their authorised managers or agents, and in the event of our receiving instructions to renew to advise you promptly of the details thereof;

6 to forward to you promptly any notices of cancellation that we receive from Underwriters; and

7 following a written application from you to advise you promptly of the premium payment situation where such premium is paid or payable through our intermediary.

If and where we are responsible for the payment of premium to Underwriters, our above undertakings are given subject to our lien on the policies for premiums and subject to our right of cancellation on default in payment of such premiums, but we undertake not to exercise such right of cancellation without giving you 10 days' notice in writing, either by letter or electronically transmitted message, and a reasonable opportunity for you to pay any premiums outstanding.

It is understood and agreed that the operation of any automatic termination of cover, cancellation or amendment provisions contained in the policy conditions shall override any undertakings given by us as brokers.

Notwithstanding the terms of the said loss payable clause(s) and the said notice of assignment, unless and until we receive written notice from you to the contrary, we shall be empowered to arrange our proportion of any collision and/or salvage guarantee to be given in the event of bail being required in order to prevent the arrest of the vessel or to secure the release of the vessel from arrest following a casualty. Where a guarantee has been given as aforesaid and the guarantor has paid any sum under the guarantee in respect of such claim, there shall be payable directly to the guarantor out of the proceeds of the said policies a sum equal to the sum so paid.

This undertaking shall be governed by and construed in accordance with English law and any disputes arising out of or in any way connected with this undertaking shall be submitted to the exclusive jurisdiction of the English courts.

This undertaking is subject to all claims and returns of premiums being collected through us as brokers.

Yours faithfully

Mutual insurance association letter of undertaking

[Name of Assignee]
[Address of Assignee]

Date:

Dear Sirs,

m.v. '*[Name of Vessel]*' – *[Name of Owner]*

We acknowledge receipt of a letter from [ ] dated [ ] enclosing notice of assignment to you dated [ ] of the insurances on the above ship. So far as this Association is concerned, the managers do not consent to such assignment for the purposes of Rule 42 other than to give efficacy to the loss payable clause set out below and subject always to the Association's rights under Rule 42(2) in setting any claim presented by the assignee to deduct or retain such amount as the managers may then estimate to be sufficient to discharge the assignor's liabilities (if any) to the Association, whether existing at the time of the assignment or having accrued or being likely to accrue subsequently.

We do confirm, however, that the above ship is entered in this Association for protection and indemnity risks on the terms and conditions set out or to be set out in the certificate of entry. Furthermore, in consideration of your agreeing to the entry or continuing entry of the ship in this Association, the managers agree:

(a) that the owner shall not cease to be insured by the Association in respect of that ship by reason of such assignment; and

(b) that, notwithstanding the ship is mortgaged to you and that no undertaking or guarantee has been given to the Association to pay all contributions due in respect of such ship, the owner does not cease to be insured by reason of the operation of Rule 37(4).

It is further agreed that the following loss payable clause will be included in the certificate of entry:

'Payment of any recovery the owner is entitled to make out of the funds of the Association in respect of any liability, costs or expenses incurred by him shall be made to the owner or to his order unless and until the Association receives notice from [*Name of Assignee*] as mortgagees to the contrary, in which event all recoveries shall thereafter be paid to [*Name of Assignee*] or its order, provided always that no liability whatsoever shall attach to the Association, its managers or their agents for failure to comply with the latter obligation until after the expiry of two clear business days from the receipt of such notice.'

The Association undertakes:

(a) to inform you if the managers give the owner of the above ship notice under Rules 11(3) and 36(1) that his insurance in the Association in respect of such ship is to cease within or at the end of the then current policy year; and

(b) to give you 14 days' notice of the Association's intention to cancel the insurance of the owner by reason of his failure to pay when due and demanded any sum due from him to the Association.

Yours faithfully,

Chapter 9

Other security

Updated by Sheila Obhrai

Introduction

As already noted, it is highly unusual for a lender to rely for security solely on a mortgage over the ship, or ships, in respect of which it is lending. As well as the assignment of insurances, earnings and requisition compensation discussed in Chapter 8, a lender will normally wish to take any one or more of the following:

- a guarantee and indemnity, usually from the parent company or ultimate beneficial owner of the borrower;
- security over the assets of a guarantor, perhaps by way of mortgages over other ships;
- security over a cash deposit or bank account balances, either with the lender or a third party;
- a charge on or pledge of the shares in the borrowing company; and
- a general debenture over the assets of the borrowing company.

Lenders will often also look for other security peculiar to the specific transaction, for example, assignments of the benefit of certain contracts, or assignments of inter-company indebtedness. In newbuilding finance, standard security will normally include an assignment of the borrower's rights under the building contract and an assignment of any refund guarantee.[1]

The guarantee and indemnity

Unless the borrower is a substantial company in its own right, which is relatively uncommon in ship finance transactions, or the lender is prepared, in effect, to limit its recourse purely to the vessel(s) being financed, a lender will normally wish to take a guarantee and indemnity from a third party. Occasionally, this may be from a party unconnected with the borrower or the transaction, which, unless the guarantor is a bank, raises awkward legal issues. Most commonly, because of the use of one shipowning company, the guarantor will be either the parent, or an associated, company of the borrower or will be the individual or individuals who are the ultimate beneficial owners of the shares of the borrower. The latter is of particular significance when lending to owning groups where an individual, or perhaps members of a family, exercise a substantial controlling influence over the fortunes of a number of one-ship companies. The former is more important where the parent company is in diverse ownership, or where it has substantial assets in its own right. Where the fortunes of the borrowing company are controlled by one or more individuals, lenders will often insist on personal guarantees even when they know that the guarantor is likely to have put his assets out of their reach, if only to exert some sort of hold on the guarantor and to ensure his continuing involvement in the future of the vessel financed. Few individuals, even those whose assets have been hidden away, like to face the prospect of bankruptcy which will be the lender's ultimate weapon (though rarely used, unless there is some element of fraud or bad faith) against a defaulting guarantor.

Apart from obvious distinctions between personal and impersonal terms ('he' and 'his' as opposed to 'it' and 'its'), and between concepts such as bankruptcy (for individuals) and liquidation and administration (for companies), there are no substantial differences in form between guarantees and indemnities given by individuals, and those given by companies, though there are some technical legal points that need to be looked at carefully where the guarantor is a company, particularly one incorporated in England and Wales or any other jurisdiction with similar company and insolvency legislation. These will be looked at more closely later.

The law relating to guarantees in England is complex, and guarantees need to be carefully drafted. Over many years, English law has tried hard to protect guarantors, with the result that there are now many circumstances where actions taken by a lender vis-à-vis the borrower could, unless the guarantee is carefully drafted, absolve the guarantor from liability. Detailed discussion of these can be found in specialist banking law textbooks, but the following should be borne in mind when taking guarantees.

- Although it is common to refer generically to 'guarantees', the lender should ensure that its document contains both guarantee and indemnity wording. The distinction is that a guarantee in the strict sense is a secondary or collateral obligation, only enforceable if and to the extent that the principal obligation (that is, that of the borrower) is enforceable. For example, if the borrower's obligations under the underlying facility agreement were held to be beyond the corporate powers of the borrower, a guarantee taken purely as a guarantee would also fall away. On the other hand, an indemnity is a primary obligation, independent of the continuing enforceability of the borrower's obligation, and is effectively a separate undertaking by the guarantor to perform the borrower's obligations if the borrower fails to do so. A sample guarantee and indemnity wording follows (with appropriate definitions contained elsewhere in the document for the terms 'Borrower's Obligations' and 'Interest'):

'Guarantee and indemnity

In consideration of the agreement of the Bank to make the Loan available to the Borrower, the Guarantor:
(a) irrevocably and unconditionally guarantees to discharge on demand the Borrower's Obligations, together with Interest from the date of demand until the date of payment, both before and after judgment; and
(b) agrees, as a separate and independent obligation, that, if any of the Borrower's Obligations are not recoverable from the Guarantor under paragraph (a) of this Clause for any reason, the Guarantor will be liable to the Bank as a principal debtor by way of indemnity for the same amount as that for which he would have been liable had those Borrower's Obligations been recoverable and agrees to discharge his liability

under this Clause on demand together with Interest from the date of demand until the date of payment, both before and after judgment.'

- A guarantee is a contract, and so subject to all the basic rules for formation of contracts, such as the need for a valid offer and acceptance and an intention to create legal relations, but, unlike most ordinary contracts, a guarantee must be in writing and signed by the guarantor. This is an obvious practical point, but it is also a legal requirement and has been under English law since 1677.[2] Frequently, a guarantee and indemnity is executed as a deed, though this is not strictly necessary. It avoids any argument about past consideration if, as is sometimes the case, it is executed after the loan agreement.

- Unless expressly excluded by the terms of the guarantee (which it always will be, if the guarantee is properly drafted), any release or variation or re-scheduling of the obligations of the borrower will potentially release the guarantor from liability. Even if this risk is excluded by the guarantee wording, it is good practice to obtain the express consent of the guarantor to any variation, however minor, of the underlying facility.

- It is essential to specify precisely what the guarantee covers. Ideally the guarantor should be contingently liable for everything for which the borrower could conceivably be liable under the underlying facility: principal, interest, costs, indemnity liabilities and so on, together with interest on the total from the date of the lender's demand on the guarantor for payment. The lender may agree that the total amount ultimately recoverable from the guarantor will be limited, but should not limit the scope (as opposed to the amount) of the guarantor's liabilities.

- It is important to make a demand by the lender a condition of the guarantor's liability, in the same way as a notice or demand should be required to accelerate the loan following an event of default under the underlying facility. If the guarantee does not provide that it is on demand, the limitation period for beginning any legal action under the guarantee will run from the date of execution of the guarantee, not the date of demand, and could easily expire before the end of the term of the loan.[3]

- A lender must bear in mind that equity allows any guarantor, at least of ongoing obligations, to terminate his obligations by giving the lender reasonable notice. The effect of giving notice is to crystallise the guarantor's obligations at the date of giving notice (or, arguably, the date of expiry of the notice). Few guarantors, particularly personal guarantors of one-ship companies, will wish to do this, but lenders should not forget that they may have the right to do so. It is worth making it an event of default under the underlying facility if notice of termination is received, so that the lender, if it wishes, can exercise all its other default rights, for example, against the vessel, if the guarantor is not in a position, having terminated the guarantee, to satisfy his obligations.

- Guarantees should contain express provisions restricting the right of the guarantor to compete with the lender in claiming against the borrower. A guarantor who has paid the lender will be subrogated to the rights of the lender against the borrower to the extent of his payment. If the guarantor has paid only part of the outstanding indebtedness, the lender will not want to have to compete against the guarantor in, for example, a liquidation of the borrower. Similarly, the lender will want the right to keep any amounts received from the guarantor in a separate account in order to enable it to maximise its dividend by proving for the full amount of the outstanding indebtedness in a liquidation of the borrower.

The above list is by no means exhaustive and contains only some of the important matters to be borne in mind by lenders taking a guarantee and indemnity. Having in mind the particular importance of the guarantee in the context of lending to one-ship companies, a lending bank should always be guided by its legal advisers as to the terms of guarantees and indemnities no less than of loan agreements.

However, including all the right terms in a guarantee and indemnity is not the end of the matter. A lender must also be careful about the circumstances in which it actually obtains the execution of a personal guarantee. The last 15 years have seen a series of cases in the English courts where guarantees, as well as other security documents, have been set aside because of the circumstances in which they were executed.[4] Most of these cases arose where unsophisticated individuals executed guarantees or other security documents on bank standard forms without (they said) appreciating the nature or extent of what they were signing. Most of the personal guarantors involved in shipping finance will, however, be relatively sophisticated businessmen who will generally be given an advance opportunity to consider the terms of the guarantee prior to execution. Ship finance lenders can derive some comfort from the decision in *Union Bank of Finland v Lelakis*,[5] where the English High Court held that a bank owed no duty of care to advise an experienced shipowner, advised by an in-house lawyer, to seek independent legal advice on the terms of a proposed personal guarantee. However, this should not make the lender complacent. There remains the risk that the guarantor will seek to attack the guarantee on the grounds of undue influence, misrepresentation or non-disclosure of a material fact. At the very least, a lender should give a personal guarantor an opportunity to take independent legal advice on the terms and effect of the guarantee and, if he declines to do so, should obtain a signed statement from the guarantor acknowledging that, having been given that opportunity, he has declined it and is fully aware of the nature and extent of the document which he is executing. If the guarantor does take independent legal advice, the solicitor giving that advice should be required to certify to the bank that he or she has explained to the guarantor the implications of signing the guarantee. Additionally, the code of banking practice in the United Kingdom makes it obligatory for personal guarantees and other third-party security documents to contain prominent 'health warnings' putting the guarantor on notice of what he is undertaking. The latest revision to the code requires these to indicate whether or not the guarantor's obligations are limited or unlimited and, if limited, what the limit is.

Corporate guarantees and indemnities present their own problems. In many ship finance transactions, guarantees will be given by companies incorporated in jurisdictions other than England and Wales, and it is imperative that lenders take appropriate local legal advice to ensure that the guarantor has the corporate capacity to give guarantees and indemnities and to ensure that all necessary formalities (for example, shareholder approvals, exchange control consents) are satisfied.

Where the corporate guarantor is incorporated in England and Wales (or any other jurisdiction likely to follow English law) the lender must consider the following.

- Does the memorandum of association of the company give it power to give guarantees? If so, is that power an object in its own right or merely an ancillary power only exercisable in the furtherance of one of the company's principal objects? If the latter, is it in this particular case being exercised in furtherance of one of those objects and in the commercial interests of the company? If the lender is on notice, or has been put on enquiry, that the guarantee is not in the commercial interests of the guarantor, the guarantee could be liable to be set aside. It is important to stress that the question is whether *this* specific guarantee in *these* specific circumstances is in the commercial interests of *this* specific guarantor. It is not sufficient just to consider the commercial interests of the group of companies of which the guarantor happens to form part: it is the commercial interests of the actual guaranteeing company which are relevant. Of course, it may well be in the commercial interests of a parent company to guarantee the obligations of its subsidiary, because by doing so it presumably intends to assist the subsidiary in making enough profit to improve the dividend return to the parent. A subsidiary guaranteeing its parent company can be more problematical, unless it can be shown that some of the benefit of the loan will pass down the chain to the subsidiary. Guarantees of each others' obligations by sister companies need to be considered very carefully.

- It is generally accepted practice that the guarantor's board minutes should set out with some precision why the directors consider the guarantee to be in the interests of the company. This may at least help the lender in showing that the directors considered and reached a decision on the point. A company only holds its directors out as having ostensible authority to bind the company to transactions within the powers of the company, as expressed or implied in its memorandum of association; if a person dealing with the company is on notice that the directors are exercising the company's powers other than for the purposes of the company, he will be unable to rely on that ostensible authority and therefore unable to enforce the transaction against the company. For example, if a company's guaranteeing power can only be exercised incidentally to one of its main objects, and a lending bank is on notice from a review of the company's objects clause that the guarantee is being given other than in furtherance of those main objects, the bank will be unable to rely on the directors' ostensible authority and will most probably be unable to enforce the guarantee. Potentially, the bank may be protected by Section 35 of the Companies Act 1985 (as amended by Section 108 of the Companies Act 1989),[6] but it would be speculative to rely on this to save a guarantee which might otherwise be open to attack.

- Once these hurdles have been crossed, a lender must also consider whether the guarantee may be open to attack as a transaction at an undervalue under Sections 238, 339 or 423 of the Insolvency Act 1986. If a company enters into a transaction for a consideration the value of which is significantly less than the value of the consideration provided by the company, the transaction is liable to be set aside by a court as a transaction at an undervalue if the company goes into liquidation or administration within two years. Many corporate guarantees are given (especially to sister companies within a group) for no consideration, either in the sense of a guarantee fee or any other tangible benefit accruing to the guaranteeing company. While Section 238 (5) of the 1986 Act prevents the court from making an order setting aside the transaction if the transaction was entered into by the company in good faith, for the purpose of carrying on its business and with reasonable grounds to believe that the transaction would benefit the company, again it would be speculative to rely on obtaining relief from the court. The company's board minutes must show that the directors had reasonable grounds for believing that the transaction would benefit the company in something more than just a marginal way. It is also worth noting that Section 339 of the 1986 Act applies the transaction at an undervalue concept to individuals also. The relevant period is five, rather than two, years ending with the presentation of the bankruptcy petition if the guarantor was insolvent when entering into the guarantee or became insolvent as a result of doing so. There is no equivalent provision to Section 238 (5) for individuals, though it would be unusual in ship finance transactions for a personal guarantor not to derive benefit from the transaction, for without the guarantee the borrowing company (which will normally be beneficially owned by the personal guarantor) would be unable to avail itself of the facility. In the unlikely event that the personal guarantor had no connection with the borrower, the risk for the lender would clearly be significantly greater.

Occasionally (and perhaps increasingly), potential guarantors will decline to give formal guarantees and indemnities and, instead, offer lenders comfort letters containing, for example, assurances that the guarantor will ensure that the borrower always has sufficient assets to meet its liabilities as they fall due. Comfort letters are generally of limited value.[7] While they may be legally binding (this will in each case depend on the interpretation of the precise terms of the letter) they will not generally satisfy the strict legal requirements of a guarantee and therefore will be vulnerable in any of the situations when a guarantee would be vulnerable if not properly drafted.

If a comfort letter is the best that the lender can obtain, and the lender wishes the letter to impose a legally binding commitment, the lender must look very carefully indeed at the precise wording of the letter on offer. For example, does it contain an ongoing commitment that the lender will be able to enforce in, say, five years' time? Or does it just contain a statement of current intention or policy, which can be changed at will without constituting a breach? A contractually binding comfort letter is only of legal (as opposed to moral) value if it contains an ongoing commitment, breach of which will give the lender something to enforce.

Lastly, it is important to be aware that proceedings to enforce a claim based on a comfort letter are likely, even if the letter does contain a contractually binding commitment, to be more difficult than a guarantee or indemnity claim. A lender suing on a comfort letter will need to prove that the loss was caused by a breach by the writer of the letter of the obligations which he undertook. A lender suing on a well-drafted guarantee and indemnity should not need to prove that the guarantor was responsible for the borrower's breach.

Security over bank accounts

It goes without saying that, at least in theory, the best form of security for any lender is cash. Cash is readily realisable and usable to satisfy outstanding indebtedness, unlike security over other assets which will need to be enforced by selling or otherwise realising the asset. Similarly, cash is of an easily determinable value, give or take a foreign exchange risk or two.

Naturally, a cash deposit is rarely available as full security for a loan, otherwise, in most situations, there would be no commercial advantage to the borrower in borrowing at all. However, a cash deposit is sometimes required as partial, often short-term, security, and is commonly called for in ship-based lending as top-up security where there is a shortfall in the loan to value ratio, or to support a counter-indemnity given to enable a bank to issue a guarantee or letter of credit. Lenders will, in addition, often require earnings and retention accounts to be secured in their favour.[8]

It may well be asked why security over the deposit is required, and why the lending bank cannot simply rely on possession of it as its security. It was Walter Wriston, the former head of Citibank, who is reported to have said, in connection with the 1979 to 1980 Iranian hostage crisis that 'when you are holding the money, you make the rules', and to a certain extent that is true. However, the right of set-off which a lending bank will have under English law will be of limited value in the absence of express security over the deposit for the following principal reasons.

- The lending bank may have no right of set-off against liabilities of the borrower that are contingent or future, for example, liabilities that have not yet crystallised under a counter-indemnity given by the borrower to the bank in respect of the bank's obligations under a guarantee to a third party, and may have difficulties exercising set-off in respect of liabilities in different currencies.
- If the borrower goes into liquidation, even though the bank's set-off rights will be wider than in the pre-liquidation situation, there is still doubt, as a result of an unfortunate piece of statutory drafting in the Insolvency Act 1986, whether set-off is available against contingent liabilities, and no contractual variation of the statutory rules is permissible.
- If the bank's right of set-off does not work, the debt constituted by the deposit will form part of the borrower's estate on insolvency, and the bank will therefore have to compete with the borrower's other unsecured creditors and will not be able to apply the amount of the deposit against the indebtedness.

To guard against these risks, therefore, banks will generally wish expressly to take security over deposits or other balances.

Under English law, taking security over bank balances became a topical issue following the decision of Mr Justice Millett in the case of *Re Charge Card Services Limited.*[9] In brief, the Charge Card case decided that a deposit held by a bank could not conceptually be assigned or charged back to that bank. The reason for this was compellingly simple, if commercially inconvenient, that a deposit with a bank is, in law, a debt owed by the bank to the depositor. Therefore, the depositor's ultimate right against the bank in the event of failure by the bank to repay the deposit would not be to walk in and recover the same pound notes or dollar bills that were deposited, but to sue the bank for repayment of the debt. If that debt was assigned or charged back to the bank, the bank becomes its own debtor and, as the bank cannot sue itself, the debt is extinguished, and the security fails.

The position is different, of course, where the deposit is placed with a third party, when there is no conceptual reason whatsoever why it cannot be assigned and/or charged to the lending bank, although naturally the lending bank will in those circumstances have no right of set-off, and no right to net for capital adequacy purposes, and the third party holding the deposit may itself have rights of set-off if owed money by the depositor.

However, in 1997 the House of Lords overturned the Charge Card ruling in *Morris v Agrichemicals Ltd* (known as BCCI No. 8),[10] dismissing the conceptual impossibility principle and stating that there was no reason why a charge over a deposit should not be legally possible so that a debtor (the bank) could have a proprietary interest by way of charge over a debt he owed the chargor (the depositor). This gave clear authority that a charge-back is effective under English law to create a security interest, although if the account is a current account then the charge is likely to be floating rather than fixed because the lender is unlikely to have sufficient control over the account to constitute a fixed charge.

Notwithstanding the Charge Card case however, lenders continued to insist on taking a charge coupled with an express contractual agreement restricting the depositor's right of withdrawal (the 'flawed asset' arrangement), as well as an express contractual right to debit the deposit at any time towards satisfaction of the indebtedness. In BCCI No. 8 the law Lords confirmed that 'the flawed asset' arrangement was effective in creating security.

The judgment in Charge Card was interesting in that, after having decided that the debt constituted by the deposit could not conceptually be assigned or charged to the debtor, Mr Justice Millett went on to say that 'it does not, of course, follow that an attempt to create an express mortgage or charge of a debt in favour of the debtor would be ineffective to create a security'. In fact, what he seems to have had in mind was that the security created would be a right of set-off which would, of course, be subject to the problems we have already seen. Interestingly, in 1992 in the case of *Welsh Development Agency v Export Finance Co. Limited*,[11] Lord Justice Dillon had 'very considerable difficulty' with the idea that a book debt could not be charged to the debtor.

Although following BCCI No. 8 a charge-back is effective, it is likely that the practice of using the 'triple cocktail' combination of charge, contractual right of set-off and a flawed asset arrangement will continue although, of course, particular transactions will need to be given specific consideration to determine the most appropriate security to use. Care should be taken where the depositor is not an English entity, for example a charge-back does not work in Scotland so local advice will always need to be sought in such a situation.

Share charges and pledges

Commonly, ship finance lenders require to take a charge over, or pledge of, the shares in the borrower as additional security, and the use of one-ship companies makes this a much more readily available form of security in shipping finance than in most other areas (though arguably of less value if the lender already has security over the company's only asset). The principal advantage in taking security over the shares of the borrower is that the bank will be able, on default, to sell the vessel-owning company, rather than just the vessel itself. While this may not always be an attractive proposition–a purchaser will often insist on paying less for a company that may have unidentified liabilities than for a vessel sold at auction free of liens and encumbrances–it may equally be beneficial if, for example, a sale of the owning company rather than just the vessel allows a beneficial charter of the vessel to remain in place so that the bank obtains a better price than if the charter had had to be terminated on the sale of the vessel or following an arrest.

There are, however, a number of negative considerations. First, taking security over shares in the borrower can involve a significant amount of additional paper work. The crucial thing to remember is that the shares are not an asset of the borrowing company itself but of its shareholders. If security is to be taken over those assets, it will be necessary to investigate the corporate powers of corporate shareholders, and to take board minutes, possibly powers of attorney and so on. If the shareholders are incorporated in a different jurisdiction from the borrowers, it may also be necessary to obtain additional legal opinions.

Secondly, there is continuing concern that holding shares by way of security will increase the risk of a lender being liable as an operator or even as the true owner of the vessel for the purposes of the United States Oil Pollution Act 1990. While the perceived wisdom is that a mere holding of a security interest in the shares will not involve the bank in liability, at least in the absence of default and exercise of its security rights, the position cannot be guaranteed. In the same way, if a borrower is incorporated in a jurisdiction to which the Insolvency Act 1986 or any similar legislation applies, there must be some (probably small) risk that a lender taking security over the shares will be considered a shadow director.

There can frequently be a degree of confusion between the use of the expressions 'share pledge' and 'share charge'. In fact, the distinction is straightforward. A pledge is the appropriate form of security where shares are in bearer form, a charge or mortgage where shares are registered. The distinction derives from the fact that title to bearer shares passes on delivery of the share certificates while title to registered shares does not, depending on express transfer (often in a set form and sometimes subject to stamp duty) and registration.

As a form of security, a pledge depends entirely on possession of the share certificates. It is thus essential that the bank obtains possession of the certificates for all the issued shares of the company in order to perfect its security. It cannot part with possession until it is repaid without risking losing its rights as pledgee.

In contrast, a charge over registered shares does not legally depend on the bank's possession of the share certificates but, without both the certificates and the appropriate executed forms of transfer of the shares, the bank will be unable to perfect its title to the shares and to sell the shares on default. As a matter of practice, a bank will always require the borrower, as part of the charge, to deposit with the bank the certificates for all the issued shares in the company, together with executed but undated forms of transfer of the shares with the transferee's name left blank. In addition, both a chargee and a pledgee will usually require the undated resignations of all the directors of the borrower to enable the bank more easily to replace the directors with its own nominees and to manage the company in a default situation.

Apart from the requirement in a share charge for the borrower to deposit blank transfer forms, share charges and share pledges will generally contain very similar provisions. In order to ensure the efficacy of the bank's security, these will include:

- a warranty by the shareholder that the pledged or charged shares represent the whole of the authorised and issued share capital of the company and that the shares are fully paid;
- a warranty that the shares are free from encumbrances, options and so on, and a covenant not to create any encumbrances, grant any options and so on;
- usual warranties as to title;
- an undertaking to procure that the borrower issues no further shares;
- either an undertaking not to exercise voting rights in a manner inconsistent with the rights of the bank or (better from the bank's point of view) a transfer of the voting rights to the bank;
- a Power of Attorney enabling the bank on default to exercise all rights relating to the shares, to put into effect the directors' resignations and to sell the shares; and
- other standard provisions of charging documents.

One question that often causes concern to borrowers is what happens to dividends during the currency of the pledge or charge. Frequently, lending banks will be content to allow the shareholder to receive and retain dividends (perhaps subject to a cap) before an event of default, but will want to receive dividends themselves to set against the indebtedness once an event of default has occurred. This is very much a matter of negotiation between the lender, the borrower and the shareholder. Other points to bear in mind in connection with security over shares are:

- the possibility of requiring the shares to be transferred at the outset into the name of the lender's nominee company: this has both advantages (for example, the lender will be sure to receive notices relating to the shares) and disadvantages (for example, the lender may assume liabilities in relation to the shares) and with a one-ship company there is probably little to be gained;
- the constitutional documents of the company may contain restrictions on the transfer of shares (for example, pre-emption rights), and, if necessary the lender should insist on appropriate changes to the company's constitutional documents to ensure its ability to deal freely with the shares on default; and finally
- where the borrower is incorporated outside England and Wales, appropriate local legal advice must be taken not only as to the capacity of the shareholder to pledge or charge the shares but also as to the suitability of an English law security document for the purpose.

The debenture

Although a standard form of security in most domestic corporate lending, the general debenture creating a series of fixed and floating charges over all the assets of the borrower is relatively uncommon in ship finance. This is because the concept of the floating charge is rarely recognised outside common law jurisdictions, and because the typical one-ship company is unlikely to have assets other than its ship and the other assets generally caught by the mortgage and assignment.

Prior to the Enterprise Act 2002 and in the less common situation where the borrowing company is incorporated in England and Wales or Scotland, or any other jurisdiction that has provisions similar to those of the Insolvency Act 1986, the taking of a general debenture was advisable, even if the owning company had no assets other than the ship, her insurances, earnings and so on, as taking a general debenture enabled the lender to prevent the appointment of an administrator of the borrower under Section 8 of the 1986 Act by appointing an administrative receiver of the assets of the borrower.

However, since the implementation of the Enterprise Act 2002, a secured lender must (subject to limited exceptions) enforce its security either by appointing a receiver of the particular asset, as it always could, or, if the lender holds a 'qualifying floating charge' (see below), by appointing an administrator who can realise the security on the lender's behalf (paragraph 14(1), Schedule B1, Insolvency Act 1986) (1986 Act).

A floating charge qualifies if created by an instrument which:

- states that paragraph 14 of Schedule B1 to the 1986 Act applies; or
- purports to empower the holder of the floating charge to appoint an administrator or administrative receiver of the company (paragraph 14(2), Schedule B1, 1986 Act).

A person is the holder of a qualifying floating charge in respect of a company's property if he holds one or more debentures of the company secured by:

- a qualifying floating charge which relates to the whole or substantially the whole of the company's property;
- a number of qualifying floating charges which together relate to the whole or substantially the whole of the company's property;
- a charge and other forms of security which together relate to the whole or substantially the whole of the company's property, at least one of which is a qualifying floating charge (paragraph 14(3), Schedule B1, 1986 Act).

The question of whether a charge over a particular asset is fixed or floating invariably arises on a borrower's insolvency. This is because on the borrower's insolvency the holders of fixed charges over the borrower's assets get paid first, out of the proceeds of sale of the assets subject to the fixed charge, and before preferential creditors such as employees and contributions to an occupational pension scheme. Until the Enterprise Act 2002 came into force, certain Crown debts such as Customs and Excise and the Inland Revenue also enjoyed this preferential status (Crown preference), but the Enterprise Act 2002 abolished this privilege. Instead, a percentage of the floating charge assets must now be ring-fenced for payment to unsecured creditors, to ensure that floating charge holders do not benefit from the abolition of Crown preference. Only after any fixed charge holders and preferential creditors have been paid in full (and subject to the ring-fenced percentage) do the holders of any floating charges get paid out of the proceeds of sale of their assets.

So, where possible, a lender will try to assert that its charges are fixed, which would put the lender ahead of preferential creditors and the ring-fenced fund, rather than floating, which would put the lender behind them.

Whether a charge is fixed or floating is not a matter of the intention of the parties, but a matter of fact: did the lender in fact have sufficient control over the charged assets to make its charge fixed? If not, for example because the borrower was free to sell the assets without the lender's consent, the lender's charge is floating.

The second mortgage

Second and subsequent mortgages in favour of other lenders are generally frowned on by lenders and most loan documents will contain a prohibition on the owner granting a second mortgage over the vessel to anyone other than the first mortgagee without the prior consent of the first mortgagee. Second and subsequent assignments of insurances and earnings will be similarly restricted.

Most lenders feel that the existence of a second mortgage (unless to the lender itself in respect of another facility to the same owner) impairs their ability to control sensitive default situations. At best, a second mortgagee will get in the way; at worst, the second mortgagee will have rights adverse to those of the first mortgagee. In the United Kingdom, paragraph 9(2) of Schedule 1 to the Merchant Shipping Act 1995 gives a subsequent mortgagee power to sell the mortgaged ship with the consent of all prior mortgagees or the leave of the court, however, few lenders will wish to see the mortgaged vessel sold from underneath them, even if the court has approved the sale and even if they have first claim on the sale proceeds.

If a lender can be persuaded to allow a second mortgage, it will invariably insist on the second mortgagee's rights (including the right to sell the vessel with the leave of the court) being contractually postponed to those of the first mortgagee by a coordination or priority agreement.

The guiding principle behind such an agreement will be that the second mortgagee will agree not to take any steps to enforce his security without the consent of the first. The second mortgagee will also generally undertake to consent to any sale of the vessel by the first mortgagee (or agree to pay off the first mortgagee's debt in lieu) and to discharge the second mortgage when required to do so by the first mortgagee against payment of, or the provision of other security for, his outstanding indebtedness.

A coordination agreement will also deal with other security (for example, a second assignment of insurances and earnings) in substantially the same manner and may also provide for a general subordination of the indebtedness due to the second mortgagee to that to the first mortgagee. The law relating to subordination agreements is complex and technical, and subordination agreements should always be the subject of specialist legal advice to ensure their efficacy.

Second mortgages to the same lender are, of course, a rather different proposition and can often be used as additional security or to aid cross-collateralisation. A lender lending to a second company in the same group may require the two facilities to be cross-collateralised, in other words, each borrower will guarantee the obligations of the other and secure those guarantees by second ranking securities: second mortgages, second assignments of insurances, earnings and so on. Naturally, the value to a lender of a second mortgage will depend very much on the amount secured by the first mortgage compared to the value of the mortgaged vessel, but a second mortgage taken some way into the life of the facility secured by the first mortgage, particularly in a rising market, may be of some useful value and does, of course, have the attraction of becoming a first mortgage once the earlier facility is repaid.

---

[1] See Chapter 3.

[2] Section 4 Statute of Frauds 1677.

[3] See Chapter 2.

[4] Far too numerous to list, but see for example *Lloyds Bank Ltd v Bundy* [1975] QB 326; *Barclays Bank plc v O'Brien* [1994] AC 180; *Banco Exterior Internacional v Mann* [1995] 1 All ER 936; and *Bank of Baroda v Rayarel, The Times*, 19 January 1995.

[5] [1995] CLC 27.

[6] Section 35(1) of the Companies Act 1985, as amended by Section 108 of the Companies Act 1989, provides at Section 35A that 'the validity of an act done by a company shall not be called into question on the ground of lack of capacity by reason of anything in the company's memorandum'.

[7] See for example, the decision of the Court of Appeal in *Kleinwort Benson Ltd v Malaysian Mining Corporation Berhad* [1989] 1 WLR 379.

[8] See Chapter 8.

[9] [1986] 3 WLR 697.

[10] [1997] 3 WLR 909.

[11] [1992] BCLC 148.

Chapter 10

The sale and purchase
of second-hand ships

Updated by David Brookes

Introduction

For the shipowner wishing to acquire a ship there are three alternatives. He may either contract to have a new ship built, purchase a ship currently under construction or buy a second-hand ship. For the purposes of this chapter, a second-hand ship means one that has already been registered. An unregistered newbuilding may be dealt with in a similar manner from a contractual point of view, but a purchaser would have to be careful to take into account the registration requirements in relation to newbuildings and the possible liens attaching to the vessel as a newbuilding. A study of shipbuilding contracts is beyond the scope of this book.

As in any sale and purchase contract, a ship sale is concerned with: identifying that which is being sold; setting out the time and method by which title is to be transferred; setting out the time at which risk in the property is to be transferred; providing for payment; and, to a certain extent, defining and/or limiting the parties' respective liabilities for any breach of the sale contract. However, in the sale and purchase of a ship the extent to which the buyer can define exactly what it is he wishes to purchase other than by merely identifying the vessel, is usually quite limited. This suits the seller but makes it very difficult for the buyer to know the condition of the ship and therefore limits his ability to recover any compensation should the vessel not be in good condition.

Under English law, the Sale of Goods Act 1979 (as amended by the Sale and Supply of Goods Act 1994) (the 'SGA') applies to the sale and purchase of second-hand vessels in the normal way[1] but can easily be excluded because the Unfair Contract Terms Act 1977 has no application (generally speaking) to such contracts. In fact, once the buyer has identified the type and age of the vessel he wishes to purchase, he is left having to rely upon an inspection of the vessel, (albeit usually fairly superficial); an inspection of its classification society's records; and such knowledge as he has of the ship's operators. On the face of it, therefore, the sale of the vessel may not fall within a 'sale by description' within Section 13 SGA – at least to the extent of the buyer's actual knowledge. Further, the sale contract will often be drafted so that it provides that once these inspections are carried out the sale is outright and the vessel will be sold on an 'as is' basis. Having said that, any buyer may, providing market conditions are in his favour, significantly improve his position by adding appropriate terms to his contract.

The memorandum of agreement (MOA) and delivery

It should be made clear at the outset that the commentary contained in this chapter assumes that the sale and purchase contract is governed by English law. Decisions of English courts may be considered persuasive by courts in other jurisdictions, because of the importance of English law in this field, but they will not be binding, and the analysis contained in this chapter will not, therefore, be directly applicable to contracts governed by any other system of law.

A contract to buy and sell a ship need follow no prescribed form and may even be oral. Accordingly, parties (or their agents, especially brokers) should be wary during contractual negotiations to emphasise that any agreement is not to have contractual force until a document is signed. Once a contract is signed there will usually be little difficulty in persuading a court that the agreement is as written down. However, where no such written form is agreed, there will be potential for disputes with one party claiming that a contract has been concluded on which the other can be liable.[2] To be on the safe side, parties are therefore advised to use words such as 'subject to contract' in all written exchanges prior to formally entering into the MOA. The buyer and seller should also be aware that even in a broker's final recap email setting out the main agreed terms of the sale, words such as 'otherwise basis Saleform 93 subject details suitably amended to reflect also the above terms' will imply that there is still, at that stage, no binding contract.[3]

In a typical ship sale and purchase transaction the parties will enter into a written contract or MOA in which one party agrees to buy and the other agrees to sell the vessel in question on the terms set out in that MOA. The parties are then immediately bound by the terms of that contract unless otherwise stated in the MOA, although it may be drafted in such a way that some obligations (such as the basic obligations to buy and sell) will only arise if certain conditions (for example, board of directors' approvals) are fulfilled first. What is important to note is that although ownership of the vessel will be transferred *pursuant to* the MOA it will not be transferred *by* the MOA. This requires a separate instrument which, almost without exception, is referred to as a bill of sale (although these may take a variety of forms).

It is only after ownership is transferred that the buyer will normally have use and control of the vessel and, generally speaking, that it will be at the buyer's risk (although it is possible to provide that the risk passes at a different time to ownership). Accordingly, it is usual that the buyer will pay for the vessel when the bill of sale is delivered to him. Of course, as with any other sale agreement, the parties may vary this if they so wish so that, for example, the vessel may be sold on credit (generally guaranteed in some way such as by a banker's letter of credit) or it may be paid for in advance of delivery. However, standard practice is to pay in return for an immediate transfer of ownership and risk.

Accordingly, the ship purchase procedure can be broken down into two main stages, namely the negotiation of the MOA and the passing of ownership in exchange for the payment. It is at the first stage that the buyer must make clear exactly what he is expecting from the seller in terms of: the identity and condition of the vessel; how he will verify these by inspection; and the supporting documentation which he will require in order to be certain of (a) the condition; (b) becoming the new registered owner; and (c) satisfying any financing bank from which the buyer is obtaining funds.

Once the MOA is signed the parties are bound by its terms (assuming there are no conditions to be satisfied first) and have no right to require anything different or additional to that which is provided for. Hence, an imprudent buyer could find himself under an obligation to pay for a vessel that it cannot register on its chosen register, or which a bank will not consider adequate security for a loan of all or part of the purchase price. Similarly, a seller should be careful not to agree to supply what it cannot provide and so, for example, would not want to agree to supply a spare propeller when the vessel does not have one, as happened in the case of the 'ALECOS M'.[4]

After signing, the parties can, by agreement, alter or amend the terms of the MOA although neither has a right to do so without the other's agreement. In practice such variation is common because, as the parties' agents (whether brokers, lawyers or bankers) attempt to arrange the details of the delivery, they act as agents of the seller and buyer. As such, they have the ostensible authority to bind their principals and, it is suggested, agreements between them as to matters such as the documentation to be supplied and the method and timing of payments are binding even if they contradict the terms of the MOA. This would mean, for example, that, where a method or currency of payment is agreed in the MOA, and the parties' bankers later agree something different, it is not open to the seller to withhold delivery on the basis that such payment is not in accordance with the MOA.

The second stage of the sale and purchase procedure is the delivery of the vessel, when ownership (or 'title') is transferred, generally in exchange for payment. Often by this stage movements in the market price of ships can have taken place that may make delivery more difficult. Where the price has risen, the buyer will be anxious to take delivery and may not be prepared to risk losing the vessel by refusing delivery, even if the seller has breached the con-tract. The seller, on the other hand, will often be uncooperative, possibly in the hope that the buyer will not accept delivery and that it will be able to sell elsewhere for more. When the market falls the roles are reversed.

From the buyer's point of view the delivery is critical, not only because the buyer then has to operate the vessel but also because the buyer will part with the purchase price. From this point on, if he has any dispute with the seller, the only option he has is to try to recover money from the seller (that is, rather than being able to withhold it). He may also lose his right to reject the vessel.[5] In other words, if the buyer subsequently discovers anything wrong with the vessel that amounts to a breach of contract, his remedy will be to try to recover damages from the seller. (For a limited period of time he may also retain the right to reject the vessel and demand the return of the price but there is no reported instance of this being done successfully.)

Prior to delivery, the buyer can, where the breach is sufficiently serious, refuse to pay the price and claim damages or, alternatively, use this option as a basis upon which to re-negotiate the price. These alternatives need to be considered in the light of the state of the market as discussed above.

Once the price has been paid, the buyer's only redress will be through legal action, which is clearly going to cost money, and even this may be thwarted if the seller can dissi-pate its assets before any action is brought. In a single-ship company, the only asset follow-ing a sale will usually be the purchase price. Accordingly, the time that this takes to dissipate (and, therefore, the time in which the buyer must take his initial steps in any action for dam-ages) can be measured in minutes, rather than the months or years that usually characterise legal actions.

The preservation and enforcement of buyers' rights are dealt with, (though not in any great detail) later in this chapter.[6] The seller's rights are much more straightforward, in that it will not deliver the vessel unless the price is tendered in full. Without payment in full, the seller can generally keep any deposit as liquidated damages and can sue to recover any excess losses.

Standard forms of MOA

For sellers and purchasers of second-hand ships the most common standard form of MOA in current use is the Norwegian Sale Form ('NSF'), which is the Norwegian Shipbrokers' Association's Memorandum of Agreement for Sale and Purchase of Ships originally adopted by BIMCO (the Baltic and International Maritime Counsel) in 1956 and now in its 1993 version (NSF 1993). There are alternative standard forms of contract available to sellers and purchasers, the most important being the Memorandum of Agreement of the Japan Shipping Exchange Inc., currently published as Nipponsale 1999, which is popular with Japanese sellers, as well as other standard forms.

It is, of course, also open to parties to produce their own agreement from scratch, although this would be unusual. In practice, the majority of transactions are carried out on the basis of the NSF, although any number of additional clauses are then added in order to cover specific requirements of the buyer or seller.

Not surprisingly, the NSF has provisions dealing with nearly all of the legal issues relevant to ship sale and purchase. Its layout, therefore, provides a useful framework within which to review these issues. Though buyers and sellers now largely use the NSF 1993, there are still some instances of the NSF 1987 (and indeed some earlier editions) being used and so it is necessary to be familiar with both the current and previous editions. For this reason, although the text of this chapter will be based on the NSF 1993 edition (published in March 1994) it will also highlight the main differences appearing in the NSF 1987 edition. The forms of the NSF 1993 and NSF 1987 can be found on the BIMCO website – www.bimco.org.

Sale and purchase within the structure of the Norwegian Sale Form

The seller

The NSF 1993 begins by identifying the seller under the contract. Usually (but not necessarily) the seller will also be the owner of the vessel and the buyer would be well advised to confirm this by examining the register of the vessel. He should certainly always do so if the deposit is being paid into an account in the name of the seller rather than the more usual joint account. A buyer always needs to be wary of contracting to buy a vessel from a non-owner because, if there is then a breach by the seller (for example, if it is unable to compel the owner to deliver the vessel to the buyer), it is possible that there will be no assets of the seller against which the buyer can recover any losses. Nor would the buyer in those circumstances be able to obtain an order for specific performance of the contract of sale, whereas this remedy is, in certain circumstances, otherwise available in contracts for the sale and purchase of vessels.[7] It should be noted that, unless the contract expressly states otherwise, the seller need not be the owner of the vessel, because by entering into the contract he is promising only that he will have a right to sell the vessel at the time when property in the vessel is to pass, namely at the time of delivery (Section 12(1) SGA). Such a right can exist without the seller ever needing to own the vessel, but the seller will be liable for any defects in the title acquired by the buyer in the same way as a seller who sells his own property. However, the actual owner will not be liable under the contract unless he is made a party to it.

The buyer

The next point covered in the NSF is the identification of the buyer. In practice this is fairly straightforward, except in cases where a buyer is named but is said to be subject to an alternative nomination (for example, 'X Limited or nominee'). When a nomination is made under such a contract there are a number of problems that can arise. These centre primarily around the question of whether or not the original named contracting party remains liable or whether, by nominating an alternative buyer, the original named party no longer has any liability.

In the case of the 'AKTION',[8] the buyers under an NSF agreement were described as 'a company to be nominated by [the company signing the MOA]'. Following a breach of contract by the buyer the company which signed the MOA as buyers (and put up the deposit 'as a security for the correct fulfilment of [the] contract') claimed that the nomination had novated the contract so that the nominated party became solely liable as buyer and the nominating party was relieved of any liability *ab initio*. If the nomination did bring about such a novation, then the buyer's assertion would be correct, with the effect that the buyer had never been under a duty to provide a deposit, and could therefore recover it. The duty to provide the deposit would fall upon the nominee. However, the court held that the novation did not take place at the moment of nomination; the time when the novation took effect was to be determined by looking at the intention of the parties and the wording of the contract. As a matter of construction (particularly in the light of the deposit being placed as security for the buyer's performance) no novation would occur until the fulfilment of the contract, that is, the transfer of the vessel. The advantage of this position is that if the buyer (the nominating party) is in breach then it remains liable under the contract up until transfer of the vessel. On the other hand, once the buyer's contractual obligations have been fulfilled, the vessel will (in the normal course of events) have been delivered to the nominated party and therefore it is essential that any remedy for breach by the seller is available to the nominee. This is the case once novation has taken place.

It is evident from the earlier case of the 'BLANKENSTEIN',[9] that the parties may agree a different position. If it appears from the face of the contract that a nominee will assume liability under the contract immediately upon nomination, then the contract will be novated at that point and the original named buyer will have no liability under it at all. This is more likely to be the case when a nomination takes place before the deposit is paid over (or at least before it is due to be paid over) or where a buyer is nominated after the deposit has been paid and that nominee puts up its own deposit so that the original deposit is repaid to the first named buyer. This latter situation would, however, be unusual in practice.

The vessel

The NSF next identifies the vessel by a series of details including name, classification, year of build, flag, place of registration, call sign, registered tonnage and register number. Clearly, it is important to identify the vessel correctly. The stated classification of the vessel has ramifications on the rest of the NSF because the buyer normally has little opportunity to inspect the vessel in any detail, and therefore usually has to rely on this classification as proof of its reasonable condition.

Under Sections 13(1) and 15A SGA, there is a condition implied that the vessel will correspond with any description applied to it in the contract. This means that if the vessel does not meet the description the seller will be in breach of contract and the buyer will be entitled to claim damages and to treat itself as discharged from its obligations under the MOA. (This applies unless the seller can show that the breach is so slight that it would be unreasonable for the buyer to reject the vessel.) Where the buyer has also inspected the vessel, he will not be able to rely on Section 13(1) as regards matters which that inspection ought to have revealed. However, he is under no obligation to carry out a 'reasonable' inspection and the seller therefore cannot argue that he should have inspected any particular aspect of the ship which, had it been inspected, would have pointed to a misdescription.

Similarly, there is an implied term under Section 14 SGA that the vessel will be of satisfactory quality (taking account of the purpose for which vessels are commonly supplied, appearance and finish, freedom from minor defects, safety and durability). Breach of this quality standard will have the same consequences as breach of the implied term relating to description. Further, the effect of any inspection is exactly the same as it is on any misdescription.

Each of the terms as to flag, place of registration, call sign, registered tonnage and official number are part of the description of the vessel and should therefore match the register of the vessel exactly, unless the MOA states otherwise. However, in the case of the 'TROLL PARK'[10] the English court held that the register and, indeed, the builder's certificate, are only *prima facie* evidence of the year in which a vessel is 'built' and that it is open, at least to the seller, to show that the vessel was built in a year other than that shown on the builder's certificate or register. So a discrepancy between these documents and the MOA will not necessarily be a misdescription resulting in a breach of contract. In the 'TROLL PARK' case, the court held that a vessel could be described as having been 'built' when it could first be said to have complied with the ordinary meaning of 'built' and it would not be necessary for all the technical specifications under the building contract to have been met.

However, whether it is, in fact, open to a buyer to prove that a vessel was 'built' earlier than is shown in the builder's certificate is untested and most unlikely. There is a view that a ship should be described as being built in the year in which ship-brokers would, as a matter of market practice, regard her as having been built. This pragmatic approach has been viewed favourably by arbitrators.

Clause 1: purchase price

This sets out the price to be paid for the vessel. It is consistently referred to as 'the purchase price' throughout the NSF 1993. This is in contrast with the 1987 edition which subsequently referred to the 'purchase money' which was undefined but was assumed to be a reference to the price set out in this clause.

Clause 2: deposit

This clause sets the time by which the deposit must be lodged. This time is a strict condition, a breach of which entitles the seller to cancel the contract.[11] However, what remedy would the seller have if, after entering into the sale contract, the buyer then failed to pay the deposit? The 'BLANKENSTEIN' case suggests that the sellers should be entitled to sue for damages equal in an amount of the unpaid deposit rather than for the amount of damages suffered. However,

258

the 'BLANKENSTEIN' sale contract was based on the NSF 1966 edition and Clause 13 thereof (Buyers' Default) only referred to a failure to pay the purchase money and made no mention of a failure by the buyer to pay the deposit. In the NSF 1987 edition as well as the NSF 1993, Clause 13 specifically states that if the buyer fails to pay the deposit, the seller may only claim for losses and expenses incurred (as well as interest) rather then the full deposit amount. It is only *after* the deposit has actually been paid that the seller may claim the full deposit as liquidated damages.

The NSF 1993 provides that the deposit should be placed in a joint account so that neither buyer nor seller can gain control of it without the consent of the other (or a court order). The choice of bank needs to be inserted. It is usually most convenient for the joint account to be established with the seller's bank so as to avoid the need to make two transfers of funds on delivery, but this should not give the seller any greater control over the funds than the buyer, assuming that the bank in question is reputable. Interest on the deposit accrues for the benefit of the buyer.

As has been touched on above, the issue of the deposit can give rise to theoretical difficulties when a nominee buyer is substituted for the original named party.[12] Usually, the original party will have made the deposit in its own name and the nominated buyer (usually controlled by the same person in reality) will purport to release the deposit. In theory, of course, the instructions on the opening mandate (under which the depositor, but not the nominee, would generally be a signatory on the account) should be strictly followed but, despite the legal difficulties to which this could give rise, most banks take a pragmatic view and it rarely causes any problems. Some banks, however, take a more cautious approach and to be on the safe side require that both the original depositor and the nominee are signatories to the deposit release letter together with the seller.

Japanese sellers have been known to insist on the joint account being released not on the joint instructions of the named buyer and seller but, rather, on receipt by the bank of a signed protocol of delivery and acceptance. (This is a standard provision in Nipponsale 1999 and applies both to the release of the deposit and the payment of the balance of the purchase price.) As the buyer will never, in practice, be allowed to gain control of the vessel without executing the protocol of delivery and acceptance,[13] this prevents the buyer gaining control of the vessel without releasing the deposit.

However, in practice the only benefit is that, on delivery, there is one piece of paper fewer to be handed over, namely the deposit release letter. In contrast, where there is a nominee buyer this method simply adds to the confusion because the deposit will have to be placed on terms providing for its release against presentation of a protocol signed by the buyer (who will not have been nominated at the time the deposit is placed). The bank holding the deposit should then, properly speaking, satisfy itself that the party named as buyer in the protocol of delivery and acceptance is, indeed, the nominee under the original sale contract. In order to do this, it will have to concern itself with the terms of that contract and the nomination. Most banks will have no desire to do this, wishing merely to have their usual form of bank mandate in place to release the deposit on the joint signatures of the account holders. Interestingly, and of rather more concern for a buyer, the 1977 edition of the Nipponsale form provided for the deposit to be released against presentation of a duplicate notice of readiness for delivery. Such a one-sided arrangement appears to put the deposit wholly in the seller's control.

On a similar note, there have been instances of an agreed form MOA providing for the deposit to be placed directly in the seller's account, albeit in return for a refund guarantee from the seller's parent company. However, it would be fair to say that this was in instances where the buyer and seller were well known to each other and had enjoyed a longstanding and good commercial relationship. Otherwise, this would not normally be a provision that would be acceptable to a buyer.

Clause 3: payment

This clause states that the 'purchase price shall be paid in full free of bank charges' but this conflicts with the deposit clause. The purchase price includes the deposit. Under the terms of the deposit clause in the NSF (Clause 2) half of any bank charges incurred in relation to the deposit are to be borne by the seller. It is, therefore, accepted practice that the purchase price, when paid, shall be made up of a sum equal to the total price less half of the bank charges relating to the deposit, the aggregate of which shall be paid free of any further bank charges.

The clause then requires that the purchase money is to be paid 'on delivery of the vessel, but not later than three banking days after the vessel is in every respect physically ready for delivery in accordance with the terms and conditions of this agreement and notice of readiness has been given in accordance with Clause 5'. Accordingly, the buyer cannot require delivery of the vessel unless he actually makes (or, at least, tenders) simultaneous payment to the seller, and for these purposes payment is taken as meaning payment of same day dollars (or the customary equivalent for settling transactions in the currency specified in the contract). However, once notice of readiness is given under Clause 5, the buyer must pay (or tender payment) within three banking days.

Unlike the 1987 edition it would appear that under NSF 1993 the seller can refuse to effect delivery until the end of the three-day period.[14] In such circumstances the buyer should only effect payment against actual delivery while being certain to tender payment before the three days expire. In contrast, the three-day maximum is a limitation imposed on the buyer so that he will be in breach if he does not tender payment within this time limit. The seller's obligation is to deliver the vessel simultaneously with the payment being made, whether this is before or after expiry of the three-day time limit.

NSF 1993 defines 'banking days' as days on which banks are open both in the country of the currency stipulated for the purchase price and in the place of closing stipulated in Clause 8. From a legal perspective this definition is fairly loose, but should be quite workable in practice. Unfortunately, there is no such definition in the 1987 edition and so it could be open to dispute (particularly as the buyer would generally want to insist that the 'banking days' were days when his financing bank is open for business). It is frequently contended that the period ends at the end of the third complete banking day after notice was served, but the exact time of expiry is more debatable. It should probably be at the end of the third relevant 24-hour period after notice was served. However, it is more commonly taken to be the last time after expiry of that deadline at which the receiving bank can accept funds and re-deposit them on the same day.

The reference to the vessel being 'in every respect physically ready for delivery' contains two important aspects, namely that the vessel is *in every respect* ready and, secondly, that the vessel is *physically* ready, and is intended to make clear that the three-day period during which the buyer must pay does not begin to run until the vessel is, save for questions of paper work, actually ready to be delivered. This ties in with Clause 5 which also makes it a precondition to service of notice of readiness that the vessel should be 'in every respect physically ready for delivery in accordance with the Agreement'. Accordingly, under NSF 1993 a valid notice of readiness cannot be served (and the three-day payment period cannot commence) if: the ship has not yet reached the delivery port; if it is in dry dock (subject to certain provisions of Clause 6); or if the ship still requires work to put it into a deliverable state. The latter leaves it open for a buyer to challenge the validity of a seller's notice of readiness in circumstances where there are any defects to the vessel, however minor and which had not previously been agreed and accepted by the buyer in return for, say, a reduction in the sale price (fair wear and tear excepted). As for any registered encumbrances on the vessel, or other outstanding documentary requirements, these would not prevent notice of readiness being given and the three-day period commencing as they do not pertain to the vessel being 'physically ready'.

Contrast this with the position under the 1987 edition which merely required that the vessel be 'ready for delivery'. In the case of the 'AKTION', the court was of the view that this should not be interpreted literally and that the notice of readiness for delivery could be given before the vessel was in fact ready, provided that it would be ready at the expiry of the three-day notice period. The court maintained that there was no commercial advantage to the buyer in knowing that the vessel was ready three days in advance of the date on which it was obliged to take delivery. In the 1995 edition of this book, it was stated that this decision was widely regarded as incorrect among practitioners, who believed that a buyer would gain considerable commercial advantage through knowing at the earliest possible moment whether or not the notice given is, in fact, valid. For example, a buyer would want certainty as to when he should make arrangements for his crew to be at the delivery port and he would also need to know when to make arrangements for the first fixture of his new vessel. Under the interpretation given in the 'AKTION' case, the buyer would not know until the very last moment whether he has to take delivery of the vessel or not. This aspect of the 'AKTION' case was, however, disapproved by the case of the 'TARIA'[15] in which it was held that the notice must be of actual readiness for delivery when notice is given, not of any prospective readiness.

In response to the decision in the 'AKTION' case, the NSF 1993 edition provides, as mentioned above, that notice of readiness can only be given when the vessel is 'in every respect physically ready for delivery'. In the NSF 1993 and under the 1987 edition as interpreted in the case of the 'TARIA', the buyer will have three days in which to determine whether or not the vessel complies with the contract before he must accept delivery and pay the purchase price. It also gives him a certain amount of flexibility as to the day on which he must accept delivery and pay over the purchase price, whereas under the old 'AKTION' interpretation of the 1987 edition, he had no flexibility whatsoever because the vessel need not be in an acceptable condition until immediately prior to expiry of the three-day notice.

That said, the problem that the 1987 edition did not distinguish between physical readiness and documentary or legal readiness remains. It has to be acknowledged that, strictly, a vessel is rarely 'ready for delivery' in all senses until the very last moment because there are usually mortgages which are only released simultaneously with payment of the purchase money.

Accordingly, it is possible to say that as a matter of practice it would be unusual for a vessel to be 'ready for delivery' in the strict sense until the very moment of delivery.

On this basis, the NSF 1987 edition is unclear, but the best interpretation would be that for notice to be capable of being served, the vessel's physical condition should be such that it is ready for delivery and that the existence of encumbrances which will be removed on or before delivery should not be regarded as contravening this clause. Alternatively, the vessel could be said to be ready for delivery as regards encumbrances once any mortgagee has confirmed to the buyer that it will release its security simultaneously with payment of the purchase price and so the mere existence of an encumbrance would not prevent it being ready. The problem does not exist in NSF 1993.

Further, under the 1987 edition the vessel need only be ready as opposed to 'in every respect ready' before a notice of readiness is given. In the 'AKTION' case, it was made clear that defects do not give rise to an absolute right to reject the vessel. Rather, each term as to the vessel's condition should be perceived as an 'innominate' term which will only give rise to a right of rejection if sufficiently serious (presumably subject to any right of rejection under the SGA). Lesser breaches give rise only to an action for damages. Thus, under the 1987 edition, where the vessel is to all intents in a deliverable state it is conceivable that a buyer may not be entitled to reject the validity of the notice of readiness or, indeed, the vessel, on the basis of minor defects.

Clause 4: inspections

This provides two alternative arrangements for inspection by the buyer of the vessel's classification records and physical condition. The first, Clause 4(a), (which is deemed to be the applicable alternative unless deleted) is a confirmation that all such inspections have been carried out before the MOA is signed and that the sale is not, therefore, 'subject to inspection'. There is no equivalent in the 1987 edition. Such a provision had to be negotiated.

The alternative, Clause 4(b), is drafted to provide that the acceptance of the classification records and satisfactory physical inspection are conditions precedent to the rest of the contract (with the exception of the buyer's liability to place the deposit into a joint account and the seller's obligation to make the vessel available for inspection,[16] so that if the buyer does not accept the vessel after the inspections, he has no liability under the contract and can demand the return of the deposit. The question of whether or not the vessel is to be accepted following the inspections is entirely within the buyer's discretion. There is no objective standard of whether or not the vessel or its records are acceptable. However, this position can be varied by using wording other than the standard NSF wording, so that the buyer may only be entitled to reject the vessel if there is objectively something wrong with it (that is, rather than him merely not liking it).[17]

The seller, on the other hand, can only withdraw from the contract if the buyer chooses to reject the vessel or fails to inspect it within the time period inserted into the clause by the parties. Accordingly, a recalcitrant seller may try to be obstructive in the hope that the buyer will be unable to carry out a satisfactory inspection and so reject the vessel. This can take the form of giving very short notice of the vessel's availability for inspection or limiting the buyer's ability to inspect, either by refusing access to parts of the ship or by, for example, allowing inspection when the holds are too full to be inspected. Such obstruction may, of itself, lead to a right of action for the buyer.

In practice, the inspection of the vessel under Clause 4 is likely to be the first physical inspection the buyer has had the opportunity to perform, and, even so, the contract does not permit anything more than a superficial inspection. It specifically provides that there is to be no 'opening up'. The only obligation on the seller is to make the vessel available for inspection and to make the vessel's log books available. It is widely accepted, though it is not specifically provided for, that the buyer can also insist on the vessel's engines being run. A buyer is well advised to provide specifically for a much more detailed examination whenever possible. The 1987 edition included an additional requirement that the vessel be afloat at the time of inspection. By omitting this, NSF 1993 probably permits inspection in dry dock (and possibly permits inspection even when aground!).

As has been mentioned above, any subsequent claim by the buyer for breach of the implied terms relating to description and satisfactory quality (Sections 13 and 14 of the SGA) may be limited by such inspections. However, this is only to the extent that defects are drawn to the buyer's attention or as regards matters that the actual examination made by the buyer (as opposed, for example, to a full inspection) ought to have revealed.

The extent to which the buyer can rely on the classification society and its records is limited and is discussed in more detail in relation to Clause 6 below.

The buyer is under a duty to notify the seller within 72 hours (48 hours under the 1987 edition) of completion of the inspection that the vessel is, in fact, accepted. If this is not done, then, according to the contract, the seller is under a duty to release the deposit and the contract becomes automatically null and void. Clearly, there is a possibility of dispute where the buyer does not reply within the required time limit, but the seller then does not immediately release the deposit. In practice, it is likely that the seller is not entitled to release the deposit and claim the contract as null and void after he has received the buyer's notice of acceptance, even if that notice is sent outside the 72-hour period. This is because, for as long as the deposit is not released, the seller can be implied to be waiving the strict time limit requirement.

Clause 5: notices, time and place of delivery

This clause is divided into four parts, the first of which deals with various notices to be given. The parties are left to insert up to three periods of notice which the seller should give to the buyer regarding: place and time of dry-docking; underwater inspection or delivery, as the case may be. Each of these is only required to be an estimate so it would be difficult for a buyer to bring a claim against the seller if any notice were to be inaccurate as to time or place. However, this may be possible if no notice was provided or if it could be shown that the information in any notice was not a genuine estimate.

It is this part of Clause 5 which also imposes an obligation on the seller to give notice of readiness when 'the vessel is at the place of delivery and in every respect physically ready for delivery'. Commentators have made much of the way in which the wording of the clause appears to imply a duty to serve this notice of readiness as soon as the vessel is in a deliverable state. However, it seems most unlikely that it would ever be so interpreted by a court, if only because to do so would be wholly uncommercial. It is more likely that the notice cannot be served before the vessel is ready but can be served at any time after, subject to the provisions relating to cancellation.[18]

The second sub-clause goes on to state that the vessel will be delivered and taken over *'safely afloat at a safe and accessible berth or anchorage* at/in: [ ].' The words in italics were not included in the 1987 edition but were probably implied anyway (and in any event were frequently added) so not much should be read into this difference. The clause is usually completed so as to give the seller a choice of a number of ports at which to deliver and a period of time in which delivery is expected to be made. There is no obligation, however, to make delivery within that period, provided that notice of readiness is validly served on or before the date of cancelling.[19] After that date the buyer has a right to cancel (governed by Clause 14 of the NSF, subject to the provisions of Sub-clause 5(c)). This provides a framework within which the seller can propose a later cancelling date.

It is open to the buyer to reject the seller's proposal, cancel the contract and claim damages; or to accept the proposal while reserving the right to claim damages (including liquidated damages) under Clause 14. The latter is favoured by the contract wording. What is not clear is whether agreeing to an extension of the cancelling date may prejudice a buyer's general right to damages (that is, damages other than those provided for in Clause 14, assuming the provisions of Clause 14 are not comprehensive (see below)).

However, should the vessel be declared an actual, constructive or compromised total loss before delivery (or, where the contract is cancelled in accordance with its terms, before the date of cancellation) then the seller incurs no liability under the contract and the buyer is entitled to a return of its deposit and interest. It is not clear, but the seller would presumably remain under a duty pursuant to Clause 2 to bear half of the bank charges associated with the deposit as it is only after the deposit has been duly returned that the agreement becomes null and void. The NSF 1987 edition does not refer to compromised total loss (being a situation where insurers agree that the value of a vessel following repair will not justify the cost of repair and so they are prepared to treat it as a total loss). Only 'total and constructive total loss' is referred to.

Clause 6: dry-docking/divers' inspection

This clause offers two alternatives, the first of which is deemed to be selected if neither is deleted. This requires the seller to dry-dock the vessel at the port of delivery to enable inspection of the vessel's bottom and other underwater parts. This will generally afford the buyer the opportunity to inspect this part of the vessel. However, the inspection procedure is very different to that provided for in Clause 4. Here, it is a representative of the vessel's classification society who is appointed to carry out the inspection and not the buyer personally (although the buyer is entitled to be present).

If the inspector is satisfied with the condition of the vessel then the buyer has no remedy, however dissatisfied he may be. Further, should the vessel not meet with the inspector's satisfaction the buyer is not, *prima facie*, entitled to reject the vessel but, rather, the seller has the opportunity to remedy any defects. The clause does not entitle the buyer to withdraw from the contract in the way that Clause 4 does. However, if the seller should fail to remedy any defects as required by the classification society's inspector, then the buyer would have a strong case for arguing that the seller was acting in repudiation of the contract and that the buyer was therefore entitled to accept that repudiation, withdraw from the contract and recover his deposit together with any damages.

Until the seller has complied with the inspector's requirements, the vessel will not be ready for delivery and therefore the seller cannot serve notice of readiness for delivery under Clause 3 and certainly cannot deliver the vessel. Should this result in the seller not being ready to deliver before the date of cancelling, then the buyer should be in a position to withdraw in accordance with the terms of Clause 14 (see below).

As an alternative to dry-docking, Clause 6(b) provides for inspection afloat by a class-approved diver under the direction of the vessel's classification society. This alternative was not included in the 1987 edition but a similar negotiated provision was often inserted by the parties in place of the dry-docking provisions.

Commentators have expressed concern that the lack of uniformity in underwater inspection standards and requirements of classification societies may make it preferable for the buyer to negotiate more specific provisions than those included in the standard form. However, this seems to move away from the two basic principles of: (a) achieving a nominally independent standard of inspection; and (b) making the contract as straightforward as possible.

Although NSF 1993 does not expressly say so, it appears to imply that the inspection afloat is to be carried out at the port of delivery. However, if conditions at the delivery port are unsuitable for such a diver's inspection, it is to be carried out at a suitable alternative place near to the delivery port. Presumably, the vessel should then be returned to the delivery port – although, of course, the vessel may be delivered at anchorage, provided it is within the delivery range (see Clause 5).

If underwater damage is found which affects the vessel's class, the vessel is to be dry-docked, unless satisfactory repairs can be carried out afloat. Once dry-docked, the vessel is to be inspected by the classification society again. The dry-docking is to be at the seller's expense. However, it would appear the buyer must pay the cost of the underwater inspection unless the dry-dock inspection also reveals damage affecting class. If it does, the seller must also repair the damage.

If the underwater inspection results in a dry-docking requirement, the NSF permits the vessel to be moved to another port (whether or not this is outside the delivery range) if facilities are not available at the port of delivery. Following dry-docking, it must then be returned to a port within the specified range for delivery. In such an event, the cancelling date shall be extended by the additional time required not only for the extra steaming but also for the dry-docking, limited to a maximum of 14 running days. This should be contrasted with the ordinary dry-docking provisions or the situation where dry-docking is available at the place of the underwater inspection. In such circumstances no extension of the cancelling date is permitted for the time required for the dry-docking, unless both parties agree to such an extension, despite the fact that extensive work may be required to put the ship into a deliverable condition.

It is important to note that under English law, in the absence of a contractual relationship, a classification society will probably not be liable to the buyer for their inspectors' negligence.[20] This is because the damage suffered by a buyer (with whom the classification society is generally not in a contractual relationship) would almost certainly fall within the classification of 'economic loss'. English courts are most reluctant to admit there can ever be any tortious liability in the absence of physical damage.[21]

This means that where there is reliance on a classification society inspection, then, in the absence of a direct contractual relationship between the society and the buyer, there is unlikely to be any remedy available to the buyer for the society's negligence or for defects in the vessel.[22] However, as the buyer is *prima facie* responsible for the classification society's costs for dry-dock or underwater inspections (unless damage is found) it may be possible for buyers to get around these difficulties by contracting with the classification society for its services. However, even if a classification society were to enter such a contract, it would almost certainly attempt to exclude or limit its liability.

Finally, Clause 6 specifically permits the buyer to clean and paint the underwater parts while the vessel is in dry dock. If the buyer's work is still in progress when the inspection is finished and the seller has completed its work (if any) the buyer will bear the continuing dry-dock expenses and the seller will be entitled to serve notice of readiness and subsequently deliver the vessel in dry dock rather than afloat. The question of whether or not the buyer's work is still in progress is presumably for the buyer to determine when the seller announces it has finished its work. It would seem unlikely, for example, that the seller could show work was in progress and therefore insist on delivering in the dry dock merely because the buyer had succeeded in painting only part of the ship's bottom, notwithstanding that the buyer was prepared to stop painting immediately.

Clause 7: spares/bunkers etc

This clause of the contract deals with the items that are to be delivered along with the basic hull and superstructure of the vessel. In particular, it deals with the inclusion of spares which, if they belong to the vessel at the time of inspection (whether or not they are on board), are to be delivered along with the vessel. However, if they are used prior to delivery, they do not need to be replaced, although the used parts will have to be delivered to the buyer.

Spare parts can give rise to a number of difficulties, particularly where the seller operates a fleet of vessels so that spares are held in some form of pooling arrangement. In such circumstances, it is very difficult for the buyer to prove that any particular spares belong to the vessel. Buyers should take this into account when negotiating the contract so as to be sure that they receive any particular spares that they want in addition to those that are on board the vessel. Similarly, a seller should be careful that he does not agree to sell something that he does not own.

Traditional legal theory would mean that when a seller contracts to provide particular spares and fails to do so the buyer could expect to recover the cost of obtaining them elsewhere, whether or not it is 'commercial' or 'practical' to do so. This position is no longer quite so clear since a 1990 decision of the Court of Appeal in the case of a spare propeller in the 'ALECOS M'[23] where the purchase contract specifically stated that the spares included a spare propeller. There was no spare propeller (there had apparently never been one) and the buyer sued for the cost of purchasing and installing one. The Court of Appeal, however, upheld an arbitrator's decision to award merely the scrap value of a spare propeller on the basis that it would be uncommercial and impractical on the part of the buyer to manufacture a spare propeller for a vessel which was already 14 years old because the chance of it being used was so remote.

In upholding this view, the Court of Appeal seemed to introduce a new concept into English law to the effect that damages for breach of contract may have to be reasonable. This view has since been supported by the House of Lords decision in *Ruxley Electronics and Constructions Ltd v Forsyth*[24] where it was said that damages were designed to compensate for an established loss and not to provide a gratuitous benefit to the aggrieved party, from which it followed that the reasonableness of an award of damages was to be linked directly to the loss sustained. That is to say, if the loss sustained did not result in a need to reinstate it may be unreasonable in a particular case to award the cost of reinstatement.

Clause 7 also allows the seller to remove a certain amount of equipment from the vessel, either by specific exclusion from the sale or because it is only on hire/loan from a third party. In these days of personal computers, where much vital information regarding the vessel's operation may be stored on such machines, this can give rise to problems. The seller may seek to remove the equipment, or, alternatively, sell it to the buyer at an inflated price. Buyers caught in such a situation often have little option but to pay over the odds for such items unless they ensure in the MOA that any hardware and/or software used in the running of the ship is to be left on board. One should particularly note that much of Clause 7 assumes the seller is the owner of the vessel (which is not absolutely necessary).[25] If this is not the case, some of the provisions may need amendment.

Finally, Clause 7 deals with the question of bunkers and lubricating oils (together with unused stores and provisions), payment for which probably gives rise to the most frequent cause of dispute, though rarely litigation, in sale and purchase contracts. Unused stores and provisions are deemed to be included in the sale price in NSF 1993, whereas in the 1987 edition they are treated in the same way as bunkers and lubes. The NSF 1993 provides that the buyer must pay 'the current net market price (excluding barging expenses) at the port and date of delivery of the vessel'. This is often altered by one or other of the parties and would appear to be open to a number of possible interpretations in most delivery situations. When these are added to the difficulty of calculating the remaining bunkers on board, and the fact that these items are all, generally speaking, being consumed right up until the moment of delivery, it is almost inevitable that there will be disagreement about them.

There is no easy way to avoid this if one of the parties does not wish to cooperate. However, it is open to the seller, once he knows the exact amount due, to hold out for that sum. Failure on the part of the buyer to tender the correct amount will be a breach of contract just as, from the buyer's point of view, a refusal by the seller to accept a tender of the correct amount due will be a breach on the part of the seller. However, whether such breaches would be sufficiently serious to entitle a seller to refuse to deliver, or a buyer to refuse to accept delivery, is unclear, although most of those involved in ship sale and purchase would regard such refusal as being the only practical remedy in such situations.

The wording of the NSF 1993 clause is slightly more specific than the NSF 1987 edition. The latter first required calculation of the market price of unused stores and provisions; and, secondly, did not state whether barging expenses for bunkers and lubes were to be included or not. Nonetheless, there is still room for debate as to exactly what other costs should be 'netted' in order to determine the market price.

Payment of the sums due in relation to these amounts can also lead to certain difficulties because of the mechanics of arranging payment of a sum which is not fixed until the last moment. Payment is discussed below,[26] but suffice it to say that in order to facilitate many 'instantaneous' payment techniques it is a significant advantage to know the exact amounts to be paid in advance and many bankers are not keen to adapt the techniques to cover situations where the amount due varies right up to the last moment.

Clause 8: documentation

Clause 8 begins by providing for the parties to agree and insert the place of documentary delivery. This is not provided for in the 1987 edition so that an additional negotiated clause is required (which helps to avoid arguments over the place of any delivery meetings, particularly if the parties are based a long way apart). It should be noted that documentary closing will normally take place at a different location to the place of physical delivery of the vessel. The venue selected will generally be chosen for a number of reasons including: ease of effecting and receiving payment; the ease of obtaining information and evidence from the ship's existing port of registration; and the ease of access to the buyer's chosen register for the purposes of registering title and, usually, registration of a mortgage in favour of a bank financing the purchase.

Otherwise, Clause 8 deals with the documentation to be provided by the seller in exchange for the purchase price. The 1991 edition of this book stated that it was in this particular area that the NSF 1987 could be significantly improved, and suggested that Part 3 of the London Ship Sale Contract 1985 offered a better alternative. However, the NSF 1993 edition largely incorporated the improvements necessary.

The clause provides a standard, but not exhaustive, list of documents to be handed over at delivery. These are intended to ensure that the buyer: (a) gets good title to the vessel; (b) can register its title under its chosen flag; and (c) receives such documentation as is necessary for the operation of the vessel.

As the deletion and registration requirements of various registries are different, the clause includes a requirement that the seller provide such additional documents as may be required by the competent authorities (of the buyer's chosen registry) in order to register the vessel. However, the buyer must notify the seller of any such documents as soon as possible after the date of the MOA.

It is worth noting that although the bill of sale must be notarised and legalised, there is no requirement that the notary must warrant the validity of the execution in the way that, for example, the standard form of notarisation on a Panamanian bill of sale requires. In the latter, the notary has to certify, *inter alia*, that sufficient proof has been produced to him:

- that the vendor was immediately prior to the execution of the bill of sale the owner of the vessel and had the right to sell the vessel; and
- that the signatories had the power to execute the bill of sale on behalf of the seller in the manner in which it was executed.

Failing this, a buyer would normally wish to be reassured on these points by being provided with legalised copies of the seller's board/shareholders' resolutions (depending on the law of the place of incorporation of the seller and its constitutional documents) and Power of Attorney, or other evidence of 'internal' authorisation.

In practice, apart from the question of seller's (and buyer's) internal authorisations, it would be very difficult for a standard form to address documentation more comprehensively than the NSF 1993.

NSF 1993 leaves open the possibility that the deletion of the vessel's registration may be carried out by the seller after delivery (a common and often unavoidable practice which the NSF 1987 edition tried to avoid by requiring deletion to coincide with delivery; this was almost always amended by the parties). This can lead to difficulties, although they may be impractical to address, particularly in a standard form. In the first place, it is not entirely satisfactory to rely on an undertaking of a 'one-ship' company which falls to be enforced when its one ship has been sold. Secondly, there may be underlying reasons (such as unpaid corporate taxes) why deletion is refused by the relevant authorities. Short of the buyer meeting the seller's obligations it may not be possible to obtain a deletion. This can have the knock-on effect of preventing permanent registration under the buyer's chosen flag.

The non-payment of corporate taxes by a Panamanian seller is a case in point. Short of demanding to see an official receipt for such taxes on delivery, it would be extremely difficult to know if such taxes were outstanding. A Panamanian 'certificate of good standing', for example, does not extend to such fees.

The buyer and seller have a contractual obligation under Clause 8 to sign a protocol of delivery and acceptance at the time of delivery.[27]

In contrast to NSF 1993, the NSF 1987 edition imposes only three obligations on the seller, namely:

- to provide a notarially attested and legalised bill of sale;
- to provide a certificate stating that the vessel is free from registered encumbrances (generally accepted to mean an official certificate from the relevant registry, although the NSF 1987 edition is silent on this); and
- to provide for the deletion of the vessel from its current registry and to deliver a certificate of deletion to the buyer.

This should always be added to through a negotiated provision so as to bring it broadly in line with the documentary requirements of the NSF 1993.

Clause 8 also provides that classification certificates, plans and technical documentation are to be handed over together with copies of the log books. Examination of the class certificates will show the buyer that the vessel is in class for the purposes of Clause 11. To prevent problems on delivery, buyers would be well advised to request copies in advance but they will in any event be reviewed on board by the new master upon delivery.

Clause 9: encumbrances

This is the seller's warranty that, at the time of delivery, the vessel is free from all charters; encumbrances; mortgages and maritime liens; or any other debts whatsoever (being debts which, at the time of delivery, have given rise to actual existing rights affecting the property in or use of the vessel).[28] There is also an indemnity against the consequences of any claims, which 'have been incurred' prior to the time of delivery, being made against the vessel after delivery. In other words, and as the Court of Appeal held, if after taking delivery of the vessel, the vessel is subsequently arrested or claims are brought against the vessel, in each case as a result of events which took place prior to delivery, the buyer is entitled to be indemnified by the seller for all costs, losses and damages resulting therefrom regardless of whether the liability asserted by the claimant exists or not.[29] The wording of the 1987 edition did not refer to charters although it was probably intended to exclude them too. Not being debts, mortgages or maritime liens they would have to fall within the description 'encumbrances,' which has been said to refer to proprietary and possibly also possessory rights over a vessel. However, there has been no direct judicial confirmation that a charter would be included (see the case of the 'BARENBELS').[30] Similarly, the NSF 1993 does not refer to trading commitments in general, but only to charters although the wider meaning is probably intended.

In any event, where the seller is a one-ship company the indemnity will probably be of little use should the warranty subsequently prove to be false. Unfortunately, there is little one can do to avoid this beyond being cautious and ensuring to the best of one's ability that the vessel is indeed free from encumbrances. It is possible to check casualty lists for the appropriate period under the various maritime conventions to see if any unexpired claims may still be outstanding. Alternatively, in jurisdictions where issue and service of the claims form (or writ as it used to be called) are separate, such as in England and Wales or Singapore, it is possible to search the claims form register to see if any are outstanding. It should be noted that a claims form issued in respect of an action *in rem* can be served on the vessel even where ownership has changed between issue and the service of the claims form,[31] so the change in ownership will not defeat the action against the ship. A third alternative or additional precaution would be for the buyer to take an assignment of the vessel's insurance policies to cover any claims and liabilities that have arisen or been incurred prior to the date of delivery.

In practice, however, buyers rarely look further than the vessel's current register in order to see if there are any encumbrances. Beyond that they usually rely on the seller's warranty, valueless though it may be. Similarly, casualty lists and claims form/writ registers are rarely checked and insurance policies are almost never assigned on sale. The warranty is, of course, repeated in the wording of the bill of sale by which title is transferred. Where a buyer suspects that a vessel may have claims attaching to it, he would be well advised not to go ahead with the purchase, unless it is bought through a court sale,[32] which will generally give him 'clean' title to the vessel. However, there are limitations on this. Although court sales in one jurisdiction are supposed to be recognised in all other jurisdictions as removing claims, this is not always the case, notably with claims arising in that other jurisdiction.[33] This is notwithstanding the fact that failure to recognise such a sale is said to contravene internationally accepted law[34] and the Brussels International Convention for the Unification of Certain Rules Relating to the Arrest of Seagoing Ships 1952.

The buyer of a newbuilding (that is, the buyer of a newbuilding from its first owner, rather than directly from the builder) is one exception to this rule. The buyer will frequently request sight of, or even an assignment of, the builder's warranty, showing that the vessel is free from any encumbrances, liens or debts. This document is generally issued by shipyards as a matter of course when delivering a new vessel to buyers.

270

Clause 10: taxes

Clause 10 apportions liability for taxes, registration fees and deletion fees. The buyer pays those connected with the purchase and registration and the seller pays those incurred in connection with the sale and deletion of the vessel. One point for buyers to be wary of is that, in certain jurisdictions, deletion cannot be obtained until the necessary tax clearance certificates have been issued by the authorities in that jurisdiction. These certify that all taxes due to the authorities in the seller's place of registration in connection with the vessel have been paid. For example, when purchasing from a Greek seller one will wish to make sure that the NAT (Greek Seamen's Pension Fund) clearance certificate has been issued, and therefore a buyer should ask to see a copy. (See also the reference to Panamanian corporate taxes referred to in the discussion of Clause 8 above.)

In the absence of all necessary tax clearance certificates being granted it is unlikely that deletion will be obtainable. The buyer could subsequently be left with the difficulty of trying to enforce the seller's obligations to pay costs associated with the deletion when the purchase price has already been paid and, in the case of single-ship companies, he could meet with little success. He would then have no alternative but to pay off the outstanding taxes himself in order to obtain the deletion certificate from the seller's registry (which he needs to acquire or maintain his own permanent registration on his new register).

Clause 11: condition on delivery

Clause 11 begins by stating that the vessel remains at the seller's risk and expense until delivery, so that: if any damage is done to the vessel it is for the seller to pay; if the vessel is lost it is the seller's loss; and if the vessel incurs any liability it will be the seller's liability. Note that where the vessel is lost then the obligation to deliver is avoided under Clause 5. This is so whether it is an actual, constructive or compromised total loss.

This clause also imposes on the seller an obligation to repair damage that is incurred after the date of the buyer's inspection because it obliges the seller to deliver the vessel in the condition in which she is at the time of her inspection, subject only to fair wear and tear. Accordingly, any damage other than fair wear and tear must be repaired at the seller's expense before delivery takes place.

To the extent that the SGA applies to the sale contract in question, one should note the way in which the provisions of the SGA regarding the description and quality of the vessel[35] impose additional obligations regarding the condition of the vessel. Clause 11 appears to say that once the buyer has inspected the vessel, the seller's only obligation is to deliver the vessel in the condition that it was in at the time of the inspection. The SGA, on the other hand, gives the buyer rights of action for defects that were not actually inspected, or for any misdescription applied to the ship by the seller which was not apparent from the buyer's inspection, and would thus appear to put a buyer in a stronger position than does the express wording of NSF.

Clause 11 imposes three further obligations, namely:

- to deliver the vessel with her class maintained (the 1987 edition says 'in class' but is often amended to read 'class maintained') without condition/recommendation (for which purpose any notes on the surveyor's report are to be ignored provided they are accepted by the classification society);

- free of average damage affecting class ('average damage' was held to mean damage which is ordinarily covered by insurance, in the 'ALFRED TRIGON' case)[36]; and
- with her classification, national and other certificates valid and unextended without conditions/ recommendations.

The requirement relating to 'average damage' does not appear in the 1987 edition, although it has been common to insert it as a negotiated amendment for many years (which is how the question arose in the 'ALFRED TRIGON' case). On the other hand, the 1987 edition imposed an additional obligation on the seller which does not appear in the NSF 1993 text. This was to notify the classification society of any matters coming to their knowledge that would affect class.

This first appeared in the 1983 edition of NSF following the decision of the Court of Appeal in the 'BUENA TRADER' case[37] which determined that there was no implied duty (owed to the buyer) for a seller to report matters to the classification society. However, subsequent cases such as the 'WORLD HORIZON'[38] and the 'NIOBE'[39] indicate that the introduction of such an obligation may have led to more disputes than it prevented. It has been necessary for the House of Lords in the 'NIOBE' to determine that the obligation to report matters that would affect class is so wide that it even includes things coming to the knowledge of the seller before the date of the contract or of the last survey of the vessel (although the Law Lords acknowledged that in practice it will not usually be necessary to go back beyond the last relevant survey).

However, the provision still leaves sellers in the difficult position of having to decide what will affect class (and therefore what to report) and the detail in which it needs to be reported. By removing the obligation from NSF 1993 the position reverts to that determined in the 'BUENA TRADER' (that is, there is no obligation, as between seller and buyer, for the seller to report defects/damage to the classification society) unless the parties introduce a negotiated amendment.

Another common amendment is to provide that the class certification should be valid for a minimum period following delivery, and/or should have been issued within a certain maximum number of days prior to delivery. The latter can cause problems as it means the certificate is only available at the last moment and cannot be examined in advance by the buyer. Knowing the vessel to be in class and free of recommendations does, of course, provide the buyer with some objective measure of the vessel's condition. (Although quite what level of reassurance this actually provides to owners nowadays is a matter of some debate, partly due to the varying standards of classification societies and partly due to the lack of redress.[40]) This obligation should be read in conjunction with Clause 8 which imposes the obligation to provide the class certificates.

Clause 12: name/markings

This requires that the buyer changes the name of the vessel and alters the funnel markings. This is generally included because owners like to retain the names of their ships when they sell them so they may use them in the future (although this is no guarantee for a seller that he will be able to re-use a name). The reference to funnel markings is to prevent a buyer operating the vessel under the seller's house colours.

Clause 13: buyer's default

This deals with default by the buyer and sets out the seller's rights against the buyer in the three different situations detailed below.

- If the buyer does not pay the deposit as required, the seller can cancel the agreement and claim compensation for losses and expenses plus interest at an unspecified rate (in the 1987 edition interest was at a pre-determined rate of 12 per cent). Neither version makes clear the date from which interest should run (for example, the last date for paying the deposit, the date expenses were incurred, the date of the claim and so on).
- If the deposit is paid but the purchase price is not, then the deposit, together with any interest earned, is to be treated as liquidated damages for the seller, who may claim all of it as well as cancelling the agreement.
- If the deposit is paid and the purchase price is not, and the deposit is insufficient to cover the seller's losses and expenses, then the seller may claim further compensation, together with interest at an unspecified rate (again, the 1987 edition provided for a rate of 12 per cent), as well as cancelling the agreement.

When interpreting this clause, it should be remembered that the buyer's duty is only to pay (or tender payment of) the purchase price when the vessel is tendered for delivery in accordance with the terms of the contract. So, if it is not properly tendered for delivery in accordance with the terms of the contract, then the buyer's duty to pay the purchase money never arises and the seller is not entitled to retain the deposit or claim damages under this clause.[41]

It has been suggested that the provisions regarding immediate cancellation and forfeiture of the deposit for late payment are too harsh. Indeed, the Nipponsale 1999 form provides for up to 10 days 'demurrage' to be payable at an agreed daily rate before the seller will have the right to cancel and the buyer's deposit is forfeited. Such a provision could form the basis of a negotiated amendment for a concerned buyer.

Clause 14: seller's default

The NSF 1993 version of this clause identifies two seller's defaults, either of which gives the buyer the option of cancelling the agreement, namely:

- failure to give notice of readiness in accordance with Clause 5(a) (which provides that 'when the vessel is at the place of delivery and in every respect physically ready for delivery in accordance with this Agreement, the Sellers shall give the Buyers a written Notice of Readiness for delivery'); or
- failure to be ready validly to complete a legal transfer by the cancellation date (as per Clause 5(b)).

There then follow the words 'provided always that the Sellers shall be granted a maximum of three Banking Days after Notice of Readiness has been given to make arrangements for the documentation set out in Clause 8'.

It has been suggested that these provisions should be re-written as:

- failure to give notice of readiness in accordance with Clause 5(a) on or before the cancellation date; or
- failure to arrange for the documentation set out in Clause 8 (including being ready to complete a legal transfer) within three banking days of giving notice of readiness.

In other words, it is the duty to give notice of readiness which is said to be subject to the cancellation date (which is supported by the second paragraph of Clause 14 under which the seller must compensate the buyer if it fails to give notice of readiness by the cancelling date). The separate obligation to be ready to complete a legal transfer is regarded as irrelevant (as it is covered by the proviso). The proviso imposes an obligation on the seller to prepare the delivery documentation within three days while making it clear that this period can extend beyond the cancelling date (implying that the contract cannot be cancelled by the buyer in the intervening period).

This is then subject to the provisions given below:

- Clause 5(d). Under this the contract becomes null and void if the vessel is lost.
- Clause 6(b)(iii). This provides that the cancelling date may be extended if dry-docking has to be carried out at a port other than the chosen delivery port.
- Clause 14. This implies that if notice of readiness is given and the vessel subsequently ceases to be physically ready for delivery, the seller's obligation to serve notice of readiness before the cancelling date merely revives, rather than there being an automatic breach on the expiry of three days from the original notice. However, this is not entirely clear as the buyer is said to 'retain' its option to cancel if a subsequent notice of readiness is not served by the cancelling date. This is impractical as one will not know if the option is retained until the cancelling date passes. It would seem better, therefore, to regard it as an option arising on the cancelling date.

However, the wording of Clause 14 of the NSF 1993 is ambiguous and the default provisions are capable of a number of other interpretations. For example, one alternative interpretation is that 'failure to serve a valid notice of readiness' could mean serving an invalid notice of readiness. If this is correct, the buyer could cancel if the seller gives notice of readiness which, for some reason, is not in accordance with Clause 5(a). The most likely instance of this would be a situation where the vessel is not physically ready for delivery when notice is given.

However, in such circumstances the notice of readiness would presumably be defective and the seller could still put the vessel in order and serve a valid notice of readiness (assuming there was no time constraint). It would, therefore, be difficult to describe the seller as having failed to give notice of readiness in accordance with Clause 5(a). It would also seem illogical to adopt this interpretation when the clause later provides that, where the vessel ceases to be ready for delivery after notice of readiness has been served, a second notice of readiness is to be served rather than the buyer being entitled to cancel straight away. Accordingly, it is submitted that failure to serve a valid notice of readiness is not the same as serving an invalid notice of readiness.

Another alternative interpretation is that the clause imposes an obligation on the seller to serve notice of readiness immediately the vessel becomes physically ready for delivery. This is because the notice is to be given *in accordance* with Clause 5(a) which provides that *when* the vessel is ready the seller *shall* give notice of readiness. This probably places undue emphasis on the word 'when' (by interpreting it as 'immediately') and also produces a result that could lead to uncertainty and litigation. It is difficult enough trying to determine whether a vessel is ready for delivery without having to determine the exact moment at which it became so. Meanwhile, the commercial benefit of such an interpretation would seem to be minimal except, perhaps, that a buyer may be keen to take delivery as soon as possible after the vessel's bottom has been inspected.

There are also further interpretations looking at the second of the two defaults (failure to be ready to complete a legal transfer by the cancelling date), seeking to explain, first, the use of the words 'maximum of three banking days' in the proviso and, secondly, the distinction between being 'ready to validly complete a legal transfer' in the default and having 'to make arrangements for the documentation' in the proviso. In the 1995 edition of this book it was mooted that these issues could be explained (at least in part) if the default provisions were re-written as three separate defaults, namely:

* failure to give notice of readiness in accordance with Clause 5(a) on or before the cancellation date;
* failure to be ready to complete a legal transfer by the cancellation date; or
* failure to arrange for the documentation set out in Clause 8 (including being ready to complete legal transfer) within three banking days of giving notice of readiness.

Using this interpretation, the buyer may cancel if the seller does not serve a valid notice of readiness before the cancellation date. The buyer may also cancel if the seller is not ready to complete a legal transfer by the cancellation date. The seller will then have three days after serving notice of readiness in which to prepare the delivery documents. (In the NSF 1987 edition it is generally accepted that, although the buyer has up to three days in which to pay for the vessel, the seller is expected to produce delivery documents upon payment being tendered, even if three days has not expired – this is despite the fact that the right to claim damages under Clause 14 may only arise on the cancellation date.)

If the seller does not arrange the delivery documents before the expiry of three days from the notice of readiness he will be in default, notwithstanding that the cancellation date may be some time away (hence, a maximum of three days after notice of readiness). Meanwhile, the seller's right to delay delivery of the documents (for up to three days) is to be read as being subject to the duty to be ready to complete a legal transfer by the cancelling date, so that if the seller serves notice of readiness on the cancellation date, the buyer can insist on taking immediate delivery (provided it pays) rather than having to wait up to three days for the seller to prepare the documents. In other words, in this interpretation, the proviso should not be read as meaning 'the seller shall always be given three banking days' to prepare the delivery documents. Rather, it should mean 'whatever the circumstances, the seller shall be granted no more than three banking days (and sometimes less)' to prepare the delivery documents.

To conclude, therefore, the seller's default provisions of the NSF 1993 edition are open to several interpretations, with many practitioners favouring the first interpretation set out above, and others subscribing to the latter. The safe course of action for any concerned seller would therefore be to seek to give himself as large a safety margin as possible when negotiating the cancellation date and to ensure that the vessel arrives at the delivery port in good time for the notice of readiness to be served well in advance thereof.

In contrast to this structure, the NSF 1987 edition identified failure 'to execute a legal transfer or to deliver the vessel with everything belonging to her in the manner and within the time specified in line 38' as entitling the seller to cancel. (The reference to 'the manner' was never explained but should probably have referred to the manner provided for in the MOA as a whole. The reference to line 38 was a reference to the cancelling date.)

The draftsman is said to have intended that damages should only be available for failure to serve notice of readiness or to effect delivery where this is due to the seller's negligence. Indeed, this was the subject of a specific amendment in the 1987 edition of NSF following the 'AL TAWFIQ' case in 1984, in which the court reached the opposite conclusion.[42] However, whether the amendment achieves this aim is open to doubt. In particular, in order to exclude the seller's *prima facie* liability for breach of contract (which does not require proof of negligence) general principles would require that any restriction be written in a manner that clearly excludes the relevant liability (any doubt being interpreted in the buyer's favour). Instead, the relevant provision in NSF 1993 merely makes clear that the seller will be liable if negligence can be proved. It says nothing about liability in these circumstances when the seller's negligence cannot be proved. Normal rules would result in the seller being contractually liable in such circumstances as well.

The NSF also remains silent on the consequences of other breaches of contract by the seller, for example, if the vessel does not comply with the terms of Clause 11. In such a circumstance, the buyer should be entitled to: refuse to accept delivery; refuse to pay the price; and to sue for damages. Alternatively, the buyer may pay the price, accept delivery and still sue for damages.

It is submitted that, if the intention of NSF Clause 14 was to restrict the availability of these remedies to situations only where there is proven negligence on the part of the seller, it has failed to do so.

Clause 15: buyers' representatives

This clause entitles the buyer to put two representatives on board the vessel for the purposes of familiarisation only. It provides that the representatives shall be 'at their sole risk and expense'. Whether this means the buyer's risk and expense or the representative's risk and expense is unclear. However, it is not possible to predetermine or restrict liability of or to the representatives by a contract to which they are not a party. Further, it is not possible to restrict the seller's possible liability for any personal injury that may be caused to the representatives (liability for personal injury cannot be excluded or limited by contract in English law). It is for this reason that an indemnity letter should be obtained from the buyer (or, better still, the buyer's P&I club) before allowing the representatives on board. It is submitted that a letter of indemnity signed by the representatives themselves, as is provided for in Clause 15, is inadequate protection for a seller unless it is clear they are signing on behalf of the buyer (and have full authority to do so).

There was no equivalent of Clause 15 in the 1987 edition although a similar provision was often added as a negotiated addendum. Now, as then, such representatives are only there for the purpose of familiarisation and as observers. However, they will no doubt surreptitiously inspect the vessel's condition. Sometimes, the seller includes clauses in the indemnity (which has to be given by the buyer before the agents go on board) to the effect that the buyer will not allow himself to be influenced as to whether or not to accept the ship at delivery by anything the agents may discover about the vessel during their period on board. This is of little practical value because every buyer is going to consider all available information in deciding whether or not to take delivery.

Clause 16: arbitration

The arbitration clause offers the parties three alternatives. If none is selected, the first is deemed to apply. This nominates English law as the governing law and provides for arbitration in London in accordance with the Arbitration Act 1996 (by virtue of this Act superseding the Arbitration Acts 1950 and 1979 to which the MOA refers). The MOA does not provide for any particular set of arbitration rules to apply. A reference to the London Maritime Arbitrators' Association terms would have better reflected market practice, though, in fact, LMAA arbitrators always accept appointments on LMAA terms.

The second option which can be selected by the parties is for the contract to be governed by, and construed in accordance with, Title 9 of the United States Code and the Law of the State of New York. Arbitration is to be in New York under the rules of the Society of Maritime Arbitrators Inc.

The third option is for the parties to insert their own choices of governing law and place of arbitration.

The 1987 edition provides for each party to appoint one arbitrator and then requires that they insert the name of a third party whose responsibility it will be to appoint a third arbitrator. All three arbitrators will then sit to hear any dispute. One fault that has occurred in the completion of this clause arises out of the provisions that apply where one of the parties fails to appoint an arbitrator. In such circumstances the NSF provides that the person entitled to appoint the 'third' arbitrator shall also appoint an arbitrator for the defaulting party. However, it is common for the parties to have agreed that the third arbitrator should be appointed by the first and second arbitrators jointly. Hence, if one party fails to appoint an arbitrator there is no one to appoint the third arbitrator and, similarly, there is no one to appoint an arbitrator in place of the one that should have been appointed by the defaulting party. Again, resort would ultimately have to be had to the court to resolve the situation. The clause goes on to provide that the MOA is to be governed by the law of the place agreed for arbitration.

Execution and additional clauses

The MOA is usually signed by both parties (or, commonly, their agents) and, unless stipulated otherwise, it will be binding on the parties from the time of signature. Alternatively, each party may sign one original and exchange it for an original signed by the other party, in which event it would normally be binding from the date on which both counterparts are delivered or exchanged.

In addition, it is fairly usual to include a number of extra clauses which are typed onto additional sheets and attached to the back of the MOA dealing with any particularly unusual aspects of the transaction, such as specific requirements for the type of vessel involved, but may also include a number of other standard provisions such as those detailed below.

- It is common for the buyer to require that the seller confirms that the vessel is not 'black-listed' and this can take a number of forms. The seller's confirmation is usually only given 'to the best of his knowledge' but the blacklisting covered by the letter may range from blacklisting by the Arab League in Damascus through to blacklisting by 'any nation or charterer' or even just 'blacklisting' as a general term.
- There is sometimes a confidentiality clause requiring each party to keep the contents of the MOA confidential.
- The sale may be subject to third-party consents being obtained, such as export or import licences. In contrast to situations where sales are subject to approvals on the part of the buyers or sellers themselves, such clauses import a duty on the relevant party to use reasonable endeavours to obtain the specified consent.[43]
- it is also frequently common for Clause 8 to be deleted and replaced by an addendum setting out in more detail all the sale and purchase documents required by the buyer and seller, taking into account (if the vessel is to change flag) any specific requirements the buyer's new intended register may have.

The standard documents

Acting for the buyer – registration, seller's authorisation and buyer's authorisation

When acting for the buyer, there are three main concerns to address regarding the standard documents. First, and primarily, one must make certain that the documents produced by the seller will be sufficient for the buyer to obtain good title and a permanent registration under the buyer's intended flag. Secondly, one must ensure that the seller, or its representatives, has the power/authority to transfer the vessel to the buyer. Thirdly, one should ensure that the buyer, or its representatives, also has the necessary power/authority to buy and pay for the vessel.

Each registry has different requirements for obtaining permanent registration and the major ones are dealt with in Chapter 11. The NSF 1993 (unlike the 1987 edition) sets out various commonly required documents that are to be provided by the seller as a matter of course. It also requires the seller to provide such additional documents as the buyer's chosen register may require, subject to timely notification of these requirements by the buyer. It is important, therefore, for a buyer to understand its own requirements in this area.

Generally speaking, in order to obtain a permanent registration on a new register, it will be necessary to obtain evidence that the old registration has been permanently deleted or closed, as well as to produce a bill of sale. These will often need to be legalised by the authorities in the new place of registration unless they are executed or issued there. The reasoning behind this dual obligation is that a new register will wish to have evidence of a good root of title on the part of the seller, and evidence that the title has been properly transferred to the buyer. If this is provided it is reasonable for the registrar to conclude that the buyer has acquired good title.

That said, it is rare for the permanent deletion documents to be available at the time of sale and much more usual for the buyer to be given evidence that the vessel is in a position where it can be deleted together with an undertaking to delete it within an agreed period of time. (This could constitute, for example, proof of all taxes having been paid and any necessary permissions having been granted before the transfer.) The period of time should be agreed between the parties, taking into account the minimum time in which deletion can be achieved in the seller's place of registration and the maximum time that will be allowed in the buyer's place of registration. The time period is limited to a maximum of four weeks in the NSF 1993. In contrast, the NSF 1987 edition implies that the deletion certificate should be handed over at delivery. Generally speaking, a seller should ensure the latter is amended before executing an MOA in the NSF 1987 edition format, as he will frequently have difficulty complying with such an obligation.

On the basis of the presentation of such evidence, together with the bill of sale, the new registry will usually issue some form of provisional registration that enables the vessel to sail, even if full or permanent registration is not yet possible. However, the buyer should always be careful to ensure that any additional required documentation is provided within the agreed time period. The essence of provisional registration is that should the required additional documents not be provided the registration will not be made permanent and could even lapse. (This is subject to certain protection given to mortgagees in most jurisdictions, although the basis of such protection is often unclear.) The time period can sometimes be extended provided the registrar is kept properly informed. Lack of a permanent registration would usually be regarded as an unsatisfactory root of title for the purposes of any future sale of the vessel, and lack of any registration at all would make the vessel practically impossible to operate.

The second concern of the buyer is to verify that the seller is duly authorised to effect the sale. This is discussed to some extent under Clause 8 of the NSF above. This is because, although valid registration of a vessel is generally accepted as being evidence of having good title to a vessel, it does not, of itself, actually confer ownership. The only real way for the buyer to acquire good title is for the seller to transfer good title to the buyer. It follows that, should the selling company not validly authorise the sale, then the buyer may not acquire good title, even though the buyer's new registry will show it as having good title. (In most jurisdictions, the fact that a party is registered as the owner of the vessel is not conclusive of title, it is merely good evidence.)

The means by which a seller validly transfers title will depend largely upon two factors: the law of the place of incorporation of the selling company and the law of the place in which the bill of sale is executed. It is the law of the place of incorporation that will generally govern the power of the company to dispose of assets (and the means of exercising that power) and this will usually depend upon a combination of the rules set out in the company's own constitutional documents and the general law of the place of incorporation. Accordingly, any buyer should ask to see the constitutional documents of the seller (or obtain copies from a public registry, if available) and may also wish to take legal advice in the seller's jurisdiction.

Generally speaking, resolutions of a selling company's directors and/or its shareholders will be required in order to authorise the sale of a major asset such as a ship. Once the buyer has identified which resolutions are necessary then he should require copies of them, which may either be certified as true by the seller or, better still, be notarised to confirm the authority and identity of any signatory and legalised to confirm the authority and identity of the notary.[44]

Shipowners often point out, not unreasonably, that they regularly enter into significant contracts such as charterparties or repair and maintenance arrangements. In doing so they would not normally expect the board of directors (or the shareholders) to authorise the contract formally, provided it is signed by a director or officer/manager of the company. Even so, they would expect those contracts to be binding on the company and not capable of being avoided for lack of authority. This is correct.

The difference is that such contracts are within the ordinary course of business for a shipowning company. As such, they fall within the ostensible authority of a director or officer/manager of the company. However, it would be very unusual for the sale or purchase of a ship to be within the ordinary business of a shipowning company. For this to be the case, the company would need to be in the business of buying and selling ships on a regular basis. Due to the one-ship company ownership structure that is generally employed by owners, this would be most unusual. However, for a large, multi-vessel company, this argument may well have some justification.

Accordingly, most owning companies, including all one-ship companies, will need formal authorisation in order to sell a vessel, whereas a large multi-vessel owning company (not a mere holding company) may find that it buys and sells ships regularly enough for a sale to fall within its ordinary business, and so it could be within the ostensible authority of individual directors or officers/managers. In such circumstances, board resolutions may be unnecessary but would still be advisable.

The reason why the law of the place of execution of the bill of sale is also relevant is because, at least under English rules of private international law, the formalities of execution of a document are generally regarded as being governed by the law of the place of execution. Accordingly, if a Liberian company executes a bill of sale in England, then the actual execution is regarded as being governed by English law even though the authorisation is governed by Liberian law. Accordingly, if the English rules governing execution are not complied with, the bill of sale may be ineffective to transfer title.

It should be noted that in such circumstances the bill of sale will usually be executed under a Power of Attorney, in which case the Power of Attorney constitutes part of the authorisation documentation. The buyer will want first to verify that the seller validly authorised and executed the Power of Attorney, and secondly to see the Power of Attorney itself (to ensure that it grants the necessary authority). Accordingly, the buyer should always have legal advice in the jurisdiction in which the bill of sale is executed and in the place where the Power of Attorney is executed (or alternatively insist that each document is notarised to say that it is valid and binding in accordance with its terms and then legalised).

The third area of concern for the buyer is to see that the buyer itself is duly authorised to carry out the transaction. As a corporate entity the buyer should be certain that any decisions are duly recorded in its minutes and that whatever meetings are required under its constitutional documents or the general law are duly held, the decisions recorded and that any necessary appointments, such as attorneys in fact, are made.

Acting for the seller – authorisation

The seller will wish to see that the buyer is duly authorised, although, in practice, provided the seller receives the money due he will probably not be too concerned with this detail. The seller will also wish to see that the seller is duly authorised to prevent any later recriminations from shareholders, investors or creditors. In practice, one-ship companies often show little concern in this area, but any shipowner of repute will always wish to see that its transactions are properly authorised and carried out.

Acting for either party – the protocol of delivery and acceptance

The one document that both parties will wish to see, to sign and to have an original of, is the protocol of delivery and acceptance. This is provided for in Clause 8 of NSF 1993 although it was not mentioned in NSF 1987. The document is used to define the exact time at which property and risk in the vessel passes. One should recall that the memorandum of agreement (which sets out the sale contract) does not operate to pass title to the buyer and specifically (at least in the case of the NSF contract) states that risk will remain with the seller until delivery of the vessel. Delivery of the vessel can be divided roughly into two parts, namely: physical delivery, where the ship is handed over and the crews exchanged; and documentary delivery, where the bill of sale is handed over in exchange for payment.

Technically speaking, it is the delivery of the bill of sale that transfers title to the buyer. However, a bill of sale does not necessarily bear the date upon which it is delivered because it can be executed 'in escrow'[45] and therefore on its face does not indicate the date on which ownership is transferred and would in any event not indicate the time of day at which ownership is transferred.

Of course, the parties will know at what moment the bill of sale was handed over but each will wish to have some written evidence of that time. Therefore, a protocol of delivery and acceptance is drawn up in duplicate and signed by each party so that each has an original record of the agreed time of delivery. One common error is to state in the protocol that title to the vessel is transferred by the protocol. This is incorrect, as it is merely a document recording between the parties the date and time at which the document transferring title, namely the bill of sale, is handed over. It merely constitutes good evidence of the time at which title is transferred.

It is also common practice for a further protocol of delivery and acceptance to be executed on board the vessel at the time when control is handed over from the seller's crew to the buyer's. Indeed, some practitioners regard this as the more important document. Generally speaking, this is coordinated so as to be simultaneous with the execution of the protocol of delivery and acceptance at the documentary closing. However, although its wording is generally identical, its purpose and effect, from a legal perspective, is probably somewhat different. By recording the time at which physical control of the vessel passes from seller to buyer it is probable that this second protocol of delivery and acceptance acts as evidence of the moment at which 'risk' in the vessel passes, and the buyer becomes responsible for insurance, whereas title may pass before, after or at the same time and will be separately recorded in the first protocol referred to above.

A further issue that commonly arises when drafting the protocol of delivery and acceptance, is the extent to which it can be used to limit the buyer's rights against the seller. For example, the protocol may be worded in such a way that the buyer acknowledges that the vessel is delivered 'in accordance with' the sale and purchase agreement. If the vessel does not 'accord' with the MOA (for example, because it is defective) the buyer would normally have a right to claim damages from the seller. By executing a protocol of delivery and acceptance in this form, such rights may be lost. In any event, there is a certain tension between the general law and the principle of signing an 'acceptance' of the vessel.

Under the SGA, a buyer is entitled to reject defective goods, even after taking delivery of them, at any time prior to them being 'accepted' by him.[46] However, the SGA makes clear that acceptance only occurs, and this right to reject is only lost, when the buyer has had a reasonable opportunity to inspect the goods. In theory, therefore, the right to reject the vessel may be retained, notwithstanding the execution of an 'acceptance,' until the buyer has had a reasonable opportunity to inspect the vessel following delivery. This does not apply where the buyer has examined the goods before delivery.

However, what is not clear is whether the right to reject the vessel after delivery will only be lost if such pre-delivery examination amounts to a 'reasonable opportunity to ascertain whether [the vessel] is in conformity with the contract' (consistent with Section 35(2)(a) SGA). The alternative to this is the right to reject after delivery only being lost in relation to defects that the actual examination carried out (rather than a reasonable examination) ought to have revealed (which would be consistent with Section 25(b) SGA). A complete pre-inspection would be practically impossible for something as complex as a vessel, which can only really be properly inspected while it is being operated. It would certainly be greater than that envisaged by Clause 4 NSF 1993 or 1987 editions.

Many practitioners would regard this right to reject after delivery as contrary to accepted market practice, as well as being very difficult to make use of (because of the difficulties of actually recovering the purchase price). Nonetheless, it may constitute an additional weapon in the armoury of the disappointed buyer.

Practical matters

Notarisation and legalisation

It is appropriate at this stage to mention something on the subject of notarisations and to point out that these can take many forms. Many notarial attestations will not make clear quite what is being attested to by the notary. Others are much more specific. One should be aware that a notary may be attesting to any one or more of the following:

- that the document was signed by a person who informed the notary that he was the person named in the document (this is a style of notarisation common in the United States);

- that the document was signed by a person who actually was the person named in the document;
- that the person who signed the document held the position he was identified in the document as holding;
- that the person who signed the document was duly authorised to sign the document;
- that the document itself is what it purports to be; and
- that the document itself is valid and binding.

Those familiar with notarisations will have observed the subtle differences between the various certificates applied by notaries. This is sometimes the result of the notary only having a limited knowledge of the accuracy of the document being notarised. On other occasions it may be related to the notary's special knowledge of the jurisdiction in which the document being notarised will be required.

Legalisation, on the other hand, is merely a governmental acknowledgement that the notary or government official who has certified the relevant document is the person he purports to be, and is known by that government to be duly appointed as a notary or to hold the official status he claims. That is to say, it is not the underlying document that is 'legalised' but, rather, the authenticity (not the accuracy) of the notarial or official certificate (or of any prior legalisation).

Where a legalisation is required, it is the legalisation of the government of the place where the document is to be produced that must be obtained. This would normally be obtained from the consulate of that country in the place where the document is executed (and may require the prior legalisation by the authorities of the place of execution). On the other hand, where the document is executed in a country that is a party to the Hague Convention of 5 October 1961 and it is to be produced in another country that is also a party to that Convention, then the authorities of the country in which it is executed can place a certificate known as an 'apostille' on the document making legalisation unnecessary.

Inspections

Difficulties with inspections have largely been dealt with when reviewing Clauses 4 and 6 of the NSF 1993, as well as in the discussion of protocols of delivery and acceptance under 'acting for either party' (above). However, when delivery is actually taking place, there will in effect be a further informal inspection as the new master comes on board. He will want to look around the vessel before confirming to the buyer that it is in order and that he is ready to accept it, and the buyer will not normally make payment until such confirmation has been received.

Before taking delivery, the buyer has to consider what (if anything) is wrong with the vessel and whether it amounts to a breach of contract. If it does amount to a breach of contract, the buyer has to decide whether he is entitled to reject the vessel and, if so, whether he wishes to do so. If not, he must decide whether there is a realistic possibility of recovering damages in respect of the breach once he has paid the purchase price. This will depend not only on whether he can prove his claim but also on whether he can seize any assets of the seller. Clearly, taking delivery and paying the purchase money is a critical moment for the buyer because, once this has been done, the remedies available to him significantly change.

Completing the transaction

By the time it comes to completion of the sale and purchase, one would hope to have agreed all the final points of the documentary completion and be left with only three outstanding items on the agenda (other than the handing over of documents). These would generally be: the discharge of the old mortgage; the registration of the ship (and any new mortgage); and payment. Prior to NSF 1993 it was standard practice to effect all of these simultaneously, at least in theory. Whether or not it was in fact simultaneous is a matter of conjecture, but it was the norm for each party to confirm that provided the other(s) went ahead as agreed then it would proceed also.

However, under Clause 8 of NSF 1993, the seller is only entitled to receive the purchase money if he tenders delivery of the vessel free from encumbrances together with a certificate of freedom from encumbrances from the vessel's registry. This would seem to have the practical effect of requiring the seller's mortgagee to release his security before receiving payment. (However, it can be left until the last minute if the seller's registry is on hand to issue a freedom from encumbrances certificate at the delivery meeting.) This is in contrast to the position under the 1987 edition where a buyer would be ill-advised to claim that a ship was not properly tendered for delivery if a bill of sale and an effective discharge of mortgage is offered against payment. That is to say, under the 1987 edition a vessel may be capable of delivery even when the register shows it to be subject to an encumbrance.

Accordingly, under NSF 1993 or NSF 1987 the seller's mortgagee will confirm that, provided payment is effected, it will discharge the old mortgage. The buyer will confirm that, provided the old mortgage is discharged and that the old registry agrees to issue the necessary deletion documents, and that the documents that have already been determined as needed to pass (and to evidence) good title and to obtain registration will be handed over, he will instruct his bank to make payment. The buyer's bank will confirm that, provided the documents that it has previously determined to be necessary to achieve the new registration of the vessel and the new mortgage as a first priority charge will be handed over, then it will effect payment. Once each of these parties has confirmed to the other that this will be done the requirements of the 1993 and 1987 editions appears to diverge slightly.

Under the 1993 edition:

- the old mortgage is discharged first;
- the bill of sale and other delivery documents are handed over upon payment being received;
- the ship is registered in the ownership of the buyer; and then
- the new mortgage is registered.

Under the 1987 edition it is a matter of conjecture whether payment is made against the first or the second of the stages, and whether the process can be stopped mid-way through. There is a practical difficulty in that, while the seller is under a duty to discharge the old mortgage before he transfers title to the ship (assuming they cannot actually be done simultaneously), the buyer is only under a duty to pay against the transfer of the ship. However, the seller will almost invariably want the purchase money in order to discharge the old mortgage.

The normal course of action is for the seller to provide for the discharge of the mortgage by lodging an executed discharge with the current registry of the vessel. Once all parties are happy that payment will be tendered, the seller's mortgagee (who will be represented at the closing meeting) will give notice to the registrar that the mortgage should be deleted, whereon the registrar can give instructions to its agent to issue a certificate evidencing that the vessel is free of encumbrances. This should satisfy the buyer (and its bank and its proposed registry) that the vessel can be registered, at least provisionally, and the new mortgagee can then advance the purchase price.

Payment

The means of paying the purchase price is frequently the cause of some difficulty although the most favoured and sensible method available these days is the 'irrevocable payment letter'. This is, as its name indicates, a simple letter addressed from the buyer's bank to the seller's bank undertaking that payment of a specified amount in same day value funds will be made on the date of the letter. Most sophisticated international banks will accept such a letter as binding and act in reliance upon it. This means that there is no need to wait for a confirmation to be passed around the banking system by telex to the effect that funds have been transferred between the appropriate correspondent banks in New York (assuming a dollar payment).

The most common alternative is to make payment by 'tested telex' or SWIFT money transfers between banks. The banker suggesting this method will normally assure the other party that it will take 'about five minutes' to confirm such a telex or trace the receipt of funds. In practice it can take anything up to eight hours because of the queuing systems built into modern day telex machines, the possibility of the telex going astray and the time taken to decode any telex 'test'. The test is merely a security device employed between banks to identify the source of the telex and so ensure that they can rely upon the instructions or information contained in any particular telex. SWIFT money transfers are also not always easy to trace.

The most significant problem with adopting the irrevocable payment letter technique arises where amounts are left to be agreed at the last moment, such as for bunkers and lubes.[47] These make it necessary either to agree a different payment method for these items (which, if tested telex is chosen, makes the use of a payment letter for the price fairly pointless) or for the attending banker to carry a letter 'in blank' so that he may complete the amount due in relation to this element of the payment when known. Many banks are reluctant to issue payment letters in blank but there is no reason why one should not be drafted specifying a maximum amount in excess of the anticipated total, and providing for the exact sum to be completed in manuscript at the delivery meeting. The risk to the bank is then capped at the level of the selected maximum amount. This allows the appropriate signatories in the bank to execute the letter before the exact amount is known and allows some other, probably more junior, representative of the bank to attend the delivery meeting in order to complete the actual amount and to hand the letter over.

A third alternative in occasional use, particularly in certain types of sale (such as vessel scrapping arrangements), is the letter of credit. These are the subject of a number of books already and cannot be covered usefully in this chapter. However, one point worth noting by a seller when agreeing to a letter of credit payment, is the danger of leaving any of the payment terms within the control of the buyer. By establishing a letter of credit the buyer will generally avoid the requirement to put up a deposit because payment is, essentially, guaranteed.

However, in the event that the market price falls or the buyer for some other reason does not wish to accept delivery, then there will be no deposit for the seller to claim as liquidated damages, as there is under the standard NSF terms. Accordingly the seller should ensure that the letter of credit is payable against presentation of documentation entirely within his own control so that, once the letter of credit is established, he no longer need rely on the buyer's cooperation in order to receive payment. The dangers of not doing this were readily apparent in the 'MESSINIAKI TOLMI' case[48] where the buyers, Taiwanese shipbreakers, refused to sign the papers necessary for the sellers to receive payment as they no longer wished to pay the contract price for the ship.

The preservation and enforcement of the buyer's rights

Breaches of contract by sellers can be divided into two types: non-delivery (possibly this would need to be by reason of the seller's proven negligence in order to be actionable – see Clause 14 – Seller's default above); and delivery of a defective or non-complying vessel. In the former situation, the buyer is, under the NSF, entitled to a return of his deposit plus interest and damages for breach of contract. However, breach of a sale and purchase contract does not give rise to an action *in rem* against the vessel (at least in English law) and therefore it can be difficult for a buyer to obtain security prior to bringing an action. (The seller can dispose of the vessel elsewhere and dissipate the money received – the right of action will not follow the vessel in the way that an *in rem* action would.)

On the other hand, the equitable remedy of specific performance can be available in the English courts to enforce a sale and purchase contract.[49] This means that, where enforcement of such a remedy is practicable, a buyer may be able to compel performance of the contract if he can show that damages would be an inadequate remedy, and persuade a judge to exercise his discretion to make the necessary order.

The second type of breach is where the seller tenders a defective or non-complying vessel for delivery.[50] Provided the buyer is aware of the breach, he must first decide whether or not it entitles him to refuse to accept delivery and, if so, whether he wishes to do so. Most breaches of the MOA will entitle the buyer to reject the vessel, and so the main consideration is whether or not he wishes to do so. If he does wish to reject, his concern is first how to recover the deposit (with interest) and secondly how to recover any damages to which he is entitled. Where the buyer still wishes to take delivery of the vessel (or where he has no choice), then the primary concern is how to obtain compensation for the breach, whether through agreement with the seller or by way of arbitration or litigation.

There is potentially a half-way house, in that the buyer may wish to prevent the seller tendering delivery and so prevent the breach arising, or at least delay it until the cancelling date. In doing so, the buyer may hope to encourage the seller to remedy the potential breach, while at the same time, by preventing the seller from tendering the vessel for delivery, avoiding any chance of being in breach of contract himself. The most likely way in which a buyer could succeed in such an action would be by seeking an injunction to prevent the seller from serving notice of readiness under the MOA. If successful, this would prevent the obligation to pay the price from arising until the injunction was lifted and notice duly served.

Once the buyer 'accepts' the vessel, whether by signing the protocol of delivery and acceptance or subsequently,[51] he effectively loses the right to reject the vessel and he is left with four options as to how to proceed.

- He can raise the issue with the seller beforehand, and either negotiate a reduction in the purchase price or agree that the seller is to put up a certain amount on joint deposit for the purpose of giving security for any possible action.
- He can accept that the selling company is a substantial company which will still have assets after the sale has gone ahead, and therefore can usefully be sued to recover damages.
- He can agree with the seller that the seller will arrange for a third party of a substantial nature to guarantee the seller in relation to any potential litigation.
- He can endeavour to freeze the assets of the seller immediately upon handing over the purchase price. In England this is dealt by means of what is now know as a Freezing Order (previously known as a *Mareva* injunction after the case in which it was first recognised), while on the continent *saisie conservatoire* proceedings are available on a similar basis. Previously the English courts developed a practice of facilitating this process much more easily than they do at present by granting *Mareva nisi* injunctions which became 'absolute' when a cause of action arose.[52] In a sale and purchase situation the cause of action arises when the contract is breached, which happens on delivery.

The availability of a *Mareva nisi* meant that, assuming that all the other requirements for *Mareva* relief could be satisfied, one was able to have an order prepared and made by the court before the delivery meeting. (This could be done in anticipation of a breach, even though no actual cause of action had yet arisen in favour of the buyer.) One could then serve it on the seller immediately after taking delivery and making payment, and before the seller had an opportunity to dissipate the funds. Unfortunately for buyers, the Court of Appeal in the 'VERACRUZ I' case[53] ruled that there was no provision in English law under which such a *nisi* (or provisional) *Mareva* injunction could be granted before a cause of action arose.

Accordingly, it is now once again necessary to rush straight to court from the delivery meeting in order to obtain the injunction and, therefore, very difficult to give notice of the injunction to the seller's bankers before there has been an opportunity for the seller to dissipate the purchase monies.

It should perhaps be stressed that when a buyer prevents the seller removing assets from the jurisdiction (by way of a Freezing Order (*Mareva* injection)) it does not mean that the buyer has failed to comply with his contractual obligation to effect payment in freely transferable funds. This was pointed out by the Court of Appeal in the 'BHOJA TRADER'[54] case. It is an important distinction, because if the buyer fails to pay it is arguable that the seller can recover the vessel in quasi-contract. If payment is made, on the other hand, the seller has no remedy against the vessel and is left either to fight the injunction or to dispute the buyer's claim, and recover whatever monies are left when judgment is obtained.

---

[1] *Lloyd del Pacifico v Board of Trade* [1929] 35 Lloyd's Rep. 217.

[2] *Rugg v Street [1962] 1 Lloyd's Rep.* 364.

[3] *Thoresen & Co. (Bangkok) Ltd v Fathom Marine Company Ltd and Others* [2004] EWHC 167 (Comm); [2004] 1 Lloyd's Rep. 622.

[4] [1991] 1 Lloyd's Rep. 120.

[5] See also under 'The standard documents – acting for either party' in this chapter.

[6] See 'Practical matters – the preservation and enforcement of the buyer's rights' in this chapter.

[7] The 'STENA NAUTICA' (No. 2) [1982] 2 Lloyd's Rep. 336.

[8] [1987] 1 Lloyd's Rep. 283.

[9] The 'BLANKENSTEIN' [1985] 1 Lloyd's Rep. 93.

[10] [1988] 2 Lloyd's Rep. 423.

[11] The 'SELENE G' [1981] 2 Lloyd's Rep. 180.

[12] See under 'Sale and purchase within the structure of NSF – the buyer' above.

[13] See further under 'The standard documents – acting for either party' below.

[14] See under 'Clause 14: sellers' default' in this chapter.

[15] The 'TARIA' [1998] 2 Lloyd's Rep. 341.

[16] The 'MERAK' [1976] 2 Lloyd's Rep. 250.

[17] Docker v Hyams [1969] 1 Lloyd's Rep. 487.

[18] See Clause 14 in this chapter

[19] See Clause 14 in this chapter.

[20] The 'MORNING WATCH' [1990] 1 Lloyd's Rep. 547.

[21] For example, Caparo v Dickman [1990] 1 All ER 568.

[22] The 'NICHOLAS H' [1995] 2 Lloyd's Rep. 299.

[23] [1991] 1 Lloyd's Rep. 120.

[24] [1995] 3 WLR 118.

[25] See under 'The seller' in this chapter.

[26] See 'Practical matters – payment' in this chapter.

[27] See under 'Acting for either party – the protocol of delivery and acceptance' in this chapter.

[28] The 'BARENBELS' [1985] 1 Lloyd's Rep. 528.

[29] Rank Enterprises v Gerard [2000] 1 Lloyd's Rep. 403.

[30] [1985] 1 Lloyd's Rep. 528.

[31] The 'MONICA S' [1967] 2 Lloyd's Rep. 113.

[32] See Chapter 7.

[33] The 'CERRO COLORADO' [1993] 1 Lloyd's Rep. 58.

[34] The 'TREMONT' [1841] 1 Wm. Rob. 163 per Dr Lushington.

[35] See under 'The vessel' above and 'Clause 14: sellers default' in this chapter.

[36] [1981] 2 Lloyd's Rep. 333.

[37] [1978] 2 Lloyd's Rep. 325.

[38] [1993] 2 Lloyd's Rep. 52.

[39] [1995] 1 Lloyd's Rep. 579.

[40] See 'Clause 6: dry-docking' in this chapter.

[41] See generally 'Clause 3: payment', particularly the discussion on notice of readiness conditions.

[42] [1984] 2 Lloyd's Rep. 598.

[43] Windschuegl v Pickering [1950] 84 Lloyd's Rep. 89.

[44] See under 'Practical matters – notarisation and legalisation' in this chapter.

[45] The 'ORO CHIEF' [1983] 2 Lloyd's Rep. 509.

[46] Section 35 Sale of Goods Act 1979, as amended.

[47] See also 'Clause 7: spares/bunkers etc' in this chapter.

[48] [1983] 1 Lloyd's Rep. 666.

[49] The 'STAR GAZER' and 'STAR DELTA' [1985] 1 Lloyd's Rep. 370.

[50] Discussed under 'Clause 14: seller's default' and 'Acting for either party – the protocol of delivery and acceptance'.

[51] See under 'Acting for either party – the protocol of delivery and acceptance'.

[52] A v B [1989] 2 Lloyd's Rep. 423.

[53] [1992] 1 Lloyd's Rep. 353.

[54] [1981] 2 Lloyd's Rep. 256.

Chapter 11

Registering the ship

Updated by Lucy French with international contributions

As has been seen in Chapter 1, there are several different types of register, all of which have different requirements for an owner wishing to register his ship. This chapter considers the requirements of certain of the most important registries, including examples of the domestic register (for example, of the United Kingdom); the international register (for example, the Norwegian International Ship Register) and the open register (for example, of Liberia and Panama). As in Chapter 7, the information relating to those registers is presented in question and answer format for ease of comparison.[1] In addition, we have included summaries of registration procedures in India and China, which we hope are of interest.

The registration of the ship is, of course, the responsibility of the owner, or prospective owner, and the financing bank is unlikely to become too involved in the detailed registration procedure. However, the bank has a very clear legitimate interest in the registration process for the simple reason that, unless the ship, which forms the basis of the bank's underlying security, is properly registered, the bank will be unable to have a properly registered mortgage. A properly registered ship is, therefore, a fundamental condition of any financing in which a ship mortgage forms part of the security and it is, therefore, important for the financing bank to know something of the requirements of the most important registries.

One of the most important points on which a lender must satisfy himself is whether the registration of the vessel is provisional or permanent. This has different consequences in different jurisdictions. In many, a vessel that is only provisionally registered may not be mortgaged until permanent registration takes place. In others, mortgaging a provisionally registered vessel is perfectly possible and, indeed, quite usual, with the mortgage taking effect from the date of its registration, whether or not the vessel was then permanently registered.

Bahamas*

A   Ownership

1   What, if any, are the restrictions on ownership of vessels registered under the flag of the Bahamas?

There are no restrictions on ownership of vessels registered under the Bahamian flag.

2   If registration by companies is limited to companies incorporated in the Bahamas, is a local 'brass-plate' company sufficient, or must there be a closer, genuine connection?

Registration of Bahamian flag vessels is not restricted to companies incorporated in the Bahamas.

3   If registration by companies incorporated other than in the Bahamas is permitted, must a local representative be appointed? If so, are there any restrictions on the identity of that representative?

No local representative of a non-Bahamian shipowning company need be appointed.

4   Please summarise any restrictions (for example, as to number, nationality and so on) on who may own shares in shipowning companies incorporated in the Bahamas.

There are no restrictions with respect to ownership of shares in a Bahamian incorporated shipowning company.

5   Please explain any exchange control or other governmental or regulatory consents required in connection with the ownership of ships registered in the Bahamas.

There are no exchange control or other governmental or regulatory consents required in connection with vessels owned either by non-Bahamian shipowning companies or Bahamian shipowning companies provided the Bahamian shipowning company is owned by a non-Bahamian.

6   Please explain any special rules for any particular type of vessel.

The only special rules with respect to vessels are that they must be under 12 years old and have a minimum of 1,600 tons.

7   Is there any mandatory registration requirement for certain owners (for example, citizens of the Bahamas)?

There are no mandatory registration requirements for certain owners.

B   Eligibility

1   Are any particular types/sizes of ship ineligible for, or exempt from, registration?

There are no exemptions from registration of vessels under Bahamian Merchant Shipping Act.

2   What, if any, is the maximum age for registration of ships under the flag of the Bahamas?

Maximum age for registration of a Bahamian flag vessel is 12 years. In respect of any vessel in excess of that age, it is possible to make application to the Ministry of Transport for permission to register under Bahamian flag.

C   Names

1   What, if any, are the restrictions on the name under which a ship may be registered in the Bahamas?

While there are no restrictions on names under which ships may be registered under Bahamian flag, our law does not permit the use of duplicate names.

2   Is there a procedure for approval of names in advance?

There is a procedure for reserving a name in advance upon making the appropriate application.

3   If so, how does it operate? Does approval confer any priority rights in the use of the name?

Application must be made to the Registrar of Ships and once permission has been granted for use of that name, permission confers priority rights with respect to its use. Permission is valid for a period of three months.

D   New registration procedure

1   Where may ships intending to fly the flag of the Bahamas be registered:

1.1   in the Bahamas?

1.2   abroad?

Ships intending to register under Bahamian flag may do so either:

1.1   in Nassau:

Bahamas Maritime Authority, Gold Circle Building, East Bay Street, P.O. Box N 4891, Nassau, Bahamas

1.2   in London:

Bahamas Maritime Authority, 2nd Floor, Latham House, 16 Minories, London EC3N 1EH, England

in New York:

Bahamas Maritime Authority, Bahamas House, 231 East 46th Street, New York, NY 10017, United States of America

2   What documents and information must be submitted to effect registration? Does the legal system in the Bahamas lay down any specific requirements as to the contents of any of these documents–for example, of Bills of Sale–and, if so, what are they?

In support of an application for registration, the following documents in prescribed form must be submitted to the Registrar either in Nassau, London or New York:

(a)   name of ship;

(b)   former tonnage certificate;

(c)   former survey certificate and/or copy of certificate of registry;

(d)   former SOLAS certificate;

(e)   passenger ship: safety certificate;

(f)   cargo ship:

(i)   cargo ship safety construction certificate (500 gt)

(ii)   cargo ship safety equipment certificate (500 gt)

        (iii)   safety radiotelegraphy certificate (1,600 gt)

        (iv)   safety radiotelephone certificate (300 gt)

        (v)   MARPOL 1973 Oil Pollution Cert (over 150 gt tankers: 400 gt other)

- (g) former load line certificate;
- (h) number of passengers (if any);
- (i) number of crew berths (including master);
- (j) Bill of Sale or Builder's Certificate (new ship);
- (k) Declaration of Ownership;
- (l) certificate of company incorporation and certificate of good standing;
- (m) managing owner;
- (n) authorised officer declaration;
- (o) oil pollution certificate (tankers only) (CLC);
- (p) registration fee;
- (q) annual fee;
- (r) particulars of radio equipment installed;
- (s) radio accounting authority identification code (AAIC);
- (t) release from foreign register;
- (u) declaration of no liens on foreign register; and
- (v) carving note returned duly completed.

3   Please identify how many originals or copies of each document are required. Are fax copies of any of them acceptable?

An original of each of the above must be submitted for a registration. It is possible to proceed with registration with fax copies but this facilitates only provisional registration. The originals must be produced within the provisional registration period of six months and thereafter full registration is achieved.

4   Are there any requirements as to the language in which documents must be submitted? If they may be submitted in a foreign language, are there any translation requirements? If so, what are they and when must they be complied with?

All documents must be submitted in the English language or must be accompanied by certified translations into English when they are submitted to the Registrar of Shipping.

5   Please identify any particular requirements of the legal system in the Bahamas with regard to the method of execution of any of the registration documents, or with regard to notarisation or legalisation.

The following registration documents must either be signed before an English Notary Public or Commissioner for Oaths or alternatively have affixed to it an apostille with respect to the person administering the oath.

- (a) Declaration of Ownership;
- (b) Bill of Sale; and
- (c) Authorised Officer Declaration.

6 If the initial registration takes place abroad, is that registration final or provisional?
Registration abroad can be either provisional or final.

7 If provisional, what needs to be done to effect final registration? When must it be done?
If provisional, in order to effect final registration, the carving note must be returned to the Bahamian Registrar duly completed.

8 If provisional, what if any are the restrictions which apply to the vessel pending final registration?
All privileges and benefits of the Bahamian Merchant Shipping Act are conferred on provisionally registered vessels.

9 Can a provisionally registered ship be mortgaged?
A provisionally registered vessel can be mortgaged and particulars of the mortgage entered in the fees and deeds books and upon final registration transferred into the register.

E Technical matters

1 Please identify the requirements of the Bahamas with regard to inspection, survey measurement and the like in respect of newly registered ships.
2 By when must these requirements be complied with?
The Bahamian Merchant Shipping Act provides that all Bahamian registered ships shall be inspected for safety before the ship is put into service or on first registry and thereafter annually. Safety inspection certificates for all Bahamian ships are required to be renewed annually. Inspection is done by the government-appointed nautical inspectors in over 200 ports worldwide. Details of such inspectors can be obtained from the Registrar in London, in Nassau or in New York. The vessel must also be in class with one of the classification societies that have been appointed to survey Bahamian ships and issue the relevant certificates. The following is a list of the seven international classification societies:

(a) American Bureau of Shipping;
(b) Bureau Veritas;
(c) Det Norske Veritas;
(d) Germanischer Lloyd;
(e) Lloyds' Register of Shipping;
(f) Nippon Kaiji Kyokai; and
(g) Registro Italiano Navale

F Transfer of ownership

1 Please answer, either separately or by reference to your earlier answers, the questions listed under Sections D and E above in respect of a transfer of ownership of a vessel already registered in the Bahamas.
For the transfer of ownership of a Bahamian vessel, the following documents must be submitted:

    (a)   Bill of Sale;

    (b)   Declaration of Ownership;

    (c)   Authorised Officer Declaration;

    (d)   memorandum of managing owner;

    (e)   certificate of good standing in respect of shipowning company; and

    (f)   copy of certificate of incorporation of shipowning company.

2   *Please explain any exchange control or other governmental or regulatory consents required in connection with the sale to a foreign flag of a vessel registered under the flag of the Bahamas.*

There are no exchange control or other governmental or regulatory consents required in connection with the sale of a foreign flag or a Bahamian vessel provided the vessel is owned by a non-Bahamian owned company.

G   Deletion

1   *Please outline the procedure for deletion of vessels from the flag of the Bahamas.*

2   *Please answer, either separately or by reference to your earlier answers, the questions listed under Section D in respect of the deletion, as opposed to new registration, of a vessel.*

The following must be submitted in support of an application for Deletion Certificate:

    (a)   written application for Deletion Certificate;

    (b)   consent of mortgagee or discharge of existing mortgages;

    (c)   name, address, nationality of new owners;

    (d)   Bill of Sale; and

    (e)   details of country for transfer of ownership.

H   Certificate/transcripts

1   *Please identify the certificates and other documents issued to an owner on registration of his ship under the flag of the Bahamas.*

On provisional registry a provisional certificate of registration is issued which is valid for a period of six months within which time final registration must be achieved and at that point a certificate of registration in respect of full registration will be issued.

2   *Please outline the procedure (including fees payable) for obtaining information on the registered ownership of and encumbrances on vessels registered in the Bahamas.*

Information with respect to Bahamian vessels is obtained by a search of the register at a cost of US$18. It is also possible to obtain a transcript of the register for the price of US$50.

I   Fees/taxes

1   *What fees are currently payable:*

    1.1   *on new registration?*

1.2   on transfer of ownership?

1.3   on deletion?

The following fees are payable:

1.1   on registration:

(a)   for ships of 2,000 nrt or less, US$2,000;

(b)   for ships of 2,001 nrt to 5,000 nrt, US$1 per nrt;

(c)   for ships of 5,001 nrt to 25,000 nrt, US$0.90 per nrt; and

(d)   for ships over 25,000 nrt, US$22,500.

Annual fees

(a)   for ships of 2,000 nrt or less, US$2,552;

(b)   for ships of 2,001 nrt to 5,000 nrt, US$2,090 plus US$0.20 per nrt;

(c)   for ships 5,001 nrt to 25,000 nrt, US$2,090 plus US$0.17 per nrt; and

(d)   for ships over 25,000 nrt, US$2,090 plus US$0.17 per nrt.

Non-commercial yachts:

On registration US$2,000

Per annum US$700 plus US$150 Radio License and US$60 Certificate of Registry

Commercial yachts' fees are to be calculated on nrt, as with other ships.

A scheme of discounts has been introduced with regard to the registration of ships:

(a)   a discount of one third off the initial registration fee will be offered to an owner registering a ship less than five years old;

(b)   a discount of one third off the initial registration fee will also be offered to an owner registering three or more ships at the same time or within a period of 12 months provided that they are less than twelve years old;

(c)   the discount will be increased to 50 per cent in respect of an owner registering 10 or more ships at the same time or within a period of 12 months; and

(d)   discounts may be available for multiple registrations where some or all of the ships are over 12 years. In such cases the BMA office should be consulted.

NOTE: Discounts are not to be applied to ships with nrt less than 500.

1.2   on transfer of ownership:

US$200 if vessel is 1,600 nrt or under and US$400 if the vessel is over 1,600 nrt.

1.3   on deletion:

US$200.

J   Parallel Registration

1   Is parallel registration permitted:

1.1   onto the Bahamas' register?

1.2   from the Bahamas' register?

2   If so, what, if any, specific governmental or other consents are required?

Parallel registration is permitted under Bahamian law and no special governmental consent is required.

3   Is the period of parallel registration limited? If so, is it renewable?
Parallel registration is limited to length of the demise charter.

4   If parallel registration is dependent on the existence of a demise charter, does the Bahamas have a specific definition of demise or bareboat charter for these purposes? If so, what is it?
The Bahamian Shipping Act provides that 'bareboat charter' means lease without master and crew and for a given period of time.

5   Please answer the questions listed under Sections A to E above with reference to application for parallel registration onto the Bahamas register.
Application for registration of dual registry would follow the same form as normal registration with the various documents and fees being applicable in this case as well.

6   Can/must mortgages on ships parallel registered into the Bahamas registry also be registered in the Bahamas?
Mortgages on ships parallel registered in the Bahamas registry are only required to be registered where the Bahamas is the primary register.

7   Under what circumstances will/may the parallel registration of a ship onto the Bahamas' register be terminated or revoked?
Parallel registration will be revoked under an application for deletion as explained earlier.

K   General

1   Please identify the principal statutes and regulations in the Bahamas governing the registration of ships.
The following are the principal statutes and regulations in the Bahamas governing the registration of vessels:

> (a)   Merchant Shipping Act 1976;
> (b)   Merchant Shipping (Maritime Claims Limitation of Liability) Act 1989; and
> (c)   Merchant Shipping (Oil Pollution) Act.

2   Are there any other matters in the context of registration of ships under the legal system in the Bahamas which you feel should be emphasised?
No

---

* Contributed by Paul Knowles of McKinney, Bancroft and Hughes, Nassau, Bahamas.

Bermuda*

A   Ownership

1   What, if any, are the restrictions on ownership of vessels registered in Bermuda?
Vessels are divided into 64 shares and the minimum requirement for registration in Bermuda is that 33 of these shares should be owned by one or more qualified persons. Companies are qualified persons if they are incorporated in Bermuda, the United Kingdom, Anguilla, Cayman Islands, Channel Islands, Falkland Islands and Dependencies, Gibraltar, Isle of Man, Montserrat, Pitcairn Islands, St Helena and Dependencies, Turks and Caicos Islands or the British Virgin Islands (the 'Relevant Territories').

Individuals are qualified if they are British citizens, British Overseas Territories citizens, British Overseas citizens, persons who under the British Nationality Act, 1981 are British subjects and persons who under the Hong Kong (British Nationality) Order, 1986 are British Nationals (overseas).

In addition to the above the following are also deemed as a qualified person for the purposes of registration: bodies incorporated in an EEA state and an European Economic Interest Grouping (being a grouping formed in pursuance of Article I of the Council Registration No. 2137/85 and registered in the United Kingdom).

2   If registration by companies is limited to companies incorporated in Bermuda, is a local 'brass-plate' company sufficient, or must there be a closer, genuine connection?
Companies which are qualified persons are also required to have their principal place of business in one of the Relevant Territories, but not necessarily the one in which they are incorporated. Broadly speaking, 'principal place of business' means the centre of management and control. There is no restriction on the nationality of the shareholders of such companies.

3   If registration by companies incorporated other than in Bermuda is permitted, must a local representative be appointed? If so, are there any restrictions on the identity of that representative?
If none of the owners of the vessel are resident in Bermuda, a representative person must be appointed. The representative person may be an individual resident in Bermuda or a company incorporated in Bermuda and having its principal place of business there.

4   Please summarise any restrictions (for example, as to number, nationality etc.) on who may own shares in ship-owning companies incorporated in Bermuda.
There are no specific restrictions, but permission is required (from the Bermuda Monetary Authority) to incorporate a Bermuda company and generally, for the issue and transfer of its shares.

5   Please explain any exchange control or other governmental or regulatory consents required in connection with the ownership of ships registered in Bermuda.
Exchange control permission is required for the issue and transfer of shares in a Bermuda company, whether a local or exempted company, involving persons who are non-residents of Bermuda. The procedure is designed to enable the Bermuda Monetary Authority to screen prospective users of the jurisdiction for respectability and responsibility. Companies exempt

from Bermudian ownership requirements and generally carrying on business outside Bermuda are known as exempted companies. Upon incorporation, an exempted company is designated non-resident for exchange control purposes and is free to deal in any currency save for Bermuda dollars.

Specific permissions of the Bermuda Monetary Authority are generally required where 5 per cent of the equity securities in a Bermuda company are issued or transferred (except in the case of a company listed on an Appointed Stock Exchange). A general permission of the Bermuda Monetary Authority is customarily given in relation to applications for permission to transfer shares on enforcement of a share charge or other security interest over securities of a Bermuda exempted company.

Registration of a vessel may be refused if, having regard (a) to the condition of the ship so far as relevant to its safety or to any risk of pollution, or (b) to the safety, health and welfare of persons employed or engaged in any capacity on board the ship, it would be inappropriate for the ship to be registered.

6   *Please explain any special rules for any particular type of vessel.*
Regulations, cannot be registered in Bermuda.

7   *Is there any mandatory registration requirement for certain owners (for example, citizens of Bermuda)?*
No.

B   Eligibility

1   Are any particular types/sizes of ships ineligible for, or exempt from, registration?
Bermuda is recognised as a Category 1 Red Ensign Group Register by the United Kingdom and as such is able to register vessels of any type or tonnage. Fishing vessels are ineligible.

2   Is there a maximum age for registration of ships under the British flag in Bermuda?
There is no maximum age, but age could be a factor in refusing registration or removing from the register. In either case, the relevant factors are the condition of the vessel so far as relevant to its safety or to any risk of pollution and the safety, health and welfare of the persons employed or engaged in any capacity on board the vessel.

C   Names

1   What, if any, are the restrictions on the name under which a vessel may be registered in Bermuda?
The name of a vessel registered in Bermuda must be in Roman letters and any numerals must be in Roman or Arabic numerals. The Registrar of Shipping will not approve the proposed name of a ship if the name is the same as a ship already registered in Bermuda; if the name is similar to that of a registered ship in Bermuda such that the result would be to deceive or cause confusion in respect of the ships; if the name would be likely to be

confused with a distress signal, or if it is a name which is prefixed by any letters or a name which could indicate a type of ship or other word, where such prefix or suffix might cause confusion as to the name of the ship. The Registrar may also refuse to approve a name which might cause offence or embarrassment or which has a clear and direct connection with the Royal family.

2   Is there a procedure for approval of names in advance?
Yes.

3   If so, how does it operate? Does approval confer any priority rights in the use of name?
The appropriate form should be completed and sent to the Registrar of Ships, Hamilton, Bermuda. Once allowed by the Registrar of Ships, the owner has priority for a 12-month period and that period may be extended if sufficient cause is shown.

D   New registration procedure

1   Where may vessels intending to fly the flag of Bermuda be registered?
Hamilton is a British Registry Port and the only Registry Port in Bermuda. Vessels registered in Bermuda fly the red ensign undefaced and not the Bermuda flag.

2   What documents and information are required to effect registration?
- (a)   Builder's Certificate and all subsequent documents of sale (if any) prior to registration of the vessel. In the case of an existing foreign registered vessel, the original Bill of Sale is required;
- (b)   Application for Name Approval;
- (c)   Application to Register;
- (d)   Certificate of Incorporation and any certificates of change of name;
- (e)   certified copy of Memorandum of Association and Bye-laws (or equivalent);
- (f)   Appointment of Authorised Officers;
- (g)   Appointment of Representative Person and/or manager (if necessary);
- (h)   radio licence;
- (i)   Declaration of Ownership;
- (j)   Declaration of Eligibility;
- (k)   Certificate of Survey; and
- (l)   evidence of marking.

3   Does the legal system in Bermuda lay down any specific requirements as to the contents of any of these documents (for example, of Bills of Sale) and, if so, what are they?
Wherever possible, the documents should follow the statutory requirements or the statutory forms. However, in the case of new registrations, Bills of Sale complying with the requirements of the vessel's existing registration and otherwise valid may be acceptable.

4   *Please identify how many originals or copies of each document are required. Are fax or pdf copies acceptable?*

One original only is required. There may be circumstances where the Registrar will accept facsimile or pdf documents against an undertaking to produce the original but this should be considered only in emergencies and documents should be cleared with the Registrar in advance.

5   *Are there any requirements as to the language in which registration documents must be submitted?*

Documents should generally be submitted in the English language.

6   *If they may be submitted in a foreign language, are there any translation requirements? If so, what are they and when must they be complied with?*

All documents should be in English, but where this is not possible they should be accompanied by a certified translation.

7   *Please identify any particular requirements of the legal system in Bermuda with regard to the method of execution of any of the registration documents, or with regard to notarisation or legalisation.*

Documents in the statutory form should be executed as required by the form. Where they are executed outside Bermuda, they should be notarised, but legalisation is not generally necessary.

In the case of companies, the appointment of authorised officers must be executed under seal and the application for registration and Declaration of Ownership must be executed by an authorised officer so appointed. The authorised officer must also be an officer of the owning company.

8   *If the initial registration takes place abroad, is that registration final or provisional?*

Normally, arrangements can be made for a certificate of registry to be issued in Bermuda and forwarded to the relevant port, but a provisional certificate of registry may be issued by the appropriate person at ports outside Bermuda.

9   *If provisional, what needs to be done to effect final registration? When must it be done?*

Final registration must be effected within three months or, if earlier, when the ship next calls at a British registry port. It should be noted that where a ship has been provisionally registered once, it shall not be provisionally registered again within one year of the date of the issue of the certificate of provisional registration, except with the consent of the Registrar.

10   *If provisional, what, if any, are the restrictions which apply to the vessel pending final registration?*

Provisional certificates will not normally be issued where restrictions would be appropriate.

11   *Can a provisionally registered ship be mortgaged?*

A registered legal mortgage cannot be effected until the vessel has been registered in Bermuda, but an equitable mortgage can be effected pending such registration.

E   Technical matters

1   Please identify the requirements of Bermuda with regard to inspection, survey, measurement and the like in respect of newly registered ships.

Application for survey for tonnage measurement for Bermuda registration purposes may be made to:

(a)   Lloyds' Register of Shipping;

(b)   The British Technical Committee of the American Bureau of Shipping;

(c)   The British Committee of Bureau Veritas;

(d)   The British Committee of Det Norske Veritas;

(e)   The British Committee of Germanischer Lloyd;

(f)   The British Committee of Registro Italiano Navale (RINA) by special arrangement.

2   By when must these requirements be complied with?

The certificate of survey must be issued and the vessel marked prior to registration.

F   Transfer of ownership

1   Please answer, either separately or by reference to your earlier answers, the questions listed under Sections D and E above in respect of a transfer of ownership of a vessel already registered in Bermuda.

A statutory form Bill of Sale is required to transfer the vessel on the Bermuda Register and has to be recorded with the Registrar of Shipping at Hamilton, Bermuda. The Bill of Sale must be dated and include the number of shares of the vessel being transferred. The Registrar will need to be satisfied that the Bill of Sale has been executed in accordance with the Memorandum of Association and Bye-laws of the company. This will usually mean that the Bill of Sale must be executed under seal and the new owner will have to swear a Declaration of Ownership. The vessel does not have to be in Bermuda for this purpose. No other documents of title are required. Items such as the certificate of incorporation and appointment of authorised officers will be required in respect of the new owner, unless they are already on file. A Declaration of Eligibility must be completed confirming that the Company is qualified to own a British ship. No new certificate of survey is required but the appropriate fee must also be paid.

2   Please explain any exchange control or other governmental or regulatory consents required in connection with the sale to a foreign flag of a vessel registered in Bermuda.

Normally, the transferor and the transferee will not be subject to any exchange control restrictions relevant to the sale. If either of the seller or purchaser is a local Bermuda company, exchange control consent may be required for payments in currencies other than Bermuda dollars.

G   Deletion

1   Please outline the procedure for deletion of vessels from the Bermuda Registry.

An authorised officer must formally notify the Registrar of Ships in Bermuda in writing of the circumstances giving rise to the deletion and the Registrar makes an entry on the register accordingly. The Registrar will then issue a closure transcript to the owner of the ship and the ship's owner shall then surrender the certificate of registry to the Registrar for cancellation.

2   *Please answer, either separately or by reference to your earlier answers, the questions listed under Section D above in respect of the deletion, as opposed to new registration, of a vessel.*

No other documentation is required.

H   Certificates/transcripts

1   *Please identify the certificates and other documents issued to an owner on registration of a vessel in Bermuda.*
    (a)   Certificate of Registration;
    (b)   Tonnage Certificate;
    (c)   transcripts are available evidencing the registered owner and evidencing any subsisting registered mortgages.

2   *Please outline the procedure (including fees payable) for obtaining information on the registered ownership of and encumbrances on vessels registered in Bermuda.*

The Register of Ships may be inspected at Hamilton, Bermuda at a cost of US$25 per folio (in practice, US$25 per entry). Application may also be made for a transcript of the register in relation to ownership and in relation to encumbrances at a cost of US$110 each.

I   Fees/taxes

1   *What fees are currently payable*
    1.1   on new registration?
    1.2   on transfer of ownership?
    1.3   on deletion?

1.1   The initial registration fee is based on net registered tons. The basic fees are as follows:

Registration fees (in force from 1 April 1999)

Cargo ships, on the principal register:

One ship – up to 10,000 tons
Registration Fee: US$3,000
Annual Tonnage Fee: US$3,000

One ship – over 10,000 tons and up to 50,000 tons
Registration Fee: US$3,000 plus US$0.30 for each ton over 10,000
Annual Tonnage Fee: US$3,000 plus US$0.22 for each ton over 10,000

One ship – exceeding 50,000 tons

Registration Fee:	US$15,000
Annual Tonnage Fee:	US$11,800 plus US$0.17 for each ton over 50,000 tons (maximum US$30,000)

In respect of a second ship, being in the same ownership or management, registered at the time of registration of the first ship or within 12 months of such registration:

Second ship – up to 10,000 tons

Registration Fee:	US$2,000
Annual Tonnage Fee:	US$3,000

Second ship – over 10,000 tons and up to 50,000 tons

Registration Fee:	US$2,000 plus US$0.20 for each ton over 10,000
Annual Tonnage Fee:	US$3,000 plus US$0.22 for each ton over 10,000

Second ship – exceeding 50,000 tons

Registration Fee:	US$10,000
Annual Tonnage Fee:	US$11,800 plus US$0.17 for each ton over 50,000 tons (maximum US$30,000)

In respect of a third or subsequent ship being in the same ownership or management, registered at the time of registration of the first ship or within 36 months of such registration:

Third or subsequent ship up to 10,000 tons

Registration Fee:	US$1,000
Annual Tonnage Fee:	US$3,000

Third or subsequent ship – over 10,000 tons and up to 50,000 tons

Registration Fee:	US$1,000
Annual Tonnage Fee:	US$3,000 plus US$0.22 for each ton over 10,000

Third or subsequent – exceeding 50,000 tons

Registration Fee:	US$1,000
Annual Tonnage Fee:	US$11,800 plus US$0.17 for each ton over 50,000 tons (maximum US$30,000)

Passenger ships, engaged in long international voyages with Class I passenger ship safety certificates:

One ship – up to 10,000 tons

Registration Fee: US$6,000

Annual Tonnage Fee: US$7,000

One ship – over 10,000 tons

Registration Fee: US$6,000 plus US$0.35 for each ton over 10,000

Annual Tonnage Fee: US$7,000 plus US$0.30 for each ton over 10,000

Passenger ships, engaged in short international voyages with Class II passenger ship safety certificates:

One ship – up to 10,000 tons

Registration Fee: US$4,000

Annual Tonnage Fee: US$4,000

One ship – over 10,000 tons

Registration Fee: US$4,000 plus US$0.40 for each ton over 10,000

Annual Tonnage Fee: US$4,000 plus US$0.35 for each ton over 10,000

Yachts (owned by a body corporate):

Up to 15 tons

Registration Fee: US$825

Annual Tonnage Fee: US$550

Over 15 tons and up to 100 tons

Registration Fee: US$1,650

Annual Tonnage Fee: US$1,375

Over 100 tons

Registration Fee: US$3,300

Annual Tonnage Fee: US$2,750

Yachts (owned by a person other than a body corporate):

Up to 15 tons

Registration Fee: US$165

Annual Tonnage Fee: Nil

Over 15 tons and up to 100 tons

Registration Fee: US$330

Annual Tonnage Fee: Nil

Over 100 tons

Registration Fee: US$660

Annual Tonnage Fee: Nil

Yachts (of 24 metres or over engaged in commercial activity):

Registration Fee: US$5,000

Annual Tonnage Fee: US$3,750

Other fees

Registration of each mortgage, transfer or discharge of mortgage; Registration of each transfer of ownership, a share or shares in a registered ship; Registration of a change of name of a ship; Registration of change of particulars recorded in the Register (except those resulting from the issue of a preliminary Certificate of Survey)

(a)   yachts not exceeding 24 metres in
             registered length: US$110
(b)   yachts exceeding 24 metres in
             registered length: US$220
(c)   other ships: US$440

Issue of a Transcript of Register relating to any one ship

(a)   for current entries: US$110
(b)   for other entries: US$110

Where application for registry is withdrawn prior to the completion of the registration of a ship

(a)   yachts not exceeding 24 metres in
             registered length: US$110
(b)   yachts exceeding 24 metres in
             registered length: US$220
(c)   other ships: US$440

Issue of duplicate Certificate of Registry: US$110

Personal Inspection of the Register: US$25

Transfer of registration to a port in the United Kingdom or a British possession

(a)	yachts not exceeding 24 metres in registered length:	US$110
(b)	yachts exceeding 24 metres in registered length:	US$220
(c)	other ships:	US$440

Documentation charges for demise charter registration out of flag

(a)	yachts:	US$440
(b)	ships other than passenger ships and yachts:	US$440
(c)	passenger ships:	US$440

For requesting a search for any document or of any Register or Index and issuing a copy thereof (applies only to a public document):	US$110
For a certified copy of any document to be produced in evidence under the Merchant Shipping Act 2002:	US$110
For the issue of a seaman's discharge book:	US$65
For the issue of a Bermuda endorsement:	US$125
For the issue of a statutory certificate of exemption:	US$125
Annual service fee for vessels over 500 grt:	US$500
Annual service fee for vessels not over 500 grt and over 24 metres:	US$250
Annual service fee for Class 1 passenger vessels:	US$1,000
Initial fee for approval of 'Approved Container Examination Programme' (ACEP):	US$5,000
Annual fee for administration of ACEP:	US$20,000

1.2 Registration of each transfer of ownership
    (a)   yachts not exceeding 24 metres in registered length: US$110
    (b)   yachts exceeding 24 metres in registered length: US$220
    (c)   other ships: US$440
1.3 None.

J   Parallel registration

1   *Is parallel registration permitted?*
    1.1   *onto Bermuda register?*
    1.2   *from Bermuda register?*

1.1   The Merchant Shipping Act 2002 provides for ships chartered-in on demise charter terms (onto Bermuda register). Persons qualified to be owners of British ships, who charter a ship on demise charter, are permitted to register a ship on the Bermuda register. In order to be chartered-in the country of primary registration must be compatible with the laws of Bermuda.

1.2   The Merchant Shipping Act 2002 also makes provision for ships chartered-out on demise charter terms. Application for the consent of the Registrar, to effect the transfer, shall be made by the owner to the Registrar. The Registrar must be satisfied that the merchant shipping laws of the country of secondary registration is compatible with the laws of Bermuda, that each registered mortgagee has consented to the charter, that the authority in the country of secondary registration has consented to the registration and that the owner of the ship has given all necessary undertakings required under the laws of Bermuda.

2   *If so, what, if any, specific governmental or other consents are required?*
The consent of owners, mortgagees and the principal or secondary registry (as applicable) is required for demise charter registration into or out of Bermuda.

3   *Is the period of parallel registration limited? If so, is it renewable?*
The registration of a ship chartered-in on demise charter terms shall remain in force for a maximum period of five years from the date of registration or, if less than five years, until the end of the charter period. Renewal is permitted with the consent of the Registrar.

4   *If parallel registration is dependent on the existence of a demise charter, does Bermuda have a specific definition of demise or bareboat charter for these purposes? If so, what is it?*
Parallel registration is dependent on the existence of a charter by demise. The definition of 'demise charter terms' means the hiring of the ship for a stipulated period on terms which gave the charterer possession and control of the ship, including the right to appoint the master and crew.

5   *Please answer the questions listed under Sections A to E above with reference to application for parallel registration onto Bermuda's register.*

(Al)   The restrictions on ownership applicable to the Principal Registry also apply to the Demise Charter Registry.

(A2)   The requirement for a principal place of business in a Relevant Territory applies in the same way as it does for the Principal Registry.

(A3)   If the charterer is not resident in Bermuda, it must appoint a representative person in the same way as for the Principal Registry.

(A4)   There is no restriction on the ownership of shares in the charterer.

(A5)   For exchange control, see entry for the Principal Registry.

(A6)   There are no special rules for particular types of vessel as far as ownership is concerned.

(A7)   There is no mandatory requirement for registration.

(Bl)   Fishing vessels and ships of less than 24 metres in length may not be registered on the Demise Charter Register.

(B2)   There is no maximum age for the registration of ships on the Demise Charter Registry.

(Cl)   The name of the vessel must not appear to the Registrar of Ships in Bermuda to be undesirable.

(C2)   There is no procedure for approval of names in advance, but in the absence of a conflict with another vessel already registered on the register or another British ship, the vessel must retain the name assigned to her under the underlying registry.

(C3)   Unlike the position on the Principal Registry, there is no formal procedure for reserving a name.

(Dl)   Vessels must be registered at the Port of Hamilton, Bermuda.

(D2)   The following documents and information must be submitted to effect registration:

   (a)   a certified copy of the agreement under which the ship is chartered by demise to the charterer;

   (b)   a certified transcript of the entries in the underlying registry including details of ownership and any mortgages, charges or liens registered against the ship;

   (c)   the written consent of the appropriate maritime authorities of the country of registry to demise charter registration;

   (d)   the current International Tonnage Certificate relating to the ship and the certificate of survey;

   (e)   the written consent of the mortgagees, if any, and the written consent of every owner to demise charter registration;

   (f)   the name and address of the individual or of the body corporate appointed as the representative person, where required;

   (g)   Appointment of Authorised Officer;

   (h)   application for registration;

   (i)   appointment of manager;

   (j)   evidence of marking;

   (k)   radio licence;

   (l)   certificate of survey; and

   (m)   such supplementary information and evidence relating to the ship and the ownership thereof as the Registrar may require to determine whether the ship may properly be registered.

(D3)   There are statutory forms for most of the documents required in connection with registration under the Demise Charter Registry.

(D4)   The position with regards to originals, copies and facsimile documents is the same as for the Principal Registry.

(D5)   The language requirements for documents are the same as for the Principal Registry.

(D6–D9) The requirements are the same as for the Principal Registry.

(D10)   There is no provision for initial registration abroad.

(E)   A certificate of survey is required as in the case of the Principal Registry and must be produced prior to registration.

(F)   If the vessel is sold the demise charter registration terminates unless the new owner consents to the registration continuing within a period of seven days.

6   *Can/must mortgages on ships parallel registered into Bermuda's register also be registered in Bermuda?*

There is no provision for registration of mortgages on the Demise Charter Registry.

7   *Under what circumstances will/may the parallel registration of a vessel onto Bermuda's register be terminated or revoked?*

There is no specific procedure for deletion, but the registry will cease if:

(a)   the foreign registry or the Bermuda registry revokes its consent to the ship continuing to be registered;

(b)   the charterparty terminates;

(c)   the charterer ceases to be a qualified person;

(d)   the ship's underlying registration is terminated;

(e)   the ship is sold without the new owner consenting within seven days to the continuance of the demise charter registration; or

(f)   the ship fails to maintain internationally agreed safety standards IMO or ILO.

K   General

1   *Please identify the principal statutes and regulations in Bermuda governing the registration of ships.*

(a)   The Merchant Shipping Act 2002

(b)   The Merchant Shipping (Registration of Ships) Regulations 2003

(c)   The Merchant Shipping (Fees) Amendment Regulations 2004

2   *Are there any other matters in the context of registration of ships not referred to above which you feel should be emphasised.*

No.

---

* Contributed by Timothy Counsell and Clive Langley, Appleby Spurling Hunter, Hamilton, Bermuda.

The People's Republic of China*

A   Ownership

1   What, if any, are the restrictions on ownership of vessels registered under the flag of the People's Republic of China (the 'PRC')?

Only the following ships can be registered under the flag of the PRC:

(a)   ships owned by a Chinese citizen who has his residence or main place of business in China;

(b)   ships owned by an enterprise established in accordance with Chinese law and whose main place of business is in China;

(c)   ships for public service purposes owned by Chinese governmental authorities or public institutions; and

(d)   other ships required by the Ship Registration Authority to be registered under the flag of the PRC.

2   If registration by companies is limited to companies incorporated in the PRC, is a local 'brass-plate' company sufficient or must there be a closer, genuine connection?

The ship to be registered under the flag of the PRC must be *actually owned* (to be evidenced by documents, see D2, below) by one of the parties mentioned in A1, above. Ships flying the flag of the PRC must be manned by Chinese crew. In case of actual need for foreign crew, approval from Ministry of Transportation must be obtained.

3   If registration by companies incorporated other than in the PRC is permitted, must a local representative be appointed? If so, are there any restrictions on the identity of that representative?

Not applicable.

4   Please summarise any restrictions (for example, as to number, nationality and so on) on who may own shares in vessel-owning companies incorporated in the PRC.

For a Chinese-foreign joint venture incorporated in the PRC, the capital contributed by the Chinese party shall not be less than 50 per cent, that is, the foreigner or foreign company can have no more than 50 per cent (including 50 per cent) shares in a vessel-owning company in the PRC.

5   Please explain any exchange control or other governmental or regulatory consents required in connection with the ownership of vessels registered in the PRC.

None, save as specified elsewhere herein.

6   Please explain any special rules for any particular type of vessel.

The registration of fishing ships, military services ships and sports ships is regulated by different rules.

7   Is there any mandatory registration requirement for certain owners (for example, citizens of the PRC)?

All ships owned by parties mentioned in A1, above are required to be registered under the PRC flag.

310

B   Eligibility

1   Are there any particular types/sizes of vessel ineligible for, or exempt from, registration?
Life craft onboard a ship and boat/craft less than five metres in length are exempt from registration.

2   What, if any, is the maximum age for registration of vessels under the flag of the PRC?
Although there are mandatory requirements for all ships to undertake special periodic surveys or to be scrapped at a certain age, there is maximum age requirement *only* for registration of vessels purchased or demise-chartered *from abroad*:

	Maximum age	
Types of ship	Sea-going ship	River ship
Passenger ship	10	10
Oil tanker, chemical ship	15	16
Liquefied gas ship	12	16
Bulk carrier, ore carrier	18	18
Roll on–roll off ship, cement carrier, reefer ship, general cargo ship, multi-purpose ship, container ship, timber ship, tugboat, push boat, barge	20	20

C   Names

1   What, if any, are the restrictions on the name under which a vessel may be registered in the PRC?
A ship can only use one name. A ship's name must not be the same or have the same pronunciation as any other registered ship. A ship's name shall consist of Chinese ideograph (the English translation of the characters shall be in the Chinese Phonetic Alphabet) or combination of both Chinese ideograph and Arabic numerals. The number of characters shall be between 4 and 14 (one Chinese ideograph is counted as two characters and one Arabic number is counted as one character).

(a)   A ship's name must not be the same or similar to the name of any country, governmental authority, party, intergovernmental organisation or head of state.

(b)   A ship's name must not contain anything of national discrimination or colonist inclination. A ship's name must not be prejudicial to social morals and must not be culturally ill-inclined.

(c)   Names forbidden by law cannot be used.

2   Is there a procedure for approval of names in advance?
Yes.

3   If so, how does it operate? Does approval confer any priority rights in the use of the name?
Before making an application for registration of ownership, the applicant shall submit the following documents to the Ship Registration Authority at the port of registry (for Use of Ship Name Board) or the State Maritime Safety Administration for approval:

(a)   an application for use of the ship's name;

(b)   document evidencing identity of the applicant such as business licence or citizen's identification card;

(c)   shipbuilding contract for newly built ship, ship sale contract for newly purchased ship or purchase invoice or other document evidencing the lawful acquisition of the title to the ship, or demise charter party for a demise-chartered ship;

(d)   written consent from the local government if the name of a province, autonomous region, municipality directly under the central government or other major city is to be used.

The Ship Registration Authority will examine the application in accordance with the Administration Rules on Ship's Names promulgated by the State Maritime Safety Administration under the Ministry of Transportation. Following a successful application, a notice will be given to the applicant allowing the latter to use the name.

After the ship's name is approved, the applicant is conferred the priority right in the use of the name for one month.

D   New registration procedure

1   *Where may vessels intending to fly the flag of the PRC be registered:*

    1.1   *in the PRC?*

    1.2   *abroad?*

Registration must be made in the PRC.

For a ship purchased from or built in a foreign country, an application must be made with the Chinese Embassy/Consulate in that country for the granting of a provisional certificate of nationality. A provisional certificate will be valid for a discretionary period of time (of up to a year) depending upon when it will be feasibly possible to effect final registration.

2   *What documents and information must be submitted to effect registration?*

The following documents/information must be submitted:

(a)   Application for Use of Ship's Name (approved by Ship Registration Authority in advance);

(b)   Application for Ownership Registration;

(c)   document evidencing joint ownership (applicable in case of joint ownership);

(d)   letter of authorisation (where an agent is appointed for completing the application formalities);

(e)   document evidencing acquisition of ownership of the ship (such as ship sale contract, delivery/acceptance document or ship purchase invoice and delivery/acceptance document);

(f)   Import Permit issued by the competent authorities for equipment and machinery and the Customs Duty Paid Certificate (applicable for ships purchased from abroad);

(g)   Certificate of Capital Contribution (applicable for Chinese-foreign joint ventures);

(h)   certificate issued by original ship registration authority certifying that the original ownership registration has been deleted (applicable for ships that was originally registered under different ownership);

(i)   certificate issued by original ship registration authority certifying that no mortgage is established on the ship or the written consent from the mortgagee to transfer of the mortgaged ship;

(j)   ship's technical data;

(k)   five photos of the ship (two for abeam, one for side bow, one for stern and one for funnel); and

(l)   other documents required by the Ship Registration Authority.

After ownership registration, the applicant shall apply for initial inspection/measurement of the ship. The applicant can then apply for flag registration by submitting the following documents to the Ship Registration Authority:

(a)   Application for Flag Registration;

(b)   Certificate of Ownership;

(c)   document evidencing the identity of the ship operator;

(d)   letter of authorisation (where an agent is appointed for completing the application formalities);

(e)   certificate issued by the original ship registration authority certifying that the original certificate of nationality has been deleted or certifying that once the new registration is effected the original Certificate of Nationality shall be deleted (applicable for ships that were originally registered under different flag);

(f)   agreement for operating the ship (applicable in case the ship is operated by a party other than the owner);

(g)   ship's technical documents/certificates issued by ship surveyors (depending on the type of ship); and

(h)   Other documents required by the Ship Registration Authority.

3   *Does the legal system in the PRC lay down any specific requirements as to the contents of any of these documents (for example, of Bills of Sale) and, if so, what are they?*

No.

4   *Please identify how many originals or copies of each document are required. Are fax or pdf copies of any of them acceptable?*

Both an original and a copy of each document is required. The Application for Flag Registration and Application for Ownership must be in two originals, however. After the original documents are verified, a stamp 'recorded' will be affixed to the original documents and a copy will be kept by the Ship Registry Authority.

Where the Deletion Certificate from the previous registry is not immediately available a provisional registration will be allowed for up to three months. The final certificate of registration will only be granted after the original Deletion Certificate is submitted.

5   Are there any requirements as to the language in which documents must be submitted?
All applications must be in Chinese. Supporting documents such as documents evidencing the acquisition of ownership and certificates issued by foreign ship registration authorities in foreign languages are acceptable, provided they are translated.

6   If they may be submitted in a foreign language, are there any translation require-
*   ments? If so, what are they and when must they be complied with?*
For documents submitted in a foreign language, a Chinese translation is required to be produced by an intermediary who has the legal qualification for producing translations. Translations shall be submitted at the time of the application.

7   Please identify any particular requirements of the legal system in the PRC with
*   regards to the method of execution of any of the registration documents, or with*
*   regard to notarisation or legalisation.*
There are no specific requirements with regards to the method of execution of the registration documents. Normally, for a document produced by a natural person, his or her signature is sufficient. For a document produced by a company, the signature of the legal representative is required and the company stamp must be affixed.

For ships purchased from abroad, the mortgage-free certificate must be issued by the original registration authority or notary public. There is no express requirement for legalisation by the Chinese Embassy/Consulate in the country where the documents are produced. In practice, the Ship Registration Authority may have a requirement for notarisation and legalisation for certificates issued from those countries that are not familiar to the Ship Registration Authority.

8   If the initial registration takes place abroad, is that registration final or provisional?
Provisional. See D1, above.

9   If provisional, what needs to be done to effect final registration? When must it be done?
Final registration is effected through the same procedures as mentioned in D2, above. Final registration shall be effected within the term set out in the provisional certificate.

10   If provisional, what, if any, are the restrictions which apply to the vessel pending final
*   registration?*
A provisional certificate of nationality has the same legal effect as the normal certificate of nationality.

In case a provisional certificate of nationality is granted for a ship purchased from abroad and which is in operation, a final certificate shall be obtained before the ships' departure from her first port of call in China unless a special approval is granted by the competent authority.

11   Can a provisionally registered vessel be mortgaged?
A provisionally registered ship cannot be mortgaged if the Certificate of Ownership has not been obtained. If it has, it is possible to register a mortgage, even if the ship only has a provisional certificate of nationality.

314

E   Technical matters

1   Please identify the requirements of the PRC with regard to inspection, survey, measurement and the like in respect of newly registered vessels.

For ships to be registered under the flag of the PRC, an application must be made to surveyors authorised by the State Maritime Safety Administration for an initial inspection and measurement to be completed, once ownership registration has been achieved, to obtain the following technical documents (for ocean-going ships):

    (a)   International Tonnage Certificate;

    (b)   International Loadline Certificate;

    (c)   Cargo Ship Safety Construction Certificate;

    (d)   Cargo Ship Safety Equipment Certificate;

    (e)   Passenger's Certificate;

    (f)   Passenger Ship Safety Certificate;

    (g)   Cargo Ship Safety Radio Certificate;

    (h)   International Oil Pollution Prevention Certificate;

    (i)   Safety Navigation Certificate; and

    (j)   other relevant technical certificates.

2   By when must these requirements be complied with?

After ownership registration is effected but before flag registration is effected.

F   Transfer of ownership

1   Please answer, either separately or by reference to your earlier answers, the questions listed under sections D and E above in respect of the transfer of ownership of a vessel already registered in the PRC.

In case of transfer of ownership, ownership registration and flag registration must be completed, following the same procedures as for a newly registered ship, but the inspection/measurement is not required to be conducted again.

2   Please explain any exchange control or other governmental or regulatory consents required in connection with the sale to a foreign flag of a vessel registered under the flag of the PRC.

No specific exchange control or specific consent required. However, in order to export the ship, if the owners are not recorded as competent foreign trade dealers, they must appoint a third party with such qualification to act as their agent in exporting the ship.

    An application shall be made to the Ship Registration Authority for deletion of both the Certificate of Ownership and the Certificate of Nationality.

G   Deletion

1   Please outline the procedure for deletion of vessels from the flag of the PRC.

The applicant shall submit the following documents to the Ship Registration Authority for deleting the ownership registration:

(a)   Application for deletion of ownership registration (in two originals);

(b)   documents substantiating the need for deletion such as, loss of ship, sale or demise-charter of the ship abroad;

(c)   documents evidencing the identity of the applicant;

(d)   letter of authorisation (applicable where an agent is appointed for completing the deletion formalities);

(e)   Certificate of Ownership and Nationality;

(f)   written consent from the mortgagee for the deletion (applicable for mortgaged ships);

(g)   written consent from the demise-charterer for the deletion (applicable for a ship that is on demise-charter); and

(h)   other documents required by the Ship Registration Authority, as the case may be.

The applicant shall submit the following documents to the Ship Registration Authority for deleting the flag (nationality) registration:

(a)   Application for deletion of flag registration (in two originals);

(b)   documents substantiating the need for deletion;

(c)   documents evidencing the identity of the applicant;

(d)   letter of authorisation (applicable where an agent is appointed for completing the deletion formalities);

(e)   Certificate of Nationality; and

(f)   other documents required by the Ship Registration Authority, as the case may be.

2   *Please answer, either separately or by reference to your earlier answers, the questions listed under section D in respect of the deletion, as apposed to new registration, of a vessel.*

Similar but simpler than that mentioned in section D.

H   Certificates/transcripts

1   Please identify the certificates and other documents issued to an owner on registration of a vessel under the flag of the PRC.

The Certificate of Ownership will be issued after ownership registration. The Certificate of Nationality will be issued after flag registration. It is valid for five years.

2   Please outline the procedure (including fees payable) for obtaining information on the registered ownership of and encumbrances on vessels registered in the PRC.

There are no specific provisions on procedure or fees payable. The practice may vary between different registration authorities.

I   Fees/taxes

1   What fees are currently payable:
  1.1   on new registration?
  1.2   on transfer of ownership?
  1.3   on deletion?

1.1   For ships with net tonnage of less than 50 tons, RMB100 plus an amount to be calculated on basis of RMB1 per net ton and on basis of RMB0.5 per net ton for the part
exceeding ten thousand in net tonnage shall be payable.

For ships with net tonnage of 50 tons or more, RMB200 plus an amount to be calculated on basis of RMB1 per net ton and on basis of RMB0.5 per net ton for the part
exceeding ten thousand in net tonnage shall be payable.

For tugs, an amount is to be charged at RMB0.5 per kilowatt.

The cost of production of certificates is RMB100 for originals and RMB50 for copies.

1.2   Same as on new registration as new registration is required.

1.3   Not applicable.

J   Parallel registration

1   Is parallel registration permitted:
  1.1   onto the PRC register?
  1.2   from the PRC register?

Parallel registration is not allowed.

Ships registered under foreign flag are not allowed to be registered under the flag of
the PRC if the original flag registration has not been deleted or suspended. For ships under
foreign flag demise-chartered into China, the original flag registration shall be deleted or suspended and a provisional flag registration shall be made in China.

Flag registration for a ship registered under the flag of the PRC shall be deleted when
the ship is sold abroad, or suspended when the ship is demise-chartered abroad.

2   If so, what, if any, specific governmental or other consents are required?
Not applicable.

3   Is the period of parallel registration limited? If so, is it renewable?
Not applicable.

*4   If parallel registration is dependent on the existence of a demised charter, does the
PRC have a specific definition of demise or bareboat charter for these purposes? If
so, what is it?*
Not applicable.

*5   Please answer the questions listed under sections A to E above with reference to
application for parallel registration onto the register of the PRC.*
Not applicable.

6   *Can/must mortgages on vessels parallel registered into the registry of the PRC also be registered in the PRC?*

Not applicable.

7   *Under what circumstances will/may the parallel registration of the vessel onto the register of the PRC be terminated or revoked?*

Not applicable.

K   General

1   *Please identify the principal statutes and regulations in the PRC governing the registration of vessels.*

    (a)   Maritime Code of the PRC;

    (b)   Maritime Traffic Safety Law of the PRC;

    (c)   Ship Registration Regulations of the PRC, the Supplementary Explanations on the Ship Registration Regulations of the PRC and the Interpretations on Application of the Ship Registration Regulations of the PRC;

    (d)   Ships Statutory Inspection Regulations of the PRC; and

    (e)   Administration Rules on Ship's Name of the PRC.

2   *Are there any other matters in the context of registration of vessels under the legal system in the PRC which you feel should be emphasised here?*

Not applicable.

---

* Contributed by Shen Xiangman of Wang Jing & Co., Guangzhou, PRC.

Cyprus*

A   Ownership

1   What, if any, are the restrictions on ownership of vessels registered under the flag of Cyprus?

A vessel can be registered under Cyprus flag if:

(a)   the majority of shares in the ship (that is 51 per cent of the shares or more) are owned by:

  (i)   a Cypriot (a citizen of the Republic of Cyprus or a person of Cypriot origin descended in the male line); or

  (ii)   a citizen of other Member State (a Member State of the European Union or other contracting party to the European Economic Area Agreement); or

(b)   the total (100 per cent) of the shares in the ship are owned by one or more companies, which have been established and operate:

  (i)   in accordance with the laws of the Republic of Cyprus and have their registered office in Cyprus; or

  (ii)   in accordance with the laws of any other Member State and have their registered office, central administration or principal place of business within the European Economic Area and which will, during the whole period of the registration of the ship in the Register, have either appointed and maintain an authorised representative in Cyprus or ensured that the management of the ship in respect of her safety is entrusted in full to a Cypriot shipmanagement company or an EU shipmanagement company, having its place of business in Cyprus; or

  (iii)   outside the territory of the Republic of Cyprus and outside the territory of any other Member State, which are controlled by Cypriot citizens or natural persons who are citizens of any other Member State and who will, during the whole period of the registration of the ship in the Register, have either appointed an authorised representative in Cyprus or ensured that the management of the ship in respect of her safety is entrusted in full to a Cypriot shipmanagement company or an EU shipmanagement company, having its place of business in Cyprus.

2   If registration by companies is limited to companies incorporated in Cyprus, is a local 'brass-plate' company sufficient, or must there be a closer, genuine connection?

The only requirement for a shipowning company incorporated in Cyprus is that it should operate under and in accordance with the laws of Cyprus and have its registered office in Cyprus. No other connection is needed. By far the majority of companies owning and registering ships under Cyprus flag are incorporated in Cyprus.

3   If registration by companies incorporated other than in Cyprus is permitted, must a local representative be appointed? If so, are there any restrictions on the identity of that representative?

(a)   A company established and operating under the Laws of a Member State or a Company under 1(b)(iii) above must either appoint and maintain an authorised representative in

Cyprus or entrust the full management of the ship to a Cypriot Shipmanagement Company or an EU Shipmanagement Company based in Cyprus.

(b)   an authorised representative may be:

(i)   a Cypriot citizen or a citizen of any other Member State who is resident in the Republic within the meaning of the Cyprus Income Tax laws; or

(ii)   a partnership which has been established and is registered in accordance with the provisions of the Partnerships and Business Names Law, having its place of business in Cyprus and which employs permanent staff in Cyprus; or

(iii)   a company which has been established and is registered in accordance with the provisions of the Companies Law, having its place of business in Cyprus and which employs permanent staff in Cyprus; or

(iv)   a branch of a non-Cypriot Company which has been established and is registered in accordance with the provisions of the Cyprus Companies Law, having its place of business in Cyprus.

4   *Please summarise any restrictions (for example, as to number, nationality and so on) on who may own shares in shipowning companies incorporated in Cyprus.*

There are no restrictions as to the legal status (corporations or natural persons) nationality, residence, majority control and number, or any other consideration regarding the question of who may own (and how many) shares in a shipowning company incorporated in Cyprus.

5   *Please explain any exchange control or other governmental or regulatory consents required in connection with the ownership of ships registered in Cyprus.*

No exchange control permission or other governmental consents are required for the acquisition of shares in a company incorporated in Cyprus which proposes to acquire and register in its ownership a ship under Cyprus flag.

6   *Please explain any special rules for any particular type of vessel.*

There are no special rules regarding the ownership of any particular type of vessel to be registered under Cyprus flag.

7   *Is there any mandatory registration requirement for certain owners (for example, citizens of Cyprus)?*

No.

B   Eligibility

1   Are any particular types/sizes of ship ineligible for, or exempt from, registration?

(a)   The following ships are exempt from registration in Cyprus:

(i)   ships not exceeding 13 metres in overall length employed solely in coastal navigation in Cyprus; and

(ii)   ships not having a whole or fixed deck and employed solely in fishing, lightering or coastal trading on the shores of Cyprus.

(b)   A fishing vessel can only be registered in the Cyprus Register of Ships if it secures, prior to registration, the written consent of the Director of the Department of Fisheries and Marine Research of the Cyprus Ministry of Agriculture, Natural Resources and the Environment.

2   *What, if any, is the maximum age for registration of ships under the flag of Cyprus?*
(a)   Ships of any size and type not exceeding 15 years of age (except cargo vessels with a grt of less than 1,000 tons and passenger vessels) and cargo vessels with GRP of less than 1,000 tons not exceeding 20 years may be registered in Cyprus without any special conditions.
(b)   Vessels over 15 years of age, cargo vessels with a grt of less than 1,000 tons over 20 years, fishing vessels and passenger vessels, can only be registered under additional conditions imposed by the Government Policy on the Registration of Vessels under Cyprus flag.
These additional conditions may include:
(i)   satisfactory entry inspection;
(ii)   management by a Cyprus or an EU shipmanagement company;
(iii)   possibility for additional inspections by the Department of Merchant Shipping.
(c)   The following vessels cannot be registered, because of their age, under Cyprus flag:
(i)   cargo vessels and ocean-going tug boats over 23 years of age;
(ii)   passenger vessels over 35 years of age; and
(iii)   fishing vessels over 20 years of age.

C   Names

1   *What, if any, are the restrictions on the name under which a ship may be registered in Cyprus?*
A ship may not be registered in Cyprus under a name which is the same as, or very similar to, the name of an already registered Cyprus ship. In practice, at least two letters or a component word or number of the ship's name must be different.

2   *Is there a procedure for approval of names in advance?*
Yes.

3   *If so, how does it operate? Does approval confer any priority rights in the use of the name?*
As a matter of practice a written enquiry is made with the Department of Merchant Shipping as to the availability of the desired name. If the name is free it is automatically reserved for the applicant for one month.
To acquire priority rights in the use of the available name either (a) it must be reserved in writing as above (without charge for an initial period of one month and on payment of a fee beyond one month), or (b) the prescribed application to the Minister of Communications & Works for permission to register the vessel under the desired name must he filed through the Registrar of Cyprus Ships.

D   New registration procedure

1   Where may ships intending to fly the flag of Cyprus be registered:

    1.1   in Cyprus?

    1.2   abroad?

Ships intending to fly the Cyprus flag may be registered either:

1.1   in Cyprus; or

1.2   abroad before a Cyprus Consular Officer (for provisional registration only).

2   What documents and information must be submitted to effect registration?

(a)   The prescribed application to the Minister of Communications & Works ('the Minister') through the Registrar of Cyprus Ships for the registration of a Vessel must contain/include the following information/documents:

Vessel Information:

    (i)   present name of ship;

    (ii)   name under which she is to be registered under Cyprus flag;

    (iii)   present flag;

    (iv)   year and place of build;

    (v)   date when her keel was laid;

    (vi)   name and address of her builders;

    (vii)   gross and net tonnage;

    (viii)   type of vessel;

    (ix)   classification society;

    (x)   present state of employment of ship;

    (xi)   present and future area of trading;

    (xii)   proposed port of delivery; and

    (xiii)   place of documentary closing/Consulate where provisional certificate will be issued (if not Limassol).

Company Documents:

For a Cyprus shipowning company:

    (i)   Certificate of Incorporation of ship-owning company;

    (ii)   Memorandum and articles of association;

    (iii)   list of directors and secretary;

    (iv)   list of shareholders of shipowning company;

    (v)   Certificate of Registered Address.

For shipowning companies registered outside Cyprus the exact company and other documentation will depend on the country of incorporation of the proposed owners.

(b)   Following the submission of the application for registration the following confirmations must be sent to and forms deposited with the Registrar of Cyprus Ships:

    (i)   confirmation from the vessel's classification society confirming that the vessel maintains her class, that her international trading certificates are in full force and effect, the vessel's degree of automation, and that it is prepared to issue new statutory certificates without any recommendations on behalf of the Cyprus Government upon registration of the vessel under the Cyprus flag; and

   (ii)   confirmation from an international radio accounting authority recognised by the Cyprus Government to the effect that they have undertaken the clearance of the vessel's radio maritime accounts.

   (iii)   ISM forms.

(c)   For provisional registration under the Cyprus flag the following documents are required to be deposited with the Registrar of Ships in Cyprus or a Cyprus Consul abroad, or partly with the one and partly with the other, at the owner's option:

   (i)   Bill of Sale (if applicable) or Builder's Certificate if the ship is a newbuilding;

   (ii)   Deletion Certificate (if applicable) or confirmation from the previous registry that the vessel is owned by the sellers and is free of encumbrances;

   (iii)   Directors' Resolutions of the shipowning company resolving purchase of the vessel, registration under Cyprus flag;

   (iv)   Power of Attorney of shipowning company;

   (v)   Declaration of Ownership;

   (vi)   Form of Registration of a Mobile Maritime Radio Station;

   (vii)   ISPS forms;

   (viii)   Form of Registration of Search and Rescue particulars;

   (ix)   Application for Minimum Safe Manning Document;

   (x)   Form of appointment of Authorised Representative (if applicable).

(d)   For permanent or final registration of a ship in the Cyprus Register the following supplemental documents must be deposited with the Registrar of Ships:

   (i)   application for permanent registration;

   (ii)   Certificate of Survey;

   (iii)   International Tonnage Certificate (1969);

   (iv)   Carving and Marking Note;

   (v)   international certificates under the Load Line, SOLAS and MARPOL Conventions;

   (vi)   Shore Based Maintenance Agreement;

   (vii)   Deletion Certificate from previous registry (if not deposited for provisional registration);

   (viii)   final CSR from previous registry;

   (ix)   International Safety Management Certificate; and

   (x)   International Ship Security Certificate.

3   *Does the legal system in Cyprus lay down any specific requirements as to the contents of any of these documents – for example, of Bills of Sale – and, if so, what are they?*

Cyprus merchant shipping law and practice lay down specific requirements as to the contents of some of the documents required to be deposited for (a) the provisional registration and (b) the permanent registration of a vessel under Cyprus flag. Thus the following documents must contain specific particulars or be in a prescribed form:

   (a)   Bill of Sale;

   (b)   Builder's Certificate;

   (c)   Declaration of Ownership;

(d)   ISM and ISPS forms;

(e)   form of registration of a Mobile Maritime Radio Station;

(f)   Form of Registration of Search and Rescue particulars;

(g)   Certificate of Survey;

(h)   International Tonnage Certificate (1969); and

(i)   Carving and Marking Note.

4   Please identify how many originals or copies of each document are required. Are fax copies of any of them acceptable?

One duly executed and legalised (where applicable) original of each document or a duly certified copy thereof (where permissible) is sufficient.

     Fax copies of documents may be accepted at the discretion of the Registrar, subject to an undertaking by the Owner's Cypriot lawyer to deposit the original within a stated period. Fax copies of documents of form (such as application for radio licence) will be accepted without more. It should be noted that this is a matter of practice and there are no fixed rules.

5   Are there any requirements as to the language in which documents must be submitted?

Registration documents are usually in English (as the international lingua franca of shipping) but may also be in Greek or Turkish, the official languages of the Republic of Cyprus.

     If any document not required to be in a specific form (for example, Bill of Sale, Builder's Certificate or Deletion Certificate) is submitted for registration of a ship under Cyprus flag and is drawn up in any other language, such document must be accompanied by a certified translation into Greek, Turkish or English.

6   If they may be submitted in a foreign language, are there any translation requirements? If so, what are they and when must they be complied with?

The translation requirements of a document submitted in a foreign language (other than Greek, Turkish or English) is that it must be a sworn or certified translation by a person so authorised under the laws of the country wherefrom the document emanates, sworn or certified before an appropriate officer (for example, notary) in the country in question and legalised by a Cyprus Consular Officer or by Apostille. Translation requirements must be complied with simultaneously with the submission or deposit of the relevant registration document(s).

7   Please identify any particular requirements of the legal system in Cyprus with regard to the method of execution of any of the registration documents, or with regard to notarisation or legalisation.

(a)   Execution:

Registration documents which may originate in foreign jurisdictions (for example, Bill of Sale and Power of Attorney, if the said bill is executed by an attorney, Builder's Certificate and Deletion Certificate) must be duly executed in accordance with the law of the foreign jurisdiction. Registration documents which are necessarily governed by Cyprus law (for example, Declaration of Ownership, Power of Attorney of Cypriot shipowning company) must be duly executed in accordance with the provisions of the relevant Cyprus statute (for example, the Merchant Shipping (Registration of Ships, Sales and Mortgages) Law in the case of the Declaration of Ownership, the Companies Law in the case of the Power of Attorney).

(b)   Notarisation and legalisation:

Registration documents executed in the Republic of Cyprus and requiring authentication or attestation of the signature(s) appearing thereon may be executed before a Certifying Officer (the nearest equivalent in Cyprus to a notary public). However, the Declaration of Ownership must be executed before the Registrar of Ships or a Court Registrar.

Registration documents executed outside Cyprus and requiring authentication or attestation may be either:

(i)   executed before a Consular Officer of the Republic of Cyprus;

(ii)   notarised and legalised by a Cypriot Consular Officer; or

(iii) notarised and apostilled, Cyprus being a signatory to the Hague Convention abolishing Legalisation for Foreign Public Documents of 1961.

It should be noted that some of the prescribed registration documents do not require any notarisation or legalisation at all, for example, documents (such as statutory certificates) issued by or on behalf of an international classification society recognised by the Cyprus government.

8   If the initial registration takes place abroad, is that registration final or provisional?
Initial registration which takes place abroad is invariably provisional registration (see D1.2 above).

9   If provisional, what needs to be done to effect final registration? When must it be done?
To effect final or permanent registration under Cyprus flag the supplemental documents set out in sub-section D2.4 above must be deposited with the Registrar of Ships.

Final or permanent registration must take place within the six-month validity of the Provisional Certificate of Cyprus Registry, or the three-month extension thereof, if such an extension is required to complete permanent registration formalities and is obtained on application to the Minister.

10   If provisional, what, if any, are the restrictions which apply to the vessel pending final registration?
There are no restrictions which apply to a provisionally registered vessel under Cyprus flag pending permanent registration.

11   Can a provisionally registered ship be mortgaged?
A provisionally registered vessel under Cyprus flag can be mortgaged and such mortgage can be recorded in the Register of Ships.

Furthermore by an express statutory provision the validity of such mortgage once recorded shall not be affecte3d by the expiry of the six-month duration of the Provisional Certificate of Cyprus Registry, or of the three-month extension thereof, and the priority of such mortgage shall be preserved upon the final registration of the vessel.

E   Technical matters

1   *Please identify the requirements of Cyprus with regard to inspection, survey, mea-surement and the like in respect of newly registered ships.*

The requirements under Cyprus law and practice with regard to inspection, survey, measurement and the like in respect of newly registered ships are the following:

(a)   pre-provisional registration requirements (inspection):

    (i)   For a vessel not exceeding 15 years of age, any pre-registration inspection is at the discretion of the vessel's classification society which is required to send a confirmation to the Registrar of Cyprus Ships regarding the vessel's status from a safety point of view.

    (ii)   For a vessel above 15 years of age (or otherwise depending on the type of the vessel), a special entry inspection by a surveyor of the Department of Merchant Shipping is mandatory as a precondition to registration under Cyprus flag. The parameters of such an inspection are set out in the current Government Policy on the Age Limit of Vessels which may be registered in the Cyprus Register of Ships ('the Government Policy').

(b)   As regards pre-permanent registration requirements (survey and measurement), in order to effect permanent registration under the Cyprus flag, the vessel must be surveyed by a surveyor of ships (either of the Department of Merchant Shipping or of a recognised classification society) and her tonnage measured in accordance with the International Convention on Tonnage Measurement of Ships, 1969. The prescribed Certificate of Survey and the International Tonnage Certificate, once completed and issued, must be deposited with the Registrar of Ships for the purpose of permanent registration.

2   *By when must these requirements be complied with?*

The inspection requirements for over-age vessels must be complied with either within three months of provisional registration at the latest (and in any case before permanent registration).

The survey and measurement requirements must be complied with prior to and for the purpose of permanent registration of the vessel, which must be effected within six months of the provisional registration. A three-month extension is legally feasible and readily granted upon submission of the prescribed application and payment of the appropriate fee.

F   Transfer of ownership

1   *Please answer sections D and E above in respect of a transfer of ownership of a vessel already registered in Cyprus.*

(D1)   The transfer of ownership of a vessel registered in Cyprus may be effected either:

    (a)   in Cyprus; or

    (b)   abroad, before a Cyprus Consular Officer.

(D2)   To effect the transfer of ownership of a vessel registered in Cyprus the following documents and information are required:

    (a)   For filing the prescribed application:

        Information:

(i)   name of the ship under which transferees propose to trade her (if change of name is to take place simultaneously with the transfer of ownership); and

(ii)   venue of completion of the transaction (place where there is a Diplomatic Mission or a Consulate of the Republic of Cyprus).

Documents:

(i)   the same documents as provided in D2 above must be submitted;

(ii)   a confirmation from an international radio accounting authority recognised by the Cyprus government to the effect that they have undertaken the clearance of the vessel's radio maritime accounts on behalf of the transferees/new owners must be sent to the Registrar;

(iii)   Bill of Sale duly executed by the transferors and attested/legalised;

(iv)   Power of Attorney (if the Bill of Sale is to be executed by an attorney of the transferors);

(v)   Directors' Resolutions of transferor company resolving sale of vessel and transfer of her ownership;

(vi)   memorandum of discharge of mortgage (if any), or written consent of the mortgagees to the transfer of ownership subject to mortgage;

(vii)   Directors' Resolutions of transferee company resolving purchase of vessel, retention of Cyprus registry;

(viii)   Power of Attorney of transferees' company;

(ix)   Declaration of Ownership by transferee company;

(x)   ISM and ISPS forms by the transferees;

(xi)   Form of Registration of Search and Rescue particulars; and

(xii)   Carving and Marking Note in respect of the change of the vessel's name (if there is such a change and it is to take place simultaneously with the transfer of ownership) or an undertaking for its submission.

(D3)   Cyprus merchant shipping law and practice lay down specific requirements as to the contents of some of the documents required for transfer of ownership (and change of the vessel's name, if applicable). Thus the following documents must contain specific particulars or be in a prescribed form:

(a)   Bill of Sale;

(b)   Declaration of Ownership;

(c)   ISM and ISPS forms;

(d)   Form of Registration of Search and Rescue particulars; and

(e)   Carving and Marking Note.

(D4–7)   The answers given above to the questions of Section D numbered 4 (number of originals or copies of each document, acceptability of fax copies), 5 (language requirements of documents), 6 (translation requirements), 7 (mode of execution, notarisation and legislation) are equally valid here and apply, mutatis mutandis, to the procedure for the transfer of ownership of a Cyprus registered vessel.

(D8)   Transfer of ownership of Cyprus registered vessel which takes place abroad before a Cyprus Consular Officer is final. Thus on receipt by the Registrar of Ships by fax or e-mail a notice of deposit of the prescribed documents with the Consular Officer whom the Registrar had authorised (on the application of interested parties) to effect the transaction, the transfer shall be deemed to have been registered as from the date of such deposit and the necessary entry shall be made in the Register of Cyprus Ships.

(D9–11) Not applicable here.

(E1)   There are no specific requirements with regard to inspection, survey, measurement and the like in respect of the transfer of ownership of a vessel already registered in Cyprus. However, if the vessel was originally registered under certain conditions imposed or registration as per the Government Policy the new owners must undertake to and must comply with such conditions. Furthermore, if there are any items relating to the foregoing technical matters which are outstanding at the time of transfer of ownership (for example, expiry of an international certificate under the SOLAS or MARPOL Conventions or non-completion of survey and measurement requirements for purposes of permanent registration of the vessel in question) these must be attended to. If the outstanding matters relate to questions of safety, seaworthiness or international conventions they must be complied with before the transfer of ownership can be effected. If, on the other hand, the outstanding items relate to matters for which the time limit prescribed by law has not expired (such as survey and measurement where the Provisional Certificate of Cyprus Registry of the vessel to be transferred has not expired) the relevant requirements can be complied with by the transferees after completion of the transfer of ownership.

(E2)   See (E1) above.

2   *Please explain any exchange control or other governmental or regulatory consents required in connection with the sale to a foreign flag of a vessel registered under the flag of Cyprus.*

No exchange control or other governmental or regulatory consent is required in connection with the sale of a Cyprus registered vessel for transfer to a foreign flag.

G   Deletion

1   *Please outline the procedure for deletion of vessels from the flag of Cyprus.*

The procedure for the deletion of a vessel from the Cyprus flag is well-defined and speedy. On deposit of the prescribed documents (see (D2) below) with the Registrar of Ships or with a Cyprus Consular Officer abroad (on the Registrar's prior authority) and on payment of the outstanding dues of the vessel to the government (if any) the vessel can be deleted from the Cyprus Register forthwith and finally.

2   *Please answer, either separately or by reference to your earlier answers, the questions listed under Section D in respect of the deletion, as opposed to new registration, of a vessel.*

(D1)   The deletion of a Cyprus registered vessel may be effected either:

(a)   in Cyprus; or

(b)   abroad before a Cyprus Consular Officer, acting on the prior authority of the Registrar of Ships.

(D2)   To effect the deletion of a Cyprus registered vessel the following information and documents are required:

        (a)   For filing the prescribed application for deletion and arranging for the issue of appropriate authority by the Registrar of Ships to a Cyprus Consulate (if deletion is to take place abroad):

                (i)   reason for deletion;

                (ii)   new flag; and

                (iii)   venue of completion of the transaction (place where there is a Diplomatic Mission or a Consulate of the Republic of Cyprus).

        (b)   For completion of the deletion procedure the following documents must be deposited:

                (i)   Bill of Sale (if applicable) duly executed by sellers and attested;

                (ii)   Directors' Resolutions of seller company resolving sale and deletion;

                (iii)   Power of Attorney (if the Bill of Sale is to be executed by an attorney);

                (iv)   Original Certificate of Cyprus Registry (or, in lieu, undertaking on behalf of owners/sellers to return the same to the Registrar of Ships for cancellation within a stated period of up to 30 days if by reason of the vessel's trading the said certificate cannot be produced for deletion at the venue of completion);

                (v)   Memorandum of discharge of mortgage (if any);

                (vi)   Protocol of delivery and acceptance of the vessel executed by sellers and buyers; and

                (vii)   Deletion Certificate from her previous registry, if the vessel is still provisionally registered under Cyprus flag and no such Deletion Certificate had been deposited with the Registrar of Cyprus Ships earlier.

(D3)   The Bill of Sale is the only document required to be deposited for the purposes of deletion on which Cyprus law lays down specific requirements as to its contents. In practice it is set out in a standard form.

(D4–7)   The answers given above to the questions of Section D numbered 4 (number of originals or copies of each document, acceptability of fax copies), 5 (language requirements of documents), 6 (translation requirements) and 7 (mode of execution, notarisation and legalisation) are equally valid here and apply, *mutatis mutandis*, to the procedure for the deletion of a vessel from the Cyprus Register.

(D8)   Deletion of a Cyprus registered vessel which takes place abroad before a Cyprus Consular Officer on the authority of the Registrar of Cyprus Ships is final.

(D9–12) Not applicable here.

H   Certificates/transcripts

1   *Please identify the certificates and other documents issued to an owner on registration of his ship under the flag of Cyprus.*

The following certificates and other documents are issued to an owner on registration of his ship under Cyprus flag:

(a)   On provisional registration:
- (i)   Provisional Certificate of Cyprus Registry;
- (ii)   written confirmation that the ship's radio licence is in the process of being issued (given by the Cyprus Consular Officer);
- (iii)   Document of Safe Manning;
- (iv)   Continuous Synopsis Record.

(b)   Following provisional registration:

Radio licence (issued by the Department of Merchant Shipping in Cyprus).

(c)   On permanent registration:

Certificate of Cyprus Registry (issued by the Registrar of Ships).

2   *Please outline the procedure (including fees payable) for obtaining information on the registered ownership of and encumbrances on vessels registered in Cyprus.*

The procedure for obtaining information on the registered ownership and encumbrances of a vessel registered in Cyprus is twofold.

(a)   An inspection of the Register may be made by any interested person on application to the Registrar of Ships and payment of a fee of C£5.

(b)   Alternatively, a Transcript of Register (or a Certificate of Ownership and Encumbrances in the case of a provisionally registered vessel) may be issued to any person on application to the Registrar and payment of a fee of C£10 or C£3 respectively.

I   Fees/taxes

1   What fees are currently payable:
- *1.1   on new registration?*
- *1.2   on transfer of ownership?*
- *1.3   on deletion?*

The following fees assessed in Cyprus currency are currently payable:

1.1   on new registration (whether provisional or permanent):

      (a)   on any ship other than a passenger ship:
- (i)   for each ton gross up to 5,000 gt: 10 cents
- (ii)   for each ton gross over 5,000 gt and up to 10,000 gt: 8 cents
- (iii)   for each additional ton gross in excess of 10,000 gt: 4 cents
- (iv)   minimum fee: C£125
- (v)   maximum fee: C£3,000

(NB C£1 (one Cyprus Pound) is divided into 100 cents.)

      (b)   on passenger ships:
- (i)   for each ton gross: 15 cents
- (ii)   minimum fee: C£250

No additional fees are payable for a provisionally registered vessel if her permanent registration is effected before the expiry of the six-month validity of the Provisional Certificate of Cyprus Registry.

Apart from the above registration fees, fees for the issue of the vessel's radio licence amounting to C£10 are also payable on new registration.

1.2   On transfer of ownership:

      (a)   on each ton gross up to 10,000 gt: 2 cents

      (b)   on each additional ton gross in excess of 10,000 gt: 1 cent

      (c)   minimum fee: C£30

1.3   On deletion: None

2   *What annual or other ongoing fees or taxes are payable in respect of ships registered in Cyprus?*

The ongoing taxes and fees payable are annual tonnage tax and radio licence renewal fees.

(a)   Annual tonnage tax:

This annual tax is assessed on two factors, (a) the gross tonnage and (b) the age of a Cyprus registered vessel.

The tax is payable to the Cyprus authorities in advance in two equal half-yearly instalments, save the first which is payable on registration of the vessel calculated from the year in which her keel was laid.

The tax for any ship other than a passenger ship is calculated as follows. The basic amount is assessed at the following tax rates:

(i)   for a ship of gross tonnage up to 1,600 gt, flat sum of C£100 plus rate per gross ton of 26 cents

(ii)   on each additional gross ton in excess of 1,600 but not over 10,000 gt: 16 cents

(iii)   on each additional gross ton in excess of 10,000 but not over 50,000 gt: 6 cents

(iv)   On each additional gross ton in excess of 50,000 gt: 4 cents

The resulting amount is then multiplied by the corresponding age multiplier as shown in the table below:

Age of ship	Multiplier
Up to 10 years	0.75
11 to 20 years	1.00
Over 20 years	1.30

The tonnage tax payable for passenger ships is double the corresponding tax for other types of ships calculated above.

Note: The word 'ton' used in the Cyprus merchant shipping legislation has been substituted with the word 'unit' as a result of the mandatory application of the 'International convention on Tonnage Measurement of Ships, 1969'. The term 'gross ton' has been retained above in line with international practice.

(b)   radio licence renewal fees:

The annual fee payable to the Department of Merchant Shipping for the renewal of the licence to install and work a wireless radio telegraphy/telephone station on board a Cyprus registered ship is C£10. Radio licence renewal fees are payable at any time before the expiry of the validity of the radio licence of the vessel, that is, before the first or subsequent yearly anniversary of the date of registration of the vessel under Cyprus flag.

J   Parallel registration

1   *Is parallel registration permitted:*
    1.1   onto the Cyprus Register?
    1.2   from the Cyprus Register?

Parallel registration of a ship is permitted both onto the Cyprus Register from a foreign register and from the Cyprus Register onto a foreign register.

2   *If so, what, if any, specific governmental or other consents are required?*

The specific governmental and other consents required are the following:

(a)   Parallel registration onto the Cyprus Register:
    (i)   approval of the Minister of Communications and Works of the Republic of Cyprus;
    (ii)   written consent of the appropriate maritime authorities of the country of the foreign register;
    (iii)   written consent of the shipowner; and
    (iv)   written consent of the mortgagees (if any).

(b)   Parallel registration from the Cyprus Register onto a foreign register:
    (i)   approval of the Minister of Communications & Works of the Republic of Cyprus;
    (ii)   written consent of the appropriate maritime authorities of the country of the foreign register, including a confirmation that the law of that country allows the parallel registration of a Cyprus ship onto its register;
    (iii)   written consent of the bareboat charterer; and
    (iv)   written consent of the mortgagees (if any).

3   *Is the period of parallel registration limited? If so, is it renewable?*

The period of parallel registration in Cyprus is limited but is renewable.

(a)   Parallel registration onto the Cyprus register from a foreign register:
    The law prescribes that the period of such parallel registration will be for such time as the Minister shall approve. In practice the validity of the Certificate of Parallel Registration is two years (or less if the bareboat charter is of a lesser duration). This can be extended by re-registration of the ship in the Special Book of Parallel Registration of the Cyprus Register.

(b)   Parallel registration from the Cyprus Register onto a foreign register:
    Such registration remains in force for the duration of the bareboat charter but in any case not longer than three years. Similarly, the period of outward parallel registration may be renewed on application to the Minister.

4   *If parallel registration is dependent on the existence of a demise charter, does Cyprus have a specific definition of demise or bareboat charter for these purposes? If so, what is it?*

Both instances of parallel registration are under Cyprus law dependent on the existence of a bareboat charter which is defined in the statute as follows:

> *'Bareboat charter of a ship*, is the charter by virtue of which the charterer shall for an agreed period of time, acquire full control and possession of the ship, have the management and operation of the ship, appoint and dismiss the master and the crew, be responsible towards third parties as if he were the shipowner, and, generally, be substituted in all respects for the shipowner so long as the charter lasts, save that he shall have no right to sell or mortgage the ship.'

5   *Please answer the questions listed under Sections A to E above with reference to application for parallel registration onto and from the Cyprus Register*

Onto the Cyprus Registry:

(A1)   For parallel registration onto the Cyprus Registry the only restriction on the bareboat chartering of vessels to be registered in parallel under Cyprus flag is that they must be chartered by persons who are qualified to own a Cyprus ship, as set out in Section A1 above.

(A2–5)   The answers to Section A on Ownership apply, *mutatis mutandis*, here by substituting shipowning companies with bareboat chartering companies.

(A6)   There are no special rules for any particular type of vessel applying for parallel registration onto the Cyprus register.

(A7)   There is no mandatory parallel registration requirement for any category of bareboat charterers.

(B1)   In theory, the types of ship which would be ineligible for parallel registration onto the Cyprus Register are those which, although registrable in the underlying registry, would not be registrable, in the ordinary case, in Cyprus.

(B2)   The same rules on the maximum age of entry of ships in the Cyprus Register apply also in the case of ships registered in a foreign registry for which an application for parallel registration onto the Cyprus Register has been made.

(C1–2)   There is a restriction on the name under which a ship may be registered in parallel in Cyprus. The name cannot be the same as or confusingly similar to the name of another ship already registered in the Cyprus Register.

(C3)   See answer to question in main Section C.

(D1)   Parallel registration of ships onto the Cyprus Register can only take place in Cyprus.

(D2)   For parallel registration of a ship into the Cyprus Register the following documents and information are required:

     (a)   Memorandum and articles of association of the bareboat chartering company (the Company);

     (b)   Certificate of incorporation, certified list of directors and secretary and certified list of shareholders of the company and of registered address;

     (c)   Directors' Resolutions of the company resolving the chartering of the ship and her parallel registration in the Cyprus Register;

     (d)   Power of Attorney of the company;

     (e)   certified copy of the bareboat charterparty;

     (f)   written consent of the shipowner;

       (g)   written consent of the appropriate maritime authorities of the country of the foreign registry;

       (h)   Certificate of Ownership and Encumbrances from the foreign registry;

       (i)   written consent of the mortgagees (if any);

       (j)   Certificate of survey and International Tonnage Certificate of the ship (or equivalents) of the foreign registry;

       (k)   ISM and ISPS forms;

       (l)   application for registration of a Mobile Maritime Radio Station;

       (m)   Form of Registration of Search and Rescue particulars;

       (n)   Form of appointment of Authorised Representative (if applicable);

       (o)   crew list;

       (p)   confirmation from the ship's classification society to the Registrar of Cyprus Ships as to maintenance of class and status of international trading certificates;

       (q)   confirmation from an international radio accounting authority as to clearance of ship's radio maritime accounts; and

       (r)   confirmation from the Master of the ship or a surveyor of a classification society as to the marking and carving of the name and port of registry of the ship under Cyprus flag.

(D3)   The following documents required to effect parallel registration must be in the prescribed form:

       (a)   ISM and ISPS forms;

       (b)   application for registration of a Mobile Maritime Radio Station; and

       (c)   Form of Registration of Search and Rescue particulars.

(D4)   One duly executed and legalised (where appropriate) original of each document or a duly certified copy thereof (where permissible) is sufficient. Fax copies of documents are acceptable in lieu of originals at the discretion of the Registrar and subject to an undertaking (where appropriate) to produce the original within a reasonable period.

(D5–7) The requirements as to the language of the documents, translation, execution, notarisation and legalisation are the same as for the ordinary registration of ships in the Cyprus Register (see answers to original Section D above).

(D8–11) Not applicable as there can be no parallel registration of a foreign registered ship onto the Cyprus Register either taking place abroad or being provisional.

(E1)   The requirements of Cyprus law and practice with regard to inspection, survey and measurement of ships which are registered in a foreign register and for which an application has been made for parallel registration in the Cyprus Register are the following:

       (a)   Before parallel registration a confirmation must be sent from the ship's classification society to the Registrar of Cyprus Ships regarding the vessel's status from a safety point of view. This may necessitate a prior inspection at the discretion of the classification society.

       (b)   No new survey or measurement of the tonnage of the ship is required for parallel registration in the Cyprus Register. The Certificate of Survey and the International Tonnage Certificate will be issued on the basis of the corresponding documents of the underlying registry.

(E2)   The above requirements must be complied with prior to parallel registration in the Cyprus Register.

Parallel registration from the Cyprus Register onto a foreign register:

Such registration will only be effected by a foreign Registry and thus most of the questions of Sections A to E do not apply. However, the Registrar of Cyprus Ships must give his prior consent to such Parallel Registration of a Cyprus registered vessel under a foreign flag (the 'Consent') and therefore the replies hereunder refer to such Consent and not a registration.

(A–C)   Not applicable.

(D1)   The Consent can only be given by the Registrar in Limassol.

(D2)   For the issue of the Consent the following documents and information are required:

(a)   Directors' Resolutions of the Cyprus shipowning company resolving the chartering of the ship and her parallel registration in the foreign register;

(b)   Power of Attorney of the Cyprus owning company in favour of the person who executed the charterparty;

(c)   certified copy of the bareboat charterparty;

(d)   written consent of the charterer;

(e)   written approval of the appropriate maritime authorities of the country of the foreign registry to the parallel registration together with a confirmation that the law of that Country allows the parallel registration of Cyprus Vessels to their Registry;

(f)   written declaration of owners and charterers undertaking that, during the ship's parallel registration in the foreign registry:

(i)   Cyprus laws will be respected;

(ii)   the ship will continue to meet the same requirements as regards compliance with international conventions as they apply to Cyprus ships, even though the state of parallel registry may not be a contracting party to all those conventions;

(iii)   a certified copy of the certificate of parallel registration issued by the foreign registry will be deposited with the Registrar of Cyprus Ships within one month;

(iv)   any changes in the name or other particulars of the ship will be communicated to the Registrar of Cyprus Ships without delay.

(g)   written consent of the mortgagees (if any);

(h)   confirmation from the vessel's international radio accounting authority that they will continue the clearance of ship's radio maritime accounts.

(D3)   None of the above documents required to effect parallel registration out from the Cyprus Registry.

(D4)   One duly executed and legalised (where appropriate) original of each document or a duly certified copy thereof (where permissible) is sufficient. Fax copies of documents are acceptable in lieu of originals at the discretion of the Registrar and subject to an undertaking (where applicable) to produce the original within a reasonable period.

(D5–7)   The requirements as to the language of the documents, translation, execution, notari-sation and legalisation are the same as for the ordinary registration of ships in the Cyprus Register (see answers to original Section D above).

(D8–11) Not applicable as the consent cannot be issued abroad or be provisional.

(E)   Not applicable.

6   *Can/must mortgages on ships parallel registered into the Cyprus Registry also be registered in Cyprus?*

Mortgages on a foreign registered ship subsisting at the time of her parallel registration in the Cyprus Register, as well as mortgages created on the ship by the foreign shipowning company after the said parallel registration, must by law be notified to the Registrar of Cyprus Ships and entered in the Special Book of Parallel Registration kept by the Registrar. However, the Cypriot bareboat chartering company is not permitted to register any mortgage on the ship in Cyprus.

7   *Under what circumstances will/may the parallel registration of a ship onto Cyprus' register be terminated or revoked?*

The parallel registration of a foreign registered vessel in the Cyprus Register will be revoked in the following circumstances:

(a)   where the maritime authorities of the underlying registry revoke their consent for the parallel registration of the foreign ship in the Cyprus Register;

(b)   in the case of termination of the bareboat charter;

(c)   pon the lapse of the period of time for which the Minister has approved the parallel registration of the ship in the Cyprus Register; and

(d)   f there exists any reason for deletion which would under the Merchant Shipping Laws be applicable in the case of a ship ordinarily registered in the Cyprus Register.

K   General

1   *Please identify the principal statutes and regulations in Cyprus governing the regis-tration of ships.*

Principal statutes and regulations governing the registration of ships in Cyprus:

(a)   The Merchant Shipping (Registration of Ships, Sales and Mortgages) Laws, 1963 to 2005;

(b)   The Merchant Shipping (Fees and Taxing Provisions) Laws, 1992 to 2004;

(c)   The Merchant Shipping (Master and Seamen) Law of 1964 to 2004;

(d)   The International Convention on Tonnage Measurement of Ship, 1969 (Ratification) and for Matters Connected therewith Law, 1986; and

(e)   The Merchant Shipping (Tonnage of Ships) Regulations, 1987.

2   *Are there any other matters in the context of registration of ships under the legal sys-tem in Cyprus which you feel should be emphasised?*

Cyprus law allows the registration of ships under construction, as well as the recordation of mortgages thereon.

---

* Contributed by Acis Montanios and Adam Montanios, Montanios & Montanios, Nicosia, Cyprus.

Greece*

A   Ownership

*1   What, if any, are the restrictions on ownership of vessels registered under the flag of
         Greece?*

Under Greek Law (LD187/1973, art. 5), there is a restriction on ownership of vessels registered under the Greek flag regarding the nationality of the owner(s). A vessel can only
be registered under Greek flag if it belongs by a percentage exceeding 50 per cent to Greek
citizens or to Greek legal entities whose share capital belongs to Greek citizens by over 50
per cent. If the owner is a member of the Union of Greek Shipowners, the evidence
required by the Greek Ships Registries is in the form of a statement issued by the Union
of Greek Shipowners, certifying the existence of the Greek interests in the vessel to be registered. If the owner does not wish to become a member of the Union of Greek Shipowners,
the Greek Ships' Registry will require a personal declaration of the representative of the
owner regarding the existence of the Greek interests in the vessel, the signature of whom
must be certified.

Notwithstanding the foregoing rule, vessels which are owned by non-Greek legal
entities (single-purpose companies or holding companies) can be registered under the Greek
flag pursuant to the provisions of the Greek Legislative Decree 2687/53 concerning investment and protection of foreign capital, as interpreted by Legislative Decree 2928/54
('LD2687/53'), provided the said non-Greek entities are beneficially owned by majority
Greek interests by a percentage exceeding 50 per cent.

*2   If registration by companies is limited to companies incorporated in Greece, is
         a local 'brass-plate' company sufficient, or must there be a closer, genuine
         connection?*

A local brass-plate company is not sufficient. There must be a genuine connection as per 1 above.

*3   If registration by companies incorporated other than in Greece is permitted, must a
         local representative be appointed? If so, are there any restrictions on the identity of
         that representative?*

In case of non-Greek legal entities which own vessels registered pursuant to the provisions of
LD2687/53 a local representative and a resident agent must be appointed.

*4   Please summarise any restrictions (for example, as to number, nationality and so on)
         on who may own shares in vessel owning companies incorporated in Greece.*

There are no restrictions apart from the above.

*5   Please explain any exchange control or other governmental or regulatory consents
         required in connection with the ownership of vessels registered in Greece.*

In general there are no exchange controls or any other governmental or regulatory consents with respect to the ownership of a vessel registered under the Greek flag. Having
said this, it should be noted that in order for a vessel to be registered initially under the
Greek flag, a Ministerial Decision in respect of that vessel must be adopted by the
Ministers of National Economy, of Finance and of Mercantile Marine, which should then

be published in the Government Gazette (that is, the official gazette of the state, where all laws are published).

6   *Please explain any special rules for any particular type of vessel.*
There are no special rules for particular types of vessels. See B1 below.

7   *Is there any mandatory registration requirement for certain owners (for example, citizens of Greece)?*
There are no mandatory registration requirements with regard to vessel owners.

B   Eligibility

1   *Are there any particular types/sizes of vessel ineligible for, or exempt from, registration?*
There are no particular types/sizes of vessels ineligible for or exempt from registration. Under the provisions of Article 1 of the Greek Code of Private Maritime Law (L.3816/1958), a ship is defined as 'any vessel of not less than ten (10) net register tons (nrt), intended to navigate at sea by its own means of propulsion'. Based on their net registered tons ships are divided into two classes:
(a)   Class B: ships of not less than 60 nrt; and
(b)   Class A: ships of not less than 10 nrt and not more than 59.99 nrt.
      Vessels of less than 10 nrt (boats, crafts and the like) and floating structures, although eligible for registration, are treated as movables, are recorded in separate Register Books and, in principle, are not subject to hypothecation.
      Ships of less than 1,500 grt may not be registered pursuant to LD2687/53.

2   *What, if any, is the maximum age for registration of vessels under the flag of Greece?*
There is no maximum age for registration of ships, except for passenger ships, which are not eligible for registration if they exceed 20 years of age.

C   Names

1   *What, if any, are the restrictions on the name under which a vessel may be registered in Greece?*
There are no restrictions with regard to the name of a vessel except for passenger ships.

2   *Is there a procedure for approval of names in advance?*
Approval of the name under which a passenger ship will be registered is required.

3   *If so, how does it operate? Does approval confer any priority rights in the use of the name?*
Approval in respect of passenger ships is obtained from the Greek Ministry of Merchant Marine ('YEN') following relevant application. Approval confers priority rights in the use of the name.

D New registration procedure

1   Where may vessels intending to fly the flag of Greece be registered:

1.1   in Greece?

1.2   abroad?

1.1   Vessels intending to fly the Greek flag can be registered at any Port Office (Harbour Master's Office) in Greece. Port Offices are divided into three categories:

(a)   Central Port Offices;

(b)   Port Offices; and

(c)   Port Stations.

Ships Register Books are also divided into three categories based on the vessel's nrt:

(a)   Register Books for class B Ships, wherein ships of not less than 60 nrt are registered;

(b)   Register Books for class A ships wherein ships of not less than 10 nrt and not more than 59.99 nrt are registered; and

(c)   Register Books for boats and crafts of less than 10 nrt.

Central Port Offices keep Register Books of all of the above categories.

Port Offices keep Register Books of categories (a) and (b) above (with the exception of the Port Offices of the islands of Hydra and Ithaca which keep Register Books of all three categories).

Port Stations keep Register Books for category (c) only.

1.2   At a Greek Mercantile Marine Service and, where such service does not exist, at any Greek Consulate.

2   What documents and information must be submitted to effect registration?

The following documents and information are required for the purpose of initial registration of a vessel under Greek flag:

(a)   Permanent registration:

(i)   Title of Ownership (Bill of Sale or other contract of sale). In case the parties to the contract of sale are legal entities, evidence is required to the effect that the person(s) signing the contract of sale in the name, stead and place of such legal entities is (are) duly authorised to act for the entity. The signatures on the Bill of Sale must be legalised and if signed outside Greece it should be notarially attested and apostille must be affixed, unless they are legalised by a Greek mercantile office outside Greece. For newbuildings the notarially attested Builder's Certificate and commercial invoice must also be submitted and a protocol of delivery and acceptance legalised by the competent port or consular authority.

(ii)   Certificate or other evidence of Greek citizenship (nationality) of the owner applying for registration. In case the owner applying for registration is a legal entity, evidence is required to the effect that such legal entity (a) is a Greek legal entity and (b) is beneficially owned by a percentage exceeding 50 per cent by Greek interests.

(iii)   Solemn declaration of the new owner applying for registration stating that the vessel (a) is owned by the owner applying for registration, (b) has not been registered at the Registry of another Greek Port, (c) has/has not received provisional ship documents pursuant to a provisional registration and (d) is/is not supplied with VHF.

In case the owner applying for registration is a legal entity, the solemn declaration must further provide for the appointment of a resident agent for service of process; the said resident agent must accept his appointment under the same or by separate solemn declaration.

(iv)   Solemn declaration of the owner applying for registration to the effect that all SOLAS certificates of the vessel shall be replaced.

(v)   Customs clearance certificate.

(vi)   Certificate of Deletion or free of encumbrances certificate from the vessel's previous flag. A Deletion Certificate is required if the vessel was registered under one of the following flags: Russia, Egypt, Germany, Italy, Cyprus, Georgia, Estonia, Jordan, China, Croatia, S. Africa, Tunisia, Bulgaria and Albania.

(vii)   Certificate of nationality and certificate of measurement of the vessel issued by its former Register together with solemn declaration of the owner applying for registration to the effect that as of the date of application for registration under Greek flag there have been no changes in the vessel's particulars described in the above certificates.

(viii)   Application to the Registrar of Ships (hereinafter the 'Registrar') requesting registration of the vessel.

(ix)   Form of Certificate of Nationality from the Greek Seamens' Pension Fund (hereinafter, the 'NAT').

(b)   Registration pursuant to LD 2687/53:

For the purpose of registering a ship under Greek flag pursuant to LD 2687/53, it is necessary that a joint ministerial decision of the Ministers of Merchant Marine, National Economy and Finance, approving the registration of the ship (hereinafter the 'Approval' be issued). The Approval is issued for ships which exceed 1,500 grt and can be granted to non-Greek legal entities provided same are beneficially owned by majority Greek interest.

Following the Approval, the documents and information required to effect registration are identical to the ones referred to under D2(a) above except that the Registrar will not request the production of the documents referred to in D2(a)(ii) above since similar documentation is one of the requirements for the issuance of the Approval (see D2(b)(vii) below). Furthermore a receipt issued by the Greek Chamber of Shipping must be submitted to YEN evidencing that the required fees have been paid.

For issuance of the Approval the following documents and information are submitted to YEN:

(i) Application, in the form required by YEN, which contains detailed information in respect of the ship and the application-corporation (hereinafter the Company).

(ii) Solemn declaration signed by the Company's representative, to the effect that (1) the particulars and information contained in the application are true and correct (2) the Company covers Greek majority interests by a rate exceeding 50 per cent and (3) YEN will be promptly notified in case such percentage becomes less than the rate referred to above. Information is also contained as to the corporate style, place and date of incorporation of the Company and as to the names, addresses, telephone numbers, profession, identification, passport numbers, and office held by each of the directors of the Company.

(iii) Declaration (Appointment) addressed to (1) YEN, (2) the Ministry of Finance and (3) the NAT whereby the Company appoints a representative in Greece, who will be personally liable as primary obligor for the prompt payment of all amounts becoming due by the ship to the Greek authorities.

(iv) Acceptance of such appointment by the aforesaid representative of the ship.

(v) Corporate resolutions approving the purchase of the ship and the registration thereof under Greek flag pursuant to LD 2687/53 and appointing a legal representative of the Company who will bind same by his signature.

(vi) Copy of the articles of incorporation, original good standing certificate, and original certificate of incumbency of directors and officers of the company.

(vii) Certification from the Union of Greek Shipowners to the effect that the Company covers Greek interests by majority (hereinafter the 'UGS Certificate').

(c) Provisional registration:
All documents referred to in paragraph D2(a) or, (if the ship is registered pursuant to LD 2687/53), in paragraph D2(b) above must be produced except that a Customs Clearance Certificate under D2(a)(v) above is not required.

(d) Registration of vessel under construction:
A vessel under construction may be registered under the Greek flag. The Registrar will request the production of the shipbuilding contract and will only register the vessel if the shipbuilding contract contains express provisions to the effect that title in the vessel under construction has passed to the owner applying for registration and a protocol of delivery and acceptance shall be executed by the builder and the owner upon completion of the construction of the vessel. The documents referred to in paragraph D2(a) or (if the ship is registered pursuant to LD 2687/53) in paragraph D2(b) above must also be produced.

*3   Does the legal system in Greece lay down any specific requirements as to the contents
        of any of these documents (for example, of Bills of Sale) and, if so, what are they?*

Standard Bill of Salle form is normally used and accepted. The Bill of Sale must evidence a contract between seller and buyer and must be signed by both parties.

Specific requirements are laid down as to the contents of all solemn declarations and also as to the contents of the application for registration and the supporting documents submitted to YEN for issuance of the Approval.

*4   Please identify how many originals or copies of each document are required. Are fax
        copies of any of them acceptable?*

One original or certified copy is required for each document submitted. However, the Appointment referred to in D2(b)(iii) above and the acceptance of same referred to in D2(b)(iv) above must be submitted to YEN in three originals. Fax copies are not acceptable.

5   Are there any requirements as to the language in which documents must be submitted?

Registration documents must be submitted in the Greek language. However, the Bill of Sale, all corporate documents (such as Corporate Resolutions, Certificates of Good Standing or Incumbency, Powers of Attorney and so on) which refer to or are issued by non-Greek legal entities, and all ships' documents issued by non-Greek authorities may be submitted in a foreign language.

*6   If they may be submitted in a foreign language, are there any translation require-
        ments? If so, what are they and when must they be complied with?*

The documents which may be submitted in a foreign language must be accompanied by certified Greek translation, certified by a Greek lawyer.

*7   Please identify any particular requirements of the legal system in Greece with
        regards to the method of execution of any of the registration documents, or with
        regard to notarisation or legalisation.*

Documents executed by individuals are executed by subscription of the individual's name.

Documents executed by legal entities are executed by subscription of the name of the individual acting for and on behalf of the legal entity beneath the corporate name.

Signatures on all documents must be legalised (authenticated) or notarised and apostilled if outside Greece.

Signatures on documents executed in Greece can be legalised, *inter alia*, by any police authority, port office authority or local consular authority.

Signatures on documents executed abroad must be notarised by a local notary public or authenticated by any other local public authority; such notarisation/authentication must thereafter be legalised by a local Greek consular authority or by way of apostille.

8   If the initial registration takes place abroad, is that registration final or provisional?

It can be final if it takes place at the Greek Mercantile Marine Services of London, New York, or Tokyo. It can only be provisional if it takes place before any other Greek Consular

Authority.

Although, New York and Tokyo can be final, it is a requirement of Greek law that ships registered thereat by way of final (permanent) registration be transcribed to a Greek port within a 12-month period. Transcription is made at the request of the shipowner who must state the Greek port to which the ship should be transcribed. It should be noted that where final (permanent) registration of the vessel is effected at any one of the Greek Mercantile Marine Services of London, New York and Tokyo, a Customs Clearance Certificate of the vessel (see D2(a)(v) above) is not required. Such certificate must however be produced upon transcription of the ship to a Greek port.

9   If provisional, what needs to be done to effect final registration? When must it be done?
Final registration must be effected within a period of three months at a port office in Greece. An extension of up to three months may be granted.

10   If provisional, what, if any, are the restrictions which apply to the vessel pending final registration?
None.

11   Can a provisionally registered vessel be mortgaged?
No.

E   Technical matters

1   Please identify the requirements of Greece with regard to inspection, survey, measurement and the like in respect of newly registered vessels.
A provisional measurement certificate is supplied to newly registered ships by the port office effecting the ship's registration under Greek flag. The said provisional certificate is issued based on the vessel's certificates (tonnage, measurement, nationality) issued by its previous flag and is valid for three months; extension of its validity can be granted for an additional three-month period whereupon it must be replaced by a final measurement certificate.

The final measurement of the vessel is made by the Merchant Marine Inspection Service ('EEP') following an application by the owner and submission, inter alia, of vessel's plans, classification society's records and previous tonnage/measurement certificates.

Upon completion of the measurement of the vessel a (new) final measurement certificate is issued by EEP.

As regards the SOLAS certificates a three-month period is granted to the shipowner within which the certificate must be replaced and new certificates be issued by the vessel's classification society which must be approved by the Greek government. The classification societies approved by the Greek authorities are:

    (a)   American Bureau of Shipping;
    (b)   Det Norske Veritas;
    (c)   Hellenic Register of Shipping;
    (d)   Germanischer Lloyd;
    (e)   Nippon Kaiji Kyokai;

(f)   Registro Italiano Navale;

(g)   Lloyd's Register of Shipping; and

(h)   Bureau Veritas.

2   *By when must these requirements be complied with?*

Please see E1 above.

F   Transfer of ownership

1   *Please answer, either separately or by reference to your earlier answers, the questions listed under sections D and E above in respect of the transfer of ownership of a vessel already registered in Greece.*

The transfer of ownership of a vessel already registered in Greece may be recorded only at the vessel's home port.

Documents required for the transfer of ownership of a vessel already registered under the Greek flag are as follows:

(a)   Title of Ownership as per D2(a)(i);

(b)   certificate or other evidence of Greek citizenship (nationality) of the person to whom ownership is transferred as per D2(a)(ii);

(c)   in case the new owner is a legal entity, (i) solemn declaration providing for the appointment of a resident agent for service of process and (ii) acceptance of such appointment by the resident agent;

(d)   Clearance Certificate from the Piraeus Tax Authorities evidencing that no taxes are due in respect of the vessel;

(e)   Clearance Certificate from NAT evidencing that no contributions are due in respect of the vessel;

(f)   Clearance Certificate from the Greek Telecommunications Organisation (OTE) evidencing that no charges are due in respect of the vessel;

(g)   Transfer Tax and VAT Return Form evidencing that transfer tax and VAT payable for the sale of the vessel, has been paid or alternatively, confirming that no transfer Tax or VAT is payable on transfer of the vessel;

(h)   the original of the vessel's certificate of nationality issued in the name of its previous owner; and

(i)   application for the recordation of the transfer of ownership.

Notes:

1   If the vessel is mortgaged, discharge of all mortgages is required. If the vessel is otherwise encumbered, discharge of all encumbrances of record is required.

2   Transfer tax amounts to US$1 per nrt. Vessels of less than 10 nrt are exempt from transfer tax but are subject to stamp duty. As per Note 4(d) below, vessels registered pursuant to LD 2687/53 are not subject to transfer tax.

3   In case of sale of a yacht or other pleasure boat registered in the name of an individual, in addition to the foregoing documents, the seller (individual) must produce a tax certificate evidencing that he has stated in his annual income tax return that he is the

owner of such yacht/pleasure boat. Such obligation does not apply in respect of professional-tourist yachts registered as such under L. 438/76.

4   Documents required for the transfer of ownership of a vessel already registered pursuant to LD 2687/53 are:

(a)   Title of Ownership as per (a) above;

(b)   solemn declaration as per (c) above;

(c)   Clearance Certificates as per (d), (e) and (f) above;

(d)   Tax Transfer Form and VAT confirmation as per (g) above. (Note: The sale of vessels registered pursuant to LD 2687/53 is not subject to transfer tax or VAT);

(e)   the vessel's certificate of nationality as per (h) above;

(f)   Government Gazette Issue evidencing the issuance of an Approval under LD 2687/53;

(g)   Declaration (appointment) addressed to YEN, NAT and the Ministry of Finance and acceptance of such appointment as per D2(b)(iii) and (iv) (in four originals);

(h)   Solemn declaration by the representative of the new owner containing the information referred to in D2(b)(ii) together with copies of the Articles of Incorporation, Good Standing Certificate, Corporate Resolutions, Power of Attorney and Certificate of Incumbency of the new owner (transferee);

(i)   the UGS Certificate; and

(j)   application to the Registrar.

2   *Please explain any exchange control or other governmental or regulatory consents required in connection with the sale to a foreign flag of a vessel registered under the flag of Greece.*

The issuance of an export licence by the Greek authorities is required in connection with the sale of a Greek flag vessel to a foreign non-European Community flag.

The issuance of an export licence by the Greek authorities is required in connection with the deletion of a Greek flag vessel. If a Greek flag vessel had been bought in euros and is being sold to a foreign flag in foreign currency (that is, other than in a member state of the European Union), the seller (transferor) is obligated to import foreign currency equivalent to a value assessed by the Greek authorities as being the market value of the vessel.

YEN's approval is required in connection with the sale of a Greek flag vessel to a foreign flag.

No exchange control or other governmental or regulatory consents including the approvals referred to above are required in connection with the sale of a vessel registered under Greek flag pursuant to LD2687/53 to a foreign flag.

G   Deletion

1   Please outline the procedure for deletion of vessels from the flag of Greece.

The procedure for deletion of vessels from the Greek flag involves, as in the case of initial registration and transfer of ownership, the procurement and filing with the appropriate port office of an application accompanied by the documents outlined below.

2   *Please answer, either separately or by reference to your earlier answers, the questions listed under section D in respect of the deletion, as opposed to new registration, of a vessel.*

Application requesting deletion of a Greek flag vessel along with its supporting documents must be submitted to the Registrar of the vessel's home port.

Deletion of a Greek flag vessel is effected on account of her sale to non-Greek individuals or to legal entities which, irrespective of their country of incorporation are not beneficially owned by majority Greek interests.

Documents and information required to effect deletion are as follows:

(a)   Deed of transfer or ownership as per D2(a)(i);

(b)   Clearance Certificates as per F1(d), (e) and (f);

(c)   Transfer Tax Form and VAT or stamp duty confirmation as per F1(g) and Notes;

(d)   original of vessel's Certificate of Nationality as per F1(h);

(e)   Export Licence;

(f)   approval by YEN for the vessel's sale to foreigners; and

(g)   Application to the Registrar.

If the vessel is registered pursuant to LD 2687/53 the documents and information required to effect deletion are identical to the ones referred to above except that the export licence referred to under (e) above and YEN's approval under (f) above are not required.

Under Section 1 of the standard form of the Approval the shipowner has the right not only to sell but also to change the flag of the vessel, without a change of ownership, without prior approval or permission by any Greek authority.

For the purpose of deleting a Greek flag vessel registered under Greek flag pursuant to LD 2687/53 on account of change of her flag the following documents are required for submission to the Ships' Registrar of the vessel's home port:

(a)   application requesting deletion of the vessel from the Greek Register on account of change of her flag. (The vessel's new flag must be mentioned in the application);

(b)   Corporate Resolutions approving the change of the vessel's flag and authorising a representative of the shipowner to sign and to submit to the Greek authorities all appropriate documents;

(c)   solemn declaration of the aforesaid representative of the shipowner stating that he is duly authorised to submit the application for the deletion of the vessel;

(d)   the original of the vessel's Greek Certificate of Nationality; and

(e)   Tax, NAT and OTE Clearance Certificates as per F1(d), (e) and (f).

Notes:

1   If the vessel is mortgaged or otherwise encumbered, discharge of all registered mortgages and encumbrances of record is required.

2   In accordance with Section 1 of the Approval, in lieu of the certificates referred to above the shipowner is entitled to submit a bank guarantee for an amount provided for in the Approval.

H   Certificates/transcripts

1   Please identify the certificates and other documents issued to an owner on registration of a vessel under the flag of Greece.

The following certificates are issued to an owner on registration:

       (a)   Certificate of Nationality;

       (b)   Provisional Certificate of Measurement; and

       (c)   Provisional Radiotelegraphy Certificate.

2   Please outline the procedure (including fees payable) for obtaining information on the registered ownership of and encumbrances on vessels registered in Greece.

The Ships Register Books and the Books of Ship Mortgages are public documents, are open to the public and can be reviewed without charge. A minimal fee (stamp duty) is charged for the issuance of certificates. Certificates concerning the registered ownership and the mortgages and other encumbrances recorded on vessels are issued by the Registrar following the filing of an application in writing.

I   Fees/taxes

1   What fees are currently payable:

       1.1   on new registration?

       1.2   on transfer of ownership?

       1.3   on deletion?

1.1   A charge of 30 euros is payable on new registration for issuance of the vessel's certificate of nationality, provisional certificate of measurement and provisional Radio Station Licence.

1.2   A fee of 90 euros is payable on transfer of ownership of B class vessels, 30 euros for A class vessels and 6 euros for boats and crafts of less than 10 nrt.

1.3   A fee of 30 euros is payable on deletion of B class vessels, 15 euros for A class vessels and 6 euros for boats and crafts of less than 10 nrt.

2   Are there any annual or other ongoing fees or taxes payable in respect of ships registered in Greece?

Yes.

3   If so, what are they? On what basis and when are they payable?

There is an annual tax calculated on the basis of the vessel's age and/or grt in accordance with the provisions of L 27/75, which came into force on 22 April 1975, concerning taxation of Greek flag vessels, establishment of foreign shipping enterprises and related matters (hereinafter 'L 27'). The taxes are payable annually in four instalments.

L 27 divides Greek flag vessels into two categories:

Category A, which includes:

       (a)   motor-driven cargo ships, tanker ships and reefers of gross tonnage 3,000 tons and above;

(b)   steel cargo ships that carry dry and liquid cargoes and also reefers of gross tonnage over 500 tons and up to 3,000 tons that extend their voyages to non-Greek ports or trade between non-Greek ports;

(c)   passenger ships that extend their voyages to non-Greek ports or trade between non-Greek ports;

(d)   passenger ships of gross tonnage exceeding 500 tons that in the preceding year and for a period of at least six months engaged exclusively in regular itineraries between Greek ports, or between Greek and non-Greek ports, or between non-Greek ports only for the entertainment of their passengers following public announcement of such cruises (touring or cruising ships); and

(e)   floating drills of a displacement exceeding 5,000 tons and also floating refineries and fuel oil depots of gross tonnage exceeding 15,000 tons which are utilised as from their construction or reconstruction for exploitation, drillings, distillation and storage of fuel oil or gas; and

Category B which includes:

All other motor-driven vessels, sailing boats and boats in general.

The vessels of category A are subdivided into (i) vessels that are registered under Greek flag following issuance L 27 and (ii) vessels that were registered under Greek flag before issuance of L 27.

Vessels of category A (i) are subject to payment of tax on basis of the vessel's age and grt as follows:

Vessel's age	Factors in US$ per grt
0-4	0.53
5-9	0.95
10-19	0.93
20-29	0.88
30 and over	0.68

The above amounts of tax are multiplied, based on the vessel's grt, by the following factors:

Vessel's grt	Factors
100-10,000	1.2
10,001-20,000	1.1
20,001-40,000	1.0
40,001-80,000	0.9
80,001	0.8

Vessels of category B are subject to payment of tax in drachmas (in practice, this is paid in euros) based on the vessel's grt as follows:

Factor in Greek grt scale	drs per grt	Total annual tax in drs	Grt	Tax in drs
20	200	4.000	20	4.000
30	230	6.900	50	10.900
50	260	13.000	100	23.900

348

Vessels exceeding 100 grt are subject to payment of tax at the rate of drs300 per grt.

Note: L 27 provides for several tax exemptions and rebates for both categories of vessels.

J   Parallel registration

1   *Is parallel registration permitted:*
       1.1   onto the Greek register?
       1.2   from the Greek register?
2   *If so, what, if any, specific governmental or other consents are required?*
3   *Is the period of parallel registration limited? If so, is it renewable?*
4   *If parallel registration is dependent on the existence of a demised charter, does Greece have a specific definition of demise or bareboat charter for these purposes? If so, what is it?*
5   *Please answer the questions listed under sections A to E above with reference to application for parallel registration onto the register of Greece.*
       5.1   application for parallel registration onto Greece's register; and
       5.2   application for parallel registration from Greece's register.
6   *Can/must mortgages on vessels parallel registered into the registry of Greece also be registered in Greece?*
7   *Under what circumstances will/may the parallel registration of the vessel onto the register of Greece be terminated or revoked?*

There is no provision in Greek law regarding parallel registration.

K   General

1   *Please identify the principal statutes and regulations in Greece governing the registration of vessels.*
(a)   Royal Decree of 10 July 1910 on ship registers and ship mortgage registers as amended;
(b)   Presidential Decree 893/1978 on Certificates of Nationality of Greek Merchant Ships;
(c)   Law 3816/58 ratifying in Greek Code of Private Maritime Law;
(d)   Legislative Decree No 187/73 concerning the Greek Code of Public Maritime Law;
(e)   Legislative Decree 2687/53 as interpreted by Legislative Decree 2928/54;
(f)   Legislative Decree 3899/58 concerning Preferred Mortgages;
(g)   Law 27/75 concerning taxation of Greek flag vessels, establishment of foreign shipping enterprises and related matters;
(h)   Presidential Decree 913/78 concerning NAT; and
(i)   Law 438/76 concerning tourist-professional yachts.

2   *Are there any other matters in the context of registration of vessels under the legal system in Greece which you feel should be emphasised here?*

Greek flag vessels are subject to contributions payable to NAT based on the vessel's crew in accordance with the provisions of Presidential Decree 913/78.

L   Greek ENE companies

1   How can a vessel be registered under a Greek ENE company?
An ENE company is a special maritime enterprise, set up specifically in order to acquire a vessel. The same registration procedure is followed as for any other foreign legal entity, but the Ministerial Decision which will be issued for the registration of the vessel under the Greek flag should make express provision to the ENE company. This is incorporated in Article 16 of the Ministerial Decision. The ENE company should acquire the vessel within 6 months from its incorporation and it is dissolved five years after its incorporation if it remains without owning a vessel.

2   Can an ENE company be controlled by foreign legal entities?
The ENE company can be controlled by foreign legal entities, provided that these foreign legal entities are controlled by majority Greek interests and if the majority Greek interests cease, the vessel would be deleted from the Greek registry upon a Ministerial Order made pursuant to Article 24 of the Ministerial Decision. However, if a mortgage exists on the vessel, the Ministerial Order allows a period of six months within which the mortgagee can arrange and secure its interest differently.

3   Do the provisions of Article 16(f) of the Ministerial Decision (beneficial ownership) also apply to non-ENE companies owning Greek flag vessels (for example, Liberian corporation)?
Article 16(f) (beneficial shareholding) does not apply to non-ENE companies owning Greek flag vessels (for example, Liberian corporations). Having said that, please note that a vessel would be deleted from the Greek registry even if it was owned by a company incorporated in any other jurisdiction (for example, Liberia/Marshall Islands), if the majority Greek interest behind it ceases to exist. Thus, the position is not much different, in this respect, with the Greek ENE.

* Contributed by Nigel Bowen-Morris and Alexandros Damianidis of Stephenson Harwood Consultants OE, Piraeus, Greece.

Hong Kong* **

A   Ownership

1   What, if any, are the restrictions on ownership of vessels registered under the flag of Hong Kong?

Registration of a ship in Hong Kong is effected under the Merchant Shipping (Registration) Ordinance (the 'MSRO'). A ship is registrable if:

(a)   a majority interest in the ship is owned by one or more qualified persons (section 11(1)(a) MSRO); or

(b)   the ship is operated under a demise charter by a body corporate being a qualified person (whether or not a majority interest in the ship is owned by one or more qualified persons) (section 11(1)(b) MSRO);

and a representative person is appointed in relation to the ship.

A 'qualified person' is classified as either an individual who holds a valid Hong Kong Identity Card and who is ordinarily resident in Hong Kong, a body corporate incorporated in Hong Kong or an overseas company registered in Hong Kong under Part XI of the Companies Ordinance. The representative person appointed in relation to a ship must be either a qualified person and the owner or part owner of the ship, or a company incorporated in Hong Kong which is engaged in the business of managing, or acting as an agent for, ships (Section 68 MSRO).

2   If registration by companies is limited to companies incorporated in Hong Kong, is a local 'brass-plate' company sufficient, or must there be a closer, genuine connection?

See A1 above. Registration is not limited to companies incorporated in Hong Kong but it is limited to companies registered in Hong Kong. However, a 'brass-plate' company is sufficient provided a representative person is appointed.

3   If registration by companies incorporated other than in Hong Kong is permitted, must a local representative be appointed? If so, are there any restrictions on the identity of that representative?

As stated in A1 above, a representative person must be appointed in relation to the ship in any event. An overseas company registered under Part XI of the Companies Ordinance must also, under Section 333A of the Companies Ordinance, have a person resident in Hong Kong at all times who is authorised to accept service of process and notice on its behalf (authorised representative).

4   Please summarise any restrictions (for example, as to number, nationality and so on) on who may own shares in shipowning companies incorporated in Hong Kong.

Where a ship is owned by a Hong Kong incorporated private company, Hong Kong company law restricts the number of members the company may have to between 1 and 50 (Section 29 of the Companies Ordinance). There are no such restrictions on the number of members a Hong Kong public company may have. There are no restrictions as to the nationality of the shareholders.

5   Please explain any exchange control or other governmental or regulatory consents required in connection with the ownership of ships registered in Hong Kong.

None, save as appear in these notes.

6   *Please explain any special rules for any particular type of vessel.*

There are no special rules for any particular type of vessel in respect of ownership save in respect of government-owned vessels. Certain vessels, for example, gas carriers and chemical carriers, have more stringent survey requirements.

7   *Is there any mandatory registration requirement for certain owners (for example, citizens of Hong Kong)?*

No.

B   Eligibility

1   Are any particular types/sizes of ship ineligible for, or exempt from, registration?

There are no restrictions on the type or tonnage of a ship that may be registered. A 'ship' includes every description of vessel capable of navigating in water not propelled by oars, and includes any ship, boat or craft and an air-cushion vehicle or similar craft used wholly or partly in navigation in water (Section 2 MSRO). The Director may, under Section 3 MSRO, provide by notice in the Gazette that certain vessels are not to be treated as ships for the purpose of any provision of the MSRO. No such notices have yet been given.

A ship may be declined registration if the Director of Marine, having regard to:

(a)   the condition of the ship so far as relevant to its safety or to any risk of pollution; or

(b)   the safety, health and welfare of persons employed or engaged in any capacity on the ship, considers it inappropriate for the ship to be registered. Furthermore, the Director of Marine may, if he is satisfied in respect of any ship or any class or type of ship that, having regard:

(i)   to the use, nature or condition of that ship or of that class or type of ship; and

(ii)   to the difficulty of providing adequate supervision and control of that ship or that class or type of ship in Hong Kong, it would be inappropriate to register that ship or ships of that class or type, direct the Registrar not to register such ships.

2   What, if any, is the maximum age for registration of ships under the flag of Hong Kong?

There are no restrictions on the age of a ship that may be registered. However, regard should be had to B1 above.

C   Names

1   What, if any, are the restrictions on the name under which a ship may be registered in Hong Kong?

Names of ships are governed by the MSRO and the Merchant Shipping (Registration) (Ships' Names) Regulations. Generally, there are no restrictions on the name under which a ship may be registered in Hong Kong, other than the fact that the name must be in English alphabetic characters which may include numerals. A Chinese name alone is not registrable, but can be registered if the phonetically corresponding name in the English alphabet is also registered.

The Registrar will refuse to register a ship by its proposed name if the name:

(a)   is already the name of a registered ship or is a reserved name, or is in the opinion of the Registrar so similar as to be likely to deceive; or

(b)   is in the opinion of the Registrar undesirable for the purposes of registration in Hong Kong.

2   *Is there a procedure for approval of names in advance?*
Yes.

3   *If so, how does it operate? Does approval confer any priority rights in the use of the name?*

An application to reserve a name for a ship which is intended to be registered in Hong Kong can be made in the specified form free of charge by a qualified person who is the owner of the ship, or by a person authorised by such owner for the purpose. If the proposed name is approved by the Registrar, the name shall be reserved to the owner for a period of three years from the date of such approval.

D   New registration procedure

1   Where may ships intending to fly the flag of Hong Kong be registered in:
1.1   Hong Kong?
1.2   abroad?

1.1   At the Shipping Registry, Marine Department, 21/F, Harbour Building, 38 Pier Road, Hong Kong.

1.2   Registration must take place in Hong Kong.

2   *What documents and information must be submitted to effect registration?*

Where a ship is owned by one or more individuals, an application for registration as owner shall be made by that or those individuals, or by an individual or individuals appointed to act on their behalf. In the case of corporate ownership, each body corporate shall authorise an individual to act on its behalf (Section 19(1) MSRO).

If a ship is to be registered under Section 11(1)(b) MSRO (see A1 above), then the application for registration must be made by both the demise charterer and the owner together. If the demise charterer and/or the owner are corporate bodies, they should authorise individuals to act on their behalf.

Where an application is made by an individual on behalf of an owner or demise charterer, the application must be accompanied by evidence in writing of that person's authority to so act (Form of Authority).

The following documents must be produced to the Registrar with an application to register a vessel under the Ordinance:

Registration document	Registration by owner(s)	Registration by demise charterer
Owner's statutory declaration in prescribed form (s.20(1) MSRO)	Yes	No
Demise charterer's statutory declaration (s.20(2) MSRO)	No	Yes
Builder's Certificate (in cases of newbuildings), Bill of Sale (in cases of second-hand ships)[1], Certificate of Ownership Free of Encumbrance (where there has been a sale of ship which is not a new ship) or court order	Yes	Yes
Evidence of deletion from old registry (in case of second-hand ships)	Yes	Yes
Certificate of survey[2]	Yes	Yes
Certificate or declaration of marking[3]	Yes	Yes
Continuous Synopsis Record[4]	Yes	Yes
Certified true copy of individual owner's Hong Kong Identity Card (where relevant) Certificate of Incorporation of corporate owner or Certificate of Registration under Part XI of the Companies Ordinance of corporate owner[5]	Yes Yes	No Yes
Certificate of Incorporation of demise charterer or Certificate of Registration under Part XI of the Companies Ordinance of demise charterer	No	Yes
Certificate of Incorporation and Memorandum of Association of the representative person appointed in relation to the ship (where relevant)	Yes	Yes

Notes:

1. The Bill of Sale must be duly executed (see D3) and accompanied by a copy of Certificate of Ownership Free of Encumbrance where there has been a sale of ship in favour of the owner.

2. The Certificate of Survey must be issued by an authorised surveyor. An authorised surveyor means one appointed by a Certifying Authority referred to in Section 2A of the Merchant Shipping (Registration) (Tonnage) Regulations. The Certifying Authorities are the Director of Marine and anyone authorised as such by him in writing. In an application for provisional registration, this certificate need not be produced until the application for full registration is being determined. In the meantime it is acceptable to produce a copy of the ship's current International Tonnage Certificate certified by the issuing authority of that certificate, the shipowner or the representative person appointed in relation to the ship (Section 27 (2) MSRO).

3. A certificate or declaration of marking must be submitted before registration can take place. However, such document does not accompany the initial application. When the Registrar has received all the other necessary documents, has satisfied himself that they are in order and has appropriated an Official Number, he will issue a standard form 'Issue of Marking Note and Certificate or Declaration of Marking' to the owner, authorised person or demise charterer as appropriate. Marking must then either be certified by an authorised surveyor or confirmed by a declaration made in Hong Kong by one or more of the owners or, in the case of a demise chartered ship, by the demise charterer. The certification/declaration must be made on the standard form which must then be returned to the Registrar.

4   The Continuous Synopsis Record (CSR) must be issued by the outgoing flag admin-
        istration including all previous CSRs issued by other flag states.
5   In the case of registration by a demise charterer, under Section 11(1)(b) MSRO the
        owner or owners of the ship need not be qualified persons. If not, a Certificate
        of Incorporation from the place of incorporation should be produced. If such a document
        is not issued in the place of incorporation, the following evidence should be produced:
        (a)   a letter from a solicitor practising in the place where the owner is incorpo-
                 rated confirming that according to the law of that place no certificate of
                 incorporation is issued; and
        (b)   a document certified by that solicitor as equivalent to a certificate of incor-
                 poration according to the law of that place. A copy of this document certi-
                 fied as true by the solicitor would be acceptable.
        In addition, the Registrar may reasonably require other documents or information as
to the incorporation or registration of an owner in the case of an application by a demise charterer (Section 21(4) MSRO).

3   *Does the Hong Kong legal system lay down any specific requirements as to the contents
        of any of these documents – for example, of Bills of Sale – and, if so, what are they?*
Many of the required documents must be in a specified form. Forms can be obtained from the
Shipping Registry in Hong Kong. Examples of the forms can also be found in the Instructions
to the Registrar issued pursuant to Section 5 MSRO in December 1990 ('the Instructions').
The Instructions also contain suggested formats for some of the documents for which there is
no specified form.
(a)   Owner's Statutory Declaration (s.20(1) MSRO):
        The declaration should be in the specified form, which includes statements:
        (i)   to the effect that the declarant is authorised to make such a declaration and
                 that the ship is registrable under Section 11 MSRO (see A1 above);
        (ii)   as to the share of the legal title of the ship vested in the declarant;
        (iii)   that to the best of the declarant's knowledge and belief a majority interest in
                 the ship will be owned by one or more qualified persons on registration;
        (iv)   that the general description of the ship contained in the application is cor-
                 rect;
        (v)   that the ship is not registered in any place outside Hong Kong or, if it is,
                 that the declarant shall secure deletion from any other such registration;
                 and
        (vi)   if the declarant is not a qualified person, that he consents to the ship being
                 registered in Hong Kong.
(b)   Demise Charterer's Statutory Declaration (s.20(2) MSRO):
        Although this declaration must contain specified information, there is no specified
        form. An example of a suggested format can, however, be found in the Instructions.
        The declaration should include the following statements:
        (i)   items (i), (iv) and (v) as for the owner's declaration detailed above;
        (ii)   that the body corporate has entered into a demise charterparty in respect of
                 the ship with the owner of the ship;

       (iii)   that, pursuant to the terms of the demise charterparty, the body corporate is able to register the ship in its name as the demise charterer; and

       (iv)   that a true, correct and complete copy of the demise charterparty and the consent of the owner of the ship to registration of the ship in Hong Kong are attached to the declaration.

(c)   Builder's Certificate:

This is a certificate signed by the builder of the ship containing a true account of:

       (i)   the proper denomination and tonnage of the ship, as estimated by him;

       (ii)   the date and place where the ship was built;

       (iii)   the name of the person on whose account the ship was built.

(d)   Bill of Sale:

If there has been a sale of the ship, a Bill of Sale containing the following particulars needs to be produced to evidence the title of the owner:

       (i)   particulars sufficient to identify the ship, that is, name, official number, gross and registered tonnages, power and engine and method of propulsion;

       (ii)   establish that a transfer on sale took place that is, acknowledge receipt of a sum of money in full settlement; and

       (iii)   identify the seller and the purchaser.

There is no specified form for a Bill of Sale, but the Instructions do contain an example for reference.

(e)   Evidence of deletion:

The evidence of deletion from a previous registry (or registries) can be in any one of the following forms:

       (i)   a Certificate of Deletion, or equivalent, from the last registry where the ship was registered;

       (ii)   a letter/telefax/telex from the ship's last registry informing the Hong Kong Shipping Registry that it has consented to the closure of registry of the ship and that steps are being taken to effect the closure; or

       (iii)   A true copy of the application made by the owner or the representative person of the ship to the registry where the ship was last registered to close the registration of the ship.

Notes:

     Where the certificate(s) of deletion cannot be produced at the time of registration, it/they must be presented to the Registrar within 30 days from the date of registration.

     If the ship is concurrently registered in more than one register, evidence of deletion from each of the registers is required.

In addition, the Registrar may reasonably require other documents or information as to the deletion of a ship from any registry (Section 21(4) MSRO).

4   *Please identify how many originals or copies of each document are required. Are fax copies of any of them acceptable?*

Except as otherwise indicated in this text, one original of each document is required. Either originals or photocopies of the Certificates of Incorporation of corporate owner, demise charterer and representative person are acceptable. Photocopies must be certified as true by the secretary or a director of the company, a solicitor or a notary public in Hong Kong.

5   Are there any requirements as to the language in which documents must be submitted?
If any of the required documents are in a foreign language, a certified translation in English must be produced by the applicant.

6   If they may be submitted in a foreign language, are there any translation require-
         ments? If so, what are they and when must they be complied with?
If a translation is made outside Hong Kong, to be acceptable it should be certified as a correct translation by either:

> (a)   a sworn translator of the court of the place where it was made;
>
> (b)   a PRC consular officer; or
>
> (c)   the translator and further certified by a notary public of the place where the translation is made that he believes that the translator is competent to make the translation.

If made in Hong Kong, it should be certified by either:

> (a)   a sworn translator of the High Court of Hong Kong; or
>
> (b)   any translator, provided that it is further certified by a notary public or a solicitor in Hong Kong to the effect that he believes that the translator is competent to make the translation.

7   Please identify any particular requirements of the Hong Kong legal system with
         regard to the method of execution of any of the registration documents, or with regard
         to notarisation or legalisation.

(a)   Evidence of Authority:

Where an application to register a ship is made by a person on behalf of an owner or demise charterer, the authority of that person shall be testified by writing:

> (i)   if appointed by one or more individuals, under the hand and seal of the person or persons so appointing him;
>
> (ii)   if authorised by a body corporate possessing a common seal, under the seal of the body corporate; or
>
> (iii)   if authorised by a body corporate not possessing a common seal, under the hand and seal of a person purporting to be authorised by the body corporate to make declarations on its behalf.

In the case of (iii) above, the person must also make a declaration that the body concerned does not possess a common seal.

(b)   Declarations:

Declarations for the purposes of registration may be made:

> (i)   in Hong Kong before the Registrar, a notary public, a commissioner for oaths or a solicitor;
>
> (ii)   in a place outside Hong Kong before a notary public or such other person as may be specified for the purpose in instructions (none have yet been so specified); and

(iii)   on behalf of a body corporate by the secretary or any other officer of the body corporate authorised by it for that purpose.

(c)   Bills of Sale:

A Bill of Sale must be signed, sealed (even by individual owners), witnessed and dated. If a corporate owner does not possess a common seal then a statutory declaration by a director or the secretary of the company confirming that the company does not have a common seal and a notarial certificate authenticating the person or persons who signed the Bill of Sale on behalf of the owner and his or their power to do so must also be produced to the Registrar.

A Bill of Sale can be executed by an attorney. If so, the original Power of Attorney must be produced to the Registrar. If the original is not available, a copy certified by the owner, a solicitor or a notary public may be acceptable. However, the ship can only be provisionally registered if the original title document cannot be produced at the time of registration.

8   If the initial registration takes place abroad, is that registration final or provisional?
As indicated in Dl above, registration may only take place in Hong Kong, the application being made in Hong Kong. It is also possible, however, to effect provisional registration of a ship in Hong Kong under Section 27 MSRO. Provisional registration is appropriate when the original title documents (for example, the Builder's Certificate, the Bill of Sale or the Certificate of Ownership Free of Encumbrance) cannot be produced at the time of registration. Provisional registration under the MSRO is a valid registration but for a limited period only (initially one month).

9   If provisional, what needs to be done to effect final registration? When must it be done?
The Registrar will only provisionally register a ship if an application for full registration has been submitted with all necessary supporting documents except the Certificate of Survey (see D2, Note 1) and the original title documents (see D8). This must be done within the period of validity of the provisional certificate. The provisional certificate is initially valid for a period of one month commencing on the date of provisional registration, but it is possible to extend validity by a further one-month period by application to the Registrar.

10   If provisional, what, if any, are the restrictions which apply to the vessel pending final registration?
Save as indicated above, there are no restrictions which apply to the vessel pending final registration. It should be noted, however, that the provisions of the MSRO apply equally to a provisionally registered ship as to a registered ship.

11   Can a provisionally registered ship be mortgaged?
Yes. Section 32 MSRO provides that, where the context allows, the provisions of the Ordinance apply equally to provisionally registered ships as to registered ships. If the provisional registration lapses and, despite an application having been made, full registration is not granted, this will not affect any existing entry in the Register so far as the entry relates to any undischarged registered mortgage of that ship or any share in it (Section 67 MSRO).

E   Technical matters

1   Please identify the requirements of Hong Kong with regard to inspection, survey, measurement and the like in respect of newly registered ships.

Where a ship is to be registered an authorised surveyor shall:

(a)   ascertain the ship's tonnage in accordance with the Merchant Shipping (Registration) Tonnage) Regulations (which follow the International Convention on Tonnage Measurement of Ships, 1969); and

(b)   grant a certificate, in the specified form, specifying the ship's tonnage and build, and such other particulars descriptive of the identity of the ship as may for the time being be required by the Director of Marine (Section 14 MSRO).

The Chief Executive in Council may, where it appears to him that legislation to the same effect as the tonnage regulations is enforced in any country, order that ships of that country shall be deemed to be of the tonnage denoted in their respective Certificates of Registry or other national papers without being remeasured in Hong Kong (Section 15 MSRO).

Every ship must also be marked, or a declaration made that it will be marked, with the ship's name on her bows and her name and Port of Registry (HONG KONG) on her stern in accordance with Section 18 MSRO.

2   By when must these requirements be complied with?

The requirements must be complied with prior to registration. If an application to provisionally register the ship has been or is to be made, the certificate of survey need not be submitted initially, but must be submitted before full registration can be made.

F   Transfer of ownership

1   Please answer, either separately or by reference to your earlier answers, the questions listed under Section D and E above in respect of a transfer of ownership of a vessel already registered in Hong Kong.

The answers under sections D and E above are also applicable for a transfer of ownership of a vessel already registered in Hong Kong. In addition:

In order to effect registration of the transfer, a Bill of Sale and a Declaration of Transfer must be lodged with the Registrar (Sections 39(1) and 40(1) MSRO). The Registrar shall then enter in the register the name of the transferee as owner of the ship, and shall endorse on the Bill of Sale the fact of that entry having been made and the day and hour of making the entry.

The Bill of Sale must:

(a)   contain such of the description of the ship contained in the Certificate of Survey as is sufficient to identify the ship to the satisfaction of the Registrar; and

(b)   be executed by the transferor in the presence of, and be attested by, one or more witnesses (Section 39(2) MSRO).

For further information as to Bills of Sale see D7 above.

2   *Please explain any exchange control or other governmental or regulatory consents required in connection with the sale to a foreign flag of a vessel registered under the flag of Hong Kong.*

There are none.

G   Deletion

1   *Please outline the procedure for deletion of vessels from the flag of Hong Kong.*

Where the owner of a registered or provisionally registered ship wishes the ship registration to be closed he should:

(a)   obtain the consent of each registered mortgagee (if any) to the closure of the ship's registration (which should be in writing, in the specified form and duly verified in the specified manner – see Note 1 below); and

(b)   give notice in writing to the Registrar and to the demise charterer (if registered) that he wishes the ship's registration to be closed.

Upon receipt of this notice, and of the consents (if any), the Registrar shall record the giving of notice and obtaining of consent in the register and the ship's registration shall thereupon be closed.

Upon closure the Registrar shall issue to the owner a Certificate of Deletion certifying that the ship's registration is closed and the date of closure. Upon the issue of the Certificate of Deletion, the owner or Master of the ship shall return the certificate of registry or provisional registry to the Registrar forthwith if the ship is in Hong Kong or as soon as practicable and in any case within 30 days, if the ship is outside Hong Kong.

The procedure outlined above relates to the situation where the owner seeks closure of registration. It should be noted, however, that the Registrar has powers to close registrations for failure to pay any fee or charge relating to a registered ship imposed under the MSRO, failure of the representative person to comply with any obligation imposed on him by the MSRO or failure to comply with MSRO provisions or, if in his opinion, the ship has ceased to be registrable. In such situations a Certificate of Deletion will be issued as outlined above and notice will be given to any outstanding registered mortgagees. If such mortgagees exist, closure will be qualified to show that the registry is closed except in so far as it relates to the outstanding mortgages.

Note: The consent granted by each mortgagee shall be verified as follows:

(a)   If the mortgagee is an individual the consent should be signed and sealed by the mortgagee in the presence of a solicitor or a notary public who shall attest the signature by signing his name and stating his occupation and address legibly.

(b)   Where the mortgagee is a corporation, the consent should be executed under seal in the presence of a solicitor or notary public who shall attest the signature as in (i) above. If no seal is possessed, the consent should be accompanied by a declaration made by one of the directors or officers of the mortgagee, or its lawful attorney if the consent is signed by an attorney, confirming that the mortgagee does not have a common seal.

(c)   If consent is given by the lawful attorney of the mortgagee, the consent shall be signed by the attorney in the presence of a solicitor or notary public who shall attest the signature as in (i) above. The original Power of Attorney or a copy certified by a solicitor or a notary public, must be produced to the Registrar along with the consent.

2   *Please answer, either separately or by reference to your earlier answers, the questions listed under Section D in respect of the deletion, as opposed to new registration, of a vessel.*

See G1 above.

H   Certificates/transcripts

1   Please identify the certificates and other documents issued to an owner on registration of his ship under the flag of Hong Kong.

Certificate of Registry.

2   Please outline the procedure (including fees payable) for obtaining information on the registered ownership of and encumbrances on vessels registered in Hong Kong.

The Registrar keeps a register of ships registered or provisionally registered under the MSRO. This contains particulars in respect of ships, owners and their respective interests in ships, demise charterers, mortgagees, and representative persons. Any person may, on payment of the prescribed fee:

(a)   inspect the register (HK$110 per ship record);

(b)   require to be furnished with a copy of, or extract from, any entry in the register (HK$110 per copy/extract); or

(c)   require such copy or extract to be certified as a true copy by or on behalf of the Registrar (HK$260 per copy/extract).

The fees are currently as indicated in brackets, but are subject to review.

I   Fees/taxes

1   What fees are currently payable:

1.1   on new registration?

1.2   on transfer of ownership?

1.3   on deletion?

1.1   The fees payable on the registration of a new ship, or for registration anew are, in addition to the annual charges (see below): HK$3,500 for a ship not exceeding 500 gross registered tons; and HK$15,000 for a ship exceeding 500 gross registered tons. If a ship is provisionally registered, the initial fee is 35 per cent of the full registration fee, with a further 75 per cent of this full fee payable on the change from provisional to full registration.

1.2   For registering a transfer of mortgage, transfer by Bill of Sale, transmission, mortgage or discharge of mortgage, the fee payable is HK$440.

1.3   There are no fees payable on deletion.

2   *What annual or other ongoing fees or taxes are payable in respect of ships registered in Hong Kong?*

(a)   Annual tonnage charges are payable in respect of ships registered in Hong Kong. The charges are currently, for a ship not exceeding 1,000 net registered tons, HK$1,500 and for a ship exceeding 1,000 net registered tons, HK$1,500, with an additional HK$3.50 payable for each additional net registered ton or part thereof up to 15,000 net registered tons and an additional HK$3 for each such ton over 15,000 net registered tons subject to a maximum aggregate charge of HK$100,000.

(b)   For a provisionally registered ship, one-twelfth of the annual tonnage charge is payable for each period of 1 month of provisional registration. If a ship changes from provisional to full registration, the annual tonnage charge under I2(a) becomes payable.

J   Parallel registration

1   Is parallel registration permitted:
        1.1   onto Hong Kong's register?
        1.2   from Hong Kong's register?

As noted above, registration by a demised charter which is a body corporate and a 'qualified person' is permitted. However, as mentioned in D3 above, the application for registration must contain a statement in the required statutory declaration that the ship is not registered elsewhere or, if it is, that such registration will be deleted.

2   If so, what, if any, specific governmental or other consents are required.
The written consent of the owner to registration in the name of the demise charterer must be attached to the demise charterer's statutory declaration.

3   Is the period of parallel registration limited. If so, is it renewable?
Registration by a demise charterer is unlimited, other than by the duration of the demise charter. Registration will terminate if the ship ceases to be operated under a demise charter by a body corporate which is a 'qualified person', whether by reason of the termination of the demise charter or otherwise.

4   If parallel registration is dependent on the existence of a demise charter, does Hong Kong have a specific definition of demise or bareboat charter for these purposes? If so, what is it?
Registration is dependent on the existence of a demise charter, but there is no statutory definition.

5   Please answer the questions listed under Sections A to E above with reference to an application for parallel registration on Hong Kong's register.
Please see sections A to E above with reference to registration by demise charterers.

6 *Can/must mortgages on ships parallel registered in Hong Kong's registry also be registered in Hong Kong?*

Not applicable

7 *Under what circumstances will/may the parallel registration of a ship on Hong Kong's register be terminated or revoked?*

Please see J3 above.

K General

1 *Please identify the principal statutes and regulations in Hong Kong governing the registration of ships.*

The principal statutes and regulations in Hong Kong governing the registration of ships are the Merchant Shipping (Registration) Ordinance (Cap. 415), the Merchant Shipping (Registration (Fees and Charges) Regulations, Merchant Shipping (Registration) (Ships' Names) Regulations and Merchant Shipping (Registration) (Tonnage) Regulations and the Companies Ordinance.

2 *Are there any other matters in the context of registration of ships under the Hong Kong legal system which you feel should be emphasised?*

There are none.

---

* Contributed by Chooi Ling Lau and Ben Harris of Stephenson Harwood and Lo, Hong Kong.

** The information in this section is based on the law in Hong Kong as at 28 November 2005.

India*

A   Ownership

1   What, if any, are the restrictions on ownership of vessels registered under the flag of India?

According to the Merchant Shipping Act, 1958 (the '1958 Act') Indian flag vessels may be owned by any of the three categories of persons, mentioned below:

    (a)   a citizen or citizens of India;

    (b)   a company or body established by or under any central or state act, which has its principal place of business in India; or

    (c)   a co-operative society which is registered or deemed to be registered under the Co-operative Society Act, 1912, or any other law relating to Co-operative Societies for the time being in force in any state.

The restriction as to number of owners of a vessel is provided in Section 25(b) of the 1958 Act. It provides that in the cases of joint owners or owners by transfer by operation of law (for example, inheritance laws), not more than 10 individuals shall be entitled to be registered at the same time as owners of any one ship.

2   If registration by companies is limited to companies incorporated in India is a local 'brass-plate' company sufficient, or must there be a closer genuine connection?

The registration by companies is limited to companies incorporated under any central or state act of India. The 1958 Act further prescribes the requirement that the principal place of business of the company should be in India. Thus a local brass-plate company will not be able to meet this requirement of the 1958 Act.

3   If registration by companies incorporated other than in India is permitted, must a local representative be appointed? If so, are there any restrictions on the identity of that representatives?

Under the 1958 Act, registration of ships by companies incorporated outside of India is not permitted.

4   Please summarise any restriction (for example, as to number, nationality and so on) on who may own shares in vessel owning companies incorporated in India.

Any company or body established by or under any central or state act which has its principal place of business in India is entitled to own a vessel and have the same registered as an Indian ship. There is no restriction regarding the number and nationality of persons who may own shares in vessel owning companies incorporated in India other than a restriction on nationals of certain neighbouring countries of India.

5   Please explain any exchange control or other governmental or regulatory consents required in connection with the ownership of vessels registered in India.

There is no other consent required under exchange control or from any governmental or regulatory authority, other then those mentioned herein.

6   *Please explain any special rules for any particular type of vessel.*
According to Section 3 (55) of the 1958 Act a vessel includes *'any ship, boat, sailing vessel or other description of vessel used in navigation'*. Accordingly, the 1958 Act deals with the registration of vessels in three parts:

    (a)   Part V of the 1958 Act applies to sea-going ships fitted with mechanical means of propulsion, as stated in Section 20;

    (b)   Part XV of the 1958 Act applies to sailing vessels. Sailing vessels have been defined in Section 3 (39) of the 1958 Act to mean *'any description of vessel provided with sufficient sail area for navigation under sails alone, whether or not fitted with mechanical means of propulsion, and includes a rowing boat or canoe but does not include a pleasure craft'*; and

    (c)   Part XVA of the 1958 Act deals with fishing boats.

7   *Is there any mandatory registration requirement for certain owners (for example, citizens of India)?*
Under Section 22 (1) of the 1958 Act, registration is mandatory for a ship owned by:

    (a)   a citizen of India;

    (b)   a company or body established by or under any central or state act which has its principal place of business in India;

    (c)   a co-operative society which is registered or deemed to be registered under the Co-operative Society Act, 1912, or any other law relating to Co-operative Societies for the time being in force in any state.

Any such ship found not registered shall be liable to detention.

B   Eligibility

1   *Are there any particular types/sizes of vessel ineligible for, or exempt from, registration?*
Any ship which does not exceed 15 tons net and is employed solely in navigation on the coasts of India is granted exemption from the requirement of registration under the 1958 Act.

2   *What, if any, is the maximum age for registration of vessels under the flag of India?*
The 1958 Act does not specifically prescribe the maximum age for registration of vessels under the flag of India. However, Clause 1.1 of the Office Memorandum No. SD-11018/1/97-MD dated 5 March 2002 provides that prior technical clearance is required for the acquisition of vessels of 25 years of age and above.

C   Names

1   *What, if any, are the restrictions on the name under which a vessel may be registered in India?*
According to Section 55 (2) of the 1958 Act, a proposed name under which a vessel is sought to be registered may be rejected by the Registrar on the following grounds:

      (a)   the proposed name is already borne by another ship; or

      (b)   the proposed name is so similar to another registered name as is calculated or likely to deceive.

2   *Is there a procedure for approval of names in advance?*

There is no provision for approval of names in advance. The owner of a ship wishing to register the ship at a port in India has to give a minimum of 14 days notice to the Registrar of the proposed name. The Registrar, before registering the ship, must obtain prior approval of the name from the Director General of Shipping (the 'DGS').

3   *If so, how does it operate? Does approval confer any priority rights in the use of the name?*

Not applicable.

D   New registration procedure

1   *Where may vessels intending to fly the flag of India be registered:*

      1.1   *in India?*

      1.2   *abroad?*

Ships registrable in India under the provisions of the 1958 Act are required to be registered only at ports designated as 'Ports of Registry'. At present, the ports at Mumbai, Calcutta, Madras, Cochin and Mormugoa have been notified as Ports of Registry in India.

      When a ship is built or acquired abroad, the owner or the Master of the ship will have to apply to the nearest Indian Consular Officer for the issue of a Provisional Certificate of Indian Registry. Such a certificate has all the force of a Certificate of Registry. It is, however, valid for a period of 6 months from its date of issue or until the arrival of the ship at a Port of Registry whichever happens first, and on either of these events happening the certificate issued by the Indian Consular Officer will cease to have effect. The provisional certificate so issued will have to be exchanged by the owner for a Certificate of Registry from the Registrar at the relevant Port of Registry.

2   *What documents and information must be submitted to effect registration?*

The owner of a ship wishing to register it under Indian flag for the first time has to submit, to the Registrar at the relevant Port of Registry, the following documents:

      (a)   original Declaration of Ownership, in prescribed form;

      (b)   certified copy of the board resolution of the owner with common seal;

      (c)   original Builder's Certificate;

      (d)   original Carving and Marking Note;

      (e)   Tonnage Certificate (Indian/International) – photocopy is sufficient;

      (f)   general arrangement plan, mid-ship section, structural profile and plan, crew accommodation plan and shell expansion – photocopy is sufficient;

      (g)   propelling machinery details;

      (h)   technical specification by class;

(i)   certified copy of the memorandum and articles of association of owner; and

(j)   original Certificate of Survey endorsed by an authorised surveyor.

In the case of a second-hand ship, the following additional documents are required:

(a)   instrument of sale/protocol of delivery (duly notarised);

(b)   original Bill of Sale with common seal or duly authenticated by Indian Consulate;

(c)   copies of previous statutory certificates;

(d)   technical clearance from the DGS for ships more than 25 years of age;

(e)   original Certificate of Deletion from previous register; and

(f)   copy of previous Certificate of Registry.

3   Does the legal system in India lay down any specific requirements as to the contents of any these documents (for example, of Bills of Sale) and, if so, what are they?

The content of the Declaration of Ownership document is prescribed in Schedule I of the Merchant Shipping (Registration of Indian Ships) Rules, 1960 read with Rule 38 thereof.

4   Please identify how many originals or copies of each document are required. Are fax or pdf copies of any of them acceptable?

Please refer to D2.

5   Are there any requirements as to the language in which documents must be submitted?

The documents have to be submitted in English.

6   If they may be submitted in a foreign language, are there any translation requirements? If so, what are they and when must they be complied with?

If the documents are in a foreign language they have to be translated into English and supported by an affidavit of the translator stating therein that the he is well acquainted with both of the languages, that is, the English language and the foreign language in which the documents were originally executed. This translation work has to be complete in all respects before the production of the same before the Registrar of the vessel's Port of Registration.

7   Please identify any particular requirements of the legal system in India with regards to the method of execution of any of the registration documents, or with regard to notarisation or legalisation.

The Declaration of Ownership can be made before a Registrar, Special Executive Magistrate or an Indian Consular Officer. Please refer to our response to D2 above.

8   If the initial registration takes place abroad, is that registration final or provisional?

If the initial registration takes place abroad, the same is provisional.

9   If provisional, what needs to be done to effect final registration? When must it be done?

Please refer to our response to D1 above.

10   If provisional, what, if any, are the restrictions which apply to the vessel pending final registration?
Please refer to our response to D1 above.

11   Can a provisionally registered vessel be mortgaged?
According to Guidelines No. SD-13/POL(5)/2001 dated 3 May 2002, provisionally registered vessels can be mortgaged.

E   Technical matters

1   Please identify the requirements of India with regard to inspection, survey, measurement and the like in respect of newly registered vessels.
The Registrar arranges for a survey of the ship by a surveyor for the determination of her tonnage in accordance with the Merchant Shipping (Tonnage Measurement) Rules, 1987 as amended from time to time, in order to issue a Certificate of Survey.

2   By when must these requirements be complied with?
These requirements relating to inspection, survey, measurement and the like in respect of a vessel have to be carried out at the time of registration and before the Registrar issues the Carving and Marking Note for such vessel.

F   Transfer of ownership

1   Please answer, either separately or by reference to your earlier answers, questions listed under section D and E above in respect of the transfer of ownership of a vessel already registered in India.
The DGS's prior approval for the sale of the ship is not required provided:

(a)   all wages and other amounts due to seamen in connection with their employment on that ship have been paid; and

(b)   the owner of the ship has given notice of such transfer or acquisition of the ship to the DGS.

Any such transfer can be affected only by an instrument in writing in the prescribed form. Such instrument has to contain a full description of the ship, as is generally contained in the surveyors' certificate, so as to identify the ship.

The owner of an Indian ship or a share therein wishing to transfer it in favour of somebody else will have to provide full particulars of the transferee to the Registrar.

Where the instrument of sale refers to consideration other than money, and if the Registrar has any doubts as to whether it constitutes good consideration, the decision will lie with the DGS to whom the matter must be referred.

If the transaction has been concluded in India, the documents mentioned in response to D2 above and the prescribed fee have to be submitted to the Registrar of the Port of Registry. The Registrar will then make appropriate entries in the Register Book and will also endorse on the transfer instrument the date and hour of the entry. The Registrar must also endorse the ship's Certificate of Registry as soon as possible. Every such transaction has to be reported to the DGS.

If a ship is acquired by way of transfer outside India, then the procedure, as mentioned in response to D1 above, shall apply.

2   *Please explain any exchange control or other governmental or regulatory consents required in connection with the sale to a foreign flag of a vessel registered under the flag of India.*

There is no other consent required under exchange control or from any governmental or regulatory authority, other than those mentioned herein.

G   Deletion

1   Please outline the procedure for deletion of vessels from the flag of India.

According to Section 39 (1) of the 1958 Act, in the event of a registered vessel ceasing for any reason to be an Indian vessel, every owner of the ship or any share in the ship shall immediately give notice thereof to the Registrar at the Port of Registry of that vessel and the Registrar shall make an entry thereof in the Register Book. Thereafter, the registry in that book in respect of the vessel in question shall be considered as closed except so far as relates to any unsatisfied mortgages entered in the register.

Section 39 (2) of the 1958 Act further provides that in the event of a registered vessel ceasing for any reason to be an Indian vessel, the Master of the ship shall, immediately if the event occurs in any port in India, or within 10 days after his arrival in port, if it occurs elsewhere, deliver up the Certificate of Registry to the Registrar of the port or any other officer specified in this behalf by the Central Government.

If the arrival is in any port outside India, then the certificate is to be delivered up to the nearest Indian Consular Officer.

If this tendering up of the certificate is not at the Port of Registry of that ship, then the Registrar, or the officer so specified or the Indian Consular Officer, as the case may be, shall forthwith forward the certificate delivered to him to the Registrar of the Port of Registry of that ship.

2   *Please answer, either separately or by reference to your earlier answer, the questions listed under section D in respect of the deletion, as apposed to new registration, of a vessel.*

The following documents are required to be submitted along with the prescribed fees:
    (a)   original notice to DGS regarding the sale of the vessel;
    (b)   original no objection certificate by Seaman's Provident Fund;
    (c)   original no objection certificate by the Port's Shipping Master;
    (d)   notarised copy of Bill of Sale;
    (e)   certified copy of the memorandum of undertaking to sell;
    (f)   Certificate of Survey;
    (g)   load line certificate;
    (h)   all safety certificates;
    (i)   Certificate of Registry;
    (j)   Tonnage Certificate (Indian/International);

(k)   original Master's Certificate; and

(l)   certified copies of the board resolution of owner.

H   Certificates/transcripts

*1   Please identify the certificates and other documents issued to an owner on registra-
        tion of a vessel under the flag of India.*

According to Section 34 of the 1958 Act, on completion of the registration of an Indian ship, the Registrar will grant a Certificate of Registry containing the particulars in respect of the vessel, as entered in the Register Book, along with the name of the Master of the vessel.

*2   Please outline the procedure (including fees payable) for obtaining information on
        the registered ownership of and encumbrances on vessels registered in India.*

According to Section 25 of the 1958 Act, every Registrar of a Port of Registry has to keep a book of containing entries relating to the vessels registered at that port which is known as Register Book, including mortgages and other encumbrances. Information on the registered ownership of and encumbrances on vessels registered in India can be obtained from the said Register Book by paying the appropriate fee. The fees which have been prescribed in Schedule 1 of the Merchant Shipping (Registration of Indian Ships) Rules, 1994 are:

(a)   for a certified copy of the particulars entered by the Registrar in the Register Book on the registry of a ship, together with a certified statement showing the ownership of the ship at that time: INR500;

(b)   for a certificate copy of any declaration document, a copy of which is made evidenced by the Merchant Shipping Act, 1958: INR500; and

(c)   for a certified copy of, or extracts from document declared by the Merchant Act, 1958, to be admissible in evidence, Declaration of Ownership, Instrument of Sale, Instrument of Mortgage, Certificate of Registry (initial issue), Provisional Certificate of Registry: INR100 per copy.

I   Fees/taxes

1   What fees are currently payable:

        1.1   on new registration?

        1.2   on transfer of ownership?

        1.3   on deletion?

1.1   On new registration, the following fees are prescribed in Schedule 1 of the Merchant Shipping (Registration of Indian Ships) Rules, 1994:

(a)   Process Fee on initial registry, re-registry, registry anew or registration on transfer of port of registry: INR500;

(b)   Registration Fee: INR1 per grt:

        (i)   for ships up to 3,000 grt subject to minimum of INR1,500;

        (ii)   Ships from 1,600 grt to 20,000 grt subject to maximum of INR15,000: INR1 per grt; and

        (iii)   Ships 20,000 grt and above: INR15,000 + INR1 per grt in excess of 20,000 grt.

1.2   On transfer of ownership, a fee of INR1,000 is prescribed in Schedule 1 of the Merchant Shipping (Registration of Indian Ships) Rules, 1994.

1.3   On deletion, a fee of INR500 is prescribed in Schedule 1 of the Merchant Shipping (Registration of Indian Ships) Rules, 1994.

J   Parallel registration

1   Is parallel registration permitted:
    1.1   onto the Indian register?
    1.2   from the Indian register?

The legal system in India does not permit parallel registration of vessel, either onto the Indian register or from the Indian register.

K   General

1   Please identify the principal statutes and regulations in India governing the registration of vessels.

The principal statute and regulation in India governing the registration of vessels are the following:

(a)   The Merchant Shipping Act, 1958 (as amended);

(b)   Merchant Shipping (Registration of Indian Ships) Rules, 1960;

(c)   Merchant Shipping (Registration of Indian Ships) Rules, 1994;

(d)   Merchant Shipping (Registration of Indian Ships) Rules, 1997;

(e)   Ministry of Shipping, Government of India Circular No. SD-11018/1/97-MD dated 15 June 2001 – Guidelines for import of all types of ships;

(f)   Ministry of Shipping, Government of India Circular No. SD-11018/1/97-MD dated 5 March 2002 – Guidelines for import of all types of ships;

(g)   Guidelines on Registration of Indian Ship in accordance with Para 1.2 of Office Memorandum No. SD-11018/1/97-MD dated 5 March 2002;

(h)   Director General, Shipping Order No. 2 of 2002 Revised guidelines for registration of ships;

(i)   SD Branch Letter No. SD-13/POL(5)/2001 dated 28 June 2002 – Guidelines for registration of ships; and

(j)   MMD Letter dated 4 June 2002 – Guidelines for registration of ships

2   Are there any other matters in the context of registration of vessels under the legal system in India, which you feel should be emphasised here?

Conscious of the global competition in the field, the government has also framed a policy according to which on the receipt of all the documents required for registration of the ship, the Registrar has to ensure that the certificate of permanent registration is granted to the ship immediately and in any case within three working days.

---

* Contributed by Pankaj Prakash of International Law Group, New Delhi, India.

Isle of Man*

A   Ownership

1   What if any, are the restrictions on ownership of vessels under the flag of the Isle of Man?
As British ships, the Merchant Shipping Registration Act 1991 (the 'Act') requires that the owner of an Isle of Man flagged vessel must be a 'Qualified Owner'. To qualify as a British ship and a qualified owner the majority interest in the vessel, that is, at least 33 out of 64 shares, must be held by one of the following:

(a)   a company incorporated in the Isle of Man and having its principal place of business in the Isle of Man;

(b)   a company incorporated in the United Kingdom, the Channel Islands, or any British Dependent Territory and having its principal place of business in any such territory;

(c)   a company incorporated in a member state of the European Union or in a European Economic Area Country and having its principal place of business in any such country (the company may be incorporated in any of the above territories or member states and have its principal place of business in any other of the above territories or member states);

(d)   a Limited Partnership established and registered in the Isle of Man in accordance with the Partnership Act 1909 and the International Business Act 1994, and in certain prescribed countries as detailed in Manx Shipping Notice No. 194 including Belgium, Bermuda, Cayman Islands, Denmark, Germany, Netherlands, Norway, Sweden and the United Kingdom;

(e)   a British citizen, a British Dependent Territories citizen, a British overseas citizen, a British subject under the British Nationality Act 1981, or a British National (Overseas);

(f)   a citizen of a member state of the European Union and European Economic Area Countries.

2   If registration by companies is limited to companies incorporated in the Isle of Man, is a local 'brass-plate' company sufficient or must there be a closer, genuine connection?
Not applicable as companies other than Isle of Man incorporated companies may own Isle of Man vessels – see above.

3   If registration by companies incorporated other than in the Isle of Man is permitted, must a local representative be appointed? If so, are there any restrictions on the identity of that representative?
It is a requirement that every merchant ship and commercial yacht registered in the Isle of Man have an Isle of Man approved ship manager or 'representative person' appointed in relation to that vessel. Alternatively, the owner can establish its own office in the Isle of Man having responsibility for the vessel. Confirmation of the representative person is made on Form REG6.

The Registry maintains a list of currently approved representative persons for merchant ships and for commercial yachts available on its website. Persons who can act as a representative person include individuals or bodies corporate. An individual must be resident in the island and the body corporate must be incorporated in the island and have its principal place of business on the island. The representative person is responsible for the statutory certification, operational safety and manning of the vessel, anti-pollution measures and the settlement of accounts in respect of survey, registration and related matters. The representative person may carry out all these required functions directly or may sub-contract all or part of these functions, but in such cases would remain legally responsible in respect of these functions and answerable as such to the Registrar in the Isle of Man.

4   *Please summarise any restrictions (for example, as to number, nationality etc) on whom may own shares in vessel owning companies incorporated in the Isle of Man?*
In general, there are no nationality or other restrictions for ownership of Isle of Man incorporated companies.

5   *Please explain any exchange control or other governmental or regulatory consents required in connection with the ownership of vessels registered in the Isle of Man.*
No exchange control or other governmental or regulatory consents are required in the Isle of Man in connection with the ownership of vessels registered in the Isle of Man.

6   *Please explain any special rules for any particular type of vessel.*
The Isle of Man has a separate register for fishing vessels which are outside the scope of this book. However, in general, fishing vessels may only be registered on the Isle of Man Register if they are locally owned and operated vessels. If there are any questions over a vessel proposed for registry on the Isle of Man flag these may be raised with the Registrar of Ships and the Principal Surveyor prior to any official application for registration being made.

7   *Is there any mandatory registration requirement for certain owners (for example, citizens of the Isle of Man)?*
There are no mandatory registration requirements for certain owners. Section 64 of the Act provides that for the purposes of the payment of dues, fees or other charges, liability to fines and forfeiture and the punishment of offences committed on board the vessel or by any persons belonging to the vessel, a vessel may be treated and dealt with in the same manner in all respects as if the vessel were a Manx Ship if the vessel is:

(a)   24 metres, or more in length, and

(b)   wholly owned by one or more persons resident in the island who are qualified to be owners of Manx Ships, but

(c)   neither registered under Part I, II or III nor registered under the law of any country outside the island.

This is the case notwithstanding that the vessel is not entitled to any benefits, privileges, advantages or protection usually enjoyed by a Manx Ship.

B   Eligibility

1   Are there any particular types/size of vessels ineligible for, or exempt from, registration?

The following vessels are not generally accepted for registry:

- (a) vessels which are not classed with one of the accepted Classification Societies;
- (b) vessels of under 500 GT unless they are operating locally in and around the Isle of Man;
- (c) vessels greater than 15 years of age;
- (d) single-hull oil tankers;
- (e) Ro-Ro passenger vessels operating outside the Irish Sea area;
- (f) passenger vessels operating outside Manx waters;
- (g) High Speed Craft operating in areas outside the Irish Sea area;
- (h) Floating Dry Docks;
- (i) harbour and estuarial craft operating outside Manx waters;
- (j) Pilgrim Vessels; and
- (k) vessels engaged in the carriage of irradiated nuclear fuel and vessels with a nuclear reactor.

It is worth noting that the Isle Marine Administration no longer accepts single-hull vessels for registration.

2   *What, if any, is the maximum age for registration of vessels under the flag of the Isle of Man?*

Vessels over 15 years of age are not generally accepted for new vessel registrations.

C   Names

1   What, if any are the restrictions on the name under which a vessel may be registered in the Isle of Man?

Every application to approve a name must specify a name which is in Roman letters and any numerals must be in Roman or European numerals.

The name will not be approved if the proposed name is:

- (a) already the name of a registered Isle of Man vessel;
- (b) a name so similar to that of a registered Isle of Man vessel that it is likely to cause confusion or is likely to deceive;
- (c) a name which may be confused with a distress signal;
- (d) a name which is prefixed by any letters or name which could be taken to indicate a type of ship or any other word, pre-fix or suffix which might cause confusion as to the name of the vessel.

The Registry may also refuse to approve a name which may cause offence or embarrassment or which has a clear and direct connection with the Royal Family.

2   Is there procedure for approval of names in advance?

It is possible to check on name availability before making the application and to reserve preferred names. This can be done by telephoning the Registrar.

3   If so, how does it operate? Does approval confer any priority rights in the use of the name?

If the proposed name is available the Registrar will reserve this name for a period of up to three months. If the name is not utilised within this period it is possible to reserve the name for a further period by simply telephoning the Registrar. While the name is reserved no other vessel to be registered on the Isle of Man flag will be permitted to register in the Isle of Man with this name.

In certain circumstances the Registry may allow reservation of a name or designation for a period of 10 years. These include where the Registry is satisfied that:

(a)   the vessel is intended to replace another of the same name which is to be registered within 10 years of the date of the application, and

(b)   the applicant is the owner of a registered vessel with the same name as that which is to be reserved and its British registration will be closed before registration of the new vessel, or

(c)   the applicant is the owner of a registered vessel with the same name as that which is to be reserved and it will be sold before the registration of the new vessel on condition that it changes its name and that its name is so changed.

Applications for a reservation such as this must be made in writing to the Registry and must be accompanied by a full statement of the circumstances of the case.

D   New registration procedure

1   Where may vessels intending to fly the flag of the Isle of Man be registered:
    1.1   in the Isle of Man?
    1.2   abroad?

1.1   Yes

1.2   The Registry do not currently permit registration of vessels other than in the Isle of Man.

2   What documents and information must be submitted to effect registration?

An owner seeking to register a vessel in the Isle of Man should initially make contact with the Registrar to ensure that there are no obstacles to registry and to arrange a suitable date and place for the initial inspection of the vessel by the Isle of Man surveyors.

The following information and documentation should then be supplied:

(a)   Apply in writing on Form REG 1 to the Registrar. This form also allows the owner to specify the preferred name for the vessel and any alternatives should the preferred choice be unavailable. There are four ports of registry in the Isle of Man. Vessels may be registered in any one of the four at the owner's preference. The options are:

    (i)   Castletown;
    (ii)   Douglas;
    (iii)   Peel;
    (iv)   Ramsey.

The most commonly used port of registry is Douglas, the capital of the Isle of Man.

(b)   Provide a Certificate of Survey to accompany the REG 1 form. This document is issued by the vessel's Classification Society and is a simple form which sets out the basic identifying parameters of the vessel which will be included in the registry details. The Isle of Man surveyor who attends the vessel for pre-registry survey and inspection can also complete this form.

(c)   When the vessel is owned by a company, provide a copy of the company's Certificate of Incorporation and a copy of Form REG 3 appointing authorised officers for the company to accompany the REG 1 Form.

(d)   When the vessel is owned by a Limited Partnership, Form REG 14 must be provided setting out details of the partnership and proof of incorporation, to accompany the REG 1 form.

(e)   Provide a Declaration of Ownership on Form:

      (i)   REG 4 for a body corporate;

      (ii)   REG 5 in the case of an individual.

(f)   Prior to registry, produce evidence of title of ownership. This can be in two forms.

      (i)   If the vessel has not been previously registered (that is, a newly built vessel), or if she has never changed hands it should be in the form of a Builders Certificate.

      (ii)   If the vessel has been previously registered, or if she has been owned by a previous owner it should be in the form of an original Bill of Sale from the last owner to the applicant.

(g)   When the vessel is registered under another flag, produce a Deletion Certificate or Closed Transcript from the other registry before final registry in the Isle of Man.

(h)   Confirmation of the appointed manager is to be provided on Form REG 6 (see A3 above).

(i)   Make arrangements with the Marine Administration for a surveyor to inspect the vessel prior to acceptance for registration to ascertain that the vessel complies with International Conventions in respect of safety, prevention of oil pollution and manning. In addition, the surveyor will conduct any survey as appropriate for the issue of International Convention Certificates.

(j)   Make arrangements with the Ship Radio Licensing Office in the United Kingdom for the issue of a Radio Call Sign and MMSI No. The MMSI Number and Call Sign will need to be advised to the Registrar before final registry.

Once the application is made the Registrar will issue a Carving and Marking Note. The vessel must be marked with the name, Port of Register and IMO number and once marked, the markings need to be verified by either the Isle of Man surveyor (if the Isle of Man surveyor is present at marking) or by the Classification Society surveyor. The verifying surveyor signs the Carving and Marking Note and it is returned to the Registrar.

Once registered on Part I of the register in the Isle of Man that registry is permanent until the owner chooses to register elsewhere or the vessel is deleted.

3   Does the legal system in the Isle of Man lay down any specific requirements as to the contents of any of these documents (for example, Bill of Sale) and, if so, what are they?

The form of the documents referred to above are as prescribed by regulation and most are available on the Marine Administration website http://www.gov.im/dti/marineadmin or from the Marine Administration.

The Builder's Certificate and Bill of Sale do not necessarily have to be in the form provided by the Registry, however, the information contained in the proposed form must be largely the same as that set out in the prescribed forms. If it is proposed that if any form other than the prescribed form is used it should be cleared with the Registry in advance of execution and registration.

4   Please identify how many originals or copies of each document are required. Are fax or pdf copies of any of them acceptable?

The Registry will generally require an original of each of the documents prior to registration. If it will not be possible to provide the originals on registration of the vessel (for example, the original Builder's Certificate, Bill of Sale or such other document that may only be available on delivery), alternative arrangements should be made with the Registry prior to registration.

If an original Certificate of Incorporation cannot be provided a certified true copy of the Certificate of Incorporation will suffice but this should be approved by the Registrar in advance.

5   Are there any requirements as to the language in which the documents must be submitted?

Registration documents should be submitted in English. Wherever possible any other documents accompanying the registration documents should, if possible, be submitted in English. Where a document, for example, a Certificate of Incorporation, may be in a foreign language, an official translation should be provided.

6   If they may be submitted in a foreign language, are there any translation requirements? If so, what are they and when must they be complied with?

Documents that are submitted with the vessel registration application forms that may be in a foreign language, for example, a Certificate of Incorporation, a Power of Attorney or notarisations, should be accompanied by an official translation. This should be provided when the document is submitted to the Registry.

7   Please identify any particular requirements of the legal system in the Isle of Man with regards to the method of execution of any of the registration documents, or with regard to notarisation or legalisation.

The Builder's Certificate, Bill of Sale and form REG 3 (appointment of authorised officer) should be executed under seal or as a deed. If executed outside of the United Kingdom they must be executed before and witnessed by a notary.

Any other documents (for example, a Power of Attorney) executed as a deed or under seal must be notarised if executed outside of the United Kingdom.

Legalisation or apostilling of documents is not currently a requirement.

8   If the initial registration takes place abroad, is that registration final or provisional?
Not applicable. Registrations can only be done in the Isle of Man. In addition, the Registry does not currently allow for provisional registration of vessels.

9   If provisional, what needs to be done to effect final registration? When must it be done?
Not applicable – see above.

10   If provisional, what if any are the restrictions which apply to the vessel pending final registration?
Not applicable – see above.

11   Can a provisionally registered vessel be mortgaged?
Not applicable – see above.

E   Technical matters

1   Please identify the requirements of the Isle of Man with regard to inspection, survey, measurement and the like in respect of newly registered vessels.
It is an absolute requirement that each vessel proposed for registration must be satisfactorily inspected and surveyed by an Isle of Man Marine Administration Surveyor ('IOM Surveyor') prior to acceptance for registration. The Marine Administration has its own teams of surveyors who conduct all inspections on vessels proposed for registry in the Isle of Man. The IOM Surveyor will travel to all major ports. Provided that sufficient notice is given to the surveyors, an inspection can generally be arranged to accommodate the vessel's schedule. Only upon receipt of a positive report from the IOM Surveyor can the Registrar proceed to register the vessel.

The initial request for survey should be followed up with copies of the vessel's general arrangement plan and, if it is an existing vessel, copies of any existing statutory certificates. The owner will also need to provide the proposed manning scales for the vessel.

The initial inspection will cover the general condition of the vessel, internal checks on selected tanks, safety equipment, MARPOL compliance, ISM and ISPS compliance, crewing, manning and certification and capability of the crew, crew accommodation and standards and crew welfare and working conditions. The IOM Surveyor will also complete annual surveys for the International Oil Pollution Prevention Certificate and SEC if necessary.

For new builds most of the work of survey and certification is carried out by the appointed Classification Society. An IOM Surveyor will be nominated as lead surveyor and will undertake approval of plans for crew accommodation. At the final stages of construction the IOM Surveyor will attend at the yard and conduct a thorough survey and inspection. He may also undertake some operational checks of ship board safety equipment and will review the vessel's ship management systems.

For existing vessels the IOM Surveyor will attend and carry out a complete inspection and review the vessel's existing certification. The IOM Surveyor will also complete any surveys that are due. He can then issue the Isle of Man certificates to replace the existing certificates.

The Marine Administration undertakes all audits for ISM and ISPS and only in exceptional circumstances will the ISM audits be delegated to the classification society.

2   By when must these requirements be complied with?

Surveys and inspections of vessels by an IOM Surveyor must be completed prior to the vessel being registered. It is possible for inspection and registration to be completed at the same time. However, for this to work there can be no major defects in the vessel and as much information as possible must be provided prior to the IOM Surveyor attending the vessel. Minor deficiencies will not stop the registration and the deficiencies will require clearing within an agreed timescale.

F   Transfer of ownership

1   Please answer either separately or by reference to your earlier answers, the questions listed under sections D and E above in respect of transfer of ownership of a vessel already registered in the Isle of Man.

The procedure on a transfer of ownership of a vessel already registered in the Isle of Man is relatively simple.

The documents which will be required from the owner (who should be a 'qualified owner') or representative are:

(a)   an original Bill of Sale (Form REG 11);

(b)   in the case of company ownership a certificate of incorporation should be provided and authorised officer(s) should be appointed (Form REG 3);

(c)   a Declaration of Ownership should be completed (Forms REG 4, REG 5 or REG 14);

(d)   form REG 6 advising of the appointment of an approved ship manager ('authorised person'). Alternatively, the owner may establish its own office in the Isle of Man having responsibility for the vessel.

The owner or representative should also advise on the location of the vessel so that arrangements can be made to have the Certificate of Registry amended.

The remaining provisions set out in section D above would apply equally to a transfer of a currently registered Isle of Man vessel.

2   Please explain any exchange control or other governmental or regulatory consents required in connection with the sale to a foreign flag of a vessel registered under the flag of the Isle of Man.

There are currently no such exchange control or other governmental or regulatory consents in the Isle of Man required in connection with the sale to a foreign flag of a vessel registered under the flag of the Isle of Man

G   Deletion

1   Please outline the procedure for deletion of vessels from the flag of the Isle of Man.

If the vessel is subject to a mortgage the mortgage must be discharged prior to its deletion. Alternatively the mortgagee's consent will be required to delete the vessel from the Register subject to the mortgage. If the vessel will be registered on another flag, the requirements as to transfer of mortgages (if permitted) on the new flag must be complied with.

The owner must provide the Registrar with written authority to close the register.

2   *Please answer either separately or by reference to your earlier answer, the questions
       listed under section D in respect of the deletion, as opposed to new registration, of a
       vessel.*

While it is preferable for the Registry to have the original authority to close the register they
will accept a copy on the understanding that the original will follow. This should, however, be
cleared with the Registrar in advance. There is no requirement to notarise instructions to close.
This applies equally to any mortgagee's consent that may be required.

H   Certificates/transcripts

*1   Please identify the certificates and other documents issued to an owner on registra-
       tion of a vessel under the flag of the Isle of Man.*

The Registrar will issue a Certificate of Registry once the vessel has been registered. The
owner will also receive the various certificates issued by the IOM surveyor as a result of the
survey and inspection of the vessel.

*2   Please outline the procedure (including fees payable) for obtaining information on the
       registered ownership of and encumbrances on vessels registered in the Isle of Man.*

Information regarding a registered vessel is not generally provided over the phone. A request
can be made of the Registrar, by telephone or in writing, for a transcript of ship register. Any
telephone request for a transcript should be followed by written confirmation of this request.
The transcript of ship register sets out, among other things, who the registered owner of the
vessel is and provides details of any registered encumbrances.

At present there is a fee of £37 payable for each transcript obtained.

In addition, a personal inspection of the register relating to the vessel can be made upon payment of a fee, at the time of writing, £21.

I   Fees/taxes

1   What fees are currently payable:
       1.1   on new registration?
       1.2   on transfer of ownership?
       1.3   on deletion?

1.1   There is a one-off registration fee on first registration of the vessel in the Isle of
       Man. This is currently £525. Any survey and inspection fees are based on an
       hourly rate for the surveyors plus the costs of travel and subsistence. There may
       be an additional charge of £525 per day if a surveyor is kept waiting and is
       unable to commence work.

1.2   A fee of £210 is currently payable on transfer of ownership by Bill of Sale. Any tran-
       script of register obtained currently costs £37.

1.3   There is no fee on deletion but if a closing transcript is required the usual transcript
       fee of £37 applies.

J   Parallel registration

1   Is parallel registration permitted:
*   1.1   onto the Isle of Man Register?*
*   1.2   from the Isle of Man Register?*

1.1   In general yes. The underlying principal Register must have legislation which permits demise registration.

1.2   In general yes. The intended demise register must have the equivalent legislation permitting demise registration onto their Register.

2   If so, what, if any specific governmental or other consent are required?

The consent of both Registers will be required. In addition, if the vessel is subject to a mortgage the written consent of the mortgagee will be required. The owner on the underlying register must also provide its written consent to register the vessel in the Demise Charter Register in the Isle of Man.

(See below)

3   Is the period of parallel registration limited? If so, is it renewable?

The period of registry would be fixed according to the charter period but subject to a maximum period of five years. It is renewable during the six-month period prior to the date of expiration of the Demise Charter Registry.

4   If parallel registration is dependent on the existence of a demised charter, does the Isle of Man have a specific definition of demise or bareboat charter for these purposes? If so, what is it?

Part IV Merchant Shipping Registration Act provides a definition of 'charter by demise'. This means the charter of a ship for a fixed period of time under which the charterer:

        (a)   has possession of the vessel; and
        (b)   has operational control of the vessel; and
        (c)   has the power to appoint and dismiss the master and the crew of the vessel; and
        (d)   is responsible to third parties as if he was the vessel owner, but has no right to sell or mortgage the vessel.

5   Please answer the questions listed under sections A to E above with reference to an application for parallel registration onto the register of the Isle of Man.

(A1)   It is the identity of the charterer and not the owner which is significant for a vessel which is to be registered in the demise charter register in the Isle of Man. The Act requires that the charterer must be a person qualified to be the owner of an Isle of Man Ship. The person to whom the vessel is chartered by demise must therefore meet the same criteria as a 'Qualified Owner' as set out in section A above for vessels which are registered as Isle of Man vessels.

(A2)   Not applicable as the charterer need not be an Isle of Man incorporated company.

(A3)   It is a requirement that a vessel to be entered onto the Demise Charter Register in the Isle of Man have an approved ship manager or 'representative person' appointed in relation to that vessel. The charterer may appoint a ship management organisation incorporated in and having its principal place of business in the Isle of Man to act as representative person or establish its own office in the Isle of Man having responsibility for the vessel. The appointment of the manager by the charterer is to be made on Form DCR 3 and is submitted to the Registry along with a copy of the Certificate of Incorporation of the appointed manager.

The Registry has a list of currently approved managers or representative persons for merchant ships and for commercial yachts available on its website.

(A4)   Please see A4 above.

(A5)   No exchange control or other Isle of Man governmental or regulatory consents are required in the Isle of Man in connection with vessels demise charter registered in the Isle of Man.

(A6–7) Not applicable.

(B1)   A vessel will not be eligible to be entered in the Demise Charter Register if the vessel is a fishing vessel or if it is less than 24 metres in length.

(B2)   The maximum age of vessels eligible for registration on the Isle of Man Demise Charter Register is 15 years.

(C1)   The vessel will retain her original name unless there is a clash with an existing vessel's name (whether that existing vessel is registered on the Demise Register or the main Part I Register) or if the applicant wishes to change the name on the underlying register. The Registry must also be satisfied that the name is not undesirable.

(C2)   Please see C2.

(C3)   Please see C3 above.

(D1)   Please see D1 above.

(D2)   The demise charterer should:

    (a)   apply in writing on Form DCR 3 to the Registrar for Demise Charter Registration;

    (b)   appoint an authorised officer(s) using form DCR 7;

    (c)   provide a Certificate of Survey by an approved Classification Society;

    (d)   provide a certified copy of the demise charterer's Certificate of Incorporation or other equivalent documentary evidence;

    (e)   provide a certified copy of the demise Charter Party under which the ship is chartered to the demise charterer by the register owner;

    (f)   provide the written consent of:

        (i)   the relevant authorities of the underlying registry to demise charter registration of the vessel in the Isle of Man;

        (ii)   the owner on the underlying register to demise charter registration in the Isle of Man using form DCR 4;

        (iii)   the mortgagees (if any) on the underlying register to demise charter registration in the Isle of Man using form DCR 5;

    (g)   provide a certified copy of the entries (a transcript) on the underlying register including details of ownership and any registered mortgages, charges or liens;

    (h)   appoint a ship management organisation to act as a representative person in the Isle of Man or establish its own office in the Isle of Man having responsibility for the ship, using form DCR 3;

(i)   make arrangements with the Marine Administration for a surveyor to inspect the vessel prior to acceptance for registration to ascertain that the vessel complies with International Convention in respect of safety, prevention of oil pollution and manning. In addition, the surveyor will conduct any survey as appropriate for the issue of International Convention Certificates;

(j)   make arrangements with the Ship Radio Licensing Office in the United Kingdom for the issue of a Radio Call Sign at the time of issuance of the Radio Licence and provide a copy of the notification letter; and

(k)   pay any fees in connection with registration and survey.

Once the application is made and the procedures completed the Registrar will issue a Carving and Marking Note indicating how the vessel is to be marked. Once marked and verified by either the Isle of Man surveyor (if the Isle of Man surveyor is present at marking) or by the Classification Society Surveyor the vessel will be registered for any period up to five years and a Certificate of Registry issued along with the necessary statutory certificates.

(D3)   The form of the documents referred to above are as prescribed by regulation and most are available on the Marine Administration website http://www.gov.im/dti/marineadmin or from the Marine Administration.

(D4)   Save as set out in (D2) above the Registry will generally require an original of each of the documents prior to registration.

(D5)   Please see D5 above.

(D6)   Please see D6 above.

(D7)   Forms DCR 4, DCR 5 and DCR 7 should be executed under seal or as a deed. If these forms are executed outside of the United Kingdom they must be notarised.

Any other documents (for example, a Power of Attorney) executed as a deed or under seal must be notarised if executed outside of the United Kingdom.

Legalisation or apostilling of documents is not currently a requirement.

(D8)   Please see D8 above.

(D9–11) Not applicable.

(E1)   Each vessel must be satisfactorily inspected and surveyed by an IOM Surveyor to ascertain that the vessel complies with International Conventions in respect of safety, prevention of oil pollution and manning prior to acceptance for demise registration. The IOM Surveyor will conduct any surveys as appropriate for the issue of International Convention Certificates.

(E2)   Surveys and inspections of vessels by an IOM Surveyor must be completed prior to the vessel being registered on the demise charter register.

6   *Can/must mortgages on vessels parallel registered into the Registry of the Isle of Man also be registered in the Isle of Man?*

There is no provision allowing mortgages registered on the underlying register to be registered on the Demise Charter Register in the Isle of Man. Any legal action to secure rights under a lien would be exercisable under the law of the underlying registry.

7   *Under what circumstances will/may parallel registration of the vessel onto the register of the Isle of Man be terminated or revoked?*

Registration on the Demise Charter Register ceases when one or other of the following occurs:

(a)   the Registry revokes its consent to the vessel being registered;

(b)   the authorities of the underlying register revoke their consent to the demise charter;

(c)   the charter lapses or is terminated by any of the parties to it – the period of registry would be fixed by reference to the charter period subject to a maximum period of five years;

(d)   the charterer ceases to be a qualified person or the charter is transferred or assigned to another person (whether qualified or not);

(e)   the vessel's underlying registration is terminated for any reason;

(f)   the vessel is sold – the new owner may, within seven days, consent to the present demise charter registration continuing;

(g)   the charterer has requested that the register be closed; or

(h)   if the vessel fails to maintain internationally agreed safety standards of IMO or ILO or no longer complies with its statutory obligations.

In addition if a registered mortgagee withdraws its consent to the demise registration the Registrar will ordinarily withdraw consent to and terminate the Demise Charter Registration.

K   General

1   *Please identify the principal statutes and regulations in the Isle of Man governing the registration of vessels.*

The Merchant Shipping (Registration) Act 1991

The Merchant Shipping (Registration) Regulations 1996

Merchant Shipping (Demise Charter Register) Regulations 1991

The Merchant Shipping (Yachts in Commercial Use) Order 2002

2   *Are there any other matters in the context of registration of vessels under the legal system in the Isle of Man which you feel should be emphasised here?*

No.

---

* Contributed by Robyn Wood of Dickinson Cruickshank, Douglas, Isle of Man.

Liberia*

A Ownership

1 What, if any, are the restrictions on ownership of vessels registered under the Liberian flag?

Generally, a Liberian flag vessel must be owned by a citizen or national of the Republic of Liberia. The term 'citizen' or 'national' includes corporations, limited liability companies formed under the Limited Liability Company Act, partnerships and associations of individuals.

The Commissioner or Deputy Commissioner of Maritime Affairs of the Republic of Liberia is authorised by statute to waive such ownership requirement, and such waiver is routinely granted, where the owner of the vessel qualifies for, secures and maintains registration in the Republic of Liberia as a 'foreign maritime entity', pursuant to Chapter 13 of the Liberian Business Corporation Act (the 'BCA') and appoints a qualified registered agent in the manner prescribed by §3.1(1) of the BCA.

A foreign entity whose indenture or instrument of trust, charter, articles of incorporation, agreement of partnership or other document recognised by the foreign state of its creation as the basis of its existence, directly or by force of law comprehends the power to own or operate vessels and confers or recognises its capacity to sue and be sued, may apply to the Minister of Foreign Affairs to be registered as a foreign maritime entity.

2 If registration by companies is limited to companies incorporated in Liberia, is a local 'brass-plate' company sufficient, or must there be a closer, genuine connection?

A corporation or partnership formed under Liberian law and maintaining a qualified registered agent constitutes a 'citizen' or 'national' for vessel registration purposes, regardless of the citizenship or nationality of its shareholders, directors, officers or partners or the existence of any other connection with Liberia.

3 If registration by companies incorporated other than in Liberia is permitted, must a local representative be appointed? If so, are there any restrictions on the identity of that representative?

A non-Liberian entity which wishes to be registered as a foreign maritime entity must designate a registered agent in Liberia upon whom process against such entity or any notice or demand required or permitted by law to be served may be served. If such entity maintains a place of business in Liberia such entity may designate as its agent a resident domestic corporation having a place of business in Liberia or a natural person, resident of and having a business address in Liberia. If such entity does not have a place of business in Liberia, such entity must designate as its agent a domestic bank or trust company with a paid in capital of not less than US$50,000, which is authorised by the Legislature to act as such. At present, The LISCR Trust Company is the only entity which has received such authorisation.

4 Please summarise any restrictions (for example, as to number, nationality and so on) on who may own shares in shipowning companies incorporated in Liberia.

There are no restrictions on who may own shares in shipowning companies incorporated in Liberia.

5   *Please explain any exchange control or other governmental or regulatory consents required in connection with the ownership of ships registered in Liberia.*

Apart from the citizenship restrictions referred to in A1 above, there are no exchange control or other governmental or regulatory consents required in connection with the ownership of vessels registered in Liberia, so long as the vessels otherwise comply with the laws and regulations of the Republic of Liberia.

6   *Please explain any special rules for any particular type of vessel.*

Apart from the size and age requirements referred to in B1 and B2 below, there are no special rules for registration for any particular type of vessel.

7   *Is there any mandatory registration requirement for certain owners (for example, citizens of your country)?*

Yes. Owners of vessels of 20 net tons and over engaged solely in domestic commerce are required to register such vessels in Liberia.

B   Eligibility

1   *Are any particular types/sizes of ship ineligible for, or exempt from, registration?*

The following vessels are ineligible for registration: any vessel of less than 20 net tons engaged solely in coastwise trade between ports of Liberia or between those of Liberia and other West African nations; unless waived by the Commissioner or Deputy Commissioner of Maritime Affairs, any sea-going vessel of 500 net tons or less engaged in foreign trade; and any yacht or other vessel used exclusively for pleasure, of less than 100 net tons.

2   *What, if any, is the maximum age for registration of ships under the Liberian flag?*

Unless waived by the Commissioner or Deputy Commissioner of Maritime Affairs, the maximum age for registration of vessels under the laws of Liberia is 20 years.

C   Names

1   *What, if any, are the restrictions on the name under which a ship may be registered in Liberia?*

While there are no legal restrictions on the name under which a vessel may be registered, as a matter of practice the Liberian Deputy Commissioner of Maritime Affairs (the 'Libdepcom') will not permit a vessel to be registered under a name already assigned to a vessel on the active register.

2   *Is there a procedure for approval of names in advance?*

Yes.

3   *If so, how does it operate? Does approval confer any priority rights in the use of the name?*

The proposed name may be cleared in advance with the Libdepcom and, if not already assigned or reserved for another vessel, may be reserved for a period of at least two years. A name which is reserved may not be used for another vessel.

386

D   New registration procedure

1   Where may ships intending to fly the Liberian flag be registered:

1.1   in your country?

1.2   abroad?

Applications for registration under the Liberian flag may be submitted to:

Vessel Registration, LISCR, 99 Park Avenue, Suite 1700, New York,

New York 10016-1601 USA

Phone: (212) 697-3434

Fax: (212) 697-5655

E-mail: registration@liscr.com

Applications may also be submitted through the Regional Offices of LISCR in London, Tokyo, Hamburg, Piraeus and Hong Kong.

2   What documents and information must be submitted to effect registration?

The following documents and information must be submitted to effect registration:

(a)   Application for registration of vessel;

(b)   authority of agent or officer of the owner to make such application;

(c)   proof of ownership as evidenced by:

    (i)   in the case of an existing vessel, a Bill of Sale;

    (ii)   in the case of a newbuilding, a Builder's Certificate or Master Carpenter's Certificate; and

    (iii)   in the case of an existing vessel transferred to Liberian registry without change of ownership;

(d)   an official certificate of ownership, transcript of register or other acceptable document;

(e)   Continuous Synopsis Record (CSR) File: The CSR is a new record keeping requirement for all SOLAS ships. It is a document upon which ownership and operational information shall be provided. It must be on board all SOLAS vessels and it must be kept up to date. Therefore vessel registration procedures shall require the submission of a copy of the vessel's current complete CSR File certified by the flag administration from which the vessel is being transferred along with an Amendment Form and a new Index of Amendments. The Administration shall in turn, upon receipt of the last CSR from the losing flag administration, issue a new CSR Document;

(f)   confirmation of class dated not more than ten (10) days prior to registration; Classification Society Statement or Affidavit, Survey Reports of Classification Society for vessels that are 15 years of age or older;

(g)   application for Minimum Safe Manning Certificate (MSMC);

(h)   ISM Code Declarations of Company and Designated Person(s): The ISM Code means the 'International Management Code for the Safe Operation of Vessels and for Pollution Prevention'. Now that the ISM Code is in effect, it is necessary for the flag State to verify and maintain company and vessel compliance. ISM and MSMC applications cannot be executed by an attorney-in-fact, but must be executed by the Chief Executive Officer and/or the Designated Person of a Company;

(i) ISPS Code Declaration of Company Security Officer (CSO): The ISPS Code means the 'International Ship and Port Facility Security' Code. The Company shall appoint a Company Security Officer and shall provide the Administration with the full name of the CSO and information to enable direct and immediate contact at all times between the Administration and the CSO with regard to matters related to the ISPS Code;

(j) proof from present state of registry of consent to transfer and freedom from recorded liens;

(k) proof of liability insurance;

(l) Oath of Owner; and

(m) registration fees and tonnage taxes.

3 *Does your legal system lay down any specific requirements as to the contents of any of these documents – for example, of Bills of Sale – and, if so, what are they?*

With respect to the documents listed in D.2 above:

(a) the Application for registration must be submitted on Form RLM 101a;

(b) the authority of the agent or officer of the owner should be submitted in the form of a Power of Attorney, or a Secretary's Certificate of Corporate Resolutions, authorising one or more named persons to act on behalf of the owner in making application for registration of the vessel and to perform all acts necessary to accomplish the same;

(c) the Bill of Sale does not have to be in any specific form except that, if it is to be recorded, it must have an acknowledgement in accordance with Chapter V, Section 2(B) of the RLM 100 and Section 15 of the Maritime Law;

(d) a Builder's Certificate or Master Carpenter's Certificate does not have to be in any specific form;

(e) the proof of ownership does not have to be in any specific form;

(f) the certificate of confirmation of class must be issued by one of the following societies:

(i) American Bureau of Shipping Bureau Veritas;

(ii) Bureau Veritas;

(iii) China Classification Society;

(iv) Det norske Veritas;

(v) Germanischer Lloyd;

(vi) Korean Register of Shipping;

(vii) Lloyd's Register of Shipping;

(viii) Nippon Kaiji Kyokai;

(ix) Registro Italiano Navale; or

(x) Maritime Register of Shipping.

(g) proof of the consent of the state of registry from which the vessel is being transferred in the form of a document approving transfer of the vessel to the

Liberian flag in the ownership of the shipowner. If actual proof of the vessel's cancellation from her present registry is submitted, then proof of consent is not required. If the government of the present registry does not issue a consent, then an affirmation to that effect, given by a person admitted to the practice of law in the state of the present registry, may be required in lieu of proof of consent;

(h)   proof that the vessel is free of recorded liens is required in the form of an official statement issued by the state of registry from which the vessel is being transferred;

(i)   proof of liability insurance may take the form of a cover note issued by one of the International Group of P&I clubs and should cover any default of the owner of its repatriation obligations under Section 342 of the Liberian Maritime Law;

(j)   the Oath of Owner should be submitted on Form RLM 103; and

(k)   registration fees and tonnage taxes are payable in US dollars.

4   *Please identify how many originals or copies of each document are required. Are fax copies of any of them acceptable?*

In order to be recordable, it is necessary to furnish four (4) signed and acknowledged originals of the Bill of Sale. If two (2) copies are signed originals, two (2) photocopies of a Bill of Sale are acceptable. If the Bill of Sale is not to be recorded, then one original thereof will be acceptable for initial registration. In the case of re-registration, the Bill of Sale must be recorded. All other application forms and supporting documents must be submitted in triplicate.

5   *Are there any requirements as to the language in which documents must be submitted?*

All registration documents must be submitted in English or, if not in English, must be accompanied by a certified English translation thereof.

6   *If they may be submitted in a foreign language, are there any translation requirements? If so, what are they and when must they be complied with?*

All documents submitted in a foreign language should be accompanied by a certified English translation thereof prepared by a certified translator or an attorney.

7   *Please identify any particular requirements of your legal system with regard to the method of execution of any of the registration documents, or with regard to notarisation or legalisation.*

All registration documents should be executed by a duly authorised signatory of the owner. As noted above, if the Bill of Sale is to be recorded it must have an acknowledgement. If a Power of Attorney authorising execution and delivery of the RLM forms and Bill of Sale is furnished as proof of authority, it should be notarised in accordance with the Liberian Maritime Regulations. There is no need for legalisation or apostille. Certain of the Liberian forms require notarisation but not legalisation or apostille.

All initial registrations, whether within Liberia or abroad, are provisional.

8   *If provisional, what needs to be done to effect final registration? When must it be done?*
A provisional certificate of registry issued upon new registration will be valid for a period of 12 months from the date of registration. A request for a permanent certificate of registration should be submitted with supporting documentation to:

Liberian International Ship & Corporate Registry (LISCR), Chief, Vessel Registration Division, 99 Park Ave., Suite 1700, New York, New York 10016-1601 USA,

or through overseas LISCR offices.

The following documents must accompany any request for permanent registration:

(a)   Certified copy of the vessel's current classification certificates. The certificates must show (i) the present name of the vessel and (ii) the home port as Monrovia, Liberia.

(b)   Liberian Certificate of Tonnage Measurement (either National or 1969 Convention). This Certificate is to be signed and accepted on the Certificate by the Shipowner, his authorised agent or master.

(c)   Liberian Load Line Certificate, which must be issued in compliance with the International Convention on Load Lines, 1966 and must be full term and valid.

(d)   Liberian certificates issued under the provisions of the International Convention for the Prevention of Pollution from Ships (MARPOL 73/78), Annexes I through V. The International Oil Pollution Prevention (IOPP) and/or the Noxious Liquid Substances (NLS) certificates must be full term and valid.

(e)   Liberian certificates issued under the provisions of the International Convention for the Safety of Life at Sea (SOLAS), 1974, as amended. The certificate covering the requirements of the Convention for Safety Construction, Safety Equipment, Safety Radio, Carriage of Grain, Bulk Chemicals and Gas and the like, must be full term and valid.

(f)   Liberian National or International Maritime Organization Code or Resolution Certificates. These certificates may be required for vessels under 500 gross tons, or non-propelled vessels, fishing vessels, Mobile Offshore Drilling Units, or other vessels not covered by the SOLAS Certificates.

(g)   Report of Satisfactory Completion of Liberian Safety Inspection. An initial Safety Inspection is required within 30 days after the date of registration or, where both the owner and management of the vessel have been changed, the date of re-registration. Application therefor may be submitted to any office of LISCR.

(h)   Liberian Ship Radio Station License. The License will be issued upon application to the Chief, Radio Communications Division, LISCR.

(i)   Certificate of cancellation of vessel's former registry. (To be submitted within 90 days of the date of the vessel's initial registration).

(j)   Civil Liability Certificate for Oil Pollution Damage (1992). (This Certificate is only required for vessels with more than 2,000 tons of oil as cargo).

(k)   Owner's Acceptance of Certificate of Tonnage Measurement (Form RLM 126). (Only required in case of re-registration of an existing vessel where ownership has changed and there already exists a Liberian Certificate of Tonnage Measurement).

(l)   Minimum Safe Manning Certificate (This document is required by Maritime Regulations 7.38(5) to be issued to each vessel at registration or shortly thereafter setting forth the required minimum numbers of officers and crew, which have been prescribed for the safe navigation and operation of that vessel).

(m)   ISM Code Declarations of Company and Designated Person. And ISPS Code Declaration of Company Security Officer. These documents are to be submitted at registration or shortly thereafter.

(n)   Continuous Synopsis Record (CSR) File: A complete CSR File consisting of a certified copy of the vessel's CSR File provided by the flag administration from which the vessel was transferred along with an Amendment Form, a new Index of Amendments and a new revised CSR Document is required.

(o)   Affirmation Re: Markings (Form RLM 106A). (Only required when the vessel has undergone a change in name).

9   *If provisional, what, if any, are the restrictions which apply to the vessel pending final registration?*

There are no restrictions that apply to the vessel pending permanent registration.

10   *Can a provisionally registered ship be mortgaged?*

A provisionally registered ship may be mortgaged.

E   Technical matters

1   *Please identify the requirements of Liberia with regard to inspection, survey, measurement and the like in respect of newly registered ships.*

Please see E2 below.

2   *By when must these requirements be complied with?*

A safety inspection is required within 30 days after either the date of registration or, if both the owner and management of the vessel have been changed, the date of re-registration. An application for safety inspection will provide the proposed port and date of inspection, estimated time of arrival of the vessel and agent identification.

The application is to be submitted to LISCR Vienna, VA Office:
Chief, Safety Division, 8619 Westwood Center Drive, Suite 300,
Vienna, Virginia 22182, USA

A Liberian Certificate of Tonnage Measurement (either national or 1969 Convention) is required at the time of registration. See D9(b) and (k) above.

F   Transfer of ownership

1   Please answer, either separately or by reference to your earlier answers, the questions listed under Sections D and E above in respect of a transfer of ownership of a vessel already registered in Liberia.

An application for re-registration of a vessel already registered under the Liberian flag should be submitted to the Liberian International Ship & Corporate Registry (LISCR) Vessel Registration at the address mentioned in Dl above. The application is to be submitted on form RLM 101A.

The following documents and information must be submitted to effect re-registration:

(a)   Certificate of Permission for Sale for the Purpose of Re-registration (issued by the Chief, Vessel Registration Division, upon application of the seller);

(b)   Application for registration of vessel;

(c)   authority of agent or officer of buyer to make such application;

(d)   if buyer is not an incorporated company, an Oath of Owner, Managing Owner or Part Owner on form RLM 103;

(e)   Bill of Sale (to which should be affixed a copy of the vessel's existing Certificate of Registry);

(f)   CSR Amendment Form and a new Index of Amendments;

(g)   confirmation of class, dated not more than ten (10) days prior to re-registration; Classification Society Statement or Affidavit, Survey Reports of Classification Society for vessels that are 15 years of age or older;

(h)   proof of liability insurance; and

(i)   re-registration fees.

The same requirements with respect to forms, numbers of copies, language, translations and method of execution of documents apply to re-registration as they do to initial registration.

2   Please explain any exchange control or other governmental or regulatory consents required in connection with the sale to a foreign flag of a vessel registered under the Liberian flag.

There are no exchange control or other governmental or regulatory consents required in connection with the sale to a foreign flag of a vessel registered under Liberian flag other than obtaining a Certificate of Permission to Transfer. See G1 below.

G   Deletion

1   Please outline the procedure for deletion of vessels from the Liberian flag.

In order to delete a vessel from the Liberian registry, a written request for a Certificate of Permission to Transfer must first be submitted by the vessel owner to:

Liberian International Ship & Corporate Registry (LISCR),
Vessel Registration, 99 Park Ave., Suite 1700, New York,
New York 10016-1601 USA or the other offices of LISCR.

The request for permission to transfer must include the name and domicile of the buyer as well as the name of the country to which the vessel's registration is to be transferred. If only the vessel's registration is to be transferred, the application should include a request 'for transfer of the vessel to [*name of country*] registry and flag without change of ownership'. If the vessel is subject to one or more preferred ship mortgages, hypothecations, or similar liens, a satisfaction, release or discharge of such lien must be recorded with the office of the Libdepcom prior to such transfer. Certificates of Permission to Transfer are issued for periods of limited validity. The cost of a Certificate for 90 days is US$250; for 180 days, US$350.

2   *Please answer, either separately or by reference to your earlier answers, the questions listed under Section D in respect of the deletion, as opposed to new registration, of a vessel.*

After a Certificate of Permission to Transfer has been issued, a Certificate of Cancellation of Registry will be issued once the following conditions have been met:

(a)   the recordation of a satisfaction, release or discharge of any existing recorded preferred ship mortgage, hypothecation or similar lien that has been recorded with the Libdepcom;

(b)   payment in full of any outstanding fees, penalties or charges of whatever nature due against the vessel or her owner to the Republic of Liberia;

(c)   submission of the following documents to LISCR, Vessel registration in New York, to a Liberian consul or to one of the Regional Offices of LISCR in London, Tokyo, Hamburg, Piraeus or Hong Kong:

   (i)   current Certificate of Registry;

   (ii)   Liberian Ship Radio Station License; and

   (iii)   three copies of the Bill of Sale, where a change of ownership has occurred.

H   Certificates/transcripts

1   *Please identify the certificates and other documents issued to an owner on registration of its ship under the Liberian flag.*

Upon registration of a vessel under the Liberian flag, the owner will receive:

(a)   Provisional Certificate of Registry;

(b)   temporary ship radio station authority;

(c)   letter to whomever it may concern relating to tonnage taxes;

(d)   CSR document for new vessels or CSR Amendment Form and a new Index of Amendments for vessels already registered with the Administration; and

(e)   combined publications folder containing Liberian regulations and forms.

2   *Please outline the procedure (including fees payable) for obtaining information on the registered ownership and encumbrances on vessels registered in Liberia.*

To obtain information on a Liberian registered vessel, an oral or written request to the Libdepcom's office may be made for a Certificate of Ownership and Encumbrance, the fee for which is US$100.

I   Fees/taxes

1   *What fees are currently payable:*

    1.1   *on new registration?*

    1.2   *on transfer of ownership?*

    1.3   *on deletion?*

1.1   Initial registration fees:

(a)	Initial Registration fee, per vessel	
	For vessels of 14,000 Net Registered Tons and above:	US$0.13
	per net ton (not to exceed US$3,900) plus	US$1,500
	Registration Administrative Fee:	US$6,500
	For vessels less than 14,000 Net Registered Tons:	US$2,500
(b)	Annual tonnage tax:	
	For vessels of 14,000 Net Registered Tons and above:	US$0.10
	per net ton plus	US$3,800
	For vessels less than 14,000 Net Registered Tons:	US$0.40
	per net ton (but not less than	US$880)
(c)	Annual fee: marine investigation, nautical training and international participation	
	For vessels of 14,000 Net Registered Tons and above:	US$0.03
	per net ton, plus	US$2,000
	For vessels under 14,000 Net Registered Tons:	US$0.07
	per net ton, plus	US$1,000
(d)	Marine Inspection (each), for vessels 500 gross tons or over:	US$1,450
(e)	Provisional Certificate of Registry:	US$250
(f)	Permanent Certificate of Registry (payable at initial registration):	US$250
(g)	Temporary Radio Authority:	US$100
(h)	Combined Publications Folder:	US$75/82
(i)	Oil Record Book:	US$105
(j)	Articles of Agreement:	US$10

1.2   Re-registration fees:

(a)	Certificate of Permission for Sale:	US$250
(b)	Re-registration charges:	US$1,500
(c)	Provisional Certificate of Registry:	US$250
(d)	Permanent Certificate of Registry:	US$250
(e)	Temporary Radio Authority:	US$100
(f)	Recording Bill of Sale:	US$200
(g)	Official Forms & Publications:	US$75/82

Note: change of name fees are also payable when the name of a vessel changes on re-registration.

1.3   Deletion
    (a)   Deletion Fee: US$750
    (b)   Certificate of Permission to Transfer (90 days validity):   US$250
    (c)   Certificate of Permission to Transfer (180 days validity):   US$350
Note: the fees indicated in (a) and (b) include the subsequent issuance of a Certificate of Cancellation of Registry.

2   *What annual or other ongoing fees or taxes are payable in respect of ships registered in Liberia?*
The tonnage taxes and fees referred to in I.1.1(b), (c) and (d) are payable annually for all registered vessels.

J   Parallel registration

1   Is parallel registration permitted:
    1.1   onto your country's register?
    1.2   from your country's register?
Parallel registration is permitted onto and from the Liberian registry provided a bareboat charter of the vessel is in full force and effect.

2   If so, what, if any, specific governmental or other consents are required?
Permission is required from the Chief, Vessel Registration Division for both (i) Liberian bareboat charter registration (into the Liberian registry) and (ii) foreign bareboat charter registration (from the Liberian registry).

3   Is the period of parallel registration limited? If so, is it renewable?
The period of bareboat charter registration is limited to two years. It may be renewed for further periods of not more than two years each but not later than the expiration date of the bareboat charter.

4   If parallel registration is dependent on the existence of a demise charter, does your country have a specific definition of demise or bareboat charter for these purposes? If so, what is it?
The Republic of Liberia does not have a specific definition of demise or bareboat charter for the purpose of bareboat charter registration.

5   Please answer the questions listed under Sections A to E above with reference to application for parallel registration:
5.1 onto the Liberian register:
Generally, in order to be eligible for Liberian bareboat charter registration, a vessel must meet all of the requirements for initial registration with the exception of ownership and cancellation

from present registry, and the bareboat charterer must meet all of the requirements for an owner of a Liberian registered vessel. The following are specifically required:

(a)   An Application for Registration on form RLM 101 must be executed by the charterer of the vessel. The information relating to the bareboat charterer should be entered in Items 8, 9 and 10 (Name of Owner, Residence and Citizenship). The application with all required supporting documents, fees and tonnage tax should be submitted to: Liberian International Ship & Corporate Registry (LISCR), Chief, Vessel Registration Division, 99 Park Ave., Suite 1700, New York, New York 10016-1601 USA, or the other offices of LISCR.

(b)   The charterer should also submit a letter of request in triplicate, typed on the letterhead of, and signed by, the charterer of the vessel requesting bareboat charter registration and setting forth:

(i)   present name and official number of the vessel;

(ii)   present country of registry of the vessel with address, telex/telefax number of the country's vessel registration office;

(iii)   names, addresses and telex/telefax numbers of the owner and vessel's manager;

(iv)   names, addresses and telex/telefax numbers of all holders of any registered ship mortgages, hypothecations or similar charges upon the vessel and the dates contemplated for commencement, and earliest lawful termination, of the bareboat Charterparty; and

(v)   effective 1 July 2004, a request for the submission of a certified copy of the vessel's CSR File to the bareboat charter registry.

(c)   A certified true copy of the bareboat charterparty together with all annexes and addenda thereto and any bareboat sub-charterparties, shall be submitted for recording in triplicate, with English translation if in any other language, and with proof of due execution. Certification may be by a notary public or any other officer authorised to take acknowledgements.

(d)   Any subsequent amendments or addenda to the charterparty or any subsequent bareboat sub-charterparties must be submitted for recording within 30 days of execution with proof of due execution and English translation, where necessary.

The following documents shall also be included with the Application:

(a)   an official certificate from the present country of registry setting forth the ownership of the vessel and any recorded encumbrances;

(b)   the written consents, with proof of their due execution, of the owner and the mortgagee (s) to the bareboat registration;

(c)   evidence that the present county of registry will withdraw from the vessel the right to fly the flag of that country while the vessel is under bareboat registration;

(d)   the charterer must also submit an Oath of Undertaking duly acknowledged which will include the charterer's undertaking that:

(i)   the vessel will not fly any flag other than the Liberian flag, nor show any home port other than Monrovia, while the vessel is subject to the bareboat charter;

(ii)   during the period of bareboat registration, Liberia shall have exclusive jurisdiction and control over the vessel, in its capacity as flag state;

(iii)   the charterer will immediately notify the Chief, Vessel Registration Division whenever the charterparty has been terminated for whatever reason or that another jurisdiction has accorded the vessel the right to fly its flag;

(iv)   within 30 days of the termination of the bareboat charterparty or the current Liberian Provisional Certificate of Registry, whichever is earlier, the charterer will surrender to the Chief, Vessel Registration Division, the Provisional Certificate of Registry and all other certificates issued to the vessel by or on behalf of the Republic of Liberia; and

(v)   that by failure to comply with any of the provisions in the Oath of Undertaking, the charterer acknowledges the liability to pay damages in accordance with Section 88 of the Liberian Maritime Law.

The registration fees and tonnage taxes are the same for bareboat charter registration as those fees charged for an initial registration listed in D2 above.

5.2 from the Liberian register:

The following conditions must be satisfied in order to foreign bareboat charter register a vessel:

(a)   Application for Permission: An application, four (4) signed originals must be submitted to:

Liberian International Ship & Corporate Registry (LISCR),

Vessel Registration, 99 Park Ave., Suite 1700, New York,

New York 10016-1601 USA, or the other offices of LISCR,

and must include the following information:

(i)   registered name and official number of the vessel;

(ii)   name, address, telex/telefax and telephone numbers of the bareboat charterer; intended service of the vessel, including nature of the cargo and geographical areas to be navigated; and

(iii)   date contemplated for commencement of the bareboat charterparty and the date contemplated for its earliest lawful termination.

(b)   Consent of Mortgagees: if the vessel is subject to one or more mortgages, the written consent of each mortgagee to the proposed foreign bareboat charter registration, usually in the form of a letter, must be filed with the Chief, Vessel Registration Division.

(c)   Charterparty: a certified true copy of the bareboat charter, along with all annexes and amendments thereto, must be filed with the Chief, Vessel Registration Division.

(d)   Owner's Oath of Undertaking: the Owner must submit a letter addressed to the Chief, Vessel Registration Division containing an undertaking to:

(i)   surrender to the Chief, Vessel Registration Division, within 60 days of the issuance of the Certificate of Permission for Foreign Bareboat Charter Registration or within 30 days of the date of commencement of the charterparty, whichever is later, any Liberian Certificate of Registry previously issued to the vessel; and

    (ii)   immediately notify the Chief, Vessel Registration Division whenever the charterparty has terminated, for whatever reason, or when the owner has otherwise retaken possession of the vessel.

(e)   Agreement between owner and charterer: the owner and the charterer of the subject vessel must enter into an agreement which contains an undertaking by the owner and the charterer (i) that they will neither permit the vessel to fly the flag of Liberia nor show Monrovia as her home port while the vessel remains in the service of the charterer under the bareboat charter; (ii) that the vessel shall be equipped, maintained and navigated to standards which are not less than those contained in the Liberian Maritime Law, Regulations and rules including the international conventions to which Liberia is a party and (iii) that failure to comply with such agreement shall be cause for the imposition of the penalties stipulated in Section 88 of the Liberian Maritime Law.

(f)   Other conditions:

    (i)   the vessel's Liberian Provisional Certificate of Registry and Ship Radio License shall be surrendered to the Chief, Vessel Document Division during the bareboat charter registration;

    (ii)   if a major casualty occurs during the period of the bareboat charter or the vessel extensively pollutes the environment, the owner and charterer shall facilitate the boarding of the vessel and/or the interviewing of the Master, officers, crew or other witnesses and the gathering of information by an investigating officer representing the Liberian registry, whenever deemed necessary; and

    (iii)   any subsequent amendments or addenda to the agreement between the owner and charterer or to the charterparty and any subsequent bareboat sub-charterparties with English translations thereof if in a language other than English shall be filed with the Chief, Vessel Registration Division together with a letter noting which sections, if any, have been changed or altered together with a letter of consent as to the amendments by the mortgagees of the vessel.

(g)   A fee of US$250 for the issuance of a Certificate of Permission for Foreign Bareboat Registration must be paid by the charterer at the time of registration.

(h)   The annual tonnage tax remains applicable to foreign bareboat charter registered vessels (as per above fee schedule; two sets of tonnage tax fees apply according to vessel net tonnage).

6   *Can/must mortgages on ships parallel registered onto the Liberian registry also be registered in Liberia?*

Without prejudice to the continuing foreign legal status of a ship mortgage, hypothecation or similar charge made and registered in accordance with the laws of the foreign state, upon compliance with Sections 85 and 86 of sub-chapter II of the Liberian Maritime law (relating to the recording of the bareboat charterparty and the undertaking of the bareboat charterer), such foreign mortgage, hypothecation or similar charge may be recorded in accordance with Liberian law and if so recorded shall constitute a Liberian preferred mortgage and shall give rise to a preferred mortgage lien.

7   *Under what circumstances will/may the parallel registration of a ship onto the Liberian register be terminated or revoked?*

The grant by a foreign state of the right to fly the flag of such state shall terminate the Liberian bareboat registration of the vessel.

In addition, if the bareboat charterer breaches the undertaking to fly the flag of Liberia and to show the home port of Monrovia, or a vessel while registered under the Liberian flag shall be found flying or pretending entitlement to fly the flag of a foreign state without the permission of the Commissioner or Deputy Commissioner of Maritime Affairs of the Republic of Liberia and the consent of the vessel's mortgagees, if any, the owner and/or the charterer shall be liable for penalties not to exceed fifty thousand dollars, which until paid shall constitute a maritime lien on the vessel.

K   General

1   *Please identify the principal statutes and regulations in Liberia governing the registration of ships.*

The principal statutes with respect to the registration of vessels are Title 21 (Maritime Law) of the Liberian Code of Laws of 1956, as amended, and the Liberian Maritime Regulations made by The Commissioner of Maritime Affairs under the authority vested in him by the Liberian Maritime Law.

2   *Are there any other matters in the context of registration of ships under your legal system which you feel should be emphasised?*

In general, the Libdepcom and its staff take a flexible and practical approach in their application of the Maritime Law and Regulations and seek to accommodate the legitimate needs of shipowners.

---

* Contributed by Hadley S. Roe, assisted by Kassandra L. Slangan and Mira Trifunovic, all of Seward & Kissel, New York, United States of America.

Malta*

A   Ownership

1   What, if any, are the restrictions on ownership of vessels registered under the flag of Malta?

A vessel registered under the flag of Malta does not suffer from any restrictions on ownership due to nationality of the owners. Thus Malta flagged vessels may be owned by:

(a)   citizens of Malta;

(b)   bodies corporate established under and subject to the laws of Malta having their principal place of business in Malta or having a place of business in Malta and satisfying the Minister for Competitiveness and Communications (hereinafter referred to as the 'Minister') that they can and will ensure due observance of the laws of Malta relating to merchant shipping (hereinafter referred to as 'Shipping Organisations'); and

(c)   a foreign corporate body or other entity which enjoys to the satisfaction of the Registrar-General (hereinafter referred to as the 'Registrar') legal personality in terms of the law under which it has been established or constituted and which has satisfied the Registrar that it can and will ensure due observance of the laws of Malta relating to merchant shipping.

If a shipowner should wish to register under the flag of Malta as a Maltese Shipping Organisation the following basic details would need to be provided:

(a)   the proposed name/s of company. The word 'Limited' is always inserted at the end of the chosen name. It is useful to provide additional alternative names (in order of preference);

(b)   the name, address, nationality, passport number/date and place of issue and date and place of birth of each shareholder (a minimum of one). In the case of bodies corporate, the name, registered office address, date and place of incorporation and registration number;

(c)   the number of shares to be held by each (out of standard 500 shares of LM1 each) NOTE: the share capital of a Shipping Organisation may be denominated in any currency which is a convertible currency;

(d)   the name and all particulars as at (b) above of the director/s (a minimum of one); and

(e)   any special instructions on company structure, voting rights and so on.

Should shipowners wish to opt for international ownership of a Malta flagged vessel the following documents would have to be provided:

(a)   if ownership is by a foreign corporate body/legal entity:

(i)   original Memorandum and Articles of Associate/Articles of Incorporation (or certified true copies attached to the legal opinion (referred to in (v) below) on the contents of the Memorandum and/or Articles);

(ii)   Good Standing Certificate;

(iii)   Original Declaration of Appointment of a Resident Agent in Malta, duly notarised and apostilled;

(iv)   Powers of Attorney (if and when required);

(v)   Legal Opinion, duly notarised and apostilled, confirming that the corporate records of the corporate body/entity have been examined and giving the details of the directors and holders of office and of persons authorised to represent the corporate body/entity and to bind it with their signature and to appoint a Resident Agent;

(vi)   Memorandum and Articles/copy of ID Card of the Maltese Resident Agent;

(vii)   Good Standing Certificate of the Maltese Resident Agent (if applicable); and

(viii) Acceptance of appointment by Maltese Resident Agent.

(b)   if ownership is by citizens of a Member State of the European Union:

(i)   certified true copy of passport;

(ii)   Original Declaration of Appointment of Resident Agent in Malta, duly notarised and apostilled;

(iii)   Memorandum and Articles/copy of ID Card of Maltese Resident Agent;

(iv)   Good Standing Certificate of Maltese Resident Agent; and

(v)   Acceptance of appointment by Maltese Resident Agent.

Note: A Shipping Organisation may also operate under a trust or be a foundation.

2   *If registration by companies is limited to companies incorporated in Malta, is a local 'brass-plate' company sufficient, or must there be a closer, genuine connection?*

Registration is not limited to companies incorporated in Malta, but if a shipowner were to opt for the establishment of a Maltese Shipping Organisation, a local 'brass-plate' company is sufficient and no closer genuine connection is required.

3   *If registration by companies incorporated other than in Malta is permitted, must a local representative be appointed? If so, are there any restrictions on the identity of that representative?*

An international owner must appoint in writing a resident agent who:

(a)   is habitually resident in Malta;

(b)   is not interdicted or incapacitated or is an undischarged bankrupt;

(c)   has not been convicted of any of the crimes affecting public trust or of theft or fraud or of knowingly receiving property obtained by theft or fraud; and

(d)   has satisfied the Registrar to be a person capable of carrying out the functions of a Resident Agent.

Note: a Resident Agent may also be a Maltese body corporate. International owners must also ensure that they have a validly appointed Resident Agent at all times. Removal or resignation of the Resident Agent must be accompanied by the giving of at least 15 days notice in writing to the Registrar and to any registered mortgagee.

4   *Please sOummarise any restrictions (for example, as to number, nationality and so on) on who may own shares in shipowning companies incorporated in Malta.*

There are no restrictions on the basis of nationality with regards to shareholdings in Shipping Organisations. Shipping Organisations may be constituted as single member companies (that is, with no minimum number of shareholders required). By law, a private company is one which restricts the right to transfer its shares and limits the number of its members to 50 and prohibits any invitation to the public to subscribe for any shares or debentures of the company. (See Regulation 6(1) of Merchant Shipping (Shipping Organisations – Private Companies) Regulations, 2004 – L.N. 223 of 2004.)

5   *Please explain any exchange control or other governmental or regulatory consents required in connection with the ownership of ships registered in Malta.*

No exchange control permission or external transaction clearance is necessary to incorporate Shipping Organisations for the purpose of owning or operating Malta flag vessels, insofar as no less than 80 per cent of the shareholding is held by nonresidents.

Notwithstanding the fact that companies exclusively owning and operating an exempt vessel are not subject to income tax, an annual income tax form needs to be filed with the Inland Revenue Department together with sets of company accounts containing details of any payments and disbursements made locally.

The new Merchant Shipping (Shipping Organisations – Private Companies) Regulations, 2004 impose the duty of keeping proper accounting records with respect to:

(a)   all sums of money received and expended by the company and the matters in respect of which the receipt and expenditure takes place;

(b)   the assets and liabilities of the company; and

(c)   all sales and purchases of goods and services by the company.

The above duty is subject to a transition period of five years. Another option to the above would be to file with the Commissioner of Inland Revenue a Declaration in Lieu of a Tax Return, however, this will only available for five years from the date from which the above-mentioned regulations came into force. It is therefore advised that for general purposes as well as those of company liquidation the first option be adopted.

6   *Please explain any special rules for any particular type of vessel.*

The following are the particular types of vessel to which special rules apply:

(a)   Laid up vessels or vessels on tow: the Registrar may grant a non-operational certificate where the vessel is not in possession of valid safety and load line certificates; or the vessel is at least classed with them or in possession of the relative towage certificate accordingly.

(b)   Fishing vessels: the registration of fishing vessels under the Malta flag necessitates obtaining the relative authorisation after application from the Department of Fisheries and Aquaculture. Prior to the provisional registration of the vessel, applicants may be required to inform the Merchant Shipping Directorate (hereinafter referred to as the 'Directorate') of the areas where they are to fish and to produce evidence that they will be duly authorised by the appropriate authorities to carry out fishing operations. Registration under the Malta flag does not guarantee authorisation to carry out fishing operations.

(c)   Pleasure yachts: the Maltese flag allows for the possibility of registering pleasure yachts. The most important consideration is that these vessels do not automatically enjoy the fiscal concessions and exemptions from the payment of income tax, stamp or transfer duty and donation and succession duty which are otherwise enjoyed by other vessels. The companies owning such pleasure yachts may however, apply for a declaration from the relevant Minister that the vessel be considered an exempted ship.

(d)   Passenger ships: these should be in possession of the relative passenger ship safety certificate from the relative classification society.

7   *Is there any mandatory registration requirement for certain owners (for example, citizens of Malta)?*

There are no mandatory registration requirements for Maltese citizens to register their vessels in Malta.

B   Eligibility

1   Are any particular types/sizes of ship ineligible for, or exempt from, registration?

Yes:

(a)   Ships under six metres in length are not registrable under the Merchant Shipping Act.

(b)   Ships registered under the Malta Maritime Authority Act, 1991 not exceeding 24 metres in length shall be exempted from registry and such ships, if not registered elsewhere and if owned wholly by persons habitually resident in Malta or by bodies corporate established under and subject to the laws of Malta and having their principal place of business in Malta, shall also be deemed to be Maltese ships.

2   What, if any, is the maximum age for registration of ships under the flag of Malta?

No ship shall be registered otherwise than by or with the express permission of the Registrar if the completion of her first construction occurred more than 25 years before the commencement of the year in which application for registration is first made under the Merchant Shipping Act.

C   Names

1   What, if any, are the restrictions on the name under which a ship may be registered in Malta?

The name proposed for a ship to be registered may be refused if it is already the name of a registered Maltese ship or a name so similar as to be calculated to deceive.

2   Is there a procedure for approval of names in advance?

Yes, see C3 below.

3   If so, how does it operate? Does approval confer any priority rights on the use of the name?

The owner of a ship intending to register that ship in Malta, may, on payment of such fee as may be prescribed on application to the Registrar, reserve the proposed name of the ship for a maximum period of three months. Once a name is reserved it cannot be used by any person but the applicant.

D   New registration procedure

1   *Where may ships intending to fly the flag of Malta be registered*

    1.1   *in Malta?*

    1.2   *abroad?*

Ships intending to fly the Maltese flag must be registered in the Registry of Ships at the Directorate, Malta.

2   *What documents and information must be submitted to effect registration?*

Registration takes place in two stages. The vessel is first provisionally registered following which it is registered permanently.

The following is a list of the principal requirements for provisionally registering a vessel in Malta:

    (a)   an Application for the Registration of a Vessel under the Malta Flag, giving the vessel's descriptive details including:

        (i)   present name, or if a change of name is intended, the proposed name (a name may be reserved beforehand);

        (ii)   propulsion (steam or motor);

        (iii)   service (dry cargo, tanker, pleasure yacht and so on);

        (iv)   has the vessel ever been registered in Malta?

        (v)   country under laws of which the ship was last documented;

        (vi)   Classification Society;

        (vii)   proposed date of registry;

        (viii)   port where ship will be at time of registry;

        (ix)   number of seamen and apprentices for whom accommodation is certified;

        (x)   gross tonnage;

        (xi)   net tonnage;

        (xii)   length (metres);

        (xiii)   breadth (metres);

        (xiv)   depth (metres);

        (xv)   framework;

        (xvi)   number of decks;

        (xvii)   number of masts;

        (xviii)   number of bulkheads;

        (xix)   where and when built;

        (xx)   full name and full address of builders;

        (xxi)   number, type and description of engines;

        (xxii)   number of cylinders;

        (xxiii)   horsepower;

        (xxiv)   full name and full address of engine makers;

        (xxv)   name and office address of ship's manager (including telephone, telex and fax numbers); and

        (xxvi)   description of stem and stern.

(b)   a copy of the proposed crew list accompanied by the Maltese Endorsements (when available) in terms of STCW 1978 (as amended); or certified true copies of the passport issued by the state of nationality of the Master and officers; or their seaman's passports; medical certificates; Master and officers' certificates of competency and relative endorsements under the said Convention; one colour photograph of Master and officers; and relative funds for obtaining the required Maltese Endorsement;

(c)   an application for the issuance of a Minimum Safe Manning Certificate in respect of a Malta-flagged vessel, duly completed;

(d)   a fax copy of the current International Tonnage Certificate in terms of the 1969 Convention (that is, the certificate of the flag prior to the Malta flag);

(e)   a fax from the vessel's Classification Society addressed and sent to the Registrar-General of Shipping and Seamen (the 'Registrar') indicating:

    (i)   the current name and Class ID No.;

    (ii)   the IMO Number;

    (iii)   the Class notation (that is, bulk carrier, oil tanker, chemical tanker or passenger vessel) held by the vessel;

    (iv)   the validity dates of all the statutory (Load Line, SOLAS and MARPOL) certificates held by the vessel; and

    (v)   a clear specification of any exemptions and/or conditions granted to the said statutory certificates; if no exemptions and/or conditions have been granted under the current flag jurisdiction, this must be clearly indicated by Classification Society;

(f)   a fax from the Classification Society entrusted with the certification in terms of the ISM Code, attaching a copy of the current DOC Certificate held by the intended technical managers of the vessel undertaking to carry out the necessary audits and to issue the relevant SMC Certificate to the vessel upon transfer of ownership or flag;

(g)   in the case of vessels intended to carry 1,000 tons of oil or more as cargo, a faxed copy of the Blue Card issued by the relevant P&I club to permit issuance of CLC Certificate;

(h)   for the Provisional Ship Radio Station Licence, the AAIC number of the Accounting Authority entrusted with the handling of radio traffic accounts;

(i)   funds for payment of registration fees and other ancillary fees and charges; and

(j)   confirmation that legal title of the vessel has passed to the owner free from encumbrances (or otherwise); a faxed copy of the Bill of Sale from the last registered owner to the present owner and a fax copy of the Transcript or Extract of Register from the out-going flag administration would normally suffice for this purpose.

3   Does the legal system in Malta lay down any specific requirements as to the contents of any of these documents for example, of Bills of Sale – and, if so, what are they?

The Merchant Shipping Forms Regulations, Subsidiary Legislation 234.04 contains the specific formats required for each document.

4   Please identify how many originals or copies of each document are required. Are fax copies of any of them acceptable?

One copy of each of the documents mentioned in D2 above is required. The application for registration of a ship needs to be signed in original by the owners or their appointed representatives in Malta as is the Declaration of Ownership. Fax copies of the load line and other safety certificates are enough. A fax copy of the confirmation by the classification society will suffice.

5   Are there any requirements as to the language in which documents must be submitted?

Applications for the registration of a ship and Declarations of Ownership should be submitted in English or in Maltese.

6   If they may be submitted in a foreign language, are there any translation requirements? If so, what are they and when must they be complied with?

Not applicable

7   Please identify any particular requirements of the legal system in Malta with regard to the method of execution of any of the registration documents, or with regard to notarisation or legalisation.

With regards to the Declaration of Ownership, such Declaration is usually signed by an authorised representative in Malta at the Registry of Ships in the presence of a Registry official.

The corporate authorities empowering representatives to carry out the registration procedures are to be signed and witnessed by a lawyer whose signature is then confirmed by an Honorary Consul of Malta. These may alternatively, be notarised and apostilled.

Bills of Sale need to be signed in the presence of a witness.

8   If the initial registration takes place abroad, is that registration final or provisional?

Not applicable.

9   If provisional, what needs to be done to effect final registration? When must it be done?

In order to qualify for 'permanent' registration status, the following requirements must be satisfied:

      (a)   Within one month of provisional registration, renewable for good reason by another one month, the following documents must be presented:

            (i)   the Deletion Certificate (original) from the previous Register, translated into the English Language as necessary;

            (ii)   the (original) Bill or Bills of Sale transferring legal title of ownership from the last registered owner appearing on the previous Register to the current owner; and

            (iii)   the vessel's Carving and Marking Note, duly endorsed as required.

      (b)   Within six months of provisional registration, renewable for good reason for an aggregate of another six months, the following documents must be presented:

            (i)   a Radio Licence Application Form, duly completed with all the descriptive particulars of the equipment installed on board, together with a copy of the current valid Safety Radio Certificate and accompanying Form R as issued to the vessel by its Classification Society;

(ii)   a certified copy of the International Tonnage Certificate as issued to the vessel in terms of the 1969 Convention on behalf of the Government of Malta and an original Certificate of Survey issued in respect of the vessel in terms of Section 14 of the Merchant Shipping Act;

(iii)   confirmation by Classification Society (by fax to the Registrar) of the validity of the statutory certificates as issued to the vessel on behalf of the Government of Malta; and

(iv)   the owners' or technical managers' undertaking to return the Provisional Certificate of Malta Registry to the Registrar as soon as possible, and, in any case, within 30 days of receipt of the Permanent Certificate.

A Permanent Certificate of Malta Registry is not quite what it implies: it is only valid for one year and is renewable annually on payment of the relative fee. A Classification Society would also be required to send a fax or telex to the Registry of Ships updating the validity dates of all the statutory (Load Line, SOLAS and MARPOL) certificates, including those required under the ISM Code. If another Classification Society is entrusted with certification under the Code, then, a separate confirmation to the Registry of Ships would have to be sent by fax or telex.

10   *If provisional, what, if any, are the restrictions which apply to the vessel pending final registration?*

No restrictions apply. But a provisional vessel should be registered permanently within six months, which period may be extended to a maximum of 12 months from date of provisional registration.

11   *Can a provisionally registered ship be mortgaged?*

Yes, a provisionally registered ship can be mortgaged.

E   Technical Matters

1   *Please identify the requirements of Malta with regard to inspection, survey, measurement and the like in respect of newly registered ships.*

Apart from the requirements mentioned in Section D above, the Directorate has introduced the following compulsory provisions:

(a)   As a rule, trading vessels of 25 years and over will not be registered while applications for the registration of trading vessels of less than 25 years will be considered subject to:

(i)   the vessel being either in class or in the process of being classed with a recognised classification society;

(ii)   the receipt of an up-to-date class survey status report or information on the validity of the current statutory certificates including details of any existing exemptions and/or conditions, relating to both class and statutory certificates.

(b)   Registration of trading vessels of 20 years and over but less than 25 years will also be subject to the outcome of a prior inspection by an authorised flag state inspector; the Directorate may require the inspection to be carried out in dry-dock; where the Directorate allows the inspection to be carried out on registration, only a non-operational Provisional Certificate of Registry will be issued.

(c)   Vessels of 15 years and over but less than 20 years shall also be presented for an inspection by an authorised flag state inspector within one moth of registration; owners may opt to have their vessel inspected prior to registration.

(d)   A negative outcome of an inspection of a registered vessel may lead to the immediate closure of the vessel's register.

(e)   Pre-registration inspections, even when allowed to be carried out on registration, are subject to a charge of LM1,000.

(f)   Inspections within one month of registration of vessels of less than 5,000 net tons are subject to a LM500 charge; there is still no charge for vessels of 5,000 net tons and over.

(g)   Payment to the Directorate of the charge must be made prior to the authorisation of the inspection; the charges quoted above are payable on a one-off basis; however, unforeseen costs not included in these amounts, such as higher inspection fees, travel expenses, supplementary inspections and the like, are charged separately by the Directorate.

(h)   The final decision on a vessel's seaworthiness and acceptability for registration remains exclusively at the discretion of the Directorate.

Note: Each Malta-flagged vessel needs to be issued with a Continuous Synopsis Record ('CSR'). Such record is not a pre-requisite to registration, however, it is in the interest of the vessel to have a valid CSR issued by the flag state as quickly as possible as the vessel will only be allowed to operate under the CSR of its previous flag for three months after its deletion from that flag. To obtain the CSR under the Malta flag the following documents are required:

(a)   copy of the valid International Safety Management Certificate issued by an authorised Classification Society following the authorisation by the Malta flag to issue the statutory safety certificates in its name (ref to H2 below);

(b)   copy of the valid International Ship Security Certificate issued by an authorised Classification Society following the authorisation by the Malta flag to issue the statutory safety certificates in its name (refer to H2 below); and

(c)   copies of all previous CSRs issued by other flag states, in particular the last CSR issued by the flag immediately prior to the Malta flag containing the date of deletion of the vessel from the Register of such flag.

2   *By when must these requirements be complied with?*
See Sections D and E1 above.

F   Transfer of Ownership

1   Please answer, either separately or by reference to your earlier answers, the questions listed under Section D and E above in respect of a transfer of ownership of a vessel already registered in Malta.

A registered ship or a share therein shall be transferred by a Bill of Sale. The Bill of Sale shall contain such description of the ship as is contained in the surveyor's certificate or some other description sufficient to identify the ship to the satisfaction of the Registrar, and shall be executed by the transferor in the presence of, and attested by, a witness or witnesses.

For this purpose, corporate authorities of both sellers and buyers will have to be produced to the Registrar. It is usual for sellers to appoint a representative to sign, execute and deliver a Bill of Sale on the basis of a Power of Attorney issued for that purpose.

The transferee shall not be entitled to be registered as owner thereof until he, or in the case of a body corporate, the person authorised to make declarations on behalf of that body corporate, has made a declaration referring to the ship and containing (a) a statement of qualification of the transferee to own a Maltese ship, or, if a body corporate, of such circumstances as prove it to be qualified to own a Maltese ship; and (b) a declaration that, to the best of his knowledge and belief, no unqualified person or body of persons is entitled as owner to any interest in the ship or share therein.

Transfer of the vessel does not affect the validity of any mortgage security attaching to it though it is clear that an unauthorised transfer usually constitutes an event of default in terms of the security documentation.

If in the mortgage, the mortgagee prohibited the mortgagor from transferring the vessel to third parties without his express consent, the Registrar is bound not to register the transfer (except in the case of a court-ordered sale).

Upon entry of a transfer of a registered ship or a share therein in favour of a person qualified to own a Maltese ship the Registrar shall notify accordingly the holder of any registered mortgage.

The vessel's official number and call sign remain the same. The only changes entered on the vessel's register are the name and address of the new owner. If the permanent registration procedure was, at the time of the registration of the transfer, still incomplete, the new owners would have to satisfy the outstanding requirements.

On transfer a new certificate of registry is usually not issued, but the Registrar does issue, on request, a certificate confirming the change of ownership.

The new owners are also bound to apply for a new radio licence by the completion of the relative survey form, regardless of the fact that a licence may still be current and valid.

The recognised Classification Societies authorised to issue statutory certificates on behalf of the Government of Malta are the following:

(a)   American Bureau of Shipping;
(b)   Bureau Veritas;
(c)   China Classification Society;
(d)   Class NK;
(e)   Det Norske Veritas;
(f)   Germanischer Lloyd;
(g)   Korean Register of Shipping;

(h)   Lloyd's Register of Shipping;

(i)   RINA; and

(j)   Russian Maritime Register of Shipping.

Requests for classification with and certification by any of the Classification Societies listed below are treated on a case by case basis. It is to be noted, however, that the grant of authorisation is closely linked to the principal place of business of the ship operators and the class of the vessel during the previous 12 months:

(a)   Croatian Register of Shipping;

(b)   Hellenic Register of Shipping; and

(c)   Polish Register of Shipping.

2   *Please explain any exchange control or other governmental or regulatory consents required in connection with the sale to a foreign flag of a vessel registered under the flag of Malta.*

No duty on documents is payable in respect of any instrument connected or involved with the sale or transfer of an exempted ship or a sale thereof.

G   Deletion

1   Please outline the procedure for deletion of vessels from the flag of Malta

Voluntary Closure of Registry:

Where the owner of a Maltese ship desires to close the register of a ship he shall make an application to that effect to the Registrar giving all such particulars and information as the Registrar may require for the purpose including the reason for closure and the new registry of the ship.

The Registrar may refuse such application if all liabilities and obligations in respect of the ship towards the Malta Maritime Authority, the Government of Malta and any body corporate established by law, whether for fees, charges, fines or otherwise, have not been paid, and shall refuse such application unless the consent in writing of all mortgagees whose mortgage is duly registered in respect of the ship is produced to him.

A copy of a valid Radio Licence must be also be presented.

Where any such application is acceded to, the Registrar shall make an entry thereof in the register and thereupon the ship shall cease to be a Maltese ship and the registry of the ship shall be considered as closed except so far as relates to any unsatisfied mortgages or privileges entered therein.

Closure of registry on sale of ship pursuant to court sale or sale by mortgagee in possession:

The register will be closed when the purchaser of a ship pursuant to a court sale or to a sale by a mortgagee in possession is not a person who is qualified to own a Maltese ship.

Compulsory closure of registry:

Registration of a ship onto Malta's register will/may be terminated or revoked in the following circumstances:

(a)   where the Minister has ordered such closure in the national interest or in the interest of Maltese shipping;

(b)   where the Registrar has directed such closure if:

(i)   the annual fees have not been duly paid in accordance with the Merchant shipping Act;

(ii)   the formalities in relation to the documents and evidence after provisional registration are not complied with within the maximum periods therein specified;

(iii)   in the event of a registered ship being either actually or constructively lost, taken by the enemy, burnt or broken up, or ceasing, whether by reason of a transfer to persons not qualified to own a Maltese ship or for any other reason, to be a Maltese ship;

(iv)   the owner fails to observe the provisions of the Merchant Shipping Act;

(v)   it is established that the ship will not or cannot be registered under the Merchant Shipping Act;

(vi)   where required, any conditions established by the Minister are not observed for a period in excess of a month;

(vii)   the owner fails to pay any fine imposed under the Merchant Shipping Act, or fails to pay any penalty within one month of their being demanded in writing by the Registrar; or

(viii)   the owner fails to be in possession of a valid certificate of registry, whether provisional or otherwise, for a period in excess of a month.

The Registrar shall give one month's notice in writing to the registered owner and any registered mortgagee of the intention of closure of registry unless the cause of such closure is remedied. The reason for closure and the expiry date for compliance will be specified in such notice.

2   *Please answer, either separately or by reference to your earlier answers, the questions listed under Section D in respect of the deletion, as opposed to new registration of a vessel.*

The documents required to effect deletion are the following:

(a)   a written application to the Registrar informing him of the nationality of the buyers and requesting closure of the register; and

(b)   a copy of a valid Radio Licence for the vessel.

Note: a Deletion Certificate is issued by the Registrar only if the original certificates issued in respect of the previously Malta flagged vessel at the time the vessel was so flagged are all returned.

A 'Deletion' Continuous Synopsis Record will also be issued.

An original request is required and the all original Provisional and Permanent Certificates of Registry issued by the Malta Registry of Ships are required (Renewals of the Certificate of Registry are not required).

The written application for deletion should be in English or in Maltese.

If the application is signed by the Maltese representatives of the Shipping Organisation which owns the vessel, the Power of Attorney empowering the representatives to sign such application must be duly witnessed by an attorney and the attorney's signature must then be certified by an Honorary Consul of Malta. Alternatively, such Power of Attorney may be notarised and apostilled.

There is no such thing as a 'provisional deletion', however, the additional requirements mentioned in the Note above are required for the issuing of a Deletion Certificate.

H   Certificates/transcripts

1   Please identify the certificates and other documents issued to an owner on registration of his ship under the flag of Malta.

On registration, the documents issued by the Registrar (provided the vessel's trading certificates are all valid) are the following:

- (a)   a provisional certificate of registry;
- (b)   a form of first ship's Carving and Marking Note;
- (c)   a standard Maltese crew agreement and list of crew;
- (d)   a Safe-Manning Certificate; and
- (e)   a log book.

Immediately upon registration, the Registrar also issues a fax authorisation to the relevant classification society authorising it to issue safety certificates, or if necessary, to conduct surveys for the purpose, on behalf of the Government of Malta, thus finalising the provisional registration process.

Once the previous copies of the Continuous Synopsis Records have been received, a CSR will also be issued showing the next consecutive number of the Record and stating the date of registration under Malta flag.

2   Please outline the procedure (including fees payable) for obtaining information on the registered ownership of and encumbrances on vessels registered in Malta.

A search over a vessel registered under the Malta flag can be freely conducted. Current fees (for legal and sundry expenses) are LM30.

I   Fees/taxes

1   What fees are currently payable:
- *1.1   on new registration?*
- *1.2   on transfer of ownership?*
- *1.3   on deletion?*

2   What annual or other ongoing fees or taxes are payable in respect of ships registered in Malta?

Initial fees

Net tonnage	Rate per net ton
First 8,000	LM0.10
Additional NT	LM0.03
Minimum Fee: LM50	

Annual fees

Net tonnage	Rate per net ton
First 8,000	LM0.15
Next 2,000	LM0.08
Next 5,000	LM0.06
Next 5,000	LM0.05
Next 10,000	LM0.04
Next 20,000	LM0.03
Excess over 50,000	LM0.02

Minimum Fee: LM75

Other than for the year of first registration, the following annual charges are also payable in respect of non-Maltese seamen serving on board:

First 30 seamen	LMl/seaman/month
Next 70 seamen	LM0.50/seaman/month
Excess over 100 seamen	LM0.20/seaman/month

The annual fee due in respect of any one year for vessels of a net tonnage of 500 and over, and of 20 years of age and over, shall be increased by LM500.

Pre-registration inspection (vessels of 20 years and over) are subject to a minimum charge of LM1,000. Inspections within one month of registration (vessels of 15 years and over but less than 20 years) are subject to a LM500 minimum charge when the total net tonnage is less than 5,000. There is no charge when the net tonnage is 5,000 and over.

Fees for Certificates and Services

Item	LM
Registry of any change in the registered ownership of a registered vessel (transfer of ownership)	100
Registry of any change of name in the registered mortgagee	100
Registration of mortgage or special privilege or registration of any transaction related to a registered mortgage or special privilege	200
Registration of discharge of mortgage for mortgages registered after 1 January 2003	Nil
Registration of discharge of mortgage for mortgages registered before 1 January 2003	100
Registry of any other change in the register of a vessel	50
Endorsement of any certificate of registry	10
Certificate denoting change in the register of a vessel	20
Reservation of name of a vessel	5
Transcript or extract of the register of any one particular vessel	10
Deletion Certificate	20
Certificate of insurance or other financial security in respect of civil liability for oil pollution damage	20
Issue of any other certificate in terms of the Merchant Shipping Act not specified above	20

In addition to the fees specified above, any service requiring the attendance of a Registry official outside the normal hours of business of the Directorate of the Malta Maritime Authority, is subject to a fee as specified hereunder:

Where the service starts during normal working hours   LM10
and finishes within one hour after normal hours
Where the service starts within one hour before normal   LM10
hours and finishes during normal hours

Otherwise, LM10 per hour or part thereof subject to a minimum of three hours; however, if
the service is given on any day between 21.00 hours and 07.00 hours or at any time on
Saturdays, Sundays and Public Holidays, the rate per hour or part thereof shall be LM20
subject to a minimum of three hours.

Additional fees for the provision of services outside the offices of the Directorate, outside harbour, or outside Malta may be established by the Registrar at his discretion.

Should one choose to establish a Maltese Shipping Organisation for the purposes of owning
or operating an exempt ship, the following fees would apply:

Initial	LM
Legal Fees for advice and assistance including drafting of Memorandum	200
and Articles of Association	
Share Capital (if minimum)	100
Company Registry Fee (if minimum share-capital	150
of the equivalent of LM500 is used)	
Registered Office Fee for the first year	200
Disbursements (Faxes, Telephone Calls and so on)	50
Company Books	25
Audit Fee	125
Annual Return	70

Annual	
Annual Return	70
Registered Office	200
Audit Fee	125

J   Parallel registration

1   *Is parallel registration permitted:*

       1.1   Onto Malta's register?

       1.2   If so, what, if any, specific governmental or other consents are required?

Maltese registered vessels are eligible to be bareboat charter registered under the Malta flag
provided that:

       (a)   the vessel is not registered under the Malta flag;

       (b)   the vessel is registered in a compatible registry; and

414

(c)   the vessel is not registered in another bareboat charter registry.

The following documents must also be submitted to the Registrar to his satisfaction:

(a)   an application for bareboat charter registration, giving the descriptive details of the vessel;

(b)   an application for issuance of a Minimum Safe Manning Certificate in respect of the vessel;

(c)   a declaration of bareboat charter made by the charterer or his agent;

(d)   a copy of the bareboat charter agreement (not to be made available for public inspection);

(e)   a faxed copy of the vessel's current International Tonnage Certificate (1969);

(f)   a fax from the vessel's Classification Society, addressed to the Registrar indicating:

    (i)   the current name and Class ID number;

    (ii)   the IMO number;

    (iii)   the Class notation (that is, bulk carrier, oil tanker, chemical tanker, passenger vessel and so on) held by the vessel;

    (iv)   the validity dates of all statutory certificates (Load Line, SOLAS and MARPOL) certificates held by the vessel; and

    (v)   clear specification of any exemptions and/or conditions granted on the said statutory certificates; if no exemptions and/or conditions have been granted under the authority of the underlying registry it must be clearly stated by Class;

(g)   a fax from the classification society entrusted with the certification in terms of the ISM Code, attaching a copy of the current DOC Certificate held by the intended technical managers of the vessel, and undertaking to carry out the necessary audits and issue the relevant SMC Certificate to the vessel immediately upon delivery to the charterer and transfer of flag;

(h)   the AAIC Number of the Accounting Authority entrusted by the charterer with the handling of radio traffic accounts of the vessel for the Provisional Ship Radio Station Licence;

(i)   funds for the payment of the bareboat charter registration fees and ancillary costs and charges;

(j)   an Extract or Transcript of Register of the underlying registration of the vessel containing the descriptive particulars of the vessel, her ownership and, where applicable, all registered mortgages and encumbrances of the vessel;

(k)   the consent in writing for the vessel to be bareboat charter registered in Malta of:

    (i)   the competent authorities of the underlying registry who may be further required by the Registrar to declare that during the period of bareboat charter registration the vessel will not be entitled to fly the flag of the underlying registry;

    (ii)   the owners of the vessel (as registered at the underlying registry); and

    (iii)   all registered mortgagees (if any).

The consent documents under this head must contain notarial certification of each signatory's identity and authority to bind the respective party on whose behalf the signatory acts.

It is important to note that (a) the operation of the vessel falls under the jurisdiction of the bareboat charter registry while (b) all matters of title over the vessel, mortgages and encumbrances continue to be governed by the underlying registry and no mortgages or encumbrances may be registered in the bareboat charter registry.

1.3   *From Malta's register?*

1.4   *If so, what, if any, specific governmental or other consents are required?*

Vessels may be bareboat charter registered in a foreign registry if the Registrar gives his consent in writing in terms of law, provided that:

(a)   the vessel is registered as a Maltese vessel; and

(b)   the bareboat charter registry where the vessel is to be registered is a compatible registry.

The following documents must also be submitted to the Registrar to his satisfaction:

(a)   an application for consent to the bareboat charter registration in the foreign registry made by the Maltese registered owners containing such information as may be required by the Registrar (for example, contact details of the Registrar in the bareboat charter registry);

(b)   the consent in writing to such registration of all registered mortgagees, if any;

(c)   a written undertaking by the owners to surrender the certificate of registry issued under the Merchant Shipping Act within 30 days from entry into the bareboat charter registry;

(d)   a written undertaking by the charterer that the vessel shall not hoist the Malta Flag during the period of the bareboat charter registration, nor show Valletta as the Home Port on her stern; and

(e)   a copy of the bareboat charter agreement.

The consent granted by the Registrar for such bareboat charter registration in a foreign registry has a maximum validity of two years, unless terminated earlier on the lapse of the charterparty; however, the Registrar may (after its lapse) extend the consent for a further period of two years.

Owners are to notify the Registrar of any amendments or modifications to the bareboat charter within 30 days of coming into effect.

No change of name may be effected in the bareboat charter registry. A change of name of the vessel under the Malta Flag may only be approved if the same change is effected in the bareboat charter registry.

The owner must:

(a)   immediately notify the Registrar upon the bareboat charter registration having been effected, and within 30 days surrender the Maltese certificate of registry and deliver an Extract or Transcript of Registry issued by the bareboat charter registry;

(b)   immediately notify the Registrar of the closure or lapse of the bareboat charter registration in the foreign registry, and within 30 days of such closure, deliver to the Registrar an Extract or Transcript of Register showing such closure of the bareboat charter registry; and

(c)   within 15 days from the entry into the bareboat charter registry produce proof to the Registrar that the name of the foreign home port has been marked on the stern of the vessel in lieu of the name Valletta; this would normally be in the form of the Ship's Carving and Marking Note issued by the Registrar of Shipping and endorsed by an attending class surveyor.

Again, it is important to note that (a) the operation of the vessel falls under the jurisdiction of the bareboat charter registry while (b) all matters of title over the vessel, mortgages and encumbrances continue to be governed by the underlying registry and no mortgages or encumbrances may be registered in the bareboat charter registry. The compatible registries for Bareboat Charter Registration are as follows:

(a)   Antigua & Barbuda;
(b)   Bahamas;
(c)   Belize;
(d)   Canary Islands;
(e)   Cayman Islands;
(f)   Cyprus;
(g)   Estonia;
(h)   France;
(i)   Germany;
(j)   Gibraltar;
(k)   Isle of Man;
(l)   Italy;
(m)   Latvia;
(n)   Liberia;
(o)   Madeira International Ship Register;
(p)   Marshall Islands;
(q)   Netherlands Antilles;
(r)   Panama;
(s)   Poland;
(t)   Romania;
(u)   Russian Federation;
(v)   Spain;
(w)   St Vincent & the Grenadines;
(x)   Turkey;
(y)   Ukraine; and
(z)   Vanuatu.

The following registries are compatible only for bareboat charter registration 'out':

(a)   Danish Register of Shipping;
(b)   Danish International Register of Shipping;
(c)   Italian International Ship Register;
(d)   Philippines;
(e)   Portugal; and
(f)   United Kingdom.

2   Is the period of parallel registration limited? If so, is it renewable?

The duration of bareboat charter registration shall be for a period not exceeding the duration of the bareboat charter or the expiry date of the underlying registration, whichever is the shorter period, but in no case for a period exceeding two years.

   The Registrar may, at the request of the charterer or his authorised agent, extend and further extend the registration for the remaining period of the charter or until the expiry date of the underlying registry, whichever is the shorter period, but in no case for a period exceeding two years at a time, provided he has not received any objections to this extension from the appropriate authorities of the underlying registry, the owners and the registered mortgagees, if any, within seven days from the Registrar having informed them of such request for extension.

3   If parallel registration is dependant on the existence of a demise charter, does Malta have a specific definition of demise or bareboat charter for these purposes? If so, what is it?

The Merchant Shipping Act in Section 84A defines 'bareboat charter' as 'the contract for the lease or sub-lease of a ship, hereinafter referred to as charter, for a stipulated period of time, by virtue of which the charterer shall acquire full control and complete possession of the ship, including the right to appoint her master and crew for the duration of the charter but excluding the right to sell or mortgage the ship;'

4   Can/must mortgages on ships parallel registered into Malta's registry also be registered in Malta?

No.

5   Under what circumstances will/may parallel registration of a ship onto Malta's register be terminated or revoked?

Parallel registration of a ship onto Malta's register will/may be terminated or revoked in the following circumstances:

   (a) where the Minister has ordered such closure in the national interest or in the interest of Maltese shipping;

   (b) where the Registrar has directed such closure if:

     (i) the annual fees have not been duly paid in accordance with the Merchant Shipping Act;

     (ii) the formalities in relation to the documents and evidence after provisional registration are not complied with within the maximum periods therein specified;

     (iii) in the event of a registered ship being either actually or constructively lost, taken by the enemy, burnt or broken up, or ceasing, whether by reason of a transfer to persons not qualified to own a Maltese ship or for any other reason, to be a Maltese ship;

     (iv) the owner fails to observe the provisions of the Merchant Shipping Act;

(v)   it is established that the ship will not or cannot be registered under the Merchant Shipping Act;

(vi)   where required, any conditions established by the Minister are not observed for a period in excess of a month;

(vii)   the owner fails to pay any fine imposed under the Merchant Shipping Act, or fails to pay any penalty within one month of their being demanded in writing by the Registrar; or

(viii) the owner fails to be in possession of a valid certificate of registry, whether provisional or otherwise, for a period in excess of a month;

(c)   a voluntary closure of registry has been requested and such request has been acceded to by the Registrar;

(d)   the appropriate authorities of the underlying registry, or the owners, or any of the mortgages, if any, have withdrawn their consent to the bareboat charter registration in Malta;

(e)   the registration in the underlying registry has for any reason been terminated;

(f)   the charter lapses or is terminated by any of the parties to it; or

(g)   the period for which the ship has been bareboat charter registered lapses and no extension has been granted.

K   General

1   Please identify the principal statutes and regulations in Malta governing the registration of ships.

The Merchant Shipping Act, Chapter 234 of the Laws of Malta is the main legislation governing the registration of ships and the Merchant Shipping (Shipping Organisations – Private Companies) Regulations, 2004 is the principal subsidiary legislation.

2   Are there any other matters in the context of registration under the legal system in Malta which you feel should be emphasised.

No

---

* Contributed by Dr David Galea of Ganada & Associates, Valletta, Malta.

Marshall Islands*

A   Ownership

1   What, if any, are the restrictions on ownership of vessels registered under the Marshall Islands flag?

Generally, a Marshall Islands flag vessel must be owned by a citizen or national of the Republic of the Marshall Islands. The term 'citizen' or 'national' is administratively construed to include corporations, limited liability companies, partnerships, limited partnerships and associations of individuals.

The Commissioner or Deputy Commissioner of Maritime Affairs of the Republic of the Marshall Islands is authorised by statute to waive such ownership requirement, and such waiver is routinely granted, where the owner of the vessel qualifies for, secures and maintains registration in the Republic of the Marshall Islands as a 'foreign maritime entity', pursuant to Section 119 of the Marshall Islands Business Corporation Act (the 'BCA') and appoints a qualified registered agent in the manner prescribed by 3.1(1) of the BCA.

A foreign entity whose indenture or instrument of trust, charter, articles of incorporation, agreement of partnership or other document recognised by the foreign state of its creation as the basis of its existence, directly or by force of law comprehends the power to own or operate vessels and confers or recognises its capacity to sue and be sued, may apply to the appropriate Registrar or Deputy Registrar of Corporations to be registered as a foreign maritime entity.

2   If registration by companies is limited to companies incorporated in the Marshall Islands, is a local 'brass-plate' company sufficient or must there be a closer, genuine connection?

A corporation or partnership formed under Marshall Islands law and maintaining a qualified registered agent constitutes a 'citizen' or 'national' for vessel registration purposes, regardless of the citizenship or nationality of its shareholders, directors, officers or partners or the existence of any other connection with the Marshall Islands.

3   If registration by companies incorporated other than in the Marshall Islands is permitted, must a local representative be appointed? If so, are there any restrictions on the identity of that representative?

A non-Marshall Islands corporation which wishes to be registered as a foreign maritime entity must designate a registered agent in the Marshall Islands upon whom process against such corporation or any notice or demand required or permitted by law to be served may be served. If such corporation maintains a place of business in the Marshall Islands such corporation may designate as its agent a resident domestic corporation having a place of business in the Marshall Islands or a natural person, resident of and having a business address in the Marshall Islands. If such corporation does not have a place of business in the Marshall Islands, such corporation must designate as its agent The Trust Company of the Marshall Islands, Inc.

4   Please summarise any restrictions (for example, as to number, nationality, and so on) on
        who may own shares in shipowning companies incorporated in the Marshall Islands.

There are no restrictions on who may own shares in shipowning companies incorporated in
the Marshall Islands.

5   Please explain any exchange control or other governmental or regulatory consents
        required in connection with the ownership of ships registered in the Marshall Islands.

Apart from the citizenship restrictions referred to in A1 above, there are no exchange control
or other governmental or regulatory consents required in connection with the ownership of
ships registered in the Marshall Islands, so long as the vessels otherwise comply with the laws
and regulations of the Republic of the Marshall Islands.

6   Please explain any special rules for any particular type of vessel.

Apart from the trading and age requirements referred to in B1 and B2 below, there are no special rules for registration for any particular type of vessel except for certain types of fishing
vessels. Only those fishing vessels that are operated by an entity resident in the Marshall
Islands and that land their catches solely in the Marshall Islands will be considered for registration. Special local regulations and licensing applies to such vessels.

7   Is there any mandatory registration requirement for certain owners (for example, cit-
        izens of the Marshall Islands)?

Not in the case of vessels not exclusively engaged in coastwise trade or transportation between
atolls, islands and/or ports of the Republic of the Marshall Islands.

B   Eligibility

1   Are any particular types/sizes of ship ineligible for, or exempt from, registration?

The following vessels are ineligible for registration under the Maritime Act 1990, as amended:

  (a)   vessels exclusively engaged in coastwise trade or transportation between
          atolls, islands and/or ports of the Republic of the Marshall Islands;
  (b)   any other vessel not engaged in foreign trade; and
  (c)   any decked commercial fishing vessel or any commercial yacht of less than
          24 metres in length, and any private yacht of less than 12 metres in length.
          The minimum length restrictions noted above may be waived at the discre-
          tion of the Maritime Administrator and vessel may be documented or re-
          documented where:
      (i)   the vessel meets all other applicable requirements for registration;
              and
      (ii)   it has been satisfactorily demonstrated that there is an absolute and
              genuine need for such waiver.

Although seemingly ineligible for registration under the Maritime Act 1990, as
amended, since they are not engaged in foreign trade, yachts have apparently been accepted
for registration on condition that they not carry passengers.

2   *What, if any, is the maximum age for registration of ships under the flag of the Marshall Islands?*

Unless waived by the Maritime Administrator, the maximum age for registration of ships under the laws of the Marshall Islands is 20 years.

C   Names

1   *What, if any, are the restrictions on the name under which a ship may be registered in the Marshall Islands?*

While there are no legal restrictions on the name under which a ship may be registered, as a matter of practice, the Maritime Administrator will not permit a vessel to be registered under a name already assigned to a vessel on the active register.

2   *Is there a procedure for approval of names in advance?*

Yes.

3   *If so, how does it operate? Does approval confer any priority rights in the use of the name?*

The proposed name may be cleared in advance with the Maritime Administrator and, if not already assigned or reserved for another vessel, may be reserved for a period of up to six (6) months for an existing vessel and up to two (2) years for a newbuilding. A name which is reserved may not be used for another vessel.

D   New registration procedure

1   *Where may ships intending to fly the flag of the Marshall Islands be registered:*
    1.1   in your country?
    1.2   abroad?

Applications for registration under the Marshall Islands flag may be submitted to:

    Chief, Vessel Registration Division,
    Marshall Islands Maritime & Corporate Administrators, Inc.,
    c/o International Registries, Inc.,
    437 Madison Avenue, 32nd Floor,
    New York, New York 10022, USA.

Applications may also be submitted to any of the other offices of the Marshall Islands Maritime & Corporate Administrators, Inc. located in Reston (Virginia), Fort Lauderdale, London, Tokyo, Piraeus and Hong Kong, Singapore and Shanghai.

2   *What documents and information must be submitted to effect registration?*

The following documents and information must be submitted to effect registration:
    (a)   application for registration of vessel;
    (b)   authority of agent or officer of the owner to make such application;
    (c)   proof of ownership as evidenced by:
        (i)   in the case of an existing vessel, a Bill of Sale;

(ii)   in the case of a newbuilding, a Builder's Certificate or Master Carpenter's Certificate;

(iii)   in the case of an existing vessel transferred to Marshall Islands registry without change of ownership, an official certificate of ownership, transcript of register or other acceptable document;

(d)   Continuous Synopsis Record (CSR) File: the CSR is a new record keeping requirement for all SOLAS Ships. It is a document upon which ownership and operational information shall be provided. It must be on board all SOLAS vessels and it must be kept up to date. Therefore vessel registration procedures shall require the submission of a copy of the vessel's current complete CSR File certified by the flag administration from which the vessel is being transferred along with an Amendment Form and a new Index of Amendments. The Administration shall in turn, upon receipt of the last CSR from the losing flag administration, issue a new CSR Document;

(e)   confirmation of class and Classification Society Statement or Affidavit, both dated not more than 10 days prior to registration; Survey Reports of Classification Society for vessels that are 15 years of age or older;

(f)   application for Minimum Safe Manning Certificate (MSMC);

(g)   ISM Code Declarations of Company and Designated Person(s): The ISM Code means the 'International Management Code for the Safe Operation of Vessels and for Pollution Prevention.' Now that the ISM Code is in effect, it becomes necessary for the flag State to verify and maintain company and vessel compliance. ISM and MSMC applications cannot be executed by an attorney-in-fact, but must be executed by the Chief Executive Officer and/or the Designated Person of a Company;

(h)   ISPS Code Declaration of Company Security Officer (CSO): The ISPS Code means the 'International Ship and Port Facility Security' Code. The Company shall appoint a Company Security Officer and shall provide the Administration with the full name of the CSO and information to enable direct and immediate contact at all times between the Administration and the CSO with regard to matters related to the ISPS Code;

(i)   proof from present state of registry of:

      (i)   consent to transfer; and

      (ii)   freedom from recorded liens;

(j)   proof of liability insurance;

(k)   oath of Owner (If the vessel owner is *not* an entity, he/she must submit an Oath of a Managing Owner or Part Owner); and

(l)   registration fees and tonnage taxes.

3   *Does the Marshall Islands legal system lay down any specific requirements as to the contents of any of these documents – for example, of Bills of Sale – and, if so, what are they?*

With respect to the documents listed in D2 above:

(a)   the Application for registration must be submitted on Form MI 101A;

(b)   the authority of agent or officer of the owner should be submitted in the form of a Power of Attorney, or a secretary's certificate of corporate resolutions, authorizing one or more named persons to act on behalf of the owner in making application for registration of the vessel and to perform all acts necessary to accomplish the same;

(c)   the Bill of Sale, a Builder's Certificate or Master Carpenter's Certificate does not have to be in any specific form except that, Bills of Sale, Master Carpenter's or Builder's Certificates which are to be recorded shall be submitted in one (1) original and two (2) duly executed and acknowledged counterparts or at least in two (2) executed and acknowledged originals and two (2) facsimile copies. If the Bill of Sale submitted for recording evidences a transfer of ownership for a vessel already registered under the Maritime Act, at least one (1) original Bill of Sale shall have a copy of the vessel's current Certificate of Registry of the Republic of The Marshall Islands attached to it. One (1) of the printed forms of a Bill of Sale commonly seen and approved by the international maritime community is acceptable for recordation;

(d)   the Certificate of Confirmation of Class must be issued by one of the following societies:

(i)   American Bureau of Shipping;
(ii)   Bureau Veritas;
(iii)   China Classification Society;
(iv)   Det norske Veritas;
(v)   Germanischer Lloyd;
(vi)   Korean Register of Shipping;
(vii)   Lloyd's Register of Shipping;
(viii) Nippon Kaiji Kyokai;
(ix)   Registro Italiano Navale;
(x)   Russian Maritime Register of Shipping; and
(xi)   Hellenic Register of Shipping – yachts only;

(e)   proof of the consent of the state of registry from which the vessel is being transferred in the form of a document approving transfer of the vessel to the Marshall Islands flag in the ownership of the shipowner. If actual proof of the vessel's cancellation from her present registry is submitted, then proof of consent is not required. If the government of the present registry does not issue a consent, then an affirmation to that effect, given by a person admitted to the practice of law in the state of the present registry, may be required in lieu of proof of consent;

(f)   proof that the vessel is free of recorded liens is required in the form of an official statement issued by the state of registry from which the vessel is being transferred;

(g)   proof of liability insurance may take the form of a cover note issued by one of the International Group of P&I clubs and should cover any default of the owner of its repatriation obligations under Section 183 of the Maritime Act 1990;

(h)   the Oath of Owner should be submitted on Form MI 103; and

(i)   registration fees and tonnage taxes are payable in US dollars.

*4   Please identify how many originals or copies of each document are required. Are fax
         copies of any of them acceptable?*

In order to be recordable, it is necessary to furnish one original and two photocopies of the Bill of Sale. If the Bill of Sale is not to be recorded, then a faxed copy of the Bill of Sale will be acceptable for initial registration. In the case of re-registration, the Bill of Sale must be recorded. One (1) copy of any instrument transferring title to a vessel is required for the purpose of a vessel's registration. Powers of Attorney or other evidence of authorisation should be submitted in the original or one (1) certified copy, plus three (3) copies. Application forms and related documents may, when time is short, be transmitted by facsimile or e-mail to any office of Marshall Islands Maritime and Corporate Administrators, Inc. Such facsimiles will be temporarily accepted upon an undertaking, which must state that the original forms will be delivered in due course, and not later than five (5) business days after their facsimile transmittal.

5   Are there any requirements as to the language in which documents must be submitted?

All registration documents must be submitted in English or, if not in English, must be accompanied by a certified English translation thereof.

*6   If they may be submitted in a foreign language, are there any translation require-
         ments? If so, what are they and when must they be complied with?*

All documents submitted in a foreign language should be accompanied by a certified English translation thereof prepared by a certified translator or an attorney.

*7   Please identify any particular requirements of your legal system with regard to the
         method of execution of any of the registration documents, or with regard to notarisa-
         tion or legalisation.*

All registration documents should be executed by a duly authorised signatory of the owner. As noted above, if the Bill of Sale is to be recorded it must have an acknowledgement. If a Power of Attorney authorising execution and delivery of the MI forms and Bill of Sale is furnished as proof of authority, it should be notarised in accordance with the Marshall Islands Maritime Regulations. There is no need for legalisation or apostille. Certain of the Marshall Islands forms require notarisation but not legalisation or apostille.

8   If the initial registration takes place abroad, is that registration final or provisional?

All initial registrations, whether at the New York offices of Marshall Islands Maritime & Corporate Administrators, Inc. or abroad, are provisional.

9   If provisional, what needs to be done to effect final registration? When must it be done?

A provisional certificate of registry issued upon new registration will be valid for a period of 12 months from the date of registration. A request for a permanent certificate of registration should be submitted with supporting documentation to:

Chief, Vessel Document Division,
Marshall Islands Maritime & Corporate Administrators, Inc.,
11495 Commerce Park Drive Reston,
Virginia 20191-1507, USA,

or any other office of Marshall Islands Maritime and Corporate Administrators, Inc.

The following documents must accompany any request for permanent registration:

(a) Certified copy of the vessel's current classification certificates. The certificates must show (i) the present name of the vessel and (ii) the home port as Majuro, Marshall Islands.

(b) Marshall Islands Certificate of Tonnage Measurement (either National or 1969 Convention). This Certificate is to be signed and accepted on the Certificate by the Shipowner, his authorized agent or Master.

(c) Marshall Islands Load Line Certificate, which must be issued in compliance with the International Convention on Load Lines, 1966, as amended by the 1969 Protocol and must be full term and valid.

(d) Marshall Islands certificates issued under the provisions of the International Convention for the Prevention of Pollution from Ships (MARPOL 73/78), Annex I through VI. The International Oil Pollution Prevention (IOPP) and/or the Noxious Liquid Substances (NLS) certificates must be full term and valid.

(e) Marshall Islands certificates issued under the provisions of the International Convention for the Safety of Life at Sea (SOLAS), 1974, as amended. The certificate covering the requirements of the Convention for Safety Construction, Safety Equipment, Safety Radio, Carriage of Grain, Bulk Chemicals and Gas, Safety Management, Security and so on, must be full term and valid.

(f) Marshall Islands National or International Maritime Organization Code or Resolution Certificates. These certificates may be required for vessels under 500 gross tons, or non-propelled vessels, fishing vessels, Mobile Offshore Drilling Units, or other vessels not covered by the SOLAS Certificates.

(g) Report of Satisfactory Completion of Marshall Islands Safety Inspection. An initial Safety Inspection is required within 30 days (90 days for mobile offshore units and support equipment) after the date of registration or, where both the owner and management of the vessel have been changed, the date of re-registration.

(h) Marshall Islands Ship Radio Station License. The License will be issued upon application to the Chief, Radio Communications Division, Marshall Islands Maritime & Corporate Administrators, Inc.

(i) Certificate of cancellation of vessel's former registry. (To be submitted within 30 days of the date of the vessel's initial registration).

(j) Civil Liability Certificate for Oil Pollution Damage (1969). (This Certificate is only required for vessels with more than 2,000 tons of oil as cargo).

426

(k)   Owner's Acceptance of Certificate of Tonnage Measurement. (Only required in case of re-registration of an existing vessel where ownership has changed and there already exists a Marshall Islands Certificate of Tonnage Measurement).

(l)   Minimum Safe Manning Certificate: This document is administered by Seafarers' Documentation in Reston, Virginia, USA.

(m)   ISM Code Declarations of Company and Designated Person and ISPS Code Declaration of Company Security Officer. These documents are to be submitted at registration or shortly thereafter.

(n)   Continuous Synopsis Record (CSR) File: a complete CSR File consisting of a certified copy of the vessel's CSR File provided by the flag administration from which the vessel was transferred along with an Amendment Form, a new Index of Amendments and a new revised CSR Document is required.

(o)   Affirmation Re: Markings. (Only required when the vessel has undergone a change in name.)

10   *If provisional, what, if any, are the restrictions which apply to the vessel pending final registration?*
There are no restrictions that apply to the vessel pending permanent registration.

11   *Can a provisionally registered ship be mortgaged?*
A provisionally registered ship may be mortgaged.

E   Technical matters

1   *Please identify the requirements of the Marshall Islands with regard to inspection, survey, measurement and the like in respect of newly registered ships.*
See E2 below.

2   *By when must these requirements be complied with?*
A safety inspection is required within 30 days after either the date of registration or, if both the owner and management of the vessel have been changed, the date of re-registration. An application for safety inspection will provide the proposed port and date of inspection, estimated time of arrival of the vessel and agent identification. The application is to be submitted to:

Chief, Safety Evaluation Division,
Marshall Islands Maritime & Corporate Administrators, Inc.,
11495 Commerce Park Drive, Reston,
Virginia 20191-1507, USA;
Telefax: 703-476-8522; Telex: 248736 or 275501

A Marshall Islands Certificate of Tonnage Measurement (either national or 1969 Convention) is required at the time of registration. See D9(b) and (k) above.

F   Transfer of ownership

1   Please answer, either separately or by reference to your earlier answers, the questions listed under Section D and E above in respect of a transfer of ownership of a vessel already registered in the Marshall Islands.

An application for re-registration of a vessel already registered under the Marshall Islands flag should be submitted to the Chief, Vessel Registration Division, Marshall Islands Maritime & Corporate Administrators, Inc. at the address mentioned in D1 above.

The following documents and information must be submitted to effect re-registration:

      (a)   Certificate of Permission for Sale for the Purpose of Re-registration (issued by the Chief, Vessel Registration Division, upon application of the seller). Although such request must be submitted in writing, no formal 'Request Form' is utilised;

      (b)   Application for registration of vessel (Form 101-A);

      (c)   Authority of agent or officer of buyer to make such application;

      (d)   if buyer is not an incorporated company, an Oath of Owner, Managing Owner or Part Owner on form MI 103;

      (e)   Bill of Sale (to which should be affixed a copy of the vessel's existing Certificate of Registry);

      (f)   CSR Amendment Form and a new Index of Amendments;

      (g)   Confirmation of Class and Classification Society Statement or Affidavit, dated not more than 10 days prior to registration; Survey Reports of Classification Society for vessels that are 15 years of age or older;

      (h)   proof of liability insurance; and

      (i)   re-registration fees.

The same requirements with respect to forms, numbers of copies, language, translations and method of execution of documents apply to re-registration as they do to initial registration.

2   Please explain any exchange control or other governmental or regulatory consents required in connection with the sale to a foreign flag of a vessel registered under the flag of the Marshall Islands.

There are no exchange control or other governmental or regulatory consents required in connection with the sale to a foreign flag of a vessel registered under Marshall Islands flag other than obtaining a Certificate of Permission to Transfer. See G1 below.

G   Deletion

1   Please outline the procedure for deletion of vessels from the flag of the Marshall Islands.

In order to delete a vessel from the Marshall Islands registry, a written request for a Certificate of Permission to Transfer must first be submitted by the vessel owner to:

      Chief, Vessel Document Division,

      Marshall Islands Maritime & Corporate Administrators, Inc.,

      11495 Commerce Park Drive, Reston,

      Virginia 20191-1507, USA.

The request for permission to transfer must include the name and domicile of the buyer as well as the name of the country to which the vessel's registration is to be transferred. If only the vessel's registration is to be transferred, the application should include a request 'for transfer of the vessel to [*name of country*] registry and flag without change of ownership'. If the vessel is subject to one or more preferred ship mortgages, hypothecations, or similar liens, a satisfaction, release or discharge of such lien must be recorded prior to such transfer. Certificates of Permission to Transfer are issued for periods of limited validity. The cost of a Certificate for 90 days is US$200; for 180 days, US$300.

2 *Please answer, either separately or by reference to your earlier answers, the questions listed under Section D in respect of the deletion, as opposed to new registration, of a vessel.*

After a Certificate of Permission to Transfer has been issued, a Certificate of Cancellation of Registry will be issued once the following conditions have been met:

(a) the recordation of a satisfaction, release or discharge of any existing recorded preferred ship mortgage, hypothecation or similar lien that has been recorded;

(b) payment in full of any outstanding fees, penalties or charges of whatever nature due against the vessel or her owner to the Republic of the Marshall Islands; and

(c) submission of the following documents to Marshall Islands Maritime & Corporate Administrators, Inc., Reston, Virginia: current Certificate of Registry; Marshall Islands Ship Radio Station License; and one copy of the Bill of Sale, where a change of ownership has occurred.

H Certificates/transcripts

1 *Please identify the certificates and other documents issued to an owner on registration of his ship under the flag of the Marshall Islands.*

Upon registration of a vessel under the Marshall Islands flag, the owner will receive:

(a) Provisional Certificate of Registry;

(b) temporary ship radio station authority;

(c) letter to whomever it may concern relating to tonnage taxes;

(d) Port Authority Letter;

(e) CSR document for new vessels or CSR Amendment Form and a new Index of Amendments for vessels already registered with the Administration;

(f) Minimum Safe Manning Certificate, a Certificate of Insurance or Other Financial Security in Respect of Civil Liability for Oil Pollution Damage (CLC) for vessels carrying 2,000 tons or more of oil in bulk as cargo, upon receipt and approval of proof of this liability insurance; and

(g) Combined Publications Folder containing Marshall Islands regulations and forms.

2   *Please outline the procedure (including fees payable) for obtaining information on the registered ownership and encumbrances on vessels registered in the Marshall Islands.*

To obtain information on a Marshall Islands registered vessel, an oral or written request to the office of the Marshall Island Maritime & Corporate Administrators, Inc. in New York may be made for a Certificate of Ownership and Encumbrance, the fee for which is US$100.

I   Fees/taxes

1   What fees are currently payable:

    1.1   on new registration?

    1.2   on transfer of ownership?

    1.3   on deletion?

1.1   Initial registration fees:

(a)	Registration fee		US$2,500
(b)	Annual tonnage tax, per net ton		US$0.20
(c)	Annual fee: marine investigation, nautical training and international participation		US$1,000
(d)	Additional for international participations and marine investigations, per gross ton		US$0.03
(e)	Marine Inspection (each)		US$1,500
(f)	Provisional Certificate of Registry		US$200
(g)	Permanent Certificate of Registry (payable at initial registration)		US$200
(h)	Temporary Radio Authority		US$100
(i)	Publications (CPF, Articles, Oil/Cargo Record Book)		US$82
(j)	Initial CSR Document		US$200
(k)	Certification of Articles of Agreement (entire set)		US$100

1.2   Re-registration fees:

(a)	Certificate of Permission for Sale		US$100
(b)	Re-registration charges		US$1,500
(c)	Provisional Certificate of Registry		US$200
(d)	Permanent Certificate of Registry		US$200
(e)	Temporary Radio Authority		US$100
(f)	Recording Bill of Sale		US$100
(g)	Official Forms & Publications		US$82

Note: change of name fees are also payable when the name of a vessel changes on re-registration.

1.3   Deletion:

(a)	Certificate of Permission to Transfer (90 days validity)		US$200
(b)	Certificate of Permission to Transfer (180 days validity)		US$300

Note: the fees indicated in (a) and (b) include the subsequent issuance of a Certificate of Cancellation of Registry.

2	*What annual or other ongoing fees or taxes are payable in respect of ships registered in the Marshall Islands?*

The tonnage taxes and fees referred to in 1.1(b), (c) and (d) are payable annually for all registered vessels.

J   Parallel registration

1	*Is parallel registration permitted:*
1.1	*onto the Marshall Islands register?*
1.2	*from the Marshall Islands register?*

Parallel registration is permitted onto and from the Marshall Islands registry provided a bareboat charter of the vessel is in full force and effect.

2	*If so, what, if any, specific governmental or other consents are required?*

Permission is required from the Chief, Vessel Registration Division for both (i) Marshall Islands bareboat charter registration (into the Marshall Islands registry) and (ii) foreign bareboat charter registration (from the Marshall Islands registry).

3	*Is the period of parallel registration limited? If so, is it renewable?*

The period of bareboat charter registration is limited to two years. It may be renewed for further periods of not more than two years each but not later than the expiration date of the bareboat charter.

4	*If parallel registration is dependent on the existence of a demise charter, does your country have a specific definition of demise or bareboat charter for these purposes? If so, what is it?*

The Republic of the Marshall Islands does not have a specific definition of demise or bareboat charter for the purpose of bareboat charter registration.

5	*Please answer the questions listed under Sections A to E above with reference to application for parallel registration.*

Generally, in order to be eligible for Marshall Islands bareboat charter registration, a vessel must meet all of the requirements for initial registration with the exception of ownership and cancellation from present registry, and the bareboat charterer must meet all of the requirements for an owner of a Marshall Islands registered vessel. The following are specifically required:

(a)	An Application for Registration on form MI 101BCR must be executed by the charterer of the vessel. The information relating to the bareboat charterer should be entered in Items 8, 9 and 10 (Name of Bareboat Charterer(s), Residence and Citizenship). The application should be signed and dated by the charterer and such application with all required supporting documents, fees and tonnage tax should be submitted to one of the offices of Marshall Islands Maritime & Corporate Administrators, Inc.

(b)   The charterer should also submit a letter of request, typed on the letterhead of, and signed by, the charterer of the vessel requesting bareboat charter registration and setting forth:

    (i)   present name and official number of the vessel;

    (ii)   present country of registry of the vessel with address, telex/telefax number of the country's vessel registration office;

    (iii)   names, addresses and telex/telefax numbers of the owner and vessel's manager;

    (iv)   names, addresses and telex/telefax numbers of all holders of any registered mortgages, hypothecations or similar charges upon the vessel and the dates contemplated for commencement, and earliest lawful termination, of the bareboat charterparty.

(c)   The original bareboat charterparty together with all annexes and addenda thereto and any bareboat sub-charterparties, shall be submitted for recording, with English translation if in any other language, and with proof of due execution. Certification may be by a notary public or any other officer authorised to take acknowledgements.

(d)   Any subsequent amendments or addenda to the charterparty or any subsequent bareboat sub-charterparties must be submitted for recording within 30 days of execution with proof of due execution and English translation, where necessary.

(e)   The following documents shall also be included with the Application:

    (i)   an official certificate from the present country of registry setting forth the ownership of the vessel and any recorded encumbrances;

    (ii)   the written consents, with proof of their due execution, of the owner and the mortgagees to the bareboat registration; and

    (iii)   evidence that the present country of registry will withdraw from the vessel the right to fly the flag of that country while the vessel is under bareboat registration.

(f)   The charterer must also submit an Oath of Undertaking duly acknowledged which will include the charterer's undertaking that:

    (i)   the vessel will not fly any flag other than the Marshall Islands flag, nor show any home port other than Majuro, while the vessel is subject to the bareboat charter;

    (ii)   during the period of bareboat registration, the Marshall Islands shall have exclusive jurisdiction and control over the vessel, in its capacity as flag state;

    (iii)   the charterer will immediately notify Marshall Islands Maritime & Corporate Administrators, Inc., whenever the charterparty has been terminated for whatever reason or that another jurisdiction has accorded the vessel the right to fly its flag;

    (iv)   within 30 days of the termination of the bareboat charterparty or the current Marshall Islands Provisional Certificate of Registry, whichever is earlier, the charterer will surrender to the Marshall Islands Maritime & Corporate Administrators, Inc. the Provisional Certificate of Registry and all other certificates issued to the vessel by or on behalf of the Republic of the Marshall Islands; and that by failure to comply with any of the provisions in the Oath of Undertaking, the charterer acknowledges the liability to pay damages in accordance with Section 263 of the Maritime Act 1990, as amended.

(g)   The registration fees and tonnage taxes are the same for bareboat charter registration as those fees charged for an initial registration listed in D2 above.

The following conditions must be satisfied in order to foreign bareboat charter register a vessel:

(a)   Application for Permission for Bareboat Chater Registration in Foreign State: No application form is used. One (1) signed original letter of application should be submitted to one of the offices of Marshall Islands Maritime & Corporate Administrators, Inc., and must include the following information:

(i)   registered name and official number of the vessel;

(ii)   name, address and telex/telefax and telephone numbers of the bareboat charterer;

(iii)   intended service of the vessel, including nature of the cargo and geographical areas to be navigated; and

(iv)   date contemplated for commencement of the bareboat charte-party and the date contemplated for its earliest lawful termination. Also, effective 1 July 2004, a request for the submission of a certified copy of the vessel's CSR File to the bareboat charter registry.

(b)   Consent of Mortgagees: if the vessel is subject to one or more mortgages, the written consent of each mortgagee to the proposed foreign bareboat charter registration, usually in the form of a letter, must be filed with Marshall Islands Maritime & Corporate Administrators, Inc.

(c)   Charterparty: a certified true copy of the bareboat charter, along with all annexes and amendments thereto, must be filed with Marshall Islands Maritime & Corporate Administrators, Inc.

(d)   Owner's Oath of Undertaking: the Owner must submit a letter addressed to Marshall Islands Maritime & Corporate Administrators, Inc. containing an undertaking to surrender to Marshall Island Maritime & Corporate Administrators, Inc., within 60 days of the issuance of the Certificate of Permission for Foreign Bareboat Charter Registration or within 30 days of the date of commencement of the charterparty, whichever is later, any Marshall Islands Certificate of Registry previously issued to the vessel; and must immediately notify Marshall Islands Maritime & Corporate Administrators, Inc., whenever the charterparty has terminated, for whatever reason, or when the owner has otherwise retaken possession of the vessel.

(e)   Agreement between owner and charterer: the owner and the charterer of the subject vessel must enter into an agreement which contains an undertaking by the owner and the charterer:

(i)   that they will neither permit the vessel to fly the flag of the Marshall Islands nor show Majuro as her home port while the vessel remains in the service of the charterer under the bareboat charter and that the vessel shall immediately revert to the jurisdiction and control of the Republic of the Marshall Islands when the charterparty is terminated or expires, or possession and control of the vessel is retaken by the owner; and

(ii)   that the vessel shall be equipped, maintained and navigated to standards which are not less than those contained in Marshall Islands Maritime Act 1990, as amended, the Maritime Regulations and rules including the international conventions to which the Marshall Islands is a party.

(f)   Other conditions:

(i)   the vessel's Marshall Islands Provisional Certificate of Registry and Ship Radio License shall be surrendered to Marshall Island Maritime & Corporate Administrators, Inc., during the bareboat charter registration;

(ii)   if a major casualty occurs during the period of the bareboat charter or the vessel extensively pollutes the environment, the owner and charterer shall facilitate the boarding of the vessel and/or the interviewing of the Master, officers, crew or other witnesses and the gathering of information by an investigating officer representing Marshall Islands registry, whenever deemed necessary; and

(iii)   any subsequent amendments or addenda to the agreement between the owner and charterer or to the charterparty and any subsequent bareboat sub-charterparties with English translations thereof if in a language other than English shall be filed with Marshall Islands Maritime & Corporate Administrators, Inc., together with a letter noting which sections, if any, have been changed or altered together with a letter of consent as to the amendments by the mortgagees of the vessel.

(g)   A fee of US$225 for the issuance of a Certificate of Permission for Foreign Bareboat Registration must be paid by the charterer at the time of registration.

(h)   The annual tonnage tax of US$0.20 per gross ton, the annual fee of US$1,000 for marine inspections, nautical training and international participations, and the additional fee for additional international participations of US$0.03 per gross ton remain applicable to foreign bareboat charter registered vessels.

6   *Can/must mortgages on ships parallel registered into the Marshall Islands registry also be registered in the Marshall Islands?*

Without prejudice to the continuing foreign legal status of a ship mortgage, hypothecation or similar charge made and registered in accordance with the laws of the foreign state, a notice may be recorded in accordance with Chapter 3 of the Maritime Act 1990, as amended, that such mortgage exists.

7   *Under what circumstances will/may the parallel registration of a ship onto the Marshall Islands register be terminated or revoked?*

The grant by a foreign state of the right to fly the flag of such state shall terminate the Marshall Islands bareboat registration of the vessel.

In addition, if the bareboat charterer breaches the undertaking to fly the flag of the Marshall Islands and to show the home port of Majuro, or a vessel while registered under Marshall Islands flag shall be found flying or pretending entitlement to fly the flag of a foreign state without the permission of the Maritime Administrator and the consent of the vessel's mortgagees, if any, the owner and/or the charterer shall be liable for penalties not to exceed US$50,000 which until paid shall constitute a maritime lien on the vessel.

K   General

1   *Please identify the principal statutes and regulations in the Marshall Islands governing the registration of ships.*

The principal statutes with respect to the registration of vessels are the Marshall Islands Maritime Act 1990, as amended, and the Marshall Islands Maritime Regulations made by The Trust Company of the Marshall Islands, Inc. under the authority vested in it as the duly appointed Maritime Administrator by the Maritime Act 1990, as amended.

2   *Are there any other matters in the context of registration of ships under the Marshall Islands legal system which you feel should be emphasised?*

In general, Marshall Islands Maritime & Corporate Administrators Inc. and its staff take a flexible and practical approach in their application of the Maritime Act 1990 and the Maritime Regulations and seek to accommodate the legitimate needs of shipowners.

---

* Contributed by Hadley S. Roe, assisted by Kassandra L. Slangan and Mira Trifunovic, all of Seward & Kissel, New York, United States of America.

Norwegian International Ship Register*

A   Ownership

1   What, if any, are the restrictions on ownership of vessels registered under the flag of the Norwegian International Ship Register ('NIS')?

Pursuant to Section 1 of the Act of 12 June 1987 No. 48 (the 'NIS Act'), NIS is open to all Norwegian and non-Norwegian shipowners. It is not necessary to incorporate a company in Norway for the purpose of registering a vessel in NIS. A vessel may be registered in the ownership of a Norwegian company or a non-Norwegian company. However, for non-Norwegian companies, certain particular rules are applicable to companies incorporated within the European Economic Area (the 'EEA'). A citizen of a jurisdiction within the EEA is hereinafter referred to as an 'EEA citizen', and a limited company incorporated in a jurisdiction within the EEA is hereinafter referred to as an 'EEA company'.

The ownership requirements applicable to Norwegian companies and EEA companies are set out in Section 1 of the Norwegian Maritime Act of 24 June 1994 No. 39 (the 'Maritime Act'). These are satisfied if:

(a)   (i)   the owner is a Norwegian company incorporated in Norway where at least 60 per cent of the equity capital and voting rights are held by Norwegian citizens and/or EEA citizens;

(ii)   its principal place of business is in Norway; and

(iii)   the Chairman of its Board of Directors and a majority of the Directors are Norwegian and/or EEA citizens, residing in Norway or in the relevant EEA jurisdiction and having been so residing for at least two years prior to the date of the company's application for registering the vessel in NIS; or

(b)   (i)   the owner is an EEA company incorporated in a jurisdiction within the EEA where at least 60 per cent of the equity capital and voting rights are held by Norwegian citizens and/or EEA citizens;

(ii)   its principal place of business is in the relevant jurisdiction within the EEA;

(iii)   the Chairman of its Board of Directors and a majority of the Directors are EEA and/or Norwegian citizens, residing in the relevant EEA jurisdiction or in Norway, and having been so residing for at least two years prior to the date of the company's application for registering the vessel in NIS; and

(iv)   the vessel is managed and operated from Norway as part of the EEA company's business activities from a permanent establishment in Norway.

If the owner does not satisfy the requirements set forth in any of paragraphs (a) or (b) above, the NIS Act prescribes that the relevant owning company (irrespective of its jurisdiction of incorporation) must appoint a Norwegian management company for the technical or commercial management of the vessel, and a legal representative in Norway or in the EEA who shall be authorised to receive, on behalf of the owner (i) legal process documents such as claims and suits, and (ii) all communication to the owner from NIS and the Norwegian maritime authorities.

2   If registration by companies is limited to companies incorporated in Norway, is a local 'brass-plate' company sufficient, or must there be a closer, genuine connection?

Registration in the NIS is not limited to companies incorporated in Norway, as described above.

3   If registration by companies incorporated other than in Norway is permitted, must a local representative be appointed? If so, are there any restrictions on the identity of that representative?

As described in A1 above, a legal representative must be appointed if the requirements set forth in Section 1 of the Maritime Act are not satisfied. The legal representative must be a Norwegian or EEA citizen, or a Norwegian or EEA company satisfying the requirements listed in sub-sections (i)–(iii) of paragraphs (a) or (b) (as the case may be) in A1 above.

Additionally, the technical or commercial management of the vessel must be undertaken by a Norwegian management company when the requirements set forth in Section 1 of the Maritime Act are not satisfied.

4   Please summarise any restrictions (for example, as to number, nationality and so on) on who may own shares in vessel owning companies incorporated in Norway.

There are no such restrictions.

5   Please explain any exchange control or other governmental or regulatory consents required in connection with the ownership of vessels registered under NIS flag.

No such consents are required.

6   Please explain any special rules for any particular type of vessel.

There are no special rules for particular types of vessel.

7   Is there any mandatory registration requirement for certain owners (for example, citizens of Norway)?

Section 11 of the Maritime Act prescribes that all Norwegian vessels with an overall length of 15 metres or more must be registered in the Norwegian Ordinary Ship Register ('NOR') or in NIS, provided they meet the registries' requirements.

B   Eligibility

1   Are there any particular types/sizes of vessel ineligible for, or exempt from, registration?

NIS is open for all self-propelled vessels except fishing vessels.

However, NIS registered vessels may not carry cargo or passengers between Norwegian ports, or carry passengers in a regular set route between Norwegian and foreign ports or between Nordic countries. In this respect, oil and gas installations on the Norwegian continental shelf are considered Norwegian ports.

2   What, if any, is the maximum age for registration of vessels on the NIS registry?
There is no maximum age for vessels in the NIS. The Norwegian authorities will, however, carefully consider whether to accept older vessels for registration and may require a survey to establish the vessel's technical standard before accepting it for registration.

C   Names

1   What, if any, are the restrictions on the name under which a vessel may be registered under NIS flag?
Pursuant to Section 7 of the Maritime Act, a vessel's name must clearly distinguish itself from the names of all other registered vessels. Vessels belonging to the same shipowner or shipowning group, may nevertheless have the same name as long as they are indicated with different numbers. Names must not interfere with distinctive naming traditions of other shipowners.

By giving notice to the Norwegian Maritime Directorate, it is possible to reserve a name for newbuildings. The reservation can be made as soon as a contract of purchase or construction is entered into. Reservations may also be made in other situations, if there are reasonable grounds for the request, and then for five years at the time.

2   Is there a procedure for approval of names in advance?
Yes.

3   If so, how does it operate? Does approval confer any priority rights in the use of the name?
The application must be addressed to the Norwegian Maritime Directorate. A reserved name has the same protection as that of a registered vessel.

D   New registration procedure

1   Where may vessels intending to fly the NIS flag be registered:
*   1.1   in Norway?*
*   1.2   abroad?*
1.1   In general, vessels intending to fly the NIS flag can only be registered at NIS's offices in Bergen, Norway. However, documents faxed or sent as pdf copies by e-mail directly from a Norwegian Consulate or Embassy to NIS in Bergen are acceptable as basis for registration. The original documents must then be sent by courier directly from the relevant Norwegian Consulate or Embassy to NIS. This procedure allows for registration of the vessel on the date of delivery of all required documentation to the relevant Consulate or Embassy.
1.2   A Provisional Certificate of Nationality may be issued by a Norwegian Consulate or Embassy upon receipt of instructions from NIS. This certificate will normally allow the vessel to fly the Norwegian flag for five months. If all requirements for permanent registration are fulfilled within this five-month period, the final Certificate of Nationality will be issued by NIS before the expiry date of the Provisional Certificate of Nationality.

2   *What documents and information must be submitted to effect registration?*

The documents and information required will to some extent depend on the specifics of the individual registration. However, for most registrations the following documents are required:

(a)   Name Certificate: the Name Certificate is issued by the Norwegian Maritime Directorate allowing the vessel to use a certain name and call sign. Such certificate is not necessary if, upon any change of ownership to a vessel which is already registered in NIS, there shall be no name change.

(b)   Provisional Certificate of Nationality: the Provisional Certificate of Nationality may be issued by a Norwegian Consulate/Embassy upon receipt of instructions from NIS. This document is not strictly necessary for re-registrations in NIS (that is, no change of flag). As described in D1.2 above, this certificate will normally allow the vessel to fly the Norwegian flag for five months. If all requirements for permanent registration are fulfilled within this five-month period, the final Certificate of Nationality will be issued by NIS before the expiry date of the Provisional Certificate of Nationality. Before issuing the Provisional Certificate of Nationality the local Norwegian Consul or Embassy representative must receive confirmation from a recognised classification society that the vessel has valid certificates. NIS only recognises the following five classification societies:

(i)   Det Norske Veritas;

(ii)   Lloyd's Register;

(iii)   American Bureau of Shipping;

(iv)   Bureau Veritas; and

(v)   Germanischer Lloyd.

(c)   International Tonnage Certificate: a copy of the International Tonnage Certificate, certified by the vessel's Classification Society as true and appropriate for NIS registration purposes, is sufficient. This requirement only applies when a vessel enters NIS from a foreign register.

(d)   The NIS Application Form: the NIS application form must be signed by the owner or an authorised representative or signatory of the owner. For a non-Norwegian owner, the form shall be signed by its legal representative (see A1 and A3 above).

(e)   Corporate documentation: for Norwegian companies, an updated company certificate ('Firmaattest') is sufficient. For foreign companies, the exact requirements vary depending on the country of incorporation, but the following aspects must be covered:

(i)   name;

(ii)   registered office;

(iii)   business address of the head office;

(iv)   type of company;

(v)   place of registration;

(vi)   share capital;

(vii)   name, address and date of birth of board members and general manager, if any; and

439

        (viii)   details concerning the authority to sign for the company with legally binding effect.

Please see D7 concerning the requirements for notarisation and legalisation of signatures.

Companies which do not satisfy the Norwegian ownership requirements described in A1 above, must also produce copies of the management agreement between themselves and a Norwegian management company and the legal representative engagement letter, duly counter-signed by the relevant legal representative.

(f)   Bill of Sale: an original Bill of Sale or, in the event of a newbuilding, an original Builder's Certificate accompanied by a copy of the duly signed Protocol of Delivery and Acceptance, must be provided. No specific form is required, but the names of the parties and particulars of the vessel must be clear. Please see D7 concerning the requirements for certification or notarisation and legalisation of signatures.

(g)   Certificate of Deletion: an original Certificate of Deletion issued by the vessel's previous registry is required. This document must show the name and ownership of the vessel in the previous registry, and also contain a notation to the effect that the vessel has been deleted from the previous registry free from registered encumbrances. As it is not always possible to obtain this information from the previous registry in one document and/or on the closing date, NIS has in practice accepted certain modifications to this particular requirement. The details in each individual case should be clarified with NIS in advance.

(h)   Declaration of Nationality: this document is required only for vessels owned by Norwegian companies or EEA companies and is a declaration to the effect that the requirements set out in Section 1 of the Maritime Act are met.

(i)   Guarantee for payment to crew: the owner must lodge a guarantee covering liability for crew wages and repatriation costs, should the owning company go bankrupt. The guarantee must be in the minimum amount of NOK2m for cruise and passenger vessels and NOK500,000 for other vessels. Under certain conditions a lower guarantee amount may be accepted for smaller vessels. The guarantee can be issued either by the Norwegian Shipowners' Association, if the shipowner is a member, or by an approved bank, insurance company or the like.

3   *Does the legal system in Norway lay down any specific requirements as to the contents of any of these documents (for example, of Bills of Sale) and, if so, what are they?*

See D2 for reference to each document.

4   *Please identify how many originals or copies of each document are required. Are fax or pdf copies of any of them acceptable?*

An original of each of the documents listed in D2(a), (d), (e), (h) and (i), and a copy of the document referred to in D2(c), should be filed with NIS before the closing date. The documents referred to in D2(f) and (g) can be faxed or sent as pdf copies to NIS on the date of closing. However, fax or pdf copies of these documents are only acceptable as basis for registration in NIS if the originals are delivered to a Norwegian Consulate/Embassy and faxed or sent by e-mail to NIS directly from the relevant Consulate/Embassy. The original documents must subsequently be sent by courier from the relevant Norwegian Consulate/ Embassy to NIS.

5   *Are there any requirements as to the language in which documents must be submitted?*
Pursuant to Section 17 of the Regulations Concerning Registration of Vessels in NIS of 30 July 1992 (the 'Regulations to the NIS Act'), the documents must, as a general rule, be in Norwegian, Danish, Swedish or English. If deemed necessary, NIS has the right to require translation of any particular document into Norwegian. NIS accepts to record documents written in a language other than those mentioned above, if a certified translation is enclosed and the registrar has no doubt about the contents.

6   *If they may be submitted in a foreign language, are there any translation requirements? If so, what are they and when must they be complied with?*
For requirements that apply for languages, please see D5. If translation of any particular document shall be required by NIS, the translation must be completed before registration of the relevant document. The translation must be done by a certified translator. Furthermore, the signature of the translator must be notarised and legalised. The registry may also approve a translation confirmed by a Norwegian lawyer or a civil servant of the foreign services.

7   *Please identify any particular requirements of the legal system in Norway with regards to the method of execution of any of the registration documents, or with regard to notarisation or legalisation.*
Signatures on Powers of Attorney or documents establishing the owner's title to the vessel such as a Bill of Sale or a Builder's Certificate must be certified.
      For Norwegian companies, the certification may be given by a Norwegian judge, Norwegian lawyer, notary public or by two witnesses of age residing in Norway.
      For non-Norwegian companies, the certification must be obtained by way of a notarial certificate, which must include a confirmation by the notary that the person signing the relevant document on behalf of the relevant non-Norwegian company is duly authorised to do so. For non-Norwegian companies, the corporate details of the company referred to in D2(e) above, must also be certified as true and correct by a notary. The signature of the notary must be legalised. If the country of jurisdiction of the relevant non-Norwegian company has ratified the Hague Convention of 5 October 1961 on Abolishing the Requirements of Legalisation for Foreign Public Documents, a convention apostille is sufficient.
      The registrar may, at his sole discretion, accept a document for registration even if a signature has not been certified as described above.

8   *If the initial registration takes place abroad, is that registration final or provisional?*

Please see above in D1, D2 and D4.

9   If provisional, what needs to be done to effect final registration? When must it be done?
The provisional registration confirmation given by NIS will normally state information both
as to what needs to be done to effect permanent registration and when it must be done. As a
minimum, NIS will require receipt of the original Bill of Sale/Builder's Certificate and the
original Free from Encumbrance Certificate/Deletion Certificate from the previous registry
before accepting permanent registration of the vessel. When these requirements are fulfilled
in a manner satisfactory to NIS, permanent registration will be effected. Should the requirements not be satisfactorily fulfilled, NIS may deny permanent registration. In such circumstances NIS will send a formal notice to the owner and the mortgagee (if any). If the matter
outstanding is not dealt with within the time period prescribed by NIS in its notice to the
owner and the mortgagee, NIS may effect an *ex officio* deletion of the vessel.

*10   If provisional, what, if any, are the restrictions which apply to the vessel pending final
         registration?*
No particular restrictions apply to a vessel pending final registration.

11   Can a provisionally registered vessel be mortgaged?
Yes, a vessel that is provisionally entered into the register may be mortgaged. However, it
should be noted that should the requirements for permanent registration not be fulfilled, as
described in D9, the mortgage will be discharged concurrently with the deletion of the vessel.

E   Technical matters

*1   Please identify the requirements of the NIS registry with regard to inspection, survey,
         measurement and the like in respect of newly registered vessels.*
Vessels registered in NIS are subject to Norwegian law. Public control of Norwegian vessels is
based on the Seaworthiness Act of 1903. As a general rule, the Seaworthiness Act applies to
Norwegian vessels in excess of 500 GT. The responsibility for the exercise of public control lies
with the Ministry of Trade and Industry and the Norwegian Maritime Directorate. However, the
Norwegian Maritime Directorate has to a large extent delegated its powers to pre-approved classification societies (being Det Norske Veritas, Lloyd's Register, American Bureau of Shipping,
Bureau Veritas and Germanischer Lloyd). The inspections, surveys, measurements and the like
must also be exercised in accordance with the international conventions that Norway has ratified.
        Vessels under 500 GT, all passenger vessels, mobile offshore units, supply ships and
stand-by ships shall be inspected/surveyed by the Norwegian Ship Control or, if authorised by
the Norwegian Ship Control in each individual case, by one of the pre-approved classification
societies. Pursuant to the Seaworthiness Act and the regulations thereto (in particular the regulations of 15 June 1987), the Norwegian Maritime Directorate and the pre-approved classification societies can carry out both announced and unannounced inspections.
        Norway has ratified international conventions concerning safety at sea such as the
SOLAS conventions, the Load Line Convention, the STCW Convention, the MARPOL convention and others. The requirements of such conventions as well as certain EU requirements

have to an extensive degree been incorporated into the Seaworthiness Act. NIS registered vessels must have valid certificates showing compliance with these regulations.

Guidelines on how to comply with these requirements can be found on the homepage of the Norwegian Maritime Directorate www.sjofartsdir.no/nis-nor/. The guidelines are in Norwegian and English. The forms in question can also be downloaded from this page.

2   By when must these requirements be complied with?
The requirements must be complied with before registration in NIS.

F   Transfer of ownership

1   Please answer, either separately or by reference to your earlier answers, the questions listed under sections D and E above in respect of the transfer of ownership of a vessel already registered under NIS flag.

Transfer of ownership when the vessel is already registered in the NIS, assumes mainly the same requirements as described above in D2. The Deletion Certificate and the Tonnage Certificate are, however, not necessary. Unless the vessel changes name, a Name Certificate is not required.

2   Please explain any exchange control or other governmental or regulatory consents required in connection with the sale to a foreign flag of a vessel registered under the NIS flag.

No such consents are required.

G   Deletion

1   Please outline the procedure for deletion of vessels from the NIS registry.
Deletion of vessels from NIS is initiated by the owner's written request for deletion. The request must state the reason for deletion request and be signed by an authorised signatory of the owner. Adequate proof of authority must be submitted together with the deletion request. Forms of request for deletion can be downloaded on the NIS homepage www.nis-nor.no.

If the deletion is in connection with a sale of the vessel, a confirmed duplicate/copy of the Bill of Sale issued to the new owner must be enclosed.

In order for the vessel to be deleted, all registered encumbrances must be discharged in advance and upon the written consent of the mortgagee/beneficiary. Such consent must be endorsed on the original mortgage or encumbrance creating document.

2   Please answer, either separately or by reference to your earlier answers, the questions listed under section D in respect of the deletion, as opposed to new registration, of a vessel.

For the questions in D2, see G1 for reference.

The documents described above in G1 must be notarised and legalised in the same manner as described above in D7.

H   Certificates/transcripts

1   Please identify the certificates and other documents issued to an owner on registration of a vessel under the NIS flag.

When provisionally registering a vessel, NIS will issue a Registration Confirmation and a Provisional Certificate of Nationality. When registration is made permanent, NIS will issue a confirmation to that effect and a Permanent Certificate of Nationality and a Certificate of Ownership and Encumbrances if requested by the owner.

2   Please outline the procedure (including fees payable) for obtaining information on the registered ownership of, and encumbrances on, vessels registered in the NIS registry.

NIS normally gives such information upon requests and payment of fees. The fee currently payable (as of 1 July 2005) for a Certificate of Ownership and Encumbrances is NOK422.

I   Fees/taxes

1   What fees are currently payable:
   1.1   on new registration?
   1.2   on transfer of ownership?
   1.3   on deletion?

A complete list of registration fees along with banking details is available on the NIS homepage www.nis-nor.no

As of 1 July 2005 the registration fees payable to NIS are:

   1.1   NOK7,321. For each following year the annual fee is NOK5,800.
   1.2   NOK1,521.
   1.3   No charge

The fees charged by the Norwegian Maritime Directorate, set out in regulations of 13 January 2002, are:

   (a)   The fee for a new registration of passenger vessels, cargo vessels under 500 GT, standby and supply vessels is as of November 2005 an amount equal to the aggregate of:
   (i)   NOK5,000, plus NOK0.50 per net tonne, multiplied with 1.1356; and
   (ii)   a flat fee varying from NOK3,690 to NOK303,063 depending on the actual tonnage of the vessel and, if the vessel is a newbuilding, where the vessel is built.
   (b)   For cargo vessels over 500 GT the fee for a new registration is an amount equivalent to the aggregate of:
   (i)   NOK12,000 plus NOK5 per net tonne for the first 5,000 GT, NOK4 per net tonne for the following 5,000 GT, NOK3 per net tonne for the following 20,000 GT and NOK2 per net tonne for the following 40,000 GT. For vessels over 70,000 net tonnes an addi-

tional NOK1 is charged per net tonne over 70,000; and

(ii)   a flat fee varying from NOK57,927 to NOK3,638,748 depending on the actual tonnage of the vessel and, if the vessel is a newbuilding, where the vessel is built.

For transfer of ownership and deletion no fees are charged by the Norwegian Maritime Directorate.

J   Parallel registration

1   Is parallel registration permitted:

1.1   onto the NIS register?

1.2   from the NIS register?

Parallel registration is not permitted.

K   General

1   Please identify the principal statutes and regulations in Norway governing the registration of vessels under NIS flag.

The principal statutes and regulations governing the registration of vessels under the NIS flag are:

(a)   The NIS Act of 12 June 1987, no. 48, and the Regulations Concerning Registration of Vessels in NIS of 30 July 1992;

(b)   The Maritime Act of 24 June 1994, no. 39;

(c)   The Seaworthiness Act of 9 June 1903, no. 7;

(d)   The Measurement of Vessels Act of 19 June 1964, no. 20;

(e)   The Registration Act of 7 June 1935, no. 2; and

(f)   The Regulations of 2 February 1996 on fees to the Norwegian Maritime Directorate.

2   Are there any other matters in the context of registration of vessels under the legal system in Norway which you feel should be emphasised here?

No, but please see the NIS homepage www.nis-nor.no, which contains useful information in both Norwegian and English.

---

* Contributed by Bernhard Haukali and Gry Bratvold of Wikborg Rein, Oslo, Norway.

Panama*

A   Ownership

1   What, if any, are the restrictions on ownership of ships registered under the Panamanian flag?

There are no nationality requirements concerning the ownership of a ship registered under the flag of Panama and the owner of a ship may be an individual or entity, either Panamanian or foreign, residing or doing business in Panama or elsewhere.

2   If registration by companies is limited to companies incorporated in Panama, is a local 'brass-plate' company sufficient, or must be there a closer genuine connection?

As stated above, there are no nationality requirements concerning the ownership of a ship registered under the flag of Panama.

3   If registration by companies incorporated other than in Panama, is permitted, must a local representative be appointed? If so, are there any restrictions on the identity of that legal representative?

Any ship that is registered under the flag of Panama must have a legal representative, regardless of the place of incorporation or formation of the owning company or entity. The legal representative must be a lawyer or law firm authorised to practise law in the Republic of Panama.

4   Please summarise any restrictions (for example, as to number, nationality, and so on) on who may own shares in shipowning companies incorporated in Panama?

In the event that a shipowning company is established in Panama, the ownership of shares thereof is not restricted either in number or nationality.

5   Please explain any exchange control or other governmental or regulatory consents required in connection with the ownership of ships registered in Panama.

There are no exchange controls or governmental or regulatory consents required in connection with the ownership of ships registered in Panama.

6   Please explain any special rules for any particular type of ship.

There are no special rules regarding the ownership of a particular type of ship in Panama.

7   Is there any mandatory registration requirement for certain owners (for example, citizens of Panama)?

There are no mandatory registration requirements for certain owners.

B   Eligibility

1   Are any particular types/sizes of ship ineligible for, or exempt from, registration?

No.

2   What, if any, is the maximum age for registration of ships under the flag of Panama?

There is no particular age restriction for registration of ships under the flag of Panama.

However, according to a new procedure established by the Panama Maritime Authority, all enrolment authorisations are granted with a note stating vessels older than 20 years must be surveyed within the first two months from the registered date. In practice, the Shipping Bureau Office is not applying any kind of sanction for the non-compliance with such deadline. We believe the measure to be a way to alert the shipowners and encourage an earlier inspection. In any event, the shipowners must coordinate the Annual Special Inspection for vessels older than 20 years within six (6) months of provisional registration of the ship.

C   Names

1   What, if any, are the restrictions on the name under which a ship may be registered in Panama?
There are no express provisions of law in respect of the name of ship. However, in practice, a ship may not be registered with a name which is identical to the name of another ship already registered under the flag of Panama.

2   Is there a procedure for approval of names in advance?
Yes. A name may be approved and reserved in advance.

3   If so, how does it operate? Does approval confer any priority rights in the use of the name?
The name may be approved and reserved in advance by lodging a request to that effect with the Shipping Bureau which is the government entity in charge of all administrative matters concerning ships registered under the flag of Panama. Such a request is either made through a lawyer in Panama or through a Panamanian Consulate abroad. Such approval and reservation confers priority rights in the use of the name.

D   New registration procedure

1   Where may ships intending to fly the flag of Panama be registered?
          1.1   in Panama?
Yes.

          1.2   abroad?
Yes. At present through a Panamanian Consulate with maritime functions abroad.

2   What documents and information must be submitted to effect registration?
(a)   The enrolment process begins with an application for registration which is either lodged at a Panamanian Consulate with maritime functions or at the Shipping Bureau in Panama through a local attorney. The following information is required to complete the appropriate application form, to wit:
          (i)   present name and former name, if any, of the ship;
          (ii)   type of ship, that is, steam, motor, sailing, tanker, barge and so on;
          (iii)   name, nationality and complete address of the owner;
          (iv)   previous country of registry, if applicable;

(v) net and gross tonnage in accordance with the 1969 International Tonnage Convention;

(vi) principal dimensions, that is, length, breadth and depth;

(vii) kind and number of engines and number and type of cylinders with an indication of their length and diameter, as well as the name of the engine manufacturers;

(viii) speed of the ship and horsepower or wattage;

(ix) nature of service or traffic to be rendered by the ship, that is, tanker, bulk carrier, passenger trade, refrigerated cargo and so on;

(x) name and address of the builder of the ship, place of construction and year thereof, and material out of which the hull was built;

(xi) name and address of the authorised accounting corporation who will be responsible for the payment of statements for radiotelegraphic services;

(xii) ship's legal representative in Panama, that is, lawyer or firm of lawyers that will represent the ship in Panama and handle the different phases required for enrolment under the flag;

(xiii) name of the authorised classification society that will issue technical certificates.

(xiv) International Maritime Organization number, that is, IMO number.

(xv) whether the ship is fitted with radiotelephony, radiotelegraphy and/or telex machine, and whether selective call letters are required (if so, the IMPIRB and MMSI numbers).

It is important to provide accurate information in respect of the above referred items. In particular, attention should be given to provide correct dimensions and tonnages as any changes will result in delays and additional expenses in obtaining statutory enrolment.

(b) At the same time that the application for registration is lodged, the interested party should be in position to settle the enrolment charges and taxes, and submit the following documents required for enrolment, to wit:

(i) A Power of Attorney or authorisation in favour of the person who completes and/or lodges the application form for registration of the ship. Said Power of Attorney should be authenticated by a notary public and legalised by a Panamanian Consul or by way of Apostille.

(ii) A Power of Attorney or authorisation in favour of the legal representative of the ship in Panama. Said Power of Attorney should be authenticated by a notary public and legalised by a Panamanian Consul or by way of Apostille.

(iii) Proof of ownership or the ship's title deed duly authenticated by a notary public and legalised by a Panamanian Consul or by way of Apostille. If the ship is newly constructed, proof of ownership thereof would consist of a Builder's Certificate or construction certificate which should contain the price of construction and description of the ship. If the ship has been transferred to the Panamanian flag on account of a sale, the Bill of Sale would constitute proof of ownership. If the ship has been transferred to the Panamanian flag without an intervening sale, proof of ownership should be established by the Bill of Sale, or construction or Builder's Certificate under which the owner took ownership thereof, and/or by virtue of a certificate of ownership from the previous country of registry and the corresponding Certificate of Deletion evidencing the cancellation of registry.

In the case of an initial registration of a ship under the flag, the builder's or construction certificate or Bill of Sale should contain a declaration by a notary public out of his own knowledge and not by way of deposition, that the seller was at the time of sale the legal owner of the ship and that the person acting on its behalf was duly authorised to do so. Furthermore, the builder's or construction certificate or Bill of Sale should also set out the acceptance of the sale or transfer by the buyer, or alternatively, a separate document containing the acceptance of sale or transfer can be attached to the corresponding document.

(iv)   Official certificate or documents, duly authenticated and legalised by a Panamanian Consul, or by way of Apostille, to the effect that the previous registry has been cancelled or closed, or a consent to the cancellation of the same. This does not apply to newly constructed ships.

(c)   Thereafter, the Shipping Bureau will issue, or authorise the appropriate Consulate to issue, a provisional navigation licence valid for six months and a provisional radio licence valid for three months. At this time, the interested party should make arrangements for the issuance of a crew roll list and for the issuance of certificates of competency.

3   Does the Panamanian legal system lay down any specific requirements as to the contents of any of these documents – for example, of Bills of Sale – and, if so, what are they?

Aside from the above mentioned requirements, there are no particular requirements as to the contents of the documents referred to save that the Builder's Certificate or Bill of Sale and acceptance should, at least, contain reference to the names and addresses of the builder or seller and the buyer, as well as the price of construction or sale, the ship's port of registry and particulars thereof, the ship's international call signal, and a description of the ship, that is, measurements and tonnages.

4   Please identify how many originals or copies of each document are required. Are fax copies of any of them acceptable?

One original of each document is required for registration purposes. In practice, a certified copy is made and retained by the Panamanian Consulate when provisional registration of the ship is accomplished through a Consulate. Fax copies are not acceptable.

5   Are there any requirements as to the language in which registration documents must be submitted?

There are no requirements as to the language of the corresponding documents to accomplish provisional registration of the ship abroad as long as the documents are submitted in a language which is understood by the officials reviewing the documents, otherwise, they would have to be translated into Spanish. In any event, the corresponding documents have to be translated into Spanish by the lawyer or firm of lawyers that will complete the enrolment of the ship under the flag of Panama subsequent to provisional registration in order to obtain the issuance of the statutory navigation licence.

6   *If they may be submitted in a foreign language, are there any translation requirements? If so, what are they and when must they be complied with?*

As stated, such documents would have to be translated into Spanish by the lawyer or firm of lawyers that will complete the enrolment of the ship under the flag of Panama in order to obtain the issuance of the statutory navigation licence, and which should be undertaken within the six months that follow provisional registration of the corresponding ship.

7   *Please identify any particular requirements of the Panamanian legal system with regard to the method of execution of any of the registration documents, or with regard to notarisation or legalisation.*

(a)   The Power of Attorney or authorisation in favour of the person who completes and/or lodges the application form for registration of the ship and the Power of Attorney or authorisation in favour of the legal representative in Panama, that is, lawyer or firm of lawyers who is to handle the various phases involved in the enrolment process, should be authenticated by a notary public as to identity of signatory and authority to act and legalised by a Panamanian Consul or by way of Apostille.

(b)   The ship's title deed as described beforehand should be duly authenticated by a Notary Public and legalised by a Panamanian Consul or by way of Apostille.

In case of the initial registration of a ship under the flag, the builder's or construction certificate or Bill of Sale should contain a declaration by a notary public out of his own knowledge and not by way of deposition, that the seller was at the time of sale the legal owner of the ship and that the person acting on its behalf was duly authorised to do so.

Furthermore, the builder's or construction certificate or Bill of Sale should also set out the acceptance of the sale or transfer by the buyer, or alternatively, a separate document containing the acceptance of sale or transfer can be attached to the corresponding document. The corresponding document should be authenticated by a notary public as to identity of signatory and his/her authority to act, and should also be legalised by a Panamanian Consul or by way of Apostille.

(c)   The Certificate of Deletion from the previous registry should be duly authenticated by a notary public as to identity of signatory and authority to act and legalised by a Panamanian Consul or by way of Apostille.

8   *If the initial registration takes place abroad, is that registration final or provisional?*

Registration abroad is provisional.

9   *If provisional, what needs to be done to effect final registration? When must it be done?*

(a)   During the period of provisional registration, the interested party should send the Power of Attorney in favour of the legal representative of the ship in Panama, proof of ownership as described above, as well as the certificate or document evidencing the cancellation of the previous registry to the lawyer or firm of lawyers that will complete the enrolment of the ship under the flag of Panama.

(b)   The interested party should arrange for the issuance or re-issuance of various technical certificates which are required by International Conventions to which the Republic
of Panama has adhered and which are described in Section E hereof under the heading of 'Technical Matters', as well as the issuance or re-issuance of a 1969
International Tonnage Certificate ('ITC') which has been issued by an authorised
Classification Society on behalf of the Panamanian government. The interested party
should arrange to obtain a certified true copy of the ITC and send it to the lawyer or
firm of lawyers that will complete the enrolment of the ship under the flag of Panama.
In addition, the interested party should complete an application for the issuance of a
statutory radio license and forward it to the Shipping Bureau in Panama through the
lawyer or firm of lawyers that will complete the enrolment of the ship under the flag of
Panama, or through the company that is authorised to handle the ship's radio accounts.

(c)   Once the lawyer or firm of lawyers in Panama receives the corresponding documents, various steps should be taken to complete the enrolment of the ship under the
flag, and the issuance of a statutory navigation and radio licences to wit:

(i)   translation, protocolisation and registration at the Public Registry of the
document evidencing proof of ownership;

(ii)   presentation of the application for the issuance of the statutory radio license
at the Shipping Bureau;

(iii)   presentation at the Shipping Bureau of the Power of Attorney in favour of
the legal representative of the ship in Panama, as well as the certificate or
document evidencing the cancellation of the previous registry and proof of
ownership as registered at the Public Registry, as well as the tonnage certificate mentioned before.

Once the above mentioned steps have been appropriately completed, the Shipping
Bureau will issue statutory radio and navigation licenses valid for four years, or two
years in case of yachts.

10   *If provisional, what, if any, are the restrictions which apply to the ship pending final
registration?*

Other than completing the above mentioned requirements, there are no particular requirements
which apply to a ship pending final registration. To the extent that the provisional navigation and
radio licences expire without the ship having been issued statutory navigation and radio licences,
these may be extended for a further period of time upon payment of renewal charges and a fine.

11   *Can a provisionally registered ship be mortgaged?*

A ship which has been provisionally registered may be mortgaged.

E   Technical matters

1   *Please identify the requirements of Panama with regard to inspection, survey, measurement and the like in respect of newly registered ships.*

Ships of twenty (20) or more years of age are subject to a special inspection during the period
of provisional registration. In practice, platforms and drilling rigs are not required to undergo

a special inspection, instead they must present a valid copy of the Mobile Offshore Drilling Safety Unit Certificate issued by a recognised organisation.

All Panamanian ships must have a 1969 International Tonnage Certificate issued on behalf of the Panamanian Government by a recognised organisation authorised by the Shipping Bureau.

In general and in accordance with International Conventions, Panamanian ships must have the following certificates (according to the ship's trade and tonnage):

(a)   Passenger Ship Safety Certificate;

(b)   Cargo Ship Safety Construction Certificate, Cargo Ship Safety Equipment Certificate, Cargo Ship Safety Radiotelegraphy Certificate;

(c)   Cargo Ship Safety Certificate;

(d)   Cargo Ship Safety Radio Certificate;

(e)   International Loadline Certificate;

(f)   Minimum Safe Manning Certificate, Certificate of Crew Accommodation;

(g)   International Oil Pollution Prevention Certificate;

(h)   International Air Pollution Prevention Certificate;

(i)   Safety Management Certificate;

(j)   Document of Compliance;

(k)   International Ship Security Certificate;

(l)   Continuous Synopsis Record;

(m)   Mobile Offshore Drilling Unit Safety Certificate.

In addition to the above, the officers and crews of all Panamanian ships must posses valid certificates of competency issued by the Shipping Bureau.

In addition, all Panamanian ships engaged in international trade are subject to an annual safety inspection which aims to verify if the ships comply with the national and international safety rules, the certification of the crew and officers and the existing living, hygienic and working conditions of the crew in accordance with International Conventions ratified by the Republic of Panama.

2   *By when must these requirements be complied with?*

Generally, the requirements should be completed during the period of provisional registration. The inspection programme is administered and controlled by the Maritime Safety and Navigation department which has a computerised record of each ship enabling the Shipping Bureau Office to be able to determine when a ship is due for inspection.

F   Transfer of ownership

1   Where may ships intending to maintain the flag of Panama be registered?

1.1   in Panama?

Yes.

1.2   abroad?

Yes. At present through a Panamanian Consulate with maritime functions abroad.

2   *What documents and information must be submitted to effect registration?*

(a)   An application has to be lodged with the Shipping Bureau requesting the issuance of provisional navigation and radio licences or requesting that a Panamanian Consulate with maritime functions be authorised to issue such documents. The corresponding application has to be lodged through a lawyer or law firm in Panama together with a certificate from the Public Registry, an agency of the Ministry of Government and Justice, that is responsible for coordinating all matters concerning the juridical status of ships enrolled under the flag of Panama, showing the ownership of the vessel and the encumbrances thereon. The following information is required to complete the application, to wit:

    (i)   name of the buyer and full address of operations;

    (ii)   name and address of the authorised accounting corporation who will be responsible for the payment of statements for radiotelegraphic services;

    (iii)   name of the authorised Classification Society that will re-issue technical certificates;

    (iv)   new name of vessel, if applicable.

(b)   The interested party should be in a position to settle the government charges for change of ownership, and submit the following documents required for enrolment, to wit:

    (i)   a Power of Attorney or authorisation in favour of the person who completes and/or lodges the application form for registration of the ship. Said Power of Attorney should be authenticated by a notary public and legalised by a Panamanian Consul or by way of Apostille.

    (ii)   a Power of Attorney or authorisation in favour of the legal representative in Panama. Said Power of Attorney should be authenticated by a notary public and legalised by a Panamanian Consul or by way of Apostille.

    (iii)   a Bill of Sale and acceptance duly authenticated by a notary public and legalised by a Panamanian Consul or by way of Apostille.

    (iv)   a discharge of mortgage or consent of mortgagee duly authenticated by notary public and legalised by a Panamanian Consul or by way of Apostille, to the extent that the ship is subject to encumbrances.

(c)   Thereafter, the Shipping Bureau will issue, or authorise the appropriate Consulate to issue, a provisional navigation licence valid for six months and a provisional radio licence valid for three months. At this time, the new owner should make arrangements for the issuance of a crew roll list and for the issuance of certificates of competency.

3   Does the Panamanian legal system lay down any specific requirements as to the contents of any of these documents – for example, of Bills of Sale – and, if so, what are they?

Aside from the above mentioned requirements, there are no particular requirements as to the contents of the referred documents save that the Bill of Sale and acceptance should, at least, contain reference to the names and addresses of the seller and the buyer, as well as the price of sale, the ship's registration details and international call signal, and a description of the ship, that is, measurements and tonnages.

4   Please identify how many originals or copies of each document are required. Are fax copies of any of them acceptable?

One original of each document is required for registration purposes. In practice, a certified copy is made and retained by the Panamanian Consulate when provisional registration of the ship is accomplished through a Consulate. Fax copies are not acceptable.

5   *Are there any requirements as to the language in which registration documents must be submitted?*
Please refer to section D5 above.

6   *If they may be submitted in a foreign language, are there any translation requirements? If so, what are they and when must they be complied with?*
Please refer to section D6 above.

7   *Please identify any particular requirements of the Panamanian legal system with regard to the method of execution of any of the registration documents, or with regard to notarisation or legalisation.*
(a)   Please see section D7 above.
(b)   The Bill of Sale and acceptance should be duly authenticated by a notary public both as to the identity of the signatories and their authority to act, and legalised by a Panamanian Consul or by way of Apostille.

8   *If the initial registration takes place abroad, is that registration final or provisional?*
Registration abroad is provisional.

9   *If provisional, what needs to be done to effect final registration? When must it be done?*
(a)   During the period of provisional registration, the interested party should send the Power of Attorney in favour of the legal representative of the ship in Panama, and the Bill of Sale and acceptance as described above, to the lawyer or firm of lawyers that will complete the enrolment of the ship under the flag of Panama.
(b)   The interested party should arrange for the issuance or re-issuance of various technical certificates which are required by International Conventions to which the Republic of Panama has adhered and which are described in Section E hereof under the heading of 'Technical matters'. The 1969 International Tonnage Certificate should be re-issued to the extent that there is change in the Classification Society. However, if there is only a change in the name of the vessel, the legal representative thereof should arrange for the issuance of a replacement certificate through the New York Office of the Shipping Bureau (SEGUMAR).
        If after the change of ownership there has been no change in the managers/agents of the vessel, the interested parties will need to present a Declaration of Designated person and Declaration of Company (in respect to ISM certificates).
        In cases that the ISPS Code is applicable, the issuance of a new Continuous Synopsis Record reflecting all changes effected over the vessel would be required.
        In addition, the interested party should complete an application for the issuance of a statutory radio license and forward to the Shipping Bureau in Panama through the lawyer or firm of lawyers that will complete the enrolment of the ship under the flag of Panama, or through the company that is authorised to handle the ship's radio accounts.

(c) Once the lawyer or firm of lawyers in Panama receive the corresponding documents, various steps should be taken to complete the enrolment of the ship under the flag, and the issuance of a statutory navigation and radio licenses to wit:

    (i) translation, protocolisation and registration at the Public Registry of the Bill of Sale and acceptance;

    (ii) presentation of the application for the issuance of the statutory radio licence at the Shipping Bureau;

    (iii) presentation at the Shipping Bureau of the Power of Attorney in favour of the legal representative of the ship in Panama, as well as the Bill of Sale and acceptance as registered at the Public Registry, and the 1969 International Tonnage Certificate as reissued.

(d) Arrangements should be made to accomplish the permanent registration of the discharge of mortgage or consent of mortgagee, duly authenticated by a notary public, both as to identity of the signatory and authority to act and legalised by a Panamanian Consul or by way of Apostille, to the extent that the ship is subject to encumbrances. Once the above mentioned steps have been appropriately completed, the Shipping Bureau will issue statutory radio and navigation licences valid for four years, or two years in case of yachts.

10 *If provisional, what, if any, are the restrictions which apply to the ship pending final registration?*

Other than completing the above mentioned requirements, there are no particular requirements which apply to a ship pending final registration. To the extent that the provisional navigation and radio licences expire without the ship having been issued statutory navigation and radio licences, these may be extended for a further period of time upon payment of renewal charges and a fine.

11 *Can a provisionally registered ship be mortgaged?*

A ship which has been provisionally registered may be mortgaged.

12 *Technical matters*

    12.1 *Please identify the requirements of Panama with regard to inspection, survey, measurement and the like in respect of ships.*

Please refer to section E1 above.

    12.2 *By when must these requirements be complied with?*

Please refer to section E2 above.

13 *Please explain any exchange control or other governmental or regulatory consents required in connection with the sale to a foreign flag of a ship registered under the flag of Panama.*

There are no exchange control or other governmental or regulatory consents required in connection with the sale of a ship which is registered under the flag of Panama, and the transfer thereof to the flag of another country.

G   Deletion

1   Please outline the procedure for deletion of vessels from the flag of Panama.
An owner wishing to delete a ship from the flag of Panama must submit an application at the Shipping Bureau through a lawyer in Panama stating the reasons for requesting the deletion of the ship.

The Shipping Bureau will issue the corresponding Deletion Certificate upon receipt of payment of the relevant fees and upon being satisfied that the ship has no outstanding debts with the Panamanian government and that ship is free from registered encumbrances or as stated below.

In addition, and of particular benefit when the ship is mortgaged, it is possible to obtain a certificate from the Shipping Bureau that there is no objection to the deletion of a ship upon submission of evidence that any encumbrances of record have been discharged or that any mortgagee of record consents to the deletion of the ship. Such a certificate may be obtained in Panama or through a Panamanian Consulate with maritime functions abroad, and is valid for thirty (30) days.

During such period, the interested party should proceed with the registration of the instrument of discharge of mortgage or the document evidencing the mortgagee's consent to the deletion of the vessel at the Public Registry in Panama and present evidence thereof to the Shipping Bureau.

In cases where the ISPS Code is applicable, the issuance of a Continuous Synopsis Record which shows that the vessel has ceased to fly the Panamanian flag should be issued once the vessel is permanently deleted from the Panamanian Registry.

2   Where may ships flying the flag of Panama be deleted?
    2.1   in Panama?
Yes.
    2.2   abroad?
No. However, the certificate that there is no objection to the deletion of a ship (mentioned above) may be obtained through a Panamanian Consulate with maritime functions abroad.

3   What documents and information must be submitted to effect deletion?
Please refer to Section G1 above and note that an original of the discharge of mortgage or mortgagee's consent would be required if there are any encumbrances of record.

In addition, and to the extent that the application for deletion is not lodged by the legal representative of the vessel in Panama, one would have to file a duly authenticated and legalised Power of Attorney in favour of the lawyer, or firm of lawyers, in Panama who applies for the deletion of a ship.

4   Does the Panamanian legal system lay down any specific requirements as to the contents
    of any of these documents – for example, of Bills of Sale – and, if so, what are they?
Please refer to Section G1 and 3 above.

5   Please identify how many originals or copies of each document are required. Are fax
    copies of any of them acceptable?

An original of each document referred to in Section G3 would be required. However, an original or certified copy would be retained by the Panamanian Consulate if the certificate of no objection to the deletion of a ship is obtained through a Consulate. Fax copies are not acceptable.

6   *Are there any requirements as to the language in which registration documents must be submitted?*

There are generally no requirements as to the language of the corresponding documents to obtain the certificate of no objection to the deletion of the ship abroad as long as the documents are submitted in a language which is understood by the officials reviewing the documents abroad. Otherwise, they would have to be translated into Spanish, and in any event, the corresponding documents have to be translated into Spanish by the lawyer or firm of lawyers that will complete the deletion of the ship in Panama.

7   *If they may be submitted in a foreign language, are there any translation requirements? If so, what are they and when must they be complied with?*

As stated, such documents would have to be translated into Spanish by the lawyer or firm of lawyers that will complete the deletion of the ship.

8   *Please identify any particular requirements of the Panamanian legal system with regard to the method of execution of any of the documents referred to above, or with regard to notarisation or legalisation.*

The documents referred to in Section G3 must be authenticated both as to identity of the signatory and authority to act by a notary public and thereafter legalised by a Panamanian Consulate, or by way of Apostille.

9   *If the initial steps in respect of the deletion of a ship are taken abroad, is that final or provisional?*

Please refer to Section G1 above.

10   *If provisional, what needs to be done to effect final registration? When must it be done?*

Please refer to Section G1 above.

11   *If provisional, what, if any, are the restrictions which apply to the ship pending final deletion?*

There are no particular restrictions, but in practice the Shipping Bureau will scrutinise any action taken in contravention of the purported intention of deleting the ship.

H   Certificates/transcripts

1   *Please identify the certificates and other documents issued to an owner on registration of his ship under the flag of Panama.*

On registration of a ship an owner is issued a provisional navigation licence with a validity of six (6) months and a provisional radio licence with a validity of (3) months. After completing the steps outlined in Section D.9., the ship will be issued with statutory navigation and radio licenses with a validity of four (4) years. In addition, an owner is issued a log book and a crew roll, and receipts evidencing the payment of enrolment charges and taxes.

2   *Please outline the procedure (including fees payable) for obtaining information on the registered ownership and encumbrances of ships registered in Panama.*

Information on the registered ownership and encumbrances of ships registered in Panama may be obtained through a search at the Public Registry Office in Panama, or by obtaining a certificate issued by the Public Registry showing the ownership of a ship and encumbrances of record. Either is usually handled through a lawyer in Panama upon payment of reasonable fees and expenses.

I   Fees/taxes

1   What fees are currently payable
    1.1   on new registration?
    1.2   on transfer of ownership?
    1.3   on deletion?

1.1   New registration

Name reservation (optional) (monthly charge)	US$20

Enrolment and annual charges:

(a)   Enrolment charges in accordance with the following scale:

Ships of up to 2,000 grt:	US$500
Ships from 2,000 to 5,000 grt:	US$2,000
Ships from 5,000 to 15,000 grt:	US$3,000
plus US$0.10 per gross ton or fraction thereof in excess of 15,000 grt up to a maximum of	US$6,500

(b)   Annual tax at the rate of US$0.10 per net ton or fraction thereof.

(c)   Annual charge for investigation of accidents and participation in International Conferences and Treaties, to wit:

(i)   tankers, drilling rigs, vessels engaged in the transportation of passengers, gas carriers and vessels engaged in the transportation of chemical products: US$850

(ii)   other vessels not specified above as follows:

(1)	with a gross registered tonnage up to 500 grt:	US$300
(2)	more than 500 grt up to 10,000 grt:	US$400
(3)	More than 10,000 grt:	US$500

In addition a US$0.03 per net registered ton charge is levied. Vessels exempted from the application of the above mentioned charge include pleasure or private use vessels and those which are not propelled (other than drilling rigs).

(d)   Annual service charges:

(i)   vessels engaged in commercial activities such as general cargo, passenger trade, fishing on the high seas, drilling rigs, tug boats, dredgers

(1)	up to 1,000 grt:	US$1,200
(2)	more than 1,000 grt up to 3,000:	US$1,800
(3)	more than 3,000 grt up to 5,000:	US$2,000
(4)	more than 5,000 grt up to 15,000:	US$2,700
(5)	more than 15,000 grt:	US$3,000

(ii)   vessels without self-propulsion, and those engaged in scientific investigations, supply, exploration, floating dry docks, submarines, crew boats or any other activity which is non-profit or which does not constitute trade.

(1)	up to 500 GET:	US$850
(2)	more than 500 GET up to 1,000:	US$1,400
(3)	more than 1,000 GET:	US$1,800

(e)   Annual inspection charges:

(i)   Passenger trade:

(1)	up to 1,600 GET:	US$900
(2)	more than 1,600 GET:	US$1,800

(ii)   Tankers and cargo vessels

(1)	up to 500 GET:	US$500
(2)	more than 500 GET up to 1,600:	US$750
(3)	more than 1,600 GET up to 5,000:	US$850
(4)	more than 5,000 GET up to 15,000:	US$1,000
(5)	more than 15,000 GET:	US$1,200

(iii)	Drilling rigs:	US$1,300
(iv)	Others not specified above:	

(1)	up to 500 GET:	US$500
(2)	more than 500 GET up to 5,000:	US$800
(3)	more than 5,000 GET:	US$1,000

1.2   Transfer of ownership

(a)	Name reservation (optional) (monthly charge):	US$20
(b)	Change of ownership documentary charges:	US$1,000
(c)	Change of ownership omitted:	US$500

1.3   Deletion

Documentary charges: US$1,000

2.   *What annual or other ongoing fees or taxes are payable in respect of ships registered in Panama?*

    2.1   Changes in respect of ships registered in Panama:

(a)	Change of name:	US$1,000
(b)	Change of tonnages:	US$1,000
(c)	Change of service:	US$500
(d)	Change of Radio Accounting Authority:	US$500

2.2 *Consular fees in accordance with Cabinet Decree No. 75 of 1990 (to be added only when the following matters are handled through a Panamanian Maritime Consulate):*

(a)	Preliminary Registration of Discharge of Mortgage:	US$750
(b)	Preliminary Registration of Title of Ownership:	US$750
(c)	Preliminary Registration of Mortgage:	US$750
(d)	Issuance of Provisional Patente (due to enrolment or change of ownership):	US$500
(e)	Issuance of Provisional Radio Licence (due to enrolment or change of ownership):	US$100
(f)	Registration of a yacht (including issuance of Provisional Patente):	US$2,000
(g)	Issuance of Authorised Certifications (Ownership/Encumbrances, Tax Clearance, Dual Registration):	US$50
(h)	Legalisation of Documents per document:	US$20
(i)	Legalisation of International or Technical Certificates:	US$50

2.3 *Special charges of pleasure vessels*

Pleasure vessels or those of private use, that is, yachts, pay a sole enrolment charge of US$1,500 or US$1,000 if the owner is of Panamanian nationality.

The said fees must be paid every two (2) years to allow the renewal of the corresponding Patente and Radio Licence. The above mentioned charge excludes the payment of any other recurrent annual charge.

2.4 *Title registration*

There are no charges in respect of registration of titles.

2.5 *Special discounts*

(a) Pursuant to Law No. 25 of 2002, the Shipping Bureau may authorise a discount on the registration charges in respect of vessels to be enrolled under the Panamanian flag in cases where significant tonnage is being transferred. A special application for discount needs to be filed with the Shipping Bureau prior to registration.

(b) Pursuant to Law No. 7 of 1988, shipowners may deduct salaries and expenses (up to a certain amount) paid to Panamanian warrant officers from the vessel's taxes and charges. To be entitled to the deduction, the shipowner must hire Panamanian warrant officers (of third rank or more) to perform services on the high seas in vessels with 1,000 or more grt.

J   Parallel registration

1   *Is parallel registration permitted*
       1.1   onto Panama's register?
       1.2   from Panama's register?

1.1   Yes.

1.2   Yes.

2   *If so, what, if any, specific governmental or other consents are required?*

    2.1   onto the register of Panama?

    2.2   from the register of Panama?

2.1   Ships registered under the flag of another country and which are chartered for a period of up to two (2) years (it may be a renewable charter) may be registered under the flag of Panama without having to waive such other registry to the extent that reciprocal arrangements are in existence in respect of the foreign registry. The Shipping Bureau will authorise the issuance of a special navigation license with a validity of two (2) years and which may be renewed upon compliance with the requirements which are set out below.

2.2   Ships registered under the flag of Panama and which are chartered for a period of up to two (2) years (it may be a renewable charter) may be registered under the flag of another country without having to waive the Panamanian registry to the extent that reciprocal arrangements are in existence in respect of the foreign registry. The Shipping Bureau would have to issue a consent to such subordinate or parallel registration.

3   *Is the period of parallel registration limited? If so, is it renewable?*

Yes, but it may be renewed.

4   *If parallel registration is dependent on the existence of a demise charter, does Panama have a specific definition of demise or bareboat charter for these purposes? If so, what is it?*

There is no express definition of the type of charter arrangements involved, and thus it may be argued that such parallel registration may also include time or voyage charter arrangements.

5   *Reply to the questions listed under Sections A to E above with reference to:*

    5.1   application for parallel registration onto the Register of Panama.

For sections A, B and C, please refer to prior Sections A, B and C above.

For sections D and E:

(a)   Please refer to section D2(a) above in respect of information required for registration.

(b)   At the same time that the application for registration is lodged, the interested party should be in position to settle the enrolment charges and taxes set out in section 11.1 and submit the following documents required for enrolment, to wit:

    (i)   a Power of Attorney or authorisation in favour of the person who completes and/or lodges the application form for registration of the ship. Said Power of Attorney should be authenticated by a notary public and legalised by a Panamanian Consul or by way of Apostille;

    (ii)   a Power of Attorney or authorisation in favour of the legal representative in Panama. Said Power of Attorney should be authenticated by a notary public and legalised by a Panamanian Consul or by way of Apostille;

    (iii)   an authenticated copy of the Charter Party pursuant to which the special registration is to be made, and which should be legalised by a Panamanian Consul or by way of Apostille;

(iv)   a document evidencing the consent of the other registry consenting to the special parallel registration under the flag of Panama, duly authenticated and legalised by a Panamanian Consul or by way of Apostille;

(v)   Certificate of ownership and encumbrances in respect of the ship, duly authenticated and legalised by a Panamanian Consul or by way of Apostille;

(vi)   document evidencing the owner's consent to the parallel special registration under the flag of Panama, duly authenticated and legalised by a Panamanian Consul or by way of Apostille;

(vii)   document evidencing the consent of the mortgagee(s), if any, to the parallel special registration under the flag of Panama, duly authenticated and legalised by a Panamanian Consul or by way of Apostille;

(viii)   technical certificates including Safety Management Certificate, Document of Compliance, Ship Security Certificate and Continuous Synopsis record (if applicable).

(c)   Once the above mentioned formalities have been accomplished, the Shipping Bureau will issue, or authorise the appropriate Consulate to issue, a special navigation licence valid for two (2) years and a provisional radio licence valid for three months. At this time, the interested party should make arrangements for the issuance of a crew roll list and for the issuance of certificates of competency, and for the issuance of a statutory radio licence.

5.2   Application for parallel registration from the Register of Panama.
Please refer to Sections A, B, C and D above, and refer to Section J2.2 above.

6   *Can/must mortgages on ships parallel registered into Panama's registry also be registered in Panama?*
No. Mortgages on ships parallel registered into the registry of Panama may not be registered in Panama.

7   *Under what circumstances will/may the parallel registration of a ship onto Panama's register be terminated or revoked?*

(a)   if the ship is in the service of a nation at war with the Republic of Panama;

(b)   if it is registered in the merchant marine of another country other than in respect of parallel registration as described above;

(c)   if it is used for contraband, illegal trade or piracy;

(d)   in the event of a serious violation of the legal provisions regarding seaworthiness, safety, sanitation, labour standards and prevention of pollution of the marine environment;

(e)   in the event of violation of International Conventions ratified by Panama, or of resolutions issued by competent organisations of the United Nations, if such sanction is contemplated;

(f)   in the event of expiration of the navigation patente without the timely renewal thereof; and

(g)   in any other cases established by law.

K   General

1   *Please identify the principal statutes and regulations in Panama governing the registration of ships.*

Legal provisions which apply to the registration of ships under the Panamanian flag are contained in various Laws, Cabinet and Executive Decrees and Resolutions, as well as in the Commercial, Labour, and Fiscal Codes. Of primary importance are Law No. 8 of 1925 and Law No. 2 of 1980 which provide the basic guidelines for registering ships under the Panamanian flag and which set out the functions of the Shipping Bureau. In addition, Law No. 14 of 1980 and Law No. 43 of 1984 regulate the preliminary registration of title and mortgages on ships enrolled under the Panamanian flag.

2   *Are there any other matters in the context of registration of ships not referred to above which you feel should be emphasised?*

(a)   There are two government entities primarily involved in the enrolment of ships under the flag of the Republic of Panama. The Panama Maritime Authority (beforehand referred to as Shipping Bureau) is in charge of all administrative matters regarding ships registered or to be registered under the flag of the Republic of Panama, while the Oficina del Registro Público (beforehand referred to as Public Registry) is the entity responsible for coordinating all matters concerning the juridical status of ships enrolled in the Panamanian Registry, namely the registration of title to ships and mortgages thereon.

(b)   These two government entities are, in turn, assisted by other government authorities in coordinating their respective services. There are several consulates of the Republic of Panama scattered around the world, (London, New York, Hamburg) that are designated by the Shipping Bureau to exercise certain functions on its behalf and thus expedite the process of registering a ship under the Panamanian flag. These consulates are also entitled to act as auxiliary registrars of the Public Registry for the preliminary registration of title and mortgages on ships enrolled under the Panamanian flag. In addition there is an office of the Shipping Bureau (beforehand referred to as SEGU-MAR) located in New York which is in charge of coordinating technical matters.

---

* Contributed by Brett R. Patton of Patton, Moreno & Asvat, Panama and London, England.

Singapore*

A   Ownership

1   What, if any, are the restrictions on ownership of vessels registered under the flag of Singapore?

A vessel registered in Singapore (a 'Singapore vessel') may be wholly or partly owned by a company and/or an individual. Subject to any exemptions that may be obtained on a case-by-case basis, the company must be incorporated in Singapore (a 'Singapore company'). The individual must be a citizen of Singapore, which term includes permanent residents in Singapore.

A Singapore vessel may be divided into 64 shares. Up to five Singapore companies and/or individuals may be registered as joint owners of a share or shares in a Singapore vessel.

There are two categories of Singapore company, namely, a 'foreign-owned Singapore company' and a 'local-owned Singapore company'. A 'local-owned Singapore company' is a Singapore company in which all or a majority of its shares are owned by persons who are (a) citizens of Singapore or (b) other local-owned companies. A 'foreign-owned Singapore company' is a Singapore company which is not a local-owned Singapore company. The main reason for this distinction is that while a local-owned Singapore company may own share(s) in all types of Singapore vessels, a foreign-owned Singapore company may only own share(s) in a Singapore vessel that is self-propelled and of at least 1,600 gross tons (GT). A foreign-owned Singapore company may not therefore own shares in, for example,, a tug which is only of 1,000 gross tons or a barge. An exemption from this condition may be obtained on a case-by-case basis, if the vessel is operated from or based in Singapore.

There are special conditions for a tug or a barge, or any vessel of less than 1,600 gross tons (each, a 'small vessel'). The registry of a small vessel owned wholly or partly by a local-owned Singapore company shall be closed if all or a majority of the shares of that local-owned Singapore company or of its holding company, if any, are transferred to a person who is neither a citizen of Singapore nor another local-owned Singapore company. Further, the registry of a small vessel owned wholly or partly by a citizen of Singapore shall be closed if any share in the small vessel is transferred to a person who is neither a citizen of Singapore nor a local-owned Singapore company.

2   If registration by companies is limited to companies incorporated in Singapore, is a local 'brass-plate' company sufficient, or must there be a closer, genuine connection?

A tug or barge owned wholly or partly by a local-owned Singapore company (which owns only tugs and/or barges) shall not be registered in Singapore unless each of the local-owned Singapore company and its holding company (if any) has a minimum paid-up capital of 10 per cent of the value of the tug or barge or S$50,000, whichever is lower, subject to a minimum of S$10,000. This restriction applies only to the first tug or barge to be registered in Singapore by the local-owned Singapore company.

A vessel, other than a tug or barge referred to above, owned wholly or partly by a Singapore company shall not be registered in Singapore unless the Singapore company has a minimum paid-up capital of S$50,000. This minimum paid-up capital requirement may however be waived for the Singapore company's related company(ies) if the Singapore company and/or its related Singapore company(ies) qualify under the 'Block Transfer Scheme'. The Block Transfer Scheme applies if the Singapore company and its related Singapore company(ies) have registered or applied to register (or have informed the Singapore Registry of Ships (the 'Registry') that they will apply to register) any of the following combination of vessels within a reasonable period of time:

      (a)   two vessels having an aggregate tonnage of at least 40,000 net tons ('nrt');

      (b)   three vessels having an aggregate tonnage of at least 30,000 nrt;

      (c)   four vessels having an aggregate tonnage of at least 20,000 nrt; or

      (d)   five or more vessels having any aggregate tonnage.

Where a Singapore company owning only tugs and/or barges (as mentioned above) subsequently registers a vessel other than a tug or barge, the amount of its paid-up capital must be adjusted to the amount required for Singapore companies owning other types of vessels.

3   *If registration by companies incorporated other than in Singapore is permitted, must a local representative be appointed? If so, are there any restrictions on the identity of that representative?*

Not applicable. Please see A1 and A2 above.

4   *Please summarise any restrictions (for example, as to number, nationality and so on) on who may own shares in vessel owning companies incorporated in Singapore.*

Please see A1 and A2 above.

5   *Please explain any exchange control or other governmental or regulatory consents required in connection with the ownership of vessels registered in Singapore.*

There are none, other than the requirements set out in these answers.

6   *Please explain any special rules for any particular type of vessel.*

Please see A1 and A2 above.

7   *Is there any mandatory registration requirement for certain owners (for example, citizens of Singapore)?*

No, save as mentioned in A1 and A2 above.

B   Eligibility

1   *Are there any particular types/sizes of vessel ineligible for, or exempt from, registration?*

A vessel which has been struck off her former registry for non-compliance with mandatory requirements will not be accepted for registration in Singapore.

2   What, if any, is the maximum age for registration of vessels under the flag of Singapore?
A vessel must be not more than 17 years old at the time of registration in Singapore unless the Registry is satisfied that the vessel is in a satisfactory condition in all respects. This means that a satisfactory special report on the condition of the vessel, issued by one of the authorised Classification Societies, would have to be submitted to the Registry. This age requirement does not apply to a vessel already registered in Singapore but is to be registered anew in the ownership of another owner in Singapore.

The following classification societies are recognised by the Registry:

(a)   American Bureau of Shipping;
(b)   Bureau Veritas;
(c)   China Classification Society;
(d)   Det norske Veritas;
(e)   Germanischer Lloyd;
(f)   Korean Register of Shipping;
(g)   Lloyd's Register of Shipping;
(h)   Nippon Kaiji Kyokai;
(i)   Registro Italiano Navale.

C   Names

1   What, if any, are the restrictions on the name under which a vessel may be registered in Singapore?
The name for a vessel to be registered in Singapore must be approved by the Registry, even in the case of a vessel which is to be transferred from another registry without any change in its name.

The name of a Singapore vessel must be in English letters and if the name contains any numerals, such numerals must be in Roman or Arabic numerals (for example, 1, 2, 3 or I, II, III).

The Registry may require the name of an existing vessel to be changed or refuse to register a vessel by a name if that name:

(a)   is already the name of a vessel which is registered in Singapore;
(b)   is, in the Registry's opinion, so similar to that of a Singapore vessel as to be calculated to deceive or likely to confuse;
(c)   may be confused with a distress signal;
(d)   is prefixed by any letters or a name which might be taken to indicate a type of vessel or any other word, prefix or suffix which might cause confusion as to the name of the vessel; or
(e)   might cause offence or embarrassment.

2   Is there a procedure for approval of names in advance?
Yes.

3   If so, how does it operate? Does approval confer any priority rights in the use of the name?
The application for approval of a name should be made in writing at least two weeks prior to the proposed registration of a vessel. Where the name is different from the existing name of

the vessel, the owner must give the Registry written notice of the existing name. More than one name may be submitted for approval but the applicant must state the order of preference for the names. A name which has been approved by the Registry may be reserved upon request, for a period of up to one year.

In the case of a change of name of a vessel already registered in Singapore, a Carving and Marking Note will be issued upon approval of the new name, which note must be certified by the vessel's Classification Society and returned to the Registry within 30 days.

A fee of S$26 plus GST is payable for each approval of name (including any change of name).

D   New registration procedure

1   Where may vessels intending to fly the flag of Singapore be registered:
1.1   in Singapore?
1.2   abroad?

All Singapore vessels must be registered at the Registry in Singapore. The Registry does not have offices outside Singapore.

2   What documents and information must be submitted to effect registration?
(a)   Application for reservation of the vessel's name;
(b)   completed Application Form;
(c)   if the owner is a company, a Business Profile computer printout on the company issued by the Accounting and Corporate Regulatory Authority in Singapore ('ACRA');
(d)   completed Appointment of Agent Form (if required);
(e)   completed Appointment of Manager Form (who must be a person resident in Singapore);
(f)   Evidence of Ownership:
    (i)   if the vessel is a newbuilding, a copy of the Builder's Certificate (and a copy of the Power of Attorney if it is executed under Power of Attorney); or
    (ii)   if the vessel is transferred from another registry, a copy of the Bill of Sale (and a copy of the Power of Attorney if it is executed under Power of Attorney) or a transcript of that registry;
(g)   evidence of value of vessel in Singapore dollars (if not reflected in other documents submitted, for example, the Bill of Sale);
(h)   Tonnage Certificate:
    (i)   if the vessel is a newbuilding, a copy of the interim tonnage certificate; or
    (ii)   if the vessel is transferred from another registry, a copy of the existing tonnage certificate;
(i)   Class Certificate:
    (i)   if the vessel is a newbuilding, a copy of the provisional/interim Class Certificate; or
    (ii)   if the vessel is transferred from another registry, a copy of the Class Maintenance Certificate, and, if the vessel is more than 17 years old, a satisfactory class survey report on the vessel.

The above documents are required for provisional registration of the vessel. For permanent registration or transfer to permanent registration, the following additional documents must be submitted:

(a)   Evidence of Ownership:

   (i)   if the vessel is a newbuilding, the original Builder's Certificate (and the original Power of Attorney if it is executed under Power of Attorney); or

   (ii)   if the vessel is transferred from another registry, the original Bill of Sale (and the original Power of Attorney if it is executed under Power of Attorney);

(b)   full-term Tonnage Certificate;

(c)   full-term Class Certificate;

(d)   original Carving and Marking Note;

(e)   evidence of cancellation of former registry (for example, original Deletion Certificate or original closed transcript of former registry);

(f)   Trading Certificates including (where applicable):

   (i)   International Load Line/Local Freeboard Certificate;

   (ii)   Safety Construction Certificate;

   (iii)   Safety Equipment Certificate;

   (iv)   Safety Radio Certificate;

   (v)   International/Singapore Oil Pollution Prevention Certificate;

   (vi)   Certificate of Fitness/Noxious Liquid Substance Certificate;

   (vii)   30 Mile/Port Limit Passenger Ship Safety Certificate;

   (viii)   Document of Compliance;

   (ix)   Safety Management Certificate;

   (x)   International Ship Security Certificate.

3   Does the legal system in Singapore lay down any specific requirements as to the contents of any of these documents (for example, of Bills of Sale) and, if so, what are they?

The documents listed in D2 above must be submitted in the prescribed statutory forms (if applicable).

4   Please identify how many originals or copies of each document are required. Are fax or pdf copies of any of them acceptable?

The documents listed in D2 above must be submitted in single originals except for the Builder's Certificate or the Bill of Sale, each of which must be submitted in an original with a photocopy (the original will be returned to the owner).

5   Are there any requirements as to the language in which documents must be submitted?

All registration documents must be in the English language.

6   If they may be submitted in a foreign language, are there any translation requirements? If so, what are they and when must they be complied with?

Where a document is in a foreign language, it must be accompanied with a certified English translation.

7   Please identify any particular requirements of the legal system in Singapore with regards to the method of execution of any of the registration documents, or with regard to notarisation or legalisation.

Any Bill of Sale, Builder's Certificate or Power of Attorney executed outside Singapore must be notarised and legalised at the Singapore embassy in the place of execution.

If the executor of any of these documents is not local (for example, a foreign company) but arranges for such documents to be executed in Singapore, the documents are to be executed before a notary public in Singapore (but no legislation is required).

8   If the initial registration takes place abroad, is that registration final or provisional?

Not applicable (the Registry does not have any offices outside Singapore).

9   If provisional, what needs to be done to effect final registration? When must it be done?

Please see D2 above on the additional documents to be submitted for permanent registration. The time period for submission of such documents to the Registry is usually 30 days from date of provisional registration but further extensions of time at the discretion of the Registry may be obtained. The provisional certificate of registry is valid for one year from the date of issue. When all the outstanding documents have been submitted to the Registry, the vessel's permanent registration will date back to the date of provisional registration.

10   If provisional, what, if any, are the restrictions which apply to the vessel pending final registration?

There are none.

11   Can a provisionally registered vessel be mortgaged?

A provisionally registered vessel can be mortgaged provided that the proper mortgage registration procedure is followed. If, at the time of mortgage registration, the original of the Builder's Certificate or the Bill of Sale, as the case may be, has not yet been submitted to the Registry, the mortgagee must confirm in writing to the Registry that the mortgagee (or its representative) has sighted the original Builder's Certificate or Bill of Sale before the mortgage will be accepted for registration. Although the vessel may be provisionally registered, the mortgage, when registered over the vessel, is a permanent mortgage.

E   Technical matters

1   Please identify the requirements of Singapore with regard to inspection, survey, measurement and the like in respect of newly registered vessels.

A newly registered vessel must have its tonnage determined in accordance with the provisions of Part II of the Merchant Shipping (Tonnage) Regulations, 1996 Edition (which applies the International Convention on Tonnage Measurement of Ships, 1969). The tonnage certificate may be obtained from the Marine Division of the Maritime and Port Authority of Singapore or one of the authorised classification societies.

The vessel must be marked permanently and conspicuously as follows:

(a)   the name must be marked on each of the vessel's bows;

(b)   the name and port of registry must be marked on the stern;

(c)   the official number and registered tonnage must be cut in the main beam;

(d)   a scale denoting the vessel's draught of water must be marked on each side at the vessel's stem and stern post.

2   *By when must these requirements be complied with?*

The vessel must be marked as per E1 before the certificate of registry will be issued. Please see D2 above for comments on the tonnage, classification and trading certificates.

F   Transfer of ownership

1   Please answer, either separately or by reference to your earlier answers, the questions listed under sections D and E above in respect of the transfer of ownership of a vessel already registered in Singapore.

The new owner must submit the following:

(a)   Completed Application Form;

(b)   if the owner is a company, a Business Profile computer printout on the company issued by ACRA;

(c)   completed Appointment of Agent Form (if required);

(d)   completed Appointment of Manager Form (who must be a person resident in Singapore);

(e)   original Bill of Sale (and the original Power of Attorney if it is executed under Power of Attorney);

(f)   certified Carving and Marking Note on the change of name if applicable;

(g)   evidence of value of vessel in Singapore dollars (if not reflected in the Bill of Sale).

2   *Please explain any exchange control or other governmental or regulatory consents required in connection with the sale to a foreign flag of a vessel registered under the flag of Singapore.*

There are no exchange control or other governmental or regulatory consents required in connection with the sale of a Singapore vessel for registration under a foreign flag except that all outstanding taxes and fees must be paid before the Registry will issue a Deletion Certificate or a closed transcript of registry.

G   Deletion

1   Please outline the procedure for deletion of vessels from the flag of Singapore.

An owner may apply in writing to the Registry to close a Singapore vessel's registry if there is/are no:

(a)   outstanding mortgage;

(b)   court order prohibiting any dealing with the vessel;

(c)   unpaid fees including any outstanding annual tonnage tax; or

(d)   outstanding claims of the Master or seamen of the vessel.

There is no prescribed format for the application for closure – a simple letter from the owner (or its lawyers, if the owner is legally represented) would suffice.

The owner must submit the following documents to the Registry:

(a)   a written application stating the reason for the closure of the vessel's registry (for example, sale/scrapping), the name and nationality of the buyer (if applicable) and the intended new registry of the vessel (if applicable);

(b)   the original certificate of registry or a letter of undertaking to submit the original certificate to the Registry within 30 days; and

(c)   if applicable, the original Bill of Sale (with a photocopy, the original will be returned upon endorsement by the Registry).

Once the registry is closed, the Registry will issue a 'closed' transcript of registry if requested, at a fee of S$14 plus GST.

2   *Please answer, either separately or by reference to your earlier answers, the questions listed under section D in respect of the deletion, as opposed to new registration, of a vessel.*

There are no additional requirements other than as set out above. The answers to questions D1, D4 and D5 apply, *mutatis mutandis*, to applications for deletion.

H   Certificates/transcripts

1   Please identify the certificates and other documents issued to an owner on registration of a vessel under the flag of Singapore.

On registration, the vessel will be issued with a Certificate of Registry. If the vessel is only provisionally registered, a certificate of provisional registry will be issued which will be replaced with a permanent certificate when the owner fulfils all registration requirements for the vessel's permanent registration.

2   Please outline the procedure (including fees payable) for obtaining information on the registered ownership of and encumbrances on vessels registered in Singapore.

Any person may apply during office hours to the Registry for a transcript of registry on any Singapore vessel. The fee payable for a transcript of registry is S$14 plus GST. In the case of a Singapore vessel which is unencumbered, the transcript of registry will contain a footnote stating that the vessel is 'free from registered encumbrances according to Registry records at the time this document is generated'.

I   Fees/taxes

1   What fees are currently payable:

  1.1   on new registration?

  1.2   on transfer of ownership?

  1.3   on deletion?

  1.4   on inspections?

1.1 The fee on new registration is calculated at S$2.50 per nrt (to the nearest ton), subject to a minimum of S$1,250 (that is, 500 nrt) and a maximum of S$50,000 (that is, 20,000 nrt).

For vessels registered under the Block Transfer Scheme, the registration fee for each vessel is calculated at S$0.50 per nrt, subject to a minimum of S$1,250 (that is, 2,500 nrt) and a maximum of S$20,000 (that is, 40,000 nrt).

1.2 The fee on change of ownership is calculated at the rate of S$1.25 per nrt (to the nearest ton), subject to a minimum of S$1,250 (that is, 1,000 nrt) and a maximum of S$6,000 (that is, 4,800 nrt).

1.3 There are no deletion fees payable on a deletion of a Singapore vessel, save that where there is a Bill of Sale to be recorded, a fee of S$50 is charged.

1.4 Additional registration fees are payable on any alteration of a Singapore vessel, for example, if major alterations are made to the hull or structure affecting the dimensions of the vessel or in the means of propulsion, the Singapore vessel must be re-registered. In such cases, the registration fee is calculated as follows:

The lower of S$2.50 x (NRTAA − NRTBA) or S$50,000 − (S$2.50 x NRTBA), subject to a minimum of S$1,250

NRTAA represents the nrt of the vessel after any alteration, and NRTBA the nrt of the vessel as at initial registration or last registration.

2 *What annual or other ongoing fees or taxes are payable in respect of vessels registered in Singapore?*

Every Singapore vessel attracts an annual tonnage tax calculated at the rate of S$0.20 per nrt (to the nearest ton) subject to a minimum of S$100 (that is, 500 nrt) and a maximum of S$10,000 (that is, 50,000 nrt). Tonnage tax is payable in advance at the start of each year and non-returnable even though the vessel's register may be closed during that year for any reason. All unpaid fees and tonnage taxes constitute maritime liens on the vessel.

J   Parallel registration

1   Is parallel registration permitted:
  1.1   onto Singapore register?
  1.2   from Singapore register?

1.1 Although statutory regulations are in place for the bareboat registration in Singapore of a vessel registered in a foreign registry ('Bareboat Charter In'), the Registry does not, in practice, accept and allow a Bareboat Charter In registration. The Registry will consider any application on a case-by-case basis.

1.2 It is possible for a Singapore vessel to be bareboat chartered-out and registered outside Singapore in the name of the bareboat charterer ('Bareboat Charter Out').

2   If so, what, if any, specific governmental or other consents are required?

For Bareboat Charter Out, the owner (or a person authorised by the owner) must submit the following:

      (a)   completed Application Form;

      (b)   certified copy of the bareboat charterparty;

      (c)   certified transcript of the foreign register or similar document stating the bareboat registration of the vessel;

      (d)   original certificate of Singapore Registry of the vessel; and

      (e)   fee of S$1,250.

If the certified transcript of registry or similar document stating the bareboat registration of the vessel, or the original certificate of Singapore Registry is not submitted together with the Application Form, the Registry may grant provisional Bareboat Charter Out and grant a provisional suspension of the Singapore vessel. The document(s) must be submitted to the Registry within 60 days, failing which the provisional suspension will be terminated and cease to have effect.

3   Is the period of parallel registration limited? If so, is it renewable?

The period of the Bareboat Charter Out will be linked to the term of the bareboat charterparty. It is possible to apply to the Registry to extend the suspension of the Singapore vessel. The owner (or its authorised person) must submit the following:

      (a)   completed Application Form;

      (b)   certified copy of the extended or new bareboat charterparty;

      (c)   certified transcript of the foreign register or similar document showing the extension of the bareboat charter registration of the vessel; and

      (d)   fee of S$1,250.

4   If parallel registration is dependent on the existence of a demised charter, does Singapore have a specific definition of demise or bareboat charter for these purposes? If so, what is it?

There is no definition of 'demise charter' or 'bareboat charter' but there is a definition of 'bareboat charter terms' as follows:

      '"bareboat charter terms", in relation to a ship, means the hiring of the ship for a stipulated period on terms which give the charterer possession and control of the ship, including the right to appoint the master and crew.'

5   Please answer the questions listed under sections A to E above with reference to application for parallel registration onto the register of Singapore.

Upon the expiry or termination of the bareboat charterparty, the owner (or its authorised person) must submit the following in order to reactivate the Singapore registry of the vessel:

      (a)   completed Application Form;

      (b)   original closure certificate or similar document for the closure of the bare boat registration of the vessel; and

(c)   copies of valid statutory certificates for the vessel which are required of a Singapore vessel.

If the original closure certificate or similar document for the closure of the bareboat registration of the vessel is not submitted together with the Application Form, the Registry may grant a provisional reactivation of the vessel's Singapore registry. If the document is not submitted within 60 days, the provisional reactivation will cease to have effect.

If no application is made to reactivate the suspended registry of a Singapore vessel within 60 days of the date of termination of the suspension or if the provisional reactivation ceases to have effect, the registry of the vessel will be automatically closed, except for any subsisting mortgages.

During the period of suspension of the registry of a Singapore vessel, the provisions of the Merchant Shipping Act (Chapter 179) and its regulations will cease to apply to the vessel except:

(a)   the provisions relating to mortgages and property in the vessel in Part II of the Merchant Shipping Act (Chapter 179);

(b)   the provisions relating to the vessel's register; and

(c)   the provision relating to the continued payment of the vessel's annual tonnage tax.

6   *Can/must mortgages on vessels parallel registered into the registry of Singapore also be registered in Singapore?*

No.

7   *Under what circumstances will/may the parallel registration of the vessel onto the register of Singapore be terminated or revoked?*

When the vessel's registry is deleted or struck off its register, or the bareboat charterparty is terminated.

K   General

1   *Please identify the principal statutes and regulations in Singapore governing the registration of vessels.*

The applicable statutes/regulations include the following:

(a)   The Merchant Shipping Act (Chapter 179);

(b)   The Merchant Shipping (Fees) Regulations, 1997 Edition;

(c)   The Merchant Shipping (Load Line) Regulations, 2001 Edition;

(d)   The Merchant Shipping (Prescribed Forms) Regulations, 1997 Edition;

(e)   The Merchant Shipping (Registration of Ships) Regulations, 1997 Edition;

(f)   The Merchant Shipping (Safety Convention) Regulations, 1999 Edition;

(g)   The Merchant Shipping (Survey of Singapore Ships) Regulations, 1996 Edition; and

(h)   The Merchant Shipping (Tonnage) Regulations, 1996 Edition.

2   *Are there any other matters in the context of registration of vessels under the legal system in Singapore which you feel should be emphasised here?*

The income derived from the carriage (other than within the limits of the port of Singapore) of passengers, mails, livestock or goods by a sea-going Singapore vessel (including the income from the charter of such vessels) is exempt from income tax in Singapore.

Companies with Singapore vessels enjoy tax exemption on the sale proceeds of such vessels. The tax exemption is from Year of Assessment 2005 and is valid for an initial period of five years.

---

* Contributed by Harold Or of Allen & Gledhill, Singapore.

United Kingdom*

A   Ownership

1   What, if any, are the restrictions on ownership of vessels registered under the British flag?
The register of British ships (the 'Register') is the responsibility of the Registry of Shipping and Seamen based in Cardiff (the 'Registry') under the supervision of the Register General (the 'Register').

The ownership of a British ship is divided into 64 shares. It is possible to be registered as the owner of all or any of the shares and any share may be owned by up to five people or companies as joint owners.

At least 33 of the shares in the vessel must be in the ownership of a person or a company fitting into one of the following categories (a 'qualifying owner'):

    (a)   British citizens;
    (b)   citizens of an EU member state exercising their rights under article 48 or 52 of the EU Treaty in the United Kingdom ('UK');
    (c)   citizens of the British Dependent Territories;
    (d)   British Overseas Citizens;
    (e)   companies incorporated in a country in the European Economic Area ('EEA');
    (f)   companies incorporated in a British overseas possession having their principal place of business in the United Kingdom or in that overseas possession; and
    (g)   European Economic Interest Groupings.

2   If registration by companies is limited to companies incorporated in the UK, is a local 'brass-plate' company sufficient, or must there be a closer, genuine connection?
Where entitlement to register arises by virtue of the qualifying owner being a company incorporated in an EEA country, that company should be resident in the UK (that is, having a place of business in the UK). Where this condition is not satisfied the ship will be registered only if a representative person is appointed (see A3 below).

3   If registration by companies incorporated other than in the UK is permitted, must a local representative be appointed? If so, are there any restrictions on the identity of that representative?
A representative must be appointed if none of the qualifying owners is resident in the UK. The representative appointed must be either an individual resident in the UK or a company incorporated in an EEA country which has a place of business in the UK.

Where more than one of the qualifying owners of the vessel is resident in the UK, one of the qualifying owners will be appointed the managing owner of the vessel and will receive all correspondence from the Registry.

4   Please summarise any restrictions (for example, as to number, nationality and so on) on who may own shares in shipowning companies incorporated in the UK.
There are no restrictions as to who may own shares in shipowning companies incorporated in the UK for vessels registered on Part I of the Register which relates to merchant ships and pleasure vessels.

476

5   *Please explain any exchange control or other governmental or regulatory consents required in connection with the ownership of ships registered in the UK.*
There are none.

6   *Please explain any special rules for any particular type of vessel.*
The rules are slightly amended for fishing vessels and for small ships as follows:

Fishing vessels

Part 2 of the Register is dedicated to fishing vessels.

In the case of fishing vessels all of the 64 shares must be legally and beneficially owned by a qualifying owner and the vessel must be directed and controlled from within the UK. Any charterer, manager or operator of the vessel must also be a qualifying owner.

For fishing vessels the qualifying owners are persons in categories (a), (b), (e) and (g) listed in Al above.

Where a fishing vessel is owned by a British company, the shares in that company must be owned by qualifying owners.

A fishing vessel may be registered either with 'full registration', where title to the vessel is registered and mortgages may be recorded, or with 'simple registration', which does not show title.

Small ships

Part 3 of the Register is dedicated to small ships. It is administered by the Driver & Vehicle Licensing Centre in Swansea. Small ships are defined as being less than 24 metres in length. For small ships the qualifying owners are:
    (a)   persons in categories (a), (b) and (c) in A1 above;
    (b)   persons who under the British Nationality Act 1981 are British subjects;
    (c)   persons who under the Hong Kong (British Nationality) Order 1986 are British Nationals (overseas); and
    (d)   Commonwealth citizens not falling within those categories.
This part of the Register does not register title and mortgages are not registrable.

7   *Is there any mandatory registration requirement for certain owners (for example, citizens of the UK)?*
There are no mandatory registration requirements other than for fishing vessels. All fishing vessels must be registered, with a few minor exceptions.

B   Eligibility

1   Are any particular types/sizes of ship ineligible for, or exempt from, registration?
No ship is ineligible for registration if it satisfies the ownership requirements.

Even if the ship is otherwise entitled to be registered, the Registrar may refuse to register it on ground that the condition of the ship or its equipment cause a risk to the safety of the ship or its crew, or a risk of pollution.

2   What if any is the maximum age for registration of ships under the British flag?
There are no age restrictions on ships registered under the British flag but vessels over 15 years old require approval from the Registry's technical experts before they can be registered.

C   Names

1   What if any are the restrictions on the name under which a ship may be registered in the UK?
A ship registered in Part 1 (the main register) or Part 4 (the bareboat ships register) may not have a name which is the same as that of another ship registered in either of those parts of the Register. The Registry will also refuse any name which is so similar to an existing ship as to be calculated to deceive or which could cause confusion in an emergency situation or which may be regarded as offensive.

A fishing vessel can have the same name as another ship on the Register so long as that name is different from any other ship registered at the port of choice of the fishing vessel.

2   Is there a procedure for approval of names in advance?
Yes.

3   How does it operate? Does approval confer any priority rights in the use of the name?
An application for approval can be made in advance to the Registry and any approved name can be reserved for a period of up to three months from notification of approval by the Registrar.

The Registrar may allow reservation of a name for 10 years if the ship is intended to replace, within 10 years of the application, another UK registered ship in the ownership of the applicant with the same name.

D   Registration procedure

1   Where may ships intending to fly the British flag be registered:
        1.1   in the UK?
        1.2   abroad?
Permanent registration can only take place in the United Kingdom by application to the Registry in person or by post. Applications in respect of fishing vessels can also be made through a local office of the Registry.

The Registry's address is: The Registry of Shipping and Seamen, PO Box 420, Cardiff CF24 5XR

Where a ship to be registered in Part 1 or 2 of the Register is outside the British Isles and at a port, an application can be made for provisional registration to:

> (a)   any British consular officer (or, in the case of a British Commonwealth country, any member of the High Commissioner's official staff) who has responsibility for that port; or

(b)   in the case of a British colony, the Governor or the relevant person appointed by the Governor.

This officer will forward documentation to the Registrar who, on being satisfied that the ship is eligible for registration, will approve the provisional registration of the ship for a period of three months. A certificate of provisional registry will be issued by the Registrar or officer.

2   What documents and information must be submitted to effect registration?

In order to complete the registration process the owner should lodge with the Registry the following documents:

(a)   an application to register a British ship;

(b)   a declaration of eligibility or if at the time the registration is made the ownership of the ship has not yet passed, a declaration of intent (which shall be followed by a declaration of eligibility on transfer of ownership);

(c)   the certificate of incorporation and any certificates of incorporation on change of name of any company mentioned in a form submitted to the Registry (or in the case of non-UK companies proof of incorporation in accordance with the laws of its place of incorporation);

(d)   where there is a change of flag from an overseas register, a certified transcript of registry issued by that register;

(e)   proof of ownership comprising of:

    (i)   for a new ship, the Builder's Certificate; or

    (ii)   for an older ship, the Bill or Bills of Sale showing the ownership of the vessel for the last five years before the date of the application or, in the event that the ship has previously been registered with full registration within the last five years, the Bill or Bills of Sale showing the ownership since the ship was last registered; and

(f)   a certificate of survey for tonnage and measurement.

3   Does the legal system in the UK lay down any specific requirements as to the contents of any of these documents – for example, of Bills of Sale – and, if so, what are they?

Documents (a) and (b) listed in D2 above are in a prescribed form.

Title documents showing changes in ownership prior to registration under the British flag will normally be in the form approved by the ship's place of registry at the time. In the event of a change in ownership of the ship or a share in the ship once she is under the British flag the Bill of Sale must be in the form prescribed by the Registry.

4   How many originals or copies of each document are required? Are fax or pdf copies of any of them acceptable?

One original of each of the documents is required other than the certificate of incorporation, a copy of which is acceptable. Faxed or pdf copies are not acceptable.

5   Are there any requirements as to the language in which documents must be submitted?

All the prescribed forms must be submitted in the English language. Other documents may be submitted in a foreign language but must be translated (see below).

6   *If they may be submitted in a foreign language, are there any translation require-
        ments? If so, what are they and when must they be complied with?*
Documents submitted in a foreign language must be accompanied by a notarised translation into English at the time of submission.

7   *Please identify any particular requirements of the legal system in the UK with regard
        to the method of execution of any of the registration documents, or with regard to
        notarisation or legalisation.*
Application forms submitted by a company must be signed by an authorised officer on behalf of the company.

        For companies incorporated in England and Wales, documents required to be exe-
cuted as deeds should be done so under seal or by a duly appointed attorney. If the company does not have seal a deed should be executed by either two directors or by a director and the company secretary. Any Power of Attorney used should be executed as a deed and should be presented to the Registrar for inspection

8   *If the initial registration takes place abroad, is that registration final or provisional?*
As mentioned in D1 above, any registration abroad will be provisional.

9   *If provisional, what needs to be done to effect final registration? When must it be done?*
The certificate of provisional registration (see D1 above) will have the effect of a certificate of registry until:
        (a)   the end of three months from the issue of the certificate;
        (b)   the ship's arrival in the UK; or
        (c)   termination of the register at the owner's request.
The full registration procedure set out above must be completed to effect permanent registration.

10   *If provisional, what if any are the restrictions which apply to the vessel pending final
        registration?*
There are no restrictions applying to the ship during provisional registration.

11   *Can a provisionally registered ship be mortgaged?*
No.

E   Technical matters

1   *Please identify the requirements of the UK with regard to inspection, survey, mea-
        surement and the like in respect of newly registered ships.*
The Maritime and Coastguard Agency ('MCA') are responsible for the technical aspects of registration. They will appoint a Customer Service Manager (who is a qualified surveyor) to guide the owner through the registration procedure. Generally the MCA require the survey to

be carried out by an MCA surveyor. In certain circumstances, arrangements can be made for the survey to be carried out by a class surveyor on behalf of the MCA (or other organisations, including the Royal Yachting Association, in respect of yachts).

Once the Registry is satisfied that the documentation produced to it is acceptable for registration of the vessel, the Registry will issue a Carving and Marking Note showing the official number and other details of the ship which must be marked on her.

The Carving and Marking Note must be signed by the owner (for pleasure vessels less than 24 metres in length) but for all other ships must be certified by a surveyor or, if the vessel is abroad, it may also be signed by a consular officer.

2   By when must these requirements be complied with?
The Carving and Marking Note must be completed and returned to the Registrar within three months of issue otherwise the Registrar may cancel it and consider the application for registration as withdrawn.

The Registrar will not normally complete permanent registration of the ship until she has been duly carved and marked and the survey has been carried out.

F   Transfer of ownership

1   Please answer Sections D and E above in respect of a transfer of ownership of a vessel already registered in the UK.
A change of ownership can only be registered in the UK at the Registry.

On selling a vessel or shares in a vessel a Bill of Sale (form MSF 4705) should be completed and presented by the buyers to the Registry. The Bill of Sale must be executed as a deed (see D7 above). The seller must also inform the Registry in writing of the sale and the name and address of the buyer and must also return the Certificate of Registry for the vessel to the Registry.

The buyers must complete a declaration of eligibility and, if they are a company, present a copy of their certificate of incorporation and any copies of any certificates of incorporation on change of name.

The application for transfer of the vessel or the shares in it must be made within 30 days of the change in ownership. If this is not done the Registry can cancel the registration of the vessel which would necessitate a new application for registration with the greater application fees involved.

Other requirements are as set out in sections D and E above.

After submission of the required documents the Registry will issue a new certificate of registry and will send this to the new owners together with an endorsed Bill of Sale.

2   Please explain any exchange control or other governmental or regulatory consents required in connection with the sale to a foreign flag of a vessel registered under the British flag.
There are none.

G   Deletion

1   Please outline the procedure for deletion of vessels from the British flag.

The ship may be deleted from the Register on the application of the owner. The Registrar will also delete the ship if she is no longer eligible to be registered or if she is destroyed.

On deleting the ship the Registrar will issue a closure transcript to the owner of the ship. On receipt of the closure transcript the owner must return the certificate of registry to the Registry for cancellation.

If there are any mortgages registered against the ship, these will be shown on the closed transcript and will remain on the Register until their satisfaction.

2   Please answer, either separately or by reference to your earlier answers, the questions listed under Section D in respect of the deletion, as opposed to new registration, of a vessel.

No other documents are required to effect deletion of the vessel. The answers set out in D above, where applicable, apply equally for deletion.

H   Certificates/transcripts

1   Please identify the certificates and other documents issued to an owner on registration of his ship under the British flag.

On completion of registration the Registrar will issue a certificate of registry to the owners showing the details of the owners of the ship and how the shares in the ship are held and showing the full technical details of the ship.

The certificate of registration will be valid for a period of five years, and the vessel's registration must then be renewed for further consecutive five-year periods.

2   Please outline the procedure (including fees payable) for obtaining information on the registered ownership of and encumbrances on vessels registered in the UK.

The Register may be inspected at the Registry by any member of the public in person. A transcript of registry may also be obtained by post on written request. The fees are set out in Section I below.

I   Fees/taxes

1   What fees are currently payable:
*   1.1   on new registration?*
*   1.2   on transfer of ownership?*
*   1.3   on deletion?*

Fees

Registration of a ship (including registration of a ship whose registry has expired): £130

Registration of transfer of ownership or of shares in a registered ship:

     (a)   one transfer   £80

     (b)   where more than one transfer in relation to a ship is logged at the same time:

        (i) two transfers: £95

        (ii) three transfers: £115

(iii) four transfers or more:	£130
Renewal of registration (without a break in registration) (before expiry):	£50
Issue of duplicate certificate:	£13
Issue of transcripts of entries in the Register relating to any one ship:	
(a) for current entries:	£13
(b) for other entries:	£25
Personal inspection of the Register:	£12
Registration of change of name of a ship:	£35
Registration of change of port of choice:	£35
Registration of change of measurement, tonnage or engine particulars recorded in the Register:	£35
Transfer to a port in a British possession:	£35
Transfer from a port in a British possession:	£115
Application to the Registrar for provisional registration:	£115
Full registration of a ship directly following provisional registration:	£55

2   *What annual or other ongoing fees or taxes are payable in respect of ships registered in the UK?*

There are no annual or other ongoing fees or taxes payable.

J   Parallel registration

1   Is parallel registration permitted (a) onto the Register, or (b) from the Register?

Part 4 of the Register is a register of bareboat chartered vessels. Parallel registration is not permitted from the Register.

2   *If so, what if any specific governmental or other consents are required?*

No specific governmental consents are required.

3   Is the period of parallel registration limited? If so, is it renewable?

The period of registration is limited to the term of the bareboat charter or the expiry of five years, whichever is the earlier. The registration is renewable during the last three months of the current registration period.

4   *If parallel registration is dependent on the existence of a demise charter, does the UK have a specific definition of demise or bareboat charter for these purposes? If so, what is it?*

A bareboat charter is defined as 'the hiring of a ship for a stipulated period on terms which give the charterer possession and control of the ship, including the right to appoint the master and crew'.

5   *Please answer the questions under Sections A to E above with reference to application for parallel registration onto the UK's register.*

The documentation required to effect the bareboat registration are:

    (a)   a declaration of eligibility;

    (b)   a copy of the charterparty (showing the name of the ship, the name of the charterer and the name of the owners and the length of the charter period);

    (c)   a Certificate of Registry from the country of primary registration; and

    (d)   a Certificate of Incorporation and Certificates of Incorporation on Change of Name for any charterers that are companies. A representative person must be appointed if none of the charterers is resident in the UK.

The requirements for registration on Part 4 of the Register are the same as those for the Part 1 of the Register as set out above, including the satisfaction of survey and marking requirements. The Registry will notify the registry of the country of primary registration of the bareboat charter under the British flag.

6   *Can/must mortgages on ships parallel registered into the UK's registry also be registered in the UK?*

Mortgages registered on the primary register of the ship cannot also be registered on the UK Register.

7   *Under what circumstances will/may the parallel registration of a ship in Part 4 of the register be terminated or revoked?*

The Registrar will close the ship's register on the application of the charterer, on destruction of the ship or on the ship being no longer eligible for registration. The register will also be closed if the certificate of registry for the ship expires and is not renewed. On closure of the register the Registrar will notify the primary registry.

K   General

1   *Please identify the principal statutes and regulations in the UK governing the registration of ships.*

The Merchant Shipping Act 1995 and the Merchant Shipping (Registration of Ship) Regulations 1993 both as amended.

2   *Are there any other matters in the context of registration of ships under the legal system in the UK which you feel should be emphasised?*

The UK has a tonnage tax regime where companies have one year from commencing the operation of ships in the UK to elect (on a group wide basis) into the regime. The election into the regime is renewable annually.

    More detailed information on registration together with the forms required for registration can be found at the MCA's website www.mcga.gov.uk.

* Contributed by Philippa Sharratt of Stephenson Harwood, London, England.

¹ As with Chapter 7, I am very grateful to my colleague, Philippa Sharratt, for helping with collating and editing the replies to our questionnaires.

Chapter 12

The role of insurance in shipping and ship financing

Graham Barnes

Insurance is the underwriting of specified risks, confined to accidents characterised by the unexpected, under which the aggregate of all premiums charged are actuarially assessed, on past experience and available data, to meet all anticipated claims on such specified risks within a class of business. Hence the requisite for full disclosure of all material facts, circumstances and claims records, as embraced in the term *uberrima fides* or utmost goodfaith, on the part of assureds and their insurance brokers when negotiating with underwriters in the placing of any insurance.

Despite periodic crises, London continues to retain its standing as being the principal centre for marine insurance, centred on the Lloyds subscription market attributed with its ability to underwrite new and innovative risks. London is estimated to insure 21 per cent of global marine business, before taking into account its preponderant position with protection and indemnity (P&I) clubs. However, London is closely followed by the Norwegian and American markets, both very competitive in underwriting the traditional risks. Asian markets are now beginning to grow with their volumes of domestic business.

Insurance has been evolving in London over the last four centuries. Each stage of this evolution was marked by some crisis resulting in new insurance laws, such as the various Marine Insurance and Life Assurance Acts, that combined to disallow wagering contracts and introduced the mandatory requirement for named assureds to have an insurable interest and, further, made all insurances contracts of indemnity, unless otherwise exempted. The most significant legislation governing marine insurance was the Marine Insurance Act of 1906 which laid down the fundamental principles of marine insurance as applied today.

The extent of new legislation and regulations governing shipping and insurance that has recently been introduced, and more pending, is unprecedented. The International Maritime Organisation (IMO), created in 1960 under the auspices of the United Nations, began with upgrading the Safety of Life at Sea (SOLAS) convention and has now implemented regulations covering everything from ship construction, carriage of cargoes, navigation, safety equipment, the all embracing International Safety Management Code (ISM) and the latest regulation being the International Ship and Port Facility Security Code Port State Control; all enforceable through Port State Control. The United States of America, with a preference for their own legislation, have effected their own equivalent to the ISPS with the US Maritime Security Act (MTSA). All this legislation bears directly on the marine insurances taken out by shipowners because compliance failure can be held to be breaches of legality and render such insurances void or voidable. P&I club rules make full compliance with SOLAS regulations a condition of cover; consequently any breach will result in claims not being payable, excepting those liabilities on which payment has to be guaranteed.

The combination of the very much higher liability limits plus the requirement for payment guarantees under the new protocols and amendments to shipowners' limitation of liability conventions put the P&I clubs' mutual system under exceptional strain. This particularly applies to the smaller clubs.

The consequences can only be ever higher premiums, or calls for protection and indemnity cover combined with the P&I clubs exercising greater selection against those operators who are deemed to be higher risk or substandard. Minor shipowners operating older vessels could find they are denied cover from P&I clubs of the International Group.

For example the conventions shown in Exhibit 12.1 have increased shipowners' liabilities by multiples.

Exhibit 12.1(a)

Shipowners' Limitation of Liability Conventions – Increases

Convention on Limitation of Liability for Maritime Claims (LLMC), 1976 – 1 December 1986, and 1996 Protocol, effective 13 May 2004

Increased by 230% to 1800% depending upon size of vessel and type of liability

The Limitation of Liability for Marine Claims 1976, limiting property damage, personal injury and death and passenger liabilities, replaced the International Convention Relating to the Limitation of the Liability of Owners of Seagoing Ships in 1986. The LLMC 1976 limits for property claims began at SDR167,000 and third party personal injury claims from SDR333,000, each with stage increases with vessel size. Passenger liabilities being limited to SDR46,666 per passenger capacity of the vessel; capped at SDR25m.

1996 Protocol to the LLMC, effective from 13 May 2004, increased these liability limits to respectively SDR1m and SDR2m, again increasing with vessel size. Passenger liabilities increased to SDR175,000 multiplied by passenger capacity, with no limitation cap.

Athens Convention relating to the Carriage of Passengers and their Luggage by Sea (PAL), 1974 – 28 April 1987, and Athens Protocol, 2002 – 1 November 2002. Pending ratification

New Strict Liability SDR250,000

Athens Convention 1974 consolidated two earlier Brussels conventions dealing with passengers and luggage.

Maximum Limit SDR400,000, or unlimited

The Athens Protocol 2002 effective 12 months after 10 national states have ratified the protocol, expected 2005. The Protocol increases liabilities per passenger from SDR46,666 to SDR250,000 on strict liability basis, to be guaranteed, and to a recommended maximum of SDR400,000.

Pending ratification

Under Athens Convention liabilities are on a per capita basis whereas LLMC calculates liabilities on a vessel's passenger capacity.

International Convention on Civil Liability for Oil Pollution Damage (CLC) 1992 – 29 November 1992 plus Amendment – Effective 1 November 2003

The Civil Liability Convention covers those who suffer oil pollution damage resulting from maritime casualties involving oil-carrying ships. The Convention places the liability for such damage on the owner of the responsible ship.

(Continued)

Exhibit 12.1(a) *(Continued)*

The Amendment increased the liability limits from 1 November 2003, as follows:

- Tankers not exceeding 5,000 gross tons, liability is limited to SDR4.51m. (Previous limit was SDR3.0m)
- Tankers between 5,000 to 140,000 gross tons: liability limit SDR4.51m plus SDR631 for each additional gross tonne over 5,000. (Previous limit was SDR3m plus SDR420 for each additional gross tonne)
- Tankers over 140,000 gross tons: liability limit SDR89.77m. (Previous limit was SDR59.7m)

CLC 1992 increased on 1 November 2003 by 50.37% from SDR59.7m to SDR89.77m

The 1992 CLC Convention has been ratified by 104 States (93.44% of world tonnage)

International Convention on the Establishment of an International Fund for Compensation for Oil Pollution Damage (FUND), 1992 – 16 October 1978
Plus 5/2003 Fund Protocol, effected 1 November 2003

IOPC Fund increased from SDR135m to SDR203m.

The International Oil Pollution Compensation Funds (IOPC Funds) is an international liability and compensation regime for oil pollution damage caused by oil spills from tankers, under which the owner of a tanker is liable to pay compensation up to the applicable CLC 1992 limit for oil pollution damage following an escape of persistent oil from his ship. If that amount does not cover all the admissible claims, further compensation is available from the 1992 Fund if the damage occurs in a State which is a Member of that Fund. Additional compensation may also be available from the Supplementary Fund if the State is a Member of that Fund as well.

Funded by companies and importers

The Fund has full recourse against shipowners

The 1992 Fund supplanted the 1971 Fund Convention on 24 May 2002.
The 1992 Fund Convention has been ratified by 91 States, representing 88.39% of world merchant shipping tonnage.

International Oil Pollution Compensation Supplementary Fund Protocol 2003 increases amounts available under the 1992 Fund Convention to an overall limit of SDR750m – effected 3 March 2005

New third tier Supplementary Fund increases compensation to SDR750m

Levels of compensation for victims of oil pollution from oil tanker accidents substantially increased on 3 March 2005 following the entry into force of the 2003 Protocol establishing the International Oil Pollution Compensation Supplementary Fund.
This new additional Fund supplements the compensation available under the 1992 Civil Liability Convention (CLC) and the International Convention on the Establishment of an International Fund for Compensation for Oil Pollution Damage (FUND) by providing a third tier of compensation. Participation is optional and is open to all States that are parties to the 1992 Fund Convention.
The total amount of compensation payable for any one incident now limited to a new combined total of SDR750m, just over US$1,145m, including the amount of compensation paid under the existing 1992 CLC/Fund Convention.
The 2003 Protocol will apply to damage in the territory, including the territorial sea and the Exclusive Economic Zone of a Contracting State.

Full recourse against responsible shipowners retained

(Continued)

Exhibit 12.1(a) *(Continued)*

International Convention on Liability and Compensation for Damage in Connection with the Carriage of Hazardous and Noxious Substances by Sea (HNS), 1996 – 3 May 1996	**New US$320m**

The Convention will make it possible for up to SDR250m (about US$320m) to be paid out in compensation to victims of accidents involving HNS, such as chemicals.

International Convention on Civil Liability for Bunker Oil Pollution Damage, 2001 – 23 March 2001	**New**

The Convention was adopted to ensure that adequate, prompt, and effective compensation is available to persons who suffer damage caused by spills of oil, when carried as fuel in ships' bunkers.

Wreck Removal Convention (WRC)	**New**

A draft wreck removal convention (WRC) is being developed by the IMO Legal Committee and it is anticipated that it will be ready for consideration by a Diplomatic Conference in the 2005–2006 biennium.

Source: Author's own.

Mandatory certificates

Under the above conventions, to which must be added the International Safety Management Code (ISM) and the International Ship and Port Facility Security Code (ISPS), the following certificates much be carried by the relevant ships. Insurance, particularly marine liability insurance in the form of protection and indemnity cover, is now compulsory.

Exhibit 12.1(b)

Insurance related certificates to be carried by ships

Mandatory certificates under SOLAS

International Ship Security Certificate (ISSC) against terrorism risks.	The International Ship and Port Facility Security Code (ISPS Code), under SOLAS	Effective for Ships & Ports from 1 July 2004
Safety Management Certificate (SMC), and Document of Compliance (DOC).	As under the International Safety Management Code (ISM) for safety and pollution prevention of vessels under (SOLAS Chapter IX).	Applies to all passenger ships, oil tankers, chemical carriers, gas carriers since 1 July 1998 and cargo ships and mobile drilling units over 500 gt since 1 July 2002.
BLUE CARD arranged by the P&I club to be carried by all tankers. Passenger Vessels – Guarantees for liabilities to passengers for injury and death to be provided by P&I clubs and/or other guarantors for liabilities arising from terrorism.	POLLUTION LIABILITY GUARANTEE per CLC 1992 Athens Protocol 2002 SDR250,000 per passenger for marine liabilities and a reduced amount for terrorism	To be carried by all tankers since 30 May 1996. To be introduced 12 months after ratification by 10 states.

(Continued)

Exhibit 12.1(b)   *(Continued)*

Equivalent mandatory requirements for the USA

US Maritime Security Act (MTSA)	Security plans against terrorism must be submitted to the US Coast Guard	No limitation of liability in event of non-compliance.
Certificates of Financial Responsibility (COFRs) under US Oil Pollution Act 1990 to guarantee statutory oil liabilities to US third party plaintiffs.	US Coast Guard approved OPA Guarantor, available from The Shipowners' Insurance and Guaranty Company Limited, Shoreline Mutual or WQIS.	Statutory Liability Limits under OPA 90 guaranteed. OPA 90 + CERCLA: • Tankers US$1,500 per gt • Dry Cargo US$900 per gt Increases proposed
Passenger Vessel Financial Responsibility guarantees. Provided by P&I clubs against a bank guarantee, or LOC, to cover liabilities arising from non-performance.	To the Federal Maritime Commission (FMC) for US$15m. FMC advise the US$15m limit to be increased.	For liabilities to passengers for injury, death or non-performance, to include return of passenger prepayment deposits.

Source: Author's own.

Marine insurances as security for ship financing

Ships carry high insurance risks by being large and constantly on the move, carrying cargoes or passengers. Similarly, aircraft are a high insurance risk relative to property or real estate.

Ships may not only have large total loss claims, which could include 'general average' contributions for any sacrificial jettisoning of cargo, but they can incur considerably larger, potentially unlimited, liabilities to third parties arising from collision and pollution, as well as passenger and crew liabilities.

Financiers of ships have to be satisfied that a financed ship is insured against all loss or damage not only to safeguard the security interest on the sound value of the ship but also to ensure that all potential liabilities of the ship are insured to sufficient limits so as to prevent a maritime lien being attached in favour of third party plaintiffs potentially ranking prior to a mortgage.

The essential criteria for all ship financing considerations are:

- that the estimated operating profit comfortably exceeds the shipowner's debt servicing obligations by way of interest and principal repayments, where the principal repayments well exceed the potential depreciation of the ship;
- that the pessimistic (forced) sale value of the ship will, at any time and in any place, exceed the outstanding debt secured on the vessel in the currency of the debt;
- that any loss or damage of the ship is fully insured on terms and for amounts that will meet either the cost of repair or, in the event of total or constructive total loss or any unrepaired damage claims, clear the outstanding indebtedness secured on the ship;
- that any liabilities for which the ship is found responsible are insured for sufficient amounts to ensure that no maritime lien attaches to the ship ranking ahead of any security interest

by way of mortgage, or more critically causes a lessor to become liable as the ultimate owner – ideally liability cover should include the provision to arrange for the release of a ship from arrest following a liability incident and hence allow the ship to continue trading; though not explicitly covered under the P&I clubs' rules this is a service the clubs habitually provide;

- that through a registered mortgage, a bank is always able to repossess a ship following default by the mortgagor, and realise a resale value in a jurisdiction of its choice sufficient to clear the debt.

Marine insurances, under one type of policy or another, can be effected to meet points 3, 4 and 5 of the above criteria and can include a contingency insurance for secured lenders against any breach of warranty by shipowners or operators or managers either under mortgagees' interest insurance or lessors' interest insurance. Loss of hire insurance covering the period a ship is out of commission, undergoing repairs, resulting from damage following a marine peril, would contribute towards point 1 above.

There are numerous classes of marine policies, each covering different perils, or risks. For example, hull and machinery marine policies essentially cover physical loss or damage to an insured vessel; general average contributions for the sacrificial jettisoning of cargo, and a proportion of damage liability to third parties following collision caused by perils of the sea. The perils insured are detailed in the policy conditions under an insuring or perils clause. The consequences of war are covered by war risks insurance, and shipowners' liabilities to cargo and crew, collision liabilities excluded under a hull and machinery policy, and other third party liabilities are covered under the protection and indemnity coverage by P&I clubs. Bankers should note that collision liabilities are insurable under either the hull and machinery insurances or by a P&I club, and are frequently insured by a combination of both.

For each class of insurance there are differing insuring conditions under numerous clauses. For example, the London Institute Time Clauses provide for three different hull and machinery insurance conditions for navigating vessels under Institute Time Clauses – Hulls (1 October 1983). Full conditions covers all loss or damage to the vessel, including general average and three-quarters collision liability; the more limited conditions cover only total or constructive total loss of the vessel but still include general average and three-quarters collision liability; and the most limited cover total loss only. Each only allow for additional hull cover up to 25 per cent of the insured.

In addition to the London Institute Hull clauses, shipowners have the option to use the American Hull Clauses or the Norwegian Plan or the German Hull Clauses, plus many other national marine hull clauses, all of which are different.

Shipowners' Marine Liability cover, insured under the 'First Party Indemnity' principal known as Protection and Indemnity cover, is recognised as being critical to ship financiers. Third party plaintiffs able to establish a maritime lien, or a promissory lien, or a statutory lien will prime the rights of a mortgagee on a mortgaged ship. For other forms of ship financing, such as unsecured corporate financing and, more critically, lease financing, non-payment in whole or in part of legal liabilities will be more serious, as detailed in Exhibit 12.2.

Exhibit 12.2

Financing risks of a shipowner failing to pay legal liabilities following a catastrophe that either results in the P&I club declining the claim, or the liabilities exceeding P&I cover limits

Type of financing	The liability risk resulting in insolvency and bankruptcy of owners/borrowers	Potential consequences
Single ship mortgage	Maritime Liens, Possessory Liens, Statutory Liens can each prime a Mortgage in favour plaintiffs, such as crew, passengers, salvors & harbour masters. Some jurisdictions provide P&I clubs with maritime liens for outstanding calls.	Default and loss of the loan
Corporate financing unsecured	All plaintiffs and creditors of all subsidiary owning and management companies will have priority over unsecured lenders.	Borrowers declare bankruptcy or file under Chapter 11. Loan default – likely to be larger than a single ship financing.
Ship lease financing	Lessors are at risk of becoming liable for outstanding liabilities for which a ship, owned by a Lessor, is found responsible which are unrecoverable from the Lessee and/or the Managers or Operators.	Lessee declares bankruptcy or files under Chapter 11. Corporate veils risk being pierced. Loss of the financing plus liability for outstanding liabilities unrecoverable from Lessee/owners and/or managers/operators.

Source: Author's own.

Summary of the marine insurances available to shipowners

A list of the principal marine risks and the type of insurance available to cover each risk is contained in Exhibit 12.3, together with the limit of indemnity under each insurance.

Insurance Covenants

Ship financiers and their lawyers first need to detail the insurances required to be taken out by the shipowner under the terms of the loan agreement or ship mortgage.

Due to the possibility of changes in the regulations governing shipping following the introduction of new laws under jurisdictions that could well come to emulate the US Oil

Exhibit 12.3

Marine insurances – arranged by owners and assignable as security

Marine insurances

Arranged by shipowners and/or managers or bareboat charterers

The Risk	Covered by (type of policy)	Indemnity or claim amount
Maritime Perils Named perils per Clause 6 of ITC plus • Collision Liability • General Average • Salvage • Sue & Labour • Agreed Insured Values	**Hull & Machinery Policy** for: • Total Loss • Particular Average (PA) partial loss and collision damage • General Average (GA) • Collision Liability (RDC) • Expenses of Salvage and Charges • Sue & Labour	• Agreed Insured Value or Cost of Repairs or unrepaired damages • General Average contributions to cargo liability (indemnity up to Hull Value, subject to any cover with P&I club) • Sue & labour
Ancillary losses & liabilities following Total or Constructive Total Loss of the Vessel.	**Increased Value,** Disbursements, Freight, Hull Interest and Time Charter Hire, following Total Loss subject to Disbursement Warranty under Hull & Machinery Policy.	Agreed sum insured not to exceed the Disbursements Warranty Limit under the Hull & Machinery policy (usually 25% of the H&M insured value), paying only upon Total or Constructive Total Loss under Hull & Machinery Policy.
War and hostilities Blocking and Trapping, Confiscation and damage from hostilities, mines, strikes, riots and civil commotion, sabotage, vandalism and malicious mischief. **Liabilities** arising from War and Terrorism (War P&I) – primary cover	**War Risks Policy** with either: • commercial markets, or • a mutual War Club Subject War Risks Trading Warranties (no trading in high risk areas without prior agreement and additional premium). **War Protection & Indemnity extension to the Risks Policy** Primary first loss liability cover limited to the Agreed Insured Value of the vessel.	Agreed Insured Value or Cost of Repairs. (Confiscation by Flag Country and loss arising from insolvency, financial default and failure to meet liabilities and pay fines are excluded.) Additional cover for liabilities arising from terrorism, insured to Agreed Insured Value with the War P&I extension, the War Risks policy can pay the agreed insured value twice – physical loss & damage and also liabilities.
	A mutual War Club, available through P&I club managers.	Cover limits either US$400m, or US$500m, or £350m for War P&I liability cover.
Loss of hire following a damage or a PA claim to the Vessel under the Hull & Machinery Policy	**Loss of Earnings or Loss of Hire Policy**	Daily Indemnity on either profit or earnings, subject to an excess – usually 14 days limited to agreed number of days – most often 180 days each accident and in all on the policy. No claim in event of Total Loss.
Passenger refund liabilities due to cruise cancellation arising from a marine peril (per H&M).	**Passenger Money Insurance** for cruise lines.	Reimbursement of passenger deposit monies. No claim in event of Total Loss

(Continued)

Exhibit 12.3   *(Continued)*

Marine liability insurances (Protection & Indemnity)

Under P&I club rules, for mutuality reasons, club managers must give written approval to a ship becoming mortgaged. Certificates of Entry are non-assignable

The risk	Covered by (type of policy)	Indemnity or claim amount
Liabilities to • passengers and/or cargo • crew • pollution • collision liabilities • damage to port installations • removal of wreck **Excess War P&I Cover including liabilities for terrorism**	**Either** Entry in a Protection & Indemnity Club which is a member of the International Group of P&I associations (Full Entry as per rules)	Maximum approx. US$4.50bn liability limit any one accident, excepting: • oil pollution which the Group P&I clubs limit to US$1bn • the legal liability limit under the applicable Shipowners' Limitation of Liability Convention • War P&I and Terrorism limited to US$500m in EXCESS of the lower amount of either: the fair market value of the ship, the hull value insured for War Risks or US$100m • liabilities resulting from a chemical, biological or electro-magnetic weapon, cover limit US$20m • new liability limits insured when notified
	or Fixed Premium Insurers (as per conditions)	Fixed Premium P&I insurers have lower limits of cover. Often not more than US$500m. No excess War P&I cover.
Legal costs and expenses	Freight Demurrage and Defence Club (FD&D) another class of P&I club cover	Costs that the club consider reasonable to enforce claims or defend actions on matters concerning the operation of the vessel.

Other marine insurances

The risk	Covered by (type of policy)	Indemnity or claim amount
Laid up **or** **working in port**	Port Risks Clauses covering: • Hull & Machinery, and • Collision Liabilities, and • Expenses of Salvage, Charges and Sue & Labour, and • Protection & Indemnity, as per clauses, and • Removal of Wreck. War risks may be included by extension. Excluding Pollution Liabilities, unless 'bought back' for certain events.	• Agreed Value for total loss or damage, plus • Liabilities up to the Insured Hull Value, or as agreed, plus • Salvage charges, plus • Removal of wreck. Always subject conditions of cover.

(Continued)

Exhibit 12.3 *(Continued)*

Oil pollution liabilities	**Excess Oil Spillage and**	Up to the Liability Limit insured sub-
excess of P&I cover limit.	**Pollution Insurance**. Rarely	ject full payment by P&I club of
	required since P&I clubs increased	underlying limit insured for oil
	their oil pollution cover limit to	pollution.
	US$1bn. More often used for oil rigs.	
Oil drilling & production	**Rig, Platform and Barge** wordings	Limited to sums insured
	All risks, loss or damage, cost of	Review special provisions relating to
	control.	Sound Market Value.
	Comprehensive General Liability	

Source: Author's own.

Pollution Act, and the further probability of insurers amending their insurance clauses and terms of cover within the loan period, the insurance covenants need to be either amendable at the discretion of lenders or sufficiently widely worded to allow lenders a substantial degree of flexibility over approval of insurance terms and conditions.

The recommended insurance covenants in Exhibit 12.4 are provided as a guide for mortgagees. Amendments will obviously be required where any financing is being made under a lease and minor amendments may be required on a case-by-case basis.

Exhibit 12.4

Insurance covenants and related undertakings

Insurance Covenants and Related Undertakings

The Borrower/Obligor/Mortgagor/Shipowner (hereinafter referred to as the Owner) covenants with the Mortgagee/Lessor/Security Agent/Assignee (hereinafter referred to as the Assignee), in respect of each Vessel that is Mortgaged or Leased to the Assignee (hereinafter referred to as the Collateral Vessel) for the duration of the Security Period, to procure at the Owner' cost and expense the following:

1 **Insurances, insuring conditions, values and amounts:**

Insurances covering physical loss and/or damage and liabilities to crew, cargo and third party interests of, or in connection with, the Collateral Vessel on terms, conditions, insured values and governing jurisdiction as expressly required by the Assignee. Such Insurances shall be underwritten a full one hundred per cent (100%) by insurers of financial standing to be approved by Mortgagees, either directly by the Owner or through the Owner's Insurance Brokers approved by the Assignee. Such approvals not to be unreasonably withheld or delayed.

Unless and until otherwise agreed in writing, the Insurances required by and acceptable to the Assignee will be:

1.1 **Hull and Machinery insurance:**

(A) on insuring conditions as wide as under the International Hull Clauses (01 November 2003), or Institute Time Clauses Hulls (1 November 1995), or Norwegian Marine Insurance Plan of 1996 as updated under subsequent versions, or German ADS and DTV conditions, or American Institute Hull Clauses (2 June 1977), or French Maritime Clauses dated 1 January 1998 as updated and amended. Other insuring conditions to be approved by the Mortgagee.

(Continued)

494

Exhibit 12.4   *(Continued)*

(B) the Value Insured shall be an agreed value that is the higher of:

(a)   the market value of the Collateral Vessel (as at the beginning of the relevant policy year), and

(b)   one hundred and twenty per cent (120%) of the outstanding indebtedness under the mortgage, or all mortgages, on the Collateral Vessel.

(C) the deductible amount, including any aggregate deductible or retained first loss limit, in respect of claims shall not exceed one hundred thousand US Dollars (US$100,000) any one accident or occurrence, or such higher amount as the Assignee may agree (such agreement not to be unreasonably withheld).

1.2 **Increased Value insurance** (total loss only, including excess liabilities):

(A) on insuring conditions as wide as the Institute Time Clauses Hulls Disbursements and Increased Value (1 November 1995), or American Institute Increased Value and Excess Liabilities Clauses (3 November 1977), or the equivalent under the Norwegian Marine Insurance Plan of 1999 or French Maritime Clause dated 1 January 1998; and

(B) for a maximum insured amount but not exceeding the limitation under the Disbursements Warranty in the applicable Hull & Machinery insuring conditions in 1.1.(A) above. (Such Disbursements Warranty limit is commonly twenty five per cent (25%) of the insured value under the Hull & Machinery policy).

1.3 **War Risks insurance:**

Either

(a)   on conditions as wide as the Institute War and Strikes Clauses Hulls – Time (1 November 1995), to include the London Blocking and Trapping Clause (LPO 444), or American Institute Hull War Risks and Strikes Clauses (1 December 1977); and

(b)   extended to include War Protection & Indemnity cover on insuring conditions as wide as that provided by the Protection and Indemnity Clubs under their excess War P&I cover, as in 1.4(B) below. Institute Protection and Indemnity War Strikes Clauses Hulls – Time (20 July 1987) extended to cover liabilities for crew, cargo and collision being acceptable; and

(c)   extended to cover 'piracy' should piracy be excluded under the Hull & Machinery Insurance insuring conditions in 1.1 above.

(d)   the Value Insured shall be an agreed value that is the fair market value of the Collateral Vessel (as at the beginning of the relevant policy year).

Or   Full entry in a recognised mutual War Risks Club or Association.

1.4 **Protection and Indemnity cover:**

The Owner, together with managers and/or bareboat charterers and/or their agents, shall be full members or joint members of a Protection and Indemnity Club that is within the International Group of Protection and Indemnity Associations.

(A) The Collateral Vessel to be entered in such Protection and Indemnity Club and thereby be covered for all protection and indemnity risks to the full scope and limits available under club rules for any one accident or occurrence. Such limits currently being 2½% of London Convention Limits for Property Damage, excepting oil pollution which is covered to a limit of one billion US Dollars (US$1,000,000,000). And

(B) Excess War Protection and Indemnity Risks, including terrorism, also to be covered to the maximum limit available under club rules; currently being US$500,000,000 in excess the primary limit for War Protection and Indemnity covered by the extension of the War Risks cover under 1.3(b) above.

(C) Where the Collateral Vessel is a tanker, or a combination vessel capable of carrying oil as cargo, protection and indemnity cover to be extended to include all voyages to and from the United States of America; in respect of which the Owner shall ensure that US Voyage Quarterly Declarations are made for each quarter ending 20 May, 20 August, 20 November and 20 February no later than six weeks after the end of each quarter to the Protection and Indemnity Club.

(Continued)

Exhibit 12.4 *(Continued)*

    (D) The Owner shall notify the Protection and Indemnity Club of the Assignee's interest in the Collateral Vessel, and procure from club managers their written confirmation that the Cesser of Insurance rule relating to the mortgaging of vessels has been waived, as provided in the club managers' Letter of Undertaking in Schedule 3 below.

1.5 **Freight, Demurrage and Defence** cover on terms and conditions under the applicable class rules of the Protection and Indemnity Club in which the Collateral Vessel is entered, if required by the Assignee.

1.6 **Loss of earnings or loss of charter hire insurance**, subject to ABS 1 October 1983 or Norwegian wordings, including war risks, if required by the Assignee.

1.7 **Additional Insurances**, which in the reasonable opinion of the Assignee become necessary as a result of: (a) any subsequent reduction or limitation in cover from that stipulated in the Insurances herein above, or (b) any change in the navigation areas or use of the Collateral Vessel as originally forecasted, or (c) any change in laws or decree or navigation rules of any sort which might result in certain risks and liabilities related to the Collateral Vessel becoming, in the opinion of the Assignee, inadequately insured.

  2 **Securitisation of the Insurances**

    Notices of Assignment, Loss Payable clauses and reinsurance Cut Through clause to secure the interests of the Assignee in the said Insurances, as follows:

2.1 Each of the Insurances referred to in paragraphs 1.1 to 1.3 and 1.6 to 1.7 above, and each of the relevant policies when issued, shall be endorsed with:

    (A) a Notice of Assignment of Insurances signed by all assureds named on the relevant policy, and

    (B) the Loss Payable Clause;

    (C) Where the Assignee is a lessor, the Assignee to be included as a named assured.

2.2 If one or more of the Insurances referred to in paragraphs 1.1 to 1.3, are not effected with insurers rated at least BBB by Standard and Poor's, or equivalent rating by another international rating agency, or are effected with a captive insurer, then the Owner shall procure documentary evidence that such insurers have effected facultative reinsurances with reinsurers and through brokers, in each case, acceptable to the Assignee. Such facultative reinsurances to be:

    (A) on same terms, conditions, agreed insured value, law and jurisdiction, period and expiry date as the primary insurances, and

    (B) fully reinsured with reinsurers of financial standing to be approved by Mortgagees, with the primary, or ceding, insurer's retention not exceeding five per cent (5%) of the insured risks, and

    (C) are assigned by the primary, or ceding, insurer in favour of the Assignee by endorsement of the Notice of Assignment, and

    (D) are endorsed with a cut-through clause on the terms set out below, or otherwise satisfactory to the Assignee:

'The reinsurers hereby agree that in the event of any claim arising under the reinsurances in respect of a total loss or other claim where, as provided by the Security Documents, such claim is to be paid to the person named as sole loss payee under the primary insurances, the reinsurers shall in lieu of payment to the reassured, its successor in interest and assigns, pay to the person named as sole loss payee under the primary insurances effected by the Assured that portion of any loss due for which the reinsurers would otherwise be liable to pay the reassured (subject to proof of loss), it being understood and agreed that any such payment by the reinsurers shall (to the extent of such payment) fully discharge and release the reinsurers from any and all further liability in connection therewith. Any payment due under this clause shall not contravene any law, statute or decree of (....name of the insurer country....).'

  3 **Letters of Undertaking:**

3.1 In respect of each Insurance referred to in paragraphs 1.1 to 1.3 above and reinsurance under 2.2 above when applicable, and for every renewal thereof, Owner's insurance brokers to provide the Assignee with the following:

    (A) Letters of Undertaking addressed to the Assignee, in a form no less wide than the Standard Letter of Undertaking 2002 recommended by London Market Insurance Brokers' Committee.

(Continued)

Exhibit 12.4 *(Continued)*

(B) Copy Cover Notes detailing cover terms, conditions and underwriting security showing net underwritten lines per insurer.

(C) Such brokers to further undertake to give immediate notice of any insurance being subject to the Condition Survey Warranty (JH.115) and/or Structural Condition Warranty (JH.722) and/or the Classification Clause (Hulls) 29 June 1989 (JH. 131) and/or any other classification clause, 30 days prior to the attachment date of any insurance bearing any of these warranties, for example,, ISM).

(D) In addition, Owner's insurance brokers to undertake that their lien on the insurance policies for premium shall be confined to premium outstanding on the insurances covering the Mortgaged Ship or to sign separate policies covering the Collateral Vessel, and

3.2 In respect of the Protection and Indemnity cover, in paragraph 1.4 above:

(A) The Owner shall procure from Protection and Indemnity Club managers the standard club letter of undertaking addressed to the Assignee. Such letter to acknowledge the Assignee's interest in the Collateral Vessel, confirm cover is maintained and further confirm endorsement of their standard Loss Payable and Cancellation Clauses to the Certificate of Entry in favour of the Assignee, and

(B) Procure delivery to the Assignee of a copy of the Certificate of Entry of the Collateral Vessel in the Protection and Indemnity Club.

(C) Where the Assignee is a lessor the Owner shall, at the option of the Assignee, either:

    (a) have the Assignee included as named assured on the Certificate of Entry without liability for premium or club calls, or otherwise indemnified by Owners, or

    (b) procure for the Assignee the benefit of what is recognised as the 'mis-directed arrow' clause.

4 Independent report:

The Assignee shall be entitled to commission an independent firm of insurance consultants to review and report upon the adequacy of the Insurances as notified in Section 3 above. The Owner undertakes to provide or cause all insurers or Owner's Insurance Brokers, Protection and Indemnity Club managers and all insurers to provide all the policies or certificates of insurance and related documents required by the Assignee and its insurance consultants upon reasonable request. The Assignee shall commission such reviews and reports on the initial Insurances and for each renewal thereof, also at any other time if, in the opinion of the Assignee, there is material change either in the Insurances or the circumstances of the Collateral Vessel or insurance market practice.

The cost of each review and report will be borne by the Owner and shall be payable by the Owner to the Assignee promptly following receipt by the Owner of an invoice from the Assignee evidencing such costs.

5 Additional Insurances for the exclusive benefit of the Assignee:

In addition to the Insurances covenanted to be effected and maintained by the Owner, in Section 1 above, the Assignee shall effect and maintain from the date of this Deed throughout the Security Period, the following:

(a) Mortgagee's Interest Insurance on terms as required by the Assignee or, where applicable, Lessor's Interest Insurance; and

(b) Mortgagee's Additional Perils Insurance, either confined to pollution and referred to as Mortgagee's Additional Perils (Pollution) Insurance, or otherwise extended to cover all P&I cover limitations under the P&I club rules, referred to as Mortgagee's Additional Perils (All P&I Risks) Insurance.

(c) Mortgage Rights Insurance, if required by the Assignee.

insurances shall be (i) for the exclusive account of the Assignee (acting on behalf and for the account of the Finance Parties), (ii) placed by the Assignee through its own appointed insurance broker and (iii) be on terms, conditions and insured amounts (being equivalent to one hundred and twenty per cent (120%) of the outstanding indebtedness secured on the Collateral Vessel/s). The cost of these insurances will be borne by the Owner and shall be payable by the Owner to the Assignee promptly following receipt by the Owner of an invoice from the Assignee evidencing such premium costs.

(Continued)

Exhibit 12.4   *(Continued)*

6 Additional covenants in relation to Insurances

6.1 **Fleet liens, set-off and cancellation**: to procure, if any of the insurances referred to in 1 above form part of a fleet cover, that the Approved Insurance Brokers shall (if so required by the Assignee) undertake to the Assignee that it shall neither set off against any claims in respect of the Collateral Vessel any premiums due in respect of other vessels under such fleet cover or any premiums due for other insurances, nor cancel the insurance for reason of non-payment of premiums for other vessels under such fleet cover or of premiums for such other insurances, and shall undertake to issue a separate policy in respect of the Collateral Vessel;

6.2 **Payment of premiums and calls**: punctually pay all premiums, calls, contributions or other sums payable in respect of all such insurances and produce all relevant receipts or other evidence of payment when so required by the Assignee;

6.3 **Guarantees**: to arrange for collision and/or salvage guarantee(s) or indemnity undertakings and/or other acceptable security to be provided to third parties when required from the Protection and Indemnity club or War Risks Association to prevent the arrest, or secure the release of the Collateral Vessel;

6.4 **Extent of cover and exclusions**: to take all necessary action and comply with all requirements which may from time to time be applicable to the Insurances (including, without limitation, the making of all requisite declarations within any prescribed time limits and the payment of any additional premiums or calls) so as to ensure that the Insurances are not made subject to any exclusions or qualifications to which the Assignee has not given its prior written consent and are otherwise maintained on terms and conditions from time to time approved in writing by the Assignee;

6.5 **Collection of claims**: be responsible for pursuing all claims under the Insurances referred to in 1 above, and do all things necessary and provide all documents, evidence and information to satisfy insurer's enquiries. Also to ensure the Assignee is simultaneously advised;

6.6 **Further insurance assignments**: not permit any insurance referred to in 1 above to include any person or entity as a named assured (other than the Owner) unless such person or entity has, to the satisfaction of the Assignee, executed a first priority assignment in favour of the Assignee of their interest in the said insurances on similar terms (mutatis mutandis) to the assignment by the Owner in this Deed;

6.7 **Renewing the Insurances**: to renew all Insurances before the relevant policies, contracts or entries expire, having forwarded the renewal terms to the Assignee at least seven (7) Business Days before each renewal with documentary evidence of the terms and conditions Insurances to be renewed.

7 Employment of the Collateral Vessel: to operate the Collateral Vessel within the confines of the cover provided by each of the Insurances referred to in 1 above. In that respect, the Owner shall:

7.1 **Insurance Warranties and Exclusions**: not make, do, consent or agree to any act or omission which would or could render any such instrument of insurance invalid, void, voidable, or unenforceable or render any sum payable there under repayable in whole or in part;

7.2 **Maintenance of class; compliance with regulations**: at all times keep the Collateral Vessel in class and maintain the Classification of the Collateral Vessel with the relevant Classification Society free of all overdue recommendations and comply with and ensure that the Collateral Vessel at all times complies with all regulations and requirements (statutory or otherwise) from time to time applicable to vessels registered under the laws of the Flag country or otherwise applicable to the Collateral Vessel;

7.3 **Surveys**: submit the Collateral Vessel to continuous surveys and such periodical or other surveys as may be required for classification purposes and, if so requested by the Assignee or if the survey report relates to or recommends or requires repairs and/or other work the cost of which will or is likely to exceed the Casualty Amount, supply to the Assignee copies of all survey reports issued in respect thereof;

7.4 **Prevention of and release from arrest**: promptly in accordance with good Collateral Vessel owning practice pay and discharge all debts, damages, liabilities and outgoings whatsoever which have given or may give rise to maritime, statutory or possessory liens on, or claims enforceable against, the Collateral Vessel, her

(Continued)

Exhibit 12.4   *(Continued)*

Earnings or Insurances or any part thereof and, in the event of a writ or libel being filed against the Collateral Vessel, her Earnings or Insurances or any part thereof, or of any of the same being arrested, attached or levied upon pursuant to legal process or purported legal process or in the event of detention of the Collateral Vessel in exercise or purported exercise of any such lien or claim as aforesaid, procure the release of the Collateral Vessel, her Earnings and Insurances from such arrest, detention attachment or levy or, as the case may be, the discharge of the writ or libel forthwith upon receiving notice thereof by providing bail or procuring the provision of security or otherwise as the circumstances may require;

7.5 **Employment**: not knowingly employ the Collateral Vessel or permit her employment in any manner, trade or business which is forbidden by international law, or which is unlawful or illicit under the law of any relevant jurisdiction, or in carrying illicit or prohibited goods, or in any manner whatsoever which may render her liable to condemnation in a prize court, or to destruction, seizure, confiscation, penalty or sanctions and, in the event of hostilities in any part of the world (whether war be declared or not), not employ the Collateral Vessel or permit her employment in carrying any contraband goods, or enter or trade to or to continue to trade in any zone which has been declared a war zone by any Government Entity or by the Collateral Vessel's war risks insurers unless the Collateral Vessel remains held covered while in that zone;

7.6 **Compliance with Laws and Regulations**: comply in all material respects with all laws (including Environmental Laws) applicable to it and/or the Collateral Vessel including, without limitation, requirements relating to manning and establishment of financial responsibility and to obtain and comply with all Environmental Approvals applicable to it and/or the Collateral Vessel;

7.7 **Inspection of class records:** use reasonable commercial endeavours to allow the Assignee access to the class records of the Collateral Vessel and all inspection reports held by the classification society for the Collateral Vessel at any time following written request of the Assignee to the Owner, such access to include the right to take copies of any such records and, if so requested by the Assignee, to use its reasonable commercial endeavours to procure that the classification society for the Collateral Vessel acknowledges to the Assignee that the Assignee has such right of access;

7.8 **ISM Code and ISPS Code**:

(a)   comply with and ensure that the Collateral Vessel and its Operator at all times comply with the requirements of the ISM Code;

(b)   comply with and ensure that the Collateral Vessel complies with the ISPS Code;

(c)   immediately inform the Assignee of any threatened or actual withdrawal of the Collateral Vessel's document of compliance or International Ship Security Certificate or any Operator's safety management certificate;

(d)   promptly inform the Assignee of the issue of each document of compliance International Ship Security Certificate or any safety management certificate or of the receipt by any Operator of notification that any application for the same has been refused; and

(e)   provide the Assignee promptly on request with a copy (certified as a true copy by the Owner) of each document of compliance and each safety management certificate.

Source: Author's own.

Schedule 1 Form of Notices issued to Owner's insurance brokers and Protection and Indemnity Club managers concerning assignment of the insurances by Owners.

1 To Owner's insurance brokers regarding Hull and machinery, War Risks and other insurances effected, for example, Loss of Hire, including Loss Payable Clause provision

By a Deed of Assignment dated [ ], [*insert name of Borrower/Obligor/Mortgagor/Shipowner Owner*] (the 'Owner') assigned to [*insert name of Assignee*] of [*insert address of Assignee*] (the 'Assignee') all the Owner's rights, title and interest in and to all policies and contracts of insurance from time to time taken out or entered into by or for the benefit of the Owner in respect of the vessel '[*here insert name of Collateral Vessel*]' and accordingly:

  (a) all claims hereunder in respect of an actual or constructive or compromised or arranged total loss, and all claims in respect of a major casualty (that is to say any casualty the claim in respect of which exceeds US$ [*here insert the Dollar figure for the Casualty Amount*] (or the equivalent in any other currency) inclusive of any deductible shall be paid in full to the Assignee or to its order up to the Assignee's interest; and

  (b) all other claims hereunder shall be paid in full to the Owner or to its order, unless and until the Assignee shall have notified insurers hereunder to the contrary, whereupon all such claims shall be paid to the Assignee or to its order.

2 To Protection and Indemnity managers

It is noted that [*insert name of Assignee*] is the first priority Assignee of the vessel and that by an assignment in writing all benefits under the Policy have been assigned to the Assignee.

Payment of any recovery which [*insert name of Owner*] of [*insert address of Owner*] (the 'Owner') is entitled to make out of the funds of the Association in respect of any liability, costs or expenses incurred by the Owner, shall be made to the Owner or to its order, unless and until the Association receives notice from the [*insert name of Assignee*] of [*insert address of Assignee*] (the 'Assignee') that the Owner is in default under the first priority mortgage in which event all recoveries shall thereafter be paid to the Assignee or their order; provided always that no liability whatsoever shall attach to the Association, its Managers or their agents for failure to comply with the latter obligation until the expiry of two clear business days from the receipt of such notice.

Schedule 2 Form of Notice of Assignment for endorsement to each insurance policy. P&I clubs decline any assignment of P&I

[Name of the Borrower/Obligor/Mortgagor/Shipowner and address], the owners of the '[name/s of Collateral Vessel's]', together with [names and addresses of all other assureds named on the Policy] HEREBY GIVE NOTICE that by a Deed of Assignment dated [date 2006] and entered into by us with [name and address of Assignee] and others there has been assigned by us to [name of Assignee] as Assignee of the said vessel all insurances in respect thereof, including the insurances constituted by the policy whereon this notice is endorsed.

(to be signed by all named assureds on the policy)

' .... '

' .... '

For and on behalf of all Assureds named on the Policy

Dated [date 2006]

Schedule 3 Forms of Letters of Undertaking required from Owner's insurance brokers and P&I club managers

Form of Letter of Undertaking to be provided by Brokers in respect of Hull and Machinery, War Risks and other insurances

To [*name and address of Assignee*]

(Date)

Dear Sirs,

m.v. [*Name of the Collateral Vessel*]

Owners: [*insert name of Owners*]

We confirm that we have effected insurances for the amount of the above Owners as set out in appendix 'A' attached. Pursuant to instructions received from the above Owners and/or their authorised Manager or Agents and in consideration of your approving us as the appointed Brokers in connection with the insurances covered by this letter, we hereby undertake:

1 to hold the Insurance Slips or Contracts, the Policies when issued, and any renewals of such Policies or new Policies substituted therefore with your consent as may be arranged through ourselves and the benefit of the insurances thereunder to your order in accordance with the terms of the Loss Payable Clause set out in appendix 'B' attached; and

2 to arrange for the said Loss Payable Clause to be included on the policies when issued; and

3 to have endorsed on each and every Policy as and when the same is issued a Notice of Assignment in the form of appendix 'C' hereto dated and signed by the Owners and acknowledged by Underwriters in accordance with market practice; and

4 to advise you promptly if we cease to be the Broker for the Assured or in the event of any material changes of which we are aware affecting the said insurance; and

5 following a written application received from you not later than one month before expiry of these insurances to notify you within fourteen days of the receipt of such application in the event of our not having received notice of renewal instructions from the Owners and/or their authorised Managers or Agents, and in the event of our receiving instructions to renew to advise you promptly of the details thereof.

Our above undertakings are given subject to our lien on the Policies for premiums and subject to our right of cancellation in default in payment of such premiums but we undertake not to exercise such rights of cancellation without giving you ten days notice in writing, either by letter, telex or cable and a reasonable opportunity for you to pay any premiums outstanding. We further undertake on application from you to advise you promptly of the premiums payment situation.

It is understood and agreed that the operation of any Automatic Termination of Cover, Cancellation or Amendment Provisions contained in the Policy conditions shall override any Undertakings given by us as Brokers.

Notwithstanding the terms of the said Loss Payable Clause and the said Notice of Assignment, unless and until we receive written notice from you to the contrary, we shall be empowered to arrange for a collision and/or salvage guarantee to be given in the event of bail being required in order to prevent the arrest of the vessel or to secure the release of the vessel from arrest following a casualty. Where a guarantee has been given as aforesaid and the guarantor has paid any sum under the guarantee in respect of such claim, there shall be payable directly to the guarantor out of the proceeds of the said Policies a sum equal to the sum so paid.

This undertaking is subject to all claims and returns of premiums being collected through us as Brokers.

Yours faithfully

Standard Letter of Undertaking from Protection and Indemnity Club Managers

[*Addressed to the Assignee*]

(Date)

Dear Sirs,

[*Name of the Collateral Vessel/s*] (the 'Ship/s')

Owners: [*Name of Entered Member and Owner*] (the 'Owner')

We acknowledge receipt of a letter dated from [*name of lawyers acting for the Assignee*] giving notice of assignment to you of the insurances on the above ship. So far as this Association is concerned, the Managers do not consent to such assignment for the purposes of Rule (....) other than to give efficacy to the Loss Payable Clause set out below and subject always to the Managers' right in settling any claim presented by the assignee to deduct or retain such amount as the Managers may then estimate to be sufficient to discharge the assignors liabilities (if any) to the Association existing at the time of the assignment or likely to accrue thereafter.

We do confirm however that the Ship is entered in this Association for Protection and Indemnity Risks upon the terms and conditions set out or to be set out in the Certificate of Entry. Furthermore, in consideration of your agreeing to the entry or continuing entry of the Ship in this Association, the Managers agree:

(a) that the Owners shall not cease to be insured by the Association in respect of the Ship by reason of such assignment; and

(b) that, notwithstanding that the Ship is mortgaged to you and that no undertaking or guarantee has been given to the Association to pay all contributions due in respect of the Ship, the Owners do not cease to be insured by reason of the operation of Rule €.

It is further agreed that the following Loss Payable Clause will be included in the Certificate of Entry:

'It is noted that [*name of Assignee*] is the first priority Assignee of the vessel and that by an assignment in writing all benefits under the Policy have been assigned to the Assignee. Payment of any recovery which [*insert name and address of the shipowner member*] (the 'Owner') is entitled to make out of the funds of the Association in respect of any liability, costs or expenses incurred by the Owner, shall be made to the Owner or to its order, unless and until the Association receives notice from [*insert name and address of Assignee*] (the 'Assignee') that the Owner is in default under the first priority mortgage in which event all recoveries shall thereafter be paid to the Assignee or their order; provided always that no liability whatsoever shall attach to the Association, its Managers or their agents for failure to comply with the latter obligation until the expiry of two clear business days from the receipt of such notice'

The Association undertakes:

(c) to inform you if the directors give the Owners notice under Rule b that their insurance in this Association in respect of the Ship is to cease at the end of the ten current policy year;

(d) to give you 14 days notice of the Association's intention to cancel the Insurance of the Owners by reason of their failure to pay when due and demanded any sum due from them to the Association.

Yours faithfully

Checking assigned marine insurances

Having established the insurance covenants under the loan agreement or the ship mortgage, bankers will need to check that these covenants are met and that the underwriting security of each insurance is acceptable. Many banks in the business of ship financing either have their own in-house marine insurance specialists or employ external marine insurance consultants to be responsible for checking the insurances initially proposed by shipowner borrowers and then recommend for approval, or otherwise, the final insurance documents submitted. Insurance consultants need to check that all the covenanted insurances are placed on the required insuring conditions and insured values and, in particular, review the underwriting security. The initial problem can be in obtaining the necessary documentation from the shipowner's insurance broker and Protection & Indemnity club managers prior to the draw-down of the loan for the purchase of the vessel.

Check lists

The following check lists should assist banks and their legal advisers to assemble the necessary documentation on insurances which are already in existence and on which cover notes and certificates of entry should be readily available. However, for new ship purchases full cover notes and other insurance documentation may not be available prior to the closing and drawdown of the loan. In these latter circumstances qualified confirmation will be required, prior to any loan drawdown.

Confirmations required on insurances prior to the closing of a ship financing transaction

1 Confirmation from the shipowner's insurance brokers, by way of letter, telex or facsimile, of:
   (a) the insurances which instructions have been received to place: (hull and machinery, war risks, increased value, loss of hire and the like);
   (b) the full insurance conditions, the insured values and the named assureds for each of the above insurances;
   (c) the sums insured on each insurance, detailing the underwriting security (names of correspondent brokers or intermediaries should be included, and details of reinsurance arrangements will be required where a disproportionate percentage of the risk is covered by a single underwriter);
   (d) their agreement to issue letters of undertaking in favour of the bank, as mortgagee and assignee of the insurances, in accordance with the recommended Lloyd's Insurance Brokers' Committee (LIBC) wording;
   (e) whether or not any of the insurances are being endorsed to attach to an existing fleet insurance policy, and if so, confirmation that the brokers' lien on the policies shall only apply for premiums due on the vessel or vessels mortgaged to the bank as if separate policies had been signed.

2 Confirmation from the Protection & Indemnity association or club, by way of letter, telex or facsimile, that:

(a) the vessel is entered with the club in accordance with the club's rules, with the mortgagee being advised of any qualifications and/or warranties on the entry;

(b) a standard letter of undertaking will be issued by the club including a loss payable clause in favour of the bank;

(c) a copy of the vessel's certificate of entry will be forwarded to the bank when issued as well as any subsequent endorsements to the certificate of entry, such as TOVALOP.

INSURANCE DOCUMENTATION to be supplied:

1 From the mortgagor or his insurance broker(s):

(a) copy cover notes covering:

(i) marine risks subject to Institute Time Clauses (Hulls) or their equivalent as issued in other markets: some markets may offer cover subject to more restrictive terms or on very different clauses;

(ii) war risks subject to Institute War and Strikes Clauses, Hulls – Time, or their equivalent;

(iii) any other risks required to be covered by the loan agreement or mortgage.

NB 1 Both marine and war risks may sometimes be covered by a mutual association or club.

NB 2 If assignment is in respect of all insurances taken out by the owner then cover notes in respect of additional total loss, insurances on increased value, disbursements, freight and so on will be required.

NB 3 Cover notes must include details of the assured(s), all terms and conditions of the policies to be issued, the period and attachment date, the insured value, the amount covered by the policies, all participating insurers and their percentage share, the agents or intermediaries used for the placing, and the basis of premium payment.

(b) Letter(s) of Undertaking in respect of each policy assigned to the mortgagee signed by the owner's broker(s) or hull or war club.

NB 1 The wording recommended by the Lloyd's Insurance Brokers Committee (LIBC) dated October 1984 should be the minimum requirement.

NB 2 Copies of the signed and dated notice of assignment and a loss payable clause in favour of the mortgagee, both as supplied by the mortgagee to the broker, must be attached.

NB 3 It is not normal to include a cancellation provision in the loss payable clause attached to the letter of undertaking.

(c) Sometimes owners place insurance directly with companies which will issue policy(ies) very promptly and undertakings are given in their own format which are usually acceptable.

2 From the protection and indemnity/third party insurers:

(a) Copies of the certificates of entry, including endorsements, giving details of deductibles, exclusions, limitations and any condition survey requirements.

(b) Letter(s) of undertaking: clubs limit their undertaking to an acknowledgement of the interest of the mortgagee and an agreement to endorse the Certificate of Entry with a loss payable clause. P&I clubs are currently reviewing their letters of undertaking with regard to their provision for discretionary cover where owners have failed to rectify defects on entered vessels.

(c) From the mortgagee's insurance broker: cover notes on any other insurances not referred to above and required by the terms of the loan, which the bank has had placed by its own appointed insurance broker.

On receipt of the necessary information, the mortgagee must check that the insured value on the principal insurances, the hull and machinery, marine and war risks, is at least equal to the minimum amount of cover stipulated in the loan and security documents. Should any of the insurances be effected on a fleet policy, the mortgagee may wish the brokers' lien on the policy to be restricted.

Insurance renewals

The collation of insurance documentation at the commencement of a new loan is relatively straightforward. Obtaining subsequent renewal documentation can be more tedious. It is, therefore, necessary to remind the owner's brokers and club(s) of their obligations under their respective letters of undertaking.

Here follow suggested draft letters for enquiring on insurance renewals. The essential enquiry is to insurance brokers or mutual hull or war clubs where standard letters of undertaking have been issued. The other draft letter to the P&I club is also necessary should the shipowner member terminate, or change the conditions, of his third party liability cover.

To: The Holding Insurance Broker

(sent between four to eight weeks before the date a policy is due to expire)

VESSEL:

OWNING COMPANY:

AGENT/MANAGER:

Dear Sirs,

Pursuant to your letter of undertaking to us as mortgagees concerning the insurance policies on the above, we hereby apply to you for notification within 14 days whether you have been instructed by your principals to renew the following insurances from the date of expiry on the same insurance conditions and values as current:

Hull and machinery: Expiring:
War risks: Expiring:
Loss of earnings/hire: Expiring:
Other

In the event of any proposal to make material changes to the conditions or placement of any of the above insurance renewals we must be advised well before attachment of the risk.

Following your receipt of instructions to renew, we shall await to receive copies of the cover notes and your confirmation that your letter of undertaking continues to apply to these renewals.

Yours faithfully,

To: the Protection and Indemnity Mutual Club or Association.

(To be sent four weeks before the end of the Club's financial year which is February 20 for all P&I Clubs that are members of the International Group.)

VESSEL:
OWNING COMPANY:
MANAGERS:

Pursuant to your undertakings to us as mortgagees of the above vessel under your letter of undertaking to us dated .... we request your confirmation that this ship shall continue to be entered in your Association for all Protection and Indemnity risks for 12 months from February 20 next, and that the conditions set out in the Certificate of Entry, including the provision of the loss payable clause shall remain unaltered, and that there are to be no changes or limitations to the rules from anniversary date.

In addition, we request your confirmation that the above vessel is also covered under club rules for pollution liabilities, as defined under the US Oil Pollution Act 1990, whilst trading in or through US waters or the US Exclusive Economic Zone.

Yours faithfully,

Underwriting security

An insurance contract is a contract by the named insurers to pay, each to the extent of his proportionate share, on the happening of an insured peril. The liability of each insurer named in a policy does not exceed his proportionate share. There is no joint and several liability on insurers named in an insurance or reinsurance policy. Failure of any insurer to pay his proportionate share of a claim, as a consequence of either inability to pay or unwillingness to pay, can cause nightmares for the assured and his insurance broker. The ability or creditworthiness of all insurers on a policy to pay and, when correlative, the willingness to pay, is referred to as underwriting security.

The ability of an insurer to pay is determined both by his cash reserves and also by his own reinsurance arrangements. The financial standing of established insurance companies can be assessed by reference to credit rating agencies or specialists of which A.M. Best, ISI, and Compass are well known for insurance. Although insurance companies' historic reports, accounts and financial statements detail their cash and financial standing, information on their reinsurances, usually treaty reinsurances, will be scant and will invariably omit the underwriting security of such reinsurances. All Lloyd's policies are guaranteed by the Lloyd's Central Fund.

The willingness to pay promptly can be determined by a number of factors, such as:

- the clarity of and circumstances giving rise to the claim, and the certainty that the proximate cause of loss falls within the specified perils insured;
- the insurer's commitment to his business and standing, to the assured and to the insurance broker; and
- the insurer's ability to meet the claim out of his cash reserves without firstly having to resort to his reinsurers.

The insurers who most often need to resort to their reinsurances before paying a claim are captive insurance companies established in tax havens, which may not have much liquidity, and also insurance companies established in lesser developed countries subject to tight foreign exchange controls, more often than not state insurance companies. The sovereign debt crisis of the world's lesser developed countries posed the threat that many state insurance companies might not be able to make prompt hard currency claim payments, notwithstanding the currency of the insurance contract. There was always the possibility of a state insurer's hard pressed central bank having higher priorities for the hard currency recovered from reinsurers and consequently offering the assured and its loss payees the insurer's local currency in settlement. This threat, or risk, brought reinsurance 'cut through clauses' to the fore.

Cut through clauses

A cut through clause is no more nor less than a loss payable clause applied to a reinsurance policy. Like loss payable clauses, cut through clauses must each be accompanied by a notice of assignment given by the assured, in this case the ceding insurer, in favour of the loss payee. For obvious reasons a cut through clause can only be applied to a facultative reinsurance covering a specific risk. No primary insurer will assign his general treaty reinsurances. Therefore, in order to apply a cut through clause to a specific reinsurance risk, the primary insurer will have to arrange for a facultative reinsurance for the particular risk.

State and captive insurance companies, not surprisingly, resent cut through clauses; they will prevaricate against the implied aspersions and against the extra work in creating facultative reinsurances. However, where such an insurer is taking 100 per cent of the risk, or even 30 per cent of a risk, the sovereign or cross border risk to a shipping bank may be unacceptable. When financing shipowners who must, by law, use a state insurer it is recommended that commitment letters, loan agreements or lease contracts make specific provisions for cut through clauses.

A recommended cut through clause is included in the example insurance covenants set out above.

Insurance claims

In the event of a claim

The leading underwriter of any insurance policy should be advised promptly of any accident that may result in a loss and a claim under the policy. Assureds should immediately inform their insurance broker of such events to obtain advice and put leading underwriters on notice. The golden rule is that the assured should take action to ameliorate or minimise the loss or damage, in other words take action to limit the potential claim – act as if uninsured.

Ship mortgagees will naturally rely on their clients, the shipowners or demise charterers, to deal with marine losses and claims through their brokers. However, a ship mortgagee should be advised of any major loss and, where there is a mortgagee's interest insurance in force, the bank must ensure that underwriters on the bank's mortgagee's interest insurance policy are also advised if there are any suspicions of difficulties in collecting a claim. No compromise settlement should be agreed without consulting mortgagees' interest insurance underwriters.

Not all marine casualties and claims are straightforward; there have been instances in the past where banks have had to step in. In all such instances the banks have only done so after taking extensive advice on the particular problem. The need to cope with potential problem claims is another reason for shipping banks to have their own appointed broker.

Claims payment orders and the broker's policy lien

Section 53 (1) of the Marine Insurance Act 1906 makes insurers directly liable to an assured for the payment of claims. When a marine policy is endorsed with a dated notice of assignment signed by the assured then, clearly, the insurers become liable to pay claims to the assignee of the policy under the terms of any loss payable clause.[1]

However, these statutory provisions can be circumvented by the assured and assignee signing a Payment Order authorising underwriters to settle their proportions of a claim with the nominated Lloyd's broker. The Payment Order wording required by, for example, the Lloyd's Claims Office specifically absolves underwriters from any further liability to the assured or assignee once they have settled their proportions of a claim with the broker nominated in the payment order (see Exhibit 12.5).

Payment orders, or collecting authorities, were originally introduced as a matter of convenience to delegate the administrative problem of collecting the various proportions of a claim from large numbers of underwriters to the broker who negotiated the claim and who invariably placed the original business. They also allow underwriters to settle claims in account with the nominated broker and potentially enable that broker to deduct the amount of any outstanding premiums due from the assured on all other policies.

Exhibit 12.5

Claims payment authority

CLAIMS PAYMENT AUTHORITY

FROM: Mortgagees & Assigners

TO: Underwriters on Lloyd's Policy No.

                  Period of Policy

LOSS: ['Name of Vessel' plus type of Loss]

                  [Date of Loss]

As assigners of the above policy under the endorsed Notice of Assignment dated and signed by the named Assureds, we hereby authorise you to pay your respective proportion of this claim to [Name of the Lloyd's Broker] for distribution in accordance with the Loss Payable Clause.

We agree that such payment, whether in account or otherwise, shall be a complete discharge to the Underwriters concerned for the amount of the claim.

Source: Author's own.

Before signing a payment order, the bank, as assignee and loss payee, should first obtain from the broker written confirmation of the following:

- that underwriters have agreed settlement of the claim;
- the amount of outstanding premium on the policy which the broker requires authority to deduct from the first part of the claim – particularly important in total loss claims where deferred premiums become payable immediately in full;
- the aggregate amount of any other deductions required to cover collision or salvage guarantees and collecting commissions;
- that the balance of the claim will be paid strictly on the terms of the loss payable clause, or alternatively as instructed by any disbursement instructions; and
- the estimated time scale of collection and payment to the mortgagees.

Usually, the broker's answers to the above will be acceptable to loss payees for them to sign the payment order as requested by the broker. However, if the answers given are not satisfactory, or the bank has doubts about the financial standing or creditworthiness of the Lloyd's brokers, advice should be sought.

Under English law, brokers are liable to underwriters for the payment of premiums, regardless of whether they have been paid by the assured and, consequently, brokers hold a legal lien on the policies for such outstanding premiums.[2] The broker's lien on the policy is merely possessory and gives no rights in the policy itself to the broker. The broker has no insurable interest so he is not empowered to collect a claim without the consent of the assured and any assignee, and he is therefore not empowered to offset premiums against claims without such authority.

Exhibit 12.6

Addendum to letter of undertaking

Addendum to Letter of Undertaking on

m.v.   A/C A.B.C. SHIPPING CO. LTD.

In addition to our letter of undertaking addressed to you concerning the insurances effected by us for the account of the above owners, we further confirm that our lien on the policies for premiums shall be confined to the outstanding premiums due on this vessel only. If required, we undertake to sign separate policies in the name of the above owners as assured.

Director of insurance broking firm

Source: Author's own.

Apart from the broker's lien the only other recourse for Lloyd's brokers with outstanding premiums is to cancel the policies under the provisions of the Brokers' Cancellation Clause, having first served notice of cancellation to assignees under any letter of undertaking. In practice, Lloyd's brokers are very reluctant to serve notices of cancellation or even advise assignees immediately when premiums become outstanding, as undertaken in the standard letter of undertaking, for fear of upsetting their shipowner client. Many brokers have anticipated eventual recovery of premiums out of a future claim, providing it is not to the detriment of a loss payee.

Clearly, the only way to minimise any potential threat of a broker's lien on fleet policies is to obtain further undertakings from the broker at the outset; either (i) by the broker undertaking that his broker's lien will be limited to outstanding premiums due on the vessels mortgaged to that bank; or (ii) by the broker undertaking to sign separate policies for each vessel.

The 'Addendum to the Letter of Undertaking' shown in Exhibit 12.6 is designed to deal with this situation and should be requested from the owner's broker at the time of notifying the owner's broker of the assignment of the insurances by the owner to the mortgagee and of the mortgagee's requirement for a letter of undertaking.

Marine mutual insurers and protection and indemnity

The marine insurance market includes a profusion of mutual insurers, or clubs, each made up of members having common insurable interests, such as shipowners, ship managers, charterers and others who effectively pool their resources and collectively self-insure. Such mutual clubs are governed by rules, run by managers, and shelter their major and catastrophic risks with reinsurance placed in the commercial insurance markets. By retaining a significant first loss proportion of the mutualised risks under a pool, funded by members, and bulk buying reinsurance in the commercial markets, the mutuals are able to obtain highly competitive reinsurance premiums. The mutuals themselves are all non-profit making.

Where a number of mutuals exist in competition, providing identical cover, they further enhance the benefits of bulk buying by further combining their purchase of reinsurance under an umbrella organisation, or mutuals' mutual, such as the International Group of Protection & Indemnity Associations that now reinsures through their Bermudian captive named Hydra, and the Combined Group of War Risks Associations.

510

This mutual system is dominant in the provision of marine liability insurance, particularly through the Protection and Indemnity Clubs within the International Group of P&I associations, or clubs, collectively insuring around 95 per cent of the world's ocean navigating, or blue water, tonnage. Further mutuals also exist for other risks.

The following are the types of mutual insurers, the umbrella organisation, insurance covered and names of each club:

1   Protection & Indemnity Clubs

      (a)   Members of the International Group of P&I Associations

These indemnify members for their legal liabilities up to approximately US$4.5bn, excepting oil pollution limited to US$1bn and other limits referred to below, arising from:

      (i)   liabilities to passengers and/or cargo;
      (ii)   liabilities to crew;
      (iii)   pollution liabilities – limit US$1bn;
      (iv)   collision liabilities;
      (v)   damage to port installations;
      (vi)   removal of wreck;
      (vii)   excess liabilities resulting from War Risks and terrorism in excess of the ship's hull value or US$100m; and
      (viii)   freight, demurrage and defence covering legal costs – optional additional cover under a different class.

The following are all members of the International Group of P&I Associations:

- American Steamshipowners Mutual Protection & Indemnity Association Inc.
- Britannia Steamship Insurance Association Ltd
- Assurance Foreningen Gjensidig (Gard Club)
- The Japan Shipowners' Mutual Protection & Indemnity Association
- The London Steamshipowners Mutual Insurance Association Ltd
- The North of England Protecting & Indemnity Association Ltd
- The Shipowners Mutual Protection & Indemnity Association (Luxembourg)
- Assuranceforeingen Skuld
- The Standard Steamshipowners Protection & Indemnity Association (Bermuda) Ltd
- The Steamship Mutual Underwriting Association Ltd
- Sveriges Angfartygs Assurans Forening (the Swedish Club)
- The United Kingdom Mutual Steamship Assurance Association (Bermuda) Ltd
- The West of England Shipowners' Mutual Insurance Association (Luxembourg).

      (b)   Other Independent P&I mutuals, not members of the International Group

These provide lower P&I cover limits, except when reinsured or co-insured by an International Group P&I club:

- China Shipowners' Mutual, known as China P&I club
- The Korean Shipowner's Mutual Protection & Indemnity Association
- Noord Nederlandse P&I club, reinsured by West of England Shipowners' Insurance Service Ltd.

(c)   Other P&I insurers that are not mutuals

These provide fixed premium P&I cover to limits where stated:

- British Marine Ltd, formerly British Marine Mutual – limit US$500m
- Ingosstrakh Insurance Company of Russia – can sometimes get co-insurance with an IG P&I club
- Intercoastal Shipowners' P&I b.v.; under the Raetsclub Insurance Group – limit US$50m
- Terra Nova – limit US$25m
- Osprey Underwriting Agencies Ltd – limit US$25m.

2   War Clubs

Members of the Combined Group of War Risks Associations to primary limits of US$500m, or £325m, irrespective of Insured Hull Values, excepting The Hellenic War Mutual which is US$400m. These cover physical loss and damage to a ship caused by war and allied perils, excluded from the Hull & Machinery insurance, to an agreed insured value, and liabilities arising from War Risks, including terrorism, through the following members:

- The Standard Steamshipowners' Mutual War Risks Association Ltd
- The West of England Mutual War Risks Association Ltd
- The Britannia Steamship Insurance Association Ltd
- The Sunderland Steamship Mutual War Risks Association Ltd
- The London Steamshipowners' Mutual Insurance Association Ltd
- The North of England Protecting and Indemnity Association Ltd
- The United Kingdom Mutual War Risks Association Ltd
- The Hellenic Mutual War Risks Association (Bermuda) Ltd– US$400m limit.

3   Norwegian Hull Club

This provides Hull & Machinery Insurance, 'A' rated by Standard & Poor's and highly regarded.

4   Through Transport Mutual Insurance Association Ltd (otherwise known as the TT Club) Insures property, equipment and liabilities of ship and transport operators, stevedores and port authorities, lessors of equipment and containers, terminal and depot operators.

5   The Strikes Club

Covers ships' daily running costs or charter hire during delays caused by onshore incidents, such as strikes, costs of delays sustained after the end of the disruption covered, and delays caused by war and hostilities.

6   International Transport Intermediaries Club Ltd

This provides credit risk cover on shipowners for service providers to ships, such as ship chandlers, ship sale and purchase brokers.

Protection and indemnity – marine liability insurance

The market

The market for protection and indemnity is dominated by the 13 clubs that are members of the International Group of P&I associations which, between them, insure approximately 95 per cent of the world's ocean navigating, or blue water, tonnage. However, within the International Group, there is a further concentration of the business held by the biggest clubs, to the extent of the four biggest clubs having 50 per cent of the world tonnage.

Outside the International Group, the market consists of some national mutuals that are sometimes able to reinsure or co-insure with an International Group P&I club, thereby providing the same cover limits through the International Group's reinsurance programme, and the much depleted number of fixed premium insurers. The British Marine Ltd, formerly the British Marine Mutual, is the most prominent independent and dedicated fixed premium insurer of protection and indemnity risks, suitably credit rated by Standard & Poor's with 'A–'.

Exhibit 12.7

Standard & Poor's P&I club statistics and ratings 2006 on the International Group

P&I club	Approximate gross tonnage	Gross income in 2004 (US$m)	Reserves 2004 (US$m)	Gross Claims Paid 2004 (US$m)	S&P rating 2006
The United Kingdom Mutual Steamship Assurance Association (Bermuda) Ltd	150	304.84	219.67	246.00	A
Assuranceforeningen Gard	130	257.85	327.84	193.46	A
The Britannia Steam Ship Insurance Association Ltd	101	209.20	261.13	114.35	A
Standard Steamship-owners' Protection & Indemnity Association Ltd	65	151.60	163.77	107.75	A
West of England Shipowners' Mutual Insurance Association (Luxembourg)	61	202.88	145.39	254.88	BBB
The Steamship Mutual Underwriting Association (Bermuda) Ltd	55	226.44	139.52	230.57	BBB
North of England Protecting & Indemnity Association Ltd	53	156.45	133.46	96.34	A
The Japan Shipowners' Mutual Protection & Indemnity Association	56	126.59	91.37	63.60	BBB
Assuranceforeningen	50	132.81	81.59	117.26	BBB+

(Continued)

Exhibit 12.7   *(Continued)*

P&I club	Approximate gross tonnage	Gross income in 2004 (US$m)	Reserves 2004 (US$m)	Gross Claims Paid 2004 (US$m)	S&P rating 2006
Skuld					
The London Steam-Shipowners' Mutual Insurance Association Ltd	32	86.64	101.85	103.49	BBB
American Steam-shipowners' Mutual Protection & Indemnity Association Inc.	19	118.96	31.95	43.53	B+
The Swedish Club	17	82.62	79.94	58.68	BBB
The Shipowners' Mutual Protection & Indemnity Association (Luxembourg)	10	101.32	10.70	54.06	A
TOTALS	800	2,158	1,788	1,684	

Comparisons between the biggest and smallest International Group Clubs

	Top 4 Clubs	Bottom 4 Clubs
Entered Tonnage	55.75%	9.75%
Gross Call Income	42.79%	18.05%
Reserves	54.38%	12.55%

Source: Author's own.

Terms of protection and indemnity (P&I) cover

Marine Liability insurance is restricted to first party indemnity cover only, not third party liability. P&I cover through the International Group clubs is governed by club rules and ship financiers should note the following key points:

The paramount rule: 'Pay to be paid'

P&I clubs are mutual, non-profit making associations of shipowners pooling the liabilities consequent on the ownership and operation of vessels (for example, liability for oil pollution, liability to third party cargo carried, liability to crew and employees on board, collision liability, removal of wreck). As indemnity associations the P&I clubs operate a strict 'pay-to-be-paid' principle; thus a shipowner member is technically required to pay third party liabilities first before being able to seek reimbursement from his club. In practice, shipowners will often be unable to pay first, so claims are settled to third parties through a joint account set up with the owner, which demonstrates the club's commitment in maintaining the first party indemnity principle under the 'pay to be paid' rule. This rule makes P&I cover a first party indemnity for members only. Since P&I clubs will not accept assignments of cover, only members can sue a P&I club.

Cesser of Insurance rule

Cover is automatically terminated in the event of either:

- an individual member's insolvency, bankruptcy or mental disorder or death;
- a corporation's insolvency forcing the appointment of a receiver, or commencing proceedings under bankruptcy; or
- upon a shipowner member mortgaging or hypothecation of an entered ship, without the written approval of club managers.

This rule makes it essential for mortgagees to receive a letter of undertaking from club managers, as explained in Exhibit 12.4 – Insurance Covenants above.

Current limitations of International Group P&I club cover

Cover is limited to US$4.5bn for any one accident or occurrence (collision being one occurrence) excepting:

- oil pollution cover is limited to US$1bn;
- war P&I and terrorism excess cover is limited to US$500m in excess of the higher amount of either:
- the insured limit for War P&I under the owner's War Risks insurance; or
- the fair market hull value up to US$100m;
- liabilities resulting from bio-chemical weapons is limited to US$20m;
- legal liability limits applicable under any shipowners' limitation of liability convention, notably CLC 1992, the LLMC 1976 plus 1996 Protocol and Athens Convention 1974, due to be superseded by the 2002 Protocol.

The implementation of the Athens Protocol 2002 will result in a new limitation of P&I cover for passenger liabilities. At the time of writing, this has yet to be determined by the International Group of P&I clubs.

Payments of premium, or calls

The cost of cover under a P&I club is not fixed, at least not for members. Membership of a P&I club entitles a shipowner to an unlimited number of claims but is accompanied by unlimited liability for the payment of additional premium, or calls. It is therefore critical to shipowners and their bankers that the clubs forecast their anticipated liabilities for all unclosed years as accurately as possible to enable shipowner members to make provision to meet the club's demands for payment of additional calls. The P&I clubs make numerous calls as follows:

- Advance Calls: each shipowner will pay an initial premium (Advance Call) at the start of the club's insurance year (all clubs have a common anniversary date on 20 February of each year). Additionally, each club will estimate an additional charge as ultimately needed to balance the year's premiums and claims.

515

- Supplementary Calls: this additional levy (Supplementary Call) is typically expressed as a percentage of the advance call, normally in the range of 20–50 per cent. Since P&I club business is medium to long-tail business the Supplementary Call can only be levied some time after the policy year expiry when the year's liabilities have matured. If there is a surplus of premium then the additional levy may not be required; if claims have exceeded premium then the additional levy may be increased from the original estimate.
- Release Calls: applies following the sale or loss of a ship and is the P&I club managers' estimate of the amount that would otherwise have been payable in respect of a Supplementary Call on the ship. Club rules stipulate that Release Calls must be guaranteed by a bank guarantee.
- Overspill Calls: International Group clubs provide cover up to 2.5 per cent of the London Convention limit for property damage, being approximately US$4.5bn, notwithstanding the clubs' reinsurance programme only provides reinsurance up to US$2.05bn. Any claim, or claims that exceed the reinsured limit results in an Overspill Claim on all members of all the International Group P&I clubs, based upon the total gross tonnage that each member's fleet is as a proportion of the total. Members of a mutual are jointly and severally liable for their mutual's solvency. Consequently, membership of a strongly credit rated mutual is recommended.

Provision of security preventing arrest or detainment of a ship held responsible for an accident

Though not included within P&I club rules, as a service to shipowners, the clubs will provide bail security to prevent arrest by local authorities of a ship held responsible for damage to port installations or other vessels – provided club managers are satisfied there are no known reasons why they might reject the liability claim following judgment. Such reasons could be for breach of the rules or outstanding calls.

Notwithstanding club managers being satisfied about the claim, before putting up bail security they require an indemnity from the shipowner for the bail amount which, for smaller owners, they may also want secured by a letter of credit from the mortgagee. For banks with large shipping portfolios, these letters of credit made out in favour of P&I clubs can accumulate.

The Pooling Agreement

The International Group Agreement (IGA), or Pooling Agreement, governs the interrelationship between the P&I clubs within the International Group of P&I clubs, which maintains the cohesion of mutuality necessary for the IG clubs to provide the highest levels of cover at the lowest possible cost. The IGA governs the club retentions, the operation and contributions to the pooling arrangements, the conformity of club rules and cover limits. Though each club has its own rules, the differences are largely cosmetic. However, there is a significant exception, with the Norwegian clubs being subject to Norwegian law under which there can be no retrospective cancellation of insurance. The International Group has recently formed the Bermuda captive 'Hydra' to handle the clubs' reinsurance programme, traditionally led in Lloyd's and the London company markets. Other reinsurance markets, including the Bermudian market, participate in the higher catastrophe layers.

Exhibit 12.8

Structure and interrelationship of the International Group P&I clubs

P&I Deductibles payable by shipowner members
(varies between types of claim, type of vessel, owner and club)

UK P&I club	Gard Club	Britannia Club	Standard Clubs	West of England	Steamship Mutual	North of England	Japan Club	Skuld Club	London Club	American Club	Swedish Club	Shipowners

Club Retention US$6m any one event

Lower Pool Retention US$24m – managed under International Group Agreement

HYDRA, Bermuda – Captive Insurer established by The International Group

Upper Pool Retention US$20m – reinsured and managed by the IG captive HYDRA, Bermuda

1st R/I layer 25% co-insured		75% of US$50m–US$550m
2nd R/I layer	HYDRA Reinsurance Programme	US$550m–US$1.05bn
3rd R/I layer	*Unlimited reinstatements, excepting*	US$1.05bn–US$1.55bn
4th R/I layer	*the 4 layer with just one reinstatement*	US$1.55bn–US$2.05bn

OVERSPILL CLAIMS from US$2.05bn to the P&I cover limit

(being 2.5% of London Convention Limit for property damage) approx. US$4.5bn.

Payable by ALL shipowner members of the International Group Clubs pro rata to entered gross tonnage

Some clubs have purchase finite risk insurance up to US$1bn

Source: Author's own.

Structure and management of each International Group P&I club

The clubs are mostly domiciled offshore – Bermuda and Luxembourg being the most favoured jurisdictions – with managers appointed to run the clubs' day-to-day business. The managers (the majority of which are based in the UK) report to a board of directors all of whose members are representatives of the club's shipowner members but, otherwise, exercise day-to-day control. This control includes underwriting, claims handling and investment. The clubs also pride themselves on providing a service to their shipowners: thus they offer legal expertise, technical ship operation expertise, a network of correspondents in every major port as well as the ability to post guarantees for shipowners in any country. They also act as a voice for shipowners and as a pressure group representing shipowners' interests on matters that might be affected by national and international legislation and, particularly, in connection with amendments to shipowners' limitation of liability conventions.

Current Issues threatening the International Group (IG) clubs

The following are all issues currently facing the IG clubs:

1 The IG clubs are a cartel and consequently require dispensation from EU unfair competition laws, under The Treaty of Rome, and are potentially in breach of US Anti Trust law. The clubs' current exemption period from the EU's unfair competition laws expires in 2009. The International Group have been negotiating with the EU for an extension of the exemption and hope renewal of the EU's exemption will be routine. Such an optimistic view is, however, far from certain without further amendments to the International Group Agreement.

2 Guarantees of claims payments undermine the clubs' cherished 'pay to be paid' rule under the first party indemnity principle and, further, deprive the clubs of all claims defences, such as breaches in club rules and warranties by the responsible shipowner. The trade-off for the clubs in agreeing to guarantee payments has been to obtain absolute fixed legal liability limits, at the levels negotiated prior to a convention being promulgated.

The requirement for liability claims to be guaranteed came with the 1969 International Convention on Civil Liability for Oil Pollution Damage (1969 CLC) that laid down strict liabilities (that is, liability even in the absence of fault) and a compulsory insurance requirement. The P&I clubs met the 1969 CLC requirements with a letter of guarantee, known as the 'Blue Card', issued to each entered tanker. The limits to be guaranteed under 1969 CLC were based on the official gold value, expressed in francs, and came into force in 1975. This was amended and increased under the CLC Protocol 1976 to a maximum SDR14m. With the subsequent CLC 1992 and the CLC amendment, effective since November 2003, the guarantee limits have increased by over 640 per cent to SDR89.77m.

Calculating the long-term fairness or otherwise of the international tanker-spill compensation regime is, however, complicated by changes to the conventions, the disappearance of the voluntary TOVALOP and Cristal schemes, as well as the need to exclude the US, which has its own, quite different, liability system.

The P&I clubs pay the first tranche of tanker-spill compensation and face a large number of claims, although the contribution to any one incident is limited by the civil liability conventions. The oil industry, through the IOPC Funds, provides additional cover for the far fewer but more costly incidents.

The total cost of the 5,800 incidents ran to about US$1.8bn but the bill would have been US$6.6bn if costs were updated to reflect the compensation available under revised conventions. The bill rises to US$7.9bn with the addition of the 'ERIKA' and 'PRESTIGE' spills. Projecting the study forward to 2012 lifts the total bill to US$10.6bn. Cargo interests would have contributed to just 61 spills but their share of the total cost would be 64 per cent.

3 The United States of America have consistently declined being a party to any international limitation of liability convention because of constitutional difficulties in pre-empting US state laws. Consequently and in response to the 'EXXON VALDEZ' spill in Prince William Sound in 1989, the USA implemented the US Oil Pollution Act 1990, which incorporated the Comprehensive Environmental Response, Compensation and Liability Act (CERCLA).

OPA 90 came into force on 28 December 1994 requiring all ships trading within the US Exclusive Economic Zone to have guarantees for the statutory liability limits under the Act from an approved OPA Guarantor and certified by the National Pollution Funds Center of the US Coast Guard with a Certificate of Financial Responsibility (COFR).

The statutory liability limits, to be guaranteed, are:

- For OPA 90   Tankers US$1,200 per gross ton for tankers, or US$600 per gross ton for dry cargoes vessels, plus
- CERCLA   US$300 per gross ton for all vessels
- Alaska   Tankers US$2,000 per gross ton. Dry cargo vessels US$1,200 per gross ton

Because the statutory liability limits were both higher and more easily broken under OPA 90 than those proposed under the CLC Protocol 1984, later superseded by CLC 1992, the International Group of P&I clubs declined to provide the guarantees. As a result, new OPA Guarantors were established to enable shipowners to obtain the necessary COFRs from the National Pollution Funds Center to be allowed within the US Exclusive Economic Zone.

The main OPA Guarantors are:

- Shipowners' Insurance Guarantee Company – SIGCo with 45 per cent; and
- Shoreline Mutual (Bermuda) Ltd with 17 per cent.

The State of Alaska increased their statutory limits by 33.4 per cent from 27 October 2002 and there are proposals for statutory limits under OPA 90 to be substantially increased throughout the US.

Though the P&I clubs are not the guarantors they remain liable to pay in the first instance.

4 The Limitation of Liability for Marine Claims 1996 has increased limits by between 230 per cent and 1,800 per cent over its forerunner LLMC 1976. Article 4 of the Convention provides that the right will not be available to a person if 'it is proved that the loss resulted from his personal act or omission, committed with the intent to cause a loss, or recklessly and with knowledge that such loss would probably result.'

The most imminent problem for the P&I clubs, a far bigger threat than OPA 90, is brewing with passenger liabilities.

Athens Protocol 2002 (abbreviated to PAL) is about to increase guaranteed passenger liabilities by 536 per cent for passengers on all types of ship, cruise ships and ferries. This increase is compounded by the increasing sizes of cruise ships and ferries now being built and the greater numbers of passengers both types of ship can carry.

A cruise ship or ferry carrying 3,500 passengers must be guaranteed to meeting strict liabilities to passengers of US$1,263,570,000 (at the SDR/US$ rate of 1.444). To this figure must be added pollution liabilities under CLC 1996, the future liabilities under the Removal of Wreck convention, crew liabilities where the crew on a cruise ship will number around 800 and, finally, collision liabilities.

Any major casualty involving a large passenger ship will, from mid-2007, under the current IG P&I club reinsurance programme, risk an Overspill Claim.

5 An Overspill Claim is a claim under IG P&I club cover that exceeds the reinsurance limit
   under the IG reinsurance programme, which is currently US$2.05bn.

   Though the IG P&I clubs limit claims arising from any one accident or occurrence to 2.5
per cent of London Convention limits for property damage, currently equivalent to
US$4.5bn, club rules avoid responsibility for recovery over and above that which is recov-
erable under the IG reinsurance programme plus the amount due from the P&I club with
the claim under the International Group Agreement. The P&I club presenting an Overspill
Claim assumes no responsibility for claims payments in excess of these limits.

   Any suggestion that International Group P&I clubs will pay Overspill Claims over and
above that undertaken under the rules of the club presenting the Overspill Claim is untested
and should not be assumed.

   It is my personal opinion that the first serious Overspill Claim will be the end of the
International Group.

6 The top four P&I clubs within the IG cover 55 per cent of the business. The bottom four
   only command less than 10 per cent of the IG's business. Fixed premium P&I insurers have
   been almost entirely driven out. The increases in the limits under the shipowners' limitations
   of liability conventions can only further accelerate the consolidation and concentration of

---

Exhibit 12.9

International Group R/I programme

Cover Limit any one event	**Overspill Claims not covered by reinsurance**	P&I club members become liable for Overspill Claims through a Catastrophe Call
(2.5% of 1976 London Convention Limits for property damage) Approx US$4.5bn US$2.05bn limit reinsured	Claims amounts that exceed R/I revert to the Pool, subsequently to *all* members of IG P&I clubs **IG Pool R/I programme made up of four layers of US$500m each layer (4 × US$500m)**	
US$20m	**Hydra Upper Pool retention**	Small clubs often reinsure their Club and Pool Retentions
US$24m	**Lower Pool retention**	
US$6m	**Club Retention**	
Varies per type of claim	**Owner's Deductible**	

Source: Author's own.

protection and indemnity insurance. If this is what the European Union do not want under their Unfair Competition laws, then, they have only themselves to blame. As things stand, I anticipate further concentration of the cartel of IG P&I clubs who are now competing directly with the commercial insurance markets on both Hull & Machinery business and War Risks.

Bankers' insurances

With the high risks associated with shipping, the assigned marine insurances form an essential part of ship financiers' security. Consequently, any possibility of the underwriters of any of the owners' marine insurances not paying a claim, or a claim being void or voidable, would seriously impair a mortgagee's security. For example, a first mortgage on a ship becomes worthless when the ship is a total loss or is subject to a maritime lien for unpaid liabilities that exceed the ship's value.

There are two insurance policies available to ship mortgagees to cover these risks. Mortgagees' Interest Insurance (MII) covers the risk of the underwriters of any of the owners' marine insurances, (that is, the Hull & Machinery insurance including, if endorsed, the Increased Value insurance or the War Risks insurance or the P&I club coverage) declaring a claim void or voidable. Mortgagees' Additional Perils (Pollution) insurance, extendible to Mortgagees' Additional Perils (all P&I risks) insurance (MAP) covers the risk of a maritime lien attaching to the ship for an amount that exceeds the limit of liability insured.

The difference between these two insurances is that MII covers the risk of non-payment by underwriters due to the claim being void or voidable and MAP covers the limits insured and paid under the owner's liability insurances being insufficient to meet the full legal liabilities to third party plaintiffs.

Mortgagees' interest insurance

Aside from insolvency of underwriters, there are some crucial reasons causing marine insurance claims to be void, or voidable. Such reasons frequently arise from the fact that insurance policies are subject to requirements of 'utmost good faith' or 'uberrima fides' between assureds and underwriters;[3] and from the fact that policies also contain covenants or warranties that must be maintained throughout the policy. The fact that a marine insurance claim might be legitimately declined by insurers seriously impairs the security interests of mortgagees, as assignees and loss payees of the insurance claims recoveries.

MII, or the equivalent lessors' interest insurance, covers the risks of non-payment, in whole or in part, by insurers of the hull and machinery insurance and/or the war risks insurance and/or the P&I club coverage (collectively referred to as 'Owner's Policies and Club Entries') caused by:

• misrepresentation or non-disclosure of any material circumstance which entitles the underwriters of Owners' Policies and Club Entries to avoid the insurance provided thereunder, whether such misrepresentation or non-disclosure arises from the shipowner or manager or any of the assured's insurance agents or insurance brokers;

- breach of any express or implied warranty or condition, including:
  - breach of any implied warranty of seaworthiness or legality;
  - breach of trading warranties or any other express warranty contained in the Owners Policies and Club Entries;
  - breach of any warranty or condition in the Owners' Policies and Club Entries in respect of the classification of the mortgaged vessel by a classification society or any failure to comply with the recommendations of such society;
  - breach of any warranty or condition in the owners' policies and club entries which requires compliance with any condition or structural or P&I club survey requirements;
- exercise by a P&I club or P&I insurer of the pay-to-be-paid rule as a result of insolvency or failure by an owner to pay a claim where such insolvency or failure is caused by an otherwise covered liability;
- failure of the assured under the hull policy or the owners, managers or superintendents of the vessel or any of their onshore management to exercise due diligence in respect of any loss or damage to the vessel where such failure to exercise due diligence entitles the underwriters of the owner's hull and machinery policy to deny a claim;
- any deliberate or fraudulent casting away of, or damage to, the vessel, inducing scuttling and arson;
- any fraudulent claim under the Owners' Policies and Club Entries which permits the underwriters to deny the claim;
- the operation of any law or provision which provides for a time limitation on the presentation of claims.

Experience of a large number of MII claims shows that shipowners are more likely to breach the warranties under their Hull and Machinery or War Risks or P&I clubs warranties when facing financial difficulties. A large proportion of mortgagees' interest insurance claims have been found by the courts to have been caused by scuttling, arson or the exploitation of a genuine accident to contrive a total loss. More MII claims are anticipated because of the much tighter classification warranties and the tougher positions now being taken by most Classification Societies.

The very nature of these risks makes it imperative for mortgagees' or lessors' interest insurance to be placed by the bank itself through the bank's own appointed insurance broker. Temptation to allow the shipowner to place this insurance through his own insurance broker could easily cause serious problems and render the mortgagees' interest insurance void for the following reasons.

- Since the majority of claims have occurred when the shipowner has been in financial difficulty, underwriters now hold any financial default by the shipowner at the time of placing, or renewing, a mortgagee's interest insurance to be material information and discloseable by the assured bank. Failure to have such financial default, or any other material information, disclosed to a mortgagee's interest insurance underwriters at the time of placing the insurance could invalidate the policy, by reason of the lack of good faith.
- Where loan agreements, or lease contracts, require shipowners to take out mortgagees' or lessors' interest insurance along with the normal shipowner's marine insurances, and con-

sequently pay the MII premiums, there can be problems in US courts. The case has been advanced that under such terms a mortgagee's interest insurance claim settlement ranks *pari passu* with all other insurance claim settlements to the extent of either redeeming the loan from default or even paying off the loan. Either way there would be no tangible sub-rogation rights to underwriters which, as a consequence, could invalidate the MII claim (see Institute Mortgagees Interest Clauses Hulls Clause 9.2).

- Conflict of interest on the part of an insurance broker when acting simultaneously for a shipowner and his mortgagee, particularly in the event of an MII claim.

Mortgagees' interest insurance is almost solely underwritten by Lloyd's and the London com-pany markets under either an amended form of the Institute Mortgagees Interest Clauses – Hull (30 May 1986) or what is known as the German wording. However, if the Joint Hull Committee's proposals for a new wording of hull and machinery conditions are adopted, a new MII wording will be required to fill the gaps. A draft of a new wording is currently in the course of preparation.

Mortgagees' interest insurance does not cover any express limitations, restrictions or exclusions under any of the Owners' Policies and Club Entries, unless specifically provided for in the MII policy. Neither can this contingent insurance for mortgagees cover financial default or insolvency of any insurer or underwriter of the Owners' Policies and Club Entries.

The essential difference with a lessors' interest insurance arises by virtue of the fact that a lessor is the registered owner of a ship. As owners, lessors require a triple indemnity against non-payment by the lessee's insurers from (i) total or constructive total loss, (ii) collision lia-bility, and (iii) general liability and removal of wreck.

Experience has shown that mortgagees' interest insurance claims are more frequent in the early part of a shipping recession when reductions in earnings cause shipowners to make impru-dent economies, compounded by a drop in the market values that can wipe out the owners' equity.

Mortgagees' additional perils (pollution) insurance

The need for this insurance arose from the realisation that US tort laws allow a wide range of third party plaintiffs to acquire a priority maritime lien on a vessel that is held responsible for damages where the consequential legal liabilities have not been paid or are unrecoverable. As noted above, the P&I clubs that are members of the International Group provide shipowner members with unlimited coverage, on an indemnity basis, for all liabilities, excepting oil pol-lution which is limited to US$1bn for any one incident. When the 'EXXON VALDEZ' oil spill in Alaska resulted in immediate liabilities of over US$3bn, mortgagees realised they faced the US tort action risk of maritime liens attaching to a mortgaged vessel in favour of plaintiffs.

Rather than have the shipowner buy a substantial level of excess oil pollution coverage, where the cost would be prohibitive and the insurable limit available always insufficient, Mortgagees' Additional Perils (Pollution) Insurance was introduced in early 1990.

Mortgagees' Additional Perils (Pollution) Insurance is designed to indemnify ship mort-gagees to the extent of their loss under a loan caused by a mortgaged vessel being held respon-sible for a pollution incident where the liabilities against owners and managers exceed the liability limit, or combined liability limits, insured by shipowners. Such loss will be caused by the arrest of the responsible vessel and, following actions by plaintiffs, the imposition of a maritime lien on that vessel. The loss could subsequently be compounded by moves to detain and arrest sister vessels under the same management or ownership. Though sister vessels are, in the US, free of the threat of maritime liens ranking ahead of the mortgage, any detention would prevent them making the earnings to service the debt. Mortgagees would, consequently, face the prospect of a loan default and loss of the collateral security on the responsible vessel.

In the event of a highly publicised major oil spill likely to incur punitive liabilities, sufficient to threaten the shipowner with bankruptcy, the proceeds from any forced sale of any sister vessels could easily be insufficient to cover more highly leveraged loans, whether on a single, large, cross-collateralised loan, or on individual loans on single ships probably with numerous banks.

All loans are different and banks should, consequently, take care when giving instructions for the placing of Mortgagees' Additional Perils (Pollution) Insurance that they are fully insured against any consequence of a shipowner mortgagor facing liabilities that may exceed his limits insured. Also, it is unnecessarily risky to allow the shipowner to place this insurance on behalf of the mortgagee since, as mentioned above, US courts have held with mortgagees' interest insurance that where shipowners have placed an insurance the policy can be deemed an asset of the shipowner, irrespective of the fact that the policy is in the name of the mortgagee.

Mortgagees' Additional Perils (All P&I Risks) Insurance

Mortgagees' Additional Perils (Pollution) Insurance only became necessary because the IG member P&I clubs limited cover for oil pollution. There are now numerous P&I club cover limits that are not all clearly defined.

Mortgagees' Additional Perils (All P&I Risks) Insurance is already in use where ships are not entered with the IG member P&I clubs but are, instead, covered by fixed premium insurers such as British Marine Mutual. The MAP (All P&I Risks) insuring conditions are identical to the LSW 489 wording for Mortgagees' Additional Perils (Pollution) Insurance but merely extended to cover, as the name suggests, all risks normally covered by P&I insurance.

Insurance of other interests (lessors, shipowners and passive investors)

From the insurance viewpoint, all other interests in a ship, and most particularly a tanker or oil rig, can be similarly insured against sequestration or confiscation by a court from failure to pay a full liability award as a consequence of an accidental oil spill. However, there is not much point in placing this insurance for account of the responsible parties (shipowners, including lessors, bareboat or demise charterers, ship managers or operators) if the claim by such assureds can be sequestered by a US court.

Where a bank is a lessor, and therefore the registered shipowner, there is a legal problem which the bank must resolve through its lawyers. On the other hand, passive investors in a shipowning company are not defined as responsible parties and, like mortgagees, can safely insure themselves against confiscation of the ship following accidental pollution to the extent of the value of their equity interest. Passive Investors' Equity Interest Insurance – Additional Perils (Pollution) is, therefore, placed on a separate insurance but alongside Mortgagees' Additional Perils (Pollution). It is very important to note that a claim under each of these insurances would trigger from the same event and, therefore, underwriters must be advised of the existence of both insurances on the same ship. For this reason it is better to have both insurances placed by the same insurance broker who must not be the shipowner's or operator's holding broker for the marine hull and machinery insurances.

Mortgage rights insurance

The risk of a ship mortgagee being unable to foreclose a mortgage in the event of default and gain repossession of the ship clear of lien presents a real cross-border sovereign risk on the flag country.

Mortgage rights insurance is effectively the marine mortgage equivalent of aircraft repossession insurance. These policies effectively insure the bank against confiscation, deprivation or diminution of their legal title and rights as lessor owners or mortgagees on the asset and also their inability to deregister the ship or aircraft from the flag or registry.

This insurance is therefore pertinent to mortgagees of ships and oil rigs flagged in third world countries with sovereign debt problems. Most bank inspectors accept that this insurance removes, or *lays off*, cross-border risk problem. Banks' insurances should be placed by brokers appointed by the banks to ensure full disclosure.

Exhibit 12.10

Types of insurances and documents on financed ships

Insurances for mortgagees/lessors/corporate lenders

The risk	Covered by (type of policy)	Indemnity or claim amount
Non-payment by underwriters of claims under any of the owner's marine policies (for example, H&M, War and P&I) due to breach of warranty, non-disclosure, failure to comply with SOLAS regulations, or illegal acts.	**Institute Mortgagees Interest Clauses Hulls** or BankServe's Mortgagees Interest Insurance conditions, or: Breach of warranty clauses but limited to policies to which they are endorsed, for example: (a) German Direct Mortgage Clause or LSW 1189, or (b) Norwegian Insurance Plan Chapters 7 and 8.4	To indemnify the Mortgagee's loss up to the sum insured as a result of non payment under Hull & Machinery, War and/or from the P&I club. (a) and (b) Cover confined to policies to which the GDMC/LSW 1189, or Chapters 7 and 8.4 under the Norwegian Plan are endorsed. **Non-payment by P&I club not covered**

(Continued)

Exhibit 12.10   *(Continued)*

The risk	**Covered by** **(type of policy)**	**Indemnity or** **claim amount**
For Lessors or Innocent Owners (for example, KG or KS investors) risks as above to include liabilities if applicable.	**Lessors' Interest Insurance**	To indemnify the assured for their loss (and/or liability as owners) up to the sum insured as a result of non-payment under Hull & Machinery, War and/or from the P&I club.
Risk of oil pollution liabilities exceeding the limit insured under the P&I cover, being: • US$1bn by P&I clubs in IGA • US$500m, or less, by fixed premium P&I insurers • Wilful misconduct causing loss of shipowner's right to limit under CLC 1992.	**Mortgagees Additional Perils (Pollution) Insurance**	Indemnifies mortgagees up to the lesser amount of: (a) sum insured, or (b) the outstanding debt under the mortgage.
Risks of liabilities exceeding any P&I cover limit resulting in a maritime lien on the vessel: • IGA P&I cover limit US$4.5bn • War P&I (hull value + US$500m) • Any new cover limit, for example, passenger liabilities.	**Mortgagees Additional Perils (All P&I Risks) Insurance** An extended Mortgagees Additional Perils policy covering all P&I club cover limits.	Indemnifies mortgagees up to the lesser amount of: (a) sum insured, or (b) the outstanding debt under the mortgage.
Automatic cancellation of Owner's insurances upon change of control for example, foreclosure by Mortgagee. Cover required when Mortgagee is in possession and Vessel LAID UP (under arrest)	**Port Risk Clauses**	Broad coverage for loss, damage and liability up to sum insured. Salvage, salvage charges, sue & labour. Pollution. War Risks should be included by extension.
Sovereign Risk of being denied the rights to repossess mortgaged assets following foreclosure. The Cross-Border risk.	**Mortgage Rights Insurance**	Inability to foreclose under the Mortgage. Loss or damage due to confiscation in Flag Country. Deprivation of Legal Title and rights. Inability to get de-registration. Indemnifies up to sum insured.
Mortgagees' P&I cover following cancellation by shipowner's P&I club.	**Mortgagees P&I Insurance**	To indemnify the mortgagee to the extent of their security interest under the mortgage against an incident giving rise to a maritime

(Continued)

526

Exhibit 12.10   *(Continued)*

The risk	Covered by (type of policy)	Indemnity or claim amount
		lien subject to conditions equivalent to P&I club rules.
Pre-existing Maritime & Statutory Liens arising from outstanding liabilities of a vendor or previous owner	**Mortgagees Pre-existing Liens Insurance**	Full indemnity up to the limit insured.
Risk of liabilities exceeding any P&I cover limit directly causing bankruptcy of the corporate borrower for unpaid liabilities, or the borrower filing under Chapter 11.	**Corporate Lender's Additional Perils Insurance** Equivalent to Excess Liabilities Insurance	Indemnifies the unsecured lender to the lesser amount of: (a) sum insured, and (b) the outstanding indebtedness under the corporate financing.

Source: Author's own.

---

[1]   Section 50 Marine Insurance Act 1906.
[2]   Section 53 Marine Insurance Act 1906.
[3]   Section 17 Marine Insurance Act 1906.

Annex A

Useful websites

Insurance markets

- Lloyds of London: http://www.lloyds.com/index.asp
- Lloyd's Market Association: http://www.the-lma.com
- Norwegian Market: http://www.northedge.no
- International Underwriting Association: http://www.iua.co.uk

P&I clubs

- The International Group of P&I clubs and links to members: http://www.igpandi.org
- Elysian Independent P&I commentary: http://www.elysian-insurance.com

Maritime Authorities

- International Maritime Organisation (IMO) Directory of Maritime Links: http://www.imo.org/home.asp?topic_id=161
- IMO Athens Protocol 2002 Correspondence Group: http://folk.uio.no/erikro/WWW/corrgr/index.html#ins
- International Oil Pollution Compensation Fund: http://en.iopcfund.org
- EU Commission: ec.europa.eu
- US Coast Guard: www.uscg.mil
- Federal Maritime Commission: www.fmc.gov
- International Convention on Maritime Liens & Mortgages 1993: http://www.jus.uio.no/lm/un.imo.maritime.liens.and.mortgages.convention.1993/doc.html

Maritime lawyers' regular circulars

- David Martin-Clarke's case notes: http://www.onlinedmc.co.uk
- International Law Office: http://www.internationallawoffice.com

Ship valuations

- Clarkson's Ship Values: www.Shipvalue.net

Credit rating agencies

- A.M. Bests: http://www.ambest.com/ratings/RatingsSearch.asp?b1=0
- Standard & Poor's: www.standardandpoors.com
- Moody's: www.moodys.com

Press and marine publications

- Lloyd's List: http://www.lloydslist.com/NASApp/cs/ContentServer?pagename=LLPortal/LloydsList
- TradeWinds: http://tradewinds.no/login/login.php/news/viewall/
- Fairplay: www.fairplay.co.uk
- Merlin Legal Publishing: maritimeadvocateonline@lb.bcentral.com
- Insurance Day:www.insuranceday.com
- Financial Times: www.FT.com

Annex B

Origins, history and fundamental principles of insurance

The Roman Emperor Claudius is credited as being the founder of insurance in the year AD 43. Serious drought had caused a scarcity of grain in Rome. A mob stopped Claudius in the forum and pelted him so hard with curses and stale crusts of bread that he had difficulty in regaining the palace by a side door. As a result he instigated steps to remedy the crisis by encouraging merchants and shipowners to continue to trade throughout the stormy winter months. To do this he insured merchants against the loss of their ships and cargoes against all marine perils throughout the year, which, on top of his offer of large bounties for every new grain vessel built proportionate to its tonnage, combined to guarantee the merchants a good return on their ventures.

However, the Chinese are credited with establishing 'general average' 3,000 years ago. General average is a marine insurance term defining the sacrificial loss by one party for the benefit of the whole; such as when cargo is jettisoned to save a foundering ship.

Insurance was originally established to cover the then very high risks associated with merchant shipping ventures. By the beginning of the fifteenth century marine insurance was the well-established means of English merchants for covering their vessels and cargoes against even greater marine perils associated with sailing ships trading worldwide, though without the potential for liabilities that shipowners face today.

Growing out of this form of protection to property was the insurance of the life of the merchant, who usually accompanied the ship, and of the captain of the vessel, both being liable to capture by Moorish and Turkish pirates. The persons to whom the premium was paid were termed underwriters, who in return agreed to pay a fixed amount, the sum insured, if the person insured died within a year; the document specifying the contract was called the policy, the name it still bears. The premium charged appears to have been not less than five per cent of the sum insured, irrespective of the age of the insured.

In 1574, Robert Chandler, under a patent granted to him by Queen Elizabeth I, established a chamber of insurance in London to regulate all contracts of insurance. This chamber was destroyed by the great fire of 1666.

The earliest life policy of which particulars have been preserved was issued on 15 June 1583, at the Office of Insurance within the Royal Exchange, London. This policy gave rise to the first authenticated disputed claim. It provided that if a certain William Gybbons should die within 12 months the underwriters, 13 in number, who guaranteed sums from £25 to £50 each, should pay to Richard Morton £383 6s 8d, the premium for which was eight per cent. Gybbons died on 28 May 1584 and the underwriters refused to pay on the grounds that he had survived 12 months of 28 days each. The commissioners appointed to determine such cases decided that the 12 months mentioned in the policy meant calendar months and ordered payment to be made by the underwriters; an appeal to the court of admiralty failed and the decision of the commissioners was upheld in 1587. Life insurance as a provision for a wife and children is mentioned in 1622. Policies as collateral security for money advanced for the purchase of appointments were much in vogue in the seventeenth and eighteenth centuries.

Lloyd's of London evolved out of Edward Lloyd's coffee house in Abchurch Lane from 1692, which was then a renowned meeting place of merchants. After several moves, by 1774

Lloyd's was established at the Royal Exchange and remained there until the fire of 1838 when it was finally removed to the site of the present building in Lime Street. Lloyd's then consisted of eminent merchant shipowners and underwriters effecting insurance on ships and merchandise, with each member of Lloyd's paying an annual subscription of four guineas. In support of their underwriting function a Register of Ships was compiled in 1764. In 1803 Lloyd's began establishing the Patriotic Funds to encourage the army and navy in times of war to protect the interests of the Lloyd's community, being merchants, shipowners and, of course, underwriters.

As the scope of insurance extended beyond marine risks to property and life insurance so a number of unscrupulous individuals tried to take advantage. In the early days, the concepts of insurance and gambling were very much entwined. Strange as it may seem, policies were once taken out on the lives of public men with reckless abandon. Life insurance policies were taken on Sir Robert Walpole by countless people unknown to him, the aggregate sum insured on his life amounting to a considerable amount of money. The premium rates increased at certain times in his political career, especially when his life was endangered by rioters and also during the period of his threatened impeachment. When George II was engaged in battle in 1743, people took out policies on the King's life, hoping to cash in if he died in the fighting. Commissions in the army and navy could often be secured by life insurance policies for those who could not otherwise afford it. Such officers tended to have been ordered to the thickest part of the battle to ensure they were killed – talk about conflicts of interest. The whole situation got seriously out of hand. The distinction between gambling, or wagering, and insurance had to be defined and legislated for.

On the face of it gambling and insurance have similarities. For a monetary stake or payment of a premium, the happening of an event results in a cash settlement. This, however, is far too simplistic and dangerously deceptive. With a wager a stake is paid to a bookmaker who pays out when the selected horse or dog wins: a clear win or lose situation. With insurance, a claim is paid when the assured provides evidence of a loss: insurance is a contract of indemnity with no theoretical winners. An insurance contract is enforceable in a court of law whereas a bet has no legal standing; though it may not be illegal to place a bet the outcome cannot be enforced at law.

In 1774 the Life Assurance Act became law, alternatively known as the Gambling Act. This law laid down that 'insurances lacking insurable interest on the life or lives of any person or any other event or events whatsoever' are rendered unenforceable. Another clause in the Act set forth that the sum to be recovered was not to exceed the value of the interest of the assured in the subject insured. Although this Act was not restricted to life assurance, it was made clear that the Act made exceptions for the insurance of ships, goods and merchandise in allowing for anticipated interest and valued policies, where the subject matter insured could be given a fixed agreed value irrespective of the market value.

The Marine Insurance Act was instated during the early part of 1906. This act is a codified statute and in it insurable interest is defined. Section 4(1) of the Act provides that every contract of marine insurance by way of gambling or waging is void. Indeed, by the Marine Insurances (Gambling Policies) Act 1909, it is made a criminal offence for anybody to fix up a marine insurance policy without interest or anticipated interest.

So much for history and the legislation established to draw the distinction between gambling and insurance. In my experience as an insurance broker, many people today still like to regard their relationship with marine underwriters as something akin to their relationship with bookmakers and appoint an insurance broker by his perceived ability to ensure that the premiums charged to shipowners are always less than the claims recovered. Such exploitation relies on excessive competition and over capacity in the insurance markets, which is sometimes possible over a short period in the insurance cycle. Such people should appreciate that in buying an insurance policy, even if there is no claim, the insured still had value in the form of insurance cover.

Fundamental principles of all insurance

The legislation in the form of the Life Assurance Act of 1774, supported by the Gambling Act of 1845 made all wagers unenforceable, and the Marine Insurance Act of 1906 established the mighty pillar of insurance – the principle of indemnity. The insured person (the insured or assured) shall be placed in the same position financially, in the event of a risk insured against, as he had been in immediately before the event or happening of the loss. This means that there should be no gain under a claims settlement yet neither should there be any loss, subject to the adequacy of the sum insured. Notwithstanding this bold principle there remains a temptation to exploit the use of valued policies.

In order for there to be an indemnity, the insured must have an insurable interest. This signifies that the insured person or entity must be in a legal relationship to that which is insured – the subject matter – whereby he will lose out financially by the happening of the event insured. Events insured under marine insurances are perils of the sea, war risks and liability insurances.

All insurance policies or contracts of insurance must, therefore, identify the assured (person or entity insured), the subject matter insured (ship, aircraft), the interest insured (the legal relationship between the assured and the subject matter insured, for example, as owners, charterers, mortgagees) and the events insured against or insured perils (marine perils, war risks, third party liabilities) which are detailed under insuring conditions, often in the form of standard printed clauses. Also included will be any material information in respect of the risk.

Utmost good faith or *uberrima fides* must be observed by both insurers and assureds under an insurance contract. The obligations and duties of disclosure obviously fall mainly on the proposer of an insurance who will have appointed an insurance broker to act as his agent in effecting the insurance. The proposer, invariably the assured, has a duty to disclose all material facts in respect of the risk being insured.

For example, in insuring a horse against death a prospective assured would have a duty to tell the insurers if the animal was suffering from a disease. But making the distinction with gambling, a bookmaker has no duty to disclose to a person betting on a horse that it has only three legs. If someone insures their life with the intention of committing suicide the claim is void. If a shipowner scuttles his ship his insurances will not pay; if he contrives a total loss by failing to take remedial action, where such remedial action was possible, his insurers will not pay a total loss claim.

The responsibilities of an assured under utmost good faith must be clearly spelt out and understood by shipowners and also by ship mortgagees where they rely upon the assignment of the shipowners' policies for the security of their loan. Failure of the shipowner to disclose material information will invalidate the owners' policies and impair the banks' security.

The legal definition of discloseable facts for insurance purposes is:

- The assured is bound to disclose every material circumstance which would influence the judgement of a prudent insurer in fixing the premium or determining whether he will take the risk.
- Every material circumstance which is known to the agent must be disclosed to the insurer (an agent to insure is deemed to know every circumstance which in the ordinary course of business ought to be known by, or to have been communicated to, him).
- Every material representation made by the assured or his agent to the insurer during negotiations for the insurance, and before the insurance contract is concluded, must be true. If it is untrue the insurer may avoid the contract.
- A representation may be withdrawn or corrected before the contract is concluded.
- A contract of marine insurance is deemed to be concluded when the proposal of the assured, as represented by the agent, is accepted by the insurer whether the policy is then issued or not.

Annex C

Summary of status of Conventions as at 31 March 2006

Instrument	Entry into force date	No. of contracting States	% world tonnage*
IMO Convention	17 March 1958	165	98.81
1991 amendments	–	92	83.55
SOLAS 1974	25 May 1980	155	98.79
SOLAS Protocol 1978	1 May 1981	109	95.35
SOLAS Protocol 1988	3 February 2000	81	66.92
Load Lines 1966	21 July 1968	156	98.76
Load Lines Protocol 1988	3 February 2000	76	66.57
TONNAGE 1969	18 July 1982	145	98.56
COLREG 1972	15 July 1977	148	97.92
SFV Protocol 1993	–	12	9.66
STCW 1978	28 April 1984	150	98.78
STP 1971	2 January 1974	17	22.85
INMARSAT C 1976	16 July 1979	90	92.58
INMARSAT OA 1976	16 July 1979	88	91.46
1994 amendments	–	40	28.95
FAL 1965	5 March 1967	104	68.19
MARPOL 73/78 (Annex I/II)	2 October 1983	137	97.65
MARPOL 73/78 (Annex III)	1 July 1992	122	93.69
MARPOL 73/78 (Annex IV)	27 September 2003	107	60.21
MARPOL 73/78 (Annex V)	31 December 1988	127	95.92
MARPOL Protocol 1997 (Annex VI)	19 May 2005	32	64.35
LC 1972	30 August 1975	81	69.31
1978 amendments	–	20	19.23
LC Protocol 1996	–	27	14.08
INTERVENTION 1969	6 May 1975	82	72.88
INTERVENTION Protocol 1973	30 March 1983	48	47.40
CLC 1969	19 June 1975	42	3.59
CLC Protocol 1976	8 April 1981	54	56.22
CLC Protocol 1992	30 May 1996	113	94.41
FUND Protocol 1976	22 November 1994	32	47.71
FUND Protocol 1992	30 May 1996	98	88.92
FUND Protocol 2000	27 June 2001	–	–
FUND Protocol 2003	–	17	13.73
NUCLEAR 1971	15 July 1975	17	19.85
PAL 1974	28 April 1987	32	38.64
PAL Protocol 1976	30 April 1989	25	38.36
PAL Protocol 1990	–	6	0.93
PAL Protocol 2002	–	4	0.13
LLMC 1976	1 December 1986	50	49.65
LLMC Protocol 1996	13 May 2004	21	20.98

(Continued)

Instrument	Entry into force date	No. of contracting States	% world tonnage*
SALVAGE 1989	14 July 1996	52	38.16
OPRC 1990	13 May 1995	87	64.52
Hazardous and Noxious Substances Convention (HNS) 1996	–	8	4.83
OPRC/HNS 2000	–	13	15.84
BUNKERS CONVENTION 2001	–	10	13.22
AFS CONVENTION 2001	–	16	17.27
BWM CONVENTION 2004	–	6	0.62

*Source: *Lloyd's Register of Shipping/World Fleet Statistics* as at 31 December 2003.

Annex D

Insurance cost increases

Vessel Type	Insurance cost % change on Opex 2003-2004	in amount 2003-2004	2004 Total OPEX US$	Insurance Costs US$	Insurance/ OPEX %	2003 Total OPEX US$	Insurance Costs US$	Insurance/ OPEX %
Handysize Bulker	8.39	17.24	1,198,647	131,923	11.01	1,108,136	112,524	10.15
Handymax Bulker	7.32	11.16	1,243,108	121,003	9.73	1,200,248	108,859	9.07
Panamax Bulker	8.37	18.99	1,521,016	167,346	11.00	1,385,308	140,643	10.15
Capesize Bulker	26.07	29.36	1,692,864	220,488	13.02	1,649,830	170,448	10.33
Product Tanker	12.29	23.93	1,607,879	148,851	9.26	1,456,851	120,113	8.24
Handysize Product Tanker	1.29	0.81	1,740,706	152,275	8.75	1,748,948	151,048	8.64
Panamax Tanker	9.46	8.62	2,104,773	223,509	10.62	2,121,028	205,774	9.70
Aframax Tanker	7.67	4.41	2,046,007	230,865	11.28	2,109,942	221,115	10.48
Suezmax Tanker	11.36	13.28	2,100,390	262,384	12.49	2,064,826	231,632	11.22
VLCC	7.82	21.16	2,658,327	479,294	18.03	2,365,611	395,594	16.72
Dry Cargo	3.13	-1.86	961,961	70,373	7.32	1,010,847	71,706	7.09
Container Feedermax	25.64	14.44	972,501	101,264	10.41	1,067,666	88,487	8.29
Container Ships	15.15	26.39	1,368,829	139,579	10.20	1,247,011	110,431	8.86
Container Main Liner	36.82	46.01	1,553,697	207,809	13.38	1,455,911	142,326	9.78
RoRo	-16.41	-19.84	1,305,363	133,463	10.22	1,361,149	166,490	12.23
Reefer	18.07	30.07	1,189,377	101,750	8.55	1,079,645	78,228	7.25
Coastal Vessels	-5.13	3.46	769,093	46,799	6.08	705,293	45,235	6.41

Source: OpCost 2005 prepared by Moore Stephens.

Chapter 13

An introduction to Islamic finance

Arlene Dourish and Struan Robertson

Islamic finance has grown at a rate of 15 per cent per annum between 2003 and 2006 and is currently estimated to be worth in the region of US$200bn.[1]

The recent expansion in the number of banks with Islamic finance practices has echoed this global growth of Islamic financial systems and interest-free banking. Throughout Asia, Europe and Africa a strong network of financial institutions has begun to develop profitable practices based on Islamic guidelines which may appear complex but are often quite straightforward.

Some basics

Islamic finance is a unique form of commerce in which financial products and services offered to investors and customers are structured so as to comply not only with English law but to comply with Islamic law too.

The canon law of Islam is called the *Shari'a*. This law regulates aspects of a Muslim's life, including their financial dealings. It derives primarily from the Qur'an and some other secondary sources, and does not exist in codified form (such as legislation) but instead is applied by Islamic law scholars who have interpreted rulings and previous judgments.

Islamic law contains some well-known prohibitions such as usury (including interest) and gambling. But it also contains other provisions that encourage trade while ensuring transactions are fair and conducted in an ethical manner. Underlying requirements are that (1) there is a true and fair sharing of risk between parties to a financial or commercial arrangement, (2) that there is no exploitation by one party of another weaker party and (3) that economically wasteful and unproductive activities are avoided while charitable conduct and social and economic development is encouraged.

By developing trade finance, equity and wholesale, retail and corporate products and services which utilise *Shari'a*'s encouragement of trade and entrepreneurial partnerships, banks and financial institutions engaging in Islamic finance have gained profitable practices which flourish as part of a US$200bn global industry. Industry project and asset finance has become increasingly popular in recent years and a number of high-profile *Shari'a*-compliant aviation, project and maritime finance transactions have been seen in the market place.

Interest (*riba*)

It is well known that *Shari'a* law prohibits the taking or giving of interest in financial transactions. The prohibition is against usury, which is broadly defined as any 'undue accretion' and one example of which is interest on monies lent. There is a great deal of uncertainty as to

537

the scope of this prohibition and the subject has been much debated for many hundreds of years. In some areas, however, there exist very detailed laws regulating the matter, which can often be employed in the structuring of modern financial products in a positive way.

The objective underlying the usury prohibition is to avoid the commercial exploitation by one party in a transaction of a party with a weaker bargaining position. The principles stem from the charitable aim of preventing moneylenders exploiting the needy. Another reason is that *Shari'a* law links the lawfulness of gain to risk-taking, thereby viewing gain as morally justified only when one faces risk to secure it.

Recent developments have made use of the allowance of contractually fixed countervalues and permissible mark-ups representing profit elements for banks to ensure that Islamic finance transactions are still profitable to enter into. *Shari'a* law fully recognises the value gained by the use of money over a time period by a borrower and the loss of foregone opportunity by the investor.

Risk (*maisir*)

The other main prohibition of *Shari'a* law in this field is against excessive risk in a transaction being on any one party. The reasons for the prohibition are much the same as those mentioned above, together with the objectives of avoiding situations where fraud, deception or undue uncertainty or speculation might result in excessive financial hardship on one party to a transaction. Gambling falls within the scope of this law.

Islamic financial instruments most commonly used for ship finance

Murabaha

Most Islamic funds are confined to short-term, low-risk investments, principally in the form of trade financing for property or goods accomplished through the mark-up contract called *Murabaha* (cost-plus finance). Here, an investor acquires property or goods from a supplier and then resells to its customer at a price (to be paid in instalments) which covers the costs incurred by the investor together with a contractually agreed sum that represents compensation for the loss of foregone opportunity by the investor. Either of these two sales can be on credit and in modern practice the second of them always is. The investor's added profit margin is completely acceptable according to *Shari'a* law. In addition to actual costs incurred in processing the deal, the investor can add a charge for the risk that the buyer will not ultimately pay, and, very importantly, for the investor's opportunity cost in having its funds tied up until the buyer pays. This last charge represents a very subtle distinction from the charging of straight interest. This type of sale contract is widely used in London and other financial centres in varied and often complex forms. It forms the mainstay of Islamic finance at present, although recently other modes of finance have started to become more popular.

Ijara

One other popular method of Islamic finance is the *Ijara* lease which is preferred by investors opting for longer-term, higher-yielding investments. Leases have some of the same advantages as sale in allowing recognition of a phased element of payment, and investors may regard leases as incorporating lower risks because the investor (lessor) retains legal title to the property until the end of the contract, assuring effective security of title. Other advantages include flexibility in payment terms and other provisions for transferability as well as the possibility of hire-purchase structures.

Musharaka

An increasingly popular method of Islamic finance is the partnership financing by use of the *Musharaka*. This Islamic financing technique involves a partnership between two parties who both provide capital towards the financing of a project. Both parties share profits on a pre-agreed ratio, but losses are shared on the basis of equity participation. Management of the project may be carried out by both the parties or by just one party. This is a very flexible partnership arrangement where the sharing of the profits and management can be negotiated and pre-agreed by all parties.

In many of the structures outlined above it is often hard to see how the product is nothing more than 'disguised' interest or a conventional loan executed in a roundabout way. However, in *Shari'a* law, if not in economics, there are substantial differences. For example, in the *Murabaha* transaction, during the interval between the two sales, the investor owns the property. During that time the investor bears the risk that it will be destroyed or damaged. These are risks that a bank would seldom face in a conventional loan. In any event, the objective of the Muslim in engaging in the transaction is to comply with religious law, regardless of tenuous economic or legal distinctions.

Market trends

Liquidity requirements can be onerous and repayment periods are usually shorter in Islamic finance transactions, but there are advantages too. Malaysian Islamic banks operating on short-term financing weathered the Asian economic crisis much better than conventional banks because they operate on a profit and loss sharing basis that forces them to evaluate the prospects of a venture diligently, rather than focusing only on the creditworthiness of the borrower. This illustrates that the principles on which the *Shari'a* requirements are founded are grounded in reality and practical in effect.

Increasingly, Western banks are opening Islamic 'windows' (that is, committing capital to Islamic business), recognising the potential of this area beyond the traditional roles of fund management and property finance to include international and domestic trade finance, aircraft, ship and other forms of leasing and capital market funding techniques and derivatives.

Detailed example structures

Certain Islamic structures are apt for ship finance. Documenting and advising on *Shari'a*-compliant financings requires careful consideration of ownership, title, risk and tax issues.

For a bank (the 'Bank') to finance the purchase of a second-hand vessel using an Islamic law-compliant structure, a *Musharaka* or *Ijara* arrangement would be most suitable. The

Musharaka can also be used for newbuilding payments whereas the *Istisna* would be used instead of the *Ijara*.

The *Ijara* model (leasing arrangement)

Under Islamic law, a lease is regarded as the sale of the usufruct (the right to use) property (for example, a vessel) for a specified period of time. Because the sale of a usufruct is permitted in Islamic law, economic arrangements whereby a Bank buys a vessel then leases it to its customer under a 'hire purchase' type scheme are allowed and, indeed, much used in practice.

There are, however, a number of conditions for lease-financing to be valid. One of the most important is that the Bank (as lessor) must own the leased property (the vessel) for the duration of the lease. This is explored more below, together with some of the other relevant issues which the Bank might need to consider if developing a structure based on a leasing contract. In essence, the Bank buys the vessel selected by the shipowner in question (the 'Company') and retains title to it, the Company makes a series of lease payments over a specified period of time and at the end of the term exercises an option to buy the vessel from the Bank (and therefore finally takes legal title to it).

The lease can be of relatively long duration such as 25 years and enables floating rates of return to be in-built in the scheme, making it ideal for long-term finance arrangements during the course of which market conditions may change.

The *Ijara* model can also be used for refinancing vessels already owned by the Company.

Model outline

The Company identifies a specified vessel (the 'Vessel') and agrees a purchase price with the seller of the Vessel (the 'Seller'). The Bank then buys the Vessel from the Seller at the agreed price (in the case of a re-financing the Bank will purchase the Vessel from the Company). This agreed price is the same amount as the amount of financing being provided by the Bank to the Company under the arrangement. Since the Bank will not wish to finance 100 per cent of the purchase price, the Company pays to the Bank a deposit against the purchase price agreed, together with closing costs incurred with the aim of leaving the Bank with the exposure of the amount it is prepared to finance.

Initial purchase

Upon the purchase of the Vessel from the Seller, when the Bank will pay the purchase price to the Seller, the Bank will be registered as sole owner of the Vessel. The treatment of the deposit will need to be considered (as mentioned below). The risk of damage to the Vessel between exchange of contracts and completion also needs to be allocated but can be minimised by careful structuring.

Grant of lease

The Bank enters into a lease (the 'Lease') with the Company which could be for up to 25–30 years duration and which will contain all the relevant provisions governing the employment of the Vessel by the Company. The Bank can pass to the Company as lessee, or as agent of the Bank, as much of the obligations as is practicable and as is compliant with *Shari'a* law. The Company agrees under the terms of the Lease to pay hire for the use of the Vessel. The aim is that the Lease rental should be reviewed periodically and the Company permitted to make 'prepayments'. Consideration will need to be given as to how these will be characterised and whether it will be a matter for the Bank's discretion whether to allow changes to the initial rent schedule agreed with the Company. Under *Shari'a* law, there must be some basis to the rent review provision other than it being in the complete discretion of one party.

Forfeiture and default

The Lease will provide for forfeiture of the Lease by the Bank in the event of a default by the Company/lessee to enable recovery of possession, subject to statutory provisions in that regard. The Bank can also have a contractual claim for any shortfall in recovery from the purchase price pursuant to an obligation on the Company to buy the Vessel from the Bank in the event of a default by the Company. This is frequently required to be kept separate from the Lease terms in order to comply with *Shari'a* requirements.

The Bank will give the Company the option of requesting a sale of the Vessel to the Company at the end of the initially agreed financing period, that is the Lease term, and also in certain other instances, such as a sale of the Vessel or refinancing. The circumstances in which the Bank will agree to this early repayment, and on what terms and at what price, can be determined by the Bank.

On exercise by the Company of its right to call for the Vessel and payment of all sums due to the Bank, or if the Bank calls upon the Company to buy the Vessel on default, the Vessel will then be transferred by the Bank to the Company.

Exhibit 13.1
Ijara **model**

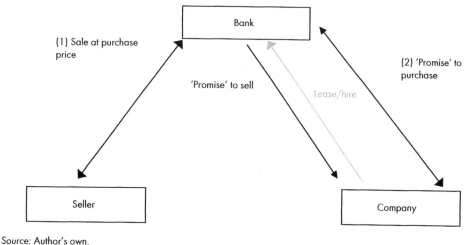

Source: Author's own.

541

The following legal issues may have consequences for the facility structure ultimately used.

Refinancing

Where the Company wishes to refinance the Vessel, repayment of the 'principal sum' due under the arrangement is required by the Bank. The issues to be considered in these circumstances include the mechanism for the Bank to sell the Vessel at the Company's request to the Company, so that he may offer security to the new finance provider; whether the Lease would be surrendered (or, if the new finance provider is also to use an *Ijara* structure, perhaps the Lease would continue) the release of the Bank's obligations as lessor; the price which the Bank would expect to receive on an early termination of this kind; what title guarantee the Bank is prepared to give as seller; and recovery of the costs of the sale.

Sale

Where the Company decides to sell the Vessel at some time before completion of the duration of the Lease, many of the same issues as mentioned for refinance apply. Also the Bank would have to enter into a sale contract at the Company's request with the purchaser, thereby exposing the Bank to contractual obligations and risks.

Minimising the Bank's obligations

The principal issue is that although an enforceable contract and lease could be prepared passing most of the risks from the Bank to the Company (although dependent on the ability of the Company to meet its obligations), if the structure is to meet the criteria required for *Shari'a* compliance, some element of risk will have to be retained by the Bank. This can be taken into account in pricing the financing. Agency provisions can be used to mitigate some of the exposure.

Subleases

The appointed *Shari'a* advisers can advise on whether the Company is entitled to take a profit income from sub-leasing the Vessel.

Other issues

Other points to be considered for the implementation of the structure include:

Rent reviews

Commercially, the Bank may like to have a review of the hire/rent. The Bank will consider whether this will be linked to known rates which might act as a benchmark identifiable in advance of entering into the *Ijara* arrangement or if it intends to try to have a variable review reflecting various expenses to the Bank, to the extent that this would be compliant with *Shari'a* requirements.

Bank accounts

Related to the above, separate accounts can be used for the deposit, rent and other payments during the term and such payments can be solely characterised as rent or partly as purchase price payments.

Lease terms

Obligations for repairs and insurance of the Vessel and its appurtenances will need to be addressed, as well as what rights the Company has to make improvements or alterations that could affect the saleability or value of the Vessel. The amount of insurance premiums will not be known at the outset and, therefore, involves a variable rent element.

Contract to buy

The Company usually identifies the Vessel to be purchased but this could also be achieved by either the Bank entering into the contract with the Seller or by the Company doing so and then sub-contracting or assigning/novating the contract to the Bank. The Bank would not be prepared to take on the purchase obligation without contractual obligations on the part of the Company to enter into the Lease and attendant documents. Cooperation of the Seller may be required at the outset to amend the sale contract accordingly.

Late payment of rent

It is necessary to establish how late payment of rent is penalised, given that default interest is not permitted under *Shari'a* law. One possibility which is sometimes used is to require the payment of a sum representing the penalty for default into a separate account, the proceeds of which are distributed to charitable causes. The Bank does not benefit from these sums but the penalty acts as a deterrent to the Company against default.

Promise to buy/promise to sell

To have a binding enforceable obligation to buy/sell, a put option and a call option are likely to be required, although the appointed *Shari'a* advisers will need to approve the terms of the obligation to buy on the part of the Company.

Re-characterisation risk

A transaction that has the same economic effect as a secured loan but which is structured as something different is at risk of being re-characterised by English law as a secured loan if the court considers that the structure chosen is a sham. This issue is relevant if the Bank's intention is to develop a structure that puts the Company as far as possible in the same economic position as if he had taken out a conventional vessel mortgage. If the arrangement were to be treated as though it were really a secured loan it would clearly become much less attractive to the Company even though its re-characterisation under English law would not necessarily affect its treatment under *Shari'a* law. It will, therefore, be important to mitigate any risk of re-characterisation in structuring the arrangement.

Documentation required

The documentation necessary for the arrangement will depend upon a number of variable factors including (1) the final form of structure agreed by the Bank in the development process and (2) the particular provisions of *Shari'a* law being followed, as recommended by the appointed *Shari'a* Committee. The documents likely to be required are as follows.

- Lease Agreement: containing the main provisions governing the arrangement and the means of determining the hire payable.
- Promise to Buy (from the Company): in order for this to be a binding contractual agreement, if this is what is required, this is likely to take the form of a put option which the Bank can trigger requiring the Company to buy for the original purchase price (together with any cost of financing which the Bank intends to recover).
- Promise to Sell (from the Bank to the Company): in order for this to be a binding obligation on the Bank to sell at the request of the Company, this is likely to take the form of a call option, exercisable either at the end of the facility term or on an earlier desire by the Company to pay off the financing on selling the Vessel or refinancing.
- Offer of Finance and Facility Terms: this governs the arrangements to be made between the Bank and the Company when the Bank agrees to acquire the Vessel for the Company.
- Service Agency Agreement: this may be required if there are obligations that the Bank wishes and is prepared to allow the Company to carry out as its agent. These might include certain obligations in relation to repair and insurance.
- Form of Contract for use in a refinancing.
- Other documents which may be required (possibly including clauses for negotiation into the sale contract with the Seller of the Vessel to enable the *Ijara* structure to be put in place, notes on how to unwind the structure on a sale or refinancing, possibly a declaration of trust in the event the deposit and amortisation payments are seen as partial payment for the purchase) (see comments above).

The *Musharaka* model (partnership financing)

This flexible structure can be used and adapted for many asset financings and has been used, for example, to finance ships on a bilateral basis in circumstances where some more heavily structured products (such as *sukuk*) are disproportionately expensive and complex for the size of deal and age and type of asset.

It is not one of the classical Islamic financing structures but due to the nature of its flexibility, has become increasingly used particularly in relation to asset finance using funds.

Model outline

The asset operator (the 'Company') and, for example, an Islamic investor group become partners. They enter into a *Musharaka* agreement (the '*Musharaka*') under which they agree to become partners and contribute agreed amounts into a fund to finance the construction and delivery of the ship which will be legally owned by the Company for the benefit of the *Musharaka*. This agreement will generally exclude the creation of a partnership under English law and the application of the English Partnership Act 1890. It will set out the basis on which profits are shared. The ratios may vary over the life of the *Musharaka*. Losses are shared on the basis of the equity participations.

The Company is appointed as the technical partner and acts as a trustee of the partners in the *Musharaka*. It is allowed to enter into agreements in its own name and on behalf of the partners. The Company may be permitted to raise monies for the benefit of the *Musharaka*, essentially a form of co-financing.

In the case of a newbuilding finance, the fund may be used to reimburse the Company for payments made by it to the shipbuilder.

The Company and the Bank participate in contributions in accordance with requests made pursuant to a schedule. The *Musharaka* is generally linked to a bareboat charter between the Company and a third party charterer. Under the charter on each payment date the Company receives the charterhire and may apply that in part to the investors to purchase their interest in the *Musharaka*. In this way the Company increases its partnership share (and, in turn, the beneficial ownership in the vessel). This entitlement may be further linked with a put and call structure.

Documentation required

The documentation necessary for a *Musharaka* facility will depend upon a number of variable factors including (1) the final form of structure agreed by the Bank in the development process and (2) the particular provisions of *Shari'a* law being followed, as recommended by the appointed *Shari'a* Committee. The documents likely to be required are as follows:

* Master Agreement;
* *Musharaka* Agreement;
* Bareboat Charter; and
* Put and call structure.

Shari'a compliance

To ensure adherence to the Islamic principles, most Islamic banks have a religious board which scrutinises proposed transactions to ensure compliance with Islamic issues and maintains an overall review of the bank's financing methods and operations. This board may be referred to as the bank's *Shari'a* board or *Shari'a* Committee. The board will comprise a number of eminent Islamic scholars, who meet at regular intervals to discuss policy and/or specific transactions.

For specific advice on *Shari'a*-compliance issues, a dialogue with the independent *Shari'a* Committee instructed on behalf of the Bank may be initiated in the process of establishing many aspects of a *Shari'a*-compliant arrangement. The School of Islamic law applied by the independent *Shari'a* Committee would have to be acceptable to parties involved. Some of these independent *Shari'a* Committees have offices that are based in London and whose boards are comprised of reputable scholars in the field of international Islamic finance.

There is no guarantee that the structuring of an arrangement will be Islamically acceptable to third parties who may be seeking to participate in a *Shari'a*-compliant manner and much depends upon the *Shari'a* Committee or Board involved.

Law and jurisdiction

The documentation for Islamic finance transactions will invariably be made subject to English law and jurisdiction. The temptation may be to include a proviso to the effect that English law and jurisdiction apply, subject to *Shari'a* law. However, *Shari'a* courts do operate in certain Gulf countries, so if jurisdiction were founded there, the proviso could have a significant effect. All clauses founded contrary to *Shari'a* would be severed, or the contract itself could be found illegal and, hence, unenforceable. Reference to *Shari'a* law in a governing role in the UK would undoubtedly cause confusion. In any case it is possible to draft agreements made subject to English law, which are nonetheless fully *Shari'a* compliant. If English law is selected as the jurisdiction then it would be applied.

Other legal issues arising when structuring Islamic finance products

Tax and capital adequacy

Tax considerations are of paramount importance. Without efficient formulation, the very object of having competitively priced Islamic alternatives is defeated.

Where tax on profits is imposed, the income derived from Islamic investment products can be treated as straight investment income, taxed at source by the bank itself. Value added taxes and duties, payable where the bank is acting as a trader, are additional costs passed on to the borrower, once again increasing costs.

Capital adequacy ratios are also relevant. The Basel Capital Accord regulates banking supervision around the world. It treats *Ijara* mortgages as being capital weighted 100 per cent, whereas conventional mortgages are at 50 per cent, requiring banks to carry double the usual capital for Islamic mortgages. This pushes up the price of the product, unless and until relaxation of the rules is granted.

Passing of title

Shari'a requirements frequently compel banks to hold title to property during transactions, so lenders seek to minimise subsequent legal liabilities arising. In *Murabaha* transactions, for the interval during the two sales, the bank owns the property and so bears the risk that it will be destroyed or damaged. Such risk must be provided for in the documentation, but *Shari'a* prescribes that certain duties, such as the obligation in leases to maintain and repair property, always rest on the owner of that property. As titleholder, a bank will frequently find itself subject to such obligations. Clauses attempting to shift repair costs will be invalid on the grounds of unjust enrichment. Circumventing the restriction using insurance policies in the borrower's name may not attain *Shari'a* Committee approval. Hence, risks for the bank could include maintenance obligations, liability for cleaning up environmental pollution regardless of fault, being left holding the goods after they have been rejected for non-conformity, or being tied as a party to a litigation where death, injury or damage has resulted from a financed product.

Although a variety of well-known Islamic instruments are available for us in finance, the precise instrument chosen must be selected carefully, as its use may invoke subtle but important distinctions. In Islamic finance of shipbuilding transactions the instrument used for financing the building of a new vessel will be different to the one used on the sale of a second-hand one. For the former, *Istisna* may be used for commissioned construction, with title passing on delivery directly to the buyer. For the latter, the object of the contract is already in existence, so *Istisna* is inappropriate. Instead *Ijara* arrangements are used, with title passing on full repayment.

Special purpose vehicles can be used to offset title-related risks but these invariably increase the complexity and cost of products.

---

[1] Statistics from the Accounting and Auditing Organisation for Islamic Financial Institutions, Bahrain.